MARINA PETROPULOS

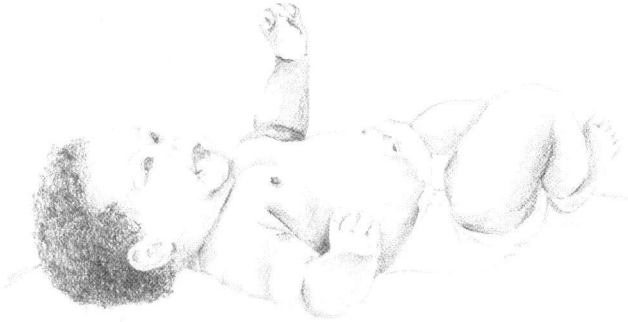

Baby &
Child Care
Handbook

MP
BOOKS

First published in South Africa by Struik in English hardcover 1980
Second hardcover impression 1983
First softcover edition 1983
Third hardcover impression 1986
Second softcover impression 1987
Third softcover impression 1989
Second hardcover edition 1989
Fourth softcover impression 1990
Second impression of the second hardcover edition 1990
Third impression of the second hardcover edition 1991
First impression of the first softcover edition published in 1992
by MP. Reg. no: 92/0311/33/07
Second impression of the softcover edition 1994
Third softcover impression 1995
Second softcover edition first impression 1997
Reprinted October 1997
New Millennium edition January 2000
Reprinted September 2000
Reprinted June 2001
Reprinted March 2002
New edition April 2003
Reprinted 2004
Twenty-fifth Anniversary Edition January 2005
Reprinted August 2005
Reprinted May 2006
Reprinted January 2007
Reprinted June 2008

The NEW Baby and Child Care Handbook
First published in English paperback 2011
Second impression 2012
Third impression 2016

BABY AND CHILDCARE HANDBOOK
First Impression January 2019

BOOKS

10 Parow Road, Maitland, Cape Town.
P.O. Box 32018, Camps Bay, 8040.
Tel. +27 21 5103844
Fax. +27 21 5101994

Photographs of Seth Leary, Luna Mbali Auchincloss and Marina Petropulos by Brooke Auchincloss
Sketches by Marina Petropulos, Chryssa Kunneke, Inge Votteler
Cartoons reproduced with permission

ISBN 978-0-6399081-0-6

Design and typesetting by Wouter Reinders
Printed and bound by Novus Print Solutions, a Novus Holdings company

CONTENTS

To my daughters Maia and Chryssa – my pride,
and my grandchildren Riley, Bay and Orion – my absolute joy;
and to Mica, Otto and Jop the strong, gentle men in my life.

Message from Marina

There are times when it feels like a lifetime ago since I was approached to write the first edition of my Baby and Child Care Handbook, and in some respects it has been, yet in others, just yesterday. Like it or not, change is ubiquitous. The fact that I have always said that babies' don't change, but circumstances do, draws closer all the time... However, I have not changed my essential philosophy on raising children. They still need tender loving care, protection and guidance above all. Yet, providing this seems to become more difficult all the time, as parents are left 'holding the baby' that arrives without an owner's manual to describe its workings, and certainly no manufacturer's guarantee!

It is my sincere conviction that parents of all shades and creeds share a common bond: that of wanting the best for their children. It is also the right of every child to be raised with enough care to nurture mind, body and soul; so that each will grow up with a good sense of self-worth, and a chance to realise their full potential.

In the newest edition of my **Baby and Child Care Handbook**, I have added **Everything You Need To Know About Pregnancy**. Pregnancy was always a part of the book, but recently there has been a great increase worldwide of various infections during pregnancy. Not only is a woman's system more than twenty per cent more vulnerable during pregnancy, but bacteria, viruses, parasites and toxins found in food are a problem. For example, even some cheeses that you enjoy will have to be avoided, and your loved cat may need to be ostracised because of the danger of transmitting toxoplasmosis infection. You will find a vast updated amount of important information, that will hopefully protect the amazing system of life developing within you.

Once the baby is born there are now a number of almost 'earth shattering' changes as to when and what to feed an infant. The well known mantra that mothers' should breastfeed for as long as possible and wait until six months before introducing solids, has now been debunked. The turnaround is due to a large increase of serious food allergies' that have affected children and restricted their lives. The LEAP (Learning Early about Peanut) study has recently and unequivocally shown that introducing allergenic foods from as early as four months, is the answer to greatly reducing the allergy problem.

In addition to my new Baby and Child Care Handbook edition, I am delighted to give you access to my website where a number of specialist paediatric colleagues speak on a variety of subjects that are of great interest; given in the form of audio videos!

MARINA PETROPULOS

Use your device to scan the QR code for free access to www.baby-childcare.com where you will be able to hear renowned Paediatric Specialists in a variety of fields give you the latest information on child care, including radical changes that have overturned previous thinking.

You will also be able to hear me answer questions from mothers and fathers on a radio programme with Nancy Richards, which was recorded many years ago. What is interesting, is that the questions they asked, are as relevant today as they were then.

CHAPTER 1

Falling in Love

'YOU ARE NEVER CLOSER TO THE MEANING OF LIFE THAN WHEN A BABY FALLS ASLEEP IN YOUR ARMS…'

These words, murmured by a man as his newborn granddaughter falls asleep in his arms – her tiny dimpled hand starfished across his chest – are a reflection of our spirituality and our deepest humanity. There is no greater measure of human civilisation than the regard we have for children.

Yet, even though parents may want to do the best for their children, it is the hardest thing to achieve – although on the surface – being a good parent should be easy. After all, procreation is said to be our single most important biological imperative. Unfortunately, there are no certain rules for a perfect outcome, no formulae that can tell you exactly how to care for the unique individual that is your child. The inherent psychological and physical complexities of being human do not make this possible…

You may think that 'maternal instinct' will kick in and tell you what to do. And it has a purpose, but it does not inform as you may hope; other than to flash neon signs instructing you to 'protect this child!' Certainly this protectiveness is the basis of parenting. Yet as instinctive as it may be, it does not come naturally to all who bear or father children. It is sometimes dormant at the time of birth and only grows with nurturance of a child. Or, it may be almost overwhelming in its intensity. Sadly, for some parents, protectiveness is not a natural urge due to their own psychological damage.

It is true that a mother often 'knows' that her child has a problem despite assurances. And she may be right. But it is a father or mother's close observation and connectedness with their child that informs their knowledge and intuition, not pure animal instinct, although we may call it that. If instinct was all it takes, then grassroots mothers would 'instinctively know' all about the most basic task of mothering – breastfeeding. Yet harmful myths abound in every culture: breastmilk can be detrimental to a child – it can be 'too salty'; or 'too weak', or even 'too strong' are common misconceptions.

Animals use pure instinct. They eat the placenta, or seek a dark hole to give birth in, and their offspring are far more sussed than ours in survival. They are also much easier to train, with a cuff here – a good example there – instinctively.

Although you are not propelled by instinct, there may well be times when you ruefully relate to animal life. Take the Arctic salmon fighting upstream, making endless heroic efforts only to slide back again, until they finally land in the pool beyond, exhausted. There to spawn, and immediately die so that their young can feed off their disintegrating carcass. You too, may feel like the Arctic salmon on occasion. You may even – heaven forbid – relate to the big grizzly papa bear who keeps his young in line with a swipe so hard it often silences them forever. No arguments about who's the boss here. And certainly, every parent will envy dolphins that can switch off one half of their brain and catch up on sleep!

It is because we are the highest form of life on earth that things are not so simple, and surely we would not want to miss the gifts this brings. Being able to consciously overcome our baser instincts to do the right thing. The exclusively human capacity to appreciate beauty: to marvel at the exquisite fragility of a baby's eyelashes fanned over translucent skin. To dream, to hope for the future. To cope with adversity; to be brave in spirit and deed.

The father of psychoanalysis, Sigmund Freud, complained that he could not figure out what it is that women want. But ask any mother and the answer is ready: she wants happiness for her children. How then, is it possible that we are so poorly equipped to do what we long for with such intensity? To nurture and protect so well that our children never feel pain, or loss, or disappointment or vulnerability; but live only in permanent happiness. Can it be that the most developed species on earth cannot succeed in achieving what it wants most?

The fact is that being a parent is unquestionably the hardest and most adult job in the world. Bar none. There are no shortcuts, no easy rides. No guarantees that what you put your heart and soul into will always turn out as you wish. *Yet there is nothing that can give more meaning to your life than raising a child.*

Like any lifelong project you must be sure of what you want to achieve. You may be hoping for an heir to take over the company you have built up. You could be dreaming of your child achieving goals you could not. Perhaps he will become a very rich sports star. Or you may believe you will get the perfect love you long for through a child.

All or any of these things may happen. But if they become the sole reason for having a child, eventually one or both of you will suffer and be disappointed.

The first thing to acknowledge is that your child will be of you, but not you – not even if the child is a clone of yourself. He or she will be a unique being entitled to their own dreams, hopes, complexities and future. You can influence, but you cannot dictate. You know this, but living it is not so easy.

IN SETTING YOUR GOALS, ASK YOURSELF WHAT KIND OF CHILDREN YOU WANT TO RAISE.

HAPPY. Certainly. Joy in living is a precious asset. It gives pleasure to those who are happy and to those who come in contact with them. It makes life worth living.

WELL BALANCED. The ancient Greek philosopher Plato cited the virtues of having a balance in life. Today we might call it yin and yang; or some such. To achieve a balance in life starts with another credo written up in the temple at Delphi: know yourself. It also requires emotional maturity, which in turn helps the capacity to live in balance with others.

MORAL. Old fashioned as this may sound, I believe that the moral values we impart are the cornerstone on which we raise our children. It is not only about the teachings of a particular religion, although this may offer much wisdom. It is based on the conviction that with a moral foundation your children will be able to achieve and enjoy all that is worth having. When you achieve your goals without honour, without morality, you always pay a price.

Note that all the above cannot be measured against the usual criteria for success. Good health, academic ability, riches, fame, a healthy sense of self esteem, sporting prowess, the ability to do good for humanity and much more – are attributes you could want for your child. None of these however, are necessary for the achievement of the first three – happiness, morality and balance. In fact, they are more than likely to be the natural outcome, than the starting point.

To raise happy, well adjusted, moral children you need to know on what to concentrate. There is no mother or father or extended family that can possibly do everything perfectly. You must decide on what is really important so that you can expend your financial and emotional resources to get the best possible return. Firstly you must have knowledge of normal child development. It is the context into which you must place your own and your child's behaviours.

Then you must beg, borrow or steal a sense of humour. Such a serious business as raising a child should not be attempted without the ability to laugh a lot – preferably at yourself. You could also do with a work mate – one who will commit to the slog as well as the fun. Common sense and a thickish skin are always useful.

Energy, a good sense of self and household help are optional extras. You do not have to be wealthy to raise children successfully. In fact, raising rich kids right can be much harder than raising poor kids properly.

Now you are as ready as you ever will be to embark on the great adventure. Your child will get 50% of her DNA (genetic material) from her mother and 50% from her father, with around 100 000 genes – of which only around 25 000 seem to have a designated function – juggled in the air and caught in a unique sequence on double helix ribbons of DNA. This genetic material contains all the inherited traits your child will receive from her parents.

What will your child be like? It is said that all newborn babies look like the father in order to entice him to stay around and not run off, as he is programmed to do, to sow his endless supply of sperm. A year later evolution presumably gives him permission to be on his merry way as the baby now starts to look like the sum of the parts of her collective gene pool. However, this does not give Dad license to sow oats in any form, unless he brings dinner home in the form of a buck slung across his shoulders and makes a fire by rubbing sticks together. *Fini*.

Above all, a child needs to interact with another human being who engages her in the process of getting to know this strange world into which she has arrived. *A child needs to become as involved with another as intensely as if she was falling in love. And in return, children need someone to fall in love with them.*

What babies do not need is an overwhelming amount of sensory stimulation. Ceaseless noise from loud music, screaming children, bickering adults, flickering television are stressful. A baby will simply tune out and turn off in self-defence. They also do not want to be picked up and jiggled all the time, although they enjoy this sometimes. It is important to learn to read your child's cues here, as in all other areas.

The other extreme is so bad it is life threatening. During the First World War (1914 to 1918) and then the great flu epidemic in 1918 in which more than 20 million people died, many babies were orphaned and had to be placed in institutional care. They had clean, sterile surroundings and enough food, yet so many of these poor 'foundlings' as they were called, died that it became an international disgrace. They simply wasted away for no apparent reason. Why? The public demanded. Doctors did tests. No, there were no dreadful bugs attacking the tiny mites. Yes, they did get all the food they needed. They were warm, well fed and protected from germs. But still they died.

And then there was Anna. Anna worked in a German home for orphans and here the babies thrived. Anna was no starched matron. She was a warm, loving mama who just could not keep her hands off the Kinder. She hugged them and smiled at them and stroked their downy cheeks. She cuddled them and cooed as she gazed in their eyes. And the babies thrived. Anna had cracked the code. Babies need to be loved! Without a loving touch and warm human interaction babies die. It is as simple and as profound as that.

Monkey babies, so often the surrogates for humans were put through an experiment. A large wire monkey mother was twisted into shape. She was equipped with a mechanical device that dispensed milk. A similar monkey mother was made and covered with terry towelling cloth to make her soft to the touch, but she was not equipped with a device for dispensing milk. The baby monkeys were kept hungry and then released. Which monkey mother would they choose? The milk dispensing mother who could calm their hunger or the soft and cuddly one who could only provide comfort? Incredibly, they chose to be comforted through touch rather than fill the very basic need for food.

Also at around the time of the same great flu disaster and the 'war to end all wars' a custom was instituted that became a form of gospel that still exists today. Babies should be fed every four hours. So here you are, watching the clock inch forward while your baby screams her head off. But it is not time! You cry back, how will you ever get her into a routine? There must be a good reason for this rule.

Well, here is the reason. Not only were mothers in short supply at this time but women in general had died in droves from the flu. Their babies had to be fed by overworked, hard-pressed nurses who worked an eight-hour shift. By feeding the babies every four hours they could get in two feeds per shift. And that is how this sacred regimen was instituted. Not on the basis of babies' needs, but on the basis of practical necessity in a time of crisis.

At this point you should have the priorities of the first year clear. It is true that food needs are also important. All you need to know about this will be explained later. But we have established that what is truly important to your baby in the first year is love. Love received and love given. The intimate human contact of one towards another.

We are talking about caring, attachment, knowing, commitment, meeting of needs, willingness to sacrifice, enchantment, delight in, pain – the full human catastrophe in fact. This may not be as immediate as you may have been led to believe. It is more likely to be a slow, incremental creep into your heart as you commit to and care for your child.

We know now that the brain is being wired for learning from before birth. All the tiny neurons and dendrons are ready to connect up with synapses to form a learned action like holding a rattle. But did you know that emotional learned reactions are also taking place?

Hard-wiring of emotional responses is being learned and fixed into the brain so that years later you may still suffer the effects of emotional neglect and abuse. While we are about it we may as well deal with the question of 'spoiling'. You may have heard that you will 'make a rod for your own back' if you run to your child every time she cries. This is true. Your child will continue to make demands by signalling you when she needs something. After all, she cannot get up and make a bottle for herself, nor change her damp nappy if it is chafing, she relies on you. And the younger she is the less she is able to delay her needs.

Babies who are repeatedly ignored when they send a distress signal will learn not to do so. They become depressed, withdrawn and ultimately waste away in extreme cases. So yes, your baby will stop crying eventually if you ignore her often and for long enough. The silent babies with haunted expressions found in the cots in Romanian institutions after the demise of communism were a terrible example of what prolonged emotional neglect can do.

Even today there are those who will tell you that children are born sinful and must have it knocked out of them. How bizarre. Could we extrapolate then that women too are inherently bad and must be tamed with regular beatings? In the early 1900s Professor Emmett Holt wrote a book, *The Care and Feeding of Children*, in which he exhorted parents never to pick up a crying child, to regulate feeding by the clock and avoid spoiling by not handling the child. Dr Truby King was a disciple who followed with similar advice.

Another academic Dr John B. Watson of Johns Hopkins University in the USA, espoused similar views based on his behaviourist concept of child development. There was a struggle of wills between parent and child, he said, and children had to be forced to be self-reliant and strong from early on or it would make the child too dependent on his parents. His treatise Psychological Care of Infant and Child (1928) admonished parents to 'never, never kiss your child.'

Certainly self-reliance and strength are desirable characteristics. But they are not developed through lack of nurturance. We are all aware of street children who are apparently self-reliant and strong, rejecting all authority while robbing, pilfering and sniffing glue. Are these spoiled children? True spoiling is another issue and it has nothing to do with being responsive to your child's needs.

In 1946 Dr Benjamin Spock caused a revolution with his book on child care. A paediatrician and psychoanalyst, he encouraged parents to be warm and flexible, and his book sold more than fifty million copies around the world. He became an all-American celebrity, only to fall out of favour with his opposition to the Vietnam War.

Sadly, the prophet could not make the leap from what he preached to what he practised, and his own children recall him as cold and unloving. He died in 1997, at the age of 94, still seeing his psychoanalyst several times a week. Thus, accepting what the mind tells us we should do, and changing all those learned responses from our own childhood, is possibly the greatest challenge in child rearing. For better or for worse our parents make us who we are. What we are, we owe to ourselves.

Let us embark on this exciting journey.

CHAPTER 2

Pregnancy
Welcome To The Miracle Of Human Creation!

Whether the news that you are pregnant is what you have been keenly hoping for, or perhaps, the last thing you want to hear; your life is about to undergo profound changes when you become a parent.

In the beginning you may be so dazed that you find it difficult to conceptualise what you are feeling – because becoming a parent is as much an experience of the mind – as of the body. It is also, the most exciting, challenging, rewarding yet complex development possible within a human being.

Which is why, the process has been delegated to the stronger, smarter sex! And when, the umbilical cord on the new-born baby drops off some days after the birth, all of us, every single human being – is left with a 'belly button' – as confirmation of our universal equality. May all go well with you on your exciting, epic journey!

WHAT TO EXPECT WHEN YOU YOU'RE EXPECTING

IN THE BEGINNING. To confirm whether you are pregnant, you could use a home pregnancy test. Some tests can establish pregnancy as early as eight days after conception, but this does not apply to all home tests, when you usually need to wait about two weeks after conception for the results.

A blood test done by a doctor for the hormone hCG (human chorionic gonadotropin) around six days after fertilisation, can tell the results immediately and establish if you are indeed pregnant. The earlier you know the better, so that you can take care of yourself and your unborn baby as soon as possible during the critical first 12 weeks, when the developing foetus is most vulnerable.

Once your pregnancy is confirmed you need to decide – if you have a choice – who will be your healthcare provider during your pregnancy, and where you will give birth.

Your choices are likely to be between your GP (general medical practitioner), gynaecologists (gynes), who offer preventative reproductive health care and treat problems in the reproductive organs – vagina, ovaries and uterus etc.; while obstetricians take care of women and the foetus in pregnancy and the birth. These days, almost all gynaecologists are also obstetricians. A midwife, is a trained professional who does routine pregnancy check-ups should there be no complications; while a nurse midwife (CNM), is professionally trained with a degree to deal with more complex aspects of childbirth. A home birth assistant may, or may not have training in childbirth. A doula is a woman companion that gives emotional and practical support during and after the birth in a non-medical capacity. Water birth is available in some medical facilities.

Keep in mind, that while giving birth is a milestone for you, it has a lifelong effect on your child. So, when choosing a healthcare practitioner it should be for his or her expertise and experience, as well as their ability to relax you. Have a written list with you, and you should be given clear and full responses to your questions. If they evade answering questions and induce labour routinely, find someone else, and note that the most 'fashionable' way of giving birth is not necessarily the best.

Your healthcare practitioner will take a blood specimen and ask for a urine sample. If you are more than six weeks pregnant you may also be given an internal examination to feel if there is enlargement of the uterus, and softening of the cervix. Although you may regard an internal examination as undignified – try and relax – as it will be clinical and detached. Your urine will be tested regularly for sugar and protein, as well as any infections. Blood specimens will be checked for anaemia, and your blood group identified. If you are Rhesus negative, more tests will be done. Later on, an internal examination will show whether your pelvic structure will allow for a vaginal birth.

Depending on your age and family history you will also be tested for various inherited disorders and possible defects. An ultrasound scan can give information regarding internal organs, and there will be checks to see if the embryo is developing in the right place.

The reason human beings are so divergent is due to the vast and varied genetic material that we have. The exception is when a single fertilised egg divides into two, resulting in identical twins. They are in effect, mirror images of each other. For example, two American tennis players, the Bryan brothers, that are the most successful doubles duo in history, are the exact image of each other, expect for the fact that the one is left handed and the other right handed. Revealing that, in effect, the egg was sliced right down the middle to become two. If two or more eggs are fertilised separately, your offspring will not be identical, even though they are born at the same time. You could have a non-identical boy and girl, or two boys and a girl, or even more.

Your baby's gestational age will be calculated so that you have an approximate due date for the birth, which is measured at 280 days after the first day of your last period. Your caregiver will usually want to see you once a month until week 28; then twice a month; until the last month, when you will be expected to come in every week. If you are expecting more than one baby, you will most likely be told to come in more often from earlier on.

PREGNANCY SYMPTOMS. During the first few weeks of pregnancy, you'll probably be feeling very tired. If you're working, use any breaks and the lunch hour to sit down with a cushion behind your back, and your feet up. The last three months can be uncomfortable, especially in summer, because you'll be feeling the heat due to an increase of up to 40 percent in your blood volume. Take every chance you can to have a rest and relax, while lying on your left side.

As compensation for the increased blood volume that you are carrying, you may be rewarded with a 'pregnancy glow'. Don't rush into maternity gear as soon as your waistline starts disappearing; nine months is a long time and you'll get tired of your clothes if you start wearing them too soon.

You're starting to feel nauseous and possibly even vomit, it's the dreaded 'morning sickness', although it doesn't only happen in the morning. Some women experience severe nausea, others only mild, while a few have none at all. The causes are mainly due to large amounts of progesterone hormones being released, and possibly low blood sugar. *If you feel nauseous when you wake up in the morning, your partner will kindly bring you a nice cup of tea, and a plain biscuit before you get out of bed…*

Should you find that you can't hold anything down, get medical advice, as the extreme type of 'morning sickness' called *hyperemesis gravidarum* can cause dehydration, weight loss and nutrient deficiency, and it may be necessary to put you on a drip to replenish fluids and correct any electrolyte imbalance that may have occurred. In the UK, the Duchess of Cambridge had this problem and was hospitalised during her pregnancy in 2017.

Your sense of smell may change, and you could have a metallic taste in your mouth that spoils the enjoyment of foods you previously liked. But, then again, you may develop an appetite for ice cream and tomato sauce with a sprinkle of chilli pepper.

So, you despatch your partner to shop for it at 10pm…

Something you might welcome is that your breasts are getting bigger, but sigh, they feel tender and your nipples are becoming sensitive and larger and darker, while you have to run to the loo all the time because you need to urinate so often. Now, you're starting to feel tired, really tired, and you have confusing mood swings.

Meanwhile, your partner scratches their head when you aren't looking…

By the time you are over the first three months of pregnancy, you'll start feeling better: less nauseous, moody and tired. You'll probably be keen to tell the world you're expecting! And, then one day, you feel a butterfly flutter in your tummy… You've experienced it before. In your finals, on your first special date, when you had to give an important seminar talk – but, somehow, this is gentler, softer – can it be? Yes, it's around 16 weeks or a little longer and your baby is moving in the womb!

THE SECOND TRIMESTER: When your nausea is over, and you're feeling more relaxed and happy, is when you can enjoy a getaway with your partner. You won't have a chance to be together this intimately for a long while: ever since you signed up for a new life. One filled with chores and delights and puppy dog fights over who gets to choose the TV programme and who's not done their homework…

Between the 18th and 30th week is a good time to take a break because your pregnancy is usually at its most stable and comfortable. If you're planning a plane trip, and been given the okay by your medical adviser, it is wise to do the following: ask whether you will need immunisation when visiting a new destination, and check if it is safe to have the necessary shots during pregnancy.

For comfort on the flight, fasten the lap belt under your bump, and drink plenty of water. Keep your blood circulation going by rolling your foot in circles five times, then point your toes down, then forward and back. Now circle your foot five times. Repeat with the other foot. Do this exercise as often as possible, and take a walk in the aisle when it's clear. Correctly-fitted 'compression' stockings are helpful in keeping your legs from swelling and possible blood clots forming (deep vein thrombosis). The stockings should be put on before you stand up in the morning.

Talking about good times you could find yourself looking forward to a bit of hanky-panky with your partner but unsure whether it's safe. Surprisingly, pregnancy may be a time when you become particularly keen on sex. That's because of increased levels of progesterone, and in particular, oestrogen hormones that stimulate the libido; bolstered by increased blood flow to the uterus and pelvis, as well as greater vaginal lubrication and heightened sensitivity in your breasts and nipples. Enjoy, after checking with your medical advisor. And no, they won't be embarrassed when you ask.

SEXUAL POSITIONING IN PREGNANCY may need to be modified. The usual 'missionary' position is out, since you don't want weight on your belly. Rather try this: your partner lies facing you on his side, on the bed, while you lie at arm's length next to him with your head on a cushion, and both your legs hung over his hip. This way you can connect without discomfort. Probably the best position, is 'woman on top' which allows you to be in control and decide how much, and when. Note, that fun tricks like your partner blowing air into your vagina, is a no, no, because it can cause an embolism (an obstruction of a blood vessel).

ON THE MORE ABSURD SIDE OF PREGNANCY, there is the latest folly-fad in which new mothers are eating their placenta. It is claimed that doing so will prevent postnatal depression, and, as Kim Kardashian says, it also gave her a huge energy boost! Well, yes, psychosomatic (mind over matter) prompting can be very effective, but consider this: the micro-biome (the multiple good/bad live bacteria in the gut/uterine/vaginal area) while not generally dangerous to adults, can be lethal in infancy. Here's a case in point. A mother who was enjoying her placenta, which, should you be interested, can be dried and made into capsules and flavoured according your preference e.g. chocolate placenta truffles and so on, or, um, neat resulted in her new-born acquiring a serious streptococcal infection. Twice.

SPEAKING OF THE PLACENTA, it is a thick, blood vessel rich, meaty area that develops during pregnancy and attaches itself to the inside of the womb. The baby's umbilical cord is joined to the placenta, where an exchange of nutrients, hormones, oxygen and blood between the mother and the developing foetus occurs. Ideally, the placenta should attach in the upper area of the uterus. However, it sometimes forms low down in the uterus, and may block the cervix through which the baby will be born, making a natural birth problematic, and a Caesarean may be needed.

PREGNANCY FOOD CRAVINGS have been with us from time immemorial, and while some are strange but harmless, others tell another story. Such is a condition known as pica, in which pregnant women crave and eat non-food substances including chalk, ice, paint chips, charcoal and the like. (It also occurs in malnourished children). This weird need is thought to be due to a lack of important vitamins and minerals in the diet. Because pregnancy significantly increases the amount of blood in the system, that, in turn, demands an increased amount of iron which is tasked to transport oxygen throughout your body.

While iron deficiency does not have obvious symptoms, it has, nonetheless, important effects. These include anaemia, feelings of weakness, irritability, anxiety, hair loss, headache and depression. All of which are common during pregnancy, and easily overlooked or misinterpreted. Incidentally, a lack of iron is the most common nutritional deficiency worldwide, with pre-menopausal women being particularly vulnerable due to blood loss during periods. In young children it can also be a factor in irritability, lack of sleep and impaired cognitive and behavioural development. If you have concerns, you may want to ask your doctor if your child should have a test, and at the same time have a blood test yourself even if you are breastfeeding.

WHERE TO FIND THE VITAMINS AND IRON YOU NEED IN PREGNANCY. There are two types of iron: **Heme iron** is found in meat, fish, seafood, poultry and eggs; thirty per cent of which is absorbed when these foods are eaten. Drinking freshly squeezed orange or other fresh juices (avoid grapefruit), that are high in Vitamin C, at the same time as eating foods such as beef, lamb or chicken (preferably free range/grass fed); or fish, salmon in particular, pushes absorption rates even higher.

Non-heme iron is mainly found in plant foods. However, only between two and ten percent is absorbed, which means that vegans and vegetarians generally need to compensate for a lack of dietary heme iron. Because of its importance, in particular during pregnancy, bread, pasta, cereals, rice and other staple foods are fortified with heme-iron.

Vegetable sources of non-heme iron are found in dark green leafy vegetables such as kale, chard and spinach, as well as beans, mange tout, dried peas and beans, mung beans, lentils, mulberries, blackberries, raspberries, tomato pastes, tofu, bell peppers, sweet potatoes (are particularly high in copper, zinc, manganese, magnesium, vitamins A, B_5, B_6, B, C, E, fibre, potassium, iron, beta-carotene, as well as unique proteins, called sporamins), coconut, dried fruit such as raisins, peaches, prunes and apricots plus numerous other fruit and vegetable sources. In many countries bread, pasta, cereals, rice and other staple foods are fortified with heme-iron. Check labels.

NOTE: Do not take or use any vitamins or supplements without consulting your medical practitioner who will advise you. (Folic acid or foliate, is considered essential from when trying to become pregnant, as It helps prevent spinal cord defects, so speak to your medical advisor if you are trying to become pregnant.)

WEIGHT GAIN IN PREGNANCY. The average amount of weight gained during a pregnancy is 12kg (26½lb). However if you go into your pregnancy at your ideal weight you should gain between 10½ and 14½kg (23–32lb). If you are underweight, you should gain between 12½ and 16kg (27–35lb) and if you are overweight when you become pregnant you should gain between 9 and 11kg (20–24lb).

If you baby weighs 3.6kg (8lb) the rest of the weight you gained during pregnancy consisted of the following: 0.9kg (2lb) was the weight of your uterus; 0.7kg (1 lb 8oz) the weight of the placenta; 0.9kg (2lb) the weight of the amniotic fluid, the weight of your breasts would have increased by 0.7kg (1lb 8oz); the volume of your blood would have increased by a mass of 1.8kg 4lb); your fat and protein store would have increased by 1.8kg (4lb); and, the fluid retention in your body would have increased by 1.8kg (4lb). It is 'normal' to gain 1–3kg (2–7lb) in the first trimester, 4–5kg (8–11lb) in the second trimester, and the balance of the weight in the third trimester.

Babies that are born LGA (large for gestational age), can weigh 4kg (8lbs 13oz) or more, which may be due to gestational diabetes in the mother. Your medical advisor may do a test for gestational diabetes mellitus (GDM), and advise you to come for follow a up visit between 10-12 weeks after the birth in order to test for type 2 diabetes, as it can cause serious health problems in the long term.

It is important that you don't diet during pregnancy, but eat a balanced variety of healthy foods, as a crash diet could stunt foetal growth and development.

SEE HOW YOUR BABY GROWS
WEEK 1 AND WEEK 2
For a woman to conceive, she must ovulate (release an egg) during her menstrual cycle (period), and the egg (ovum) must move into one of her fallopian tubes where it will wait for up to twenty-four hours, for at least one of the many millions of sperm that are released during male ejaculation to find their way to meeting the tiny egg cell.

From the minute that you partner's genes penetrate the waiting egg, a unique being will be on the path of creation…

If you have regular periods, you may be aware that your period is late; but you could still be unsure if you are pregnant due to bleeding (spotting). This is not unusual however, as more than twenty percent of women experience spotting in the first six to twelve days after conception. (Contact your medical advisor if the bleeding is causing concern).

Should the egg and sperm not meet – the lining of the uterus that had prepared a 'bed' for a fertilised egg – will shed, and menstrual bleeding will take place.

Unlike the mindboggling number of functional sperm available in males through to old age – as a woman – you have a limited amount of eggs. Therefore, your chances of becoming pregnant in the years in which you are young enough to be fertile are limited.

If the egg and sperm do meet, the egg will be fertilised, and by the fifth day the fertilised egg will have grown to a large number of cells and is called a blastocyst, even though you may not yet be aware that you are pregnant.

Over the next few days the blastocyst travels down the fallopian tube and into the uterus where it divides into two parts: the one half becomes the placenta that attaches to the uterine wall and the other half, now known as the embryo, miraculously becomes your developing baby!

WEEK 3
The embryo divides into three layers that will eventually become the organs and tissue of all the parts of the developing foetus. The inner layer contains the gut, bladder, stomach and lungs which will became the breathing and digestive system. The middle layer becomes the heart, blood vessels, bones and muscles. While the outer layer of cells develop the neural tube that becomes the brain and spinal cord.

A water-tight sac forms around the embryo which fills with amniotic fluid which protects and cushions the embryo.

WEEK 4
The nervous system, the lens of the eyes, skin, nails and tooth enamel will begin forming.

The heart, which is only the size of a small seed, will begin to beat and pump blood, and very soon it will be beating at an amazing 150 beats per minute.

The blood vessels that connect the embryo to the mother via the placenta, are shaped into a simple tube-like structure, the umbilical cord, which is already hard at work. This transfers nutrients from the mother to the embryo.

The head is still very large in proportion to the body while facial features are beginning to develop.

You baby is now about 6mm in length.

WEEK 5

The embryo makes its first movements now, although you won't feel them yet. They can, however, be seen by means of an ultrasound scan.

The arms and legs are beginning to form as well as the ears and the internal organs such as the kidneys, lungs and liver.

WEEK 6

By now it may be possible to detect the heart beat by means of ultra-sound.

The brain is continuing to develop into its complex structure and the jaw, nose, internal ears and palate are being formed.

WEEK 7 AND WEEK 8

This rather strange embryonic creature that will become your beautiful child has 'paddle like' hands and feet, with slightly webbed fingers and toes. The ears, nose and palate are forming, and all the main internal parts as well as sexual organs are starting to develop.

The embryo is now about 25mm in size.

WEEK 9

The embryonic 'tail' has disappeared and the foetal period begins. Muscles, internal organs and nerves are starting to form, and from now on, especially between weeks 9-18 growth is rapid, with the foetus already doubled in length. While the head, which is almost half the size of the body, grows less rapidly. All the main organs such as kidneys and liver are developing – the ears, nose, fingers and toes – as well as sexual organs have formed, although you cannot as yet determine the sex of the embryo.

WEEK 10

Although the foetus cannot hear yet, the inner ear is fully developed; while the vocal cords are also starting to form. The external genitalia have developed and been defined between male ♀ and female ♂. Unfortunately it's too late now to wish for a baby boy or girl…

WEEK 11

At around this time, the human foetus will be doing something never to be repeated after the birth. Because your girl or boy to be, is now surrounded by 'water' in the form of amniotic fluid and the urine they have passed. They will be surrounded by it, and swallow it happily.

WEEK 12

The twelve weeks milestone has been reached! This important milestone will tell your medical advisor a great deal about your baby's developmental progress.

WEEK 13

This is the last week of your first trimester and all of your baby's vital development has taken place and your baby is fully formed. The face begins to look more 'human' and your baby may even seem to smile. Nerve cells have been multiplying rapidly and neurological impulses in the brain (synapses) are forming. The foetus has discovered that by touching the palms of the hands, it causes a reflex that makes fingers close, and a touch on the soles of the feet makes their toes curl down! Your baby is now between 65 and 78mm long.

WEEK 14

The second trimester begins. Your baby's unique human fingerprints have formed, and if you gently press your bump and your baby feels it, he or she will instinctively start rooting to find a nipple. If your baby is a girl she will already have 2 million eggs in her ovaries, but by age seventeen this will have dropped to a about five hundred. Your baby is now between 80 and 93mm in length.

WEEK 15

The baby's body is growing faster than the head now, and the baby's skin becomes covered with lanugo, an ultra-fine, un-pigmented downy hair surface that looks a bit like the fluff on a peach. Lanugo helps keep the baby warm. Eyebrows and hair on the head are beginning to grow, but this will change after the birth with a genetic colour and texture taking root. The bones are hardening and retaining calcium, and your baby may be able to suck a thumb, grasp, squint and frown. Your baby is now between 93 and 103mm long.

WEEK 16

Between weeks 16 and 20 you will start to feel the excitement of your baby moving within you! And, if your baby co-operates, an ultrasound scan will be able to tell if you are expecting a boy or girl! All the joints and limbs can move and the legs are growing longer than the arms. While the fingers and toes have their own, exclusive fingerprints! Your baby is between 108 and 116mm in length.

WEEK 17

Your baby will now be doing something that can never be replicated outside the womb; because he or she is breathing in amniotic fluid and then exhaling it through the lungs! The sensory system and urinary tract are in full working order, and your baby may be exploring by grabbing and pulling at the umbilical cord. Your baby is now about 150mm long.

WEEK 18

The brain stem is the first part of the brain to develop. It monitors basic vital functions such the heartbeat from the time it is merely the size of a small seed. By week eighteen, a fatty substance called myelin is insulating a neuron's axon which is the long fibre that delivers impulses to other neurons. A neural pathway sends electrical impulses in a series of synapses that form a network in the nervous system in the brain. So why is it so important?

Because, the cerebral cortex, one of the four parts of the brain, controls most of our conscious, voluntary actions. Unfortunately, however, the cerebral cortex is not fully mature until the mid-twenties.

A fact that will explain a lot, when your lovely baby becomes a teenager...

WEEK 19

Your baby is going through a tremendous growth spurt and will double her weight in the next few weeks. The chest is moving up and down mimicking breathing, however, your baby is not breathing air, but effluent, including amniotic fluid, together with urine, hair, and skin...

Your baby is now between 150 and 180mm long.

WEEK 20

Your pregnancy is halfway there! Sensory development peaks this week, as the five senses sight, taste, smell, hearing, seeing and touching develop. Your baby will also be having fun *in utero,* twisting, turning, kicking and somersaulting inside you while there is still room to move. But soon, in the next few weeks there will be a lack of space in the womb, and less fun to be had. Your baby is now about 16cm long and weighs about 300g (10.5oz).

WEEK 21

Considering how long a baby spends in a 'water' environment while in the womb, it's understandable that their skin needs protection. Vernix caseosa is a white, fatty cheese like substance that coats your baby's skin for warmth and protection during the long immersion in amniotic fluid, and it also eases delivery. Vernix has many other protective benefits. Your baby is now between 190mm and 200mm long.

WEEK 22

Magically, your baby can hear now, so it's time to start singing and talking to your unborn child, who will soon become familiarised with the sound of your voice. Regardless of whether you sing out of tune, or talk baby talk, it will encourage recognition and emotional attachment with your baby. Your baby will also begin to have a sleeping pattern, waking and sleeping at more regular times, although they may not be the same as yours! Your baby is now between 200mm and 210mm long.

WEEK 23

Your baby now has the proportions of a new-born, but is still very thin as fat has not developed yet. You will begin to put weight on more steadily, averaging about 300g (10.5oz) a week. Your baby is now between 210 and 220mm long.

WEEK 24

Your baby's hearing and blood vessels in the lungs are developing rapidly. Due to advances in science and technology, chances of survival for a baby born now would be about 85% with specialised care.

WEEK 25

Your baby's breastbone is the first to turn into bone and the other bone centres will soon follow. Your baby is about 240mm long. *Your gums may bleed when you brush your teeth and your belly button will probably protrude.*

WEEK 26

Your baby may now respond to touch and turn their head if you shine a light on your abdomen. Sweat glands have formed, and your baby is now about 300mm long.

WEEK 27

It seems incredible that the 'eyes' which in the early embryonic stage, were merely dark blobs situated far back on the very large head, are now beginning to open! More amazing, is that your baby is having REM (rapid eye movements), and may be dreaming…

WEEK 28

You and your baby have reached the beginning of the third trimester and the lungs are almost ready to do the remarkable job of being able to breathe air outside the womb if they are born early. But they will still need help in the form of surfactant lecithin that is working to prevent the lungs from collapsing. The characteristic grooves on the brain's surface start to appear and more brain tissue develops. If you feel a rhythmic movement or gentle twitches you could be feeling your baby's hiccups! You could be short of breath, because your lungs are cramped by the baby that has not dropped down yet. Your baby is now about 325mm long and weighs about 1kg (2lb 3oz).

WEEK 29

If you could look inside your womb and see your baby, you could find them doing something that you may not approve of later on. Because they may be happily sucking their thumb! Your baby is about 350mm in length and weighs about 1.5kg (3lb 5oz).

WEEK 30

From now on your baby's nutritional needs are at its peak, as the body starts plumping out. The skeleton hardens, and the brain, muscles and lungs continue to mature. On your side, you may experience Braxton–Hicks contractions. These are painless, irregular contractions practicing for labour in preparation for when it's time for the birth.

WEEK 31

Your baby's arms, legs and body are becoming plumper and the head no longer looks too big for the body. The lungs and digestive track are almost fully developed, and your baby is growing faster and fatter, making it difficult to move in the uterus.

WEEK 32

If this is your first pregnancy your baby will probably remain high up in the womb until close to the birth. If is not your first child, your baby may have already 'lightened' and dropped head down into the uterus and nestled into the cervix, which should give you more breathing space.

WEEK 33

Don't expect to have a lot of activity, but enough to feel that there is some movement. Your caregiver will want to see your once a week for a check-up. Your baby is about 430mm long and weighs between 1.8 and 2.1kg (3lb 15oz and 4lb 10oz). Do keep in mind that a baby's weight and length also depends on what they have inherited.

WEEK 34

Your baby's skin that was transparent, blue veined and fragile in the early weeks is smooth and baby like now, helped by the vernix that has been protecting the skin. By this time your baby may even have a full head of hair – or perhaps – just a few wisps. This hair isn't permanent though, and the colour may change in the months after the birth. Your baby is about 440mm long.

WEEK 35

Your baby's central nervous system has not fully developed yet, although all areas are maturing and making progress. You baby is about 460mm in length.

WEEK 36

The fine slightly 'furry' hair called lanugo that covered your baby's body has disappeared, confirming that your child is almost ready to be born. Your baby is now about 470mm in length and weighs between 2.2kg and 2.9kg (4lb 11oz and 6lb 6oz)

WEEK 37 – WEEK 40

From the 37th week your baby will be deemed to be sufficiently developed to be born. He or she will be about 480mm in length and still gaining weight, and acquiring immunity to protect them from their future in the outside world. Most of the vernix has disappeared, and meconium, a blackish substance will become your baby's first bowel movement. Ideally, it should be contained in the bowel until the birth when it will be excreted.

For the lungs, breathing outside the water in the womb is a new challenge, and the lungs may need a few hours to master breathing air. Its forty weeks now, and your baby is full term, and about 500 to 520mm in length – or more – depending on the family build, and weighs between 3.2kg and 3.4kg (7lb 1oz and 7lb 8oz).

PROTECTING YOUR UNBORN CHILD

THE FIRST 12 WEEKS OF PREGNANCY are when your baby's vital organs are formed: therefore your first concern now is to protect the foetus that is developing within you. Strangely, pregnancy is also a time that your system is particularly vulnerable to infection and other problems.

What you read below is not meant to stress you, but inform you, so that you know what to avoid if possible.

Stay away from alcohol, cigarettes, or recreational drug usage as they can all cause long term harm to your unborn child. Smoking reduces the oxygen supply to the foetus which can affect brain and physical development. Alcohol intake during pregnancy can cause **foetal alcohol syndrome (FAS)** that can result in physical and mental defects: including poor impulse control and serious learning difficulties. Drug usage has potential negative effects for both the foetus and the mother.

If you are on prescribed medication, or taking over the counter products ask your doctor as soon as possible whether they are safe. For obvious reasons, medicines are not tested on pregnant women; but they will have undergone safety tests that are mandatory for all prescription drugs.

However, it does not generally apply to 'natural', 'herbal', homeopathic, organic and other alternative treatments as they are not required to be safety or content tested. Herbs such as St. John's Wort, Kava kava, Ginkgo biloba and others have been banned from use in many countries due to possible serious side effects. Yet, they are still easily available, and many people consider them safe in pregnancy. Liquorice root should also be avoided during pregnancy as it can mimic the effects of oestrogen (the female sex hormone) and induce early labour and miscarriage.

ASPIRIN is one of the oldest medications still used. It was originally made from willow bark by Hippocrates of Kos in Greece (born 460 BC), who is known as the 'father of medicine', from whom the doctors' oath: *'first do no harm'* is taken. Recently, it has been shown that early miscarriage can occur due to the regular use of aspirin or ibuprofen in pregnancy. To confuse matters, low doses of aspirin are used to help certain problems in pregnancy.

The takeaway message is: avoid anything 'natural' or medicinal that has not been discussed with, and sanctioned by your medical practitioner. **Headaches are not uncommon during pregnancy, so consult your doctor before taking aspirin, ibuprofen or other medications.**

The strange danger of eating some kinds of fruit: The last thing you might expect is for a nutritious fruit such as grapefruit, to have the potential to cause serious medical damage. Yet, according to recent Canadian research published in the CMAJ (Canadian Medical Association Journal), eighty five prescription medications may interact with grapefruit or grapefruit juice; with forty three being dangerous – resulting in too little or far too much of the drug – being retained in the users' system. **Read all medicine leaflets, and consult your medical advisor.**

Another unexpected problem is that your system in pregnancy is far more vulnerable than usual to bacteria, viruses, parasites or chemicals and toxins found in food.

LISTERIA MONOCYTOGENES is a food borne bacterial infection that in young healthy men and women does not generally cause serious illness. However, in pregnancy, listeria infection can be very dangerous as it may result in miscarriage, stillbirth and neonatal death. This is because in pregnancy, you are 20 times more vulnerable to infections, as your immune system is suppressed. Symptoms of listeria infection may appear soon after you've eaten contaminated food or it may take a month before the first signs of fever, muscle aches, nausea and diarrhoea appear. If the mother is infected, unborn babies can contract listeria infection via the placenta.

Listeria infection is most often contracted by eating improperly processed and stored deli meat products and unpasteurised milk. Foods that are packaged or processed in unsanitary conditions are also dangerous. The bacterium can be carried by animals, including new born lambs, and it is also found in un-purified water or contaminated soil when manure (animal dung) has been used as a fertiliser.

Although listeria bacteria are destroyed by pasteurisation and cooking at high heat, what makes this bacterium different is the fact that it can live and multiply in refrigerators and even freezers, in which other food borne bacteria cannot.

NOTE: If you think that you may have eaten infected food, contact your medical practitioner or hospital immediately, so that blood tests can be done and treatment given.

So this is a time to be very fussy about what you eat. Cook all food thoroughly, and keep your refrigerator set at 4°C (40°F), and the freezer below zero. As always, be sure to wash your hands frequently – with hot soapy water (not sanitiser) – and use separate boards for preparing raw and cooked foods.

Avoid anything made from unpasteurised cows', or goats' milk including soft cheeses such as Camembert, Brie, Danish blue, gorgonzola and other blue veined and mould-ripened chesses. Hard cheeses and cheese made from pasteurised milk such as Cheddar, Gouda, and Parmesan are usually considered safe. Undercooked or raw foods such as Carpaccio, oysters, steak tartar, sushi and sashimi are best avoided, unless you are certain it has been frozen for at least four days.

DO NOT EAT UNDERCOOKED MEAT, POULTRY AND FISH. To avoid infection, cook all food to at least 71°C (160°F). Raw vegetables, grown in soils that may have animal dung, should be scrubbed with a clean brush in running water before use; and stay away from prepared salads, including coleslaw and bean sprout. Avoid ready to eat deli meats and meat sandwiches, fermented meat and sausages, frankfurters, all meat spreads including livor pâté, hot dogs, cold meats such as 'polony', salami, Parma ham, pepperoni, chorizo and smoked seafood, unless you reheat them to steaming hot: at least 71°C (160°F). Ice cream may also be associated with possible listeria infection.

In 2018 South Africa experienced what is considered to be the largest documented listeriosis outbreak ever. The illness is said to have been caused by the biggest processed meats and chicken producers in the country, who also distribute to bordering countries. Their best selling products include 'polony' and processed sausages known as 'Vienna's', 'Russian's and 'kota', as well as the local iconic sandwich, the 'Gatsby'.

Professor Mark Nicol, a medical microbiologist has said that inadequate cleaning of surfaces where raw food has been placed, can spread the disease. Surfaces where raw meat is prepared must be kept separate, and any utensils used must be well washed and kept separate.

Juno Thomas of the National Institute for Communicable Diseases has stressed that using hand sanitisers is not the answer when handling food, as you will often come into contact with grease, oil, dirt and food particles which can harbour the bacteria. These tiny particles are not effectively removed by using hand sanitises as they may not reach areas behind rings or under fingernails. Washing your hands frequently, and thoroughly, with soap and hot water is essential.

LISTERIA INFECTION OCCURS ALL OVER THE WORLD. Recently, Australian rockmelon (cantaloupe) that was exported to more than ten countries, was found to be contaminated with low levels of listeriosis bacteria that had survived the washing process. A number of people were hospitalised, and seven deaths and a miscarriage were reported. In 2015, the United States experienced a multistate outbreak of listeria contaminated ice cream. Another outbreak was at a hospital in Washington State, at which milkshakes contaminated with listeria bacteria, were served to patients. In the United Kingdom ready-to-eat sandwiches of ham and cheese, and chicken, where found to be contaminated with listeria. In the Hellenic market, cooked ham and bacon cut in cubes and then packaged were said to be easily contaminated due to a great deal of handling. Belgian produced and retailed mayonnaise-based deli-salads and cooked meats were classified as medium risk foods, while smoked fish was classified as high risk.

TOXOPLASMOSIS is a single cell parasitic infection that is found worldwide, with more than 100 million people affected yearly. People with healthy immune systems are not likely to have notable symptoms. However, women that are infected with toxoplasmosis just before, or during pregnancy, when their immune system is particularly vulnerable, can result in serious problems for the new-born child, or even much later. Occasionally a new-born may have serious eye or brain damage. Symptoms in the mother may not be obvious, or seem like part of pregnancy symptoms, because they can include nausea, vomiting, diarrhoea, fever, swollen lymph nodes and an aching body.

If you are trying to become pregnant, or are already pregnant, you may want to discuss any concerns you may have with your health care provider, who may order a blood test.

The infection is spread through cysts that can sometimes be seen on raw or undercooked meat especially, venison, lamb, pork, goat and less often, beef. It can also be transmitted through contaminated water.

Toxoplasmosis is also commonly transferred when handling cat faeces.

This does not mean that cats should be avoided entirely, but their faeces (poo, poop), should be. Wash fruit and vegetables grown on open land and avoid changing cat litter. Wear disposable gloves when gardening as the soil might be contaminated with cat faeces.

Wash your hands frequently with hot soap and water for two minutes before preparing food, and wash chopping boards and knives thoroughly after preparing meats. If you are at all concerned that you may have been contaminated with toxoplasmosis, consult your doctor who can do tests to establish whether you have been infected, and provide treatment.

SALMONELLA is a major cause of food borne bacterial infections worldwide that are said to cause around 94 million cases of severe diarrhoea annually. Symptoms include fever, severe diarrhoea, cramps, nausea and vomiting: with raw and undercooked eggs amongst the most common sources of infection. Homemade mayonnaise, salad dressing and ice cream made with raw egg can be a problem, so avoid. Raw meat, chicken, dairy products and eggs can also be carriers. Cook meat well, and make sure that the eggs you eat are cooked until solid. Always wash hands thoroughly and often – with hot soap and water – not sanitisers.

NOTE: In 2017 Salmonella infection contaminated a variety of brands of infant powdered milk formula manufactured in France, resulting in a recall of more than 12 million products in 83 countries worldwide. In 2018 the US experienced a multistate outbreak of Salmonella. Fortunately there were no deaths.

SIGNS IN PREGNANCY WHEN SPEEDY FOLLOW UP IS NEEDED

POSSIBLE SIGNS OF EARLY BIRTH. If your 'water breaks' spontaneously before the 37th week of pregnancy it is known as premature rupture of membranes (PROM). Your medical advisor will evaluate all possibilities. If you're between 24 and 34 weeks they may try and delay delivery until your baby is more developed. It is also important to try and avoid infections, and you will possibly be given antibiotics to prevent infection, and steroids to assist your baby's lung development.

ECTOPIC PREGNANCY. Severe pain and bleeding in the early weeks can be a sign of an ectopic pregnancy. This is when the fertilised egg has not been embedded in the uterus, but possibly in the fallopian tube where it cannot survive.

MISCARRIAGE – which is more common than generally thought – usually occurs in the first 13 weeks, together with mild or severe backache, bright red or brown bleeding with possible blood clots and significantly, regular, birth like, contractions. **Contact your doctor immediately.**

At each check up your medical practitioner will check your blood pressure, urine, protein and other regular tests; and may also do blood clotting and kidney tests for **preeclampsia,** which is generally more common during a first pregnancy. This is a condition that can cause serious problems. Should you experience sudden significant weight gain, swelling, vision problems and severe headaches – **don't wait – contact your doctor immediately.**

PLACENTA PRAEVIA is when the placenta is implanted partially or totally over the cervix, thus obstructing the birth canal. The main symptom is painless vaginal bleeding around the 32nd week of pregnancy. In some instances the placenta moves out of the way later in pregnancy, however if this does not happen, a Caesarean delivery will likely be done.

A serious complication that may occur from the 20th week or later in pregnancy is **placenta abruption –** which means that the placenta, to which the baby's umbilical cord is attached – has become partially or completely detached from the inner wall of your uterus. Symptoms associated with this are major bleeding, a tender and very painful uterus, dizziness, clammy skin and sweating.

As a result the foetus could be deprived of oxygen as well as essential nutrients. Your waters may break; you could have pain, cramping, contractions and stiffness in your abdomen, with or without traces of blood. **Contact your doctor immediately!**

DISCOMFORT IN PREGNANCY

YOU ARE LIKELY TO FEEL THE NEED TO URINATE FREQUENTLY, especially in the very early weeks of pregnancy. This is due to the hormone hCG (human chorionic gonadotropin), and extra blood flow that makes your kidneys produce up to 25% more urine than usual. The weight of the baby on your bladder and sagging of the muscles of the pelvic floor can also increase the need to urinate. By the time you feel your baby moving in the womb, urine production should start settling down. In the last trimester you could experience stress incontinence when you sneeze, laugh or cough.

These somewhat embarrassing incidents are caused by pressure on your bladder. Wear a panty liner or pad to absorb any leakage, and don't drink fluids close to bedtime, or you could be running to the bathroom for half the night. **Note:** Your urine should be a clear pale yellow. If your urine burns, or is dark and/or cloudy, it can indicate a urinary tract infection. Contact your medical advisor.

HEADACHES during your first trimester are often due to increasing hormonal and blood levels. Later on, low blood sugar levels can also be a factor, as well as many other reasons.

Do not take any headache medication without consulting your pharmacist or doctor, as commonly used products can cause problems in the foetus and mother. See the information on Aspirin and Ibuprofen in pregnancy.

CONSTIPATION can be due to the relaxant effect of pregnancy hormones on the intestinal muscles. Make sure that you eat plenty of high fibre foods such as split peas, lentils, beans, Brussels sprouts, wheat grain cereals, bran flakes, multi-seed bread, and whole wheat pasta. Fruit, including pears, apples, raspberries, and in particular, prunes or prune juice can ease the release of retained stools. Consult your pharmacist or medical practitioner.

VARICOSE VEINS on the legs can be thin blue veins; or swollen, twisted, blue lumpy, veins that sometimes appear due to hormones and poor blood circulation in pregnancy, especially if you are overweight. Try not to stand for long periods as your blood will collect in your legs. Whenever possible, sit with your legs propped higher than your heart so that any pooled blood can drain and circulate. Compression stockings prescribed by your doctor can be helpful. Do not use elastic bandages as they can cut off blood flow.

HAEMORRHOIDS (PILES), are, quite frankly a pain in the ass. These 'very cross veins', are swollen blue veins that have enlarged due to the volume of blood flowing through them, causing bulging and anal discomfort. Speak to your pharmacist, who will advise you what the best remedy is in pregnancy.

ANAL FISSURES (tears in the anal tissue), can result from pressure while trying to have a bowel movement when constipated. You could experience bright red bleeding and pain. Your midwife or doctor will advise you regarding pain relief and may suggest a sitz bath, topical anaesthetic ointment to apply to the rectal area, nitro-glycerine ointment or other relief.

HEARTBURN can cause discomfit due to progesterone and oestrogen hormones relaxing the muscles between the stomach and oesophagus (food pipe). During pregnancy, hormones relax the food pipe, allowing food that has been swallowed to flow up again (acid reflux). This can result in inflammation and unpleasant heartburn. You will need to avoid highly spiced and strongly seasoned foods, acidic fruit, vinegar in salads, fried foods and any other substances that give you the 'burn'.

Don't eat just before going to bed, as you'll need to sit fairly upright until the food is digested, so that you don't have acid reflux flow up from your stomach. There are over the counter antacids which can be used, so ask your doctor or pharmacist to recommend a heartburn product that is safe in pregnancy.

You could experience **dizziness** as a result of changes in blood circulation. Not only do you have a far greater amount of blood circulating, but hormonal changes and reduced tone can lower your blood pressure. If you feel faint, be sure to sit down; or lie down on your left side.

LABOURED BREATHING. As your uterus enlarges to about the size of a watermelon, your lungs are pushed up, and your breathing may become somewhat laboured. If it is your first pregnancy, the baby settles into the pelvic cavity earlier, so your breathing could become easier. In future pregnancies your baby may 'drop' into the pelvic cavity later.

NOSEBLEEDS are not unusual during pregnancy. Besides the effect of hormonal changes, the tiny blood vessels on the inner surfaces of the nose are easily damaged, especially since there is an up to 50% increase in blood circulation and pressure.

HOW TO STOP A NOSEBLEED
- Lean forward and breathe through your mouth. **Note:** Leaning back will drain blood down the back of your throat.
- Sit down and pinch your nose closed just above the nostrils. Hold for at least 10 to 15 minutes.
- If possible get someone to bring you an icepack, or pack of frozen peas wrapped in a kitchen towel, to hold on your nose. The cold should help the bleeding stop.
- Don't pick any scabs, or blow your nose when the bleeding stops.

Throughout pregnancy, avoid blowing your nose vigorously. Do not use nasal sprays without informing your pharmacist that you are pregnant. **Heavy nose bleeds must be referred to your doctor.**

SLEEPING POSITIONS. Sleeping on your left side increases the amount of blood flow and nutrients that reach the placenta and the developing baby. When lying on your side put a comfortable soft pillow between your arms and another between your knees. If necessary you can put a small pillow or rolled up towel under your tummy to raise it slightly. Another way to lie comfortably during pregnancy is to put your underneath arm behind you and lie with your chest, head and uppermost arm on a pillow, putting a comfortable pillow or two between your knees.

BACKACHE is a common ailment in pregnancy due to weight gain in the mother and baby, posture problems, and pressure on the pelvis and nerves, as well as various hormonal factors that are the arbiters of physical and emotional changes. The hormone relaxin, loosens the ligaments and joints in the pelvic area in order to make them more flexible during the birth. Other physical changes in the way you stand, walk and sleep can stress bones and ligaments causing back pain.

THE RIGHT SHOES. Wear comfortable shoes with a slightly elevated heel, and whenever possible, sit with your feet resting at a comfortable height.

HOW TO AVOID STRAINING YOUR BACK

SITTING. When sitting at your desk for any length of time, you need to keep your feet resting at a comfortable height. If necessary, use a box or a brick. Occasionally, lift one foot at a time and circle it to keep the circulation flow. Never do any exercises that require you to lift your legs together, as it can put strain on your back and the abdominal muscles, and joints can be damaged.

If your chair has a high back, you can add a small cushion behind your neck. You can place a little cushion in the small of your back. Don't use large cushions because they will simply push your spine the wrong way.

AVOIDING BACK STRAIN WHEN DOING CHORES. The strain on your abdominal muscles due to the weight of the enlarged uterus can cause severe back pain, especially if your posture is not correct.

CARRYING. Keep your shoulders straight when carrying things with one hand; don't lean to one side twisting your spine. See sketch.

LIFTING AND CARRYING. When picking up a basket, or bucket from the floor do not bend forward, but keeping your back straight, bend your knees and lift. See sketch.

CORRECT STANDING POSTURE. When standing, you should be able to drop an invisible line from a point in the middle of the top of your head, straight through to your feet.

Stand as though there is a long thread running through the body, pulling up toward the ceiling.

To check your posture, stand with your feet slightly apart, squeeze your buttocks together and draw your bottom down, keeping your knees straight – the baby is now lying comfortably in the basket of your pelvis and not hanging over the edge.

Pregnant women that have to stand for prolonged periods often get cramps and varicose veins as a result of poor circulation. To prevent and alleviate these problems shift your weight from one foot to the other, curl your toes under, then release down into your shoes and rise up, lifting your heels off the ground. When standing on the same spot for long

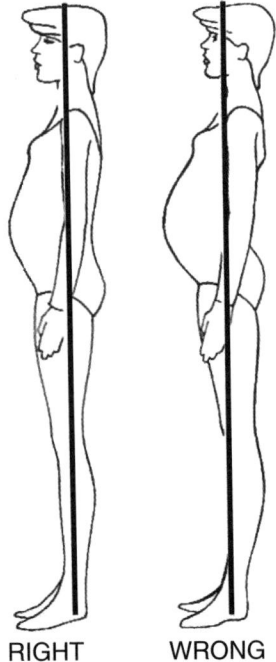

RIGHT   WRONG

periods, rest one foot on the bottom rung of a barstool approximately 10 centimetres (4 inches) off the floor.

Doing exercises under the supervision of a certified pregnancy exercise provider can be helpful in developing the right posture and easing the pain.

THE BIRTH

LABOUR is said to have started when contractions lasting about 20-30 seconds and coming regularly every 15 to 20 minutes begin. The uterus hardens, and usually there is some pain. Most medical advisors are likely to instruct you to be at the nursing home when contractions come regularly at about ten-minute intervals. In some cases, labour can be heralded by a sudden breaking of the waters. In this case it is important to get to a hospital immediately. Another sign that labour has begun is the passing of the 'plug' or operculum which is a think, pink-tinged mucous substance that has protected the mouth of the womb and is known as the 'show'.

THE FIRST STAGE OF LABOUR is the longest part, and covers the time from the start of regular contractions until the cervix (mouth of the womb) is fully stretched (dilated to 'five fingers'), so that the baby's head can pass through. This is when the ability to relax between contractions can help you to conserve energy. If you have been to antenatal classes you will have been taught breathing techniques to aid relaxation.

A **doula** is a woman who 'mothers the mother' and whose job is to give you practical assistance, encouragement and helpful support during labour and the birth. It is not to take the place of the medical experts, but to comfort you, and assist your partner – who has understandably forgotten everything he was taught at antenatal class. He will thus be able to concentrate on the birth experience with you – encouraging you and loving you – as you both marvel at the miracle that is the birth of your child…

THE SECOND STAGE OF LABOUR begins when your baby's head descends into the vagina, then moves down until it reaches the pelvic floor. Sometimes vomiting may occur during the transition between the first and second stage, and you may feel an overwhelming urge to push now. However, your midwife or gynaecologist will direct you when to hold back to ensure that your baby's birth is safe. If you have been to antenatal classes you will have been taught how to hold back the 'bearing down' urge: by panting and directing the force into the fists.

The second stage of labour may continue for too long and your medical professional may consider it better to use forceps or ventouse (vacuum) extraction to deliver the baby.

In a normal delivery 'crowning' is the stage when the baby's head first appears. As soon as the head is born, contractions stop for a short while and then begin again when the first shoulder, then the second shoulder is born until the rest of your baby slips out!

The umbilical cord will be cut, and your doctor or midwife may place your baby in your arms straight after the delivery so that you can have the unequalled experience of the first moment in your child's life…

GO TO www.baby-childcare.com TO WATCH THE FOLLOWING VIDEOS THAT ARE APPLICABLE TO CHAPTER 2

PROF CLAUDIA GRAY	Allergy prevention stategies
EMMA NUMANOGLU	Common birthing fears
DR SIMONE HONIKMAN	Anxiety disorders and pregnancy
	Management of anxiety disorders
ANEL ANNANDALE	The psychology of pregnancy
DR. NICOLA DUGMORE	Sibling rivalry
	Fathers
DR BAVI VYTHILINGUM	Prenatal depression

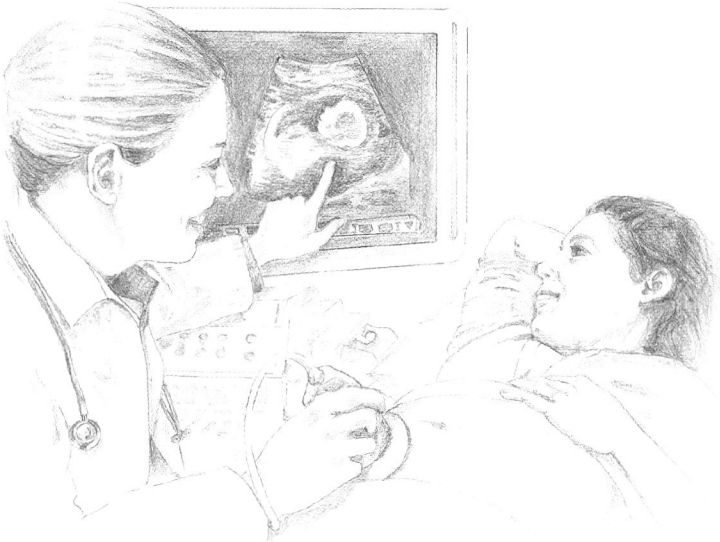

CHAPTER 3

Preparations to make before birth

DECISIONS TO MAKE BEFORE THE BIRTH

A PLACE TO NEST. Early on in your pregnancy your doctor will make a booking for you at a hospital or nursing home, or birthing centre – you may even be asked what your preferences are – but doctors usually recommend the hospital most convenient to them or to which they have some form of affiliation. If you are being seen at a public hospital you will most likely have to give birth there. You should, however, be ready with your questions. Of course, many towns have only one maternity home or hospital, or your area may only be served by a mobile unit, or you may even be having your baby at home with a midwife. If you have a choice however, this is what you should look for in the place where you are to have your baby.

CHOOSING A MATERNITY HOSPITAL

It should have good facilities for the emergency treatment of mother and child. If at all possible you should consult a child specialist (paediatrician) before the baby is due so that you can get to know him (or her) and decide if they are the kind of person you would like to care for your baby. Let him know when your baby is expected so that he or she can be on call. If circumstances permit it, you should have a paediatrician present at the birth to assess the child and if the need arises give emergency treatment.

If there is any suspicion that the baby may be born prematurely or that it will be a complicated birth, a hospital which has a neonatologist (a specialist who cares for the newborn) available would be ideal. These precautions are not necessary for most births that are straightforward and uncomplicated, but if you are particularly anxious or have had complications during pregnancy they are desirable.

Equipment such as foetal monitors can provide information that is a useful indication of the baby's welfare during labour. But their use has taken away some of the personal monitoring of mother and baby, and the usefulness of the data they provide depends on the expertise of the person reading it. These days ultrasound scanning is considered almost mandatory, although not all facilities have the equipment to do it. Scanning can tell the baby's sex, position, size and general health. It is an excellent tool in experienced hands.

If you have any choice in the matter, go for a place that has a reputation for sensitive handling of both mother and child. This could be an alternative birthing centre staffed by midwives or a hospital with every technological facility. It is the attitude to labour and birth that matters. After all giving birth is not – unless something goes wrong – a medical procedure, but a miracle of nature. You will probably never be more vulnerable than when you are in labour... at this time a gram of empathy from those around you can be worth a ton of impersonal equipment.

SHOULD THE FATHER BE AT THE BIRTH?

Having the child's father near you is probably worth ten ton of equipment – especially if he has been to antenatal or Lamaze classes with you and understands what is happening. Even if he has not been to classes, as the person closest to you and the child, he can give help and encouragement better than anyone else. So make sure the hospital allows fathers to be present at the birth, even if you are having an epidural Caesarean.

Some men are reluctant to be in on the actual birth because they are afraid they might find it unnerving or embarrassing; or even that they will make fools of themselves and may not be able to handle it. Their feelings are understandable, women have imbued the role of motherhood with such mystique for so long that men feel out of place in an area that seems sacrosanct. But once in, they cope remarkably well, and few men who participate in the birth of their child would deny it was an overwhelming and magnificent experience. An enlightened midwife or obstetrician will encourage the father to help in the actual delivery if all is well, even if you are having an epidural

Caesarean. It is no surprise that men who participate in it show a far greater interest and affinity, or paternal bonding, with their children, than those who have been left out. If the father of your child cannot, or does not want to be there a doula (trained birthing companion) can be a great help.

A WORD TO FATHERS

If you do undertake to be there during labour, this should be an act of love and commitment. You cannot spend half the time in the coffee shop reading the paper even if things seem to be slow. The mother of your child is engaged in the most momentous task imaginable. Another human being has grown with in her and is about to enter the world. Half of that new person's genetic data comes from you. Both your hopes, fantasies and fears are imbued in this event – be there in body, soul and spirit.

GOOD TO HAVE ON HAND DURING LABOUR

- Take a clean facecloth or wet wipes with you so that the birth attendant can wipe your face (giving birth is hard labour).
- Chipped ice in a flask.
- Glucose tablets for energy – you'll both need it – but check with your doctor before you have any.
- Have a camera on hand to capture the moment your baby is born.
- A doula can be of great assistance.

These are the kind of services that no machine can provide and nurses are too busy for – and that help enormously during labour.

FASHIONABLE HOSPITALS OR BIRTHING CENTRES

Fashionable hospitals are not necessarily the best. Speak to someone who has had a recent confinement there and ask these questions about their stay:

- Was the baby allowed to stay with the mother and father for a while after the birth? Sometimes there might be reasons why a baby might be taken away immediately, but unless there is an urgent need for it, the infant should be left for mother, father and child to become acquainted. After all, the child has been the centre of so many fantasies and fears for so long, that you deserve time to get to know the object of this much effort and speculation.
- If the birth was by Caesarean section, or the baby was premature, was the mother shown the baby as soon as it was feasible, and was she encouraged to touch the child, even if it was in an incubator?
- Do babies 'room in' with the mother? These days, rooming in with the mother has virtually become the norm. Although you may feel that all you want after the birth is

to rest for a week, especially if it is your second child and you know what is ahead of you, there is a good deal of evidence to support the idea that keeping the baby with the mother promotes the process of attachment or 'bonding'.

BONDING

THE TIE THAT BINDS. In the animal world, infants removed from their mothers straight after birth are likely to be rejected if they are returned later. While a mother would not reject her baby consciously, early contact with her infant appears to strengthen the mother's 'identification' with her baby and fosters nurturing. This initial attachment between mother and child is the start of a lifelong relationship. Mothers of premature babies often feel as though the baby is not theirs but 'belongs' to the nursing staff. This is mainly because the mother has not gone through the process of getting to know her child through touch and through nurturing her needs. A good hospital does not isolate mothers from their premature babies but encourages as much physical interaction as possible.

ROOMING IN

Rooming in allows the mother to feed on demand so breastfeeding can become established. She also gets to know her baby's behaviour patterns sooner than if she were isolated from her except for feeds. The main disadvantage of rooming in is that the mother may get very little chance to rest, particularly at night.

These days the normal hospital stay is short, and babies are almost always kept with their mothers. The other, somewhat outdated, method of caring for babies in the hospital is the communal nursery in which babies are kept and brought to the mother only for feeds, usually every four hours. Some of the disadvantages of this system, besides hindering bonding and breastfeeding, lie in the greater risk of cross-infection in the nursery. There is also only a slim chance of establishing breastfeeding successfully, since the four hourly routine is not enough to get the milk flow going, and the baby is likely to have cried herself asleep and be too exhausted to suck properly. You can get around this, however, if you are allowed to go to the nursery and feed your baby whenever necessary. Talk to the person in charge; and if you are sure that this will be strictly adhered to, you will have overcome some of the disadvantages of the communal nursery.

If you prefer privacy, find out if the hospital has private rooms. Many women enjoy the camaraderie that develops amongst new mothers sharing a room, but if you would rather be alone, make sure you can be accommodated. A private room may also make it easier for you to receive visitors. And these days, some rooms have an extra bed allowing the father to stay throughout!

SORT THESE THINGS OUT BEFOREHAND

- Some hospitals are still sticky about allowing children into the wards, but make sure there are facilities for you to see your other children during your stay, or they may think you have disappeared forever. They should also be able to see the baby, in order to make the adjustment of meeting their new sibling and having you home all at once, a little easier.

- If you want to have your son circumcised (*see p. 446*) make sure the hospital has the facilities for doing so.

- If you do not wish to have any of the routine procedures done, such as shaving of pubic hair, get permission from your doctor and tell the chief nurse so that you do not have a confrontation when you are in labour. Clear any other 'unusual' requests beforehand such as wanting a waterbirth.

- If you are having an epidural for pain relief the doctor who is going to administer it should be on call, and should preferably have met with you beforehand to discuss it.

- If you want a water birth, or active birth, it should be arranged at this meeting. Explain that you have cleared your requests with your doctor and try and get him or her to write them on your card so that there is some record of your arrangements.

- You may want to stipulate that you want an entirely 'natural' birth and that no procedures such as an episiotomy should be done. It is a good idea to discuss all this beforehand with your doctor or midwife, but your goal should not be a birth according to a preset definition of what is desirable or 'natural', but the birth of a healthy baby regardless of what it takes. Giving birth is a time when the best laid plans may go awry. Make allowance in your mind for this and do not feel guilty or a failure if events do not meet your own expectations. The birth is only one part of the process of becoming a mother.

- You will be given a list of items to bring with you to the nursing home. Find out if necessities such as sanitary pads are charged for as extras. You are often given a bag of necessities by the hospital for which you are charged. If you would rather make up your own pack, ask for a list and buy your own beforehand. Adhesive pads are now available in maternity size, but you will have to use the sterile hospital pads for the first few days.

- Once you have decided on a place, phone them beforehand and ask to be shown around so that you can orientate yourself before the big day. While there, find out if there is a night entrance, and make sure you know where it is. You may also be able to fill in pre-admission forms so that you do not have to do this when you are in labour.

CIRCUMCISION

One of the other questions that should be settled before you give birth is whether you want your baby to be circumcised if it is a boy. Consult your doctor and discuss it fully. Many men who have been circumcised are strongly in favour of their sons following suit. Arguments such as what the boy's reaction will be if he notices that he is different from his father arise. The trend recently has been not to circumcise except for religious reasons, but new medical reasons are coming into consideration. See the section on circumcision (*p. 446*) and make your decision.

WHY YOU SHOULD CONSIDER BREASTFEEDING

An important issue you must decide on is whether you intend breastfeeding your baby. Most hospitals, in particular those designated as 'baby friendly', and doctors as well as nurses have a keen awareness of its value and try to encourage it, but unless you have the right kind of help and information it may not be easy. If you are not sure why you should try and what it is about, consider the following:

- Colostrum and mature breastmilk contain antibodies against diseases that the mother has had, or has been inoculated against. These will most likely include gastroenteritis, whooping cough, polio, tetanus, flu and other infectious diseases. Since your baby's own immune responses only start working months later or when the child is immunised, knowing that she is protected helps provide valuable peace of mind. You may still worry about her not getting enough milk, about sleeping patterns and colic, but at least you will know that whatever the problem may be, a lot of nasty possibilities have been lessened because you are breastfeeding.
- Cows' milk can be altered to approximate breastmilk in the ratio of fats to protein and the number of vitamins and minerals, but the way these are programmed to function in breastmilk differs from cows' milk and cannot be altered except superficially. Scientists are slowly unravelling the meaning of these differences and what is coming to light makes breastmilk even more remarkable than was previously imagined. It appears that the biological cycle which starts at conception does not end at birth, but should continue with breastfeeding to be satisfactorily completed.
- Colostrum, the yellow substance that is available before your milk comes in, is a valuable food and also has a laxative effect helping to clear the baby's intestine of meconium, the sticky, tar-like substance that it contains at birth. It also breaks down mucus that can interfere with breathing in the early weeks.
- The protein in breastmilk is whey predominant which makes it more digestible.
- Enzymes such as lipase and amylase enhance absorption of many vitamins and trace elements.
- From the preventive angle, the reasons for breastfeeding are impressive and convincing, particularly in areas where good hygiene is difficult to maintain (and this includes any place where hot weather allows germs to multiply quickly). Gastroenteritis, a diarrhoeal disease which results in the death of thousands of babies every year, is less likely if the mother breastfeeds.

- The organisms which cause the illness are prevented from multiplying by factors known as macrophages and lysozymes (cells that 'eat' bacteria), which are found in breastmilk. The acid pH of breastmilk, too, results in different flora (digestive organisms) in the intestines of breast fed babies, making the growth of dangerous bacteria difficult.
- Respiratory diseases and gastric disturbances such as colic are also less frequent in breast fed babies.
- Allergy to cows' milk and its derivatives can cause endless problems, expense and ill health in an infant. Except in the very rare conditions such as galactosaemia, and congenital primary lactose intolerance, babies are always able to tolerate mother's milk. (In secondary lactose intolerance caused by an infection that damages the lining of the baby's gut, healing is likely to be far sooner than if she was bottle fed).
- New research indicates that the higher cholesterol levels in breastmilk may accustom the body to coping with it in some way, so protecting against future heart disease. Studies have shown that adults who had been breast fed for six months showed significantly lower serum cholesterol levels than those who were breast fed for two months or less.
- The incidence of coronary artery disease is lower in people who were breast fed. The risk of developing insulin dependent diabetes is also lessened.
- Because nutrients in breastmilk are utilised efficiently and the baby is not encouraged to take more than she needs, extra fat cells are unlikely to develop in infancy.
- The sudden infant death syndrome is thought to be less common amongst breast fed babies.
- Because breastmilk contains the ideal balance of nutrients to fluid there is little danger of convulsions due to an imbalance of calcium, sodium or other minerals.
- Mistakes in the making up of formula are common and can have serious consequences. Non-sterile bottles, even in hospitals can be the cause of serious illness in babies.
- For the mother, other pluses in favour of breastfeeding include the fact that every time the baby sucks, the uterus contracts so that it returns to its usual size more quickly and her body returns to normal sooner.
- Fat accumulated during pregnancy is easier to get rid of because breastfeeding burns kilojoules.
- Breast fed babies are unlikely to suffer from constipation and their stools do not have an unpleasant smell.
- Nappy rash is unlikely to be severe and thrush is less common.
- From the convenience point of view, breastmilk requires no preparation, and it is always available and at the right temperature.
- Children who have been breast fed for more than three months have been shown to have half as much tooth decay as bottle fed babies.

- Malocclusions of the jaw and faulty mouth development that result in misplaced teeth are higher in bottle fed babies, possibly due to the abnormal sucking and swallowing mechanism promoted by bottle feeding. However, breastfeeding rather than bottle feeding, is not a certain way to prevent malocclusions (misshaped teeth), as there are a number of other causes.
- Breastfeeding is much cheaper than formula, even taking into account the slightly increased amounts of food the mother needs.
- The amino acids which make up proteins are significantly different in breastmilk and are thought to promote brain development in the first year.
- Although small, the iron content in breastmilk is bound to the protein lactoferrin which enables it to be absorbed easily. Lactoferrin also works as an antibacterial agent, effectively 'starving' germs.
- Above all, breastfeeding promotes an intimate relationship between mother and child. Few mothers who have spent hours nursing their baby can fail to get to know their child and respond to her needs.

BREASTFEEDING – FOR AND AGAINST

Even if all the philosophical, psychological and medical reasons for breastfeeding don't impress you, do it simply for the peace of mind of knowing your baby is protected against many diseases. That it is convenient, and for the pleasure you will get after any initial problems have been sorted out. There is nothing quite like the feeling that comes from having a tiny head snuggled close against you, eyes closed, jaw moving rhythmically while emitting primal sounds of satisfaction… it's the stuff that feeds the myth of blissful motherhood. It is marvellous – there are few experiences to equal it – but it can involve tears and toil.

Be prepared, if you have made up your mind to breast feed, for well meaning 'friends' and relatives who may try to discourage you. Women who have not breast fed are often threatened by, or feel guilty subconsciously, and you can be put off if you pay attention to their talk. Even some doctors may have ambivalent views, either because their wife did not breast feed, or because they do not want to be disturbed by too many calls asking for help on a subject they may not know much about.

But the sentiment towards the promotion of breastfeeding is so strong today that you should have plenty of positive reaction to counterbalance any flack you may get.

One person whose support is vital for successful breastfeeding is the child's father. If he is in favour you are well away. The 'breastfeeding father' must be prepared to share proprietary rights over his wife with his child. The man who is jealous of the time and attention his wife gives their child is short-sighted. After all, anything that will benefit the baby must in the final analysis, make life better for the whole family.

Breastfeeding does not have any disadvantages for the baby; unless there are dangerous substances in the milk – these include untreated HIV infection and certain drugs. It does however impose strictures on the mother, since the baby is entirely dependent on her except for the odd bottle of formula or expressed breastmilk.

The father cannot help with feeding (especially at night), and if the mother does not receive proper help when problems arise, she could develop an abscess or become tense and frustrated.

One of the reasons why women sometimes reject the idea of breastfeeding is that they are afraid that it will ruin their breast shape. Being a lactating mother means that you will have to put up with soggy breasts, but not necessarily sagging breasts. You should wear a well-fitting bra from the time your breasts begin to enlarge during pregnancy to prevent Cooper's droop even if you don't breastfeed.

Women who live in deprived circumstances – without access to clean water and sanitation for example – can not do anything more valuable than to breast feed.

For some women breastfeeding has an animalistic quality about it that makes them uncomfortable and possibly even slightly revolted. In this case, there is no point in pursuing a practice that may hinder the mother-child relationship rather than benefit it.

If you cannot, or definitely do not want to breast feed, do not feel guilty. There are many ways to nurture your child through bottle feeding. (*See pp. 156-184*)

PHYSICAL REQUIREMENTS FOR BREASTFEEDING

TOUGHENING OR CONDITIONING THE NIPPLES. There is no real need to toughen or condition your nipples for breastfeeding, and certain practices can be harmful. Do not brush alcohol, spirits, cologne or anything similar on your nipples to 'toughen' them. It will just dry them out, making them more likely to crack. Wash with water only as soap can be drying.

Creams and lotions are not necessary, and can interfere with the normal secretions from tiny glands in the areola that lubricate the nipples.

Do not roll or pull the nipples vigorously towards the end of pregnancy as it can stimulate contractions through the release of hormones.

CORRECTING FLAT OR INVERTED NIPPLES. Flat nipples protrude only slightly from the contour of the breast, while inverted nipples turn inwards. Although most women's nipples stand out more as pregnancy progresses, some women have persistently

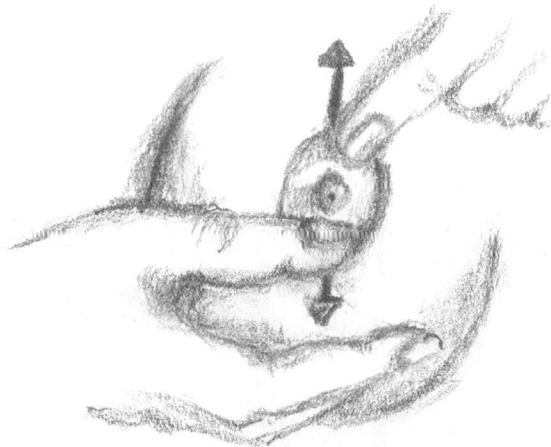

Exercise for inverted nipples

inverted nipples that require help to protrude sufficiently for the baby to latch on. This is best done before the birth. An exercise known as the Hoffman technique can help, as can wearing a glass or plastic breast shell or shield during pregnancy. A baby who sucks vigorously will often improve the nipples.

HOFFMAN TECHNIQUE

From about the 34th week of pregnancy do the following exercise five times on each side, once a day (in your bath perhaps), and you should see a marked improvement in inverted or flat nipples by the time the baby is born.

With your thumb and forefinger as shown in the sketch, stretch gently, dragging outwards from the nipple. Do this five times working your way around the nipple and away from the brown area (areola). This exercise has the effect of loosening the connective tissue that holds the nipples in.

BREAST SHIELDS. Wearing a breast shield for a few hours every day is also effective in drawing out the nipple. The shield is worn inside the bra and has a hole in the middle. The shield exerts pressure on the areola and the nipple is drawn towards the hole making the nipple protrude. A newer device works on a suction pump action to draw the nipple out. Both are obtainable from pharmacies, medical supply companies, or baby speciality stores.

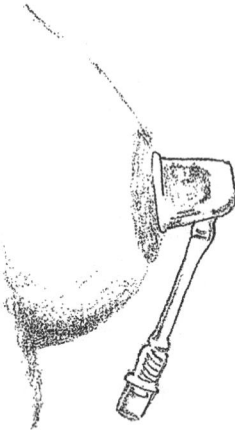

This is a device that helps draw out inverted nipples. It should be used before, or during pregnancy up to the last two months

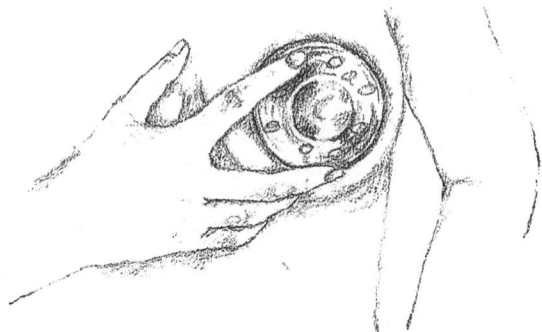

Breast shield

COLOSTRUM. You may find a yellowish substance secreted from the nipples during pregnancy, especially in the last few weeks. This is called colostrum and you can express it by squeezing gently around the sinuses on the outer edge of the areola, although this is not really necessary except to familiarise you with the technique of expressing milk. If you do not produce colostrum during pregnancy, it does not mean that you will not produce milk. Any colostrum on the nipples should be washed off with plain water (soap is drying).

BREAST SIZE. The size of your breasts is no indication of the amount of milk you will produce. Large breasts are made of fat tissue, not milk ducts and this can mean less milk is made. Women who have had plastic surgery to enlarge their breasts are often able to breast feed if the nipples have not been repositioned or the ducts cut. An operation to reduce the size of the breasts makes it more difficult. (*See p. 126*)

CAESAREAN SECTION. If you know you are having a Caesarean, tell your doctor that you intend breastfeeding so that you are not given an injection to stop your milk without your being aware of it. (*See p. 120 Breastfeeding after a Caesarean.*)

WHAT TO DO BEFORE THE BIRTH TO SAVE YOUR SANITY AFTERWARDS

DOMESTIC HELP. Depending on your lifestyle and where you live, or even if you think you will not need a domestic helper, consider looking into the various options before the birth. If you are lucky enough to have domestic help, discuss the forthcoming arrival with her and make her duties and remuneration clear. Having someone who can keep the house or apartment in order is a great luxury, especially when you have a new born baby.

If you don't have someone to help in the house, talk to friends who have a domestic helper and take the details. There are also numerous websites that have listings of women seeking domestic helper positions who may be suitable. As in all work settings, you will need someone that has experience and a good work reference. You will also need time to have a few trial runs before you hire somebody that suits your needs the best. There is nothing like another pair of willing hands when you have a new baby, so treasure them.

Having someone who can do the chores will give you a chance to be close to your baby and get used to the huge new experience of motherhood. You will also, hopefully, be able to rest so that you can give your system time to catch up with the physical changes.

One of the areas that will need good help, is doing the laundry. Especially because washing baby clothes have different requirements than that of adults. Baby clothes should be washed separately as a baby's skin is very sensitive, and new clothes may be pretty, but they will have been exposed to many hands and a variety of products that contain skin irritants. Stick with pH-neutral, non-soap cleansers (pH neutral is 7);

and avoid sodium laurel sulphate and anything that contains fragrance. There's a lot of time before she needs perfume! And, whoever washes the baby clothes should wash her/his hands first.

NURSES/NANNIES/AU PAIRS. The other kind of help you may consider is that of a trained person who will come either during the day or night, or live in and be on call round the clock. This service is very expensive, and if she is allowed to take over completely it could disturb the emerging mother/child relationship. On the other hand, if you are terribly nervous, or not well, or the baby is ill, a trained person could be of great help. It is worth finding out all particulars from an agency anyway, and to have them on hand in case you need them.

RELATIONS. You may find that a member of your family offers to come and lend a hand in the early weeks. This can be a delicate issue unless you have a particularly fine rapport with her. You will probably feel awkward taking a nap or playing with your baby while she cleans the house, yet the last thing you want anyone to do is take over the care of the baby while you clean the house. You will feel much happier if you know you have paid someone to peel the potatoes and clean the bath.

New mothers are also the most sensitive of creatures and accepting advice no matter how good or well meant, is difficult when you are in an emotional turmoil. However, if you are really close to your mother or mother-in-law or whoever offers – set a tactful limit on her stay beforehand. If it isn't working well at least you will be able to look forward to the date of departure, and if it is a success you can always persuade her to stay a while longer. New mothers also have a great need to be 'mothered' themselves. In the best of circumstances this will be the case between mother and daughter, and the new baby. New fathers can also do with tender loving care.

CARING FOR SIBLINGS WHILE YOU ARE AWAY. If you have other children who need to be looked after while you are in hospital – and your partner cannot get time off, although these days paternal leave is standard – get someone they know to come to the house. Children need the emotional security familiar surroundings provide, especially when their life is disrupted by their mother's absence and the arrival of the new baby.

Fortunately, some companies are realising the value of paternity leave, and many fathers today are highly involved in all aspects of caring for their children. Whatever your reality, do not underestimate the value of enlisting all the help and time off you can get.

FILL THE FREEZER. On the totally practical side, you should stock up with cleaning materials for at least six weeks if possible, and fill your freezer with as many homemade or convenience meals as you possibly can. If you can heat and eat in those early weeks, you will be so grateful that at least one burden is taken care of. Stock up on disposable plates as well if you do not have a dishwasher. Baby shower gift idea: ask your friends to make their favourite dish for your 'freezer fund'.

WHAT YOU NEED FOR BREASTFEEDING

CHAIR. Relaxation is vital when breastfeeding, especially before you gain confidence. You will need a comfortable chair or you will become tense from the strain of trying to support the baby correctly. The chair should be low and it should have an armrest able to accommodate a cushion for you to rest your arms on while you hold the baby. An armchair or rocking chair with an adjustable back and footrest is ideal, but any chair that is comfortable will do. A footstool is a great help.

NURSING/MATERNITY BRAS. It is not always easy to predict what size you will be when you are feeding, so don't buy a feeding bra before the birth. Wait and see what size you settle into about three weeks after the birth. Until then a comfortable ordinary bra that does not constrict will do. Breastfeeding bras come in various styles. Some have a flap that opens downwards on each cup, but although convenient, the fabric around the cup can constrict the breasts and cause congestion. Another type hooks in the centre front, opening completely, and this is better. There are also stretch bras' that are designed for maternity and breastfeeding use which are wire free, seam-free and can provide good comfort and support.

Make sure there is no plastic lining (if there is, remove it) because this can keep your nipples damp. Choose cotton or a cotton mixture fabric that is cooler and absorbs moisture better. The straps should be wide or they will cut into your shoulders, and there should be an elastic gusset under the arms for expansion as your breasts fill. You will need three bras, one to wear, one in the wash and one ready to wear.

NURSING/BREAST PADS. Breast pads are necessary to stop leaks from spoiling your clothes. Packs of disposable pads are available. Don't use anything with a plastic backing as it will keep the nipples damp and prevent air from circulating, making them soft and tender. There is also a vast choice of products for use during breastfeeding/ nursing. Some products have washable cotton pads, others have a contour shape with a multi-layered surface for absorbency. Then there are bamboo reusable nursing pads that are said to be leak free, ultra-soft, waterproof, hypoallergenic pads for when you are breastfeeding. These are but a snippet of the variety available. Make choices carefully, and discuss with your breastfeeding advisor if possible, who will tell you what would work best for your needs.

NIGHTIES. You will need front-fastening nighties for the nursing home and it is wise to plan your post-maternity clothes with easy access to the milk bar.

PREPARING A PLACE FOR THE BABY AND CHOOSING EQUIPMENT

Most women feel well and energetic in the middle period of their pregnancy and this is a good time to get things ready. Even if you are superstitious it is sensible to plan beforehand.

WHERE WILL THE BABY SLEEP? There is something to be said for keeping the baby in your room for the first month or two, especially at night, when you want to get the whole feeding performance done with as little disruption of your sleep as possible.

But if the presence of the little stranger is going to make you listen nervously to every grunt she makes and tiny babies do make an awful lot of old man snuffling and wheezing noises in their sleep; then you will all be better off if you can give her a separate place to sleep. It doesn't have to be a room of her own, just somewhere out of draughts and within hearing.

THE NURSERY. If you are going to set up a nursery, you will want everything of the best. Luckily the best need not be the most expensive, and you can often get the top results by being inventive and practical.

Basically a baby needs something to sleep in. Moses baskets or wooden cradles allow the air to circulate and in this regard are preferable to plastic. But a carry cot (bassinet / cradle), pram, or even a drawer, will do until the child outgrows it and moves to a cot / crib. The room should be warm and draught free and you will need a suitable surface to use as a changing area, and space for clothes and toiletry items.

STORAGE. Baby compactums with drawers and a bath that folds away are tempting, but expensive, and unless you have money to spare you will be better off spending your money on something that will be useful when the baby grows up. Some baby compactums are dangerous. *See www.cpsc.gov/*

If you don't have a built-in cupboard to store nappies and baby clothes, an inexpensive chest of drawers in unpainted pine or similar wood can be made to look attractive quite easily.

CHANGING TABLE AND BATH. A place to change and bath the baby is essential and should be at elbow height to avoid back strain. Although you can wash your young baby in the sink it is better to get a washtub or baby bath. If you do not have a bath stand you can rest the bath on top of a sturdy table. If there is a bed or divan in the room you can use that for changing the baby if you work sitting down, but make sure the cover is washable.

When planning the nursery layout think of the order in which you will be doing things and plan for convenience. Everything you need should be within reach so you do not have to leave the baby for an instant! Babies learn to roll over suddenly and without warning.

When choosing a changing table make certain it is sturdy and has a guard rail of at least 10cm or 4 inches around four sides. If the changing mat is thicker than 4cm the safety rail should be higher. Place the table against a wall, not a window.

CHANGING MAT. You will need a covered changing mat that fits the size of the surface you will be using it on, preferably not less than 100cm × 75cm. A mat with a raised edge of at least 10cm is best.

BABY PRAMS/PUSHCHAIRS/CRIBS/COTS

New born babies usually sleep in a pram, crib, bassinet or carry cot. If your baby is going to sleep in a pram, you will have the advantage of being able to rock or at least move it rhythmically which is soothing.

A crib or basket is likely to be made of wicker and left plain or covered in fabric. It may be on a wheeled base or have handles for carrying. A carry cot is usually made of plastic and is similar to the body of a pram with handles for carrying. Optional extras may include a wheeled base or wheels that convert it into a baby pram.

What you choose depends on your taste and pocket. Covered wicker cribs are pretty and romantic, but they are soon outgrown and dust in the fabric can cause allergies. Moses baskets are made of softer cane and can be carried around; they are also useful afterwards, but cannot be secured in the car.

It is an advantage to have a carry cot or crib that you can take the baby about in while she is asleep, especially if it fits into a car easily. If the baby will be travelling in the car while lying in a carry cot, you should have a special safety harness that is attached to the car and buckles over the cot to keep it secure.

If you choose a pram/baby carriage that converts into a pushchair and has a lift-off carry cot, you have probably got the most practical item. When buying a pram go for the best you can afford – there is always a market for it later on – or start with a good second-hand one.

POINTS TO LOOK FOR WHEN BUYING A PRAM/PUSHCHAIR/STROLLER

- Make sure the chassis folds easily and will fit into your car, and is easily manouverable on stairs. The sides should be high enough to prevent an active infant getting a leg over and toppling out.
- It should be well balanced so that it does not tip easily.

A 'baby buggy' fold-up pushchair or stroller is light, compact, and handy if you are going to be travelling on buses and trains a lot. You can put your baby in it from about six months or earlier if you wedge a small cushion in the back so that she does not sit in a slumped position. Be sure that she is strapped in well.

NOTE: It is important to open the push chair completely before you put the baby in it, as children have caught the tip of their fingers in the frame as it is pulled open.

THE COT OR CRIB. Once a baby grows too big to sleep in the pram or bassinet – some time between three and six months – the next step is usually a cot/crib. The best buy is a large, sturdy cot that will accommodate the child for the first few years. International specifications for cot safety standards have been compiled, and these are some of the points to look for:

- A heavy cot/crib that cannot be moved about by an active toddler bouncing up and down against the rails. In this way the child could manoeuvre the cot into a potentially dangerous position, for instance within reach of medicines, glass and so on.
- The mechanism on which the sides slide up and down should not be able to be manipulated by a child. This mechanism should not be able to fold open as serious accidents have occurred. See www.cpsc.gov/
- There should also be nothing on which the child could hook her clothes. The horror of the child who is strangled by her clothes hooking on to an exposed bit of metal or wood was tragically common before design changes were demanded. If you make sure of no other safety factor, be sure to preclude this danger.
- The slats should not be too wide apart. Safety regulations suggest a maximum space of 7cm or 2½ inches. The danger here is that children have the uncanny knack of getting into amazing situations such as putting their heads through bars and not being able to get them out again.
- Cots with net sides are not suitable because legs and arms are apt to get hooked in the netting and the child could climb out.
- Fastening devices for the cot's dropside should be at least 850mm apart to prevent the child from lowering it unaided.
- With the dropside lowered, the depth of the cot should be at least 250mm; with the dropside raised it should be at least 600mm.

- If castors are fitted they should be fitted on two legs only; or if fitted on all legs at least two should be capable of being locked.
- No horizontal openings, slots or rails that could provide a foothold for a child to climb out of the cot should be included in the design.
- All metal parts should be corrosion resistant.
- These days many cots have a wooden base with holes in it for air circulation. You will need to check under the mattress for damp during usage, as mould can develop.
- The other important point to watch out for is lead-based paint, particularly if you are buying second-hand equipment. The teething eight-month-old will gnaw anything including the woodwork. New items should not present a danger theoretically, but remember to ask for non-toxic, lead-free paint when doing a repaint job. If you are not sure what paint has been used and you are repainting, you should not sandpaper or strip woodwork if you are pregnant. Lead poisoning is insidious and cumulative.
- The mattress should be washable, firm and made of non-allergenic material and should fit snugly so that there is no space between it and the sides of the cot. Avoid coir or feather type mattresses as they commonly cause allergies.
- A special technique in which the mattress is wrapped in clear polythene is claimed to prevent cot death. There is no conclusive evidence however. (*See p. 496.*)
- Avoid second-hand mattresses.
- Cot units of some compactums have proved to be dangerous, as are drop side cots.

SAFETY ADVICE. See also the Consumer Safety Commission of the United States *www.cpsc.gov*

TO MAKE UP A PRAM/BASSINET. If you are not using high quality disposable nappies, that do not leak, cover the lower three quarters of the mattress with a flannel-backed waterproof sheets. Now cover the whole mattress with a fitted sheet, or a smooth cloth nappy (*see nappies p. 51*), or use an adult sized pillow slip. Fitted cot or pram sheets are also available. Babies spit up a lot and lying in a damp patch for even a short time can give your baby a rash so stretch a one-way nappy liner under the head area well, tucking and pinning securely under the mattress.

PILLOWS/CUSHIONS. Never use a pillow for a baby or young child. Even a safety pillow can smother, so avoid altogether. Soft baby cushions that are loosely filled with plastic pellets or beads are extremely dangerous and have been responsible for a number of babies suffocating.

SHAPED BABY SUPPORT CUSHIONS. These hold the baby in place when lying on her back. They are not a necessity and will soon be outgrown.

BLANKETS. Cotton wrapping or receiving blankets can be used to cover the baby, followed by a blanket or two if necessary. (*See p. 50.*) Duvets are potentially dangerous and are not recommended as they can slip up over the baby's head, and also cause overheating.

COT BUMPERS. Although it is not necessary, you can use a 'bumper' to pad the inside of the cot to make it cosier when the baby is small and prevent the child from bumping her head against the slats. Make sure it is well fastened to the rails.

MOSQUITO NETS. In tropical or high insect areas, a net to cover the baby's sleeping place is useful to protect against flies and mosquitoes. In malaria areas it is essential. It may also act as a deterrent if you have a cat.

INFANT SEATS/BABY CHAIRS. Infant seats are a good way of keeping your baby with you when you are busy and the upright position helps get the winds up and stops a lot of the 'posseting' or spitting up of milk that is common after a feed. No safety standards have been set so you need to be extra careful when making a choice.

- Look for a wide base so it doesn't tip easily.
- It should have a strap to secure the baby, and there should be a rubber fitted to the base so that it does not slip. If not, glue a piece of rubber to the base.
- The very simple plastic types do not have a padded surface and this makes the baby sit in a slumped position. The more costly type is padded and has a deep seat which is far better.

Baby chair

WARNING: Never use these seats as a substitute for a car seat. Keep the seat on the floor as soon as your baby becomes active to help prevent accidents.

BABY CARRIERS. A baby carrier, pouch or sling that you wear on your back, side or front is an excellent way of keeping your baby near you while leaving your hands free. Front carriers/slings are for younger babies and are generally outgrown after the first three months.

Choose a type that has good support and will not cut into your shoulders when it has a weight in it. The baby should be well supported especially at the back and head. Leg holes should not be so large that the baby could slip through. Any aluminium parts should be padded so that they do not chafe.

Low sided moulded baby chairs for sitting in have been banned for sale in the USA after claims that they can cause injury if they are placed on a table or countertop: should the baby arch her back she could fall out onto the floor.

HIGH CHAIRS. High chairs are useful from around six months when the baby is able to sit properly. Although not a necessity, they can be useful. Make sure the chair does not overbalance easily even if the child stands up, and most importantly, it should have a harness to strap the baby as falls are the greatest danger (you can buy these separately). Check for safety as many high chair styles have been proven to be dangerous. *See www.cpsc.gov/*

Baby carrier

The distance between the seat and the top of the backrest should be more than 350mm. Some high chairs can be converted into a low chair with a tray or table. If your baby gets used to having her meals in her high chair it can make things easier for you as she will not be able to run around at mealtimes. You can also draw the high chair up to the table so that she can be with the family at meal times.

For outings a chair that locks onto a table is useful. Make sure the table is heavy enough to support the chair and that the child's feet do not touch anything that can be used to push against as she may then be able to dislodge the chair.

WALKING RINGS AND BOUNCERS. Despite their popularity with mothers and babies, walking rings, and bouncers that hang from a door-frame are **not recommended** and are banned in some countries. (*See p. 231.*)

CHOOSING A LAYETTE

Buying baby clothes is exciting and fun, but do not get carried away and spend money needlessly – you will be glad you bought sensibly later on.

POINTS TO REMEMBER WHEN BUYING A LAYETTE

- Baby garments should be safe, with no ribbons or cords that could choke; and they should be easy to put on – the less fussing to get the garment on and off, the better.
- Snap closures or zips down the front, or down the legs make changing easier, than back closures.
- Clothes should be easy to launder – preferably in the washing machine – and they should not stretch or shrink with frequent washing. Go for pure cotton, or the newer mixtures of cotton and polyester, or cotton and wool. Wool breathes well and absorbs moisture but can shrink and discolour unless carefully handled. And, some babies are allergic to wool. Drip-dry fabrics save you ironing sheets and other baby items.

BASIC LAYETTE. The items specified will cover the needs of a winter baby adequately, but you need not buy all the items at once as you will most likely receive some gifts as well. Summer babies need the same basic layette but buy some of the items with short sleeves and short pants. Think in terms of dressing your baby in one more layer of clothing than you would wear.

- 2-6 second size vests or T-shirts with envelope neck or wrap-over closing. Vests that have snap closures at the crotch prevent the garment from creeping up.
- 3-4 onesies, stretch suits, or rompers in pure cotton, or cotton mixture. Two first and 2 second size. These all-in-one outfits have almost become a uniform for babies, and many mothers use them from birth.

- Some mothers prefer to put a tiny baby in the classic nightie and booties or top and leggings. It is a little easier to change the nappy and the whole outfit does not have to be removed if it becomes damp.
- If you use stretch suits make sure they do not constrict the child's feet as she grows. Should this happen, cut the foot end off the garment and hem to give it longer life. Check the shape of leggings and other garments. Babies have large tummies and there should not be tight elastic at the waist. Some leggings have tiny shaped feet. Avoid!
- 4 unisex 'nighties' (if you don't use stretch suits or rompers)
- 2-3 matinée jackets or baby sweaters. Hand knitted or machine knitted in cotton, synthetic mixture or wool.
- 3-4 cotton knit tops with separate leggings.
- 4 large towelling bibs.
- 4 pairs socks or booties.
- 1-3 knitted bonnets for winter outings in very cold areas.
- 2-3 wrapping (receiving) blankets in cotton.
- 1 large knitted shawl (optional).
- 3 large towels (preferably with hoods).
- 2-3 blankets. Cellular wool or pure cotton is light and warm. Don't get anything fluffy as babies soon get the hang of picking at them and end up with a fistful of fluff.

For information about nappies see below.

Pram/carry cot sheets can be made from a large used sheet (it will be softer and all the starch will be washed out, but do wash again in pure soap). Simply cut to size leaving a good bit to tuck under, and hem all round. Or, use a large pillow case to cover the mattress. Or use bought fitted sheets. Do not use a pillow.

NAPPIES (DIAPERS)

THE BOTTOM LINE. By the time your baby outgrows them she is likely to have had more than 4 000 nappy changes, so you can see why the subject deserves a good airing. There are several alternative methods of dealing with this mammoth task so weigh up your priorities and particular circumstances before you decide what is best for you.

CONSIDER THE FOLLOWING BEFORE PURCHASING

Cloth nappies do not pose a direct threat to the environment, are less expensive, and can be used for other purposes such as wiping up possets, or protecting your clothes when burping the baby. But they do involve far more labour. Ecologically, both cloth and disposable nappies affect the environment negatively in different ways. Chlorine free disposable nappies are available at some outlets, but are more expensive.

DISPOSABLE NAPPIES. Many mothers use disposables these days for convenience. Disposable nappies keep the baby's skin dry because the urine forms a gel once it goes through to the thickened part of the nappy. The more expensive the nappy the more effective this is likely to be. If the nappy has been soiled flush the soiling away and fold the nappy closed, before disposing with the garbage. Do not flush nappies down the toilet as this can block the system. Although more expensive than fabric nappies, disposables have the advantage that you can buy as needed or you can keep them for travelling or other special occasions. Disposables are also available for preterm babies and for swimming and potty training.

TOWELLING CLOTH NAPPIES. Cloth nappies come in three basic types: Towelling, twill-back and shaped cloth.

Terry cloth or towelling nappies are made from pure cotton or cotton and viscose. Cotton and hemp, or cotton and bamboo are newer alternatives. Cloth nappies are usually squares approximately 60cm × 60cm.

SHAPED CLOTH NAPPIES. Specially shaped with a thicker portion at the crotch. Sometimes a disposable pad is inserted into a pouch in the crotch section.

TWILLBACK CLOTH NAPPIES. Twillback nappies are made from woven cotton, twilled so that they are smooth on one side and mechanically fluffed on the other. They absorb well, and will last a long time if they are made from pure cotton. Twillback nappies are ideal for young babies as they are not as bulky as towelling and do not become hard after repeated washing. Twillback nappies can be used as pram or carry cot sheets. Later on a twill nappy can be combined with a towelling nappy to provide extra absorbency at night.

NAPPIES FOR PRETERM BABIES. It is important that a preterm baby's hips are not held apart by the bulk of a too large nappy. Tiny disposable nappies are available.

IMPORTANT POINTS TO REMEMBER WHEN SELECTING CLOTH NAPPIES

ABSORBENCY. Nappies are meant to absorb liquid, and their ability to do this depends largely on how much cotton they contain. So choose towelling nappies by weight; the heavier they are the better they are likely to be. Viscose adds to the bulk but is not as absorbent as cotton. Therefore, choose the heaviest pure cotton cloth nappies, even if a viscose mixture appears to be thicker.

FINISH. Make sure the edges are well seamed as they will have to withstand frequent harsh washing. There should be no faults in the fabric.

NAPPY SERVICE. A nappy laundry service can be useful, however this service has largely been outdated by disposable nappies.

DISPOSABLE NAPPIES. Disposable nappies are very convenient as they do not need to be laundered, but they are expensive. Quality in terms of comfort and absorbency depends largely on cost. They usually have a liner that allows moisture to go through onto the nappy, thus helping to prevent discomfort and nappy rash.

DISPOSAL Flush soiling down the toilet, then fold closed and discard in rubbish bin. Do not flush the nappy down the toilet as this causes blockages. In countries with a high usage, disposing of disposables has unfortunately become an environmental problem.

NAPPY LINERS. Liners are used inside cloth nappies to protect the baby's skin.
- Ordinary disposable liners save soiling of the nappy.
- One-way disposable liners save soiling of the nappy and keep the baby's skin dry.
- One-way fabric liners work the same way as one-way disposable liners but can be washed and re-used indefinitely.

Ordinary disposable nappy liners are about the same size as a man's handkerchief and are made from fibre. Their main purpose is to keep the nappy from becoming too soiled, and may be kinder against the baby's skin than a nappy. They are flushed down the toilet after use, leaving the nappy easier to clean. One-way disposable nappy liners are made from non-woven fabric with tiny holes in it and treated to make it water repellent. The urine passes through the perforations into the nappy and is held there because of the water repellent coating on the liner. In this way irritation from bacteria in the urine is cut down, helping prevent rashes. Do not use cream on the baby's skin when using a one-way liner as it blocks the perforations in the liner and prevents it from functioning properly.

Although disposable liners are meant to be used only once, they can be washed at least once and reused if they are not too dirty. You can also cut a liner in two when the baby is very small. Like ordinary nappy liners, they save on soiling of the nappy. Some mothers use these together with a disposable if they think the baby will soil the nappy, as it saves soiling an expensive disposable.

One-way washable fabric liners are made from an open-weave knitted fabric that lets urine through into the nappy, keeping the baby's skin dry. They are meant to be washed and reused for a long time. In many respects they work like one-way disposables, but may be more efficient.

Initially they are fairly expensive, but should last as long as your nappies. Keep in mind the extra work and cost as they will have to be laundered, but they are still less expensive to use than disposable liners.

Never use borax as a rinse for nappies or nappy liners — it is highly poisonous and can be absorbed through the skin. Fabric softener makes cloth nappies less absorbent.

SUGGESTED SHOPPING LIST WHEN USING CLOTH NAPPIES

- 2 dozen towelling nappies
- 4 curved pins with safety catch, or a set of plastic nappy clips
- 1 pack disposable liners or 2-3 one-way washable liners
- 2-3 waterproof pants to wear over the nappy
- 1 pack disposable nappies for emergencies and outings
- Large pail with lid for holding dirty nappies (2 is better — 1 for wet and 1 for soiled).

Your baby will use about 70 nappies a week

WATERPROOF PANTS FOR COVERING NAPPIES. Waterproof pants are worn over cloth nappies. The least costly are made from plastic but if you can afford something better it will be worth it, because plastic is non-porous and does not allow the skin to breathe. It also keeps moisture trapped inside which promotes nappy rash.

Pants made from doctor's flannel (pure wool) or synthetic flannel mixtures are best for use over nappies particularly when the baby is small. The advantage of flannel is that it absorbs moisture and allows the skin to breathe, all of which helps prevent nappy rash. Some pants have studs that close in front, others are shaped like pants with elastic at the waist and around the legs, while others have Velcro fastening — which can chafe — and make sure any elastic is not so tight that it causes redness.

When laundering flannel follow instructions on the label carefully. If the wool content is high do not use water that is too hot or it will shrink, and do not dry in direct sunlight or it will yellow. Do not use bleach or put flannel pants in a nappy sterilising solution. Undress and expose your baby's bottom to the air as often as possible to heal and prevent rashes.

HOW TO LAUNDER CLOTH NAPPIES. It is important to wash and rinse nappies thoroughly to kill germs. This can be done by using high temperatures, or by sterilising in one of the nappy sterilising chemicals. You should follow the manufacturer's instructions about changing the solution or it will lose its efficacy. After you remove the nappy, flush any stool down the lavatory and drop the nappy into the solution and leave overnight or as instructed.

Although most manufacturers state that nappies can simply be rinsed and hung up after being in the sterilising solution, most mothers find they need to wash them either by hand or washing machine afterwards.

Never use detergents or products that contain enzymes for your baby's nappies, bedding or clothes as they can cause a severe rash. Use a gentle soap and rinse at least twice. Do not use fabric softener on nappies as it can make them less absorbent and may affect sensitive skin. Drying in the sun whitens and sterilises nappies, but ironing hardens them.

However, if you live in a subtropical area, it is necessary to iron nappies and baby clothes because of the danger of the Putsi fly laying its eggs in them (*see p. 371*).

A strong ammonia smell in the nappy indicates that bacteria have changed the urine into ammonia that causes a severe rash known as ammonia dermatitis (*see p. 366*). A final rinse in a white vinegar solution – add ½ cup to the rinsing water – will counteract the ammonia (in nappies and nappy liners) by neutralising it. Strict attention must also be paid to washing and rinsing nappies thoroughly.

VARIOUS WAYS TO FOLD A NAPPY

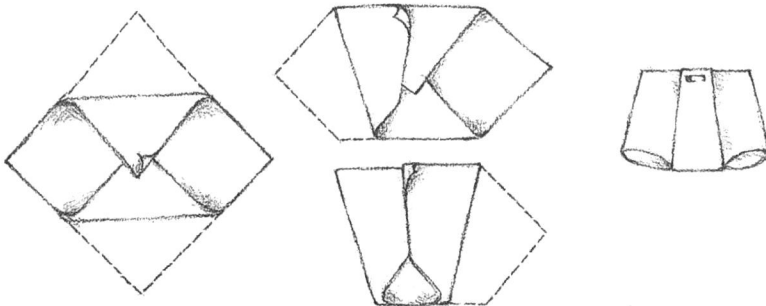

1. This method is suitable for small babies as it uses only one pin.

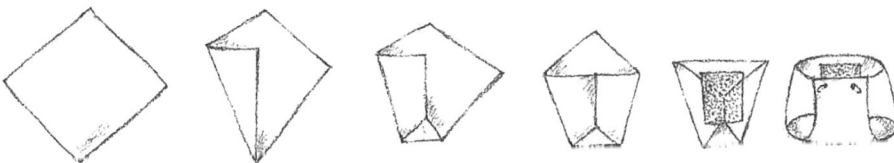

2. This method is a good way of folding a nappy because it holds together well and gives a snug fit.

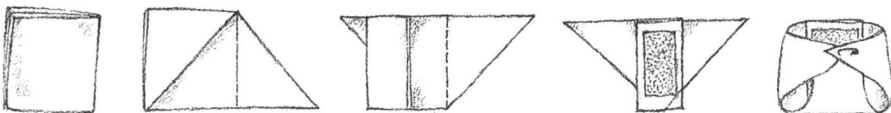

3. This method is particularly suitable for boys because it has an extra portion at the crotch. The shaded areas show where the nappy liner goes.

GENERAL CARE OF BABY CLOTHES

Wash all items before use, especially sheets which may contain starch. Always use pure soap for washing anything that comes into contact with your baby's skin, as allergic reactions and rashes are common if soap with enzyme additives is used. Drip-dry fabrics save ironing time, and airing in the sun has a mild sterilising effect. Gentle liquid soaps are available for hand or machine wash. Fabric softener is unnecessary.

TOILETRIES, BOTTLES AND SUNDRIES

BOTTLES. Choose from toughened glass; boil proof polycarbonate, polyethylene or plastic with a disposable liner. Concerns regarding polycarbonate bottles have emerged recently as some have been shown to leach Bisphenol-A; a compound used to harden plastic, when milk or other liquids are heated in them. BPA is a chemical that, at high levels, can cause harm to the heart, liver and endocrine (hormonal) system in laboratory animals. Although there is no general agreement on the level of potential danger to humans, you might want to check bottles for BPA levels. Some well known brands have low levels while some are high in BPA's. Polyethylene bottles made from non-shiny polyethylene plastic that is often coloured or decorated to make it more attractive, generally have no BPA content. Polyethylene is labelled #2 in the recycle triangle at the base.

- 2 – 6 wide-necked (for easy cleaning) boil proof bottles. Six bottles are more convenient, but you can get by with fewer. If you intend breastfeeding, you should have one or two on hand in case you need to give expressed breastmilk or other liquids.

Various teats/nipples are available. The rounded teat with a wide flattened nipple is said to approximate the effect of the breast, while the smaller ones with the firm ribbed edge seem to work well for some babies. Some teats claim to be anti-colic, others peristaltic, others orthodontic etc. Teats come in yellow latex rubber or clear silicone. Latex gets sticky after use and can harbour germs; silicone lasts longer but can be bitten through fairly easily.

The perfect shape teat for your baby is the one she gets used to and likes best. Most babies will be perfectly happy with an ordinary inexpensive teat, but it is important to have the right size hole. Discard teats as soon as they get soft and sticky, or show signs of cracking.

HOLE IN THE TEAT. The hole in the teat should be large enough for the milk to drip out rapidly when the bottle is held upside down, but it should not come out in a steady stream, or drip too slowly. A rate of 1 drop per second is usually right. Too large a hole will make the baby choke and splutter, while too small a hole will tire the child and make her swallow a lot of air. You can enlarge the hole by sticking the eye of a large needle into a cork and holding the point over a flame until it is red hot, then plunging it into the original hole. Many brands come with different size holes for various age groups.

Bottles with lids to cover the teat and a measuring jug.

TOILETRY EQUIPMENT
- Small round ended nail scissors
- Baby hairbrush
- Breast pads if you are going to breastfeed
- Large roll of cotton wool.
- Box of tissues.
- Unperfumed wet wipes.
- Two facecloths. You can make them from a double thickness of muslin which is soft and does not accumulate soap residue. Mark the cloths to keep one for the face and one for the rest of the body. Or buy two soft baby face cloths in different colours.

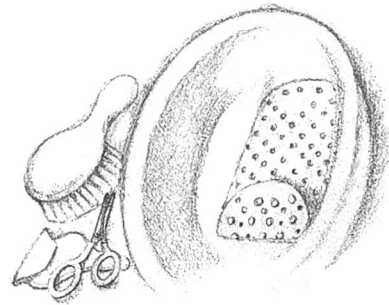

Small round ended nail scissors and a soft brush. Bath with rubber suction mat.

The most important item is soap for washing your hands before you touch your baby, in order to prevent infection. Many soaps, bubble baths, shampoos and aqueous creams contain sodium lauryl sulphate, which because it foams gives the impressions that it cleans the skin, however it is an irritant that should be avoided, so check labels carefully. Washing hands is the single most important thing you can do to prevent infection in your baby.

USEFUL THOUGH NO ESSENTIAL ITEMS
- Baby monitor. These carry sound from the baby's room to you so you can respond quickly. If you are anxious, or your baby has been ill, it can help bring you some peace of mind. They are expensive so you may want to 'inherit' one from a friend whose child has outgrown the need for it.

- Eye dropper, medicine dropper, or miniature feeder for administering drops or medicine.
- Small bottle surgical spirits for use if the cord stump has not dried up completely.
- Cotton buds are useful for hard to reach areas or dabbing on medication. Never stick a cotton bud into a baby's nose or ear, as the mucous membrane is extremely delicate and can easily be broken leaving a site for germs to enter. Shaped cotton buds which only allow a very small part of the bud to enter the cavity may be used.
- Wet wipes are handy for a quick clean up. Use unperfumed to avoid sensitising your baby.

See p. 389 for medical equipment.

TOILETRIES

Babies' skin is thin and whatever you put on it is absorbed. Skin rashes and dry patches are often caused by toiletries. Only use products that are meant for use on babies and are allergy tested. They should preferably have a pH 5.5 the same as baby's skin so that they do not dry or strip the skin of its natural lubricants. Products that say pH balanced are not the same pH as a baby's skin, they are usually pH 7. Too much cleaning and application of products can do more harm than good. A young baby's skin is best cleansed as simply as possible. Avoid products that contain colorants and perfumes. Many babies are highly sensitive to smells and can become over stimulated. Aromatherapy oils should be used with caution as their content is not regulated and anything massaged into your baby's skin will be absorbed.

- Aqueous cream BP (British Pharmacopoeia) has had the same formulation since 1958. One of the ingredients is sodium lauryl sulphate, which is a known skin irritant, and yet it is still generally prescribed and used as both a soap substitute and leave-on emollient. Users of aqueous cream have reported high rates of skin irritation, with the result that the National institute for Health and Clinical Excellence (NICE) in the United Kingdom, removed it from being used for eczema in 2007.

    New research by the *British Journal of Dermatology* has shown that aqueous cream causes skin irritation, and the skin's protective structure did not function as a protective barrier. In a nutshell, avoid products that contain sodium lauryl sulphate, such as aqueous cream, as a leave-on emollients can damage skin rather than assist in protecting the skin.
- Shampoo that does not burn eyes. Or you can use a body wash that serves as shampoo and skin wash in one.
- Baby lotion is used for cleaning the creases in the skin and for moisturising. Not really necessary, avoid under six months.

- Baby oil can be irritating or drying if it has a harsh mineral oil content. It is not really necessary.
- Barrier or healing cream for the protection of baby's bottom. The best products have skin soothing properties, and form a barrier that does not clog pores. Use only when indicated by redness in the nappy area. Your pharmacist can recommend a zinc and castor oil cream that is highly effective for nappy rash.
- Sun protection cream must be used on older children. Look for products that are allergy tested. Reapply often and do not rub in. (*See p. 237.*)
- The use of baby talc or corn-starch has become controversial due to concerns that they may be carcinogenic (cancer causing), and cause respiratory problems. The European Union has banned talc in health and beauty products. The Center for Disease Control and Prevention, and the Occupational Safety and Health Administration have said that repeated inhalation of talc might harm the lungs.

AROMATHERAPY MASSAGE OILS. These oils are sometimes promoted for various uses including helping babies to sleep, although there is little empirical evidence to substantiate this claim. Nonetheless, when it is correctly done, massage can be an excellent way of promoting intimacy and stress relief in both mother and child. Great caution must be exercised however, as any product used on a baby's skin will be readily absorbed. The oil used must be of a very high quality and the plant extracts of high purity. Unfortunately the quality of these products is not generally regulated worldwide, other than those that have the BP mark.

In Europe, the centuries old tradition has been to massage and even dose babies with the first cold pressed olive oil of the season known as *per mio figlio* (for my child) in Italy.

SUNDRIES IF YOU ARE BOTTLE FEEDING
- Liquid washing up soap.
- A bottle brush. And a small brush for the teat (optional).
- Coarse salt for cleaning the teat.
- A graduated measuring jug for making up formula, if you intend making it up in bulk.
- Bottle warmers are unnecessary and can encourage growth of bacteria if the milk is allowed to stand in them for long periods.

HOW TO CLEAN BOTTLES AND TEATS

- Bottle brush and optional teat brush.
- Coarse salt and liquid soap.

After use, bottles should be rinsed with cold water then scrubbed with liquid soap and very hot water. After thorough washing and rinsing, sterilise. Teats should be rubbed inside with coarse salt to remove the milk coating. Or use a little brush specially made for cleaning teats. Sterilise.

STERLISING EQUIPMENT AND USAGE OPTIONS

- A steam sterilising unit is ideal though expensive. Generally steam sterilising or boiling is the best way of preventing the development of thrush in your baby.
- Or, sterilising liquid or tablets can be used according to the instructions on the pack.
- Or, cover bottles with water and boil for 20 minutes in a large pot. Keep covered in water until needed. Boil teats for only 5 minutes after cleaning as they perish.
- Microwave steamers are another option. Follow all packaging instructions carefully.

GO TO www.baby-childcare.com TO WATCH THE FOLLOWING VIDEOS THAT ARE APPLICABLE TO CHAPTER 3

EMMA NUMANOGLU	Why you should do a hospital tour
	Breastfeeding questions before the birth
	The father's role
JOANNA WILSON	Causes of childhood overweight and obesity

CHAPTER 4

The Birth and Afterwards

THE MAGICAL MOMENT OF BIRTH

TRANSITION INTO LIFE. Nothing can surpass the moment when your child gives the first lusty cry of life. Wet and warm, crumpled like a butterfly emerging from a cocoon, your baby unfolds into the earth's atmosphere from an environment so nurturing a moment before, yet impossible to return to or survive in again. Perhaps birth resembles death in the passage from one dimension into another... And just as the baby cannot foresee survival outside the darkness of amniotic fluid, so we too may pass into an environment in which we do not need oxygen and amino acids to live – but some other undreamed of synthesis to sustain our being.

Dr Frederick Leboyer, the French obstetrician and gynaecologist, has suggested that birth is a traumatic experience for the child, and that the infant should be introduced to the world with gentleness. His way of doing this includes soft music, semi-darkness and an immediate re-immersion in water – a kind of return to the amniotic fluid of the womb.

I applaud his sensitivity: our methods of delivery will probably seem barbaric in time to come. But our 'backwardness' is understandable when you consider that medicine has only made childbirth relatively safe for mother and child in the last 60 years or so–a mere speck in our evolutionary history. Integrating the advances of medical technology with our psychological and emotional needs will surely be the challenge of the future.

Until recently infants were regarded as having little ability to perceive much by way of sight, sound, touch or emotion. We now know, however, that infants deprived of personalised care and touch, unlulled by the human voice, often fail to thrive, even if adequately fed, and may even waste away and die. We know too that carefully nurtured, the human intellect can be stimulated to blossom and grow.

Although I do not believe that immersing the baby in water straight after birth is a good idea – or that piped music is that important – I do think that those in attendance at the birth should go about the task gently and with great reverence for a new life.

The care of mother and child should never become a showpiece of mechanisation. So often the depersonalisation of the human being begins at birth, when instead we need to bring warmth, worth and empathy to our regard for the mother and child entity.

AFTER THE BIRTH. Occasionally a baby will cry as soon as the head is delivered, but most lie quietly for up to half a minute before they shiver into life and utter their first sound. During this period the nurse will check that there is no obstruction in the nose or mouth. If there is any mucus she will suction it away gently so that breathing is not hindered.

Once your baby is breathing, your caregiver may place her on your abdomen while the cord is being clamped and cut, a procedure that is quite painless for both mother and child. You or your partner may even do this. It is important that the baby does not become chilled so she will be taken to a heated area in the room and dried, weighed and given an identification tag on her ankle or wrist.

An injection of vitamin K to prevent bleeding is given to the baby and medication should be put in the eyes to prevent infection. She will also be quickly examined for any obvious abnormalities, and will be given a rating on the Apgar scale, named after an anaesthetist, Dr Virginia Apgar who developed the scoring method in 1953. The Apgar score measures five vital functions. This is done twice, one minute after birth and again five minutes later (*see p. 66*).

She should then be put in your arms for you and her father to savour for as long as you wish. If you feel up to it, put your baby to the breast now as the sucking instinct is strongest right after birth, and the baby highly alert. Simply put your baby near your breast, touch her lips with the nipple and she will automatically 'root' towards it and latch on. The baby's sucking at the breast causes the uterus to contract and if the placenta has not been expelled yet, it should come away easily. Separation of the placenta is not painful and is usually achieved spontaneously when the uterus contracts minutes after birth, even if you have not nursed the baby.

You may not feel like putting your baby to the breast straight away – birth is such an enormous physical effort and so emotionally charged that you could be too confused, tired, angry or ecstatic to handle another big experience so soon. Do not worry – there is nothing you should feel you have to do at this time. After the placenta has been expelled it will be examined, and if you have had an episiotomy (a small cut to help the baby through the perineum), you will be given a local anaesthetic and the cut or tear will be stitched.

You and your partner should then be given a nice cup of tea, before you are taken to your room for a thorough wash to freshen up. Then it will be time to relax, reflect and adjust.

Some mothers instantly 'recognise' their baby and say they feel immediate love; many feel nothing but exhaustion and a little startled by the stranger they have produced. Mother love is not instant, nor inevitable – and you will probably not feel very much of it straight after the birth. It grows and matures as you nurture your baby.

If the birth has been straightforward, and unless arranged otherwise, your baby will be taken away to a nursery for observation and a clean-up. Afterwards she will be brought to you if you are rooming in, or taken to the nursery if you are not having your baby with you, although this is unusual these days.

This period of separation should be as short as possible so that you can interact with your baby when she is at her most alert, and will most readily nuzzle at the breast. The father, too, should have the opportunity to hold and examine his baby as soon after birth as possible.

TESTS AND PROCEDURES AFTER THE BIRTH. While your baby is in the observation nursery or while she is with you, she will be examined for congenital defects, either by your paediatrician or by the hospital staff. Blood tests for anaemia and Rhesus incompatibility (Coombs test) will be done if problems are suspected, and her reflexes and muscle tone will be checked for any signs of damage or congenital abnormality. Her legs should be examined for any signs of 'clicking' in the hip which could indicate congenital hip dislocation. If detected early this condition can usually be treated successfully before the child begins to walk.

Depending on the country and hospital policy certain tests for inherited disorders may be done. Between the sixth and fourteenth day the Guthrie blood test for phenylketonuria (PKU), a rare metabolic disorder, may be performed to ensure that affected children are put on a special diet immediately to prevent brain damage. This test is compulsory in the United Kingdom and the United States, but not in South Africa. If you are of white descent, and in particular, Irish or Celtic origin, you should ask your doctor to do the test. It is not expensive and is simply done. Unless put on a special diet, children with PKU suffer progressive brain damage as a result of an inability to metabolise protein. Their urine has a characteristic 'mousy' or musty odour. Another rare, metabolic error that is sometimes tested for is galactosaemia.

In some countries such as the United States blood tests are done for hypothyroidism, which occurs in approximately one in 4 000 babies, and can lead to a type of mental retardation known as cretinism. In some US states, tests for sickle-cell anaemia, a blood disease found mainly in African-Americans is also done.

The staff will fill in a card with details of your pregnancy and labour, blood groups and any complications that may have arisen. Your baby's temperature and breathing will be checked and your baby will be observed for the least sign that all is not well.

WHAT HAPPENS AFTER A CAESAREAN SECTION

ELECTIVE CAESAREAN. Most Caesarean sections these days are planned beforehand (elective) and performed under spinal or epidural anaesthesia. This deadens feeling in the lower half of the body so the C-section can be done while the mother is awake. Giving birth this way allows the mother and father the opportunity to experience the moment of birth, and start getting to know their child straight away. Depending on the baby's condition the same procedures as for a vaginal delivery will be followed after the birth.

Some hospitals keep the baby in the observation unit for 24 hours, but you should ask for your child to be brought to you as soon as possible. If you put her to the breast before the epidural has worn off you will probably find it easier. In order to avoid your stitches, tuck her under your arm on the side from which you are feeding (American football hold) and begin the long exciting journey of getting to know her. (*See p. 120.*)

UNPLANNED CAESAREAN. When a Caesarean section is performed under general anaesthetic it is usually because an emergency has arisen during labour and there is no time to spare in getting the baby delivered. Although you will be relieved that it is over, you may also feel rather cheated of the experience of childbirth. It is normal to have somewhat mixed feelings – excitement and gratitude that you and the baby have come through it – but a little disappointed and angry that you were not able to have a perfectly natural birth. Talk about your feelings, but there is no need to feel that you have failed, or that you will be an inadequate mother. The birth is but one tiny fraction of the experience of motherhood as you will soon discover.

After a general anaesthetic you will be sleepy and somewhat nauseous for the first 24 hours, and your baby may be put in an incubator and kept under observation for 12–24 hours. You should see your baby as soon as possible after the birth even if you have to be wheeled to the incubator. Your baby should be taken out so that you can hold her for a while and she should also be given to you for breastfeeding (*see p. 120*). If your baby's condition is good you can ask for her to be left with you if hospital policy allows this.

A Caesarean is a major operation and you can expect to experience pain from the incision and cramping from medication to shrink the womb, and discomfort from winds.

Ask for pain relief and do not be surprised if you feel shaky when trying to get up. Do not overdo things but do move as much as you feel up to, standing straight so that you can get back to normal quickly.

EXCERCISES AFTER A CEASARIAN SECTION
TO CLEAR THE CHEST OF MUCUS
Immediately you come round from the anaesthetic you must try and clear the chest of mucus. Rather than coughing which is not always successful, try this. With your hands supporting your stitches, take a deep breath and force the air out of your lungs making a sharp 'ha-haaa' sound. If you hear a rattling noise in your chest there is still some mucus left. Repeat the exercise until the chest is clear.

FOOT CIRCLING
It is vitally important to get the blood circulating in your legs if you are not walking about. Lie in bed with a cushion under your calves. Circle your left foot ten times to the left and repeat ten times to the right. Repeat with the other foot.

LEG SLIDING
This helps to get the blood circulating after a Caesar and helps healing. Lie in bed with your knees bent, then slide one leg down, slide up again. Repeat with the other leg.

WHEN A BABY IS BORN PREMATURELY
BORN TOO SOON. When born before 37 completed weeks a baby is classified preterm or premature.

Giving birth before your expected date of delivery is always a shock. You will have dreamed and fantasised about what it will be like to give birth, and suddenly you are faced with a new reality. You may feel that you have disappointed your partner and let everyone down. Although great strides have been made in caring for women in pregnancy, many babies are nonetheless born before their time. We know some of the reasons, but often thore is no seeming reason why labour begins before the allotted time. Throughout history many famous people were born prematurely including Sir Winston Churchill, war time Prime Minister of the United Kingdom, who lived to be 91! No one is to blame, and fortunately great strides have been made in caring for fragile babies, some born months too soon.

Because the medical team will have to intervene and take over the care of your baby it may feel as though she does not need you. Nothing could be further from the truth. No one can ever give your baby the depth of caring that you and her father can. Go to her as soon as possible and touch her in the special care unit she is in. Talk to her – she can hear you – stroke her, send her your love and strength. The huge emotions you feel are there for a reason. Use them positively. The healing power of your touch is vital for a premature baby. She will probably have tubes and even needles attached to her tiny frame, and she will look wrinkled and unlike the baby you dreamed of. Although she needs the sensitive care and expertise of the doctors and nurses, she needs to feel your touch just as much. As soon as you are allowed to, put her against your naked chest and make her part of you once more. This 'kangaroo care' allows her to hear your heartbeat like she did in the womb, she keeps warm, and your breathing action helps to regulate her breathing. Tiny babies nurtured this way grow faster and better and you will feel that you are doing something vitally important in her care. Fathers too, can 'kangaroo' their babies, and in the case of multiple births it is not unusual to see burly men cosseting their babies – two, or even more at a time – in the sharing of loving care.

You may be able to express breastmilk for your baby, and this is the best medicine for the prevention of certain serious complications of early birth. Preterm babies have a higher incidence of problems than full term babies, and there may be setbacks, but many go on to develop very well. When judging your baby's development you should measure it by the child's corrected age. That is, calculate her developmental age from the date she should have been born, not the date she was born.

SMALL FOR DATE BABIES. Babies with a mass below 2 500g are also kept in a special care area even if they are not premature. They need to be observed and to be kept warm because their temperature regulating mechanism is particularly inefficient.

EXAMINING THE NEWBORN
APGAR TEST
Sixty seconds after your baby is born the midwife or doctor will assess her condition according to a standard method known as the Apgar score. This test will be repeated five minutes later. Five vital signs are tested and the baby is given 0, 1 or 2 points for each.
Heart rate:
1 point is given if it is below 100 beats a minute, and 2 points are given if it is over 100 beats a minute.
Respiratory effort:
If breathing is slow or irregular and the baby does not cry 1 point is given. If the baby cries and her breathing is regular, 2 points are given.

Muscle tone:
If the baby makes some movements 1 point is given. If there is good muscle tone with the baby making active movements, 2 points are given.
Reflex activity:
If the baby responds by grimacing when the nose is suctioned to clear it of mucus she scores 1 point. If she sneezes, coughs or cries she gets 2 points.
Colour:
The tongue should be pink. Pink skin tone with blue tinges on the hands and feet would score 1, while pink all over scores 2.

The individual scores for each test are tallied and then totalled out of a possible 10.

Most babies score 8 or 9 out of 10 on the first scoring as the limbs are usually a little blue during the first minute. A score of 8/10 or more indicates that the baby has not suffered respiratory distress and has received sufficient oxygen during and before birth. A score of between 4 and 7 indicates some breathing difficulties and the baby will be given oxygen (some doctors do this routinely for all babies). Other mild stimulatory measures may be undertaken.

A score of 3 or less indicates severe asphyxia (lack of oxygen) and calls for swift action.

If the first four signs are missing and the baby is blue all over she would not get any points out of a possible 10, and if not helped to breathe the child would be stillborn.

YOUR BABY'S FIRST PHYSICAL

WHAT IT REVEALS. Every new born baby should have a thorough examination by a suitably qualified person within 24 hours of birth. This should preferably be done when the mother and father are present. The general body tone of the baby, that is, if she is firm and able to do certain reflex actions, or if she is limp and floppy is a good indication of whether the nervous system is functioning as it should. The doctor is also able to judge whether the baby was born prematurely and by how many weeks.

- The spine will be examined to make sure it is straight and that there are no abnormalities.
- The testes will be examined in a boy to see that they have descended into the scrotum or that they can easily be made to move into the scrotum. The opening to the urethra, the meatus, will be checked to ensure that it is correctly positioned and patent (open).
- In a girl, the vaginal area is usually enlarged and there may be a discharge from the vaginal opening. This is normal and due to the effects of the mother's hormones.
- The anus will be checked to ensure that it is open and normal.
- The baby's ears will be checked internally and externally. There may be a great deal of wax but this works its way out on its own. The shape of the outer ear and its placing on the head can tell the doctor if there is a possibility of certain internal defects. In a premature baby the folds of the ear are not fully formed and the ears are softer than those of a full term baby.
- The femoral pulse in the groin is felt to make sure there is no narrowing of the main blood vessel leading from the heart to the lower limbs (coarctation of the aorta). The groin is also examined for signs of an inguinal hernia.
- The collar bone which is easily damaged during birth will be felt for any displacement or fracture.
- When forced open, the arms should return firmly to a position close to the body, indicating good reflex and tone. The baby's chest is felt to see if there is any enlargement of the heart. The liver and spleen are felt for correct position and size.

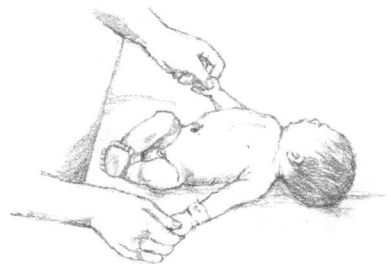

- The lungs and heart are listened to through a stethoscope. Heart 'murmurs' are common and are not an indication that there is something wrong except in rare instances.
- For the important examination of the hip joints the doctor will splay the child's legs in a frog – like position with a special grip to see if the hip bones fit into their sockets as they should. If there is a click when the examination is done or the bones are not in the correct position, the child could have dislocation of the hip which needs early treatment.
- The hands are checked for normal palms as a child with certain chromosomal abnormalities such as Down syndrome would have unusual crease marks. If the child's palm is pressed with the thumb she should close her fingers into a fist.
- The feet are stimulated to see if the child curls her toes inwards in a normal reflex. Premature babies do not have well defined lines on the soles of their feet. The ankles are bent to check for signs of clubfoot.

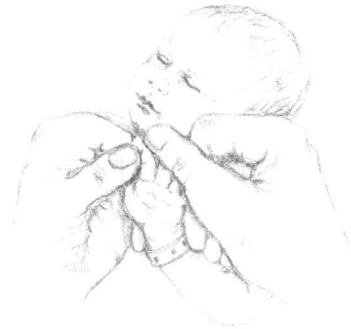

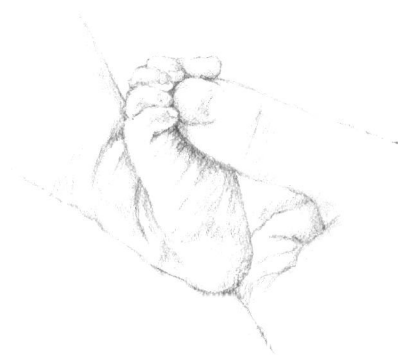

- The eyes will be examined for defects such as cataracts, possibly caused by German measles during pregnancy. The roof of the mouth will be felt for any opening that would mean the baby has a cleft palate. At the same time the doctor will test the sucking reflex. A strong sucking reflex is a sign of a healthy mature baby.
- The soft spot or fontanelle on the top of the baby's head will be checked for any signs of bulging which could indicate pressure in the brain; if it is sunken it could mean that the baby is dehydrated or has lost a lot of weight after birth.

- The baby's head will be measured around the widest part which averages 35cm in a full term baby. The baby's length will also be measured – the average is 52cm so that growth can be checked against these measurements later on if necessary.

REFLEXES IN THE NEWBORN

MORE THAN A KNEE JERK REACTION. All babies are born with autonomic primitive reflexes that help ensure survival. For example, closing the eyes in bright light, or rooting towards the nipple when the cheek is touched. These are some of the reflexes babies are born with, but keep in mind that not all babies acquire and lose them at the same times indicated.

- The Moro *reflex*, when the baby throws out her arms and legs in a startled response, then brings them together quickly and cries, is at its peak at one month and disappears at two months. This reflex occurs when a sudden loud noise is heard or when the head moves suddenly or falls backward as though the baby is falling, and it is an indication to the doctor of the condition of the baby's nervous system.

- The grasp reflex is a primitive response in which the baby grips tightly if something is placed in her hand. It is thought by some to be a throwback to a time when babies clung to their mothers' fur. This peaks after the birth and disappears at five months.

- The walking or stepping reflex shows itself in the first two months when the baby places one foot in front of the other if she is held so that her feet touch a flat surface.

- The tonic neck reflex is subtle but can be seen when the head is turned to one side. The arm on that side is stretched out, and the opposite arm is bent at the elbow so she looks like a miniature fencer. Look for it when your baby lies quietly until sometime between five and seven months of age.

- The rooting reflex promotes feeding. If the baby's cheek or lips are touched she'll automatically turn towards the source of the stimulus and 'root' for the nipple. In the

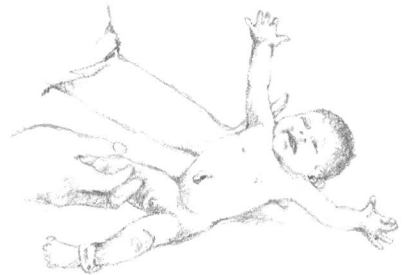

first weeks she'll move her head from side to side searching, but by three weeks she'll zone in and go straight for the nipple. This reflex disappears at four months.

- Perhaps the most important reflex is that of sucking which is there from before birth. Ultrasound and fibre optic photographs have shown babies sucking their thumb in the womb. This reflex serves to promote feeding and is also an important source of comfort. When a nipple touches the roof of the baby's mouth she automatically begins to suck. The whole procedure required for sucking, swallowing and breathing is not always mastered in the beginning, which is why some babies are not very efficient at the breast early on.

NOTE: These responses should be elicited by a trained person only.

WHAT THE NEWBORN BABY LOOKS LIKE

FULL TERM VAGINAL DELIVERY. Your full term baby will have had time to put down a layer of fat, and she will be covered by a cheesy white substance called vernix that has formed a protective layer against the long immersion in amniotic fluid and made her slippery for the birth. She may be a little bloody if you've had an episiotomy, and her hands and feet may be a little blue. Her face will be puffy and wizened and she will gaze at you quizzically with the wisdom of the world she has come from and the questioning of who you are.

Her head will be misshapen from its long journey down the birth canal, and it will take several weeks before it looks round and smooth again. She may have red pressure marks from the birth on her face and even in her eyes, and white milia spots on her nose and cheeks. They will disappear without treatment. Fine downy hair called lanugo covers her shoulders and back, more so if she was born a bit early. It will fall out in a few weeks' time. Her breasts and genital area look enlarged and swollen due to maternal hormones, but this will pass. She will be your beautiful baby...

CAESAREAN AT FULLTERM. You may not have had the experience of a 'natural' vaginal delivery, but your baby will have the advantage of not being forced through the birth canal with its pressures. Her head and face will be smooth and well shaped. She will have the vernix covering and lanugo of the newborn, but unless you were in labour before the C–section she will have none of the bruising. She will be your beautiful baby...

PRETERM. The earlier she arrives the thinner and smaller she will be and the longer her head will be in relation to her body. Babies born before term do not have the fat layer that is put down in the last weeks of pregnancy and thus you will be able to see the blood vessels beneath the skin. She will have missed out on the covering of white vernix but she may have a covering of downy hair. She will not cry lustily and her breathing may need assistance. She will be very susceptible to cold because she has no insulating layer of fat, and she must be kept warm. She will look tiny and fragile and frog like. She will be your beautiful baby...

COMMON COMPLICATIONS

JAUNDICE. One of the more common minor complications in the newborn is jaundice which affects up to 50% of babies and an even greater number of premature infants. Physiological jaundice occurs on the third or fourth day and is caused by the baby's liver being unable to cope efficiently with the breakdown of the extra load of red blood cells in the baby's circulation before birth. The child is not ill, gains weight and has normal stools. She will look yellowish though, starting with the face, abdomen and then the legs.

The condition usually rectifies itself without treatment within a week. Tests will be done and if the level of unconjugated bilirubin (unconverted waste) is above a certain level (the danger level is lower in premature infants), the baby will be put under special fluorescent lights for about 48 hours until the liver is mature enough to cope. Exposure to these lights converts the unconjugated bilirubin into a harmless form that is then excreted through the urine and stools, which is why the urine of a baby who is under the lights is brownish, and the stools appear green and loose. The baby's eyes will be protected from the harsh light and she will be brought to the mother for feeds. There are no known after-effects from this kind of jaundice and its treatment.

BREASTMILK JAUNDICE. Breastmilk sometimes interferes with the baby's ability to process bilirubin and may prolong physiological jaundice. Your doctor may recommend that you stop breastfeeding for no more than 48 hours to give the baby's liver a chance to cope. Most often it is possible to continue breastfeeding without resorting to this as the baby needs to suck on the mother's breast to keep her milk flow going.

Jaundice on the first or second day of life may be a sign of a more serious condition, such as rhesus incompatibility (*see p. 387*).

'THIRD-DAY BLUES'. By the third day you, too, may be feeling somewhat off-colour. If you have had a Caesarean, you will probably be in pain from wind and the wound, and no matter how your baby was delivered your breasts will be starting to fill with milk, unless you have had an injection to stop it. *See p. 117* for advice on engorgement, and how to breast feed in the first days. Besides discomfort from episiotomy stitches, you may have difficulty with bowel movements and suffer other indignities that are part and parcel of motherhood. Not surprisingly, you begin to feel the romance has gone out of having a baby.

In addition, your hormonal secretions – those arbiters of female equilibrium – are sending out messages in scrambled code. No wonder you are alternately laughing and crying. New fathers have been known to mutter that they can't do anything right. If they pay too much attention to the baby the mother's feelings are hurt; and if they don't fuss over the baby they are accused of not caring about their child. It is normal, it is to be expected, but you will need the diplomatic skills of a statesman to do the right thing when a new mother is in the grip of the notorious 'third day blues'.

Very few women escape the experience altogether, even though it does not always happen on the third day. Sometimes it happens sooner, sometimes later; either way some form of postnatal depression is a grim reality for most women. It even affects adoptive mothers for reasons other than hormonal changes. Some women are lucky; they settle down after a while, maybe in a day or two, but occasionally it takes much longer and it can become so serious that women have been known to contemplate suicide when those around have not realised the severity of the depression.

Firstly, the condition must be recognised for what it is. Simply knowing that the other mothers in the ward are also weeping into their pillows at the slightest provocation can be a comfort. Talking to them and sharing your misery will help you get it in perspective. But most of all you need the understanding of your baby's father who will be at the receiving end of your confusion, even though he may be feeling somewhat neglected himself. A lot of patience and sympathetic handling are needed to help restore a depressed woman's equilibrium.

Sometimes a mild anti-depressant is all that is needed; sometimes it takes stronger drugs, with counselling. Postnatal psychoses is the most serious form of depression after a birth and the woman may need to be hospitalised for her safety and recovery. Partners of depressed women often become depressed themselves and this takes away an important safety net. The problem with depression is that it takes away the ability to do something about it. Therefore outside intervention may be necessary in order to recognise it and to do something to help. Both partners need support and possibly professional counselling. Women who have experienced depression during pregnancy or previously, are most at risk for serious postnatal depression.

HOW PHYSICAL DISCOMFORT ADDS TO THE PROBLEM. It is often a rude shock to find that having a baby can leave you feeling battered and bruised. Episiotomy stitches can be painful. If your doctor isn't against it – some feel it restricts blood flow – ask for an air ring to sit on. Add salt to your bath water and use a local anaesthetic spray or gel such as 5% lignocaine if you have painful stitches. An ice pack is a simple and useful pain reliever, but its effects are limited. Some women find relief from herbal preparations such as arnica (leopard's bane) tablets. There is no harm in trying them although tests have shown lignocaine to be the most effective form of pain relief of episiotomy stitches. Enzyme preparations made from extract of the Hawaiian pineapple plant appear to be effective in helping swelling and pain, but tests are not conclusive. If stitches hurt for longer than a week or two get medical advice as there could be a pinched nerve.

If you have severe after pains (*see p. 116*) in the uterus when the baby sucks, take a pain killer 15 minutes before feeds (codeine can be constipating – paracetamol is best). If your breasts are hard and sore, follow the procedure explained under Engorgement on *p. 117*. If you have been shaved and the area is itchy, an application of the preparatory shaving cream men use (not foam) will relieve it.

HAEMORRHOIDS (piles) can be an unpleasant legacy of pregnancy; use an air ring if your doctor approves. Piles usually subside fairly quickly after delivery; however, if you have had several children you might have to have an injection to cure them, although this is usually given only after a few months.

EMOTIONAL TURMOIL IN THE EARLY DAYS. Chances are feeding problems will be your main concern. Hospital routines are not always conducive to the establishment of breastfeeding and you will probably get a lot of conflicting, if well-meant advice. You could be worried sick because your baby is too sleepy to suck or still in an incubator. Most of all, if you are worried about the baby, do not be afraid to discuss your fears with your doctor.

You may even feel that the staff is not handling your precious baby with the deference she deserves, or you may be feeling inadequate to the task that awaits you. Your baby may not be like you had expected her to be in your fantasies, and you will need time to adjust to this. Becoming a mother or father is scary and this new responsibility may overwhelm you at times. Coming to terms with the loss of freedom to go where you please when you please is a major adjustment for anyone.

It is important to talk about your feelings to someone who understands. You will probably cry buckets but you need to release the tension of the climatic build-up of birth. You will adjust to your new life, and the trade-off between what you lose when you have a baby and the fulfilment and meaning you gain, will add immeasurable value to your life.

PRACTICAL POINTS. On a practical level, if your room is flooded with bouquets of flowers, make sure they are removed at night and bear in mind the fact that the 'cold' you have developed may be an allergic reaction to the flowers. If your baby is in a communal nursery you will have one big advantage – being able to rest. Do not spend your time wandering around the corridors; write your thank you notes and rest as much as you can. Take the opportunity of asking the nurses about anything that worries you.

If you are rooming in with your baby you will be expected to bath and care for her after being shown how. Not all hospitals that keep babies in communal nurseries teach the mother about looking after her child and you may go home never having seen how your baby is bathed or changed. Whether your baby is with you all the time or not, take every opportunity you get to have her close to you. Hold her in your arms or tuck her in next to you in bed. She wants and needs to be close to her mother.

WHEN SOMETHING GOES WRONG. What if your baby is among the small percentage that are not perfect at birth? Perhaps she has a cleft lip or clubfoot or some other more serious problem. Who will tell you and how will you handle it?

No one but the parents can fully appreciate the shock of discovering their baby is less than perfect; but one would have to be callous indeed not to break the news as gently and compassionately as possible. Your doctor will be the first person to talk to you about it and hopefully he or she will do so patiently and fully. Although you will most likely be too confused and upset to think of all the questions that need answering.

Happily, there are many organisations and support groups that do splendid work in helping parents cope with such problems. If and when a child is born with a congenital abnormality, a social worker as well as a suitable person who has coped with a similar experience should be on hand as soon as possible to offer parents the kind of personalised information they thirst after.

When you meet someone who has been through what you are experiencing it makes coping with the crisis so much easier. A mother who has a baby with Down syndrome wants to hear about it from another mother. Simply seeing a child with a repaired cleft lip is sure to cheer the parents of a child with a similar defect. Too often parents are given expert medical attention but are left to flounder emotionally. The mother, especially, may have guilt feelings or become severely depressed – but the whole family needs help to come to terms with reality.

GOING HOME. You will be discharged anything from 48 hours to a week after the birth although the average stay is more likely to be three days or until your baby regains her birth weight. Before you leave, you will be given a chart with details of your baby's short history, her birth weight and her weight on discharge. If she is not breastfed, the formula she is taking will be noted, with the number of feeds she is taking in a 24 hour period.

Thus armed and with the pathetic remains of your flowers stacked in the car, you bid an emotional farewell to the staff and sundry personnel. Your baby will be dressed in her own clothes for the first time (most nursing homes provide garments for use in the hospital), and you will be in non-maternity clothes at last (even though you may still look four months pregnant).

On the way home, your partner drives the car as if the road is paved with eggs, while you watch your precious bundle, tensed against the slightest bump, in case, like a soap bubble, she should disintegrate and disappear… Finally, you make it home to a welcoming committee of relatives and friends, and your initiation into motherhood begins. What you really need is a nice cup of tea, time alone with your partner and, with any luck, a baby that will sleep for an hour or two longer. But what do you get? A lot of oohing and aahing and poking between the blankets, while you are going crazy worrying about germs and cringing at the idea that 'she's got Uncle Eric's nose'.

What can you do? You could say it is time for a feed and retire to the sanctuary of your bedroom, door closed firmly behind you. But some tactless soul may simply march in after you. Ideally, whoever has been holding the fort while you have been away should gently persuade visitors to leave the presents and move on, reminding them that they should telephone before dropping in again. Someone who will fend off visitors when you don't want to see them can be of real service and save you a lot of stress. If you have always been well groomed and meticulous, you will really hate being caught in your dressing gown at noon, without make-up and smelling of stale milk. Because that's the way it is… for the first six weeks or so anyway.

ADJUSTING TO LIFE AT HOME. No matter how 'good' your baby is in the nursing home, you will probably find she changes after the first 10 days. All of a sudden the rather placid sleepy mite may start to wake at odd hours and generally give you a hard time. If you are bottle feeding you will wonder what has happened to the four-hourly schedule she was supposed to be on, and your partner is likely to come home at night to find all that is left of you is a puddle of sweat and tears.

If I am painting a dark picture it is because too many relationships have been irreparably damaged, too many women have had their egos so badly dented that even psychiatric panel beating has not put them together again, and too many babies have been bashed by mothers and fathers who have snapped under the strain, to pretend it is roses all the way.

No one should underestimate the impact that the addition of an infant will have on their life. Mother love and maternal instinct are often either non-existent or come much later – when you are relaxed and experienced. When you really need them, it is like pulling rabbits out of a hat – easy when you know how but a mystery when you don't.

And this applies to all women. Those placid mothers in the bush don't cope alone, they have the best possible system working for them – a covey of old matriarchs who move in and take over supervision of the new mother. Leave your 'instinctive' tribal mother in the city with no one to turn to and she is in as much trouble as the next woman.

Time was when we had tradition and extended families to take care of a new mother's teething troubles. Now the nuclear family is thrown into the suburban jungle without a child care compass and we are expected to find our way alone.

Because this situation is so new in our evolution most people have not realised its implications. That is why a man who remembers his mother as a ministering angel may not appreciate the stress his wife is under. Imagine how you would feel after a major abdominal operation (if she has had a Caesarean section) or even just stitches in your seat; being woken between three and 10 times a night (a well known form of torture); after being on the go all day carrying buckets of water, doing the laundry, producing milk (it takes a great deal of energy); changing nappies, wiping possets of sour milk; in between cleaning a house and making supper, while worrying yourself silly wondering if you are doing the right thing for your child…

Until recently mothers had no doubts about the handling of their children – they did as their mothers did – while blissfully ignorant of bogeys like psychological trauma and the advantages of early mental stimulation… But things are different today, and far more is expected of parents.

No wonder she is crying. If you give it some thought you won't say: 'I don't know what you're making such a fuss about, millions of women have had babies before you…' and you will ignore the burnt toast and dust on top of the fridge. Come to think of it, you could be making the toast etc. (Okay, I know a lot of you new age men do, but what about the others?) And remember she probably finds smelly nappies just as revolting as you do. So lend a hand and tell her you think she is great. It is the one thing that will give her the confidence she needs to help her relax, and after that, all else should follow.

DOWN TO THE NITTY GRITTY OF THE DAILY ROUTINE. Your baby is probably going to wake up during the night for a feed. Forget about water or any other sop that has been suggested. What your baby needs in the early weeks is food and that is what she must get.

A dimmer switch is a useful gadget, because you can turn the light up just enough to be able to see without flooding the room with brightness and making your baby think it is time to get up. If you are breastfeeding, simply reach for her and let her latch on. Some babies do not like to feed with a wet nappy, in which case you will have to change it beforehand. Make sure you have a nappy and all you need on hand ready from the night before, or else change her at the end of the feed because she is likely to soil her nappy during the feed anyway. Burp her and put her back to sleep with as little fuss as possible, hopefully for another few hours… then go back to sleep yourself. Do not think of the day ahead and what you are going to cook for supper… go straight to bed and collect some sleep.

If you are bottle feeding the same routine applies, except that you will have to warm a bottle. Some mothers give the bottle straight from the fridge but it can cool her down and a lot of energy will have to be used to get her body temperature up again, so do not do it in the early months. You can keep hot water in a flask so that it is ready to heat up the bottle at night, or heat for a few seconds in a microwave, but do not leave the bottle in a bottle warmer for hours as this creates an ideal medium for germs to multiply. Do not use leftover milk because saliva will have mixed with it and it will not be sterile. If you heat in a microwave shake the bottle afterwards and test on your wrist as the centre of the milk heats more than the outside.

Get up when you really have to and bring some semblance of order to the house. A lick and a promise will do. You must have a proper breakfast or you will be weak and weepy from low blood sugar (hypoglycaemia). You need protein as well as starch and sugar to keep you going, so have an egg or yoghurt or cheese with your toast or coffee. If you're breastfeeding have decaffeinated coffee.

BATHING YOUR BABY

It is a good idea to have a regular time for bathing your baby so that she gets used to a routine and you can plan around it. It is probably easier in the morning because you will be even busier in the evening, but do what is the most convenient; you can even bath mid-afternoon, and she does not have to be bathed every day. It is not essential, although your baby is likely to feel fresher after it, especially in summer. You can just 'top and tail' her by wiping her face and washing the nappy area if you do not bath her.

Start about an hour before your baby's next feed is due so that she does not become ravenous halfway through. This could be before the midmorning feed or before the six o'clock feed at night. Bathing your baby at night gives the father a chance to become involved, but it is also a very busy time for you so you will have to work out what suits you best.

PREPARING THE BATH. Close all the windows and make sure the room is reasonably warm if the weather is very cold. Get your baby's clean clothes ready in the order you will be putting them on. Attach any pins to your clothes so that you do not mislay them, and fold the nappy, or open out the disposable. Fold the top of the towel – or the hood – back about 30cm and keep it handy. If you are bottle feeding make sure you have a bottle warming as she is sure to be ravenous after the bath.

Put the bath or basin on a steady surface in a draught-free place. Place a suction rubber bath mat or folded nappy in the bottom of the bath to

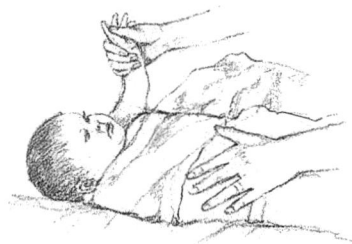

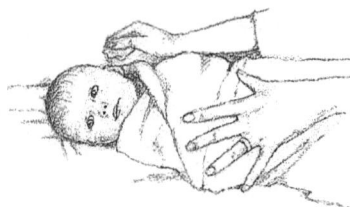

stop the baby slipping. Put cold water in the bath, and then add the hot water. Test with your elbow – it should be warm, not hot.

Very young babies are inclined to cry when they are being handled, but they soon learn to enjoy it. Some hate their tummies being exposed; you can try bathing her in her vest if this seems to be the problem.

Undress your baby, leaving the nappy on. Now wrap her in the towel. The hood, or the part that is folded back should be on the outside. Wrap her securely by taking the left side of the towel across her body and tucking it in under her arm. Fold the bottom part of the towel up over her feet, and then take the remaining part of the towel over the exposed arm and tuck it around her to make a neat 'parcel'.

Wipe her face with a soft cloth using a non-soap product. Keep this cloth separate from the one you use for her bottom – you can mark it with a piece of coloured tape, or buy two different colour cloths.

Holding the baby securely under your arm, with your fingers gently but firmly over her ears, wash her hair with a gentle shampoo formulated for babies. Do not be afraid to touch the soft spots on her head, it will not harm her. Rub her hair dry by folding up the towel. Babies sweat a lot from their scalps, so you can wash it every day, however twice a week will do if this is not practicable.

Now take off her nappy and wipe away any soiling with cotton wool or a wet wipe. When cleaning your baby, always wipe from the front to the back as germs can easily enter the urethra, and cause an infection. Lather her all over, preferably with a non-soap baby wash, making sure you get into all the creases at the top of the legs, around the buttocks and under the arms, or do it in the bath so that she does not feel cold.

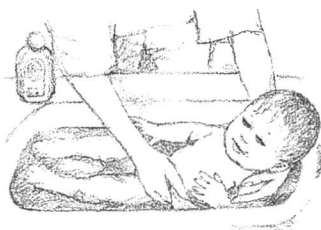

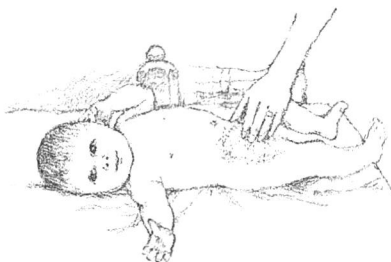

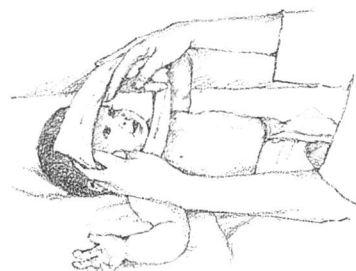

Holding her securely with your arm supporting her head and your fingers gripping her upper arm put your baby in the bath and rinse off. Very young babies like to be held very firmly or they become frightened in the water. You can also put a wash cloth over her tummy to make her feel more secure if she appears afraid.

Pat her dry while cuddling her in your arms or dry her on the changing mat but keep her covered with the towel. Make sure you dry very well in all the creases, especially around the neck. The use of baby talc or corn-starch has become controversial due to concerns that they may be carcinogenic (cancer causing), and cause respiratory problems. The European Union has banned talc in health and beauty products. The Center for Disease Control and Prevention, and the Occupational Safety and Health Administration have said that repeated inhalation of talc might harm the lungs.

Dress your baby quickly on a dry surface. Never leaving her for a second as you never know when she will acquire the ability to roll over. Gather garments that go over her head up in your hands and slip over her head as shown. Do not try and pull her arm through the armhole. Put your hand inside the sleeve and grasp your baby's hand before pulling it gently through.

DRESSING. Do not overdress your baby. Cool hands and feet are not a sign that she is too cold because most of the blood flow is directed to the stomach for the digestive process, leaving the hands relatively cool. Feel her forehead (it should be comfortably warm) to see if she is warm enough. Babies sweat mostly from their feet and scalp so it is wise to put on booties if your baby is not wearing something that covers the feet, for instance a stretch suit.

When putting on booties always make sure that you do not tie the ribbons too tightly around the leg as this can restrict the circulation. Stretch suits should never pull tightly across the feet – this can be as damaging as wearing too small shoes.

Bonnets or hoods are not really necessary unless it is terribly cold or you are going to take her out in the wind. Generally speaking your baby does not need more than three layers of clothing in winter: vest or T-shirt, nightie and matinee jacket or vest and stretch suit, unless it is very cold. One blanket is usually enough although you will have to use your own judgement. In the early weeks a baby's internal temperature control mechanism is not very stable so it is wise to keep the room at a fairly even temperature, not below 16°C (60°F).

In an atmosphere that is too cold your baby will be using energy that she needs for growth, to keep warm. But do not make the mistake of dressing your baby so warmly that she sweats and develops a rash. Babies with heat rash look like miniature cases of teenage acne with raised spots around their necks, and sometimes all over the face and body as well. The solution is obvious: take off some of her covering and dab her spots with calamine lotion and add a tablespoon of bicarbonate of soda to her bath water to soothe her skin.

Do not tuck blankets around her head. Overheating has been associated with cot death.

SWADDLING. Wrapping the baby closely in a cloth or blanket – is an old custom still practised in some cultures. Although I do not routinely recommend it after the first weeks when it becomes important for your baby to have her hands free to explore, it can help to give a feeling of security and settle a restless baby, for instance one with colic (*see p. 99*).

METHOD. Fold over the top 30cm or so of a light wrapping blanket and place the baby in the middle with her shoulders inside the top edge. Take the one side of the blanket across her body and tuck it in under the opposite arm. Take the blanket at the bottom and fold it up over her feet. Tuck the last piece of blanket over the exposed arm and in around the back to make a neat 'parcel'.

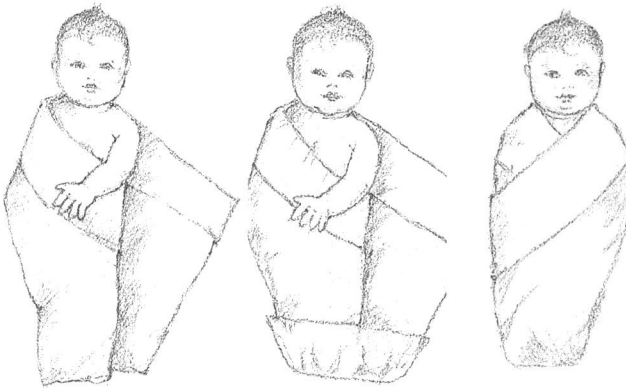

ESTABLISHING A SLEEPING ROUTINE

THIS IS IMPORTANT! In the beginning your baby will not know the difference between night and day, and will need a feed at least every three or four hours throughout. Keep the night feeds as low key as possible – use a dimmer switch or small night light – and do not use this time to play with her no matter how excited you are with your new toy. The delight will soon wear off when you wear out.

If she falls asleep during the feed, try and rouse her a little before you put her down. Putting her down sleepy but awake will help her learn to soothe herself to sleep. Feeding her, rocking her, driving around the block, swinging from the chandelier, or other fun things… may be undertaken when you are desperate but it is essential for your future sanity that you try and get your baby to learn to fall asleep without your direct involvement. A musical box, or better still a recording of you singing a lullaby, or other music that promotes alpha brain wave patterns like soothing music by Mozart or Vivaldi will be far easier than having you or dad pacing the floor every night.

CONFUSING DAY WITH NIGHT. If she sleeps longer than four hours during the day wake her so that she saves her long sleeps for the night. (*See also p. 484*) How to avoid and treat sleeping problems.

SLEEPING POSITIONS

ON THE BACK IS BEST. It has recently been found that babies who sleep on their tummies are far more susceptible to SIDS (sudden infant death syndrome). Although this is only one of a number of factors that seem to be involved, possibly because the baby breathes in the same air depleting it of oxygen when lying on the stomach; this new advice has cut the incidence of SIDS by more than half. It is therefore advisable to lie a healthy baby on her back for sleeping unless otherwise advised by your doctor.

Place her so that her feet almost touch the bottom of the bed so that she cannot slide under the covers if she moves down.

SLEEPING ON THE SIDE. In certain medical conditions or other circumstances, you may be advised to put your baby down to sleep on her side. Ensure that her arm she is lying on is well forward to prevent the rolling over onto her tummy. Put your baby down to sleep with her head facing a different way each time so that it does not become flattened on one side. You can use a bought 'wedge' behind her back so that she does not roll over, or make a roll with a small towel.

ADDITIONAL SAFETY. Do not cover your baby too warmly for sleep, as overheating has also been associated with cot death. Pillows are unnecessary and dangerous. Do not use them until your child is three or four years old. Do not use duvets or quilts as they can cover a baby's face and make breathing difficult. Do not allow anyone to smoke in your baby's presence. Tuck her bedding in well. (*See p. 47 for how to make up a baby's bed.*)

HOW TO CARE FOR SENSITIVE AREAS

MINIMUM INTERFERENCE. The key throughout is minimum interference – the less you fiddle in these areas, the better. Remember too that your baby's skin is extremely thin and what you use on it will be partially absorbed into the system.

EARS. Try to avoid getting water into your baby's ears and do not stick cotton buds into the ear canal. Excess wax will work its way out. If crusts form behind the ears, wipe the area with a piece of cotton pad dipped in boiled water that has cooled.

EYES. If there are any crusts use clean water and cotton pad to wipe from the nose outwards, using a clean piece of cotton pad for each eye. Otherwise leave them alone and simply wipe her face with a clean cloth or cotton pad.

SCALP. Although you may wash and brush your baby's hair frequently, she may develop a thick, scaly layer on her scalp. This is caused by still circulating hormones from the mother producing excess sebum (oil), and it is called cradle cap. If it is mild you can mix a teaspoon of bicarbonate of soda to half a litre warm water (not hot), and rinse her hair with it before washing. If the cradle cap is thick you will have to use another solution (*see p. 364*), to treat it, or you may want to consult your doctor if it spreads to her face and neck when it is known as seborrheaic dermatitis.

GENITALS. Girls should not be washed inside the lips of the vulva. This area often has a whitish coating in the first few weeks that should be left alone, as it will disappear by itself. A clear, white or slightly bloody discharge is also possible and it is not a cause for concern as it is due to maternal hormones from the pregnancy. It should clear up by itself.

FORESKIN. The foreskin on a baby boy is not retractable at birth but detaches itself gradually from the glans over the first two to four years of life. If you force the foreskin back you can tear it and the scar tissue that forms may then hold it to the glans so that retraction becomes difficult or impossible.

All that is required when washing your baby is to pull the foreskin back very gently as far as it will go and wash underneath. Later on the child should be taught to do this himself as a regular part of his hygiene so that problems can be prevented.

See a doctor if a sore develops at the tip of the penis or if there is ballooning of the foreskin when the child urinates. Urine should come out in a stream and not in a trickle.

CIRCUMCISED PENIS. A light dressing will probably have been placed over the head of the penis. When the baby urinates this will probably come off. Your doctor or whoever did the circumcision will instruct you as to how they want you to proceed. It is important to keep the area clean. The tip of the penis may look quite red and there may be a yellow secretion. This should disappear within a week. Any swelling, sores, redness after this should be reported as there may be an infection.

CORD. You can bath your baby before the cord has fallen off, but dry the area thoroughly. If the navel area is a little damp and sticky clean it with a cotton ball dipped in surgical spirits (rubbing alcohol). Any smelly discharge or redness must be reported to your doctor or clinic immediately. If there is any dry blood at the base of the cord, do not dislodge it as this can make it bleed again, although you can expect a few drops of blood when the cord falls off. Apply one or two drops of friar's balsam or other antiseptic as recommended by your doctor to the spot and keep it uncovered. It is not necessary to bind the cord or navel.

NOSE. Do not push a cotton bud up your baby's nostril because you can easily damage the delicate tissue. Use it to clean mucus at the opening only. If your baby's nose is blocked, take a clean piece of cotton wool and roll and twist it into a cone so that you can reach into the nostril. Dampen it with clean water before using.

HELPING YOU COPE

FEEDING CAN BE FRAUGHT. An area mothers often find difficult to cope with is feeding, especially breastfeeding. It can take up to six weeks or more to really get it going satisfactorily, so don't despair; consult the chapter on breastfeeding (*see p. 106*).

Remember that all things being equal, if your baby is gaining weight steadily and looks well, even if she does have periods of fretful crying, chances are she is thriving and well, though you may be a little ragged.

If you are bottle feeding *see p. 156* for details and then re-read the previous sentence – it still applies.

DEMAND OR SCHEDULE FEEDING? Another subject that attracts a barrage of conflicting advice is when you should feed your baby. Some will tell you to feed every four hours on the dot and that you will soon have a predictable schedule worked out. Others will suggest you feed your baby as near to four hourly as you can, while others will say feed any time your baby demands it.

Certainly we would a like our babies to be fed at exact intervals of four hours. But babies are not motor cars that run out of fuel every four hours; they are tiny humans and like the rest of us they have varying appetites at different times.

So if you want to get your baby to take a feed at exactly four hourly intervals you are going to have to be prepared to have her crying desperately for possibly an hour or more. You will probably be near to tears yourself while you sit watching the clock until it strikes the magic hour and you can feed her. I consider this a fundamentally wrong approach and one which furthermore can have very negative consequences.

Put yourself in the child's place: you are hungry, your body cries out for food, you cannot get it yourself so you send the only signal you know. You niggle then you cry, then you scream for food. And nothing happens. Then, when you have cried yourself to exhaustion and have learnt your first painful lesson of life – that the person who should satisfy your needs is not going to help – she appears and gives you a feed. What have you learnt? That your mother is not on your side, that she does not care about your needs; and that help is not forthcoming from the one person who you should have been able to trust. No wonder there is a generation gap. People who have used this method will tell you smugly that if you persevere and stick to the time table your baby will soon 'learn' to be 'good' and wait for her feeds.

What will happen is that she will soon discover that asking for something in the only way she knows, does not bring results. It is true that children of mothers who do not respond to their needs cry less than babies whose needs are met as soon as is reasonably possible. Babies in understaffed institutions do cry less than most other babies after a while. They too have been trained to be 'good' – but are they good or are they confused and eventually apathetic?

A human baby is a budding life with all the complexities of the human psyche, and it needs to be nurtured to develop strong and upright and confident of its own worth. From the above you will have deduced that I am against the rigid 'four hourly schedule'. It upsets the mother and it hurts the child, to say nothing of the rebound effect it has on the poor father.

How then, you may well ask, am I going to get any kind of order into my life?

PREPARE FOR A SIEGE. This is why you should prepare for a siege well beforehand. You need to have as little else to worry about as possible while you and your baby get to know each other, develop a rapport, and get some sort of system going.

Before long you will see a pattern emerging, in which you find your baby sleeps for a reasonable length of time between certain feeds so that you can get things done.

If you are bottle feeding, your baby will be able to go longer between feeds before she feels hungry, because the curds formed by cow's milk are larger and take longer to digest so she feels full for longer. Here you can use the four hourly schedule as a guide. If she wakes earlier and she is not starving, get everything ready, take her nappy off, expose her bottom to the air and have a little fun talking to her. Then as soon as she needs it, give her a feed.

If you are breast feeding and your baby wakes after three hours she is probably going to be yelling for food pretty soon. Breast milk is easily digested so her tummy will feel empty quicker than if she were bottle fed. So feed her as soon as she is ready; but if you have time, go through the same routine as described above for a bottle fed baby.

If your bottle fed baby is screaming and yelling after two hours and you remember she didn't take all of her previous feed – then she may be hungry – so feed her. In the early weeks your breast fed baby may even want to feed after less than two hours. Give it. It will soon sort itself out into a more predictable pattern with longer intervals in between as your breasts produce more milk and your baby gets stronger and can suck more vigorously. Remember, breastfeeding requires work on the part of the baby. Check out the breastfeeding section if your baby constantly demands a feed at very short intervals as she may be getting the fore milk only.

Even with demand feeding there are going to be times when you really don't know what your baby is trying to tell you. You feed her, she takes it, and then 20 minutes later, she is crying again. This is the kind of stress that gives mothers grey hairs before their time – if not worse. There is proof that some babies are just more difficult to satisfy than others regardless of who takes care of them. If it is your first baby, then you are having a baptism of fire. If it is your third, at least you know it is not really your fault. (*See 'Crying in the first weeks', p. 93, and different temperaments p. 521.*)

WHEN YOU FEEL YOU CAN'T COPE. Blaming yourself for not being able to keep your child happy all the time can do a great deal of harm, with many mothers becoming anxious and depressed. When you are depressed you feel closed in and despondent. You feel as though you cannot cope with your new life and although you are exhausted you cannot sleep. You may stop eating or eat compulsively and sometimes you become incapable of performing even simple tasks.

If you are a perfectionist, perhaps someone who has had a successful career, you could feel shattered to find that your previous competence counts for nothing and you cannot live up to your image of what a mother should be. Some mothers become obsessed with the thought that there is something wrong with their baby despite their doctor's assurance to the contrary. Sometimes you are so tired and unhappy being stuck at home with a baby who seems to depend on you so much, that you wish you never had her. You feel that other mothers cope so easily and you wonder if you will ever get back to being yourself again. You even wonder if your child will survive with you caring for her, and you sometimes feel like lashing out and beating her until she is quiet.

All mothers experience some of these feelings at times, but when you feel like this all the time, you need help urgently. You may not even realise what is wrong, or be able to bring yourself to do anything about it. It is up to those around you, your husband, or a close friend to see that you get the help you need. Being given a pep talk and told to snap out of it will do no good, and will probably make matters worse.

Becoming a mother puts enormous psychological, emotional and physical stress on a woman, besides playing havoc with hormonal activity. After all, the foetus is able to attach itself to the lining of the uterus, and go through all the other processes that must take place for it to grow primarily because of an alteration in hormonal secretions. After delivery, hormonal activity should return to normal fairly quickly, but fluctuations are common and you could have mood swings for some time, especially if you are breastfeeding. Anaemia and the depletion of trace elements can complicate matters and add to a general feeling of tiredness, so you should continue taking the multi-vitamin and iron supplements you were given during pregnancy for at least three months afterwards. Lowered thyroid function especially after several pregnancies may also be a contributing factor in making you feel tired and depressed.

Oestrogen supplementation and vitamin B6 have been used to good effect. But large doses will decrease your milk supply if you are breastfeeding. If you feel you cannot cope phone your doctor.

THE NEONATE

WHAT THE NEONATE IS LIKE. (A neonate is a baby less than four weeks old).

The average mass of white Anglo-Saxon babies is between 2.7kg and 3.8kg, with boys being slightly heavier. African and Asian babies tend to be lighter on average. Factors such as the nutrition and age of the mother, as well as her size and that of the father affect birth mass. Smoking results in a lighter baby, while certain conditions like pre-diabetes or uncontrolled diabetes usually mean a very heavy baby (over 4.5kg). Infants that are born at term (a full 40 weeks) but are much smaller than average are known as small-for-dates babies.

Most babies lose about one tenth of their weight in the first five days of life. This is due to the passing of meconium (dark black or greenish slimy stools which contain waste matter accumulated before birth) and the fact that they do not take sufficient feeds to meet their full requirements. From the fifth day there is usually a gradual increase and the child should regain her birth weight between the end of the first week and the beginning of the third week. Most babies grow quickly after regaining their birth weight – about 20–30g per day. Breast fed babies lose more weight because the flow of milk is inadequate in the first few days, but they usually catch up by the sixth day, unless they have not been demand fed.

The newborn baby is not always attractive, especially if forceps have been used or labour has been difficult. Babies born by Caesarean section are usually better looking as there is no moulding of the head or bruising in the birth process, however, in a week or two there should be little difference.

CORD. The umbilical cord by which the baby has been joined to the placenta is clamped and cut at birth. Within a few weeks the stump dries and falls off, leaving the navel. The stump must be kept clean and dry, so dab the base with a cotton bud dipped in surgical spirits or rubbing alcohol. If the area is damp, red, discharging, or has a bad smell, a doctor must be seen immediately as it could be infected. If the cord area swells out when your baby cries it could be an umbilical hernia. This is not serious and is caused by a small opening in the abdominal wall. This usually closes without treatment in the first eighteen months. If not, it can easily be repaired (*see p. 383*). Binding does not help healing.

EYES AND VISUAL ABILITY. At birth Caucasian babies have slate blue eyes until they gradually change to their permanent colour between three and six months. The colour at six months is likely to be permanent. Babies of African heritage have dark brown eyes and they remain that colour for life. Your newborn can see light and shapes and movement. And she focuses best on objects at a distance of between 20cm and 30cm (8 and 12 inches), just about the distance your face is when you feed her.

After about four weeks of life she should be able to follow a bright light with her eyes, and watch a patterned object that is not too big or too small and contrasts well with the background. More specifically, a strongly patterned disc between 18cm and 36cm wide, held between 20cm and 35cm away from her face moving from left to right at a speed of 30cm per second should attract her attention. The newborn's preference for strong black and white patterns and pale yellow and dark red show how perfectly nature has primed your baby to prefer the human face above all.

It is important that the child practices focusing, and a mobile hung over the cot can provide entertainment as well as visual stimulation. (*See p. 219*) for sketch and instructions.

Young babies cannot tolerate bright light, so don't put her where she will be staring into a light source like a window, or she will close her eyes. In the first few weeks babies' eyes are inclined to wander or squint when focusing, because they have not perfected the ability to co-ordinate their eyes so they work simultaneously. This tendency usually passes but if the eyes wander in different directions (walleye) or the squint does not correct itself by the fourth month a specialist should be seen. Sometimes a patch is placed over the good eye, or drops are inserted, in order to make the weak eye focus. Or, an operation may be needed to correct the problem, and this is usually done between six and eighteen months. More than one procedure may be necessary and the child may still need to wear glasses, but treatment is improving all the time.

Occasionally the epicanthic folds in the inner corner of the eyes wrongly make it seem as if the child is squinting, but it is nevertheless important that she be examined. In the first month babies do not cry tears but make enough to wash the eye. 'Real' tears are seen from around seven months. A blocked tear duct is common and can result in a discharge and excessive watering (*see p. 375*). Red spots may appear in the eye from pressure during birth but also disappear in time.

FONTANELLES. These are four areas on a baby's skull – at the top, sides and back – which are not covered by bone but by a tough membrane so that the bones can shift together when the baby passes through the birth canal. The fontanelles at the temples and behind the ears disappear after 14 days, while the one at the back of the head should disappear at two to three months. The anterior fontanelle that is at the top of the head closes between the ages of six and 18 months. Most mothers notice the anterior fontanelle because the area is soft and the pulse can sometimes be seen beating through the skin. This can be frightening, but there is no danger of hurting the baby when washing her hair. A bulging fontanelle, however, is a danger sign and could mean that fluid is causing pressure inside the skull; while a sunken fontanelle after vomiting and diarrhoea is a sign of dehydration and should be regarded as an emergency. The fontanelle is normally slightly sunken, anyway, so it is only when it becomes more so, and is associated with the symptoms above, that it need cause alarm.

LENGTH. The average length of the newborn is 52cm and doubles by age five years.

MOUTH AND THE SENSE OF TASTE. Contrary to what many people think the taste for sweetness is not learned, but innate. Even newborns prefer sweet tastes like mother's milk, to salty or sour tastes, although the degree of sweetness preferred is affected by conditioning over time.

Babies sometimes develop a blister on their top lip from sucking, but this is of no significance and should be ignored. White flecks inside the mouth that cannot be removed are caused by a fungus, candida albicans, and produce an infection known as thrush or monilia. If the mother has vaginal thrush it is easily transferred to the child at birth. Other sources of infection are nipples or teats, dummies and contaminated sterilising liquid. *See p. 367* for the treatment of thrush. Teeth are sometimes present at birth. These are either primary teeth or extra teeth. Primary teeth are firmly attached and should not be removed. Extra teeth are very small and usually very loose. They can be easily removed by a doctor.

NOSE AND THE SENSE OF SMELL. A baby's nose is usually flattened at the bridge and the sense of smell is not fully developed, although she can easily identify her mother's smell and prefers the smell of her breastmilk to that of other mothers. She dislikes sharp smells like vinegar, but the warm rich smells of vanilla and banana are attractive.

Young babies sneeze a lot but this does not mean they have a cold; it is a way of clearing the nose of mucus. Babies breathe through the nose which makes for noisy snuffly sounds if the nostrils are not clear. Do not use cotton buds to clear your baby's nostrils; roll a small piece of cotton to a thin twist and gently remove any mucus at the outer edge of the nostril. A cool mist humidifier and gentle suctioning of the nose with a special little apparatus may also be useful.

PENIS AND TESTES. If the child has not been circumcised it is natural for the foreskin to still be attached to the glans – in other words it doesn't slip back from the tip of the penis. However during the first 12 months it should gradually become more retractable until it is fully retractable by the age of three or four. Never force the foreskin back because it can cause damage. Any scar tissue which forms may result in adhesions which will make subsequent retraction very difficult. Urine should emerge in a strong stream and not dribble, even in a very young child. See a doctor if it does dribble out, or if the tip of the penis 'balloons' when urine is passed. Unless the baby is premature, in which case the testes may not have descended, they should be contained in the scrotum at birth or not later than six weeks afterwards (*see p. 385*).

VAGINA. Vaginal discharge, occasionally blood-stained, is not unusual in the neonatal period, owing to the effects of the mother's hormones still circulating in the baby's body. A thick white substance or vernix is present between the folds of the vagina; do not try to wipe it off because it will disappear naturally.

BREASTS. The breasts of boys and girls may be swollen from the effect of hormones from the mother which are still circulating in the baby's system. Do not squeeze or handle the nipples as this can easily result in an infection. Occasionally a baby's nipples appear to be secreting milk. This is caused by the factors which make the breasts enlarge and they should be left strictly alone. The effects will subside in a few weeks. If there is any sign of inflammation of the baby's breasts see your doctor.

SKULL. Your baby's skull may look asymmetrical with one side flat or otherwise slightly out of shape from pressure on it during birth. It should become more rounded within a week or two. Babies born by Caesarean section do not have moulding of the head though the bones in babies' skulls are purposely not joined together so they can overlap to fit through the birth canal.

Always support your baby's head when picking her up until she can support it herself at around three months.

SKIN. You may be disappointed to find that far from having a perfect complexion, your baby's face is marred by blotches or spots. Bruising and red marks on the nose or eyelids are often the result of pressure on the head during the birth and will disappear naturally. 'Stork bite' naevi (birthmarks) are common and are usually seen at the back of the neck or on the face. They look like a blotch of reddish spots and will disappear in the first year. Tiny white spots on the nose and cheeks are called milia and are caused by cysts that have formed in the oil glands. They require no treatment and will disappear in the first weeks. Occasionally, especially if the baby is born preterm, you may notice a change in shade between two parts of the child's body, almost a two-tone effect with one side being darker than the other. This is known as the Harlequin colour change caused by the flow of blood and has no sinister significance and will disappear quite soon. A mottled effect in which the skin looks 'marbled' with light and dark areas is simply due to the transparency of the newborn's skin and the effect of temperature changes. 'Mongolian spots' or bluish patches on the lower back are sometimes seen in dark skinned babies. They are of no significance and disappear by the time the child is around five years old (*see rashes p. 366, and birthmarks p. 443*).

The newborn baby's skin is covered with a greasy white substance known as vernix caseosa that has protected it from the effects of lying in the amniotic fluid during pregnancy. It disappears within days. There is thus, no need to bath a newborn baby to remove the vernix. Babies born after their due day often have dry, peeling vernix. All babies' hands and feet are sometimes blue, and their lips may become blue when crying – this is not a problem so long as the normal colour returns when she warms up or stops crying. If your baby's colour seems to be persistently blue, the heart and lungs may not be functioning as they should and she needs medical attention.

NAILS. The newborn infant's nails are soft and flexible yet sharp enough to scratch, especially if the baby was overdue. In the hospital her hands will probably be covered with cotton mittens to stop her scratching herself. Do not cover your baby's hands at home, she needs to be able to touch and explore with her fingers.

Cutting the finger nails is difficult and is best attempted when she is asleep. If there is an edge that is rough and has started to come off, pull it away gently. Or use an emery board to smooth the edge or a baby scissors to cut them, being very careful not to nick the flesh behind the nails as it can cause an infection. Toenails should be cut straight across but this is not usually necessary for many months. Any redness or tenderness around the nails might be an infection and must be seen to.

HAIR. Although some babies are born bald, most have a light fuzz of hair, and others have a thick mop. This first hair will fall out gradually and will be replaced by new hair that is usually darker in colour. Preterm and sometimes full term babies have very fine downy hair and this may extend over their forehead, ears and back. This downy layer of hair, known as lanugo falls out in the first months.

HEARING. Your newborn baby hears well and should respond when she hears sounds. Even in the first month your baby will know and respond to voices, especially the high tones of her mother making 'baby talk'. She will startle at loud noise levels and may even start crying, but she will love to hear the familiar tones of the voices and sounds she heard while still in the womb. Gentle music, lullabies, familiar stories grab her attention and she should respond with alert attention. She does not need absolute quiet in order to sleep, but loud throbbing sounds will disturb her.

ABDOMEN. Babies have large abdomens especially after a feed. However any hardness or unusual swelling, possibly associated with a lack of bowel movement, or vomiting must be reported to your doctor.

ROOTING. Sucking is instinctive in the newborn and if you touch your baby's cheek she should turn towards the side you touched, in a movement known as the rooting reflex, and begin to suck.

HICCUPING. Babies hiccup frequently due to the immaturity of their digestive tract. It is of no significance, but can disturb feeding. If you wish you can try giving a little cooled, boiled water to which you have added a half teaspoon of sugar.

LEGS. A baby's legs are naturally bowed in infancy and straighten as the child grows unless there is an underlying cause such as rickets (vitamin D deficiency), or if bowlegs run in the family. A baby's feet should not toe in or out. If you have doubts, consult a doctor as soon as possible, since corrective treatment works best when started early. (See club feet p. 379 and bow legs.)

PERSONALITY OF THE NEONATE. In the first few weeks after delivery, your baby will be trying to adjust to life outside the womb, and you will also be feeling your way towards becoming a mother with all its implications. For your baby, life outside the womb is almost more restricting than before. She cannot turn over or reach out with any precision, and she has to let you know when she needs food. Her eyesight is fuzzy and not precisely focused, and her nervous system so immature that she trembles and jerks easily. Her digestive system is still unsettled and she has to get used to having nourishment through her mouth instead of directly into her bloodstream as before.

Because all her systems are not yet synchronised, she hiccups easily and is likely to start crying if she is startled by a sudden noise. You may occasionally get a glimpse of a smile, but it is as likely to be caused by a grimace from a wind as a real response to your face. Towards the end of the first month you may experience the joy of your baby's first real smile directed at you. You will now know why you would walk barefoot over broken glass to protect your baby.

NEEDS OF THE NEONATE. In order to thrive and develop well in the first four weeks of life, a baby needs sufficient warmth, nourishment and love. Warmth is easily supplied through adequate, though not too much covering, and heating of the room in very cold climates.

The only nourishment the neonate needs is breastmilk or substitute milk. See Chapters five and six for quantities. No added vitamins, foodstuffs or water are required in the first four weeks unless your baby was born prematurely when vitamins and iron may be prescribed, and breastmilk may be enriched with a special formula.

By love, I mean close physical contact and comfort. If the baby is breast fed she will be having skin-to-skin, as well as eye-to-eye contact with the mother several times a day; this kind of interaction is vital even if the baby is bottle fed. Cuddle and hold your baby often, not only when feeding. Touch is so important a need that without it babies will not thrive and grow as they should.

CRYING IN THE FIRST WEEKS. There is no such thing as a young baby 'crying to exercise her lungs', or because of temper or naughtiness. These are convenient ways of dodging the issue of why she is crying, but they don't do anything to comfort the child. Very few mothers can calmly listen to a baby 'exercising her lungs'. You may feel like crying yourself when you have done everything you can think of to comfort your baby and she still remains distressed. You wonder desperately if she is ill, or hungry or even dying... You may feel so inadequate because you cannot soothe her that you sometimes become angry and resentful. This is a natural reaction, and there is no need to feel a failure because of it, every mother feels this way sometimes.

TEMPERAMENT AND CRYING. Keep in mind that some babies are naturally more easily distressed than others, and that they would probably carry on crying even if they were in other hands. If you become tense you can transmit the feeling to your baby, making matters worse. Rather leave your baby with someone you can trust and take a soothing bath, or a walk. Your baby is not angry with you personally, nor are you a bad mother because you can't seem to console her. Newborn babies cry for up to four hours a day – it's part of the adjustment to living outside the womb. Whatever you do, do not shake her to get her to be quiet. Shaking can damage a baby's brain, cause blindness or even death.

INTERPRETING A BABY'S CRIES. You may have heard that you will soon get used to your baby's cries and will be able to interpret them so well that you will know what is needed straight away. In actual fact, spectrogram studies (analysis of the frequency range of sound) have shown that while there are differences in the pattern made by babies with conditions like Down's syndrome, serious illnesses and brain damage, the crying pattern of normal babies does not vary according to a specific cause. Therefore, although the baby may give a full-throated cry when she is in pain and a niggly cry when she is hungry, the wave pattern will be the same.

The fact is, parents have to decipher what their baby is trying to tell them from obscure information. What happens with experience is that the spectrum of possible reasons for the crying is gone through quickly by the mother and she is more likely to make a correct, educated guess.

Generally, a hungry baby will start niggling before she gives the short, low pitched rise and fall… ah laa, ah laaa… of a hunger cry. If not fed soon the cry will develop into the full throated angry and hungry cry, which is similar but louder and more ragged at the edges. Pain is usually heralded with an immediate frantic high pitched shriek followed by an intake of breath and then a long, flat wail… The tired and cranky cry, which says 'I need to get away from it all and rest' is easily confused with the hunger cry.

While all babies are different, it helps to know the baby's background as well as the immediate experiences before the crying started. Therefore the more intimately you are involved with your child the better you are able to read her distress signals.

Certain distinctive cries that sound cat-like, hoarse, very high pitched or feeble can be a sign that all is not well. The child who is weak may also cry very little or only feebly.

WHY BABIES CRY AND WHAT YOU CAN DO ABOUT IT. Firstly, it cannot be over-emphasised that by handling your baby, holding and loving her as often as you wish, while responding to her needs as soon as possible, you are not spoiling her. You are doing the natural, normal thing and setting the foundation for a sound relationship in the future.

CRYING FOR A FEED. In cultures where babies are carried on the mother's back, they are fed as soon as they begin to grizzle, regardless of the time that has elapsed between feeds. Babies who sleep with their mothers go to the breast as often as every 20 minutes during the night.

Happily, there has been a growing trend to carry infants in specially designed slings either on the back or in front. This is a perfectly acceptable way of keeping your baby near you, giving her the warmth and comfort of close contact, as well as the lulling effects of your movements.

The child is then also able to hear the mother's voice and the comforting sound of her heartbeat as she did in utero – an excellent way of bridging the gap between life in the womb and independence. It has been shown that babies carried on the mother's back do not lag behind in motor development and learn to walk at the same average stages as babies who have been brought up in the usual Western manner.

If your baby is breast fed, it is worth putting her to the breast even if only one and a half hours have elapsed since the last feed if you have any indication that she may be hungry. Studies have shown that there will be far less crying – regardless of the original cause – after a feed than before a feed in both breast and bottle fed babies and even in babies who have been tube fed.

Unfortunately there is the danger of causing discomfort from overfeeding especially if your baby is bottle fed. If your baby is breast fed you can feel easier about frequent feeds, although you do not want her to be getting fore milk only so do not change breasts until the one side has been emptied. In general, if you find frequent feeds reduce the crying, then give frequent smaller feeds to the bottle fed baby by dividing the day's feeds into smaller amounts given more often.

WARMTH. It has been shown that tiny babies who are kept in a warm room are likely to sleep longer and cry less than babies in a cold room. Premature babies have been found to grow faster when held against her skin by the mother in what is known as 'kangaroo care'. Rather than heating the room, which is really not necessary except in very cold climates, you can make sure the baby is kept in a sunny room free of draughts for the first few weeks. Beware of overheating as this makes babies wake and it has also been associated with cot death.

WET OR SOILED NAPPIES. This is unlikely to wake a baby unless the wet nappy has been exposed to the air and has become cold. Cold hands do not mean she is cold; rather feel her feet or the back of her neck. After the first weeks fresh air and sunshine are desirable.

UNDRESSING. Very young babies almost invariably cry when they are undressed, even in a warm room; they seem to need the feeling of something close to the skin, particularly over the tummy. So don't be upset if your baby screams at bath time – it is normal and it will take a while before she enjoys the freedom of being without clothes and splashing in the water. You can bath her with something covering her tummy and see if this calms her.

SWADDLING. An old practice that has been shown to have a definite calming effect on a new born baby is swaddling. Because small babies thrash their arms and legs in an uncontrolled way, they tend to overstimulate themselves. Correct swaddling can comfort the newborn by providing a feeling of being touched and prevent her from becoming agitated by her own movements (*see p. 81*).

DUMMIES (PACIFIERS). Sucking is a great means of comfort to babies and this is where the judicious use of a dummy can be of great help. The sight of a two-year-old with a dummy plugged into her mouth is not attractive, and dummies can be a source of infection, but if it is used with care there is no reason why your child should be denied the comfort unless you have a strong personal objection. Some nursing homes refuse to allow dummies in the belief that it will cause 'nipple confusion' and discourage breastfeeding. There is no scientific evidence to support this.

Choose a dummy with a large base so that the child cannot get half or all of it into her mouth. If the dummy is made of rubber only it will not hurt if the child lies on it. Buy two or three so that you always have a sterilised one on hand. Prolonged boiling perishes rubber so immerse in boiling water for only three to five minutes. Dummies can be sterilised in the same chemicals you use for bottles, but it is common for the solution to become contaminated with thrush. Should your baby develop thrush, it is wise to buy new dummies and boil them. After you have sterilised the dummies, keep them in a clean, dry container in the fridge. Tiny dummies are available for preterm babies, and they can provide comfort and assist with the development of sucking. You will have to ask your doctor about this as they are not available directly to the public.

Some babies, particularly breast fed babies, are loathe to take a dummy because of its unfamiliar taste and texture but can usually be persuaded to take it in time. Dipping a dummy in breastmilk to help encourage the baby to take it in the early weeks should do no harm. Do not make a practice of dipping the dummy into the gripe water bottle as germs could multiply in the liquid. Do not dip in honey as it is dangerous for babies due to the possibility of botulism, and never tie a long cord to the dummy as the child could choke on it. Often a baby who is already screaming will not take a dummy, so give it while she is still only niggling. Sucking on a dummy relaxes the muscles of the gut so if the child is having cramps from colic it helps ease the pain.

SUCKING FOR COMFORT. One of the most confusing things about interpreting your baby's wants in the early weeks is the need for sucking comfort. You will find that she takes a bottle or breast eagerly, especially if she has been crying, with the result that you may give her a feed when sucking on a dummy will really be the answer. You will have to use your discretion about this, keeping in mind your baby's feeding pattern and weight gain. Copious 'explosive' stools can indicate overfeeding.

Regardless of whether you give your baby a dummy or not she may discover her thumb as a source of sucking comfort. Once this happens there is not very much you can do about it and you should not use any methods such as the wearing of mittens or other forms of restriction to prevent it. You may be able to persuade her to take a dummy instead of sucking her thumb, but there is not much to choose between the two. Thumb sucking can persist for a long time, however, even after the child has begun school, and this can add to displacement of the teeth if there is already a tendency to this in the structure of the jaw. You may also have the minor problem of a callus forming on the thumb, and you will not be able to throw it away as you might a dummy.

Dummies can be very unhygienic, even more so than thumbs, and you could end up getting up countless times a night to replace it when it falls out of her mouth. At least the thumb is always there. On the other hand, if you do use the dummy to get your baby over the three-month colic period and discard it as soon after this as possible, you might be able to escape thumb sucking or a dummy problem later on. However, there is really no need at any stage to force the child to give up either habit, since pressure is likely to make the need for its comfort even greater. Tactful encouragement should be sufficient – never make it into a drama – it is not worth it to either of you. Some parents make giving up the dummy a special event with a suitable small reward to mark the occasion.

There is reason to believe that the denial of the need for sucking comfort may be harmful, and some say this is the reason why some adults smoke cigarettes! If you are breastfeeding and you allow your baby to suck for as long as she wishes, you will be satisfying this need easily and naturally.

Sucking provides a great and necessary source of gratification to a child, but it should never become the child's only means of gaining comfort.

ROCKING AND OTHER MOVEMENT. Another 'old fashioned' practice that has been proven to have a definite calming effect on the new born is rocking. Cradles that rock are a rarity today but it seems that whoever phased them out wasn't aware of a baby's needs. What is really required, experiments have shown, is a rocking motion of 60 rocks a minute with a swing of 7cm (3inches). As anyone who has ever 'walked' a baby to sleep, or noticed the magical effect of a ride in a motor car on a restless baby will testify: the hand that rocks the cradle lulls the baby. A baby swing can be useful, but be sure the child is not slumped and safely strapped in.

BOUNCING CAN BE A VERY EFFECTIVE WAY OF SOOTHING A BABY TO SLEEP. A large ball that you can sit on – such as those used for Pilates exercise – is perfect. Dim the light, or put it off and leave only a passage light on. Sit on the ball with your back straight and your feet on the ground. Whilst cradling your swaddled, or loosely covered baby – according to her preference – bounce or roll the ball gently and rhythmically until she falls asleep. The effect is similar to that of taking a baby for a ride in the car.

SOUND. Most people believe that newborn babies need dead silence or they will wake. Young babies do startle and cry at sudden loud noises, but they don't like total silence either. The ideal background noise is the sound they hear in the womb. The swish of blood through arteries and veins, and the regular thumping of the mother's heart. Instinctively, mothers make a susshing sound similar to this when trying to soothe their baby. Recordings of womb sounds to play to the newborn infant have been made, but like the clock and hot water bottle trick for a kitten, they have a limited use.

Sing to your baby or make a recording singing a lullaby – record it with your baby in your arms so that you do it with feeling – and play it if you can't be with her. Experiments show that babies respond to music, especially classical music such as that of Vivaldi and Mozart, and that it promotes brain development. Babies are soothed by slow, soft music with gradual changes in tempo like rhythmic classical music and traditional lullabies. They become attentive and alert when they hear bright tempos with high notes – not loud – and with a clear rhythm such as nursery rhymes. A number of recordings of music for babies are available and they can be useful.

On a more primitive level, white sound, which is a monotonous tone without variations in pitch like the sound made by a vacuum cleaner or telephone dialling tone, seems to be effective in soothing babies to sleep. The England national team soccer player Wayne Rooney reportedly used to fall asleep to the sound of a vacuum cleaner. And some parents swear by the effectiveness of a radio tuned between stations to lull their baby, even though it is an irritating noise to adults. The tinkle of a musical box can also be effective. There is no research to prove the effectiveness of these tricks, or whether they have any potential for harm.

WARM BATHS AND MASSAGE. You may find it relaxes your baby if you take a warm bath with her. Many babies do not enjoy this in the early weeks however. A gentle massage using a suitable lotion, or oil can be soothing. Working in a circular movement with warm hands slowly stroke your baby's back then her abdomen, then with long smooth strokes working from the outside towards the body glide your hands up her limbs. You need to be relaxed to do this effectively or you will transfer your tension.

OSTEOPATHIC AND CHIROPRACTIC REALIGNMENT. Osteopathic and chiropractic manipulation in which the spine and pelvic area is 'realigned' has been promoted as a remedy for incessant crying. It is difficult to recommend this procedure without the strong caveat that any manipulation of an infant's fragile bones has the potential for serious injury. Explore this route only if you are absolutely convinced of the expertise of the practitioner and the safety of the process.

> **FRAGILE: HANDLE WITH CARE!**
> There will be times, not least of all when your baby cries incessantly, that you may be tempted to shake her to stop the crying. Don't do it! A baby's brain is more fragile than an eggshell. Blindness, bleeding around the brain, learning disabilities, paralysis and even death can result. Your baby is not 'spoiled', or crying to be annoying, or to get attention. Colic is a very painful condition, and even babies without colic cry an average of one to four hours a day. If you can't control yourself, leave the room.

HERBAL REMEDIES. Only use products that are manufactured under controlled circumstances. Natural does not necessarily mean safe. Like all medicines there may be side effects, in particular damage to the liver (Comfrey tea is not recommended) or ingredients like alcohol, which are often high. Check labels.

WHEN DOING LESS IS MORE. Some babies simply need to cry a while to release tension before they fall asleep. Check your baby for anything obvious that may be causing pain, and then try leaving her alone. Experiments have shown that when some distressed babies are handled, they simply become more agitated. Turn the lights down, close the curtains and walk away. Come back in ten minutes to check her if you must, then leave her alone. Fifteen or even twenty minutes of crying may almost finish you off, but is unlikely to harm your baby.

THE CURSE OF COLIC. Characterised by bouts of crying sometimes for hours on end, infantile colic is unnerving and exhausting for parents, and obviously painful for the baby although she gains weight and appears to thrive in other respects. Because colic, like the common cold, has no real cure or even a certain cause, some experts have tried to pretend it doesn't exist or else blame it on a 'nervous' mother. What mother wouldn't be a nervous wreck with a baby who screams for hours?

I wish we could say that tribalised mothers do not have this problem, then we could look to them for a cure, but unfortunately their babies, too, have periods of fretfulness in the early months in spite of the advantage of being kept close to their relaxed and 'natural' mothers. They, too, find that not all their children are afflicted and that they mercifully grow out of it by about three to four months of age.

A baby, who has colic draws up her legs, clenches her fists and screams in apparent agony, usually at a particular time of day. In really bad cases the child stiffens her legs and arches her back. Whereas most crying babies will stop when picked up, the child suffering from colic continues to cry unabated and may do so for hours on end. The fists are forced into the mouth and sucking is the one thing that seems to alleviate her suffering.

Most babies cry like this after the six o'clock feed – the so-called 'evening colic' – which has led people to blame a low milk supply if the baby is breast fed, or, if the baby is bottle fed, to transferred tension from a harried mother because of suppertime activity. Or else, on mismanagement of the child. Certainly, the milk supply may be low in the evening, but why do bottle fed babies suffer even more from colic? Tension can be transmitted to a baby, but placid mothers have had colicky babies while nervous mothers have been spared. As for mismanagement of the baby, colic sometimes starts in the nursing home and it happens to nurses', doctors' and psychologists' children as well.

Colic, as stomachache used to be called, is just that. A gripping, cramp-like spasm of the gut that causes a lot of pain. There are very few adults who do not know how awful a severe stomachache can be, and certainly no woman who has ever experienced severe menstrual cramps will be unsympathetic to the plight of a tiny mite with a pain in the belly. When the spasm locks in an air bubble (as X-ray pictures of the lower bowel have shown), it is doubly painful.

GAS BUBBLES. When babies drink they swallow a lot of air as well. This gas or wind is usually brought up when the baby burps after a feed, but some babies have difficulty getting up the wind and then the gas bubbles are passed into the bowel where they can cause pain, especially if they are trapped in between spasms. Evening colic may be an accumulation of wind that has built up during the day. No one has established for certain why some babies are affected and others not, but it may simply be that some babies' bowel muscles are more relaxed than others and they can pass wind more freely.

FEEDING TOO SLOWLY OR TOO QUICKLY. If the milk flows too quickly and the baby gulps it down it can cause cramps. Too slow a flow from the bottle or breast will also be a problem. Make sure the hole in the teat is the right size, (*see p. 165 and Gulping at the breast p. 137, 143*).

SENSITIVITY TO MILK OR OTHER FOODS IN THE DIET. The most common foods being cow's milk, eggs, peanuts and wheat. Occasionally, babies are sensitive to these foods, either in the formula or solids they are having or, if they are breast fed, to these foods in the mother's diet. The breastfeeding mother can try cutting these foods out one by one from her diet and if there is an improvement in the baby, it could be that her baby is allergic to cow's milk or whatever has been cut out of the diet. If it is dairy products the mother should keep up her fluid intake and replace the calcium that she would have been getting from milk and other dairy products, either through a calcium supplement or through other calcium rich foods. If your baby is bottle fed, *see cow's milk allergy pp. 144, 195 and 422. See p.144* for foods to avoid when breast feeding, as there are other substances that may be causing the problem.

INFECTION. Urinary tract infection is a possible medical cause of colic-like pain. If your baby has a low grade fever and feeds poorly, have her urine tested. So long as your baby gains weight well, the crying is unlikely to be due to illness.

REFLUX. Some babies regurgitate their feeds because the muscular valve at the top of the stomach does not close properly. This results in posseting or bringing up some of the feed, either fully through the mouth, or partly, into the oesophagus (food pipe). The acidic digestive juices cause burning of the food pipe and this raw, red area is extremely painful. (*See oesophageal reflux p. 381*) and consult your doctor.

WHAT YOU CAN DO. First read the section on *Crying starting on p. 93* and try the recommendations given there.

Also try to get your baby to bring up wind during a feed as well as afterwards. Some babies are better at this than others, but there are medicines that can be given before a feed or added to the bottle that help break the gas bubbles. Most of these contain dill and bicarbonate of soda and your pharmacist will be able to recommend a suitable product. (Some 'natural' remedies and gripe waters have high alcohol contents so check labels on all products.) Simethicone antacid works well for some infants Consult your doctor.

It you can, get the wind up after every 25ml or so, and when the baby changes breasto, but don't fuss for long because if the baby starts crying she will swallow more wind.

BRINGING UP THE WIND. Because winds – from both top and bottom – so often cause discomfort, getting them out often brings relief. There are several ways of getting up a burp after a feed, and you will have to experiment and see what works best for your baby.
■ Lie your baby on the changing mat, and two or three times a day do deep clockwise massage of the abdomen using small circles. Then bend your baby's knees right

up to her belly button. Do this four to five times. Then lift your baby up while holding her under the arms and let her feet touch the mat. Lower her to bend her legs until her knees touch right onto her tummy. Follow with another four our five massage circles on the abdomen. You should soon be rewarded with a loud passing of the troublesome wind.

- Rest your baby over your breast with her head tucked under your chin, then rub her back gently or give little pats on her bottom. Or, you can hold your baby against your chest with her head over your shoulder.

- Another way is to sit your baby on your knee and hold her head up by resting her chin between your thumb and fingers while supporting her back with your other hand. This has the effect of stretching the oesophagus, giving the wind a free passage to the mouth.

- Lying on the tummy seems to help some babies pass wind. Sit comfortably, and lay her on her tummy over your lap. Rub her back gently in a circular movement.

- A change of position by lying the baby down on her back for a few minutes after a feed and then picking her up again sometimes has the magical effect of bringing up the burp. You would never believe that this sound could be so eagerly welcomed until you have paced the floor and thumped the bottom of a colic-prone baby like a tomato sauce bottle trying to get the windup!

- Raising the head of the pram or crib also helps bring up winds, but never use a pillow for a baby; even a safety pillow is risky. Do it by folding a towel or blanket under the mattress. If you find your baby is inclined to slide down the slope, wedge a folded blanket at the bottom of the pram for her feet to rest against. When putting her down to sleep lie her on her right side so that winds can come up easier. Change her to her back after 10 minutes.

- A baby chair, especially the well padded reclining type can be useful as the baby is held in a semi-upright position which helps bring up the winds. You can put your baby in these chairs from the first few weeks if you support her by tucking a towel or blanket around her.

- Check that her bottle does not have too large or too small a hole in the teat as this can cause her to swallow a lot of air. When the bottle is turned upside down the milk should come out in quick, steady drips.

- Heat applied to the stomach can help relieve spasms, and you can try putting a warm water bottle near her tummy if you are very, very careful not to make it too hot and to cover it with a blanket or towel before putting it near your baby. Do not overheat your baby!
- Turn down the light and lie down comfortably next to your baby on the bed. Place your hand firmly over your baby's tummy. Hold it there creating warmth and support while you work at relaxing yourself and your baby through your empathy and closeness. It does not work quickly but it can be a way of helping both of you.
- Because the colicky baby forces her fists into her mouth and takes the breast or bottle eagerly, you could think she is hungry, but feeding could aggravate the problem. Sucking on a dummy is often the answer. Besides the comfort that sucking provides, it encourages peristalsis (the natural movements made by the bowel when passing food along) so it helps pass the wind. You will have to get her to take the dummy before she is really screaming, because by that stage there is little that will get her to stop. Sugar has been shown to alleviate pain, so there may be a case for trying a scant quarter teaspoon of glucose or sugar on the dummy. Do not use honey because of the danger of botulism. Do not under any circumstances use sugar as a panacea for all crying. It must only be used when all else fails and you need her to take the dummy.
- Distracting the baby from her pain can help for a little while, so hold her up and attract her attention with a toy. If she gets irritated stop immediately, as she could become over stimulated which will make matters worse. Some babies are extremely sensitive to stimulation through smell, sound and bright light. As a result they become unhappy and cannot relax. Even your perfume may be a factor. These babies need calm, neutral, darkened surroundings to avoid sensory overload.
- A ride in the car can be soothing, and rocking a well-swaddled baby or pushing her in the pram can help her relax. Or gently bounce on a Pilates ball.
- Take care to read your baby's reaction. If she does not appear to be soothed by your handling rather leave her even if she is crying. Doing too much can be counterproductive. Studies show that leaving a colicky baby to soothe herself is one of the best ways to shorten bouts of crying especially if you swaddle her.

MEDICINES THAT RELIEVE COLIC. As described earlier, medications which contain dill or an antacid which break the surface of the bubbles can help in mild cases. Simethicone is an antacid that is available under numerous brand names for babies and helps break gas bubbles. Use all medications only as instructed on the bottle, and by your medical advisor.

Gripe waters contain varying amounts of alcohol. Ask your pharmacist for the brand with no alcohol content. Many herbal and alternative remedies also contain large amounts of alcohol. Check labels, if the content is not specified, avoid.

There are a number of prescription medications that are being used for colic that are meant for other indications. Some of these are potentially harmful. They also do not work very well. Obtain your doctor's assurance that there are no potential harmful side effects. Colic is one of nature's more cruel quirks because it comes at a time when you are still adjusting to motherhood and feeling the strain of the new responsibility. Try not to become demoralised. It is not your fault – you are not an inadequate mother. It happens to experienced mothers too. Get out of the house when you can, and do something that is just for you in order to relax you and renew your spirit, and remember as long as your baby is gaining weight and she has been checked by a doctor then it is unlikely that the screaming is caused by anything other than colic. It will stop, and your baby will thrive. Some of the most colicky babies become easy, adorable children – survive as best you can and it should pass after three months – although it does sometimes last a little longer – it will ease off. Take consolation in the popular belief that colicky babies usually turn out to be very bright!

GO TO www.baby-childcare.com TO WATCH THE FOLLOWING VIDEOS THAT ARE APPLICABLE TO CHAPTER 4

PROF CLAUDIA GRAY	Colic
	Sleep in babies and children
	Common skin conditions
	Developmental milestones
	Stools
	Rashes
DR ANUSHA LACHMAN	The first 1000 days of life
	Good enough parenting
	The role of care givers
	Bonding with a premature baby
DR BAVI VYTHILINGUM	Can fathers experience postnatal depression?
	Postnatal depression
	Prenatal depression
EMMA NUMANOGLU	A message to new mothers
	Birthing options
	Preparing for a ceasarian
	Common birthing fears

What happens if things do not go as planned
The hours after your baby is born
Breastfeeding questions after the birth
Giving your prem baby the benefit of breast milk
Taking your baby home
Induction
Circumcision
Take home info when you are discharged
The father's role

DR SIMONE HONIKMAN   Management of anxiety disorders

ANEL ANNANDALE   Traumatic birth
Brain boosters
Attachment bonding
Brain development
Neuroplasticity

DR NICOLA DUGMORE   Parental self reflection
Transitional objects
Fathers

CHAPTER 5

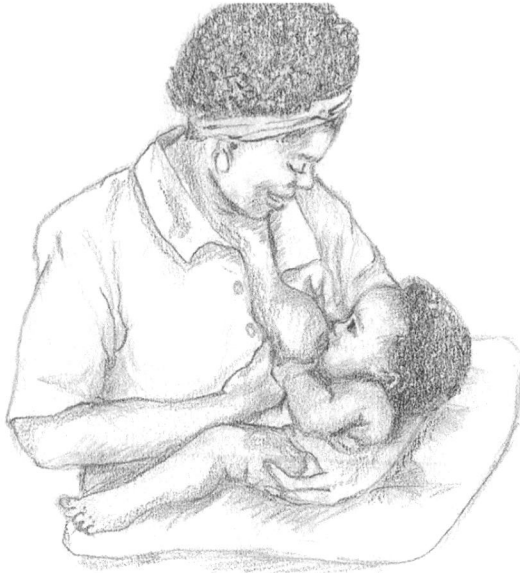

Breastfeeding

DECIDING WHETHER TO BREASTFEED. If you have read Chapter 3, you will be aware of some of the reasons why there is no exact substitute for breastmilk.

You may now be keen to try breast feeding but you may have heard so many conflicting stories about what happens, and how things can go wrong, that you are uncertain and confused. You could also be worried that your milk will be 'too weak' or that you will not have enough milk, or about breast abscesses. You may be going back to work and so you think it is better to get your baby started on formula feeds straight away, or perhaps someone has told you that mother's milk does not 'agree' with all babies.

Perhaps you are going to have a Caesarean and you think this means you cannot breastfeed. Maybe your breasts are large or very small and the nipples inverted, and this makes it seem as though you will not manage. You may be a vegetarian, or your biggest fear may be that you will lose your figure and your breasts will sag.

Let's go through some of these points individually so that you have the facts clear in your mind before you make your decision.

- It is true that you could develop a painful breast abscess and it could require surgical drainage. However, the likelihood of this happening is remote, and if you have good advice it is very unlikely indeed that things will get to this stage.
- There is no chance that your milk will be 'too weak' or 'too strong' for your baby. Mother's milk is always perfectly balanced and absolutely ideal for your baby, except in certain illnesses, such as galactosaemia, primary lactose intolerance, and other metabolic disorders.
- You may not have enough milk, but this can be remedied. Women who are physically unable to breast feed are very rare.
- A previous breast abscess should not deter a woman from breastfeeding although careful supervision is advisable so that she does not become engorged. Premature babies, and those born by Caesarean section can and should be breastfed even if the milk has to be expressed while the baby is in ICU or cannot suck. The mother's milk may need to be fortified for preterm babies.
- Women who have had a mastectomy can, and have breastfed successfully from the unaffected breast. Even adoptive mothers can produce milk if they are determined and correctly supervised (see p. 124).
- Even a few days on breastmilk is better than nothing because of the antibodies against germs that are transferred to the baby. As for working mothers, when you get back to work you can still feed at certain times, or express. It is far better to breastfeed for a while and then to change to formula, than to not breastfeed at all.
- The size of the breasts is not an indication of the amount of milk you will produce. Milk is made on a supply and demand basis. Large breasts have a lot of fatty tissue and can hinder the baby's breathing while she is feeding, but this can be overcome. Small breasts often produce more milk.
- Inverted nipples are a nuisance but can be corrected in most cases (see p. 39).
- Breastfeeding will not ruin your figure if you take care of your breasts (see p 38). It is pregnancy itself that can have an effect on breast tone and shape.

WHEN BREASTFEEDING MAY NOT BE THE BEST WAY. Certain medical conditions such as active tuberculosis, cancer and HIV infection, as well as medications the mother needs to be on can adversely affect the baby through the milk (see p. 119 and 145). Never let anyone else breastfeed your baby as you cannot be sure that her milk will be good for your baby.

WHEN BREASTFEEDING IS NOT FOR YOU. Despite everything in its favour, some women find the whole concept of breastfeeding repulsive and 'animal-like'; their feelings should be respected. Other mothers do not have success even after a determined effort. Still others may not be able to for medical reasons in the mother or baby. A happy mother/child relationship is vitally important, and breastfeeding is only one part of mothering. No woman should feel a failure or be tormented if she does not breastfeed. You can give the bottle in the same close way, especially if you open your blouse and allow your baby to nestle her cheek against your skin. Try to ignore pressure or remarks made by other men and women intended to make you feel guilty.

BREASTFEEDING AND THE MAN IN YOUR LIFE. If you are determined to breastfeed, you need good advice, encouragement and support, particularly from your partner. Some men resent the idea of a baby taking over their 'territory', but this is short sighted since it is only a temporary loan and the dividends are high.

EQUIPMENT FOR BREASTFEEDING. Breastfeeding requires no equipment except that supplied by nature. But there are a few extra items that you might want to use.

A BREASTFEEDING BRA IS USEFUL (*see p. 43*). Breast pads prevent any leakage of milk coming through on your clothes. These are obtainable from supermarkets and chemists. Some breast pads have a plastic lining which is unsuitable as the plastic holds the moisture against the skin and you could get very tender nipples as a result. So either make sure the bought pads do not have plastic linings or remove them.

Never put cotton wool or a tissue against your nipples as it can stick and hurt when you pull it off. You can even wedge a folded white tissue behind a piece of disposable one-way nappy liner to absorb moisture. The reason for using a one-way liner against your skin is that moisture will pass through it and leave your nipple dry.

In the hospital you may be given a bowl of sterile water with some cotton wool to wipe your nipples before a feed. You can do this at home if you like, by pouring cooled water from the kettle into a clean container and wiping your nipples before and after the feed, but it really is not necessary except if you have had cream on your nipples as it can make it slippery for the baby to latch on. All you should do before a feed is to wash your hands well so that you do not transfer any germs to your nipples.

There is no hard evidence to show that 'conditioning' the nipples before the birth is necessary, although certain procedures can be harmful like 'hardening' the nipples with spirits or alcohol. *See p. 39* for some procedures that may be useful.

If your nipples are dry, lanolin cream made up in a water base by your chemist is cheap and a good lubricant, but once again you will do well enough without it, and some babies are allergic to lanolin. Commercial creams for lubricating the nipples are also available, but they are not really necessary unless problems arise, when their use will be explained.

WHAT HAPPENS DURING PREGNANCY. One of the first things you will notice when you are pregnant is that your breasts become tender and enlarge as the months go by. This is caused by the increased blood supply and the growth of milk-producing glands inside the breasts. The areola, the dark area around the nipples, becomes larger and darker and the oil producing glands that look like tiny bumps on the areola also increase in size. These glands lubricate or oil the nipples while the baby sucks, as well as killing germs, so you can see why there is no real necessity for using creams.

CARE OF THE NIPPLES DURING PREGNANCY. During the last few months of pregnancy the breasts begin to produce colostrum. This is a yellowish fluid and you may find that a little leaks from the nipples. Simply wash it off with water in the bath or shower. Soap can be drying so don't use it. Rather use a non-soap skin wash or plain water. Even if you do not see any colostrum it does not mean that it is not being produced or that you will not have milk. If you like, you can try and express colostrum in the bath just to get used to the technique and clear the ducts from around the 34th week (see p. 118).

INVERTED NIPPLES. If your nipples do not stand out, do the exercise described on (p. 39), or use one of the devices like the breast shield to draw out inverted nipples.

TOUGHENING THE NIPPLES. Do not use spirits or alcohol on your nipples. This will not toughen your nipples, it will make them dry out and crack; so will scrubbing. Simply wash with water and expose to the sun whenever you can, as the ultraviolet rays will toughen them. Remember ultraviolet light does not penetrate through glass.

COLOSTRUM. This is the first secretion from the breasts and it lasts for the first two or three days after which it changes gradually from a yellowish colour to the bluish white of more mature breastmilk.

Colostrum contains seven times more protein but less carbohydrate and fat than mature milk and is easily digested. It also contains valuable protective antibodies against disease, and essential vitamins and minerals for growth and development and the specific function of its constituents is now being more fully appreciated for its unique qualities, such as the way they prevent allergy response mechanisms from developing.

HOW MILK IS MADE. The formation and secretion of milk is the result of the action of the hormone prolactin which is secreted in the brain by the anterior pituitary gland and oxytocin which is formed by the posterior pituitary gland. When the level of progesterone and oestrogen hormones decline after birth, prolactin comes into effect. This aids the formation of fat, carbohydrate and protein in the alveolar cells in the breast. These grape-like cells store the milk until they receive the signal to release it. When the baby sucks on the nipple or occasionally even when the mother hears the baby crying or even thinks about feeding, the hormone oxytocin is secreted and this signals the alveolar cells in the breast to release the milk into the ducts and sinuses around the areola (brown area circling the nipple). From there it flows into the baby's mouth.

COMPOSITION OF BREASTMILK. One of the marvels of breastmilk is that its composition changes throughout a feed. When the baby first sucks the milk is bluish and looks watery. This is the foremilk which was stored in the sinuses in the breast. It contains a higher proportion of water and less protein and fat than the hindmilk milk that is released later in the feed. In this way the baby's thirst is slaked before more concentrated food is offered. After about one to two minutes of sucking the 'let down' reflex may be felt. This is the result of the hormone oxytocin signalling the release of hindmilk from the alveolar cells. Hindmilk is richer and creamier in appearance because it contains more fat, as well as all the other constituents in milk in the following proportions:

- 1.1 to 1.5% protein;
- 7.0% carbohydrates;
- 4.0% fat;
- 0.2% mineral salts; and
- 87.3% water.

The portion and actual composition of the protein, fats and other constituents of breastmilk are significantly different from cow's milk.

THE 'LET DOWN REFLEX'. The release of oxytocin and its effect on the milk is known as the 'let down reflex' and the mother usually feels it as a sharp, tingling sensation from under the armpits down towards the breasts. Occasionally this is very uncomfortable or painful and a hot-water bottle on the breasts or a painkiller such as paracetamol is necessary. Because oxytocin does not function properly when the hormones of pregnancy are still circulating, it may take a while for the let down reflex to work efficiently.

FACTORS THAT AFFECT THE PRODUCTION OF MILK

HOW DIET, MEDICINES AND THE MIND AFFECT MOTHER'S MILK. Suitable fluids are necessary to supply the water needed for breastmilk, but this does not mean that you have to take anything more than your thirst dictates. Fluids can be taken in any form the mother desires, although excessive tea (except for rooibos), coffee and cola drinks in particular are not recommended as they can cause restlessness in the baby due to their caffeine content. Certain herbal teas contain similar 'natural' stimulants and these should be avoided. Citrus and acidic juices can irritate the baby's digestive system. Forcing the intake of too much fluid can cause discomfort.

The mother's diet should be well balanced with meat, fish, milk, cheese and legumes supplying protein; and bread, potatoes, samp or rice supplying the carbohydrates. Vitamins and minerals are found mainly in fruit and vegetables. They are best eaten raw, but cooked vegetables will also satisfy some of these needs.

Quality and quantity of breastmilk will only be adversely affected if the mother takes less than 60% of the required daily nutrients. Australian women appear to have 'richer' breastmilk in terms of fat content. While the fat content of women from Hong Kong was found to contain 0.56% of a substance known as Omega-three, which is a fatty acid vital to early brain growth that also reduces the risk of heart disease. The average amount of these fats in mothers' milk is 0.32%. A diet including lots of fish rich in Omega-three fatty acids was found to be the reason for this substance occurring in Hong Kong women's milk.

Omega-3 is known as an 'essential fatty acid' because it cannot be made by the body and is only obtained through the food we eat. EPA and DHA, the healthy fats in Omega-3 and Omega-6 rich foods, work together in the body and each fatty acid has unique benefits. These essential fatty acids are said to help prevent heart disease and promote healthy blood circulation, and can be beneficial for autoimmune and inflammatory conditions. During pregnancy they are needed for the baby's brain growth and development in the womb, as well as future mental and nervous system functioning.

If they are part of a mother's diet they will be available in her breast milk, transferring benefits to the baby. Because essential fatty acids helps regulate mood, a shortage of Omega-3 in a mother's diet may be a factor in the development of serious postnatal depression.

Omega-3 is found in cold water oily fish including salmon, halibut, mackerel, kippers, pilchards and sardines. Shark, swordfish, mackerel and marlin are likely to have a high mercury content and should be avoided at all times. Because mercury contamination is prevalent in many lakes and seas there are some concerns regarding eating fish during pregnancy. Speak to your medical advisor for direction on which fish are safe to eat where you live.

Omega 3 supplements made from marine plants are available, while vegetable sources of omega-3 include kale, spinach, walnuts, pecans, tofu, soya beans, fresh basil, and ground flaxseeds and their oil. Meat, and chicken also contain essential fatty acids and other important fats, but they must be pasture fed grass (not grain), and free range. Omega-3 eggs from chickens that are free range are also a good source.

Vegans need vitamin B_{12} supplements. If you have not gained extra weight during pregnancy you will need to eat approximately 2 000 kJ extra every day.

DIETING WHILE BREASTFEEDING. It is also possible to diet while breastfeeding, but this must be medically supervised and weight reducing medicines should never be taken unless prescribed by your doctor. Reputable organisations for weight reduction also have special diets for feeding mothers.

It is important to continue taking your multivitamin and iron supplements as you did during pregnancy so that you do not become run down. Confirm this with your medical advisor, as they may suggest a different product.

You may have heard that there are certain foods and especially drinks such as stout, ginger beer, champagne or milk that make milk. Liquids are necessary, and as such they fulfil a need, but there is no reason to suppose that they promote lactation in themselves.

Alcohol has traditionally been recommended as an aid to making milk but research has shown that while infants sucked more vigorously, they took in significantly less milk than babies whose mothers had not taken alcohol. The changes in the taste of breastmilk after the mother consumed alcohol took place between 30 minutes and an hour afterwards.

Prolactin, the hormone needed for the formation of milk is particularly well – secreted during sleep. Adequate rest for the lactating mother is essential, although not easy to achieve.

Tension can affect milk secretion and the let down reflex, so try to ensure a calm, relaxed atmosphere at feeding time.

Sucking provides the stimulus for milk to be released. The more often the baby sucks, the more milk will be made.

If the mother has been sedated during the birth it may take longer for the milk to be produced initially, probably because the baby is drowsy and does not stimulate the nipples effectively.

HORMONAL CONTRACEPTIVES. Before using any form of contraception it is essential to consult your medical advisor, as they can have interactions and side effects.

The dual or combined contraceptive pill, commonly known as 'the pill' is convenient and effective, but it contains both progestogen and oestrogen hormones. Oestrogen can interfere with milk production making it unsuitable. The so-called 'mini-pill', which does not have oestrogen may be prescribed. As it has a low level of active ingredients the 'mini-pill' must be taken at the same time daily for it to be effective. If you have diarrhoea or are on antibiotics it can make the mini-pill ineffective, so you will need to use extra protection.

The contraceptive injection Depo-Provera contains progestin only and it may be recommended. Pregnancy protection lasts for three months, and it does not affect the milk supply.

A device known as the 'Implant', is progestin only and it is inserted under the skin. It is effective for three years.

There are other devices and contraceptive methods available that do not contain hormones. It is not true that you cannot become pregnant while breastfeeding, although less likely. It is possible if you do not use contraception.

BREASFEEDING IN MATERNITY WARD. As discussed on *p. 62* the baby's sucking reflex is strong immediately after birth, but not all babies are ready to do more than nuzzle at this time. Do not fret if your baby seems reluctant. Remind the nursing staff that your baby should not be given anything to drink in the nursery if she is taken away from you after birth. You should really have arranged this with your doctor beforehand, and you must get him or her to write a note on the baby's card stipulating no bottle feeds. There is no evidence to support the idea that giving extra fluids to breast fed babies helps prevent physiological jaundice. Colostrum is all she needs in the first few days.

If she is in a communal nursery make it clear to the nursing staff that your baby is not to be given feeds of sugar water or formula in the first few hours after birth, unless you cannot feed her yourself. It is also possible that too many sugar water feeds could stimulate the pancreas to start producing insulin too soon, while a milk formula could sensitise your baby's digestive system and produce an allergic reaction.

If your baby is not with you and the hospital has a four-hourly feeding schedule you will have to get your doctor to order that she is brought to you when she cries, or at least every two to three hours. This makes more work for the staff but you must insist or your chances of breastfeeding successfully will be poor. Four hours between feeds is too long to get the milk supply going. It encourages engorgement, and your baby will probably be exhausted from crying or full of sugar water by the time she is brought to you. She will then take too little and be crying again in an hour or two, starting a vicious cycle that is bad for both of you. If your baby is rooming in with you, put her to the breast as often as she cries for a feed. The average newborn feeds 8-12 times in 24 hours.

THE FIRST BREASTFEED. Newborn babies have been shown to try and work their way to the breast within 30 minutes of birth as they recognise the smell of their mother's milk and gravitate towards the source.

You will be helped to put her to the breast and she may even latch on. The baby's sucking reflex is typically strong immediately after birth, but not all babies are ready to do more than nuzzle at this time. It's important not to feel disheartened if at first the baby doesn't latch on, or you feel awkward and unnatural. With practice, you and your baby will get the hang of it soon enough. This is only the beginning of a very special symbiotic relationship…

An important factor in the establishment of successful breastfeeding is the quality of the help a mother gets with the baby's first proper feed. Having the assistance of a knowledgeable and empathetic breastfeeding advisor to guide you in the beginning makes an enormous difference. Keep this in mind when deciding where to give birth.

PUTTING THE BABY TO THE BREAST. It is extremely important for the baby to fix properly on the breast or you could get very sore nipples and the baby will remain hungry. Make yourself comfortable in bed by packing cushions behind your back and under your elbows so that your baby is raised to the level of your nipples, and you do not feel strained when holding your baby.

If your episiotomy stitches hurt ask for an anaesthetic spray or cream to use. (*See 'Breastfeeding in Special Circumstances' p. 119 for Caesarean and other specific needs.*)

FIXING THE BABY ON THE BREAST. It is extremely important that your baby is lying with her mouth on a level with your breasts. She must not drag on the nipples at all! If necessary put a cushion underneath to raise her. If your nipples do not stand out properly, hold a cold wet cloth over them before feeding. This will make the surrounding brown area shrivel and the nipple will stand out.

- Hold your baby level with her head, neck and whole body lying horizontally across you. Tuck her lower arm around your waist, and pull her close to you. Cup your hand under your breast and touch her lips with your nipple. She will turn towards the nipple and open her mouth. You need to aim well below the back of her mouth. Her lips must not fold inwards. If she does not get a good grip repeat the process. She must latch on strongly. If she slips off easily she has not gripped the breast properly. The milk will not flow and your nipples will become sore.
- In order to make the milk flow the nipple and the brown part of the breast must be in the baby's mouth over the lower gum and tongue. The lower and upper lips must be spread out not be tucked under. The nipple must not move in and out of the mouth as this friction is what causes injury.
- The baby who is sucking well makes a strong movement with her jaws and the swallowing action can be clearly seen. If she drifts off to sleep before the feed is over, chuck her under the chin to get her going again.

You will probably feel very tense if it is the first time you are breastfeeding. Try and relax your shoulder and neck muscles. Breathe in and out slowly as you were taught in antenatal classes, or think of anything that will keep you calm. You may feel awkward and all thumbs; remind yourself that all mothers feel like that at first. Breastfeeding is an art that is learnt with practice even among tribal people.

Never allow anyone else to breastfeed your baby; even though you may be worried that she may not be getting enough milk.

REMOVING THE BABY FROM THE BREAST. If your baby is well fixed on the breast it will be difficult to break the suction, unless she has had enough and falls asleep letting the nipple slide out, or if she is still sleepy from the birth, or tired from crying. Never flick a sleepy baby's feet to wake her or make a loud noise, a cool cloth on her face is all that is needed, or lying her flat and changing her nappy.

- Gently insert a clean finger into the corner of her mouth to break the suction, when you want to take her off the breast.
- Never pull a baby off the breast; you could graze your nipples painfully.
- After you have fed your baby dry your nipples with a clean tissue or cotton wool and leave your bra open so that air can circulate around your nipples. No creams are necessary, and make sure you do not use plastic lined bras or breast pads. Your nipples must not become soggy.

TIME AT THE BREAST. You may be admonished to put your baby to the breast for only two or three minutes every four hours in the first few days. This is far too little to stimulate the milk flow and prevent engorgement. The theory behind putting the baby to the breast for slowly increasing periods of time is that it will prevent your nipples from becoming sore. Your nipples are far more likely to become tender from incorrect fixing of the baby and from pulling her off the breast.

Although most babies feed infrequently in the first two days she must be put to the breast as often as she seems to need it. From the third day demand for a feed is likely to increase greatly. Frequent sucking stimulates the hormones that produce milk and this, after all, is likely to be your biggest concern – that you will not have enough milk. So feed your baby as often as she demands it. If she is sedated from the birth, she will have to be woken if she sleeps for longer than four hours at a stretch, and may suck poorly at first.

Another important reason for not limiting time at the breast is that the composition and rate of flow of the milk changes during the feed. During the first part of the feed tho baby gets a lot of thin foremilk. Towards the end of the feed the fat rich, hunger satisfying hindmilk flows. Babies who do not get hindmilk feed more frequently because they are not well satisfied. Do not change her to the other breast until she has clearly had the creamier hindmilk. When babies are left to regulate how often and for how long they feed they grow better.

TO BEGIN WITH: DAY ONE. Without watching the clock, allow your baby to nurse for about five minutes on each side whenever she wants a feed during the day. Five minutes is only an indication of how long she may want to suck in the early days. It is not a set time span. If your baby is in a communal nursery, have a note pinned to her crib saying she is breast fed and must be brought to you every time she cries.

Even though the milk will not have come in yet she will be getting valuable colostrum and the emptying of the breast will help prevent engorgement. Always start with the alternate breast at the next feed: if you started with the right breast, then at the next feed start with the left.

AFTER-PAINS. You may get unpleasant after-pains in your abdomen when your baby nurses especially if it is your second or subsequent child. This is because the uterus contracts every time she sucks. These 'after-pains' are caused by the contraction of the uterus and will wear off in a week or two, but if you need something to relieve the cramping, speak to your medical advisor. They mean you will be getting slimmer sooner than if you were not breastfeeding.

NIGHT FEEDS IN THE MATERNITY HOSPITAL. Prolactin is secreted during sleep and you need it to make milk. However if you are rooming in with your baby, you will be expected to give night feeds around 3 am. By 5 am you will probably be woken again for washing and other hospital routines. You will also be giving a feed at about 11pm and possibly 9pm So you will be getting very little sleep during this Chinese torture routine! You will be giving night feeds at home but you will not have all the interruptions of hospital routine to cope with as well. Labour is extremely tiring, and you need to get as much sleep as possible to recover from the birth and the restless nights in the last weeks of pregnancy.

WHEN A FORMULA FEED BECOMES NECESSARY. Although this should be avoided as a routine, there may be a compelling reason why your doctor feels that your baby should have a bottle feed. If there are allergies in the family the baby should not be given a regular cow's milk formula at any time, as even a single bottle can sensitise a baby who is prone to allergies. Even humanised formulas have protein that is different to breastmilk so if you have a family history of allergy, such as asthma, hay fever, eczema or urticaria, your doctor may prescribe a hypoallergenic formula (*See p. 159*). Allergy to soya bean milk is on the increase so you are better off avoiding it. Goat's milk can also sensitise an allergy prone baby. These formula recommendations apply only if the medical staff feels a bottle is absolutely necessary.

BREASTFEEDING: DAY TWO. Same as day one, but she may now be wanting a little longer on each side. If she does not want to take the other side, leave it and start on that side next time. By now your breasts should be enlarging as the milk comes in. If they feel lumpy, give your baby a feed even if you have to wake her.

BREASTFEEDING: DAYS THREE AND DAY FOUR. If you are demand feeding as you should be, your breasts should not be engorged although they may feel full. Full breasts are normal; they feel uncomfortable but are relieved when the baby sucks. However, if you do become engorged, the milk will not flow due to a build-up of tissue tension and you could feel thoroughly miserable particularly if you are experiencing 'third day blues'. Oxytocin, the hormone that is produced to signal the release of milk, may not be flowing adequately because of the presence of the hormones of pregnancy, progesterone and oestrogen. As a result of this hormone cocktail carousing through your system, days three and four are often grim. To prevent engorgement, the baby must be put to the breast frequently to stimulate the release of oxytocin and get the milk flowing. If the baby is properly fixed it should not hurt your nipples, although engorgement is an important reason for faulty fixing.

SYMPTOMS OF ENGORGEMENT. The breasts are hard, lumpy and tender and the skin is pulled taut. The milk does not flow, but barely drips out in small quantities and the nipple is flattened because of the pressure in the breasts. Do not allow the baby to suck on a nipple that is flattened because of engorgement; she will not be able to grip properly and you will get sore nipples.

Although the breasts must be drained to ease the engorgement, they must first be softened before the baby is allowed to suck.

TREATMENT OF ENGORGED BREASTS. Oxytocin drugs are sometimes used but recent trials have shown that they are not more effective than simple draining of the breasts.
- You may have to soften the breasts so that your baby can get a good grip if the nipple is flattened.
- Stand under a hot shower and allow the water to splash on your breasts. Soap your hands well and massage gently with the palm of your hand in a downwards direction, from your armpit towards your nipple.
- Lean forward as you massage so that the milk can drip out. It may take quite a while and be initially painful, but persevere until your breasts are considerably softer and the nipple is no longer flattened. If showering is not possible, apply hot wet cloths to the breasts before expressing.
- Do not pummel or pull the skin of the breasts as you could cause damage. The soap is to make your hands glide easily and prevent dragging. Do not soap your nipples. As soon as your breasts are no longer painful and the area around the nipple is pliable again, feed your baby to help drain the milk (*see p. 114 for how to position correctly*). Frequent feeding is the best way to relieve engorgement.
- For relief from pressure and pain express a small amount of milk between feeds.

- If your baby will not take a good feed, or hand expressing does not seem to help ask for an electric breast pump so that you can express some milk.
- If your breasts are painful you can take an analgesic such as paracetamol. Avoid codeine and aspirin.

Feed your baby as often as possible and feed during the night as well. Severe untreated engorgement can cause the milk producing and expulsion cells to become damaged or to atrophy so that they no longer function properly. Therefore it is vital to treat engorgement properly and urgently since successful breastfeeding may depend on it.

BREASTFEEDING: DAY FIVE. With luck and good management any engorgement will have subsided and hormonal function will be stabilising. If not, continue with the above.

You may now be feeling the let down reflex described on *p. 110*. Emotional factors can inhibit the let down reflex and if you are in pain you may be too tense for it to function. Try to relax – the worst should be almost over – and get medication for pain if necessary.

BREASTFEEDING: DAY SIX. From now on your baby should be gaining weight properly, but it can take up to three weeks for her to regain her birth mass. Do not pay too much attention to reports that you have no milk. If there are no medical reasons for your baby's failure to gain, it may be because you have not fed often enough, or you have not had a chance to get the milk supply going because of inadequate rest or stimulation of the breasts or most likely, she is not getting the creamy hind milk. After she has had a feed, squeeze a little milk from the breast. If it is thin, not creamy, then she has probably only had foremilk. Try and keep her on one breast until she is having creamy hind milk. Consult a lactation consultant or your clinic if you are concerned. Feed as frequently as needed. Even every one-and-a-half hours if necessary.
- Do not limit the number of feeds or the length of feeds.
- Allow your baby to finish the first breast first. Do not take her off and deliberately change breasts. She must get the foremilk and the hindmilk from at least one breast.
- Make sure she is correctly positioned. You will soon build up your milk supply and your baby will gain weight. (*See p. 114.*)

HOW TO EXPRESS YOUR BREASTMILK

HAVE A PRACTICE RUN. To avoid a panic when you need it, practice expressing so that you get used to how it is done. Doing it in the bath or shower is good as the warm water helps the process. Massage the breasts gently towards the nipple with soapy hands to get the flow going. (*See p. 117 Treatment of engorged breasts.*)

- Wash your hands well, and have a sterilised wide mouthed container ready.
- Place your thumb at the outer edge of the areola, and cup your hand under the breast with your forefinger at the bottom of the dark area.
- Squeeze gently but firmly together. Picture the tiny tubes that carry the milk. You want to coax the milk along these tubes.
- Do this by pressing back towards your chest and at the same time squeezing the fingers and thumb together. Work your way like this all around the edge of the areola. As you squeeze you will suddenly find the right spots and the milk will squirt out.

BREAST PUMPS. You can also use a manual or electric/battery powered breast pump which is much easier. If you think you will only need to express occasionally get a manual pump as they are cheaper. If you will be needing it frequently, it may be worth getting an electric or battery breast pump as they are easier to use. Electric breast pump hire is expensive, and some companies have discontinued it because of the danger of contamination.

STORAGE OF EXPRESSED BREASTMILK. Collect it in a sterilised container.
- Breastmilk can be stored at room temperature for between four and five hours.
- Can be stored for up to six days if it is kept in the fridge.
- Breastmilk can be stored in the freezer for up to six months.
- And for one year in the deep freeze.

As always, wash your hands well and ensure it is stored in a BPA free freezer bag.

Never refreeze milk after it has thawed. Microwave heating can be problematic because it does not heat the milk evenly. (*See p. 208.*)

BREASTFEEDING IN SPECIAL CIRCUMSTANCES
AIDS (ACQUIRED IMMUNE DEFICIENCY SYNDROME). The AIDS virus can be transmitted through breastmilk and can infect the child. HIV positive women should receive counselling on whether it is best for them to breastfeed or bottle feed their baby. New options include offering the mother medication from before pregnancy throughout exclusive breastfeeding for at least the first six months. The baby will also receive medication and both mother and child will need to make regular clinic visits. In all cases, the wishes of the mother, after she has been properly informed of her options, should be respected.

JAUNDICE. Up to 50% of full term and a greater number of preterm babies, including babies whose birth has been induced, develop some degree of jaundice on the third or fourth day after birth. This is known as physiological jaundice and appears as a yellowing of the face and whites of the eyes at first, and progresses to the lower body. This can be aggravated by infrequent breastfeeding in the early days. The baby should be put to the breast often and water supplementation should be avoided as it has not been shown to have a positive effect. Your doctor will monitor the baby's bilirubin levels carefully to assess whether intervention is necessary. 'Breastmilk jaundice' is usually self-limiting and seldom requires discontinuation of breastfeeding. (*See p. 72.*) The assistance of a midwife or lactation specialist can be helpful, especially if you are having difficulty with feeding your baby, as jaundice is aggravated by a lack of fluid intake.

CAESAREAN. Before you have the operation remind your doctor that you intend breastfeeding so that you are not given an injection to stop your milk. Breastfeeding successfully often has a particularly important meaning for mothers who have had Caesareans because they may feel a sense of failure at not being able to have a 'natural' birth.

Modern hospital practice is to bring the baby in the incubator to the mother within three hours of the birth for a breast feed if the baby is healthy. She may however be kept in an incubator for up to 12 hours after the birth for observation if you do not ask for her to be brought to you earlier.

You will have pain after the Caesarean just as after any abdominal operation. You will also have had an anaesthetic. (The effects will be less if you have had an epidural Caesarean.) However, your baby needs only tiny amounts of colostrum in the first few days. Even a teaspoonful at a time is enough, so try and make the effort to breast feed from the beginning even though it is hard to focus on your baby when you have just had major surgery.

You will need help to find a comfortable position. Lying on your side is probably the easiest. Lay the baby on a pillow so that you don't have to lean over too much and get someone to help you get onto the other side. Don't hesitate to call for assistance for anything if you have had a Caesarean.

You will probably find things easier if you have had an epidural Caesarean. This is done without a general anaesthetic. Only the lower half of your body is anaesthetised so you do not feel the after-

A good position for breastfeeding after a Caesarean

effects of a general anaesthetic. You may even be able to put the baby to the breast straight after the birth.

The first few days after a Caesarean under a general anaesthetic are difficult. You could have referred pain in your shoulders from trapped gas in the abdomen; you will have a catheter tube to empty your bladder for the first 24 hours, and it may be hard to pass urine afterwards.

Drink plenty of fluids to clear your bladder and to help make milk. An intravenous drip will be attached to your arm so that you get fluid directly into your bloodstream and do not become dehydrated.

Pain from winds on the third day may make you feel extra miserable. Don't drink fizzy drinks and stick to a soft diet. You could need medication to open your bowels which will help release gas. Do not hesitate to take pain killers prescribed by your doctor. This will not affect your baby and will make it easier to breastfeed. It takes more than a week for most of the discomfort to pass. You should also have help with the baby when you go home – at least someone to do the heavy lifting and carrying.

The vaginal flow (lochia) after the birth will be the same as for a vaginal delivery. Maternity pads that stick on to your panties are more comfortable than a sanitary belt that can chafe your stitches.

Full rooming in with the baby may be too much of a strain. Arrange to see your baby whenever you feel up to it and see that she is brought to you whenever she cries for a feed.

Having a Caesarean is not a failure because it will have helped you produce a live healthy baby, yet it could be so contrary to your expectations that you and your partner have feelings of inadequacy. Talk about your feelings to each other so that you can adjust to the situation. You must accept what has happened and go on from there. Bringing up a child involves more than a single experience. *(See p. 64.)*

Possibly because many Caesarean mothers (other than epidural Caesarean), do not see their baby immediately after the birth, and the fact that there is considerable pain and discomfort after the baby is born, many mothers find it hard to relate to their child. Everything possible must be done to facilitate intimacy between mother and child.

PREMATURITY, AND BABIES IN INTENSIVE CARE. The baby who is born early is put in an incubator, or an Isolette to keep her warm, regulate her breathing and prevent infection. Babies with a mass of 2 500g and under are called 'small for dates' even if they were born at the expected date of delivery. They may also be put in an incubator.

If the baby was born before 36 weeks, she could have a weak sucking reflex and may have to be tube fed. A baby not born preterm may also need to be put in an incubator or special intensive care unit for medical reasons. Either way you should also try and have as much contact with her as you can, and if possible initiate breastfeeding by expressing.

If you have colostrum, even a small amount, you should let your baby have it because of the valuable antibodies it contains. Even a teaspoonful is worth giving. Ideally, you should be allowed to give it, but you may be too nervous, in which case the nurses will do it for you. If you do it yourself, make sure the spoon is over the tongue and fairly far back in the mouth or the baby will simply let it run out of her mouth. Or you may be given a syringe to use.

Breastmilk from mothers who give birth prematurely has higher protein content than usual, so it could supply all the necessary nutrients. If not, there are special supplements that can be added. If she is too weak to suck on the breast she can be given expressed breastmilk from a syringe or tube.

Babies less than 1 200g need more kilojoules than usual because their growth needs are greater. These babies are usually fed through a tube on a special formula or enriched expressed breastmilk.

If you intend breastfeeding your preterm baby – and it is well worth persevering because the rewards are great for mother and child – you must get your milk supply going by expressing frequently, even if your baby is not getting the milk in the beginning. An electric breast pump is ideal for expressing, but it can be done by hand (*see p. 118*). If your baby is in intensive care there will probably be an electric breast pump for mothers to use.

It is possible to keep the milk supply going in this way for weeks and even months, but you must express often and keep up your intake of liquids.

SLEEPY BABY. Some babies are very tired after a long and difficult delivery, or they are sedated due to drugs the mother has taken during labour. Wake her up by changing her nappy or wiping her face with a cool cloth if she sleeps for longer than four hours. Do not flick her feet or make a loud noise to wake her. If she falls asleep during the feed, chuck her under the chin to get her going again.

THRUSH, ALSO CALLED CANDIDA, MONILIA OR YEAST INFECTION. This is a fungus infection that shows itself as a white coating on the inside of the baby's mouth and on the tongue and cannot be scraped off. If severe, it can make the baby reluctant to feed. A mother's nipples may carry the thrush spores invisibly and you could be passing the infection back and forth between you and the baby. Feeding need not be discontinued but the infection must be treated in both mother and child (*see p. 367*). Thrush can also cause very sore nipples.

INTERRUPTED BREASTFEEDING (RELACTATION). If you have had to stop breastfeeding for any reason, no matter for how long, it is possible to start again. This can be done by putting your baby to the breast frequently, and by following the procedure for inadequate lactation (*see p. 133*), and the use of S.N.S. (*see p. 125*).

TWINS. Breastfeeding twins is surprisingly easy once you have got used to the idea. If the babies are very small and have to go into an incubator, milk can be expressed for them until they can be put to the breast. In small, underweight babies particularly, the digestibility of breastmilk and the antibodies it contains make it the ideal food. Breast milk for babies that are born very preterm, will probably be enriched with special nutrients, but it will still provide antibodies and the other unique breast milk properties. If one of the twins comes out of the incubator before the other, put her to the breast in the underarm position shown in the sketch so that she gets used to feeding in that position.

When you have two babies to feed, make a comfortable 'nest' of cushions on the bed or on the floor. Settle the babies in position, then squeeze yourself in between, and scoop them up under your arms. In the first week or two you will need help to fix the babies on the breast, but before long their rooting instinct will guide them and they will attach by themselves. To wind them, take one baby off the breast and hold her against your shoulder or seat her in a baby chair in front of you. Due to the frequency with which the breasts are stimulated, an inadequate milk supply is seldom a problem when feeding twins, particularly in the first few months. It is advisable to feed both at the same time or you will be feeding round the clock. Other complications such as mastitis are uncommon when breastfeeding twins, and once you have got it going it is a great labour and cost saver, besides being ideal for the babies, and giving them a special opportunity to bond with their mother.

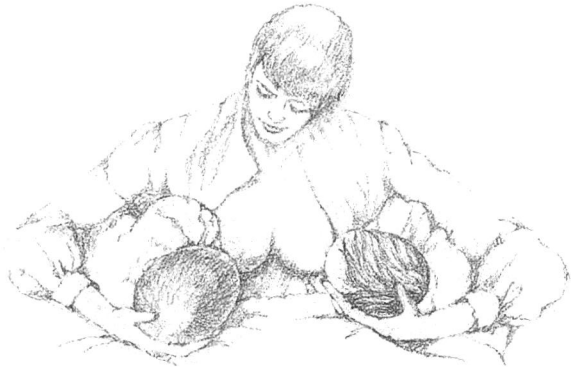

TRIPLETS. Breastfeeding triplets is not as impossible as it sounds. You may wish you were an octopus at times but that would apply even if you were not breastfeeding. And think of the saving in formula and the health benefits to your babies. The basic technique is the same as for feeding twins, but you will have to seat one of the babies near you in an infant chair and have another chair for winding.

The baby who was fed first at the previous feed should be fed last the next time. To keep track of the rotation order you could mark little safety pins with a coloured ribbon, say, red for first and blue for second, and pin it to the babies' clothes after the feed.

The baby without a tag would automatically be the last one fed. If one of the babies is screaming for food you would of course feed her first, regardless of the pecking order. If all three are screaming, hold one at bay with a dummy or bottle of cooled boiled water. Breastfeeding triplets has been done successfully and your local breastfeeding association will offer advice and support.

RHESUS INCOMPATIBILITY. It is possible to breastfeed because the dangerous antibodies in your milk will be rendered harmless by the baby's digestive system. Remember that she may be sleepy if there is jaundice.

ADOPTION. Yes, it is possible to breastfeed even if you have never had a baby. If you have carried a baby, even if it did not go to term, you have an even better chance of succeeding.

Depending on the average length of time it takes in your area to get a baby – it varies according to your specific preferences – once you have been put on the adoption list, you should have a practice run so you are well experienced and know you can do it. It will also give your breasts a chance to build up the tissue needed for the production of milk. If you are told it will take two years after you have been put on the adoption list to get your baby, start the process six months after you put your name down. You could tell the adoption authorities once you have got the flow going (they will probably have to see it to believe it) and they may then give you some idea of when you could expect your baby.

It is possible to start when you get your baby, but it takes a long time to produce the necessary amount of milk to fully breast feed your baby, so it is better if you start ahead of time. Once you have really seen that you can produce milk, not matter how little, you will feel more confident about the whole business. Contact the nearest breastfeeding advisor in your area because you will need their advice and support throughout.

You will also need the help of a doctor who is sympathetic to what you are trying to achieve, as certain drugs will have to be prescribed. Sulpiride is the one usually used and the dosage is 1×50mg tablet three times a day for three weeks, although some doctors prescribe it in larger doses initially, plus a cellular yeast and liver extract tonic: three×5ml teaspoons (15ml) three times a day. (The tablet form of this tonic has a higher caffeine content and may keep you awake at night) Note that sulpiride is normally used in certain psychiatric conditions and the stimulation of lactation is a side effect. **You must discuss the implications of the use of this, or other medication fully with your doctor.**

You should also be expressing your breasts at least five times a day (*see p. 118 How to express*). At first, you will not produce any fluid when you express unless you have had a recent pregnancy – even if it did not go to term – or the reason for your infertility is a high prolactin production. After about two weeks however, you may produce a little milk.

If you can get the use of an electric pump this will be more effective in stimulating the breasts.

Once you have initiated the first stages of lactation, reduce the sulpiride dosage slowly until you are not taking any drugs except the yeast tonic. Continue expressing three times a day until you hear that you are going to receive a baby. Get your doctor to prescribe sulpiride again, in the original dosage, and go back to expressing five times a day until you get the baby.

When you have your baby, put her to the breast at every feed for about five minutes before you give her a bottle, and follow the routine for inadequate lactation (*p. 133*). If she is frustrated because the milk flow is not adequate give the bottle first. It is important that your baby is not underfed. You can let her suckle on the breast later for comfort and the closeness this brings both of you. You may also find a breastfeeding supplementer (S.N.S.) helpful.

S.N.S. (SUPPLEMENTAL NURSING SYSTEM) is a gadget that allows your baby to suck on the nipple while getting milk formula. It consists of a bag filled with formula or mother's milk. A thin tube leads from the bag across the breast and is taped down so that the opening of the tube is in line with the nipple. The baby is put on the breast and while sucking on the nipple gets the formula that is in the bag. In this way the nipple is stimulated and milk production encouraged. Under the supervision of the doctor or counsellor who is advising you, you can slowly reduce the amount of milk in the S.N.S. until you feed your baby entirely yourself or with an occasional supplementary formula feed. Some mothers find this gadget tricky to handle. In this case it is better to do without it. Breastfeeding an adopted baby is not easy. Besides the fact that you will not have had nature's help in preparing your breasts, the baby will have been given a bottle in the nursing home which means that she may not be keen on taking the breast as it requires a different sucking action. However even partial breastfeeding will give you a sense of satisfaction.

CLEFT LIP AND/OR CLEFT PALATE. It is always a great shock to the parents when their child is born with an obvious physical deformity such as a cleft lip, and it may be difficult for the mother to bring herself to breast feed. She may be afraid of hurting the child if she puts it to her breast, but this will not happen particularly since any breastmilk that may get into the nasal passage will not be irritating. Even if you cannot feed straight away keep your milk supply going by expressing, and let your baby have it from a bottle with a specially shaped teat (the hospital staff will guide you), or even from a teaspoon.

A plate – similar to an orthodontic device – is sometimes fitted so that the cleft is closed and easier feeding can take place. Try feeding your baby in a semi-upright position and stop frequently to give her a chance to swallow.

Most doctors prefer to wait three months or at least until the baby is thriving before they operate to repair the cleft lip (*see p. 375*).

DIABETIC MOTHER. Although some diabetic mothers have difficulty getting their milk supply going, many do very well. However, you may have to alter your food intake to provide the kilojoules needed for making milk. Your sugar level will have to be checked regularly, but less insulin than usual may be needed for control when you are breastfeeding – discuss this with your doctor. Although small amounts of anti-diabetic drugs pass into the milk they are neutralised in the baby's digestive tract. Consult your medical advisor.

DOWN SYNDROME. The emotional trauma of discovering that her baby has Down syndrome may make it difficult for a mother to begin breastfeeding. But even if she makes a late start the result in terms of mother/child bonding and less susceptibility to disease makes it worthwhile. Down syndrome babies can be rather sleepy and limp, and you will have to be extra patient when feeding. Fixing may be difficult and you need empathetic help in the beginning. If she does not wake for feeds, wake her at least every three to four hours.

MASTECTOMY. Women who have had a breast removed and are not on cytotoxic drugs may be able to breast feed their babies successfully from the unaffected breast.

BREAST AUGMENTATION. Breast implants for the enlargement (augmentation) of the breasts does not mean you will not be able to breast feed.

BREAST REDUCTION. Having an operation to decrease the size of the breasts can make breastfeeding difficult. Depending on the procedure used it is possible for some women to fully or partially breastfeed however.

TUBERCULOSIS. If the mother is being treated for tuberculosis, but is no longer considered infectious or has been free of the disease for two years, she may be allowed to breast feed. The BCG injection should be given to the baby as soon as possible after birth.

LACTOSE INTOLERANCE. Primary lactose intolerance is a very rare congenital disorder caused by the absence of the enzyme lactase in the gut. Lactase is used to convert lactose (the sugar in milk) into glucose and galactose. Because lactase is absent, lactose passes unconverted into the gut where it causes smelly frothy stools with the release of carbon dioxide gas. Diarrhoea develops in the first week and the baby fails to gain weight. Stool tests confirm the diagnosis and the child is put on a lactose-free diet for at least the first two years of life. A special lactose-free modified cow's milk or soya milk is necessary and breastfeeding is not possible.

ACQUIRED LACTOSE INTOLERANCE. Acquired lactose – the 6-7% sugar in breast milk – intolerance, is not an inborn condition, but a relatively common after-effect of damage to the lining of the small intestine. Bacterial or viral infections such as gastroenteritis (diarrhoea) or rotavirus infection, can damage the 'brush' cells in the small intestine. This causes a temporary lack of lactase enzyme production. The undigested lactose results in loose stools, gas and cramping. In severe cases it can result in weight loss and muscle wasting.

Your doctor will assess the underlying causes and advise you if the baby should be taken off the breast and fed soya milk, or one of the special lactose-free cow's milk formulas until the gut has recovered. Because of its advantages you are likely to be advised to continue with breast feeding.

A few weeks on a lactose-free regimen is usually sufficient for the gut to recover and start producing lactase. While the baby is off the breast you can express in order to keep your milk supply going and store the milk in the freezer. (*See p. 118*.) The cause of the diarrhoea is due to the destruction of the 'good' bacteria in the gut. The use of probiotics (lactobacillus reuteri) helps protect the gut and restores the good bacteria. Probiotics are found in some yoghurts, and are also available in tablet or liquid form. Not all the probiotics that are contained in products are effective. Talk to your medical advisor.

NOTE: Lactose intolerance and allergy to milk are different conditions.

GALACTOSAEMIA. This is a rare inherited genetic condition, more common in people of Irish decent, in which the child's liver does not produce the enzymes needed to break down galactose which is made up of two milk sugars: galactose and glucose. Galactose accumulates in the body. The child fails to thrive on breast or formula and suffers from jaundice, vomiting and listlessness in the first weeks. The condition is diagnosed by urine tests and the infant is on a galactose free diet for life, so breastfeeding is not possible. (*See also Phenylketonuria (PKU) p. 63*.)

TEETH. Occasionally a baby may be born with one or two teeth. If they are superficial and the doctor is sure there are other teeth below them they may be removed. The presence of teeth does not mean that you cannot breast feed. When your baby normally gets her teeth, at about six months, she may try a few bites, especially at the end of a feed. Biting the gland that feeds her is ungracious and she will have to be discouraged firmly. Because of swelling and pain in the gums a baby may not be keen to suck when she is teething. Rub some teething jelly on her gums before a feed to ease any pain but note that some 'remedies' may be potentially harmful, so get medical advice before using a teething product.

HEART DEFECTS. It is often possible to breast feed a baby with a congenital heart defect. Discuss it with your doctor.

HOW PERSONALITY AFFECTS BREASTFEEDING. There is no doubt that successful breastfeeding depends largely on your state of mind. It requires determination to succeed, but it is also essential that you have the right advice at the time you need it, or even the most highly motivated mother can give up.

Ironically, certain personality traits that help you succeed in a career may mean lack of success in breastfeeding. Breastfeeding is giving, intuitive and sensual (after the initial period it can even be pleasantly stimulating sexually). But if you pride yourself on your independence and expect breastfeeding to be established and accomplished by the same forces that make for success in the market place, you could become frustrated and give up too soon. You should also be entirely honest with yourself about breastfeeding. If you feel it is not for you, make your decision and do not be pressurised into feeling guilty. Breastfeeding resentfully defeats much of its purpose, while giving a bottle in a warm loving way will give your baby many of the advantages of breastfeeding.

PRACTICAL BREASTFEEDING

HOW TO DO IT. Wash your hands thoroughly. Make sure you have somewhere comfortable to sit or lie when breastfeeding (*see p. 43*). This is important because if you are not relaxed the let down reflex will not work efficiently. A low armchair with a footstool is ideal.

- You will probably become very thirsty while you are feeding so have a glass of water or milk or whatever you fancy handy.
- Acidic fruit juice such as pineapple or orange could affect the baby. Don't have anything hot to drink in case it gets knocked over and burns the baby. Coffee and cola drinks contain stimulants that will come through the milk.
- If the baby is screaming from hunger don't waste time changing her nappy first, she will probably soil it during the feed anyway.
- Wrap her firmly in a wrapping blanket leaving her hands free. Most babies like to latch on to something when they suck, so give her one of your fingers to hold or let her grip onto your clothes.
- There is no need to clean your breasts before a feed unless you have had cream on them. Wipe this off with a clean tissue or cotton wool dipped in cool boiled water.

- If your nipple does not stand out hold a cold cloth to it before you start feeding to make the nipple protrude.
- Sit comfortably with a cushion on your lap and lie your baby across it with her nose level with your nipple. She must be high up and very close to you, and you must raise her up to the breast. You must not pull your breast towards her, or she will drag on the nipple and it will hurt! Your baby's back and neck should be in a straight line facing you.
- Holding her in the crook of your arm, tickle her lips or cheek with your nipple and she will turn towards it – in an action known as rooting – and open her mouth wide. With your free hand, cup your hand under your breast and let her take as much of the breast and areola in to her mouth as possible. Her lips should be folded outwards and cover as much of the areola (dark area) and breast as possible. She must use her lower jaw and tongue to press on the breast and draw the nipple and breast far back into her mouth. She should not chew on the nipple – she is breastfeeding not nipple feeding.
- If the baby has not latched on properly it will be easy to slip your breast out of her mouth. Repeat the procedure until she gets a good grip. You should not feel any pain while the baby is sucking. Some women feel a sharp sensation at the start of a feed but this should not last for more than a few seconds. The let down reflex which releases the milk into the ducts is felt as a tingling from the armpits into the breasts.

Improper fixing at the breast is one of the main causes of sore nipples and failure to breast feed successfully, so make sure you do it correctly (*see p. 114*) and if at all possible get an experienced lactation consultant to guide you. If your baby is sucking well – you will recognise this by the quick sucks at first followed by deep swallowing action and rhythmic movements of her jaw. She will suck for a while then pause, then suck again. If the milk flow is particularly strong at first she may come off the breast and need to catch her breath. Burp her and put her back.

She will slow down her sucking as the feed progresses until she is ready to come off. It is not normally necessary to take a baby off the breast manually.

At first feeding can make you feel tense and anxious. But do not worry about whether she is getting enough milk or what to make for supper. Chant a mantra, practice your antenatal breathing or yoga, switch on your favourite music, or simply breathe slowly and regularly. But do try and relax.

If you have older children and you are still unsure of yourself when breastfeeding, persuade them to stay out of the room, but do it tactfully. (They can listen to a favourite CD, or story you have recorded for them, or watch a DVD.) If you have someone who will distract them for you, don't tell the children it is because you are feeding the baby, or they will get the idea that the baby is taking you away from them.

If you do not have anyone to care for them, have a few special toys they can play with only when you are feeding or play the recorded story while keeping them in the room with you. Later on you can read them a story when you are feeding. Once you are relaxed about the technique of feeding, you will manage even in the middle of a three-ring circus!

- Without watching the clock give your baby as long as she wants on each side. Do not change sides unless your baby is clearly finished on one side. She will set her own pace which will vary according to her needs and capacity to empty the breast.
- She must empty the first breast before changing so that she gets the fat rich hindmilk that comes at the end of a feed. Burp her and change her if you like, then put her on the other breast for as long as she wants. Babies suck at an uneven rate and so you can wait until she eases off by herself.
- It is not generally necessary to take a baby off the breast, but if you must, do it correctly or your nipple will be hurt. Slip your finger into the corner of her mouth to break the suction and gently take the breast away.

It is not necessary to spend more than about five minutes winding your baby (*see p. 102*), then put her on the other breast and always begin a feed on the alternate side.

If you have felt the let down reflex (usually a tingling sensation from under the armpits towards the nipples) your second breast will probably have started to leak. Have a cloth ready to mop up any overflow. (This 'drip' milk can also be collected for feeding if you can cope with the gymnastics.)

The let down reflex occurs when the hormone oxytocin is released into the bloodstream after one or two minutes of sucking. This stimulates the cells that store the 'hindmilk' to release it into the ducts and sinuses around the nipple. Extrasensory stimulation such as the baby crying can stimulate the let down reflex as well.

FOREMILK AND HINDMILK, THE PERFECTLY BALANCED BABY FOOD. The first milk the baby gets at a feed is called foremilk and it has a large volume. It is watery and bluish in colour because it contains little fat and protein. This can lead mothers to believe their milk is 'too weak' because it looks thin and the baby is hungry again soon after a feed.

FOREMILK slakes the baby's thirst and it is rich in the milk sugar lactose that is attractive to the baby. However, if the baby does not empty the breast and only gets the low calorie foremilk, she will not gain weight properly and will be restless and hungry again very soon. She may also have greenish loose stools and experience discomfort from the imbalance of her feed. This will make everyone unhappy and you may want to give up breastfeeding in the belief that your milk is not right for your baby. Do not!

HINDMILK is rich in fat and protein which gives it its creamy appearance. It becomes available after the foremilk – usually after the letdown reflex – and is less in volume so the feeding rate is slower. This high calorie food satisfies hunger and gives the baby energy for growth and activity. If your baby does not get both hindmilk and foremilk she will not be getting the balanced feed she needs.

It will all work well if your baby is well fixed on the breast and allowed to empty the breasts and suck until satisfied. You may find that after five or 10 minutes her deep sucking and swallowing movements have become small and quick as though she were sucking on a dummy. She has probably emptied the breast and is having a blissful time sucking for satisfaction.

If you have the time and you are comfortable, let her carry on. She will eventually fall fast asleep and let go the nipple. Our younger daughter got the nickname the 'Tick' because she used to suck until she was bloated and then fall off! Sucking at the breast like this is a wonderful comfort for a baby and must give a great feeling of emotional security, to say nothing of the satisfaction it brings to the mother.

The extra sucking helps digestion because it promotes peristalsis (the natural movement of the bowel) so wind is passed and not bottled up to eventually cause pain and colic.

Breast fed babies often pass a stool while they are feeding. Change the nappy between breasts or at the end of the feed.

Time at the breast is approximate, and should be taken as a general indication only. Clock-watching is the worst possible way to get breastfeeding going in an easy natural manner. You should expect to spend about an hour on each feed in the beginning. It is not a question of filling up the baby like the tank of a car. When the flow becomes established and her sucking stronger, the time she needs to get enough milk will be 10 minutes or less, but you will both enjoy the extra time together whenever you can allow her to go on sucking.

AFTER THE FEED. If your baby is asleep after a feed, burp her gently – do not spend too much time on this – and tuck her in her crib. Putting her down sleepy but awake is even better because she will learn to go to sleep by herself.

Then, if you can, expose your nipples to the air for a while after the feed to prevent them getting sore. Change breast pads frequently so that your nipples do not become soggy.

There is no need to cream your nipples after a feed, but if you really want to, put on a thin layer of breast cream containing vitamins A and D. Never put on a thick layer, it will cut out the air and light and make the nipples soft.

- Time between feeds. It isn't always easy to tell whether your baby is ready for a feed, but one thing you can be sure of it will not be at exactly four hourly intervals. Until you get to know your baby's ways of letting you know she is hungry – try changing and cuddling her – perhaps this is all she needs.

- Breastmilk is absorbed more quickly because the protein is more digestible, so the breast fed baby is likely to feel hungry before a bottle fed baby does – even in one or two hours in the very beginning.
- It is not always easy to decide whether it is hunger that is making a baby cry, but you can take it that if it is three hours since her last feed, she is hungry.
- She may be uncomfortable because of trapped gas – pick her up and see she if she needs to burp.
- A hungry baby usually starts to whimper and grizzle a while before she gives it full throat.
- After the first few weeks you can try to stretch the time between feeds if she is gaining well, by giving her a dummy for half an hour or so. But never let her 'cry it out' in the belief that it will make her go for longer periods between feeds.

NIGHT FEEDS. Once breastfeeding is established, do not wake your baby for the night feed unless you want to give it before you go to bed. You need only wake a baby at night if she is gaining poorly, not well, or your breasts feel too full. When your baby wakes at night change the nappy, then feed. You do not want your baby to associate waking at night with the pleasure of a feed!

THE BABY WHO SLEEPS DURING THE DAY AND IS OFTEN AWAKE AT NIGHT. If your baby is sleeping for a reasonable period during the day but waking frequently at night she will have to be persuaded to change her schedule around.

To do this, wake her for feeds during the day as often as she is waking at night; that is, if she was waking every two and a half hours at night, wake her by wiping her face with a cool cloth at the same intervals during the day. She may not be too keen, but she will take a feed. Keep feeding her through the day, and don't wake her for a feed at night, unless she wakes by herself. Keep it up until she develops a more acceptable routine. The room must be dark at night.

HOW TO TELL IF SHE IS GETTING ENOUGH. Weight gain is the most important indicator. Another way of finding out if your baby is getting enough milk is to count the number of times she wets her nappy. If it is wet between six and eight times in 24 hours, and her urine is light yellow and odourless you can be pretty sure she is having enough milk. She will also pass soft mustard yellow stools that are not offensive.

WEIGHT GAIN. She should be gaining between 100g and 180g a week. Some weeks she may gain more, some less. In two weeks she should gain 250g or more. A satisfactory monthly average would be 450g. Although you may have to feed as often as 15 times in 24 hours in the very beginning, she should settle down to about six-eight feeds in a 24 hour period by the fourth week.

TEST WEIGHING is sometimes done to determine the amount of milk a baby takes on during a feed. This is done by weighing the baby immediately before a feed with her clothes on, then, weighing again immediately after a feed with exactly the same clothes on, without changing her nappy. The difference is the amount she has taken.

Remember that the breast fed baby needs less than she would if she were bottle fed – between 500ml and 600ml in 24 hours.

Test weighing one feed will not give you an indication of how much milk is being produced because your baby will vary her intake at every feed. To get an indication of how much she is having you need to test weigh every feed for three days, and this is obviously impractical unless you have scales. Even then I don't think you should do it. It is so easy to make a mistake and get upset when there is no need for it. Test weighing is not advisable unless supervised by someone with a positive attitude and in any event it will not show the essential data of whether she is getting any hindmilk which is the most probable cause of lack of weight gain.

INADEQUATE LACTATION

NOT ENOUGH MILK. Chances are that if you give up breastfeeding it will be because you believe that you do not have enough milk to feed your baby. Yet this is almost always a problem that can be sorted out, and the sooner the better before other factors get in the way. Once you start supplementing, restricting time at the breast or you become convinced that you do not have enough milk it makes success more problematic.

SIGNS OF INADEQUATE LACTATION. The signs that will tell you your baby is not getting enough milk are:

- Lack of weight gain, dark, strong smelling urine with few wet nappies (less than six in 24 hours) and a baby that cries after a feed – not through colic, and small greenish stools. If the baby is grossly underfed she may become lethargic and not cry much.
- Weight gain of only around 100g a week in not necessarily a sign of under- feeding, if it is consistent. A gain of 150g a week is preferable.
- The underfed baby's stools are usually small and greenish. Not all babies who cry after a feed are hungry; in fact this is seldom a cause of crying after a feed. The hungry baby does not cry lustily, but is somewhat niggly, so don't confuse this with the baby who is crying because of colic. Colicky babies really yell their heads off and appear to be in pain (*see p. 99*).

- Don't be misled into thinking your baby is hungry when she 'eats' her fist. This is not a sign of hunger, only that she is trying to suck for comfort and may have colic.
- The underfed baby usually has a poor sucking action at the breast, 'chewing' weakly and falling asleep. She may not cry very much.

MEDICAL REASONS. Only in very rare cases is the cause medical. One such cause is agalactia, when damage to the pituitary gland or a deficiency in the pituitary's prolactin production secretion results in the failure or absence of milk production secretion which prevents lactation.

Thyroid gland function is important for breastfeeding, and an underactive thyroid as well as an over active thyroid function can co-exist after the birth. Post-partum thyroiditis is an autoimmune disease that can occur in the first year after birth. During pregnancy the immune system is suppressed so that it does not harm the foetus. After the birth the immune system becomes active again. Because thyroid hormones regulate many functions and have a wide variety of symptoms – including apparent postnatal depression, and difficulty with the let-down reflex – it is important to consider possible thyroid problems when emotional or breast feeding problems occur. **Consult your doctor.**

NON-MEDICAL REASONS. Women whose breasts have not enlarged at all during pregnancy and who cannot express any milk in the first week after delivery may have a physical reason for not being able to breast feed.

- Incorrect positioning at the breast is the most common cause of a baby not getting enough milk *see p. 114* for correct positioning.
- The baby gets the foremilk only. Anxiety and tension as well as contrary hormonal influences can inhibit the let down reflex so that the baby only gets the foremilk which is low in fat and protein. The result is a restless baby who does not gain weight. She seems to want to feed continuously but is never satisfied.
- Insufficient stimulation by not feeding often enough or for long enough is one of the main causes of inadequate production of milk. Remember, the more you feed, the more milk is made to meet the demand. Never miss a feed in the belief that you will 'store' up milk for later.
- Taking the baby off the one breast before she has emptied it and had the rich hindmilk will leave her dissatisfied.
- Low fluid intake can affect the milk supply. Drink according to thirst – there is no need to force fluid intake.
- As I have already said faulty feeding technique can result in incorrect or no stimulation of the milk-producing glands.
- The combined (dual) contraceptive Pill reduces the milk supply after a few weeks; although the contraceptive injection and the mini-pill do not appear do so. You can

become pregnant while breastfeeding so you need some form of contraception. (*See p. 212 for other means of contraception*.) Although your periods may not return at all while you are breastfeeding, you could become pregnant because you could be ovulating but you may not realise this because it happens before you start menstruating.

- Your periods could return six weeks after delivery even if you are breastfeeding and your milk supply may be lower when you are menstruating. Some babies are reluctant to breast feed at this time due to the diminished output and the frustration they experience as a result. If your milk supply is lower you should feed more frequently and possibly give a complementary feed from a bottle after the ten o'clock feed at night if she is restless. (*See complementary feeds p. 149*.)
- Lack of rest can mean that your body is not able to produce enough prolactin hormone to make milk. Rest as much as possible during the day, and if you have older children get a friend to look after them if possible so that you can sleep when the baby sleeps.
- Rigid feeding schedules that do not allow for sufficient stimulation of the breasts can result in too little milk being produced.
- Incomplete clearing of the breast because of engorgement or a defective let down reflex can harm the milk-producing cells and inhibit the production of milk.
- Certain drugs such as those used for colds and flu can also adversely affect milk production.
- The baby may not be using the right sucking action. (*See negative 'flutter' sucking p. 144*.)

HOW TO MAKE MORE MILK. A great deal of what has been said in the previous section has a bearing on this and so it is worth reading it again.

- Feed more frequently. If you have been feeding every four hours and possibly giving a complementary bottle feed too, feed at least every two hours and reduce the complementary feed until it is no longer necessary.
- Do not miss out any breast feeds by giving a bottle feed. If the baby is losing weight – and she should never be allowed to lose more than one tenth of her body mass – give formula after the breast feed until you have built up your milk supply again. (*See pp. 156-184 for various formula milks*.)
- Try to promote an efficient let down reflex by getting into a routine procedure before you feed, either by playing music you like, or getting a special drink you enjoy, or simply try going through the feeding process in your mind.
- Pain from sore nipples or other sources can make you tense. See how to deal with sore nipples (*p. 138*) and take a painkiller 15 minutes before you start feeding (not codeine, it is constipating).
- Do not forget that lactation takes about three weeks to become established, so keep up frequent feeds in the beginning to get a really good flow going.

- Get as much rest as possible – prolactin is secreted in larger quantities during sleep. If possible you should go to bed with the baby for a few days.
- Drink enough fluids according to your thirst. Ceylon tea, and especially coffee are not recommended as they could over stimulate the baby, and coffee acts as a diuretic drawing water from the tissues. (Rooibos tea or the new low-caffeine Ceylon tea is in order.) Do not drink alcohol as studies have shown that this reduces the amount the baby takes in spite of sucking more vigorously. Eat a well balanced diet. Garlic in the mother's diet seems to encourage babies to take the breast keenly!
- Herbal remedies are sometimes recommended. Schlehen elixir is a berry extract taken 5-10ml three times daily. Its high fruit sugar content makes it unsuitable for diabetics. Fenugreek is widely recommended today often without warning of its possible interaction with essential medications such as warfarin, glipizide, heparin, insulin etc. The FDA does not recommend fenugreek for children, during pregnancy or breastfeeding. Chinese star anise, also known as Chinese badian, is commonly used in foods, and is safe for human consumption. A tea made with Chinese star anise is recommended by some suppliers for use during breastfeeding. However, it can be dangerous due to contamination by Japanese star anise, a highly poisonous substance that is burned as incense. Chinese and Japanese star anise look similar, and are easily confused. Japanese star anise is rated as highly poisonous and not fit for human consumption. Problems have arisen when Chinese star anise has been contaminated by, or confused with, Japanese star anise, and come though breast milk causing seizures, abnormal eye movements and vomiting. Because of this danger, Chinese star anise is only allowed to be imported into the European Union under very strict certification. So keep this in mind if you are on medication. Vitamin B complex often has a beneficial effect on lactation – probably because it helps the mother relax. The dose is two brewer's yeast tablets three times a day. Vitamin B_6 (pyridoxine) should not be taken in large amounts as it can reduce the milk supply.
- Certain medications have been found to increase the milk supply, and they may be recommended once all possible causes have been checked and other methods tried. The most prominent are two drugs that have been found to stimulate lactation markedly, although this is not their primary function, they are metoclopramide, and sulpiride. Both are only obtainable on prescription and must be taken strictly under a doctor's supervision. Metoclopramide, a drug normally used for gastric problems stimulates prolactin release by inhibiting prolactin-inhibiting factor through dopamine antagonism. It generally takes between two and five days for milk production to increase but the increased lactation is sustained once the drug is stopped. The small amounts that pass through the milk are not regarded as a problem as the drug is used in infants. Sulpiride which is a psychotropic normaliser (drug that affects the

mental state) is more problematic in action and should not be used for longer than a few weeks unless under strict medical supervision, as psychological dependency may result. It is this anti-anxiety effect which is an important reason for its popularity amongst mothers and its lactation enhancing properties.

- S.N.S. is a lactation aid gadget that is sometimes useful in getting the breasts stimulated while at the same time providing the baby with a supplementary formula (*see p. 125*).
- Psychological support and encouragement of the mother is extremely important as breastfeeding is extremely demanding emotionally as well as physically.

THE BREAST FED BABY'S STOOLS

In the first three days all babies pass sticky greenish black stools known as meconium. This consists of vernix, enzymes, bile and other substances the baby has ingested in the womb. Once these stools have been passed (about two or three a day), they gradually change to the normal breast fed baby's stool which is soft and mustard yellow in colour.

One of the joys of breastfeeding is the fact that you have very little cause for concern regarding your baby's stools. The breast fed baby's stool is not hard and it does not have an unpleasant odour. Normal stools are mustard in colour and consistency and may have white flecks like curdled milk. They may also vary from a pasty consistency like peanut butter to a small watery blob in the nappy because all the solids have been digested and absorbed. Small green stools can be a sign of under feeding.

Small amounts of blood may come through in the stools if the baby sucks on a cracked nipple but it will not harm the baby. Larger amounts of either black or red blood, or excessive mucus or a foul smell should be reported to your doctor.

An irritable baby who passes a lot of flatulence with frothy, loose watery stools may be getting too much foremilk and therefore have an excess of lactose. (*See hindmilk and foremilk p. 130.*) Consult your medical advisor.

FREQUENCY OF STOOLS. It is normal for a breast fed baby to pass a stool every time she feeds in the early weeks. At around six weeks she will have a bowel motion once a day or less frequently. She may even go without passing a stool for days or even a week. Because breastmilk is so completely utilised, there may be very little residue to pass in the stools. So long as the stool is not hard she is not constipated. Variations in the colour of a breast fed baby's stool can often be traced to the mother's diet.

DIARRHOEA is unusual in breast fed infants, and is characterised by frequent, copious, greenish, loose stools that smell different. (*See p. 178.*)

If the mother has taken medicine for constipation the baby's stools may become loose as well. This is not serious although no one should habitually take laxatives.

CONSTIPATION in babies who only receive breastmilk is most unlikely and they may go for up to six days without a stool. Very hard, infrequent stools with straining can be treated with extra fluids such as plain water or juice or extra breast feeds. When solids or other milks are added to the diet the colour of the stools darkens and the smell changes. (*See also p. 176.*)

LARGE STOOLS DUE TO OVERFEEDING. This can be quite a problem in breast fed babies since you may misinterpret your baby's cries in the beginning and feed more often than necessary.

Very frequent, large, 'explosive' stools after the first six weeks can mean your baby is getting too much milk and may be uncomfortable because her digestive system is working overtime. Cut down the number of feeds to six a day, if necessary giving about 100ml cooled boiled water to a big baby and about 50ml if the baby is small, before or between feeds. Or use a dummy to help her go for longer periods between feeds.

Occasionally breast fed babies gain weight too rapidly because of too frequent feeding or overfeeding, but do not worry about this as long as the baby is content.

A change of feeding position can help regulate the milk flow and lessen the chance of overfeeding.

By lying the baby across the breast and having her feed against the force of gravity as it were, the milk flow is not so strong. You can also feed from only one breast at each feed allowing the baby to suck on it as long as she wishes, then starting with the other breast at the next feed. For comfort, express a little from the 'unused' breast after the feed. Do not let the milk supply dwindle too low. Check by having her weighed at the end of a week. Do not feed the baby for short periods from both breasts as she will only get the foremilk which is not satisfying.

Position for overfeeding or gulping/choking at the breast. This position is especially useful for a baby who chokes on a fast flow.

BREAST PROBLEMS
SORE NIPPLES

This is one of the most common problems when breastfeeding and can put you off if not correctly handled. Fair or red-headed women often have a sensitive type of skin that chafes and cracks easily, but it can happen to anyone, especially in the first weeks.

CAUSES

- Incorrect fixing at the breast (*see p. 114*). This is by far the most likely cause.
- Incorrect removal of the baby from the breast (*see p. 115*).
- Tongue tie can result in incorrect fixing at the breast. This can be a cause of sore nipples. It is often not recognised for what it is. Referral to an experienced ENT (ear, nose and throat) specialist is likely to sort it out.
- Engorged breasts if the nipple becomes flattened making it difficult for the baby to secure a proper grip (*see p. 117*).
- Sore nipples in the first weeks are sometimes caused by the strong suction the baby exerts before the milk starts flowing. Keep yourself warm because cold constricts the blood vessels and ducts, and get the milk flow started by expressing before you put the baby to the breast.
- Thrush infection can also make nipples tender. Other than redness, this will not be visible.
- Cleaning, or previous 'toughening' with a brush or the use of drying substances such as alcohol can cause sore nipples.
- The interval between feeding is too long. Frequent feeding helps prevent sore nipples.
- Sore nipples can be as a result of eczema.

CRACKED NIPPLE

Occasionally a sore nipple can become cracked and bleed. Blood then swallowed by the baby is not of any consequence and will not harm her.

The cracked nipple looks red and grazed and may have a blister or fissure. It is usually the result of incorrect treatment of a sore nipple and is more likely to happen during the first week or two of nursing. Germs can enter the cracked nipple and cause a breast infection so strict hygiene by washing the hands carefully before touching the breasts is vital.

TREATMENT. If the crack is severe and feels too painful for the baby to suck on, milk should be expressed from the affected side, and given from a cup, spoon or syringe. If there is insufficient breastmilk, give a complementary feed of formula milk (*see p. 158*). Express either by hand or with an electric or manual breast pump. Some manual breast pumps can cause more damage to injured nipples and they should be used only if no pain is felt.

Your medical advisor may prescribe a suitable preparation to apply. Simply wipe off excess when you put the baby back to the breast. Breastmilk dabbed on to the crack is also a very good healer. About 24 hours after beginning treatment, you can put the baby back on the breast. The baby should feed on the least affected side first so that the milk begins to flow on the painful side before you put the baby to it.

Laser treatment by a physiotherapist aids healing of cracked nipples. Help the healing process by exposing your nipples to sunlight – not through glass as the ultraviolet rays do not penetrate it. Length of exposure to the sun would depend on time of day, season and sensitivity of the skin. Use your discretion (about 10 minutes would be an average time on a mild day) and take care not to burn yourself. Do this twice a day and dab on breast milk afterwards.

When using creams spread very thinly so that the air is not shut out. Do not use baby oil. If the crack is severe and there is no response to simpler remedies, your doctor may prescribe a corticosteroid cream. Make sure that there are no plastic linings in your bras and breast pads and keep the nipples dry. If possible leave your bra open for a while after a feed so that the air can circulate around the nipples. Do not use anything that has a drying, astringent effect on the nipples – a dab of breastmilk is the best.

Do not put the baby on a very full or engorged breast when you return the baby to the breast because it will damage the nipple further. Be sure to position properly as this is the main cause of sore nipples. After one or two good feeds the nipples should feel better.

A local anaesthetic jelly (1% lignocaine) applied 20 minutes before a feed and wiped off immediately before feeding, has an immediate soothing effect on sore nipples.

You can also ask your doctor for an oral painkiller such as paracetamol to be taken every four hours for the relief of pain.

If the nipple is not cracked you can try feeding the baby through a 'nipple shield' which is made from a flange teat with a hole cut in it. The mother needs to have a good milk supply for this to work, and the teat should be boiled until it is soft.

Try and express milk into the teat to make it easier for the baby to get going.

NOTE: Nipple shields are also available from your pharmacist and these are used over the nipple in order to protect it from further injury. The use of nipple shields is somewhat controversial as some mothers find that the baby gets used to the artificial teat and does not want to take the breast afterwards. Make sure that you are measured for the correct size, as too big and the baby will not be able to latch and if it is too small the nipple will be damaged. Ensure the nipple shield is always washed and store in an airtight container.

THRUSH, OR YEAST (CANDIDA) INFECTION

Nipples that are sore during and after a feed may be due to thrush in the baby or the mother. The nipple looks raw and pink and may be cracked. The baby could have white spots in her mouth and a red sore bottom. Both mother and child must be treated or the infection will be passed back and forth between them (see p. 367). Men can have thrush without symptoms and they also need treatment. This is easily treated in both partners. Talk to your doctor.

BLOCKED DUCT

SYMPTOMS. The breast is tender and a lump may be felt which is not relieved after suckling or expressing. The mother feels 'fluey' and may have a temperature.

CAUSES. Engorgement or inadequate drainage may result in a blocked lobe because of spasm of the myoepithelial muscles. Pressure from the bra as the breasts fill can also result in milk collecting in a duct and not being released.

But the prime cause of a blocked duct is a long gap between feeds and the breast is not being emptied properly, for instance when the baby sleeps through from six at night to six in the morning.

TREATMENT. A blocked duct must be treated urgently as it could develop into mastitis if the trapped milk becomes infected. Proper emptying of the breasts after every feed is important – express after a feed if necessary. Check for tight bras and feed from the affected side first for a few feeds.

Hot compresses and the treatment outlined for engorgement (see p. 117) should help get the duct unblocked. Laser treatment by a physiotherapist can be helpful. The use of hot or cold cabbage leaves as a compress is sometimes recommended.

If this is not sufficient, take medication prescribed by a doctor followed by a painkiller such as paracetamol. Then get the circulation going by swinging the arm on the affected side round and round like a windmill.

Feed the baby frequently, from the affected side first, or use an electric breast pump to drain the milk.

Go to bed with a hot-water bottle, and if you are not better within 24 hours call your doctor as he may recommend a course of antibiotics to prevent an infection. Carry on feeding even if you are on antibiotics.

MASTITIS

SYMPTOMS. Mastitis has all the signs of a blocked duct, but the breast is red and possibly shiny. The mother feels as though she has a bad dose of flu and her temperature is usually raised but she does not have a sore throat.

CAUSES. These are the same as for a blocked duct, but the milk may have escaped into the surrounding tissue and bloodstream leading to infection.

TREATMENT. If the milk has become infected – in severe cases there may be pus cells in the milk – and the surrounding tissue is inflamed, you must contact your doctor immediately as you need an antibiotic and possibly buccal pitocin or a nasal spray of oxytocin. Continue treatment as for a blocked duct. It is important to express from the affected breast because an abscess could form if the milk is not drained. The baby can usually be put back on the breast after 24 hours on an antibiotic.

Neither mild mastitis nor a blocked duct are reasons for taking your baby off the breast, although in the case of infective mastitis you must express milk from the affected side and discard it. Remember you can carry on feeding normally from the unaffected side.

Do not be perturbed if your baby's urine smells strongly or is discoloured by the antibiotic you are taking. Sometimes the infection is caused by germs in the baby's nose.

NOTE: **Consult your medical advisor.**

BREAST ABSCESS
SYMPTOMS. These are the same as in mastitis but there is also a very tender lump on the breast.

CAUSES. Neglect of a blocked duct or mastitis, particularly if you do not drain the breasts.

TREATMENT. This is a rare problem but it needs medical attention immediately. Initially the treatment may be the same as for severe mastitis, but it is usually necessary for the abscess to be opened by a doctor and drained. It is vitally important that milk flowing from the affected side is expressed. You can let the baby on to the breast again once the infection subsides.

BREASTFEEDING PROBLEMS
REJECTION OF THE BREAST can be very off-putting to a mother who is breastfeeding. At around eight to 12 weeks a baby sometimes begins screaming and fighting as soon as the mother takes her in her arms and holds her horizontal for feeding. It is very easy to feel rejected and lose confidence if your baby does this, but a bit of shrewd manipulation for a week or two will usually cure the problem. Put a little gripe water in a cup and dip a dummy into it. Put the dummy into the baby's mouth while you hold her in the feeding position. Wet your nipple with gripe water and quickly slip out the dummy and replace it with the breast. Repeat the trick when she gets agitated again.

Colicky babies may need an antispasmodic. Discuss it with your doctor.
You may also need to try a new position when feeding. Holding the baby upright, slide her down your body and let her feed in as upright a position as possible.

A blocked nose can cause the baby to 'fight' at the breast. Use a special baby syringe to clear the nose or put a few drops of saline solution from your chemist at the opening of the nostrils to help clear them.

Ear infections can cause severe pain when the child is lying on her side and this may be the reason for the fighting and crying when she is feeding. Sucking also causes pressure changes in the ears and this can cause pain. The child should have her ears checked by a doctor for otitis media. Another reason why a baby may break off feeding and cry is frustration because there is too little milk. Soothe her after she has drained the breast and distract her by playing with her. If she remains agitated, a bottle of water or diluted fruit juice may satisfy her between feeds until your milk supply builds up in a day or two. Increase your own fluid intake, feed more frequently and if you have been missing out night feeds reintroduce one of them. Within a few days your milk supply should have increased and you can cut out the extra night feed. But keep up your fluid intake.

On the other hand your baby may be getting all she needs in a few minutes, especially as she gets older and is able to suck strongly.

Babies who are very active at the breast often take their feeds better if they are sleepy.

CHOKING AND GULPING AT THE BREAST in the early weeks can happen if the let down reflex is too strong.

Try feeding against gravity by laying the baby over your tummy as shown in the sketch. (*See p. 138.*)

If your baby breaks off at the breast and refuses to continue feeding she probably has a wind. Lie her down for a few minutes then pick her up and burp her.

TEETHING AND THRUSH are other possible causes of reluctance to feed.

SIGNS OF FRUSTRATION. Even if your baby does not show signs of frustration at the breast, you may find that your milk supply appears to be low around eight to 12 weeks. This is probably because your hormones are becoming active again, from menstruation, or its suppression because of breastfeeding. All that is needed is to feed more often

POSSETING (SPITTING UP) OR VOMITING after a feed is common and the amount brought up usually appears to be more than it is. Even if it is quite a lot, don't worry about it if your baby is gaining well. Once she has settled after posseting don't give her any more milk as she was probably overfull anyway.

If she is inclined to posset regularly after a feed, change her nappy during the feed instead of after a full feed, and handle her very gently, taking care not to put pressure on her tummy. Keep her upright for a while after a feed in a padded baby chair.

You should be concerned about posseting after a feed if your baby starts to vomit with great force after every feed around the age of three to six weeks and also loses weight. See a doctor immediately as she may have pyloric stenosis (*see p. 385*). *See also Common feeding problems p. 142. See also oesophageal reflux p. 381.*

NEGATIVE OR FLUTTER SUCKING occurs when the baby uses the wrong sucking action. This results in frustration as only a little milk is obtained. In a correct sucking action the baby's tongue is wrapped around the nipple from below and pushed against the roof of the mouth. The sucking action should move in a wave like motion from front to back.

Wash your hands well. Using your index finger, stroke your baby's cheeks and gums. Then insert your finger into her mouth. Move your finger with the pad up against her palate gently rubbing from front to back. As the baby starts to suck press your finger down on the tongue, allowing the baby to suck against your finger. Rub against the palate for a short while, then press downwards against the tongue with your finger. Repeat both movements a few times. Do this before every feed so as to train the baby in the correct sucking action. If your baby breaks off during a feed, repeat the procedure. Until the baby learns the new technique supplement feeds from a spoon or S.N.S (*see p. 125*). It may take up to two weeks to correct negative or flutter sucking.

FOODS TO AVOID WHEN BREASTFEEDING

HOW WHAT YOU EAT AFFECTS YOUR BABY. If there is a history of allergies such as asthma, hay fever and eczema on both sides of your family, your child may turn out to be allergic too. By breast feeding you are doing the best thing to prevent your baby from developing allergies, since cow's milk is the most common cause of allergy in infants (*see p. 195*).

If you think your baby needs extra protection it may be better to avoid dairy products in your diet when breastfeeding and even during pregnancy (this is unproven however), as the allergens may pass unaltered into the baby's system and sensitise her. Replace the protein you would have been getting from milk by eating more legumes (peas, dried beans, lentils), eggs, meat and fish. Calcium supplements should be taken if no milk is included. However, remember to keep up your fluid intake in other ways.

Acidic foods and drinks such as orange or pineapple juice taken in large quantities can give your baby nappy rash or spots. There is no reason to avoid other foods as they are unlikely to affect your baby. The colour of your baby's stools may be altered according to your diet, but this is of no importance.

Chocolate can cause stomach cramps and restlessness because of the theobromine content, so don't have chocolate and chocolate drinks in large quantities.

Tea, coffee and cola drinks can have a stimulating effect on the baby and keep her awake and restless because of the caffeine content, so cut out or cut down. Low-caffeine tea, and herbal or rooibos teas as well as decaffeinated coffee are fine in moderation. Always check the labels.

Cigarette smoking also causes restlessness and can reduce your milk supply.

If you have been drinking a lot of milk and your baby is showing signs of allergy, with restlessness (not colic), try cutting dairy products out of your diet and see if there is any improvement. (*See p. 422.*) Occasionally eggs and wheat in the mother's diet can be a problem.

DRUGS AND BREASTFEEDING

NOTE: This list should not be considered as complete, consult your pharmacist or doctor.

MEDICINES AND OTHER SUBSTANCES IN BREASTMILK. Nicotine comes through in large quantities in breastmilk so cut down on smoking, or give it up altogether if you possibly can as it can cause colic and restlessness. Cot death is also associated with smoking. Contrary to the popular view, alcohol consumption reduces the amount of milk the baby takes, as does smoking.

NOTE: Alcohol intake during pregnancy can result in foetal alcohol syndrome, causing permanent and intellectual and behavioural problems in the child.

Aspirin taken by the mother can cause a rash in the baby and possible gastric bleeding so it is best avoided. Codeine should also be avoided. Ask your pharmacists or medical advisor for suitable painkillers.

Women on cytotoxic drugs for cancer, or those with active breast cancer should not breast feed. However, women who have been cleared of active carcinoma, and even if they have had one breast removed can breast feed, and have done so successfully for long periods.

Always inform your doctor that you are breastfeeding when medicines are prescribed. The following drugs are not recommended: Antineoplastics; radio-pharmaceuticals; chloramphenicol; iodides; gold salts and phenindione.

These drugs, should be used with caution: Antihistamines; aspirin in high doses; carbimazole and propylthiouracil (anti-thyroid agents); central nervous system depressants; corticosteroids; prolonged use of ergot alkaloids; laxatives containing stimulants such as senna, cascara or phenolphthalein; lithium; opioid analgesics; high doses of propranolol; tertracyclines (may cause discoloration of the teeth in the neonate). Certain anti-convulsants and medication for heart conditions, bronchodilators, high doses of oestrogens. Vitamin B6 can reduce milk supply.

Drugs such as heroin, cannabis ('dagga', marijuana), 'Tik', LSD and cocaine all come through breastmilk with ill effects. Alcohol crosses into breastmilk freely and can affect the child. Research has shown that the THC (Tetrahydrocannabinol) in marijuana remains in the breast milk for up to 6 days. Research is being conducted as to how this affects the development of the brain in the infant.

Medicines are best taken just before a feed or immediately after a breast feed so as to avoid peak concentrations of the drug at feeding time. Before taking any 'over the counter' or herbal preparations consult your pharmacist. If you take regular medication consult your doctor before you have your baby so that he can advise you about breastfeeding. In many instances he or she may be able to prescribe an alternative drug if the one you are taking is not safe for use when breastfeeding.

THE FOLLOWING MEDICATIONS CAN BE PROBLEMATIC
This list should not be considered definitive or complete. Before taking or eliminating any medication it is essential to consult your prescribing doctor.

- Antineoplastics
- Radio-Pharmaceuticals
- Chloramphenicol
- Iodides
- Gold Salts
- Phenindione
- Aspirin in high doses
- Carbimazole and propylthiouracil (anti-thyroid agents)
- Central nervous system depressants
- Corticosteroids
- Prolonged use of ergot alkaloids
- Laxatives containing stimulants such as senna, cascara or phenolphthalein
- Lithium
- Opioid analgesics
- High doses of propranolol
- Tertracyclines (may cause discoloration of the teeth in the neonate)
- Certain anti-convulsants

- Heart medication
- Bronchodilators
- High doses of oestrogen
- Vitamin B$_6$ (may reduce milk supply)
- Antihistamines (Some antihistamines are heavily secreted into breast milk so consult your pharmacist or doctor)

ADDITIONS TO BREASTMILK
NOTE: CONSULT YOUR MEDICAL ADVISOR

FULL TERM BABY. Breastmilk contains all the nutrients necessary for growth in the first few months. While the baby is having breastmilk only, and the mother has a well-balanced diet, no additions are necessary, except for vitamin D, and later on, iron. Strict vegetarian mothers may need an extra B-complex supplement.

VITAMIN A: Large quantities are available in a fat soluble base in breastmilk. No supplement is needed as an overdose can be harmful.

VITAMIN C: This is a water soluble vitamin and is not stored in the system, thus a daily intake is necessary to meet bodily needs. If the mother's diet contains at least 60 mg vitamin C daily her milk supply should contain enough vitamin C for her baby. However, surveys show that many mothers do not have enough vitamin C containing foods in their diet.

Foods which are richest in vitamin C are citrus fruit such as oranges. Unfortunately these are acidic and can affect the baby so it is better to get it from other sources such as guavas, broccoli, potatoes, and tomatoes. The herbs, fresh parsley and thyme have good amounts of vitamin C. A vitamin C and calcium supplement or a multi-vitamin supplement (the kind taken during pregnancy is suitable) is probably the easiest way of ensuring a good supply of vitamin C for your breastmilk, but a good diet is important as well.

Vitamin C can also be given directly to the baby, by means of a vitamin supplement, or by giving vitamin C fortified juice between feeds, if recommended by your paediatrician.

Some commercial juices and fruit syrups contain preservatives and added sugar which are not desirable and should be avoided as they can rot teeth rapidly, especially when sucked through a teat. Rather give juice from a cup or spoon when the teeth come through, or let the older child use a straw. Freshly pressed juices can be given, but they will not have added vitamin C which is the main reason for giving them. Note that all fruit juices contain fructose, the sugar in fruit and can occasionally cause cramping in a baby. Check juice labels, and dilute with water.

CALCIUM is needed for bone development and is an important element in the diet together with vitamin D. Calcium is found in milk, cheese and other dairy products. In communities in which milk is not a part of the diet when breast feeding ceases, children can become severely calcium deficient, and also lactose intolerant.

VITAMIN D is needed for normal bone development and the prevention of rickets (bowed legs and knock knees), and for the absorption of calcium from food. It may also help to prevent diabetes and certain cancers and other serious illnesses later in life. Vitamin D is available in breastmilk if the mother's diet contains sufficient quantities (200 I.U. daily) either from food sources, sunlight or from a vitamin supplement. However very few mothers have sufficient intake of vitamin D, in particular vegans. Vitamin D sources include fortified milk, cheese, and yoghurt. Also egg yolks, liver, fatty fish such as fresh salmon, and canned light meat tuna, sardines and pilchards. Vitamin D is also manufactured by the skin when it is exposed to sunlight. Exposing your baby to at least fifteen to thirty minutes or more of direct sunlight a week should produce the necessary vitamin D. However, depletion of the ozone layer makes exposure to the sun more dangerous than before and it is not recommended. The American Academy of Paediatrics has increased their recommendation of vitamin D, and your doctor may advise a vitamin D supplement for your baby of 400 I.U. daily from birth to the age of at least a year. Premature babies or twins need 800 I.U. daily.

VITAMIN K is needed for the prevention of bleeding disorders and is not found in sufficient quantities in breastmilk. In most countries babies routinely receive vitamin K at birth.

VITAMIN B$_{12}$ The breastmilk of strict vegetarians (vegans) can lack vitamin B$_{12}$, and these babies must receive a supplement. Consult your medical advisor.

IRON: Iron is an extremely important element in infancy, with iron deficiency anaemia now known to be the most common nutritional lack in children world-wide. Although small, the amount of iron in breastmilk is well absorbed and probably sufficient for the child's needs in the first few months together with iron stored in the body from before birth. Delayed clamping of the umbilical cord after the birth, transfers additional blood that may increase iron levels in the child. Iron is generally added to formula milks and baby cereals.

Iron is needed for the red blood cells (haemoglobin) which carry oxygen to all parts of the human body. A lack can have a detrimental effect on all areas of development, including intellectual and behavioural.

It is sometimes recommended that full term, breast fed babies receive 1 mg per kg ferrous sulphate (iron) drops daily from four months or as soon as solids are introduced, as solids can inhibit iron absorption from breastmilk. Do this only on your doctor's recommendation as some iron supplements are not well tolerated. Iron drops must not be given with a feed as this will also hinder absorption. An iron and vitamin preparation for infants is less likely to cause upsets. Give iron between feeds together with juice as iron absorption is better in the presence of vitamin C. Iron rich foods should also be included in the baby's diet. These include iron-fortified cereals, liver and red meat. Calcium inhibits iron absorption.

FLUORIDE: Fluoride is a natural element found in water which strengthens teeth. Depending on whether the water where you live is fluoridated – or if not, what the natural levels are – you may need to supplement. Check with your doctor or dentist before supplementing as there are various views on this. Some recommend that babies who are solely breast fed and do not receive additional water be given a fluoride supplement from birth – 0,25mg daily, as the concentration in breastmilk is low even if you live in an area where the water has adequate fluoride. Simply squirt the required dose under the baby's tongue, or in water. Consult your dentist.

WATER. In normal circumstances breast fed babies do not need water because the foremilk quenches the thirst. In hot weather you can offer the older baby a bottle of plain, cooled boiled water between feeds.

SOLIDS. The introduction of solids to the diet depends on readiness defined by a number of factors, rather than solely on age. (*See p. 151.*) However, if solids are not introduced by six months the child will no longer sustain adequate growth.

ADDITIONS TO BREASTMILK IN PREMATURE BABIES.
Depending on your baby's prematurity and health, she may be kept in ICU and given breast milk that has added health requirements. Both you and her father will be encouraged to spend time with your baby, and hold her close to your skin. Once your baby is able to drink from the breast, you will probably soon be able to take her home…

COMPLEMENTARY AND SUPPLEMENTARY FEEDS IN A BREAST FED BABY

Complementary feeds are given in addition to the breast feed, while supplementary feeds are given in place of a breast feed, for example while you are it work or if you have not been able to express and store sufficient milk.

If you do not have enough milk to express, you can make up a feed to be given from a bottle if the need arises. If you are confident your child will not be allergic, you can use a cow's milk formula. However, if allergies run in the family use a milk formula recommended by your doctor or clinic.

Breast fed babies over the age of three months are sometimes difficult about taking a bottle so you will have to have a trial run to see whether she will co-operate. Let someone else feed her because she will usually not accept anything less than breastmilk from you as she will be able to smell it.

If your periods start and you find that your breastmilk supply is low, feed more frequently and give a complementary bottle, possibly after the 6pm or night feed, if she is clearly not satisfied. Keep in mind that the breasts make milk according to how often they are stimulated so keep on offering the breast before the bottle.

Remember that breastmilk is sweet and she may turn up her nose at other feeds at first. The hole in the teat should be small and you should not add sugar to the formula she is given unless specified. Always give the complementary feed after the breastfeed.

FOR HOW LONG SHOULD YOU CONTINUE BREASTFEEDING?

NO SET TIME. One of the beauties of breastfeeding is that it becomes easier the longer you do it. Once you have got over any initial problems it is very convenient and, of course, cheap. Ideally you should feed for as long as you and your baby wish. You will have given your baby an excellent foundation and all the factors which make breastfeeding so important will have been covered in the first six months. So if you want to give up after six months for any reason you will still have given your baby the best possible start.

Some babies seem to lose interest in their feeds around this time, but others are reluctant to give up the breast.

There is absolutely no reason why you should not continue to breast feed for as long as you and your baby like, especially if the baby is thriving. In poor socio-economic conditions it is often vital for the baby to be breast fed for as long as possible. However, if solids are not introduced by four to six months, the baby may no longer gain weight as needed.

Be aware too, that if you continue breastfeeding after the first year it may be difficult to get your baby to give up the breast. This can be a problem if there is another baby on the way or if you do not want to carry on feeding.

PREGNANCY. If you become pregnant it is better to wean your baby from the breast over a period of four to six weeks. This is advisable because your milk supply will usually diminish and to allow your body to build up colostrum for the new baby in the last few months of pregnancy. Your older child should not still be dependent on the breast when you have another baby to feed. If your older child is not weaned always feed the younger child first.

RETURNING TO WORK. You may have to go back to work soon after your baby's birth. If you cannot arrange flexi time so that you can be home for feeds you can still give her a good start for the first few weeks when you are at home and then continue with as many feeds as you can fit in. You can also express milk to give her when you are away.

You can feed before you leave for work, at lunchtime if this is possible, and in the evenings. During the weekends you can give all the feeds. In order to maintain your milk supply it is better to express milk during the day. Express directly into a sterilised bottle or other sterile container, seal well and store in the fridge. You can use it within 24 hours without boiling which destroys the 'live' cells that give breastmilk its unique properties. You can freeze breastmilk but this will destroy the macrophages and lysozymes and the other factors that provide protection against disease. After freezing, breastmilk should be reheated to 80°C that is until it just starts thickening on top, before use. This would be sufficient to kill most organisms without destroying all the milk's properties. When stored breastmilk 'separates' out, simply shake before use. See the section below on how to prevent and treat refusal of the bottle.

HOW TO PREVENT AND TREAT REFUSAL OF THE BOTTLE. Whoever looks after the baby should give complementary feeds as outlined on *p. 149*, or the expressed breastmilk. If your baby is younger than three months when you return to work she will usually adjust to the new caregiver without any trouble and take a bottle with ease. However if she is older she may refuse to take the bottle. It is wise, therefore, if you intend returning to work, to accustom your baby to the bottle by giving her a milk feed from it occasionally. She may refuse to take the bottle if you give it, because she will smell the breastmilk and associate it with you. You will then have to get someone else to offer it.

If she still refuses put a little breastmilk on the teat, or dip the teat in a little sugar (not honey) or gripe water. You could also try giving her breastmilk and formula mixed to get her accustomed to the taste. Gradually increase the amount of formula. Stop all these tricks once she gets used to the bottle.

If she is around 6-8 months when you go back to work, you must introduce her to her caregiver gradually and gently as this is when stranger anxiety may first become apparent.

Let her meet the caregiver without her trying to pick up the baby or feed her the first few times. Your baby must get used to her gradually and build up a relationship before you leave her alone with her caregiver.

THE INTRODUCTION OF SOLIDS
BREAST FED BABIES AND SOLIDS

After six months breast milk alone is unlikely to provide sufficient iron, or kilojoules to fuel growth. A lack of iron results in anaemia, with susceptibility to infection, developmental lags, weakness and poor appetite.

The timing of the introduction of solids has, until recently, been carefully prescribed to be from six months, and it is still prescribed as such, by the World Health Organization, and many mothers have followed this mantra religiously.

However, there has been a big change in the last few years, after a ground breaking study by medical experts, with the LEAP study (Learning Early about Peanut Allergy). (*See page 420.*)

The results of this study is that it is advisable to introduce a variety of solids from not later than four months as this is likely to prevent allergies!

WEANING FROM THE BREAST

STOPPING SUDDENLY. Should you become ill or have to be away from your baby suddenly without any possibility of reintroducing breastfeeding, you will have to suppress your milk supply so that you do not become engorged.

Restrict your fluid intake, and wear a firm bra. Express whenever your breasts become too full – just enough to relieve the tension. The lack of stimulation to the nipple by sucking will also diminish your supply. Do not allow yourself to become engorged as you could develop mastitis.

If you have to wean suddenly, your baby may refuse to take a bottle if she has not had one before. Get someone else to feed her as she will most likely accept nothing less than breastmilk from you. If she refuses to suck at first, you should use a pliable plastic bottle so that you can squeeze milk into her mouth. Or, feed milk from a cup, and increase solids if she is on them.

Bromocriptine, a prolactin suppressor, is no longer recommended for the routine suppression of lactation, or to treat engorgement. Your doctor will advise you on which, if any medications to use to inhibit your milk supply.

NATURAL WEANING FROM THE BREAST. There is no set time when you should stop breastfeeding your baby. All things being equal, you should ideally allow your baby to indicate when she is ready to give up the breast. Ignore pressure to take your baby off the breast because of social convention. Keep in mind, however, that if you will not be able to – or do not wish to – continue breastfeeding in the second year, it is easier to wean at the end of the first year. Toddlers are notoriously difficult to wean from the breast during the second year or later, and she will be able to climb on your lap and demand a feed in a loud voice!

WHAT KIND OF MILK? If your baby is under six months it is preferable not to wean her on to plain cow's milk, especially if there are allergies in the family. Rather try to breast feed for a longer period or choose one of the modified milks detailed on *p. 158.*

Behaviour such as 'fighting' at the breast which is common around eight weeks, or the reluctance to take the breast which sometimes happens around the 12th week, is not an indication that your baby desires to be weaned. These are management problems and can be coped with effectively (*see p. 142*).

From about six months onwards your baby may show a real lack of interest in her breast feeds, taking a few sucks and playing the rest of the time. If you want to give up– and you will probably feel a great sense of loss at the thought of forgoing the warm and special relationship of breastfeeding – you can start cutting out feeds, when your baby is well settled on solids.

Remember, however, that by this time your baby could be getting up to 300ml in less than five minutes (your breasts may appear smaller and softer – this does not mean you have less milk).

She may not want to give up the feed before she goes to sleep, but the early morning feed is often the last to go because she will be thirsty and there are fewer distractions.

If you wish, you can continue giving her whichever feeds she seems to want and need for as long as you like even if you have weaned her off the day time feeds, as long as you do it gradually. It is best to give a vitamin and iron enriched formula milk rather than fresh cow's milk if she is under a year old.

CUP OR BOTTLE? You may have strong feelings about not giving a bottle at all, but the fact is that there are few babies who are content to take all their milk from a cup at an early age. If she is happy to have milk from a cup, well and good, however, sucking is such an important source of pleasure and comfort that I wouldn't deny it to a child. Beside there is very little chance of a baby taking the amount of milk she needs from a cup.

REFUSAL TO DRINK MILK FROM A BOTTLE. Some older babies, if they have been entirely breast fed, refuse to take a bottle. This can be a problem if she is really stubborn about it and also refuses to take the breast again. You will have to make up the loss of milk by giving it to her in the form of cheese, milk soups, puddings or yogurt, and increase her liquid intake in the form of water or fruit juice. Do not give juice from a bottle as this contributes to tooth decay.

If the older child still refuses to take milk from a cup or a bottle you can flavour it temporarily with one of the puréed fruits like strawberry, peach or banana. Do not put tea or coffee in her milk as they contain caffeine that can make her wakeful and irritable. Make a point of reducing the flavouring in her milk gradually, but as soon as possible, until she is drinking plain, unflavoured, unsweetened milk.

Some babies are put off the bottle by the chemical smell of steriliser. Use another method to sterilise. (*See p. 60.*) Follow the general rules for bottle feeding (*p. 165*).

Milk is the main source of calcium in a baby's diet and if she does not get it you may need to use a calcium supplement.

BABY LED WEANING. If you are prepared to continue feeding until your child 'gives you up' then do so.

HOW TO WEAN

TIMETABLE. If you are going to take your baby off the breast entirely, do it over four weeks so that you do not have problems.

FIRST WEEK
- Breast feed in early morning
- Breast feed at mid-morning
- Bottle after lunch
- Breast feed at bedtime

SECOND WEEK
- Breast feed in early morning
- Bottle at mid-morning
- Bottle after lunch
- Breast feed at bedtime

THIRD WEEK
- Breast feed in early morning
- Bottle for the rest of the day

FOURTH WEEK
- Bottle feeds throughout the day unless you feel very full. Reduce your fluid intake. It is not unusual to be able to express a little fluid from the breast for many months after you have stopped feeding. Or you can carry on giving the early morning or evening feed as long as you wish.

GO TO www.baby-childcare.com TO WATCH THE FOLLOWING VIDEOS THAT ARE APPLICABLE TO CHAPTER 5

PROF CLAUDIA GRAY	Reflux and vomitting
	Stools
	Rashes
	Milk and weaning
	Introducing solids
EMMA NUMANOGLU	Breast feeding concerns
	Expressing breast milk
	Giving your prem baby the benefit of breast milk
JOANNA WILSON	Responsive feeding

CHAPTER 6

Bottle Feeding

There are a number of reasons why a mother may not be able to breastfeed despite a desire to do so. These include having to return to work early and leave the baby in the care of others, ill health, physical restrictions, medication and a lack of success despite a fair attempt. Although breastmilk is the perfect food for babies, mothering a child is a long term commitment that involves every facet of human interaction, and no mother should be made to feel guilty because she was unable to breastfeed.

ADVANCES HAVE BEEN MADE. There are many kinds of milk formulas available today, and these will be described. Amongst these are highly specialised feeds that are mainly used in hospitals for particular conditions.

COLOSTRUM. In the first few days after the birth, colostrum is produced by the breasts. This yellowish substance provides antibodies against disease, and is high in protein and other nutrients. Even though you are not going to be breastfeeding it may still be possible to give your baby the benefit of the unique properties of colostrum. You can either put your baby to the breast in the usual way for the first two days or you can express the colostrum and give it from a teaspoon or syringe (*see p. 118 for how to express*). Exceptions to this would be if you are HIV positive, or have certain other medical conditions, in which case you will have to make a decision based on your circumstances and with information supplied by your medical advisor.

HIV AND BOTTLE FEEDING. If you are HIV positive and you are in a position to bottle feed your baby without a problem; and you have decided to do so in consultation with your medical advisor, then you should not put your baby to the breast at all. Your expressed breast milk or colostrum should also not be given. In this way, if your baby is not HIV positive you will hopefully safeguard her from HIV infection. **No one else should be allowed to breastfeed your baby.**

THE FIRST BOTTLE FEED. If you decide to start bottle feeding straight away you will be given a bottle of formula in the nursing home to feed your baby. Unless your doctor has reason to believe that your baby will be allergic to cow's milk, the formula will be one of the standard brands preferred by your hospital. (*See p. 85 for demand feeding*).

TYPES OF MILKS

WHAT'S BEST IN YOUR CIRCUMSTANCES? Most babies will thrive on any of the usual formulas based on cow's milk, and it is wise to continue the formula your baby was taking in the nursing home if she was doing well on it. Considerations which might affect your choice of formula are the price, storage facilities (powdered milks can be kept safely without a fridge); and the ease with which a feed can be made up (you will need a fridge to store fresh cow's milk and then boil it, while you need only boiled water to make up powdered milk). Because of modifications, starter milks (whey predominant usually labelled No1) are more digestible, but some babies may find them less satisfying after about the fourth month. Choose the milk that meets your baby's needs as well as your pocket unless otherwise indicated. Read labels carefully for how to make up feeds.

Do not chop and change milks simply because your baby is restless or spits up a little. There is very little difference between brands in the same category of milk. If your baby is settled on a formula, stick to it unless advised otherwise by your doctor or clinic. There are many new types of milk on the market today for specific conditions. Do not be tempted to try them without professional advice and recommendation. Many seeming 'conditions' in the first three months are normal and do not require special, and expensive milks.

Generally speaking the more highly modified a formula is – that is the more the components of fresh cow's milk have been changed to try and approximate the protein/fat/carbohydrate composition of breast milk – the more expensive it is. But many cheaper and less modified types of milk are suitable.

THE MEANING OF LOGOS ON SOME LABELS. You may notice that some products have logos on the tin with letters and possibly numbers. These are codes for additions to the milk that are claimed to be beneficial. They include Bifudus BL 'active cultures' (probiotics), which are said to boost the immune system against problems such as diarrhoea. LC-PUFA stands for long chain polyunsaturated fatty acids to 'modulate immune function, and provide DHA Omega 3 and Omega 6 fatty acids 'needed for brain functioning'. 'ARA Opti Pro™ stands for 'reduced protein with better utilisation, less waste nitrogen and so less stress on the kidneys'.

'Prebiotics' or 'Prebio' comes up on labels too, not only on baby milk products.

Some yogurts also have added probiotics, *see p. 207*. Probiotics are 'good' bacteria that normally live in the gut, which help 'fight bad bacteria'. They need prebiotics as food to grow and multiply. Since a great deal of our immune system is based in the gut, the 'good' bacteria (probiotics) are important as well as their food source, prebiotics. While these elements may possibly be desirable they add to the cost of the product. Itis essential that a milk has the correct added vitamins and minerals because if it does not you will have to add them to your child's diet separately. This is one of the reasons that using fresh cow's milk or other unmodified milks is not a good idea.

INFANT FORMULAS ARE CLASSIFIED INTO BROAD CATOGORIES ACCORDING TO THEIR AGE USAGE

Bottle feeding milk formulas vary from country to country and are marketed under different brand names and with different formulations. The information below is a profile of the types available in general and their uses. Check labels for suitability as infant formulas, nutritional content, how to make up and how much to give. Follow your paediatrician's recommendation for your child.

FORMULAS FOR HEALTHY FULLTERM INFANTS

- Starter formulas, usually labelled '1', for use between birth and six months are either whey (the 'watery' part of milk) predominant, or casein predominant (the thicker 'curd' part of milk).
- Follow On formulas '2', for use between 6–12 months. These are usually casein predominant.
- Growing up milks '3', for use between 1-3 years.

WHEY PREDOMINANT 'STARTER' FORMULAS FOR HEALTHY FULLTERM INFANTS (above 2.5kg). Like breast milk, these milks contain a higher proportion of whey to casein to make them more digestible. They are fortified with all the necessary minerals and vitamins including iron. All have essential fatty acids and trace elements added. Babies who gain well and are content can stay on them until a year old. However, some babies do not find them sufficiently satisfying after about eight to sixteen weeks, and they can move on to a casein predominant starter formula, but most infants remain contented until at least six months.

CASEIN PREDOMINANT 'STARTER' FORMULAS FOR THE LARGER, 'HUNGRY' FULL TERM INFANT. Like fresh cow's milk these milks have a larger proportion of casein to whey milk protein. Casein takes longer to digest and so the baby remains satisfied for longer. These milks are suited to the larger full term baby and the 'hungry' baby, until one year or longer. They are fortified with all the necessary minerals and vitamins including iron.

'FOLLOW-ON' FORMULAS. These can be used for babies from six months who do not gain well, or who become hungry while on starter formula. They contain more protein, as well as vitamins and minerals including calcium and other elements. Some have added polyunsaturated fat, as well as trace elements, probiotics and other elements.

ACIDIFIED COW'S MILK FORMULA. Based on cow's milk that is acidified to make it more digestible, and more difficult for bacteria to grow. Casein to whey ratio is 50:50 and the milk can be given from birth without changing at six months. Acidified milks may be useful from birth in situations where there is an increased danger of infection such as daycare, or less than optimal hygiene, or for babies with mild digestive problems. It is fortified with all the necessary vitamins and minerals including iron.

HYPOALLERGENIC FORMULA FOR ALLERGY PREVENTION. Lactose free partially hydrolysed cow's milk formula for use from birth to 1 year (halaal and kosher). These formulae are said to contain all the necessary vitamins and minerals, plus trace elements. Hypoallergenic starter and follow up infant formulas based on partially hydrolysed whey protein from cow's milk may be recommended for the prevention of allergy in high risk babies. If the baby has already had an allergic reaction it may be necessary to use a semi-elemental formula before going on to hypoallergenic formula. **Use under doctor's supervision.**

HYPOALLERGENIC AMINO ACID-BASED FORMULA. Contains no cow's milk protein. May be useful in non-IgE-mediated allergy. Is lactose free and maybe recommended for cow's milk allergy. **For use only under medical supervision.**

SOYA MILK FORMULAS. These feeds are soya bean based and are free from lactose and cow's milk protein. They are suitable for use from birth. Iron, vitamins and trace elements have been added. Concerns regarding compounds found in soy plants have made for some resistance to the use of soya milks in infancy. This is due to the high level of isoflavones found in soy plants, which classifies them as phytoestrogens; meaning that they are structurally and functionally similar to oestrogens (hormones) in humans. They also contain phytates that might interfere with iodine metabolism. Soya based milks contain more sugar from non-milk sources and can result in cavities in teeth. Soya milk may cause windiness, and the iron may not be so easily absorbed. In some Soya brands, the vitamin C content has been increased in order to aid iron absorption. It is not preferable to give soya milk rather than cow's formula unless there is good reason for it, for example lactose intolerance. There is no role for soya formula in allergy prevention. **Consult your medical advisor.**

SOYA MILK FOLLOW ON FORMULA. These are similar to the above but contain more carbohydrate and protein. For use from six months should the baby be unsatisfied. Consult your medical advisor.

POWDERED GOAT'S MILK. Goat milk formula has not been available in a number of countries due to concerns regarding its suitability as an infant food. In some countries it is obtainable, but without the addition of the essential nutrients not found in goat's milk. The UK Department of Health deems goat's milk formula unsuitable for infants and does not approve goat's milk formula for use. In the USA goat's milk formula is only available as a feed for toddlers. While in some EU countries such as Austria and the Netherlands goat's milk baby formulas have long been available.

One of the reasons regulations have been changed to allow the sale of registered goat's milk formulas in the US is because people are making goat's milk formulas in their kitchens, and regulators have expressed concerns that they may not have the correct nutritional balance. Consult you medical advisor. Goat's milk contains less sodium (salt), more potassium and chloride and more beneficial fatty acids than cow's milk, and it is slightly more digestible. Some people believe that babies who are allergic or intolerant to cow's milk can have a goat's milk formula. Goat's milk contains lactose and is not suitable for use in lactose intolerance, and it is common for babies to be allergic to both cow's and goat's milk.

Goat's milk formulas are not suitable for babies who are allergic to cow's milk.

Feeding babies unmodified raw (fresh or unpasteurised) goat's milk is part of some cultural practices, and interest has developed though the internet recently. However there are real dangers when using any raw or unmodified milk for babies, and goat's milk is no exception. Do not use unpasteurised fresh goat's milk, as it can harbour parasites and brucellosis (Malta fever), a serious illness.

In infants under a year the incidence of metabolic acidosis (kidney problems) increases with high protein intake, while the capacity to secrete salt is only fully functional at the beginning of the second year.

Fresh goat's milk lacks iron (folic acid), and vitamins, B_6, C and D amongst other nutrients essential for health and growth. Iron deficiency is associated with poor cognitive (brain) performance and development in infants. Powdered goat's milk lacks folic acid, iron and vitamins D and C, which must be supplemented. **Medical supervision is required.**

FORMULAS FOR TODDLERS. Growing up milks. These milks are similar to cow's milk but have iron as well as vitamins and trace elements added. Some have added 'immune boosters', although claims by some manufacturers that they prevent illness have been disputed. If cost is not a factor, and the child is not having a well balanced diet, there may be benefits. However, there is a danger children will not take the necessary solids because they prefer the pleasant taste of some of the milks. Give from a cup other than at sleep time and keep milk intake for children over 12 months to around 400ml in 24 hours. Limit fruit juice intake, as this too, can spoil the appetite.

POWDERED FULLCREAM MILK. These products are made from full-cream powdered cow's milk and are slightly less allergenic than fresh cow's milk due to the heat processing. Vitamins A, E and D as well as calcium, zinc, iodine and iron are added. They can be given after the age of a year.

SPECIALISED FORMULAS TO BE USED UNDER MEDICAL SUPERVISION FOR BABIES WITH PARTICULAR NEEDS.
These include:
- Preterm and low birth weight babies
- Acidified milks (*See p. 159*).
- Milk for healthy babies with regurgitation (vomiting within 2 hours after a feed)
- Milk for diarrhoea
- Milk for constipation
- Milk to minimioe wind
- Amino-acid based formulas
- Milks for babies with sensitive digestions
- Lactose and sucrose free milks
- Semi-elemental formulations
- Elemental formulations
- Milk for children who need to gain weight
- Highly specialised feeds for older children in hospital

FORMULAS FOR PRETERM AND LOW BIRTH WEIGHT INFANTS. These products are for full-term or preterm babies with a low birth weight (1 500g – 2 500g or under 1 500g) who require a special milk in order to grow well. There are also formulations used to fortify, or supplement breast milk in the case of very small babies. These products are mainly for hospital use, and are only used until the infant is doing well enough to go onto breastmilk only or starter formula. **Medical supervision is required.**

ANTI-REGURGITATION FORMULA. Used for the treatment of gastro-oesophageal reflux, in which milk is vomited by otherwise healthy infants. These formulas become thicker in the stomach and are used to help prevent regurgitation (bringing up) of feeds. There is a thickener that is added to feeds, not a formula. **Only to be used under medical supervision.**

HYDROLYSED FORMULA FOR COW'S MILK ALLERGY AND SEVERE MALABSORPTION. For use in rare cases of growth retardation associated with allergy, and severe malabsorption. **These are expensive amino-acid based formulas for use only under medical supervision.**

SEMI-ELEMENTAL HYPOALLERGENIC FORMULAS. These products are sometimes used for the treatment of chronic diarrhoea, cow's milk allergy with rash or respiratory symptoms and malabsorption. Some are lactose and sucrose free and may be used for the treatment of food sensitivity and acute diarrhoea. Some are low in lactase and extensively hydrolysed (the whey is modified) for the treatment of allergies. **These are all to be used only under strict medical supervision.**

FORMULA FOR SENSITIVE BABIES. From birth for babies with 'mild digestive problems such as colic, constipation, posseting and abdominal distension'. Reduced in lactose and slightly thickened, it contains all the necessary vitamins and minerals, including iron, as well as added trace elements. The milk is partially hydrolysed which is said to make it less likely to cause allergies. It also contains structured lipids said to help the absorption of fat and calcium. **Consult your medical advisor.**

FORMULA FOR CONSTIPATION. These claim to soften and assist in the movement of stools. High in lactose. **Use only under a doctor's supervision.**

LACTOSE FREE INFANT FORMULA. These formulas may be prescribed for babies who are sensitive to whey protein, lactose intolerance, and after gastroenteritis. Some formulation claim it is specially adapted to provide for the baby's particular needs after a bout of severe diarrhoea, and is higher or lower in vitamins, minerals and trace elements to aid healing of the gut. Unless the condition is permanent, these products should not be used as a substitute for the regular formula milk or breast milk. **Consult your medical advisor.**

FOR CHILDREN WHO NEED CATCH UP GROWTH. Specialised formulas are available. **Use only under medical supervision.**

HIGHLY SPECIALISED MILK BASED FEEDS FOR CHILDREN IN SPECIAL CIRCUMSTANCES. These highly specialised products are for use in hospitalised children with special nutritional needs. **Only to be used under strict medical supervision.**

MILKS THAT ARE SOMETIMES USED AS INFANT FEEDS

There are a number of other milks that are sometimes used as breast milk replacements. None of them are ideal for use as infant feeds and some should be avoided in the first year. Their use is often based on cost, or misplaced 'health' benefits. Breastfeeding is always the most cost effective and healthy option.

Amongst these are:

- Fresh cow's milk
- Fresh soya milk
- Powdered full cream milk
- Tinned evaporated milk
- Powdered and fresh goat's milk
- Long life milk

FRESH COW'S MILK. Fresh cow's milk from a dairy, even though pasteurised, is unsuitable for a young baby because it contains fat and protein which are difficult to digest and more likely to sensitise the baby towards an allergic reaction. The mineral content, especially sodium (salt), is too high, and the sugar (lactose), iron and vitamin content too low. While the proportion of protein, sodium and other elements differ considerably from breast milk. It is also the most likely to cause an allergic reaction, and can cause gastric bleeding due to irritation of the stomach lining if taken in excess (more than 1 litre a day). It is grossly lacking in iron, vitamins C, D and trace elements, and these must be supplemented. It is better not to use fresh cow's milk as a breast milk substitute until after the age of a year if possible when a good mixed diet will help make up for some of the milk's deficiencies.

Unpasteurised milk can harbour dangerous organisms such as tuberculosis (TB) and brucellosis (Malta fever). Do not buy fresh milk from unregulated sources. Do not give low fat (2%) or skim milk to children under 2 years as they need the essential fatty acids.

FRESH SOYA MILK. Does not contain the necessary vitamins, minerals and trace elements and is unsuitable as a baby formula. **Some long life soya milks have added vitamins and minerals but should only be used under medical supervision.**

GOAT'S MILK. Fresh goat's milk is similar to cow's milk although it contains less sodium (salt) more potassium and chloride and more beneficial essential fatty acids. It is slightly more digestible. It lacks folic acid, iron and vitamin D which are essential for health and growth. Tinned powdered goat's milk is sometimes used for babies who are sensitive to both cow's milk and soya milk. Powdered goat's milk does not have any added vitamins or minerals, which must be supplemented. Do not use unpasteurised fresh goat's milk as it can harbour parasites and brucellosis (Malta fever) a serious illness.

SHEEP, BUFFALO, HORSE MILK AND UNMODIFIED SOYA AND RICE MILK. These milks are not nutritionally adequate and are unsuitable for human babies. In terms of allergic reactions, there is also a lot of cross reactivity between the proteins in cow's milk and other mammalian milk proteins. Rice milk in particular is lacking in essential elements.

DONKEY MILK. Donkey's milk has been used since ancient times – Cleopatra bathed in ass's milk – and there has been renewed interest ever since Pope Francis received two donkeys Thea and Noah, as a gift. The pontiff shared the story of how he was fed donkey milk by his mother as a child in Argentina, when she did not have enough breast milk.

Donkey milk has some similarities with breast milk in that it may be less allergenic than cow's milk but is not nutritionally comparable to breast milk. A three-month-old, who had cow's milk allergy, did not thrive when fed unmodified donkey milk. At five months she was underweight, pale, had a distended tummy and poor muscle tone. Tests showed she was anaemic due to lack of iron and other essential nutrients and was getting only 42% of the recommended food caloric intake causing her to become malnourished. She gained weight quickly when put on a cow's milk protein free milk product.

Cultural familiarity such as the use of donkey milk in southern Italy, and camel milk in some North African and Arabic countries as well as buffalo, goat and sheep milk in Mediterranean regions – well known for cheeses such as mozzarella and feta – do not have an unpleasant taste as some highly modified formula 'milks' do; but they do not meet the needs of infants without modification and the addition of a range of vitamins and minerals.

TINNED EVAPORATED COW'S MILK. These products have half the water content of fresh cow's milk removed by a process of evaporation. No vitamins iron or other minerals are added and this makes them unsuitable as an infant formula, as is indicated on the label.

Nevertheless, some doctors do prescribe them and you must dilute and add sugar according to your doctor's instructions. Minerals and vitamins must be supplemented as they are lacking.

FULLCREAM LONGLIFE HEAT STERILISED MILKS. These milks are similar to fresh cow's milk but may be more digestible because they have been heat treated. **Folic acid, iron, and other trace elements and vitamins need to be supplemented.** It is preferable not to use them before the age of a year.

WARNING!
PRODUCTS THAT SHOULD NOT BE USED. Coffee creamers and 'dairy blends' should never be used as a feed. They are not made from milk. Rooibos tea, or other teas or coffee should never replace a feed. Coffee and Ceylon tea should not be given to children at all. They contain stimulants and the tannin in Ceylon (ordinary) tea, prevents proper absorption of iron. Rooibos tea has very little tannin (1%). Two percent milk and skim milk should not be used for children under the age of two as they do not have the necessary fats, vitamins and energy content necessary for proper growth and brain development. Sweetened condensed milk is not suitable as an infant feed unless prescribed by a doctor for a specific purpose.

EQUIPMENT FOR BOTTLE FEEDING
START WITH THE BASICS. Four to six simple, boilable, unbreakable glass or plastic bottles with wide necks for easy cleaning. The Cancer Association of South Africa, along with many international agencies have warned against baby bottles made from polycarbonate plastic saying that they contain chemicals that could cause cancer. When heated bisphenol-A chemical molecules in polycarbonate are released which may be damaging to the young, although any such damage is not conclusive in humans. Fortunately some manufacturers no longer use bisphenol-A, so look for these products, or polyethylene or glass bottles. Avoid bottles marked with the letters PC or a triangle containing the number 7. (See p. 56.)

Teats como in various shapes. You might want to buy a few in different shapes to see which suits your baby best, although most babies get used to whatever is offered. Teats, in particular, those made of rubber perish quickly and should be discarded before they become sticky and harbour germs, or lose their shape. (See p. 56.)

HOLE IN THE TEAT. The hole should not be too big or too small. Too big, and your baby will choke and gulp air, too small and your baby will get tired and frustrated. Milk should drip out fairly rapidly when the bottle is held upside down – about one drop per second. You can buy teats with holes in various sizes, usually marked according to the age for which they are meant.

TO ENLARGE THE HOLE. Push the blunt end of a thick needle into a cork and hold it over a flame until it is red hot, then plunge the point into the hole in the teat to enlarge it as required. A small hole is better for water and multiple holes or a slightly larger hole is better for milk.

You will also need a measuring jug marked off in millilitres, a straight knife or spatula to level off the powder if you are going to use powered formula; a fork or whisk for mixing; teat covers for each bottle and a bottle brush. Keep all this equipment covered on a clean tray.

YOU WILL ALSO NEED STERILISING EQUIPMENT. Either chemical steriliser, or a pot for boiling or a steamer (*see p. 60 for equipment and how to use*). The easiest is an electric streamer/steriliser or microwave steriliser. They are expensive but you may be lucky enough to 'inherit' one from a friend.

MAKING UP BOTTLE FEEDS

HYGIENE IS PARAMOUNT. It is vitally important to be meticulous about hygiene when making up a baby's feeds, because germs can multiply easily in milk. Most cases of gastroenteritis are caused by germs transferred from unwashed hands. Wash your hands well with soap before making up feeds and before giving the bottle.

- You can either make up one bottle at a time if you do not have a fridge, or you can make up all six bottles giving you enough for approximately 24 hours.
- Follow instructions on the label using the scoop that is in the tin. Measure out the required amount of water exactly. The boiled water should be allowed to cool in the kettle before making up the feed or the micronutrients will be damaged.
- If you are using powdered milk, only measure out the powder with the scoop provided in the tin, and do not heap it. Never use the scoop from another brand of milk to make up formula as it will not be the same and will give an incorrect and potentially dangerous mixture. Do not add an extra scoop if you think your baby is hungry, rather make up the correct mixture and give more of the feed. Do not make the feed weaker for any reason.
- Do not use tap water to rinse bottles that have already been sterilised with a chemical sterilising mixture unless the water has been boiled. Some babies are upset by the smell of the sterilising solution and you can rinse it off with cooled boiled water before use. Always rinse teats.
- Use bottles sterilised by boiling straight from the pot or store in the fridge until needed.
- Level off the mixture in the scoop with a knife or spatula. Then add to the cooled

boiled water. Allow the water to cool first so that the nutrients are not damaged. Do not pack the powder into the scoop or add 'one for the pot'. The feeds must be made up strictly according to the manufacturer's instructions. Adding extra powder will make the mixture too strong and could damage your baby's kidneys and brain. Too weak, will result in malnourishment and poor growth.

- Put the cover over the teat and keep the made-up bottles in the fridge, or keep the made-up mixture in a covered jug in the fridge, if you do not have enough bottles.
- Rinse bottle with cold water after a feed, then brush thoroughly with a bottle brush and liquid soap. Be sure to get rid of any left over milk as this is where the germs grow. Rinse in very hot water and sterilise as described on *p. 60* or put in a dishwasher.
- Rub the inside of the teats with coarse salt to remove any milk residue.
- Squeeze water through the teat hole and unclog with a toothpick if necessary.
- Rinse with hot water and sterilise as usual.

PREPARING FOR THE FEED. Wash your hands thoroughly, and warm the milk by standing the bottle in a jug of hot water, being very careful to keep it out of the reach of children and far from your baby. You can use a bottle warmer but do not leave the milk in it for long periods. Microwave heating makes the centre of the milk very hot and can easily scald your baby. **Be sure to shake the bottle** before testing it on your wrist. It is also possible that the molecular structure of the milk is altered. *See p. 56* for bottles that should not be microwaved with milk in them because of bisphenol-A.

If you change your baby before the feed, wash your hands well before you touch the bottle. Shake the feed to mix, and test the temperature by shaking a few drops onto your inner wrist – it should feel pleasantly warm. Some babies will take their feeds straight from the fridge and there is no harm in this after the first six months. Before this age your baby will use too much energy to get warm again after a cold feed.

GIVING THE FEED. Hold your baby close as if you were breastfeeding, opening your blouse so that she gets skin to skin contact if possible. With the teat touch her cheek and she will 'root' towards it and open her mouth. Hold the bottle fairly upright so that the teat is full of milk or she will suck in air.

If the teat booomes flattened by the suction, take it out of her mouth and allow it to expand again, or just loosen the lid slightly so that air can get in. (There are teats that claim to prevent this occurring.) Screwing the teat on too tightly can make it difficult to suck against the pressure. Make yourself comfortable when feeding. You can even do it lying on your bed, but never be tempted to prop the bottle because not only could your baby choke, she will miss the vital human contact.

If you prop the bottle there is also the possibility that liquid will run from the back of her mouth into the Eustachian tubes in the ear and collect there and form a source of infection.

Doctors operating on babies' eardrums have found stagnant milk that has resulted in a temporary hearing loss. Because the child's hearing is impaired in this way, she could lag in learning to talk and other areas of development.

Try to make a point of giving your baby her feeds yourself so that you can foster a warm close relationship in which she feels secure. Your partner can do night and other feeds occasionally so that you can get some rest.

HOW MUCH? HOW OFTEN? If your baby weighs over 3 400g you will probably be told to feed her every four hours. Babies weighing under 3 400g are usually given a feed every three hours during the day and every four hours at night. These times are only approximate and you should feed whenever your baby demands it (*see p. 85*).

- As the child grows and develops, demand feeds should gradually progress to a more regular feeding routine that meets both the parent's and the child's needs.
- You can expect to feed six to ten times in 24 hours in the first four weeks; five to six times between one and three months; four to five times between three and seven months, and three times a day with an early morning feed between seven and nine months. At the end of the first year three bottles of milk should be sufficient making up a total of between 500-600ml in 24 hours.
- Do not be upset if your baby does not take all her milk at every feed, she will probably take more at the next feed or need an earlier feed.
- Never keep left over formula to offer later. Germs breed quickly in milk and your baby could easily become ill because the milk will no longer be sterile.
- A bottle feed should take about 20 minutes. If it takes much longer, the teat hole may be too small, or the baby may be ill. If she stops feeding during a feed she may have a wind. Lay her down for a minute then try and burp her.
- The nursing home will advise you on your particular baby's needs but the average full term baby will need 150ml for every kilo of her body weight when she comes out of the hospital. That is, if she weighs 4kg she will require 600ml milk in a 24 hour period. So if she has five feeds in 24 hours each bottle will be 120ml. If she has six feeds in 24 hours she should have 100ml at each feed. Remember that if you feed your baby on demand she may take more than the six feeds in 24 hours.
- If you want to keep track of how much she has during a 24-hour period you can make up the total amount she should have in 24 hours and keep it in a closed jug in the fridge. If you do not have a regular schedule, fill the bottle with as much as you think she might take. When the jug is empty you will have some idea of what she has had during that period. Don't hesitate to give your baby more if you think she needs it in the early weeks. She will soon settle into a more predictable routine.

- Don't force your baby to finish a feed if she does not want it. Overfeeding can be a problem in bottle fed babies who are inclined to get fat. Fat babies are more prone to chest problems and colds than normal weight babies.
- As your baby increases in weight you will need to work out how much milk she should be getting. Do it on the same basis as before, that is, 150ml a kilo body mass every 24 hours. All you do is multiply the number of kilos she weighs by 150, then divide it by the number of feeds she has in 24 hours to get the amount of each feed, up to a maximum of 1 000ml (1 litre). Always follow the directions given on the formula label as they may vary from this according to the type.
- A baby should not have more than 1000ml milk in 24 hours as this can cause gastric irritation and bleeding. If more is demanded, and she is over four months and has doubled her birth weight, you might need to begin solids. Consult your medical advisor. Decrease milk intake after six months to a maximum of 500-600ml in 24 hours, between 300-500ml is sufficient from the second year. Or she may need to change to a more satisfying milk.
- From about six to eight weeks some babies are no longer satisfied by a 'starter' milk formula as they are usually whey based. In this case you may need to change to a formula with a smaller whey component. These are usually labelled No 2. Do not make the formula stronger.
- It is not advisable to change to fresh cow's milk until your baby is at least six months old. And it is much better to wait until she is a year old as fresh cow's milk does not have all the vitamins and minerals needed and it is also less digestible. If she seems hungry and cries between feeds, or does not gain weight consult your doctor or clinic. (*See Colic p. 99*).
- If you need to change feeds, choose a feed from a different category or it will not make any difference.
- In hot weather your baby may be thirsty and can be offered a little plain, cooled, boiled water between feeds. Do not add sugar, or worry if she does not want it.

SOLIDS. If your baby is not gaining weight and is clearly dissatisfied you should consult your medical advisor. After six months breast milk alone is unlikely to provide sufficient iron, or kilojoules to fuel growth. It is advisable to introduce a variety of solids from not later than four months. (*See page 187.*)

STERILISING BOTTLES. Milk is an ideal medium for breeding germs so it is wise to continue sterilising bottles until she stops using them, or at least until the end of the first year.

Or wash thoroughly with an anti-bacterial, or other good liquid washing up soap if heat sterilising is not possible. (*See p. 60*).

NIGHT FEEDS

WHEN TO STOP THE NIGHT FEEDS. Your baby will need to be fed at night until she is able to go for longer periods without nourishment. In the early weeks she will probably need a feed around ten at night and then again around two. She will also wake for an early morning feed. Don't wake your baby for the night feeds unless you want to give her a feed before you go to bed. She will gradually sleep for longer periods during the night and will eventually drop the night feeds. The 10pm feed is usually the first to go, if you are lucky, between six and eight weeks, but she could go on needing it for much longer. Try and stretch the time between night feeds by patting her or giving a dummy or water in order to get her to go for longer between feeds. If your baby starts waking again at night after sleeping through do not give a milk feed. Check for other causes such as illness, teething, being too hot or cold etc. before assuming she is hungry. She may be hungry due to a growth spurt, in this case increase her food intake during the day, not at night!

CONFUSING NIGHT AND DAY. If you find your baby is waking more often at night than during the day, give her more feeds during the day even if you have to wake her so that a gets into a more acceptable rhythm. Never keep left over milk warming in a bottle warmer during the night to give later. It is the ideal medium for germs to breed. Instead, keep boiling water in a flask so that you can warm up a bottle quickly. Do it where there is no danger of accidentally burning the baby. (*See warming the bottle in a microwave p.208.*)

BASIC DAILY NUTRITIONAL REQUIREMENTS FOR FULL TERM INFANTS UP TO ONE YEAR

The range – which is extensive – is not complete but the most important elements are shown to give you an idea of the complex nutritional needs of early childhood.

- Energy: 420-500 kilojoules per kilo of body mass
- Fluid: 150-200ml per kilo of body mass
- Protein: 2-3g per kilo of body mass

Fat soluble vitamins

- Vitamin A: 1 500 international units
- Vitamin D: 400 international units
- Vitamin E: 5 international units

Water soluble vitamins

- Vitamin B (thiamine): 0.4mg
- Vitamin B_2 (riboflavin): 0.6 mg

- Vitamin B_6 (pyridoxine): 0.3mg
- Vitamin B_{12}: 2–5 micrograms
- Folic acid: 1-2 micrograms
- Nicotinic acid: 4.0mg
- Vitamin C: 40mg

Minerals
- Calcium: 500mg
- Phosphorus: 400mg
- Iodine: 40 micrograms
- Iron: 12mg
- Magnesium: 60mg
- Zinc: 3mg

BOTTLE FEEDING AND VITAMIN, FLUORIDE AND IRON SUPPLEMENTS

WHAT THEY DO. Your baby needs vitamin C to promote healthy gums, and prevent bleeding from body tissues. Vitamin A is needed to prevent 'night blindness' and other problems involving the eye. Vitamin A also helps children recover from illness. While vitamin D is needed to prevent rickets and promote healthy bone and tooth development. Iron is an important component of healthy red blood cells, and a lack can result in iron deficiency anaemia which is the most common nutritional deficiency worldwide. (*See p. 430*). Most importantly, iron is critical for brain development. A lack of iron in the first three years can adversely affect a child's intellectual performance, behaviour, and physical development.

Recommendations for iron supplementation vary depending on the country, socio-economic conditions, customary feeding practices and the levels of iron enrichment in foods, including formula milks. Iron levels during pregnancy are important and appear to affect the amount of iron stored by the unborn child. There are also different recommendations for preterm and low birth weight babies as they are the most vulnerable. Consult your medical advisor.

Even if your baby's formula has vitamins and minerals added your doctor may advise you to give a water based multivitamin and iron preparation. Water-soluble drops are not dangerous if inhaled, unlike oil-based preparations. Continue for the first year or longer if the child does not have a good diet.

Fresh cow's milk needs to be supplemented by vitamins C, D and iron. Although most formula milks contain adequate amounts of vitamin A some do not have sufficient vitamin D. Vitamin D is manufactured by the body in sunlight, so if your baby has parts of her body exposed to the sun regularly – a total of 30 minutes a week – she will probably be manufacturing sufficient quantities. The darker the baby's skin the less vitamin D is made in sunlight. In view of the fact that skin specialists discourage exposing children to the sun at all, you may need to add vitamin D. Speak to your doctor as this is an important element.

Do not add vitamins to the milk because some may be destroyed if the formula is left for a long time before it is taken.

Vitamin C is destroyed by heat, so although it is added to most formulas, you should allow the water to cool to body temperature before making up the feed.

Vitamin C is obtained naturally in tomatoes, oranges, lemons, and especially guavas. The first three contain a lot of acid and can cause stomach upsets in young children so it is not advisable to give them in the natural form. Unsweetened fruit juices made for babies do not need diluting, and contain added vitamin C. However because they can affect the appetite it is a good idea to dilute with cooled boiled water. Fruit juice concentrates for infants also have added vitamin C and are diluted one part juice concentrate to two parts water or as much water as desired. Once the teeth come through it is not advisable to give fruit juices from a bottle as they can rot the teeth. Rather use a cup or spoon, or let the older child drink through a straw.

Iron is an essential component of blood and a shortage can have serious consequences for physical and mental growth. Most full term babies have sufficient stores of iron to see them through the first three to four months. After that iron needs to be supplied through the diet or by means of an iron supplement. It is recommended that iron fortified formulas be used from birth until the end of the first year. Nevertheless some babies do become anaemic and your doctor may advise you to give a supplement. Iron-fortified cereals and red meat, as well as green leafy vegetables are good sources of dietary iron. Vitamin C helps the absorption of iron so give any drops between feeds together with a juice high in vitamin C. The calcium in milk hinders the absorption of iron, as does the tannin in Ceylon tea, rooibos has very little tannin. Iron drops can stain the teeth and cause stomach upsets so use only on the advice of your doctor. For convenience, iron is available together with vitamins in liquid form. Iron alters the colour of the baby's stools, making them blackish or dark green, and can cause constipation. Like all medicines, iron should be kept out of the reach of children as it is poisonous in excess.

PRETERM AND LOW BIRTH WEIGHT INFANTS' IRON AND VITAMIN D REQUIREMENTS. Babies born prematurely and other low birth weight infants such as twins need extra iron and vitamin D because they have not had a chance to store it before birth. Your doctor may recommend that iron supplements be given from the second month or from birth. The usual daily requirement is 1.5mg to 2mg per kilogram body weight. The daily vitamin D requirement is also greater, 800 units for the first six months and 400 units thereafter.

FULL TERM INFANTS. Iron can be added to the diet of the full term baby if it is not supplied in the formula, or if the diet is poor. The usual daily dose is 1mg ferrous sulphate or ferrous gluconate to a kilogram body mass. For convenience, iron is available with vitamins in liquid form. A minimum of 1mg per kilo body weight is needed daily. If vitamin D is prescribed, the dose is usually 400 units a day.

IMPORTANT NOTE: Iron, vitamins A and D can be harmful in excess so follow your medical advisor's instructions carefully. (*See iron deficiency anaemia p. 430*).

FLUORIDE. Some areas have a high naturally occurring fluoride content. Do not give additional fluoride without consulting your doctor, dentist or local water authority. While fluoride can significantly reduce tooth decay, too much fluoride can cause brown spots on the teeth and weaken enamel. Do not encourage your child to swallow toothpaste that contains fluoride as it could result in her getting too much. Fluoride is easily added to the diet by means of drops. Speak to your dentist or pharmacist.

COMMON FEEDING PROBLEMS

POSSETING AFTER A FEED. Posseting, spitting up or bringing up a little milk after a feed is very common. In its simplest form it is due to the baby having taken more than her stomach can hold. This is easy to understand since the oesophagus (gullet or food pipe) is relatively short in infants and the stomach small, so food overflow is easy if the closing mechanism at the top of the stomach is not working well. These sphincter muscles at the top if the stomach are often slightly immature and do not close efficiently, (*oesophageal reflux, see p. 381*).

Milk brought up in this way often looks far more than it is, and you need not feed her again to try to make it up unless she has brought up a large amount. She will demand a feed earlier if she needs it. Milk brought up by bottle fed babies often smells sour and looks curdled. This does not mean the milk does not agree with her. It simply means stomach acids have begun digesting it. Milk brought up by breast fed babies does not smell as sour.

In its mild form babies do not appear to be distressed by it, and continue to thrive, although it makes them unpopular for the extra laundry it generates. They usually grow out of it in the second year when they take more solid food and are upright most of the time. It has become common to put all infant crying down to reflux, but this is sometimes overstated.

Vomiting can also occur if the feed is too concentrated (incorrect making up of the formula), too rich a formula, or the hole in the teat is too big or too small causing the baby to swallow a lot of air.

WHAT YOU CAN DO. If your baby does not seem distressed by it, and continues to thrive, simple measures can help. Change her before feeds or in between so that you do not put pressure on her stomach when it is full. You should handle her gently, and feed in a semi-upright position and burp often so that the stomach is emptied of wind. Seat her in a baby chair for a while until the feed settles, and raise the head end of the mattress by putting a folded towel or book underneath. Never use a pillow for a baby.

PRODUCTS THAT CAN HELP. A thickening agent that is added to feeds can be very useful to settle the stomach contents and help prevent regurgitation and the potentially serious effects of acid burns to the oesophagus. Ask your doctor or pharmacist about it. There are also milks that are slightly thickened and your doctor may prescribe a change of milk.

REGULAR VOMITING. GERD (gastro-oesophageal reflux disease) occurs when the milk brought up contains enough stomach acid to damage the lining of the oesophagus (food pipe) causing severe irritation. This is a more forceful expulsion of the contents of the stomach than posseting or spitting up, and it causes the baby distress. She may have a cough without having a cold and there may be signs of blood in the vomit due to acid burns on the oesophagus. There are many possible causes including oesophageal reflux, hiatus hernia, pyloric stenosis, urinary tract and other infections as well as physical abnormalities. (*See pp. 381, 382, 384, 385*).

Occasionally vomiting may be due to a hiatus hernia in which a portion of the stomach protrudes through the diaphragm. The baby vomits as soon as she is laid flat after a feed. Therefore she should be kept fairly upright during her feeds and propped in a baby chair afterwards. See the recommendations under 'posseting' for more hints.

When vomiting starts suddenly or builds up over a period and shoots out forcefully, or even if it is regular though not forceful, the child may have pyloric stenosis, a narrowing of the food pipe. This prevents milk from passing through or allows only a small amount through. The child loses weight slowly or rapidly according to the amount of food getting through, and must have medical attention immediately. This condition usually manifests itself around the second or third week of life and is more common in boys than girls. (*See p. 385*).

Vomiting which is due to an infection can be serious and must be attended to immediately. The signs could include poor feeding, diarrhoea, failure to gain weight and sometimes, but not always, a raised temperature.

Consult a doctor as soon as possible if your child shows any or a combination of these signs.

Excessive persistent vomiting may have a number of other causes such as bowel obstruction, or an incorrectly joined oesophagus, or a metabolic disorder, and can lead to dehydration which is serious. If the vomit contains blood or bile you should save it for the doctor to examine.

FAILURE TO THRIVE

BABIES WHO DO NOT GROW WELL. Sometimes a baby will fail to gain weight even though she shows no signs of disease and does not vomit or have diarrhoea. In preterm infants a possible cause is acidity of the blood. Your doctor may prescribe sodium bicarbonate to be added to her feeds for a few days, and improvement will be rapid. An underlying infection, hidden physical defect, metabolic disorder or allergy could be the reason why a baby fails to gain, but your doctor will have to do tests to establish the cause.

In past times babies reared in institutions sometimes failed to grow although there was no sign of illness or other apparent reason. Studies have shown that what these babies lacked was frequent person to person contact, love and handling, which was not possible when a great number of babies were looked after by a small staff. So don't hesitate to handle your baby, talk to her and let her know she is not alone in the world. Your child needs your tender touch as much as food in order to grow.

THE BOTTLE FED BABY'S STOOLS

It is easy to become greatly preoccupied with the frequency, colour and consistency of your baby's stools. It is true they can reveal a great deal, but don't let it become an obsession as it is normal for babies' stools to vary from day today.

Bottle fed babies have a far greater range of stool colours and consistencies than breast fed babies because of the variety of formulas and their effects. The most important thing to remember is that diarrhoea (frequent watery stools) can have rapid, serious consequences.

The usual stool produced by a cow's milk formula is yellowish brown and firm. Some formulas, in particular the 'humanised' or starter type, can produce a dark greenish stool especially if they have iron added. Bottle fed babies may pass only one stool a day or many more. As long as they are not large and watery, frequent stools should not be considered as diarrhoea.

Bits of undigested food like pieces of carrot are often seen in the stools and should not be considered as abnormal.

ABNORMAL STOOLS

CAUSES AND APPEARANCE. A small amount of mucus may be due to gastric irritation if the baby is colicky, and is not a sign of disease. Teething can also result in mucous in the stools due to the amount of saliva swallowed. Blood in the stools can either show up bright red if it is fresh blood or black if it has been through the digestive system. Black stools caused by bleeding are tarry and should be reported to your doctor. They should not be confused with normal dark stools caused by iron or other substances in the diet. In the first few days after birth babies' stools are black because they consist of meconium which has collected before birth. They gradually change to a normal yellow colour. Bright red blood in the stools can also be caused by bleeding from a fissure at the anus or a small polyp in the gut. In more serious cases, bleeding may be caused by a disease or deformity of the digestive tract, and prompt medical attention must be sought in all cases to establish the cause. Whatever the case, blood in the stool must be reported to your doctor immediately.

Certain diseases produce distinctive stools which are often foul smelling or bulky. Your doctor will order tests to establish the exact nature of the problem.

CONSTIPATION. It is easy to become overly concerned about the frequency of a baby's stools, but unless they are very hard and cause distress on passing it is not likely to be a problem. Hard, dry stools can be due to overly concentrated feeds, a need for extra fluids, or iron that has been added to feeds.

Occasionally a small split may form at the anus and this can make it more difficult and painful for her to pass a stool. Heal and lubricate the anal area with a suitable product – consult your doctor – and increase her fluid intake in the form of water or fruit juice.

Prune juice is a natural laxative but gives some babies cramps. If it does not affect your baby badly, give between feeds or when she is restless. You can make a prune puree by soaking organically grown prunes (most packaged prunes are dipped in preservatives) overnight in water or rooibos tea, then boil until soft in a little brown sugar water. Remove pips and puree. Offer a few spoonfuls after meals.

If your baby does not have sugar added to her feeds add a flat teaspoonful of brown sugar to each feed. If she already has sugar added to her feeds try using brown sugar instead of white sugar and increase the quantity by half to a full teaspoon with every feed. Stop as soon as the stools return to normal. Prunes and figs are natural laxatives and there are natural products made with these ingredients obtainable from health food stores that are suitable for older children. Cereal with added prunes is also available.

Rooibos tea with brown sugar can loosen your baby's stools. Make a fairly strong brew using two teaspoons rooibos tea to three cups water. Mix 60ml tea with a teaspoon of sugar, cool, and give it to your baby. Do not use ordinary tea or honey. For older children malted porridge or bran cereals are also good for adding bulk and relieving constipation. Serve her cooked, unpeeled fruit and vegetables. A lactulose product from your pharmacy is useful when dietary changes do not have the desired effect. Glycerine suppositories are also useful if you need a quick result. Your doctor may advise the use of an infant enema when all else fails.

NOTE: Constipation with or without bloating can have more serious implications, such as a physical deformity, sluggish bowel due to hypothyroidism, obstruction or worms. (*See pp. 345, 383 for constipation in older children*).

DIARRHOEA. Frequent, slimy, large stools, which may be yellow, white or greenish in colour or, if the diet is mixed, brownish, may be a sign of diarrhoea. In the newborn baby diarrhoea can be a sign of serious infection and your doctor must be contacted immediately.

The most common cause of diarrhoea in bottle fed babies is gastroenteritis, and other infectious diseases like that cause the death of thousands of children every year, particularly in hot climates. Besides having frequent stools the baby may vomit, thus increasing the risk of fatal dehydration. The front fontanelle (soft spot on the head) and eyes may become sunken, urine output is reduced, pulse is rapid and the child loses weight while the skin loses its elasticity.

Gastroenteritis, often caused by E. coli bacteria that live in the stools is highly infectious and easily spread by flies or germs from the stools, so it is vital to maintain strict hygiene and wash your hands before touching your baby or her food. The human rotavirus is also a common cause of diarrhoea especially in winter and is easily spread from person to person. Parasitic and fungal infestation also cause diarrhoea and are common particularly in older children. (*See under the various illnesses, Chapter 13.*)

Medicines to bind stools can be dangerous for children and should not be used without prescription. Antibiotics can do more harm than good, except in certain cases, for example in babies under three months when the diarrhoea may be due to another source of infection. Although most cases of diarrhoea are self-limiting and pass with no specific treatment other than extra fluids, your doctor will identify the cause of the diarrhoea and prescribe appropriate medication if necessary. Offer the usual feeds as soon as the child will take them in addition to the extra fluids. Bananas are a good source of potassium which is often depleted by diarrhoea.

WHAT TO DO AT THE FIRST SIGN OF LOOSE STOOLS. Offer extra fluids immediately to prevent dehydration. (This is over and above the usual daily intake of liquids.) You can do this best by giving her a solution to replace the liquid and minerals necessary to keep the body fluids balanced. Known as electrolyte or rehydration solutions, you can get them without a prescription from your pharmacy and make them up according to the instructions, or you can make your own in an emergency although it does not contain all the necessary elements such as potassium.

DO NOT STOP FEEDS. Many children go off their food when they are suffering from diarrhoea, however, if the child is breast fed give her feeds more frequently; if bottle fed, continue to offer bottle feeds and solids if she is interested. Rice, or rice cereal are particularly suitable. Do not force the child to eat if she does not want to, but you must ensure that she continues to receive liquids; preferably breast milk and an oral rehydration solution that contains all the necessary elements, even if she is vomiting.

ELECTROLYTE SOLUTION (ORAL REHYDRATIONSOLUTION)

Wash your hands and all utensils well. You can make up the full amount or half.

- 2 litres boiled water (use a large milk bottle as a measure if necessary)
- 16 level teaspoons glucose or ordinary sugar
- 1 level teaspoon salt

Mix all ingredients together until dissolved. For children younger than one year give 50 to 100ml (about a quarter of a teacup) after every loose stool. For children older than two years give 100 to 200ml or more after each loose stool or at least every two hours. If she vomits up the electrolyte solution wait 10 minutes then try again. If she refuses it you can flavour the solution by adding a little orange squash (but not fresh orange juice).

Some mothers believe in offering flat cola drinks to children with diarrhoea. Although this is better than nothing because it contains sugar and water, but it does not contain salt and should not be used. It also contains caffeine which removes fluid from the body. Weak tea and sugar may also help a little but it is far from ideal and should not be considered as medicinal in any way. Rooibos tea, juice, and very sweet liquids can aggravate the problem and should not be given to a child with diarrhoea.

DEHYDRATION. The important thing is to prevent the child from becoming dehydrated. Children become dehydrated more quickly than adults because they have comparatively greater fluid needs and their body surface area is proportionately larger than that of an adult. It is extremely important for all children with severe diarrhoea to be seen by a doctor but, if this is not immediately possible, you must see that the child receives the electrolyte solution. If there is vomiting as well, hospitalisation may be necessary so that fluids can be replaced intravenously.

DIARRHOEA IN BREASTFED BABIES. It is very unusual for a baby on breast milk alone to develop serious diarrhoea. Breastfeed more frequently, give an electrolyte solution and treat as described on above. Certain drugs, including some antibiotics, can cause diarrhoea, and foodstuffs such as spinach, if it is not freshly cooked, or orange juice, can also cause loose stools. If the mother of a breastfed baby has taken a laxative it may also affect her baby's stools. But these causes are unlikely to result in severe, prolonged diarrhoea, and usually there will not be a foul smell.

FROTHY, FOUL STOOLS. Congenital or primary lactose intolerance is a very rare disease in which the baby is born without lactase enzyme needed to digest milk sugars. It results in loose, frothy, foul-smelling stools during the first weeks of life and the baby does not gain weight. Special formulas that do not contain lactose (a milk sugar) are available and the baby will be taken off the breast or cow's milk formula and given soya bean milk or a special cow's milk formula which has the lactose replaced. The inability to digest sucrose (sugar) is a rare condition with similar symptoms.

Secondary lactose intolerance is the more common form of lactose intolerance and occurs after an infection in which the baby's ability to digest lactose is inhibited due to damage to the gut lining (*see p. 126*). Although this condition is temporary the child will also have to be taken off the breast or bottle and given a lactose-free formula of soya milk or specially formulated cow's lactose free milk formula for a short period. This does not mean that you will have to stop milk feeds permanently because your baby will gradually be allowed back on the breast or usual bottle feeds. You will have to keep expressing in the meantime if you wish to continue breastfeeding. In mild cases your baby could be back on the usual bottle or breastfeeds in 24 hours. But in severe cases it could take up to a month before the lactase level (the enzyme that digests lactose) returns to normal, and then it could be more than three months before a normal diet can be introduced. Fortunately, medication that replaces the lactase enzyme is now available.

Gluten enteropathy (intolerance) (coeliac disease) also produces frequent, foul, bubbly stools, or even constipation (*see p. 196*) once wheat is introduced into the diet.

UNUSUAL STOOLS. There are a number of conditions that produce stools that may be putty coloured, or clearly different from the norm. Occasional variations in stools should not be a cause for concern, but if you are concerned consult your doctor.

Cystic fibrosis and certain malabsorption conditions also result in excessive, bulky stools, often without a foul smell (*see p. 386*).

A baby who is having phototherapy for jaundice usually has dark, loose, greenish stools but they return to normal when the baby is removed from the lights.

VARIOUS TYPES OF MILKS USED AS BABY FORMULAS

TYPE OF MILK	AGE	HOW TO MAKE UP	ADDITIONS	FREQUENCY OF FEEDS	AMOUNT	GENERAL REMARKS	WEIGHT GAIN
No 1 'Starter' whey predominant cow's milk formula	For the healthy full term baby (over 2,5kg) from birth until 4 months or longer, or when the baby is no longer satisfied.	Follow instructions on label. Level the scoop and add to cooled, previously boiled water. Never pack scoop or add extra water or powder. Do not use the scoop from other feeds.	Has full range of vitamins and minerals added. Some also have added elements claimed to promote immunity and gut health. Check label. Your doctor may nevertheless recommend a vitamin or iron supplement until one year. Ask your dentist about adding fluoride if you live in a low fluoride area.	Not less than 6 feeds in 24 hours in first 4 weeks. Five feeds in 24 hours or as demanded after that. No more than 1000ml in 24 hours. From six months 3 – 4 milk feeds in 24 hours.	150ml per kilo body weight to a maximum of 1000ml in 24 hours. E.g. A baby weighing 4kg would need 150ml × 4 = 600ml in 24 hours.	Whey to casein ratio 60:40, or 70:30. Whey protein is more easily digested than casein protein.	Should regain birth weight in first two weeks. Thereafter between 20-25g per day in first four months. Consult your clinic and Road to Health Card/ Growth Chart.
No 1 'Starter' Casein predominant cow's milk formulas.	For the larger full-term baby (over 2,5kg) from birth and, the 'hungry' baby to four months or until the child stops using formula milk.	As above	As above	As above	As above	Casein to whey protein ratio usually 80:20. Casein is digested more slowly so the baby feels satisfied for longer.	As above
No 2. 'Follow-up' cow's milk formulas.	From 6-12 months or when solids are introduced around four to six months.	As above	As above	3 or 4 feeds in 24 hours or as demanded to no more than 1 000ml in 24 hours.	As above	Contains more protein, calcium, phosphorus etc to complement solids. Add solids as advised by doctor or clinic.	Should double birth weight by six months. Consult clinic and Road to Health Card/Growth Chart. Should gain approximately 250g per month between 5 months and a year.

TYPE OF MILK	AGE	HOW TO MAKE UP	ADDITIONS	FREQUENCY OF FEEDS	AMOUNT	GENERAL REMARKS	WEIGHT GAIN
No 3 cow's milk formulas. 'Growing up' milks.	From 12-36 months.	As above	Follow instructions on label for making up formula.	Two feeds in 24 hours. Too much milk can spoil the appetite for solids.	As advised by your doctor or clinic.	Use if suggested by doctor or clinic.	Follow Road to Health Card/Growth Chart.
Acidified formulas. (Casein predominant acidified formula).	Full-term babies from birth onwards. No need to change if child is content.	As above	As above	As above	As above	Pre-acidified so may be more digestible. Said to prevent the growth of bacteria, thus especially useful in crèche situations, or where hygienic conditions are difficult.	Should regain birth weight in first two weeks. Thereafter between 20-25g per day in first four months. Should gain approximately 250g per month between 5 months and a year.
Hypoallergenic partially hydrolysed cow's milk protein formula.	From birth onwards or as advised by doctor or clinic	Follow instructions on label. Never pack or heap scoop or add extra water or powder. Do not use scoop from another product.	As above	Follow clinic or doctor's advice	150ml per kilo body weight, or as advised by doctor or clinic.	Used to prevent and treat cow's milk or soya allergy. Make up bottles only as needed. Keep in fridge if not used immediately. Should be used only on doctor's recommendation.	Consult clinic or doctor. Check Road to Health Card/Growth Chart.
Powdered unmodified full cream milks.	From 8 months if advised.	Check label. Usually 1 part powder to 3 parts previously boiled cooled water.	Has vitamins A, D and iron added. Your doctor may prescribe additional vitamins and minerals.	Three times a day after solids.	No more than 500-600ml total in 24 hours after 6 months.	Similar to, but preferable to fresh cow's milk because of some added vitamins and minerals.	Should gain 250g per month between five months and a year.

TYPE OF MILK	AGE	HOW TO MAKE UP	ADDITIONS	FREQUENCY OF FEEDS	AMOUNT	GENERAL REMARKS	WEIGHT GAIN
Pasteurised fresh cow's milk (dairy milk). Never use unpasteurised milk. Spoon cream off farm milk (Jersey).	Under six months. Not really recommended under a year, but if used must be modified.	1 part milk to 2 parts boiled water plus 1 level teaspoon sugar to every 100ml made up feed to a maximum of 6 teaspoons. Bring to boil for a few seconds to make protein more digestible. Cool rapidly so that skin does not form (stand in bowl of ice water). Strain through fine sieve into sterilised bottles.	Needs addition of vitamins, iron and trace elements. Fluoride if you live in low fluoride area. Ask doctor or clinic for vitamin and iron supplement as this is essential.	Not less than 5 times in 24 hours or more frequently as demanded to a maximum of 1 000ml in 24 hours	As above	The milk most likely to cause an allergic reaction. Very different composition to breast milk. Better if introduced after six months. If allergies run in the family, better after a year. World Health Organization recommends use from age of one year only, due to vitamin and mineral deficiencies. Organic pasteurised is best.	Between 20-25g per day in first four months; 250g per month between 5 months and a year.
Pasteurised fresh cow's milk (dairy milk). Never use unpasteurised milk. Spoon cream off farm milk (Jersey).	Over six months	Do not dilute or add sugar. Bring to boil and strain as above.	As above	3-5 feeds as demanded to a maximum of 500ml in 24 hours	500-600ml in 24 hours. More than a litre can cause gastric irritation and bleeding.	Bottle can be given straight from the fridge if previously boiled and strained. Organic pasteurised milk is best.	250g per month between 5 months and a year.
Pasteurised fresh cow's milk (dairy milk). Never use unpasteurised milk.	Between 1-5 years.	Not necessary to boil after first year.	Vitamin and mineral additions can be discontinued if child is on a good mixed diet. Continue if poor eater. Fluoride supplementation to continue if living in low fluoride area.	As desired	Not more than 400-500ml in 24 hours or appetite will be spoiled.	Should be given after meals or not less than 1½ hours before meals so that appetite is not spoiled. Give skim milk or 2% milk only after age two and only if doctor recommends. Children need the essential fatty acids found in full cream milk.	Consult clinic.

TYPE OF MILK	AGE	HOW TO MAKE UP	ADDITIONS	FREQUENCY OF FEEDS	AMOUNT	GENERAL REMARKS	WEIGHT GAIN
Full cream long-life heat sterilised bottled or packaged milk.	Under six months. Not generally recommended but if used must be modified as per fresh cow's milk.	Same as for fresh cow's milk.	Supplement with multi-vitamins and iron, as it is deficient in many essentials. Ask your doctor. Ask your dentist regarding flouride.	Same as for fresh cow's milk to a maximum of 1 000ml in 24 hours.	150ml per kilo body weight.	Same as fresh cow's milk. Slightly less allergenic and more digestible than fresh cow's milk due to heat sterilisation process. Opened bottles or cartons should be stored in fridge. Does not need to be boiled before mixing with water (boil water). Do not use milks that contain preservatives. Check labels.	Consult clinic.
Full cream long life heat sterilised bottled or packaged milk.	Over six months	Same as fresh cow's milk.	Same as for fresh cow's milk.	Same as for fresh cow's milk.	Same as for fresh cow's milk.	Same as above but no water added.	250g per month between 5 months and a year
Soya milks sold as baby formulas.	From birth onwards.	Follow instructions on label.	Has full range of vitamins and minerals added. Add fluoride if you live in a low fluoride area. Ask your dentist. Most have added vitamins and minerals, but your doctor may recommend the addition of vitamins and iron.	Same as for 'starter' formulas before 6 months. After 6 months 3-4 feeds in 24 hours after solids.	150ml per kilo body weight to a maximum of 1 000ml in 24 hours before 6 months. After six months 500ml in 24 hours.	Contains no lactose or cow's milk protein. Suitable where milk allergy or lactose intolerance is proven. Also avoidance of allergic reaction in breastfed baby. Should not be used in preference to cow's milk formula if no medical reason. Some babies are allergic to it as well.	Should regain birth weight in first two weeks thereafter between 20-25g per day in first four months. Consult clinic and Road to Health Card/Growth Chart.
Powdered goat's milk. Do not use fresh unpasteurised goat's milk.	As recommended by your doctor.	Follow instructions on label. Ask pharmacist for medical measuring spoon if not supplied.	Needs full range of vitamins and minerals including iron, to be added. Consult your doctor.	Consult your medical advisor.	150ml per kilo body weight to a maximum of 1000ml in 24 hours. After six months give a maximum of 500ml.	Consult clinic or doctor before using. May be useful in some cases of sensitivity, but better options available if a true allergy. Has more essential fatty acids than cow's milk.	Consult clinic or doctor.

GO TO www.baby-childcare.com TO WATCH THE FOLLOWING VIDEOS THAT ARE APPLICABLE TO CHAPTER 6

PROF CLAUDIA GRAY
Reflux and vomitting

Rashes

Stools

Milk and weaning

EMMA NUMANOGLU
Bottle feeding

CHAPTER 7

Introducing Solids

AN EXCITING MILESTONE. One of the major differences between humans and other species is our ability to eat and enjoy a wide variety of foods. Starting your baby on solid foods is the beginning of this lifelong relationship with food that carries with it so many implications for future emotional and physical well being. Even your baby's brain development and IQ is partly due to the food she eats. All this can be rather intimidating. Fortunately, by following sensible, practical guidelines and adapting them to your particular baby's needs you will not go far wrong. Your first decision will be whether your baby is ready for her first taste of solids.

Milk is the most important element in a baby's diet for the first to four to six months, after this it becomes less important as a variety of solids take its place. The purpose of solids is to provide nutrients not available from milk, and to increase the quantity and type of nourishment that is needed for the rapid growth that takes place in the first year. (Babies treble their birth weight in the first year, and their small stomach capacity cannot hold the amount of milk that would be needed to fuel this growth.)

THE DEVELOPMENT OF TASTE PREFERENCES. The development of a taste for certain foods is an important concern for many parents who feel that certain tastes – such as that for sweet things – should be discouraged from the beginning. A baby's sense of taste develops over time but infants are naturally programmed to prefer certain tastes and to reject, or to be indifferent to others.

A preference for sweet tastes is the one response evident from before birth and continues into the second year. In others words, it is innate. Bitter and sour tasting substances are rejected, while there is indifference to salty tastes which gradually changes to liking. Savoury flavours as defined by the taste of 'umami' or monosodium glutamate (a naturally occurring substance in many foods) is another natural preference in certain contexts. All this makes sense when you consider that sour and bitter tastes are often associated with food that has gone off; and that breastmilk, the natural food for babies is sweet. Early exposure to sweet tastes does not however, seem to influence the later encouragement of a 'sweet tooth' which is a more complex phenomenon.

Breastmilk is also flavoured by foods in the mother's diet, so pungent odours and tastes like garlic or curry come through and predispose babies to the flavours of their cultural heritage. This is evidenced by the fact that breastfed babies take to new foods easier than babies who have been exposed to the unvarying flavour of formula. As disagreeable as garlic flavoured milk seems, babies take it readily and suck for longer when the mother has consumed it!

THE ROLE OF SMELL. The smell of food influences our experience of its taste, and defines the flavour we perceive. We all know how tasteless food seems when we have a cold and cannot smell it. Newborns can identify and prefer the smell of their own mother's milk to that of other mothers. And even bottle fed babies gravitate towards breastmilk odours.

TIMING IS IMPORTANT. Babies are also receptive to new tastes and textures at a particular stage – if this is missed – they become very reluctant to change their routine. This 'window of opportunity' when they open their mouths like hungry little birds is generally between four and six months. Later than this and the curiosity to try new tastes seems to dissipate and they cling to the ease of the bottle or breast.

FEEDING STAGES IN THE FIRST YEAR

OVERVIEW. A cereal that is unlikely to cause an allergic reaction such as maize or rice is introduced first. Followed by very smoothly pureed, single variety fruits and vegetables, allowing three days between them to see whether there is any adverse reaction. They are then mixed as desired, and meat in various forms is added, the amount increased and the texture made less smooth.

From six months chewing is encouraged by making food coarser with visible pieces in a smooth base and the range is widened to include wheat, oats and other cereals.

Variety is encouraged and small amounts of liquid are taken from a cup. Milk feeds are given after solids now as it is assuming less importance in the diet.

By nine months a broad range of foods is offered while still avoiding preservatives, monosodium glutamate (MSG), colourants and processed foods. Self-feeding in the form of suitable hand held foods is encouraged and although the bottle or breast is still needed, drinking from a cup is more proficient.

By the age of 12 months modified family food should be enjoyed but this does not include highly spiced, processed, preservative, MSG or colourant containing foods. Foods should still be soft and easily digestible with bigger pieces. Finger foods are enjoyed. Three meals with two small snacks in between are needed. She still wants her milk feeds as much for the comfort of sucking as for nourishment, but she is growing up fast. In these 12 months your baby has trebled her birth weight and developed from a helpless, supine creature into an animated doll. Enjoy her!

HOMEMADE OR COMMERCIAL BABY FOODS? Having decided that your baby is ready for solids and knowing the various stages you need to take her through, you will have to decide whether you are going to cook your baby's food yourself or use ready made foods. Some mothers have the time, inclination and knowledge to make all their baby's food themselves, but this is not a realistic option for many parents today. Most mothers are happy to combine some home cooking with commercially prepared baby foods, while others use only bought baby food. (See the section on making your own baby food, and commercial food *p. 199.* If there are allergies in the family see the section on food allergy *p. 194.*)

GENERAL RULES FOR STARTING AND FEEDING SOLIDS

IN THE BEGINNING. Choose a period when your baby is well. If she has a cold or has had a recent vaccination she will not be ready for a new experience. The same applies if she is very tired or hungry.

- You can start with solids at the 10am or 2pm feed as this is usually a less harassed time, but it does not have to be at either of these times.
- In the first months offer milk before solids, after this, solids before milk.

- If your baby is hungry offer a little breastmilk or formula milk before you offer solids or she will not be receptive. Get any winds up and seat your baby on your lap or in a suitable baby chair.
- The first food you offer your baby should preferably be, an iron and vitamin enriched rice or maize cereal. Iron is critical for neurodevelopment (brain development) and needs are higher between 6-12 months than during any other period of life. Wheat, which is high in gluten can cause an allergic reaction so it better not to use it as a first cereal. Wheat and mixed cereals can be given at around six months if your baby does not have allergic tendencies, and takes other foods well.
- Fill a teaspoon with cereal and hold it above her eye level, this should make her drop her mouth open. Put a little taste on her tongue and let her get used to it. Next place a teaspoonful of cereal well into her mouth and see her look of puzzled amazement! Most of it will probably be pushed out again because she's used to the action of pushing the tongue forward when sucking. She'll soon learn that a different action is needed to swallow solids.
- When introducing solids offer a small amount – one or two teaspoonfuls and build up gradually. If your baby has not had a full milk feed, give the rest of the milk feed after the solids. When a baby has had enough she shuts her mouth firmly and turns her head away. Because your baby is unlikely to finish the food you offer in one feed, rather decant small amounts at a time into a bowl and discard any that is left over. Saliva will make it watery and unsuitable for later use.
- It doesn't matter whether you start with fruits or vegetables. Some babies prefer vegetables others like fruit. Both have similar nutrients, although they do contribute various vitamins and minerals. See the section on taste *p. 183* for natural preferences and why bitter vegetables take time to accept.
- Once your baby has settled on cereal you can offer single variety fruits and vegetables such as butternut, carrots, peaches, guavas, pears and apples so that she can experience a variety of tastes. Introduce each new variety after three or four days so that you can see how your baby reacts. Once she has tried a food you can start adding another variety until she has mixed meals.

Do not despair if your baby does not take to solids immediately. Some babies take to them with gusto; others need to be given a little time to adjust. What is important is that you continue to offer a variety of solids without pressuring your baby.

AT FOUR TO SIX MONTHS your baby should be having cereal, mixed pureed vegetables and fruit, pureed meat and vegetables. Vitamin C rich fruit juice and deserts are optional and can be given occasionally.

LEARNING TO CHEW FROM SIX MONTHS. Your baby reaches another developmental stage at around six months. Coping with coarser textures and learning to chew. Just as your baby goes through the various developmental stages of crawling, standing, walking… so should a child be encouraged to go through the stages from sucking to chewing increasingly coarser food until a mature eating pattern is acquired.

Even if your baby has no teeth you should gradually start offering rougher food or she will not get used to chewing. If you make your baby's food yourself, puree until there are obvious, small pieces, or simply mash with a fork. Use the large jars of commercial baby food. A child who refuses rougher textures by nine months should have a developmental assessment as this can sometimes indicate a problem.

By the time your baby is nine-months-old she should be having three small bowlfuls of solids a day, as well as around 600ml milk. She can have suitable snacks between meals.

From nine months your baby should cope well with lumps and can have family food if it does not contain preservatives and artificial additives. Commercially prepared baby foods are suitable if they do not contain preservative, colourants or artificial additives. It is possible to get products made from organic ingredients, as well as fresh food.

A BALANCED DIET. A balance of foodstuffs is needed for proper growth and the maintenance of health. This is especially important in infancy and childhood when growth is at its most rapid. The essential components of a balanced diet are:

PROTEIN (BODY BUILDING FOODS)

Meat, chicken, fish, dried beans and peas, soya beans, liver, cheese, milk, egg (avoid egg white before the age of a year). Samp and beans eaten together can also serve as a protein food.

CARBOHYDRATES (STARCHES) AND FATS (ENERGY GIVING FOODS). Cereals, mielie-meel, bread, rice, pasta, couscous, bulgur wheat, potatoes, samp, mealie rice, margarine, butter, oil, sugar.

VITAMINS AND MINERALS (PROTECTIVE FOODS). A wide variety of fruits and vegetables are needed to provide the various vitamins and minerals not found in the other food groups, as well as to add fibre and bulk to the diet.

Servings from all the food groups are needed daily from the time solids are introduced to provide a balanced diet. The highest proportion should be carbohydrates (starches), followed by protein, and protective foods, plus a small amount of fats. Milk is also required in varying amounts.

GENERAL INFORMATION. You need patience and a sense of humour when feeding a baby. You shouldn't expect to shovel it down in seconds. Sometimes a little bit of bright chatter or distraction with a picture book will keep her occupied so that she does not play with her food. Don't make this routine, however, or you will have to do a song and dance act every time you want your toddler to eat!

Give solids after a bottle or breast feed in the first four to six months when milk is still the staple food. After six months it is better to give the bottle after solids as it could spoil her appetite if she has a lot of milk first. Some babies need to suck before they sleep, so giving her solids first and then the bottle or breast gives her longer sucking comfort and helps her relax into sleep.

- Do not add more than a pinch of salt to your baby's food, if at all. Too much can place a strain on the still immature kidneys. A too high concentration of protein in the first months can also place a strain on the kidneys.
- Do not add a lot of butter or margarine to your baby's meals because the liver cannot cope with too much fat in the first year.
- Fruit juice can cause tooth decay. Give juice from a cup or straw when the teeth come through.
- Keep your baby's utensils clean but it is not necessary to sterilise them.
- Bottles need to be sterilised until the baby stops using them because of the many crevices in the bottle area in which germs can grow and because milk is the ideal medium for bacteria to multiply.
- When cooking baby food use as little water as possible so that you do not have to pour off nutrients unnecessarily.
- Beans, peas, cabbage and cauliflower are inclined to give babies wind so introduce with care.
- Spinach can become toxic to a small baby if left for more than 24 hours after cooking so serve the day you cook it.
- Some babies gag on potato, especially if it is mashed, and are very wary of jelly! Every new taste is a mind-blowing experience when you have only known milk before.
- Let water or milk cool before adding it to cereal or the mixture will form lumps.
- Fried foods should not be given in the first six months and after that only occasionally if at all in the first year. Fried fast foods are not suitable.
- Pork, beef and chicken should be well cooked.
- Egg white should be introduced with care, after the age of ten months, because the high concentration of protein can result in a severe allergic reaction. If she shows signs of allergy to other foods leave until later.
- Egg yolk is rich in iron, vitamin A, thiamine and phosphorous and is a useful addition to the diet from around five months. It should be hard cooked and sieved over her food. It can also be added to custard, vegetables or any other dish. Unless your baby

has been put on a low cholesterol diet because of hyper-cholesterolemia in the family she can have an egg yolk a day, although you will probably not want to give this much in the first year. (*See eggs p. 202.*)

- Solids should not be added to your baby's bottle unless a doctor has ordered it, as it can adversely change the fluid to solids ratio.
- If you are breastfeeding, use expressed breastmilk or formula milk to make up cereal.
- Vitamin C enriched fruit juice or puréed fruit mixed with cereal will make the iron in the cereal 3-4 times more bio-available (easily absorbed.)
- Give your baby a balanced diet but you don't have to think of something different every day. When she gets tired of a food she will let you know. In other words provide variety, but don't think she needs soufflés and sabayon – if she hates a particular meat or vegetable don't give it. There is always a substitute. Your aim is to bring her into the family circle gradually so that she will be eating only slightly modified family food during the second year.
- It is also true that it can take many an offering for babies to take to a new food and acquire a taste for it. So persevere but don't pressure. Gradually the range of foods she has will widen, which is what is needed.
- It is normal for bits of undigested vegetables to be passed in the baby's stools.
- If there are food allergies in the family, consult a paediatric specialist for advice when your baby is four months.

FEELINGS ABOUT FOOD

Feeding is an area of child care that causes many mothers great concern. They wonder what to give their child to promote healthy development and how to encourage good eating patterns – but most often their biggest worry is that their child is not eating enough.

Food and what it conveys has great significance in most cultures. In the West it is very often seen as a means of expressing love. And love is the one thing a mother wants to show her baby. It is also true that preparing food with thought and care is a loving thing to do and when it is rejected, spat out and pushed away by your baby it takes a lot of self-control not to lash out or feel personally affronted.

So let us get things into perspective because battles over food are a great waste of energy and emotion and if you inform yourself properly you will most likely find that you are worrying needlessly and creating a problem where none exists.

Remember that all children are individuals and need to be acknowledged as such. Your placid baby who took her bottle without trouble at three months, will be developing her own personality with likes and dislikes at eight months. Because your baby rejects the food you give her it does not mean she is rejecting you. She may no longer enjoy foods she relished before, so try a change of menu and keep your sense of proportion and humour!

On the other hand giving your baby something to eat every time she grizzles can lead to a life-long dependency on food as a panacea. Propping a biscuit in your baby's hand when she is niggly may keep her quiet, but it does not prove she was hungry. After the first few months she is more likely to be bored and frustrated than starving. In later life she could continue reaching for food every time she is unhappy, frustrated or under stress. Rather look for the real need and try and fill that.

HOW DO PARENTS PROMOTE HEALTHY, AGE-APPROPRIATE FEEDING?

The development of healthy eating behaviour among infants and toddlers depends on both the provision of age-appropriate food and on responsive feeding practices by parents. Nutritional recommendations that focus only on food, and not on the behavioural aspects of feeding ignore the major role which both the child and parent play in the feeding process.

WHAT IS RESPONSIVE FEEDING?

Responsive feeding simply means that there is a level of reciprocity between child and parent during feeding. During their first year, both infants and parents begin to identify and interpret both verbal and nonverbal signals from each another. The ability of a parent to recognise and respond to verbal and non-verbal feeding cues from their child forms the basis of responsive feeding practices.

Responsive feeding can be described in stages. First, parents provide a structured and pleasant mealtime environment for their child. Second, the child is encouraged to communicate feeding cues of hunger or satiety. Third, parents respond in an appropriate manner to these cues, and finally, children learn to expect consistent responses from their parents.

Responsive feeding practices have shown several benefits, including: promoting children's interest in feeding, increasing their attention to their own cues of hunger and satiety, allowing them to effectively communicate their needs to their parents, and to progress successfully towards independent feeding.

In short, responsive feeding is having the ability to recognise a child's verbal and non-verbal cues and to respond to them in an appropriate way. A child's demands are not always complied to, but are acknowledged in a supportive and firm environment.

WHAT IS NON-RESPONSIVE FEEDING?

Non-responsive feeding is characterised by a lack of reciprocity between parent and child, where a child's cues are overridden, overindulged, or ignored. This can take the form of:

CONTROLLING OR DOMINANT FEEDING

This is when parental concern over their child's intake leads to their need to exert control over the pace of meals, volumes eaten, and what is eaten. This creates a pressured environment for children, in which mealtimes become about performance. As a result, mealtimes become stressful for both parents and children, children's internal hunger and satiety cues are overridden, and emerging feeding independence is hampered.

INDULGENT FEEDING

This is characterized by parental responses that indulge a child's every request, even when inappropriate. For example, parents who respond to their child's cries by offering treat foods teach their children that crying in an effective means of eliciting their favoured food. This feeding style lacks firm and supportive parental boundaries.

UNINVOLVED FEEDING

This feeding style is characterised by a parent's lack of attention to their child. Children as result resort to inappropriate behaviour to attract their parents' attention such as food refusal, or throwing food.

WHAT ARE SOME STRATEGIES WHICH PROMOTE RESPONSIVE FEEDING?

ESTABLISH A ROUTINE. Toddlers and young children respond well to a feeding routine which includes three meals and 2 small snacks per day. Parents can aim to offer meals and snacks at similar times, in similar settings. In this way, mealtimes are predictable, and are given when children are neither too tired nor too hungry.

PROVIDE COMFORTABLE SEATING. Parents can ensure that their child is comfortably seated in an age-appropriate chair, preferably with a tray or table in front of them. In this way, children are able to visualise and engage with the food on offer.

REMOVE DISTRACTIONS. Distractions must be minimised as much as possible. This includes TV's being turned off, and toys being put away. In this way children can learn to communicate to their parents during their mealtimes, take note of what they are eating, and to be more mindful of when they have had enough.

PERSISTENTLY OFFER A VARIETY OF AGE-APPROPRIATE FOODS

Over time, it is important to progress infants and toddlers onto foods of different texture and tastes. Ongoing, persistent exposure to a variety of healthy, age-appropriate foods will encourage acceptance of these foods over the long term. However, these foods cannot be forced on to a child. They must simply be offered on an ongoing basis.

ENCOURAGE MESS AND SELF-FEEDING

Infants and children need to be provided with the opportunity to engage with their food. In this way, mealtimes become more of a proactive activity rather than a passive one. Touching, making a mess, and attempting to self-feed increases interest in food and makes mealtimes seem more appealing.

SHARE FAMILY MEALS

Shared family meals are an essential part of developing healthy eating behaviours among children. Infants and toddlers learn by watching parents and siblings, and they need to be offered the opportunity to do so. Shared family meals exposes little people to a relaxed, social mealtime environment in which their parents model the behaviour that they are gradually learning. Wherever possible, parents can plan as many meals a week where the whole family eat together.

Parents need to respond promptly to their child's cues during mealtimes. If children turn their head away, close their lips, become unhappy or appear disinterested, they have had enough. Very little benefit is gained by trying to persist beyond this point, and the meal should be stopped. Children develop a sense of trust in their parents and in the mealtime environment if their satiety cues are responded to without more food being forced upon them.

FOOD ALLERGY

An area of feeding that you may be concerned about is allergies. Although up to 20% of adults believe they suffer from food allergy, the true incidence is much lower. This is because similar conditions such as toxic reactions to foods, food phobia and food intolerance are often confused with true allergy.

It appears that the child's immune system samples the food that is taken and adapts its immune response in order to be able to tolerate the food.

The tendency towards allergy is inherited. If both sides of the family have allergies then your child has a very high chance of being allergic as well. Babies can be sensitised while still in the womb through food the mother eats, and allergens (allergy causing substances) are transferred through breastmilk.

MOST COMMON INFANT ALLERGENS. Breast fed babies are seven times less likely to develop allergies and they are not sensitive to their mother's milk except in the rare instances of lactose intolerance or galactosaemia – although allergens may pass into the mother's milk. Allergy to cow's milk is very common and is possible even if the formula has been modified, evaporated or humanised. It is far more likely if ordinary pasteurised diary milk is used.

If you have a family history of allergies delay the introduction of solids until at least the fourth month, or later and avoid the common allergens listed above. Start with a rice or maize cereal as these are unlikely to cause problems. Allow three days between the introduction of each new food so that you can see how each is tolerated.

SYMPTOMS OF FOOD ALLERGY IN INFANTS. A baby who is allergic to milk may have all or some of these symptoms in the first weeks of life. These include: restlessness; persistent watery discharge from the nose; rough dry patches of skin on various parts of the body – most commonly the face, arms and legs. There may be crying as with colic, but there is usually diarrhoea as well and the restlessness is not confined to a particular time of day. The baby does not gain weight adequately and may have wheezy breathing. Earache caused by the excess secretions in the nasal area may cause complications, and occasionally gastric bleeding may occur and blood is seen in the stools. (*See allergies p.417.*)

All these symptoms can occur in infectious diseases or deficiencies and if there is not a rapid improvement after the removal of the allergy-forming substance, such as cow's milk, other causes for the symptoms should be sought.

Occasionally a breast fed baby may show mild allergic reactions because of allergens in the mother's diet. The most likely causes are unboiled cow's milk (boiling makes the protein in cow's milk easier to digest), chocolate, orange juice, wheat and eggs. Elimination of these or other allergens from the mother's diet should result in a quick improvement if the problem is in fact caused by allergy.

TREATMENT OF COW'S MILK ALLERGY. All forms of cow's milk are eliminated from the child's diet and substituted with either a hypoallergenic milk or a casein hydrolysate formula or a hydrolysed whey formula. Allergy to soya milk and to goat's milk is not uncommon, so preference is likely to be given to a safer alternative although they are more expensive. Once a child is sensitised to cow's milk a semi-elemental whey hydrolysate feed may be necessary before going on to the hypo-allergenic milk (*see pp. 159 and 422*).

If the problem is sensitivity to milk sugar (lactose) then a lactose free formula (possibly soya) will be prescribed. Cow's milk allergy and lactose intolerance are not very common (under 10% of babies) so beware of jumping to that conclusion when the problem may have another cause. When cereals are introduced they should not be the ready cooked kind to which only water is added, because they contain powdered milk. Check all labels for milk when buying baby foods. Terms such as whey, lactose, casein, caseinate, lactalbumin and lactoglobulin indicate the presences of cow' milk protein. Certain creams used for nappy rash contain milk derivatives such as lactic protein and in infants allergic to cow's milk these can make the nappy rash worse.

OTHER FOODS WHICH MAY CAUSE AN ADVERSE REACTION

FRUIT JUICE. Orange juice can cause a rash around the anus and mouth, eczema and diarrhoea. Other very acidic juices like pineapple, may also cause similar reactions.

GLUTEN ENTEROPATHY OR INTOLERANCE (COELIAC DISEASE IGA AND IGG MEDIATED). Gluten allergy or coeliac disease is a more lasting and serious problem, and is due to an intolerance to gliadin (the 'sticky' binding agent in wheat, rye, barley and oats). The child will be thin and small with a big tummy and small buttocks. Large, bubbly, foul smelling stools are produced. These children will have to be changed to a gluten-free diet permanently. Celiac disease was believed to be a rare condition but new methods of diagnosis have increased the number of those who are affected.

WHEAT ALLERGY (IGE MEDIATED). Introduce cereals containing wheat with care. Can cause stomach, skin and nasal symptoms and is a reaction to gluten, the protein in wheat, and often to oats, rye and barley. Be careful of products containing modified food starch, vegetable gum, starch and 'natural flavouring'.

NUTS. Allergy to nuts – peanuts in particular – is on the increase and it can be very serious. The general symptoms of allergy apply and an anaphylactic shock is possible. If diagnosed, strict avoidance is necessary and it is usually not outgrown. A method of desensitising for nut allergy is being tested and shows promise. Check labels as some cereals contain nuts without it being obvious. Allergy to sesame seeds is common in Middle Eastern countries such as Israel.

COLOURING AGENTS. Colouring added to some vitamin drops and other foodstuffs can occasionally cause an allergic reaction. Many medications and other products no longer contain colouring and preservatives so check labels. Tartrazine, a yellow colourant used in food is often blamed for allergic reactions. This is not nearly as common as is popularly made out and easily avoided by checking labels. Avoid MSG. European Union countries require a warning on food labels containing some artificial dyes that states: 'May have an adverse effect on activity and attention in children'. This is in response to studies published in medical journals including The *Lancet that* found a connection between some food colourants and ADHD in children. Check all labels and consult with your doctor.

PRESERVATIVES. Preservatives in cold drinks, fruit squash, fruit syrups and other foods can cause an allergic reaction. Sulphites (sulphur dioxide) stop food and other products including cosmetics, medicines, and wine from 'going off'.

One of the most troublesome reactions is asthma attacks which may be increased by up to 20% due to sulphur dioxide gas that is produced when sulphide containing foods interact with acid in the stomach. The gas is released up the airway causing irritation and constriction. Allergic rhinitis (hay fever like allergy) and a worsening of urticarial rash can also occur. Sulphite content has to be cited on product labels in the UK and many other countries so check labels for this and other preservatives such as sodium benzoate, sulphur dioxide, sorbic acid and potassium sorbate if you have concerns. Fresh fruit such as grapes is sometimes preserved with sulphur dioxide.

SUGAR. Allergy to sugar with resultant hyperactivity and attention deficient syndrome has become a popular concept but there is no real scientific evidence to support this, despite claims to the contrary. It is true that children who have a high sugar intake often have a poor diet and this in itself can contribute to making them 'out of control', and ratty. Refined sugar goes through chemical processing in order to render it white, and some children may be sensitive to these chemicals. (*See page.409.*)

EGG WHITE. Egg white can cause an allergic reaction because of its high protein content which the child may be unable to digest. Never give egg white to a child under six months and preferably not before the end of the first year. Symptoms may include swelling of the face and generalised urticaria. (*See p. 426.*) Never use egg white as a treatment for nappy rash. It can cause such a severe reaction that the baby may have to be hospitalised.

CHOCOLATE AND FISH. Chocolate, and occasionally fish, can cause allergic reactions with symptoms of urticaria, hay fever, diarrhoea or cramps. (*See p. 417 for other causes of allergy.*)

ALLERGIES AND BEHAVIOUR PROBLEMS. Allergies to colourants, preservatives and sugar have been blamed for behaviour problems in children. Elimination diets such as the 'Feingold' diet are sometimes recommended but there is no hard scientific evidence that their basis is sound. Giving these children the apparently offending substance in a gelatine coated capsule has not resulted in negative behaviour and there is evidence to suggest that children often respond to the extra attention that being on a special diet affords them, rather than the actual elimination of a particular food. Real illness after taking certain colourants, preservatives or foodstuffs does have a basis and must be investigated.

NOTE: Proper tests should be done by an allergy specialist before you put your child on a restrictive diet which should be described and monitored by a dietician.

WHEN IS ALLERGY OUTGROWN? By the age of three only 10% of children still have milk allergy, and 30% are still sensitive to eggs. Only 1% of children cannot tolerate fish by the age of six.

Comprehensive information on allergies is on *pages 417-428*.

FEEDING IN THE FIRST YEAR

HOMEMADE BABY FOODS. It is more economical to prepare your own baby foods if you are able to freeze what you do not use immediately. *See p. 199* for details on preparing your baby's meals. If you do not prepare all your baby's meals yourself it is sensible to have a supply of bought foods on hand as well.

BOUGHT BABY FOODS. Cereals, fruits, vegetables, meat and desserts are available commercially and are a convenient form of baby food. Baby foods are available dried, bottled, or fresh, thus they have a varying shelf life. The main difference between brands lies in the level of strict adherence to any form of additive and to farming methods. Freshly prepared foods are generally the most expensive and taste the closest to homemade. Organically produced and free-range products generally do not have any salt, sugar or modified starch added. Some use only organically grown (without the use of pesticides and chemical fertilisers) fruits and vegetables, and free range livestock. Foods are slow cooked. New regulations are being mooted in the USA in order to make labels on baby foods more transparent regarding their content.

Check labels if your child is allergic as all ingredients are listed.

POINTS TO REMEMBER. When buying bottled foods ensure that the seal on the lid is unbroken and the 'safety button' on the lid is down. There should be a 'pop' sound when the jar is opened. Do not feed your baby from the container unless you are sure she will finish the contents because saliva will quickly spoil any leftover food. Take out what you need and put it in a clean cup or empty baby food jar. Stand in hot water to make the food lukewarm. Remove from the hot water, stir and give to your baby. You can then store the jar of unused food in the fridge for as long as homemade food. (*See p. 208 for how to heat in a microwave.*)

READY COOKED COMMERCIAL CEREALS. Pre-cooked cereals are convenient to use and are often fortified with added vitamins and iron. They may need only the addition of water (the kind that have added milk powder) or milk. Always use cooled liquids to mix cereals because they are inclined to become lumpy. Rice or maize cereals are excellent first foods for your baby as they are unlikely to cause an allergic reaction.

JUICE, TEA AND OTHER BEVERAGES. Many babies enjoy juice and it contains vitamins and fruit sugars which provide a certain amount of energy. Juice can be given if your baby is thirsty between feeds but in excess it can spoil the appetite for food and cause tooth decay if allowed to wash over the teeth for prolonged periods. In extreme cases too much juice can cause loose stools and malnutrition. It is best to offer it diluted with cooled, previously boiled water – the younger the baby the more water – at least half and half.

Ceylon tea, coffee and cola drinks are not suitable for babies and should not be given. Rooibos tea is fine but an excess can also spoil the appetite and it can hinder the absorption of iron, to a small degree.

FRUIT. Fruit provides fibre, vitamins and energy through the natural sugar and starch content. It provides a moderate amount of energy. Most babies enjoy fruit purees and they can be used after the introduction of cereals and vegetables or as advised by your doctor or clinic. Always start with one kind at a time in case she has an adverse reaction and introduce new varieties after three days.

Strawberries, papayas (pawpaw), Kiwi fruit, guavas, tomatoes, cantaloupe (sweet melon), blueberries and mangos are fruits that contain generous amounts of vitamin C. They can be mashed fresh, or simmered in a little plain water until soft and the water is absorbed.

VEGETABLES. Vegetables are useful for acquainting your baby with new tastes, adding variety to her diet and providing fibre, minerals and vitamins. Plain vegetables are relatively low in energy value. Many babies reject vegetables at first, and there is no need to force the issue. Try again a little later or use a different method of preparation, for example, mixing them with fruit purees; adding a little grated cheese or making a thick vegetable soup, possibly with the addition of pasta.

MEAT AND FISH. Meat and fish provide protein, iron and B vitamins, all essential in the diet of the growing child. These forms of protein are relatively high in energy value and protein is an essential building block needed for growth.

Fish is a good source of protein and adds variety although some children are allergic to it. Liver is an excellent source of iron which is essential in the production of red blood cells and the prevention of iron deficiency anaemia, although many babies do not enjoy its strong taste at first. Chicken is likely to be a firm favourite from the beginning.

MAKING HOME COOKED BABY FOOD. Choose very fresh, young ingredients and peel or scrub vegetables and fruit very thinly as most nutrients are near the skin. Use as little water as possible so that you do not have to discard any nutrients. Simmer until soft.

Do not use more than a tiny pinch of salt if at all, and only use sugar when absolutely necessary, for instance, to modify acidic fruits.

When making up baby food it is easier and more economical to prepare it in bulk once you know what suits your baby. Cool after cooking and pack into individual plastic containers with lids or pour into an ice tray. When set, pop cubes out of the tray and freeze in a dated and labelled plastic bag. Take out as many as you need and thaw in the fridge or covered out of the fridge. Use as required. Do not refreeze after defrosting.

If you do not freeze the food after cooking you can keep it covered in the fridge for two or three days. Take out what you need and heat it up in a pot or, if you think she will only take very little, put it in a cup or clean glass jar and immerse in hot water, (remove from water before feeding to prevent accidents) or microwave very briefly. Be sure to stir all food, especially microwaved food and test on the inside of your wrist, before use.

FRUIT PURÉES. Cut a peeled apple, pear or peach into pieces, removing the stone or core, and place in a pot with very little water – just enough to prevent the fruit from burning.

If you have a heavy-bottomed saucepan with a lid, bring the mixture to the boil and switch off the heat but leave the pot on the plate; or simmer for about five minutes or until soft. Mash with a fork until smooth without discarding the cooking liquid unless there is too much; or press through a plastic sieve so that the purée does not become discoloured from the acid in the fruit reacting on a metal sieve. You can also blend the food in a liquidiser or food processor, or baby food grinder. Serve cool or slightly warm.

Guavas can be stewed in the same way and put through a plastic sieve. Unless they are very ripe bananas may be slightly indigestible to babies before the age of six months but later on they are a good source of nutrients, especially potassium which is depleted after a bout of diarrhoea. Choose ripe bananas with black spots on the skin and mash very well, adding a little previously boiled water or milk if desired. Later on, ripe bananas fried in a little butter are naturally sweet and a favourite with most children. Papino or pawpaw is served mashed or sieved through a plastic sieve. Do not give very acidic fruits such as pineapple to a baby as they can cause a rash around the anus.

Pureed fruits can be mixed with cereal for variety or you can add vegetables to a fruit base if she will not take them plain. Dried fruit such as prunes, apple rings, pears and apricots, which are a good source of iron, can be stewed and puréed in a blender, or sieved. Use organically grown products if possible as they will not have been dipped in preservatives. Soak overnight in water and simmer in the soaking water until soft. If your baby is inclined to be constipated, you can add a little brown sugar to the fruit while it is stewing. Do not make this routine. Soft stewed prunes are helpful for relieving hard stools without the addition of sugar.

VEGETABLES. Carrots, pumpkin, green beans, squash, butternut, parsnips, beetroot, sweet potato, turnips and potatoes can be prepared in the same way as fruit by boiling for five to eight minutes then sieving or liquidising. Brussels sprouts, broccoli, and other slightly bitter vegetables may need to be offered many times before your baby gets to like them. Gem squash is often given as a first vegetable – it has little food value however.

An excellent way of cooking vegetables is in a small bamboo steamer available from Oriental suppliers. Simply place the steamer in a pan on the hot stove with water half way up the sides. Put sliced vegetables or fruit in the steamer and cover with the lid. In a few minutes the vegetables will be soft and juicy and ready to serve.

A lot of babies do not like the taste of vegetables in the beginning and there is no reason to force your baby to have them. Remember, milk is the main food during the first six months and for both your sakes you should not turn feeding time into a battle.

Try adding the tip of a teaspoon of meat or yeast and vegetable extract to make vegetables more palatable. Do not add butter to vegetables in the first six months and thereafter use sparingly. Milk can be mixed with vegetables or combined with fruit. Most babies enjoy a thick meat and vegetable soup and this is a good way of getting her to take what she needs without bothering with several separate vegetables every day.

COOKING HINTS

When preparing legume foods for your baby you can help reduce the formation of intestinal gas (flatulence) by the cooking method you use. To prepare legumes change the soaking water several times, and use fresh water to cook. Slow simmering until tender makes them easier to digest. Do not add salt or acidic vegetables such as tomatoes at the beginning of cooking as they can make them tough. Beans are cooked when they can be easily mashed with a fork.

Chopped onion sautéed in butter until golden brown gives any dish a delicious caramel taste. Add well washed, finely chopped fresh parsley into as many foods as possible when almost cooked. Parsley is an excellent source of iron, folate, Vitamins A, C, and K as well as a host of other important nutrients.

MEAT CONTAINING DISHES. From around five or six months you can make your baby a nourishing thick, minestrone type of soup or stew.

- Simmer a beef or veal shin or knuckle bone, or even a lamb chop with enough water to cover until tender (lamb will be quicker). If possible, use free range meat. Skim off any scum that has formed. Add diced or coarsely grated vegetables near the end of the cooking time. Carrots and potato are good to start with. Do not overcook vegetables as they lose nutrients.

- To vary, add any vegetables to which she has not previously had an adverse reaction. Peeled, seeded tomato, small amount of onion, clove of garlic, parsnip, peas, celery, butternut, beans, broccoli, cauliflower and so on, in any combination you prefer.
- Add pasta, rice, noodles, barley, lentils or pea flour to thicken.
- Purée the mixture or use a baby food grinder at first. Gradually make the mixture less fine until she is taking it mashed with a fork.
- To enrich the food you can grate a small amount of fresh Parmesan (not the ready grated kind) over the food and even drizzle a little extra virgin olive oil over it.
- Because chicken livers are very rich in iron it is worth trying to get your baby to accept their rather strong taste. Sauté in a small amount of fresh sunflower or olive oil for a few minutes. Do not overcook as it will toughen them and make them bitter. Add to rice and vegetables. Purée until smooth or leave it coarser according to your baby's capacity to cope.
- When cooking chicken or a tender piece of meat for the family, cut off a piece, wrap in film and store in the freezer for use in the baby's food.

A great dish to offer that incorporates meat and vegetables is cottage pie, made as follows: Sauté finely diced onions in butter until golden brown, add a little tomato paste, or a little beef stock or chicken stock. You can mix some peas and grated carrot into the mince mixture. Thicken with cornflower if necessary. Top with mashed potato or sweet potato to which a beaten egg has been added. If she hates vegetables, you can slip a few peas or grated carrot into the mince mixture. Bake until golden brown.

FISH. Fish is an excellent source of protein, and in addition, oily fish is a prime source of omega-3 fatty acids that are needed for brain development. Not all babies like it at first, and some are allergic, but it is worth introducing it so that your baby gets used to eating it for its excellent nutritional value.

Steam a little skinned and filleted fish by placing on a plate over a saucepan of boiling water covered by a lid or another plate. Cook until the flesh becomes opaque – this will only take a short while, then mash together with potato and any vegetables of your choice. Add a little milk or a very small amount of virgin olive oil or butter. Or grate a little sweet milk (Gouda) cheese over it. Or make a plain white sauce, or enrich it with grated mild cheddar cheese and flake fish into it. As she gets older you can add vegetables and put it to brown under the grill.

EGGS. Eggs are rich in protein, iron, vitamin A, D, E, K, thiamine, B_6, Folate, B_{12}, (often lacking in the diet of vegetarians), phosphorous, calcium, riboflavin, zinc and many other nutrients making them an excellent nutritional addition to a growing child's diet. Egg yolk is high in cholesterol, but according to the Harvard School of Public Health an egg a day can be part of a healthy diet and it does not increase heart disease risk in healthy individuals. Keep eggs in the fridge and if possible use free range eggs as they have a higher amount of important nutrients. Eggs can cause allergies but latest advice is to give them by four months.

Be sure to get your paediatrician's go ahead before introducing eggs in her diet. Even if your baby is having an iron supplement you can give egg yolk from the fourth or fifth month or whenever she starts on solids. Start with half-a-teaspoonful of cooked egg yolk mixed into her cereal or food and increase until she has had the whole yolk. If she likes it you can give the yolk plain after cooking it for seven minutes. If you do not want to go to the trouble of making a baked egg custard from scratch you can also beat a raw egg yolk into homemade custard, return to the heat and stir until cooked.

Custard with egg and fruit can be a meal in itself on occasion. From about 12 months you can give your baby a taste of a lightly scrambled whole egg. Only give her a teaspoonful to start with in case she has an allergic reaction.

If she shows any sign of allergy stop giving her egg white in any form. Try again in a few months time. Remember many ice creams and cakes contain egg white. Meringues are made from concentrated egg white. Most children over a year can tolerate egg white and you can serve whole eggs in many different ways.

NOTE: Raw egg may be a source of bacterial infection (salmonella) and it is recommended that boiled eggs be well cooked (seven minutes) before serving. Well cooked protein is also easier to digest.

GRADUATING TO COARSER FOODS AT AROUND SIX MONTHS. The introduction of coarser foods is an important developmental stage and should not be missed or there will be resistance. Homemade foods can gradually be made coarser by mashing instead of puréeing or by cutting down the time in the food processor or blender. If your baby gags on the coarser food, make it a little finer.

Do not leave the introduction of coarse foods too late or your baby may reject them altogether. On the other hand, don't force it if your baby is not ready. Leave it and try again in a few weeks' time. A baby who rejects all coarse food by nine months should have a developmental assessment.

All babies have their own individual needs and preferences which should be respected. What you are trying to do when weaning is gradually to introduce your baby to a balanced mixed diet.

FINGER FOODS. At six months, your baby should be eating a variety of foods in a less smooth form. Be able to hold a piece of food and guide it to her mouth. You can give her an unsharp bone with the meat removed so that she does not choke to suck, or a rusk to gnaw, especially if she is teething. Never give anything like apple, banana or bread that could break off and get stuck in her throat.

Homemade rusks are cheap and easy to make. Slice wholewheat or enriched white bread about 2cm to 3cm thick and dry out in a warm oven (100°C) for a few hours.

VEGETARIAN DIETS. Many parents are vegetarians today and want to raise their children as vegetarians. This is possible, but great care is necessary as the needs of children are more complex than those of adults, and growth in the first two years may be compromised. Various classifications are made depending on what is included in the diet. Vegetarians do not eat meat, fish or poultry but they do eat eggs and dairy products, and some include fish. Ovo-vegetarians allow eggs but no animal or dairy products. Lacto-vegetarians take milk and dairy products but not eggs, fish or meat. Pescatarians eat fish but not meat, and vegans exclude meat, fish, poultry and eggs and dairy products from their diet and this is not recommended for children. Complete proteins (those containing all the amino acids), iron, calcium, folate and vitamin B_{12} are the elements most likely to be lacking in vegetarian diets.

COMPLETE PROTEINS are found in animal sources such as milk, eggs and meat and fish. The single source of first class high quality protein from plant sources is soya beans.

Soya milk formulas are modified to include all the necessary elements. Combining incomplete vegetable proteins such as dried peas, beans and lentils with whole grains such as wheat and maize (samp) taken at the same meal can provide the necessary amino acids – the components of complete proteins.

IRON is found in beans, lentils, wholewheat flour, green leafy vegetables, iron fortified baby cereals, egg yolks, dried fruits, in particular apricots, and nuts. Iron deficiency anaemia must be guarded against in vegetarians. Iron, in particular, that from plant sources is better absorbed when it is taken in the presence of foods that contain vitamin C, so include vitamin C rich fruits and vegetables with protein meals. Iron fortified bread, cereal and other iron enriched grain products can supply about half the dietary iron needed. Recommended Dietary Allowances (RDAs) for iron intake: Birth to 6 months 0.27mg, 7-12 months 11mg, 1-3 years 7mg. Richest dietary sources of iron include lean meat and seafood.

CALCIUM is found in fortified soya milk products, tofu, almonds, sesame seeds, sunflower seeds, dark green leafy vegetables, cheese and cow's milk. Exposure to sunlight and vitamin D helps with the absorption of calcium.

FOLATE It is necessary for normal cell development and repair, and it must be included in the diet. It is obtainable from green leafy vegetables, including broccoli, Brussels sprouts, soya bean sprouts, green peas, spinach, Romaine lettuce, legumes, beans, lentils, chickpeas, mung beans, avocado, papaya, tomato juice, mango, oranges, tofu, eggs, yeast extract, as well as folic acid enriched cereals, bread, rice, pasta, bulgur, barley, millet. Check labels. As well as cheese (especially whey cheese), yoghurt and cow's milk.

Folate needs are higher during pregnancy and breast feeding, in particular the first month of pregnancy as folate deficiency in early pregnancy may result in serious birth defects.

VITAMIN B$_{12}$ is found in eggs, fortified cereals, milk and dairy products. Iron deficiency anaemia and a lack of vitamin B$_{12}$ must be guarded against through supplements and careful attention to diet. A vegan diet is the most difficult for children and care must be taken to ensure that all the elements of a well balanced diet are provided through careful planning and supplementation. The high fibre intake in vegetarian diets can lead to trace element deficiency and reduced food absorption.

QUESTIONS ABOUT FEEDING

WHEN CAN YOU STOP NIGHT FEEDS? If she was a big baby and takes her feeds well, she may start sleeping through from after the 10pm feed to the 6am feed between six and 12 weeks. Breastfed babies, however, may need one night feed for at least the first three months. There should not be a break of more than eight hours at a stretch or the mother's milk supply could be affected, or she could become engorged. After the first three months you need not wake your breast fed baby for a feed. Bottle fed babies who are gaining well should not be woken for night feeds, but all babies must be fed if they are hungry at night in the first four months. If she just seems niggly during the night, check to see if she is warm enough, try patting her for a while and she may go back to sleep. If she is hungry she will wake again soon and you must food her. This applies to the first three months. After this bottle fed babies should be taking enough during the day to last them through the night, although breastfed babies may continue to wake at night for a feed. Do not encourage it! Increase the number of feeds during the day.

DOES ADDING SOLIDS HELP BABIES SLEEP THROUGH? The bad news about breastfed babies is that they do wake more frequently and this is likely to persist for as long as they are breast fed. Adding solids at an appropriate stage can increase the time between feeds, but it will not necessarily make your baby sleep though.

WILL A BOTTLE OF WATER HELP A YOUNG BABY SLEEP THROUGH THE NIGHT? Water will do nothing to help your baby sleep through – it will just give her a wet nappy. If she is awake and yelling for food you must give her a bottle or breast feed. She needs it and you will not be achieving anything by denying it to her in the first weeks. If your baby seems to be waking from hunger after the first few months increase her food intake during the day, and try and stretch the gap between night feeds to as long as possible.

IS THE BABY WHO VOMITS WHEN GIVEN CERTAIN FOODS JUST BEING DIFFICULT? No. It means she is not ready for them. Cut them out and try them again at a later stage.

SHOULD YOU BE FIRM AND INSIST WHEN A CHILD BECOMES FINICKY AND REFUSES HER SOLIDS AFTER TAKING THEM WITHOUT TROUBLE BEFORE? Babies develop their own tastes which change from time to time especially after the first six months. Teething or illness can affect her appetite and put her off her food. Her appetite and food needs will also vary from day to day. Never force your baby to eat if her weight-gain is satisfactory. She should put on about 250g a month in the second half of the first year. If she does not regain her appetite fairly quickly, make sure she has daily vitamin supplements and don't fuss about her eating, unless she appears ill or is losing weight, when you should see a doctor immediately. She will develop a more natural attitude to food if you treat it in a matter-of-fact way rather than if you allow it to become a battle of wits. Too much milk or juice can spoil the appetite for solids.

WHAT CAN YOU DO WHEN A BABY REFUSES MILK? Milk is needed for its protein and calcium content. Protein can be obtained from meat sources, but calcium may need to be supplemented if she does not take the other forms of milk suggested. From six months onwards your baby needs 500-600ml milk a day and this can be in any form she likes. A fruit shake made with fresh fruits like banana, strawberries, peaches etc is delicious and highly nutritious. Simply liquidise the fruit together with milk and give from a cup, or with a thick straw. Do not flavour milk with tea or coffee as they contain stimulants (rooibos tea does not).

Although it has largely be supplanted by yoghurt, junket is easily digested and is made with rennet tablets or liquid which can be bought from your pharmacy.

JUNKET. Heat milk to lukewarm and add sugar and rennet according to the directions on the container. Place in a glass bowl. After an hour or two the milk becomes thick and makes a palatable 'pudding' that is nutritious and digestible.

EGG CUSTARD. If your child is underweight and not eating well, a nourishing egg custard can be made with egg yolk and milk. Make custard with bought custard powder or cornflour and milk, flavour with vanilla and sugar. Sprinkle sugar over the top to avoid a skin forming. Remove from heat and mix in a beaten egg yolk. Serve plain or with fruit.

CHEESE. Cheese is an excellent substitute for milk; 25g full-cream cheese is equivalent to 225ml milk. Cottage cheese is also fine but has a lower kilojoule value. You can serve cheese grated over fruit, cereals, vegetables or meat, or let your baby pick up finely grated cheese with her fingers. Milk can be added to soup but do not cook for long as it will make the milk separate (this will not affect its food value). You can use milk powder to enrich many dishes.

YOGHURT is high in calcium, vitamin A and B group vitamins and is often enjoyed by children who do not like milk. It is useful in the prevention of yeast infections like thrush, and if the child is on antibiotics. When choosing commercial yoghurt, pick the kind made with AB cultures ('good bacteria') and made from full-cream milk. It can be bought with a variety of fruits added. Products that are labelled Howaru™ (pronounced how-are-you), contain high levels of probiotic cultures that are said to assist in lactose digestion, stimulate the immune system and improve general health.

HOMEMADE YOGHURT. Bring two litres of full-cream milk to boiling point but do not allow to boil. Remove from heat and cool to blood heat. Put a small carton of plain commercial yoghurt in a clean glass bowl and pour the warm milk over it very gently. Preheat the oven to l00°C, switch off and put the bowl with the yoghurt covered with foil in the oven. Leave overnight to thicken. Strain through a muslin cloth or skim off the liquid (whey) with a spoon. Refrigerate. Next time you make yoghurt reserve half a cupful as a 'starter', then you do not need to use bought yoghurt. You may want to sweeten the yoghurt with a little sugar before serving, or add fresh fruit such as thinly sliced bananas, pureed apple, peaches, etc.

MILK JELLY. Milk can also be added to jelly. Make commercial jelly using a quarter of the water specified and substitute milk for the rest of the water. Yogurt can be added to jelly made in the usual way, by beating it in as it begins to set. You can add well mashed banana at this stage for greater food value.

NOTE: Always give extra liquids in the form of water or fruit juice if your baby is not taking milk in the usual way to prevent constipation and to keep up her fluid intake. (*See p.153 for more ideas.*)

WHEN SHOULD I STOP GIVING A VITAMIN AND IRON SUPPLEMENT TO MY BABY? Generally speaking it is recommended that you continue giving a supplement for the first year. However, if your baby is on a good mixed diet rich in iron in particular, then it is probably not necessary. If you are at all worried about your child's eating habits then give a vitamin and iron supplement for the first year or two or until your child's diet is satisfactory.

CAN I HEAT MY BABY'S FOOD IN A MICROWAVE? Yes. Place food in microwave container. Glass is preferable because of possible leaching out of bisphenol A from plastic. For 125g food microwave on high (100%) power for 15 seconds. Stir again and allow to stand for 30 seconds. Stir. It is very important to test food on your wrist before feeding as it may be too hot. Food should be lukewarm. Do not microwave meats and eggs as the fat can cause splattering and overheating. Do not reheat food.

CAN I HEAT MY BABY'S BOTTLE IN THE MICROWAVE? The greatest danger when heating milk and other foods in a microwave is that of burning your baby. When milk is microwave heated in the bottle, heat accumulates near the top. Heat at full power for 30 seconds. Allow to stand for one minute. After heating shake well and test the temperature by dropping milk on the wrist or back of the hand. Remove lid and teat before heating. Or heat water in the microwave and stand the bottle in it afterwards. Shake and test before feeding. Never reheat milk that has been in a bottle from which your baby has previously been fed. (*See p. 165 for information on bisphenol A in baby bottles.*)

MY BABY IS OVERWEIGHT, SHOULD I PUT HER ON A LOW FAT DIET? No. unlike adults, babies need the essential fatty acids found in full cream milk and other sources. These elements are necessary for brain development and they also need the energy that fats provide in concentrated form. Children under the age of two should not have skim milk, or low fat milk. If she is overweight encourage your baby to be more mobile by playing with her on the floor, putting toys just out of reach and so on. Avoid giving her something to eat in order to keep her quiet. Sweetened biscuits do not have much food value and spoil the appetite for the real food she needs.

HOW IMPORTANT IS FIBRE IN MY BABY'S DIET? High bulk fibre foods should not be given to babies as they can interfere with absorption of micro nutrients. Babies need highly concentrated nutrients and small bulk because of their high energy needs and restricted stomach capacity. This is not to say that foods should be highly refined, but that fibrous bulk should be avoided. Brown rice and wholegrain pasta are good. Brown bread, or 'best of both' is better than wholewheat or high bran bread for babies. Check labels for added vitamins and minerals.

MY BABY IS USED TO BOTTLED BABY FOOD AND WON'T TAKE MY COOKING. Some bottled foods do have a different taste to regular home cooked foods, and babies get used to it. Mix your homemade food with the bottled baby food, gradually reducing the amount of bottled food.

GO TO www.baby-childcare.com TO WATCH THE FOLLOWING VIDEOS THAT ARE APPLICABLE TO CHAPTER 7

PROF CLAUDIA GRAY

Introducing solids

Rashes

Milk and weaning

Gluten free

CHAPTER 8

Mother and Child:
the First Year

THE EFFECT OF BIRTH ON THE MOTHER

IT'S NOTHING LIKE THE ADVERTS. Some women feel ghastly throughout their pregnancy but most find that they 'bloom' after the first few months. By the last few weeks, however, the combined effects of general discomfort, heartburn, tiredness and the inability to get a good night's sleep, make the prospect of giving birth and returning to normal highly attractive.

Unfortunately getting back in shape mentally as well as physically after the birth is not as easy as you might have imagined. Firstly, you will be tired. Tired beyond anything you have known before. Once you have had the baby you will get even less sleep than while you were pregnant. Your chores will increase and you are going to suffer from nervous tension worrying about whether you are doing things right. Your judgment may be affected and you could feel that you cannot think straight. Even driving a car may seem strange.

Most new mothers feel like this for a while, and there is a very thin line between the expected natural effects of lack of sleep, hormonal imbalance and normal tension in the face of the new stresses placed on you and more serious depression. If you feel that you will never be well again, or that you cannot cope and may harm your baby, you may be verging on puerperal psychosis and you must get help. Women who have experienced depression previously, or during pregnancy, are particularly vulnerable to postnatal depression. Because medication taken during pregnancy can be problematic, non-medicinal treatments for depression, during and after pregnancy (if you are breast feeding) are preferable. **Do not hesitate to contact your medical advisor.**

GETTING BACK IN SHAPE

EXERCISES TO DO AT HOME. You may also be disappointed to find that your body does not return to normal as quickly as you had hoped, but it will take months before you can expect to be really flat around the tummy again.

You may be able to attend postnatal exercise classes but in all likelihood you will have neither the time nor the energy. There are, however, a few things you should do that will make a big difference to your physical recovery after the birth.

As soon after delivery as possible get into the habit of 'pinching in' your muscles around the pelvic floor.

You can do this exercise sitting, standing or lying down. Make a practice of doing it whenever you can… while waiting at a traffic light, feeding your baby, or watching TV. The action will tighten the muscle tone of the perineum and your sex life will benefit. It will also help prevent the embarrassing problem of incontinence, that is, difficulty in holding urine.

To locate the muscles used, stop yourself midstream when urinating – you will feel the action of the muscles that need to be strengthened after birth. Practice pulling them up slowly through several 'layers' like an elevator going up through several floors, then release downwards after a few seconds. Repeat five times.

To strengthen the muscles of the rectal area, pull up slowly around the anus, hold, then release through the muscle layers.

This feels very similar to the previous exercise for the vaginal area but you will soon be able to differentiate. If you do these exercises faithfully you will trim your bottom and tone up your sex life.

Remember, too, that good posture is nine-tenths of getting and keeping in shape. Pull in your tummy muscles or you will never flatten your abdomen and don't allow yourself to stand sloppily with a baby on your hip. It will strain your back and ruin your look.

If you have gained a lot of weight during pregnancy do not go on a crash diet in an attempt to get rid of it quickly. You need your strength to cope with looking after the baby, but you can go on a slimming diet provided it is supervised by your doctor or a reputable organisation that specialises in helping people lose weight. Don't pop pills in an effort to curb your appetite or you could end up floating on an artificial 'high' and come crashing down with a bang. Breast feeding uses up a lot of stored body fat and kilojoules, but if necessary you can still go on a suitable diet under supervision. Never take diuretics when breast feeding as the body needs fluid to make milk. Exercise does not seem to detrimentally affect the amount of milk breast feeding mothers produce.

ANAEMIA AND HYPOTHYROIDISM. Occasionally a woman may become anaemic after the birth of her baby. The symptoms are paleness, shortness of breath and tiredness. Although these symptoms are common to all women after delivery, the possibility that they may be aggravated by anaemia should not be overlooked. Folic acid, zinc and other trace elements may also be depleted after pregnancy, so it is a good idea to keep on with the multivitamin and iron tablets you were taking during pregnancy for a few months after the birth. Hypothyroidism, a common medical condition, also causes tiredness, memory loss and weight gain all of which you may have thought of as normal after giving birth. Only tiredness through lack of sleep can be considered normal, so have a check-up. If your thyroid levels are low the solution is likely to be a course of thyroxin which is very effective.

BLADDER. You will find it difficult to pass urine for a few days after the birth, and the urine may burn your episiotomy wound. Try doing it in a half standing position so that the flow does not run over the stitches, and rinse the area with clear water afterwards. Always wipe from the front towards the back after going to the lavatory so that germs do not enter the vagina or urethra. There is nothing more important in preventing infection in your baby than washing your hands well after going to the toilet.

BLEEDING AFTER THE BIRTH. The lochia or vaginal bleeding that follows birth even if you have had a Caesarean usually starts off bright red and gradually turns brownish. A sudden rush of red blood or clots ten days or more after the birth could mean that part of the placenta has been retained and you must contact your doctor at once. During the first few days after delivery you should use sterilised maternity pads. Internal sanitary protection is not recommended until you have had your first period. If the lochia has an offensive smell or you feel ill, see your doctor.

CONTRACEPTION. Discuss contraception with your doctor at the six-week check-up after the birth and remember that you can become pregnant even if you are breast feeding. If you have been using the diaphragm it will have to be refitted. You will also need a new intrauterine device. Although there is only a slim chance of pregnancy occurring it is wise to use a contraceptive like the condom or sheath before you decide on the method you will use regularly after your six-week check-up. If you are not breast feeding you can choose any method of contraception. While you are breast feeding it will be necessary to avoid the contraceptive pill in certain forms.

THE PILL. The combined oestrogen and progestogen contraceptive pill is effective and convenient, but do not take it if you are breastfeeding as it can decrease your milk supply.

The 'mini-pill' does not contain oestrogen and has a low progestogen content. The failure rate is slightly higher than that of the combined pill and there may be slight breakthrough bleeding because of the low hormone content. The mini-pill should not affect lactation but if your milk supply is not ample it is wiser to use some other form of contraception. The Pill should be taken at approximately the same time every day and if you have diarrhoea or are on antibiotics it can make the Pill ineffective, so use additional protection.

DEPO-PROVERA. Is a contraceptive injection given every three or six months. It has a low failure rate and works well in women who have medical conditions such as diabetes, tuberculosis, high blood pressure and heart problems. There may be menstrual irregularities such as spotting or absence of periods, as well as drying of the normal vaginal secretions. The contraceptive injection can be used while breast feeding and may even increase lactation. All women on the Pill should have their blood pressure checked at least once a year.

THE DIAPHRAGM. This is a rubber cap used in conjunction with contraceptive jelly. Your doctor will need to measure the cervix at your six-week check-up after the birth or, ideally, 12 weeks after the birth (even if you have had a Caesarean). He or she will then give you a prescription for the correct size.

The failure rate is slightly higher than that of the various pills, but there is no chemical interference with the body's chemistry and so it does not affect lactation.

INTRAUTERINE DEVICES (IUDS). An IUD (this term includes loops and coils) may be inserted after the birth and remains in place until removed, although it is occasionally ejected without the woman being aware of it. The failure rate is relatively high (up to five per cent) and it can cause discomfort and bleeding problems. It does not affect lactation, however, and is suitable when chemical methods are not appropriate. Should pregnancy occur with the IUD intact there is a slightly increased risk of ectopic (tubal) pregnancy. However there is no reported risk of abnormality in the child although there is a risk of prematurity. Many doctors remove the IUD as soon as pregnancy is confirmed.

CONDOM. This is a rubber sheath that is used by the male or female partner and is effective when used correctly. It helps prevent the spread of infection, including AIDS, but sensation is reduced. When the male condom is used one or both partners may find it a little off-putting because it needs to be applied during love-making. The female condom can be applied privately before intercourse.

FOAM AND JELLY. These chemical spermicides are introduced into the vagina before intercourse and kill the sperm before they penetrate up the cervical canal. Used on their own, spermicides have a high failure rate (between 14 and 24 per cent), but when used with a condom or diaphragm they provide effective protection.

RHYTHM METHOD. This method relies on abstaining from intercourse during the fertile period of the woman's menstrual cycle. Details of the cycle must be kept for three to four months so that the time during which ovulation occurs can be noted. There are also devices that can indicate the fertile period. This method is unreliable with a failure rate of up to ten per cent. If your periods are irregular it can be even more difficult to establish the exact date when ovulation will occur.

BILLINGS OVULATION METHOD. This method relies on recognising and interpreting changes in the cervical mucus during each menstrual cycle. During the fertile period couples abstain from intercourse. It can also be used to establish the fertile period when a woman wants to become pregnant. To work properly the woman must be taught to recognise changes in the cervical secretions.

VASECTOMY. This safe and simple operation is performed on the male partner, does not affect sexual performance and is usually done under a local anaesthetic. The vas deferens, the duct along which sperm travel to the penis, is cut and tied. Although the operation should be considered irreversible, it is sometimes possible to rejoin the vas. This does not mean that fertility will automatically be regained however, as the sperm may no longer be viable.

As long as there are no undesirable psychological effects on the man, vasectomy is an excellent solution if permanent sterility is desired by both partners. Proper counselling before the operation is vital.

STERILISATION. This is a sure method of ensuring permanent contraception if both parents are certain they do not wish to have any more children. A woman can be sterilised within 24 hours of giving birth, or during a Caesarean section. There should be no alteration in the periods, menstrual cycle and sex drive, although psychological factors can have an effect. The menopause will occur as usual, but you must think carefully before consenting to sterilisation because there is very little chance of successfully reversing the operation at a later stage.

COITUS INTERRUPTUS. Other methods of contraception such as coitus interruptus (withdrawal before ejaculation) have an extremely high failure rate and impose an unhealthy restraint on both partners.

PERIODS. If you are not breast feeding your first period may return around 28 days after the birth and could be heavier than usual. If you are breast feeding you may have a period, but in most cases this does not happen until after you stop breastfeeding. Remember you can become pregnant even if you have not had a period (*see p. 112*).

PILES. If you have developed piles (haemorrhoids) during pregnancy this should improve quickly after the birth. Lie on your back with your feet raised a little, cross your legs at the ankles and holding a tissue coated with petroleum jelly against the piles, draw in the muscle around the anus and vagina. Repeat as often as possible. Occasionally an anal fissure may form and this can cause great pain when passing a stool. Lubricate the anus with petroleum or water based lubricating gel and see your doctor if the condition does not clear up within a few days. Ointment applied externally may be prescribed, or a suppository that melts and heals internally may be ordered. In severe cases an injection can be given to provide rapid relief.

SEX. During the first few weeks after the birth, your perineum will be tender especially if you have had stitches. There will inevitably be some bruising. You can resume sexual intercourse as soon after birth as you like after the six weeks checkup, but it is advisable to use a sterile glycerine based lubricating jelly as the normal secretions take some time to flow properly again. If intercourse is resumed before the lochia flow has stopped, it is advisable for the man to use a condom (sheath) as there is a slight danger of infection. It is not uncommon for the woman's libido to be lowered after the birth due to tiredness, hormonal fluctuations and stress. Patience and consideration will go a long way towards preventing a build-up of tension and resentment between the partners.

The nursing mother's breasts may be tender and uncomfortable, especially in the beginning, but thoughtfulness and a sense of humour should overcome any frustration.

THE SIX-WEEK CHECK-UP. It is essential to have a medical check-up six weeks after the birth so that your doctor can make sure that everything is as it should be. The uterus should have returned to its normal size, shape and position (or at least be on its way to complete recovery). Urine and blood pressure tests will be done, and the muscles of the abdomen examined to see if they have regained their strength. Although the body does not return to its non-pregnant state for at least six months after delivery or three months after stopping breast feeding, the examination can establish whether there are likely to be any future problems. Most doctors advise mothers to continue taking their iron and vitamin supplements for at least three months after the birth to prevent anaemia and the effects of vitamin deficiency.

HAIR. In the months after delivery your hair may be rather unmanageable and fall out in unusually large amounts. This is normal and due to hormonal effects. Use a conditioner if it is dry and do not have a perm until it settles down.

SKIN. The brown pigmentation or chloasma, also known as the 'butterfly mask', of pregnancy that sometimes discolours a woman's face, is caused by the extra hormones circulating and should fade gradually after the birth. Do not try to bleach the marks as the light parts will become lighter and make the dark patches show up more. When the hormonal levels return to normal after pregnancy the brown blotches will fade. Exposure to the sun during pregnancy and the use of oral contraceptives afterwards can aggravate the problem, especially the blotches over the upper lip. Wear a good sunscreen at all times.

The linea nigra (the brown line from the navel to the pubis) should also fade after delivery. The hair on moles often becomes darker, and is unlikely to change back to its former colour after the birth. Many women find that their skin is unusually dry after the birth; it will gradually return to normal, but meanwhile use a good moisturising cream. Tiny red marks on your face or shoulders are caused by increased pressure in the blood vessels and will disappear in time. Folic acid and vitamin E may help return the skin to normal sooner, so take your multivitamin tablets as described on *p.87*.

STRETCH MARKS. Stretch marks can occur almost overnight during pregnancy when they appear as red lines on the abdomen, breasts or thighs. They are thought to be caused by stretching of the skin if you gain weight too rapidly, in addition to the effects of hormonal changes. Although they fade gradually to silvery whiteness after the birth, they don't disappear completely. Creams and lotions, oils etc, used to prevent stretch marks lubricate the skin and possibly make it more elastic thus less prone to stretch marks, but they seldom make them disappear or prevent them forming altogether. Plastic surgery can remove stretch marks.

SWEATING. You may notice that you sweat a lot after the birth. You will also be thirsty. Drink as much as you like – water or fruit juice is best – to help flush out your system and make milk.

TEMPERATURE. If you have a raised temperatures at any time after the birth call your doctor because you could have an infection in the bladder, uterus, breasts (mastitis) or elsewhere.

TENSION. This is perhaps your biggest enemy and the most difficult to combat. Everything about having a baby conspires towards it. The pain, the tiredness, the responsibility, the feeling of being tied down, even the visitors… What is more, the tension you feel is likely to be reflected in the baby, making for a vicious cycle with little release.

Firstly you must keep up your strength as described at the beginning of this chapter, then you must learn to recognise when you are becoming particularly tense and take steps to relieve it.

I do not recommended the use of tranquillisers because they dull your perception without really helping you come to grips with problems. However, if you have reached such a pitch that you cannot help yourself and chemical means to break the cycle is necessary, only use medication prescribed by your doctor. Do not take pills that were previously prescribed, unless he or she recommends it. But hopefully you will save yourself getting to that point by using some of these simpler means.

Try to get out of the house at least once a day, if possible without the baby, even for a quick trip to the shops. Feeling trapped builds up resentment and this creates tension.

If you have managed to save money, spend it now on a trip to the hairdresser, something new to wear, or a dinner date with your partner. He should really be providing these sanity savers, but if he is too wrapped up in himself to see the need or too broke after paying confinement bills, you will have to take the lead. Learn to relax when there is a lull in the baby's routine. Don't rush around with a duster – take a nice relaxing bath and pamper yourself, and sleep when the baby sleeps. You will be doing everyone a greater service than if you provide them with polished surroundings.

Care for your baby, but don't worry yourself silly – see a doctor to put your mind at rest if there is something troubling you – don't brood on it. Some perfectly healthy babies cry a lot especially during the first months. Colic is usually the culprit (*see p. 93*). If you cannot bear it any longer, ask someone you trust to stay with her while you get out of earshot.

Do these tension relieving exercises whenever you feel muscle tension or a headache coming on, and take heart, the worst is usually over by three months.

Lie on your back with your knees over a cushion. Focus on your body and become aware of the muscles in your feet, hands, legs, trunk and face. Close your eyes and take a few slow deep breaths ending with a deep sigh. Your whole body should be fully supported so that it can relax completely. Concentrate on your feet, feel if they are tight or tense in any way. Allow the pressure to flow out until they are floppy and loose. Do it with your whole leg now. Follow with your hands and arms and your whole body. Your face is often very tense. Feel your face loosen up and hang apart. Allow your jaw to relax.

Make your eyelids melt into your face. Relax. Even after ten minutes you should feel refreshed if you have really let go.

To ease tension in your neck sit comfortably and rotate your head in a circle five times to the right and five times to the left. Then stand up and flop forward like a rag doll, allowing your arms to swing loosely in front of you.

The other marvellous way of relaxing is to get your partner to give you a full body massage. Use oil or cream so that his hands glide smoothly, then do the same for him (well, sometime).

VAGINA. If you have had an episiotomy, the cut that is made in the perineum to ease the delivery of the baby without risking tearing, you will be particularly sensitive around this area. If you have had a forceps delivery the cut will be large and may have involved muscle layers as well as skin so healing will take longer. Initially the episiotomy stitches will pull and later on may itch as they heal. An ice pack made by putting ice cubes in a plastic bag and holding it to the perineum helps reduce swelling and eases the pain. (Put a cloth around the ice bag or you could get an ice burn.) If the discomfort interferes with your ability to relax, especially when breast feeding, use an analgesic spray or jelly, such as one per cent lignocaine, on the area.

Once the stitches are removed or have dissolved (if soluble stitches were used) the discomfort should ease. If you still have pain in the area weeks after the birth see your doctor, because a nerve end may have been trapped in the scar, making it ultra-sensitive. Showering may be more comfortable than bathing at first, but make sure you clean the perineum well.

Pour salt water (1 teaspoonful to about 250ml water) over the area to help heal the wound. Observe strict hygiene so that there is no risk of infecting the area.

VARICOSE VEINS. Varicose veins developed in pregnancy should improve after delivery. But they may not disappear completely and are likely to get worse with each subsequent pregnancy. Sit with your legs up as often as possible, for instance when feeding, and see your doctor if there is no improvement.

CARING FOR YOUR BABY

NOT JUST A PIECE OF CLAY. In recent years there has been a great deal of research into the psychological and intellectual development of the child.

Far from being a dull, semi-formed creature that cannot perceive very much beyond feelings of hunger or cold, the human infant has been found to respond to mental and physical stimulation from the first few weeks of life, and can, in fact, hear and respond to stimuli while still in the womb. Many experts have also come to the conclusion that most, if not all, future abilities are influenced by the child's experiences during the first three years of life.

While it is generally agreed that no one can develop beyond a genetically determined capacity, much can be done to stimulate children's innate capabilities so that they can develop their potential fully.

Like all parents you want your child to function well, achieve some success in life and be happy and well adjusted, but you may be confused about how to achieve this goal.

You may have been brought up to believe that children should be seen and not heard; that babies should sleep most of the time, and that too much attention will spoil an infant and make her impossible to live with. As a result you could feel you need to stifle the instinct to go to your baby when she cries, to play with her, or even keep her near you.

It is my belief that you cannot spoil a child by giving her attention, comfort, interest and love. You may find you have a more demanding baby. A child who is not content to lie in her cot and stare at the ceiling for hours – but you should be rewarded with an alert; responsive child who will eventually have far fewer problems because she is competent, less frustrated and has a good self-image. Of course, the way you provide this attention is important. No parent should become a slave to a child – this does not encourage healthy development, but manipulative skill – which is dishonest and self-defeating. The way we can interact with our child in a mutually beneficial way becomes clearer if we know something about how a baby develops.

REFLEXES. In the first six to nine weeks of life the newborn baby shows a number of reflex actions that disappear with age. (*See p. 70*).

Because your baby is largely a bundle of reflexes during the first six weeks you may feel there is nothing you can do to provide her with positive stimulation. Although the cognitive abilities of the very young child are limited, you can start to build up the network of information in the brain and initiate the use of facilities needed for learning.

LEARNING TO FOCUS. Your baby needs something to practice her focusing on and if she lies in a pram without anything to look at but white walls or her sheet she will not have anything to attract her eye. Visual discrimination helps develop some of the skills needed for reading. You can easily and cheaply make a mobile that will help your baby track objects which enter her field of vision.

MAKING A MOBILE
YOU NEED: a few sheets of tissue paper like that used for kites. (Choose a number of bright colours.) A wire coat hanger. Thread.

Cut the paper into pieces approximately 20cm × 30cm and twist in the centre to form a butterfly shape. Tie with thread in the centre and suspend from the coat hanger. Hang the other 'butterflies' at varying lengths from the hanger and suspend the hanger from the ceiling so that it is slightly to the right and in her line of sight. Make sure it is well out of her reach! The mobile will spin and move in the gentlest breeze and will attract your baby's gaze, helping her learn to track and focus with her eyes.

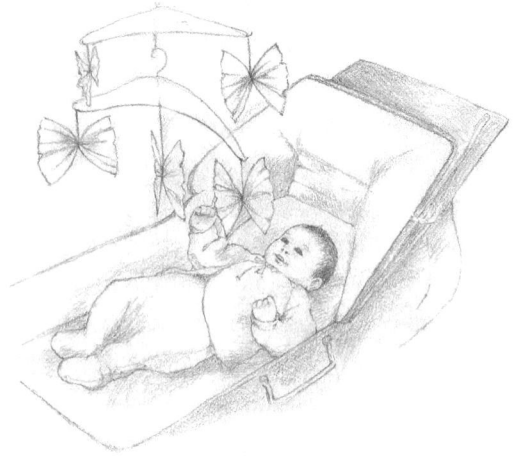

ENCOURAGING MOTOR DEVELOPMENT. Gross motor development, or the use of the large muscles of the body, is important for mastering activities like walking, jumping and skipping, while fine motor coordination allows the child to control the small muscles that are needed to write, thread beads and do other precision work.

The stimulation of motor development will play an increasing role in the months ahead during free kicking or exercise time. Even though your tiny baby may enjoy being cosily swaddled for sleep she should not always be tied down in a little bundle, especially after the first six weeks.

Once your baby has settled into some sort of routine and you find her lying awake although apparently not hungry, you can take her out of her pram or cot and give her time to stretch and exercise her muscles.

FLOOR TIME. Find a warm, draught-free spot and put a blanket on the floor. Cover it with a piece of waterproofing and a cloth nappy. Switch off any unnecessary sound, like the TV, and if you like, put on some soft, relaxing music. Take off the garments covering your baby's legs and bottom and leave her naked from the waist down. (Exposure to the air is an excellent way to reduce and heal nappy rash.) Some small babies dislike having their tummies exposed so lay a folded cloth nappy over her abdomen if she is unhappy. (You may need it to stop yourself getting an unexpected shower from your little boy, too.) Now get down and have a good time!

Do not try to communicate with your baby in this way if you feel tense and edgy, unless you find that it relaxes you. Even tiny babies respond to tension around them. Talk gently to her, look her in the eyes, stroke her limbs. If she is constipated, move her legs as though she is riding a bicycle, pedalling slowly round and round. This is good exercise at any age to strengthen your baby's muscle tone or to aid peristalsis and improve bowel action.

While your baby is on the floor play with her, indulge in skin-to-skin contact with her. It will not be long before you are rewarded with a toothless smile! (*See also Tummy Time p.225.*)

THIS IS WHAT YOU CAN EXPECT FROM THE NORMAL INFANT BETWEEN BIRTH AND SIX WEEKS.

- She will startle easily at the sound of a sudden loud noise.
- She will avoid bright lights by closing her eyes.
- She sneezes and hiccups often.
- She sucks her fists.
- She will have very little head control. You should support her head when you pick her up.
- A high-pitched noise near her should elicit a startle reflex action, blinking, or obvious concentration.
- She should follow a bright object held between 20cm and 30cm away from her eyes when it is moved across her line of vision.
- She should make some 'baby' sounds.
- Near the end of this period she should show some sign of recognising her mother when she talks to her, usually by becoming quiet and attentive.
- She should start to smile occasionally. She will lie with her head to one side and her arm on that side extended when placed on her back.

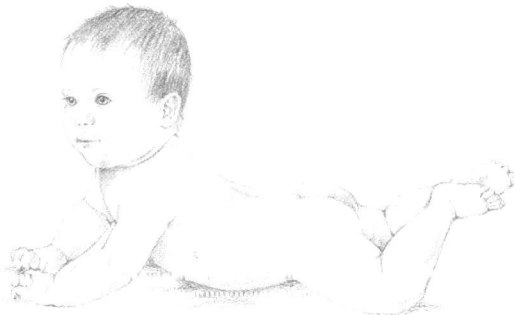

THIS IS WHAT YOU CAN EXPECT FROM THE NORMAL INFANT BETWEEN TWO AND FOUR MONTHS

STARTING TO TAKE SHAPE. Between two and four months your baby should be growing out of 'her newly hatched' state and behave in a less automatic way. She will be stronger and able to hold her head up for longer periods, although you should still support it.

- She should be smiling regularly and at the beginning of this stage will smile at anything resembling a face – even a simple line drawing showing two eyes in an oval with hair – if it is held about 30cm from her eyes.
- Her hands will fascinate her, and she will watch them move through her line of vision with great interest. She will also be able to bring her hand to her mouth with greater accuracy and may suck her fingers or fist. Her hands will slowly unclench so that they are open or slightly closed most of the time.
- Her neck muscles will gradually become stronger and she will be able to turn her head round when she lies on her back until she is able to hold it in line with the centre of her body.

Your baby will probably spend longer periods awake every day and will no longer seem to be in a perpetual state of half-waking, dozing or crying. She will have periods when she is fully awake and alert, and she will need to be amused or she could get bored and niggly. This is not to say you have to bombard your baby with sensory stimuli at all times; she will simply switch off if there is too much going on. But if she is developing normally she will need and enjoy your company and love watching what is happening around her.

From three months her field of vision will have increased to almost the same as that of an adult, and she will characteristically focus on something briefly and then look away, unlike the fixed staring of the newborn baby. This is the stage when you should start really enjoying your baby. Her ecstatic response to your presence, her gurgles and smiles for all who communicate with her, provide parents with the emotional feedback that makes up for a lot of sleepless nights!

Now your playtime will have more meaning and a clearer direction. Your aim should be to build up your baby's physical capabilities, stimulate her mental development and strengthen the emotional bond between you.

Left to their own devices most mothers will do this naturally, but there have been confusing 'fashions' in child rearing and you may not be confident that your approach is right. You might have heard that you will damage your baby by encouraging her to progress 'too soon'. That her bones will 'not be able to take it' or that her mind will become 'overloaded'. Let me assure you that your baby will not walk before she is ready and able – no matter what you do – and that she will not develop mental attitudes that will harm her in any way. As long as you never try to force her to do anything or become angry or tense because you expect her to do something she does not want to do, or is not ready for, she will benefit. As long as your baby is happy and eager to play along you will know that all is well. Some babies are extremely sensitive to overstimulation from smells, movement and sound. Be alert for this and stop.

Remember that while your baby is a relatively helpless creature, not able to move about on her own, and unable to communicate what is in her mind – she is ready and waiting for you to feed her information. Colour, shape, touch, sound, verbal communication – all the marvels of human perception are new to her.

How you introduce these wonders to her will influence her reactions. Learning can be a wonderful and exciting experience – or a painful and dull one. The more she learns the more she will want to know… and informed curiosity is the key to knowledge.

USE IT OR LOSE IT. Latest scientific research on the brain shows that the 'wiring' between neurons which forms the basis of our learning is formed through use. In other words even if a baby is born with the ability to see perfectly, if you blindfold her for the first few months she will lose the capacity to see. If you tie an arm down she will lose the ability to move it. Incredibly, emotional reactions are also developed through this kind of learning. So good experiences are vital to your child's healthy emotional development.

- From about three months your baby will delight in making sounds with her voice or playing with her saliva, or shaking something to make a noise.
- She will enjoy kicking her legs and moving her arms about actively while lying on her back.
- She should start to swipe at objects held in front of her, and her aim when she reaches out will improve gradually.
- She will explore with her fingers by touching your clothes when you feed her, by pulling on her blankets, by grabbing your necklace or whatever is within easy reach, and she will be able to bring her hand to her mouth at will.
- Towards the end of this phase she should be able to lift her head up while lying on her tummy and leaning on her elbows.
- When she is held upright she should be able to hold her head up by herself.
- Socially she will be a charmer, smiling and gurgling at all and sundry.
- A musical toy will attract her attention and amuse her.
- Playtime on the mat is even more exciting as new abilities emerge.
- Rolling over from her tummy onto her back is great fun. Help her master it by holding an attractive object just out of reach above her. She will soon make a determined effort to get it by lifting up on her arms and eventually flopping over.

'Gumming' becomes a great game, with anything and everything she can reach going into her mouth. Some of the attraction of this activity may be due to teething, but a lot is learning by exploring with a very sensitive organ, the mouth. Provide her with different tactile experiences – hard, soft, rough, smooth – so long as it is not dangerous. Unfortunately there has been an upsurge in dangerous toys since manufacturing has become global.

DANGEROUS TOYS. Lead is an extremely toxic metal that accumulates in the system and can cause brain deterioration. Many commonly used items and even jewellery can contain lead. Lead is also found in some pottery glazes, and some say that the Roman Empire declined due to lead leaching out of the glaze on urns used to store wine.

Toys that are painted with lead based paint, and even some fabrics or plastic can contain toxic levels of lead. This is potentially very serious as babies inevitably put everything within reach into their mouths. The Disney Company recently recalled some 35,000 toys – including soft blocks due to their high lead content. In South Africa wooden toy blocks has been found to have been painted with lead based paint. Unfortunately, as we have seen with melamine contaminated baby milks, the world is not a moral place – two people in China were executed for their part in this scam – but it is too late for the babies who died.

It is difficult for parents to be sure that what their baby plays with or even what they consume is uncontaminated. Many internationally famous brands have been implicated. For the brand names of toys, and child related equipment that has been recalled in the US, and information on any deaths and injuries that have been reported: go to the website of the Consumer Product Safety Commission of the United States of America. *www.cpsc.gov/*

Also, look out for any loose parts on toys, the eyes on Teddy bears must be sewn on not stuck on for example. Squeeze, poke and pull before purchasing.

STIMULATING YOUR BABY'S MENTAL AND PHYSICAL DEVELOPMENT

FOOD FOR THOUGHT. You don't need to be highly educated or rich to provide your child with the best start in life. You need interest and empathy. You have to be able to put yourself in your child's place and understand and feel what she is experiencing. To grow and develop to the best of her capacity your baby needs food for her mind as well as her body.

When she is awake and alert you can seat her in a reclining baby chair and place her where she can see the top half of your body clearly, so that she can 'read' your body language as well as see and hear what you are doing.

If you will be moving about a great deal or going out while she is awake, you can put her in a baby carrier or blanket strapped to your back or front and let her see the world go by. This allows her to view things the right way up – not just the tops of trees and telephone poles as she would lying down in a pram (stroller). The close physical contact with you will be a great source of emotional security to her – the best possible climate for getting the most out of new experiences.

Toys or equipment that assist her in practising eye-hand coordination are always good. Some bought toys are suited to this purpose but you can adapt or fashion your own. String very large plastic or wooden beads or other shapes (the greater the variety the better as long as they are not sharp), on a piece of elastic 0.5cm wide (narrower elastic will be too bouncy). Now stretch the elastic taut across your baby's crib or pram so that she can reach it comfortably. Don't hang anything on a cord or narrow elastic as it will be almost impossible for your baby to catch hold of and will only frustrate her.

Another suitable item for this stage that will serve its purpose for many months is a 'baby gym'. These toys have firm pulleys and levers on which the baby can exercise her new skills by making things happen – an early lesson in cause and effect as well as eye-hand coordination and motor development As your baby grows your special 'playtime' with your baby will start to take on a more exciting direction as her physical and mental skills develop rapidly. Take off as many of her clothes as the temperature allows and be sure to take off her nappy, protecting the carpet or blanket with a waterproof sheet.

TUMMY TIME. Ever since it has become accepted practice to put babies to sleep on their backs, rather than on their tummies as a prevention of cot death, less time has been allotted to this important aspect. Lying babies on their tummies encourages the development of important neck muscles and nerves, as well as the ability to roll over. Some babies resist being placed on their tummies. You can help her get used to it by putting her on her tummy across your lap at first.

When she is on her tummy on the floor, have a selection of bright 'toys' ready to attract her attention. They need not be toys in the strict sense of the word, merely a collection of brightly coloured items that are not dangerous, so they should not have sharp edges, be painted with toxic paint, or be small enough to swallow. A squeaky toy, a ball, a rattle, a set of measuring spoons, beans or small stones sealed in a tin or plastic bottle for example, are fine.

Place your baby on her tummy and hold one of the toys in front of her, high enough off the ground for her to have to lift her head to see it. Holding it close to her face, make a noise and wave it to attract her attention. At first her head will bob up and down because she will not have the strength to hold it up for long. This is an excellent natural exercise for strengthening the neck muscles and soon she will be able to hold her head up for longer periods. Encourage her to propel herself forward by placing a toy just out of reach in front of her. She will try to get it if the bait is tempting enough. It is amazing with what dedication and determination most babies practise new skills. Encourage and enthuse with her and you will be preparing her for learning in future. Never persist with any activity after your child loses interest or becomes tired.

If she is tense, give her a relaxing massage. Move your hands over the trunk and shoulders, in slow circular movements, talking or singing to her softly. You can play your favourite relaxing music in the background if you like.

It is also a good opportunity to play one of the special recordings made for babies that are said to stimulate or calm. Many are based on the great composers such as Mozart and there are claims that they are designed to stimulate the brain, or calm according to the metre of the music.

Allow her free kicking time while she is lying on her back. Hold an eye-catching object above your baby's head so that she can practise swiping at it, but don't pull it away just as she is about to get it. Give her the satisfaction of achievement.

Hold a 'conversation' with her. If you say something and look at her directly, she will respond with gurgles. When she stops, it is your cue to carry on the conversation.

You will find that as you talk to her she becomes excited as the pitch of your conversation rises and flows rhythmically. So do it and enjoy it – it's fun.

In this way she will be learning the art of human conversation which is a highly complex form of two-way interaction that will become one of the most important tools in her life. The art of real communication is delicate and needs great skills. It is easier if you learn it from the cradle, in fact babies who are brought up in isolation or left for long periods without being talked to may never develop the skill adequately.

BABY SIGNING. A number of programmes have been developed that purport to train parents and infants to communicate through 'signing' before the baby with normal hearing and cognitive abilities learns to talk. Many benefits are claimed, from decreased infant frustration, to advanced language development. Unfortunately these claims do not appear to be supported by properly conducted scientific trials. Specialised signing for babies with developmental problems may serve a purpose.

FOUR TO SIX MONTHS

By now your baby should be achieving some conscious control of her movements. She will be able to hold her head up unaided and should be able to propel herself forward to some extent by wriggling on her tummy.

This is usually one of the most delightful stages of babyhood and you will probably find your baby wakes cheerfully instead of crying.

Even more than before, she will delight in practising her repertoire of sounds, which up until now have been a variation of vowels. Keep up your conversations. Do it the way mothers have always done by repeating phrases of 'Who's a pretty girl? Who's mummy's baby?' Indulge yourself in schmaltz – it is learning as well as loving and it helps a baby grow into a well adjusted adult.

It is too late to start trying to bridge the communication gap when she is 16 – you have to start when she is six months – and you can never hope to be as effective again if you miss out on laying the foundations.

Around this period your baby will become more active physically and will spend a lot of her time exercising the skills which encourage motor development. New frolics like learning to roll over are repeated with gusto, while fine motor coordination is promoted with great dedication when your baby plays with her fingers, exploring whatever is within reach and feeling different textures and shapes with intense concentration. Watch your baby as she scrutinises her fingers – her single-mindedness will give you some indication of the depth of her concentration.

About this time she should discover a new set of playthings that have the advantage of always being within reach – her feet! Brand new and wriggly, they make marvellous toys – tasty too! Changing a nappy is not so easy now, especially as she will probably insist on grabbing a free foot while you are fumbling with a fastener.

Although all babies have different sleep needs, a lot of mothers are surprised if their six-month-old is happy to spend half the day awake. Do not try to force your baby to sleep more than she needs. She could then start waking during the night simply because she has slept too much during the day.

I would not call a six-month-old baby who sleeps a lot and is happy to spend most of her time staring at the ceiling 'good'. Some mothers confuse what is convenient for them with what is right for a baby. A so-called 'good' baby may be less trouble to the mother, but that is all. Babies are neither good nor bad. They may be difficult, they may be fractious, they may be placid or they may be active according to their temperaments but they cannot consciously be 'good'. You will simply have to go along with the child's personality. (See p. 521 for various baby temperaments.)

I would be inclined to worry about the overly 'good' baby. There may be no cause for concern, but the baby who shows no inclination to explore and experience appropriately for her age should be investigated. At the other end of the scale, babies who are continually on the go are being labelled hyperactive and sometimes given medication even before they are a year old. I would be very wary of pinning this kind of label on an infant, or even a toddler without a thorough investigation of her food intake, general management behaviour pattern, and certainly avoid medication.

BOUNCING. Around six months most babies enjoy really active kicking and bouncing on their legs. You may find that when your baby stands with her feet resting on your lap she bounces up and down. Her obvious delight in this activity should tell you that it is part of nature's way of strengthening her muscles in preparation for walking. Encourage it, it will not hurt her legs in any way. The delight babies take in this activity points to the reason for the popularity of contraptions that are hung from door-frames in which the baby bounces.

These devices work on springs and can bounce the child with some considerable force that might possibly lead to damage of blood vessels in the brain. Bouncing on the mother's knee is far better.

Suggestions for providing playthings for your baby should not make you think that buying expensive 'educational' toys would make your baby brighter. Many so-called educational toys are nothing of the sort and are designed to appeal to adults who are the spenders of the cash. In the USA the marketers of the Baby Einstein range of 'educational' DVD's which were promoted as being able to improve infant intelligence, have been forced to offer purchasers a $15.99 refund on any item since studies showed that the products did not deliver. Even if you don't provide your baby with the equipment I have suggested, but simply see that she is not left alone for hours in an uninteresting environment, you will be doing enough to ensure adequate development at this stage. (See Dangerous Toys www.cpsc.gov/)

ROLLING OVER. Another skill that should be emerging now is rolling over from her back onto her tummy. This requires a little more effort, but offer her a bit of bait in the form of an attractive toy and she will soon master it. You can help a little by putting a supporting hand under her shoulders while holding her thigh as she starts to go over.

SITTING. To learn to sit by herself your child needs to acquire balance, as well as strength in the abdominal muscles. The various exercises you have been doing will have been strengthening the muscles needed, but balance will have to be promoted. When your child shows signs of being ready to sit by herself from around four to six months, you can help her gain balance with this exercise. Lay her on a mat on the floor and place your right hand firmly on her right upper arm and shoulder. Lift her up while holding her legs down with your other hand, allowing her to lean on her left elbow as she moves upright into a sitting position. Support her in the sitting position for a few minutes. Do not tire her and stop immediately if she is unhappy. Lie her down by letting her lean on her elbow for support as she did to get up. Do the same on the other side. She will need supportive cushions wedged around her before she is able to maintain a sitting position alone. Do not try and force sitting too soon.

CRAWLING. Sometime from about six months onwards your baby will start to propel herself under her own steam. Before that she will be strengthening the muscles and mastering the rather complex coordination required to move legs and arms in the correct sequence for crawling. You can help your baby learn to crawl by looping a towel around her tummy and gently lift her off the floor – which should not be slippery – by holding the ends up. Put your foot behind her heels to give her traction and encourage her to move forward by putting something tempting just out of reach.

The sequence in which a baby learns to crawl and to sit alone varies. Some babies learn to sit first, others crawl first. Occasionally babies learn to get around by sliding on their bottoms or even moving backwards. It makes no difference and as long as it works you should not force her to do it your way although you can show your baby by holding her and moving her limbs in a crawling action. Babies who seem to drag their legs when crawling should have their hips checked. Babies who do not crawl at all sometimes have a developmental lag and should be assessed. Do not put your baby in a walking ring to encourage mobility. She needs to do it herself to develop neurologically as well as physically.

BATHING. Bath time is fun time and your baby should be enjoying it immensely. You will probably find the baby bath is too small to contain all the splashing, but the big bath is too big for comfort. Why not put the baby bath in the big one? To prevent slipping use a rubber bath mat with suction cups at the bottom of the baby bath. Never leave your baby for a second in the bath even when she can sit by herself, and be careful of scalding – never put the hot water in the bath first — or leave your baby where she could open a tap. Floating toys, plastic cups and bottles she uses for pouring water make great educational toys. When holding a 'conversation' now don't forget to repeat key words – 'water', 'hands', 'feet' – talk to her about what you are doing, as you dress and undress her, it will all be computerised in her receptive mind.

SIX TO NINE MONTHS

BECOMING MOBILE. While the activities and abilities of the various age groups overlap to some extent there should be a general progression towards independent locomotion and increased all round ability at this stage. During this period the child will discover tiny particles, which she scrutinises with intense interest and will delight in manipulating things with her hands, tearing paper, banging a plastic cup on a table and generally manhandling anything she can get hold of.

Another important discovery is cause and effect. The baby who drops a toy over the side of her cot and then yells for you to retrieve it is experimenting, not being naughty. (This doesn't mean you have to go on doing it until you drop!) Peek-a-boo is another popular learning game. You hold a cloth in front of your face, then pull it down quickly and reappear. Your baby will be fascinated. Now try holding it in front of her and say something like 'where's she, where's ?' using her name and she will soon learn to pull the cloth away by herself, usually laughing delightedly at her ability to make things happen. An unbreakable mirror hung on the inside of her cot will also give her a lot of fun.

Around this time your baby will be starting to understand certain words that are often used around her such as 'Mummy', 'Daddy' and the names of others in the household. Also food or bottle, and similar words.

LANGUAGE DEVELOPMENT. Babbling, the beautiful noise which sounds the same no matter what the child's future language, is practised at various pitches using b's, p's and m's as well as vowels, in preparation for the complexities of speech. From around six months of age babies imitate the sounds they hear. Thus Japanese babies would not differentiate between the 'r' and 'l' as this is not done in the Japanese language.

Gradually, babbling becomes 'lalling' – the repetition of heard sounds and sound combinations. Practising phonemes – the vowels and consonants – that make up a particular language gives a baby as much pleasure as it does to her parents. Many languages share the same basic sounds for the key words in an infant's life – milk, daddy, mama… Eventually she will utter a sound that approximates a recognisable word in her language, like 'da-da' and her delighted parents will reinforce her learning by repeating it whenever daddy is near.

The parents' role in helping a baby learn to talk is that of tutor. By responding to your baby's lalling she learns which sounds have a particular meaning. Although at first she may say 'dada' to all men she will eventually fine down her perception until her reference will be accurate. But she needs reinforcing and response for her to make sense out of the strange code with which we communicate.

Although there is no need to become serious simply because you are trying to teach your baby language, she will find it difficult to copy or understand if you flood her with baby talk. Talk to her clearly, repeating the words you want to convey, pointing to the person or object and respond positively and enthusiastically when she makes an attempt at imitation. Use the correct word the first time you teach it to her or she will have to relearn it. This does not mean you should never indulge in loving 'baby talk'.

MOBILITY. At this stage most babies will be sitting up or starting to crawl, or both. Some adventurous souls may even take their first steps at nine months, but this is unusual. Generally, however, you will have a more mobile infant than before, who will complicate your life and expose herself to new dangers. If you have to confine her use a playpen. Do not put her in a walking ring. (*See p. 49, 233*).

THE EMERGENCE OF SELF. In some ways, the 'honeymoon' is over by the time your baby is seven or eight months old. The period after three-month colic, before teething and crawling, when your baby smiled at all and sundry and stayed in the same place has gone forever. (It is this 'honeymoon' period around five or six months that traps many mothers into thinking it would be nice to start another baby. But remember that by the time the next one is born this one will be an 18 month-old terror.)

SEPARATION ANXIETY. By seven or eight months your baby will probably start crying when you leave the room. She will probably become very wary of strangers and possibly of people she has seen quite regularly; even her father may seem to frighten her. Don't be alarmed. It is a sign of normal development. She has discovered that her mother is separate from herself and her anxiety at being parted is understandable. She has also become aware of the 'strangeness' of people who are not primary caregivers in her life. It may be embarrassing to your friends and relations, who mean well, but you can console yourself that your cautious baby is showing signs of healthy development.

NINE TO TWELVE MONTHS

THE THINKING BEING EMERGES. The last quarter of your baby's first year of life sees the continued maturation and development of skills acquired in the preceding months. By their first birthday most children can pull themselves up into a standing position and take their first steps. Although early walking and generally advanced motor or physical development is a fairly sure sign that all is well with the parts of the central nervous system which control these functions, it does not necessarily indicate advanced intelligence.

However, it is the stage when a baby should begin using the rudiments of intelligent thought. Instead of interacting with objects in an obvious way, she is starting to work out the means to an end. For example, if something she wants is out of reach, she will try to get it by manipulating her environment, say, by climbing onto something to reach the desired object or by moving something out of the way to get to what she wants. The evolution of this stage from the development that has gone before is the beginning of what many consider to be the most vital part of a child's life.

PHYSICAL DEVELOPMENT IN THE FIRST YEAR

The newborn baby is unable to support her head in the midline when lying on her back.

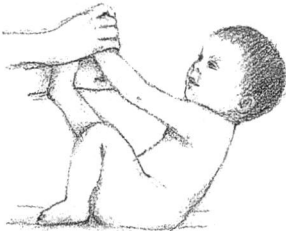

The three month old baby can hold her head upright even though it may be a little wobbly.

By six months babies love to be pulled up into a sitting position even though they may not be able to sit unaided.

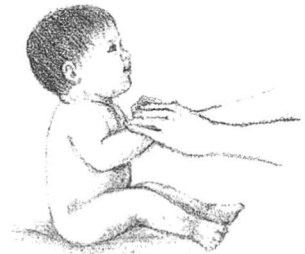

By nine months most babies are able to sit without support.

By their first birthday many babies are able to get around by holding on to something with only one hand.

DANGER. The crawling baby is highly vulnerable to danger. But how can you protect her? If you could grow an extra pair of eyes, ears and arms it would help... failing that you will have to remove as many dangers as possible. All sorts of objects that are not normally dangerous become hazardous when they are within reach of an infant.

There is no point in leaving something you value where your baby can reach it, and then getting cross when she goes for it. Keep it well out of her way until she is old enough to understand why it is something she is not allowed to explore. If you frustrate her as little as possible now she will be more cooperative later on.

It is also natural for a baby to keep on going back to things you have told her not to touch. She is not being naughty – she just wants to make sure that she is never allowed to touch it. So you have to be consistent. Don't hesitate to take her away and repeat 'no' every time she does it. It is only through endless repetition that messages get imprinted in children's minds.

If an object is dangerous, you will have to be very firm. Show by your voice and your face that you get very distressed when she goes near the fire, for example. Grab her and say something like, 'No! No! Don't touch; it will hurt... (her name)!' Be adamant about it, and look cross. There is really no need to smack her – your anger and displeasure should be enough.

PLAYPENS. What about the use of playpens to harness your child? Ideally a child should not be restricted in a playpen or cot. But the ideal situation is rare, and mothers have needs of their own plus other members of the family to care for, so playpens can be useful for times when you really cannot have your child roaming at liberty. But don't use a playpen as a handy way of restricting her for extended periods. She should be exploring and experiencing, not be imprisoned behind bars.

WALKING RINGS are not a good idea although they are popular because children enjoy the mobility it gives them. Babies need to be active and use all the muscles in their bodies at this age in order to develop neurologically as well as physically. Children deprived of this exercise may have developmental problems such as lack of co-ordination and even learning problems. Walking rings are also dangerous – every year children are injured

tumbling down stairs in walking rings – and they do not encourage early walking, they also develop the wrong muscles.

Walking rings are banned in some countries and this is a strong message being sent out by those who have experience of the effect they can have on children. If you still decide to use one however, put a gate across the top of the stairs and make sure it has no sharp edges, does not pinch, and is sturdy enough not to topple over easily.

To encourage your baby in walking, rather get a sturdy trolley that she can stand against and push.

KEEP YOUR CHILD SAFE

CHILDREN SHOULD BE SEEN AND NOT HURT. Accidents are a prime cause of death in children – particularly between the ages of one and four. Even before the age of one year, there is danger if the child is mobile. Accidents usually happen at times of stress, such as the early evening when everyone is tired and hungry; when the normal routine is disturbed such as when moving house, and at weekends.

- Many accidents occur when the young child is learning to pull herself up into a standing position. She is likely to grab the edge of a tablecloth and pull whatever is on the table over her. In this way she could be severely burnt or injured by falling objects. She may also try to pull herself up onto something that can topple over when she leans against it, for instance an umbrella stand.
- As soon as they are able to crawl and climb, babies are likely to get into dangerous situations.
- Never leave a chair or stool near a window, or the railings of a balcony.
- Most accidental injuries in the home result from falls, so a reasonably tidy home is safer than an untidy one.
- Old empty refrigerators can be death traps. Keep them locked or remove the door as children love getting inside confined spaces, and many tragedies have occurred.
- Washing machines, spin dryers and automatic wringers can mangle hands and fingers.
- Electricity can be extremely dangerous. Cover all unused plug points with tape or a special plug. Never allow anyone to probe into a plughole.
- Putting young children in the care of older siblings, unless they are over the age of fifteen is dangerous. A seven, ten or even twelve year old does not have the judgment to care for a child. Drowning and falls from balconies occur frequently due to lapses in concentration or judgment.
- Make sure all cords are sound and not frayed. If the wires we visible, buy a new cord because a fire or electric shock could easily occur.

- Never allow water to run over electric wires. And do not take electrical appliances like a heater into the bathroom.
- Warn older children not to touch wires that have come down from electric poles in the street and are hanging loose.
- Lightning strikes the highest point in an area so do not shelter under a tree. Do not stand near a large expanse of water like a pond or pool. Take shelter in a car or house and if you are out in the open, crouch down near the ground and allow yourself to get wet.

CHOKING AND ASPHYXIATION

- Children love putting things into their mouths, noses and ears. Never leave marbles, pins, peanuts, small sweets or any other object a child could put into her mouth or other orifice lying around. Toys with small parts that could break off are not suitable. The eyes of dolls and Teddy bears must be sewn on not stuck on.
- Never give your baby hard fruit to eat or anything else that could break off and cause her to choke. Sweets such as jube-jubes and jelly beans are not suitable for children under two. Peanuts are also dangerous. Always keep an eye on her when she eats. Chocking is silent!
- Make sure the cot or pram has no parts on which clothes can be caught.
- Do not dress your child in clothes that have ribbons or strings in front which could be pulled or caught and drawn tight.
- Do not use a pillow or duvet in a baby's cot or pram. She will not need one for the first three years or longer.
- Never leave plastic bags lying around. A child could pull one over her head sand asphyxiate.
- Learn to do the Heimlich hug and how to treat a choking child. (*See p. 397.*)

POISONING

Household cleansers, paint stripper, pesticides, washing soda, oven cleaners and cigarettes are among the items that should be kept away from children. **Never** put paraffin, benzene, petrol or other poison into cold drink bottles, and store these products far out of reach of children. They are **NOT** put off by the smell or taste.

All medicines and poisons should be locked away. Do not keep medicines in your handbag, because children love scratching through mummy's things. When you go visiting, especially to grandparents, be aware that they may have unguarded medicines, on bedside tables for example.

- Iron tablets taken for anaemia or during pregnancy are poisonous to small children. Keep them locked away.
- Do not refer to medicine as 'sweets' to encourage children to take it.

- Boric acid is poisonous and should not be used as an antiseptic.
- Regard all plants as poisonous. Rhubarb leaves are highly poisonous, for example, as are the 'eyes' on potatoes.
- Children love to brew 'tea' from leaves. They should not drink it. For instance, the common flowering oleander bush is poisonous.
- Leaking gas stoves or cylinders are extremely dangerous. Never keep all the windows closed when using gas.
- Never sit in a car with the engine running in a closed garage. The carbon monoxide gas from the exhaust is poisonous.
- Old batteries are dangerous and contain harmful acid and lead.
- Swimming pool chemicals give off irritating and potentially dangerous fumes.
- Lead-based paint is a common cause of poisoning. Old buildings, with layers of paint going back to the days when paints commonly contained lead, are particularly dangerous. Children often pick at this flaking paint and may eat the chips because lead has a slightly sweet taste. When buying baby equipment or toys, always make sure they are painted with non-toxic paint. (See www.cspc.gov/). Lead based paint is cheaper and many countries do not have legislation against its use. You should not even breathe in the dust raised when lead-based paint is sanded.
- Pesticides are dangerous, and can have long term ill effects. Never buy unlabelled pesticides from street sellers. Regulated pesticide manufacturers will soon have to display labels that are colour coded according to their degree of danger. The message is clear: all pesticides are harmful, especially to children.
- Keep children away from anywhere pesticides are being sprayed or mixed. The poison can be breathed in or absorbed through the skin. Alternatives to the use of pesticides are a safer option. Bedbugs: wrap the mattress in plastic and put in the hot sun. Moths: Air clothes in the sun, and scatter lavender between stored clothing. Ants: Mix half vinegar and half water, and spray on ants. Cucumber peel on the window sill will help deter ants. Crushed eggshells help keep snails away.

BURNS AND SCALDS

- Most accidents that happen to children occur in the kitchen so be particularly vigilant there.
- Always turn the handles of pots inwards so that your child cannot reach them.
- Young children have been severely burned when they have turned on the hot tap in ordinary or spa baths. Never leave them unattended. Always put the cold water in first and then add hot water.
- Fires give off poisonous gases. Never leave a fire burning without opening a window slightly unless there is a chimney above the fire.

- Never place a gas cylinder on a stove or in a hot place as it could explode.
- Cover cooking fires with water not sand, as soon as you take the food off – a child could easily pick up an apparently cold piece of coal and burn herself, or walk on still hot coals if they are covered with sand.
- Teach your child that the whole of the stove area is likely to be hot. You can convey the meaning of hot by letting her feel something uncomfortably hot but obviously not hot enough to harm her.
- Steam can cause extremely painful burns. Make sure the spout of the kettle points towards a wall or away from possible contact with a child and keep the cord short.
- Primus stoves are easily knocked over. Always keep them well out of reach of children. Do not use an overly large pot on a Primus as it could easily over balance.
- All open fires and heaters should have guards. The round plastic encased heaters or oil heaters are best. Children are likely to poke sticks or pieces of metal into bar or fan heaters.
- It is extremely dangerous to hang clothes in front of a heater to dry. Hanging clothes or nappies over an asbestos heater is also dangerous.
- When buying clothes, especially nightclothes for your child, avoid highly flammable fabrics. Pure cotton, wool or mixtures are better, and pyjamas are safer than nighties.
- Matches have a fascination for many children. Keep out of their reach. Never use flammable liquid or alcohol to make braai fires burn more quickly. Many children are terribly burnt by the sudden flare, or by pouring flammable liquid on the fire.
- Many fires are started by candles falling over. But for people without electricity, or when a power cut occurs, candles are often the only answer. Light a candle safely by cutting a candle in half and standing it in a large glass jar which has been half filled with dry sand. The wick of the candle must be below the rim of the glass. This way, if the jar is knocked over the candle will go out.

SUNBURN

- Don't think children can 'take the sun' because they are young, or because they may have a dark skin – their relatively large skin surface area in relation to their weight makes them particularly vulnerable. There is a reluctance to recommend any sun exposure for children today in view of the danger of skin cancer. Although vitamin D is found in some foodstuffs, it is also made by the body through exposure to sunlight. Rickets which causes bone softening and deformities such as bow-legs is a result of a lack of vitamin D, and it is affecting children once again. Therefore, either Vitamin

D must be supplemented, or some sun exposure allowed. (*See recommendations for Vitamin D supplementation p. 148*).

- If your child is exposed to the sun – and it is recommended that babies and very young children not be exposed to direct sunlight – you must use protection.
- Always use a sunscreen cream made especially for children, and apply liberally and frequently. Do not rub the cream in; it needs to form a protective layer on the surface. Some new products will soon be brightly coloured so that you can easily see if you have not covered an area of skin. Your child should have extra fluids if she is in the sun. Tablets against sunburn are not recommended.
- Even when protected by a sunscreen, children should not be left for long periods outdoors, especially on the beach where there is reflected sunlight from sea and sand. Children should always wear a wide brimmed hat and loose cotton top. Sunburn that produces blisters can lead to a serious form of skin cancer many years later. (*See also sunstroke and heat exhaustion p. 402*).

DROWNING

- Never leave your child alone in the bath. Two-year-olds have drowned in a few centimetres of bath water even though they were capable of lifting themselves out. Children should not bath unsupervised before the age of six.
- Slipping and scalding accidents are common in the bathroom. Use a rubber mat in the bottom of the bath and always put the cold water in first. Do not let young children bath the baby.
- Children have drowned in the water in a nappy pail. Always keep it covered. Buckets and pools of water in the garden should be covered.
- Drowning accidents in swimming pools can happen within minutes. Always keep the gate locked and do not leave anything around that the child could use to climb over the fence. Make sure you always have children in sight if there is a pool, even if it is fenced.
- Even children who have been 'drown-proofed' through special instruction in infancy should not be considered pool safe. Their reaction when the real thing happens cannot be predicted.

SAFETY IN THE CAR

CARS FITTED WITH AIRBAGS IN THE FRONT. Children under 12 can be severely injured by the impact of an inflating airbag. The younger the child the more dangerous it is. They should travel in a suitable car safety device in the back seat.

It is vital that all children travelling in a car are protected from injury caused by sudden stops or impact. An unrestrained child in a motor car is like an egg in a tin can – fragile and easily crushed by any impact. Don't take chances with your child's safety. Travelling without a suitable safety device in the back of a station wagon or 'bakkie' is very dangerous. Most injuries to toddlers in car accidents are to the head – half of them fatal – while many of those who survive have permanent brain damage. So follow these guidelines for travelling safely with your child, and note that the driver of the vehicle is legally responsible for ensuring that children travelling in the car are suitably buckled up. Never leave small children alone in the car, even for a minute. Children have died of heatstroke, and others rescued just in time.

SAFETY RULES FOR TRAVELLING WITH CHILDREN.

- Never allow a child to stand on a front seat or behind the driver. Use a suitable car seat or seatbelt.
- Never put your seatbelt around yourself and your child. Should there be a crash, your force against the child will be equivalent to that of 30 adults. Never buckle two children using one seatbelt.
- An adult holding a child does not offer protection. Even at reasonably slow speeds, a 14kg child exerts a force of 445kg in the event of a sudden stop.
- Only soft toys should be allowed in the car. Pencils, sticks, metal toys and other items that could injure if the car should halt abruptly should be forbidden.
- Do not put a car seat in the front if there is an airbag, as an expanding airbag can seriously injure a small child.
- If you make it an unbreakable rule to put your baby in a car seat every time you go out she will get used to it and there should be no problems. Some children become difficult about sitting in a car seat later on, but in an area as important as this you will have to be unflinchingly firm. If you never fail to use your seatbelt you will have set a strong example and have a ready ploy to counter difficult behaviour. Remember it is up to you to make sure the rule is never broken, even if you have to stay home or leave the child behind if she will not co-operate. Say the car does not work if she is not buckled up.
- All cars the child travels in regularly should be fitted with a suitable safety device. If it is unavoidable that the child travels in a vehicle which does not have a car seat use a seat belt on the back seat. If you live near the sea check the anchor points on the car regularly for rust.
- Safety devices are made to withstand a single impact. If an accident occurs the seat should be replaced.
- Never leave groceries, tools or other items that could become lethal missiles in a sudden stop, in the car. A 500g tin of jam attains a mass of 10kg after a stop at 60km/h, enough to kill should it hit a passenger.
- Children under the age of 14 sitting in the front passenger seat are the driver's legal responsibility and she must ensure that they wear seatbelts. From the age of 14 the

onus is on the passenger to follow the regulations for wearing safety belts. However it is not a good policy for any child to sit in the front as the safety belt passes across the neck and on impact serious injury is possible.

- Safety locks on the back doors must be used.
- To keep children from becoming bored on long trips and distracting the driver, make frequent stops.
- Dried fruit or other suitable snacks can help keep them quiet.
- Take a wet cloth in a plastic bag, or wet wipes for wiping sticky hands.
- Bits of wool, crayons and drawing pad, soft doll or finger puppets can be the basis for stories and games. A CD with sing-along songs for children is a good distraction.
- A child who suffers from travel sickness is less likely to become ill if she can see out of the car window. For long trips ask your doctor or pharmacist to recommend a suitable product to prevent nausea. A light meal before leaving is better than an empty stomach and boiled sweets or plain digestive biscuits to eat in the car are fine. Take a flask of cold water or, cold fruit juice as well. Ginger is a natural remedy for nausea. Try ginger biscuits or ginger tea. Have a change of clothes and wet wipes handy.

BETWEEN BIRTH AND SIX MONTHS

- Before the child can sit, strap her carry cot (piccolo) to the back seat with a special harness as shown.
- Never place a baby in a plastic or canvas chair in the back or the front seat. A sudden stop or swerve could fling the chair forward and throw the child out.
- Babies in a car on a hot day, even with the windows open, can suffer heat stroke.
- Car seats suitable from birth to five years are available, and comply with safety requirements.

AFTER SIX MONTHS OR WHEN THE CHILD HAS A MASS OF ABOUT 9KG AND CAN SIT UNAIDED

The child should sit in a safety seat strapped to the back seat using the seat belt provided. When shopping for a car safety seat look for the following features:

- The seat should have the official government safety agency stamp of approval.
- Never use a car seat that only hooks over the seat or slides between seats. On impact it could act as a catapult or come loose.
- The 'bucket' style seat protects the head

The 'bucket' style seat protects the head and body

and body and because it is strapped using the seat belt it cannot come loose on impact.

- The buckle should be easy for an adult to manipulate but not so large that it will hurt the child.
- You should be able to fit two fingers under the harness when the child is in the seat. Adjust if necessary for thicker clothes.
- The best position for the car seat is in the centre back or diagonally behind the driver so that you can stand on the pavement side when seating the child.
- The seat should be high enough for the child to see out of the window.

This seat is slightly raised so the child can see out the window

- A sheepskin cover is comfortable and stops the seat from becoming uncomfortably hot.
- These car seats are suitable for use until the child is about four years old or has a mass of about 18kg.
- Never leave small children alone in the car, even for a minute.

SAFETY DEVICES FOR CHILDREN FROM FOUR ONWARDS OR WHEN THEY HAVE A MASS OF MORE THAN 18KG.

- The seat should have a certified government safety agency stamp of approval.
- A lap belt that has a plastic-lined table which fits over it making a surface that the child can play on, is suitable for children between the ages of four and ten years or until they attain a mass of approximately 35kg.
- A three point safety harness like that of adults is suitable for children with a mass of over 36kg. A firm cushion for the child to sit on will make her comfortable and help her to see out of the window when she is still small. However the cushion must have strong loops for the straps to pass through so that it cannot dislodge on impact as the safety belt would then be too loose and the strap would pass across her neck.

A suitable safety device for children with a mass of more than 18kg

GO TO www.baby-childcare.com TO WATCH THE FOLLOWING VIDEOS THAT ARE APPLICABLE TO CHAPTER 8

PROF CLAUDIA GRAY   Sleep in babies and children

Developmental milestones

Potty training

Bed wetting

DR NICOLA DUGMORE   Toilet training

DR ANUSHA LACHMAN   The first 1000 days of life

The role of care givers

Modern moms

Technology

Dealing with conflict

Shared pleasures

Is it okay for my child to be bored?

Toys – less or more?

ANEL ANNANDALE   Developmental delays

Reading with your child

Seperation anxiety

Understanding babies social development

What babies need in their first few months of life

Autism spectrum disorder

Single parent

The stages of play for babies

The importance of play

Developing intelligence

Difference between the adult and the child brain

DR NICOLA DUGMORE   Play

Transitional object

JOANNA WILSON   Causes of childhood overweight and obesity

Parent creating healthy homes

Responsive feeding

CHAPTER 9

The toddler and beyond

BETWEEN ONE AND TWO YEARS

AN INTRIGUING CHALLENGE. The way a child is handled, directed and allowed to interact with people and her environment during this period is of great significance to her future development.

Yet it is often a testing time for parents who are faced with the challenge of relating to a little human being who is trying to make sense of the world around her and find her place in it. Because of the inevitable conflicts that result, this period has become known as the 'terrible two's'. Yet there are ways of keeping clashes to a minimum. As always in interpersonal relationships, empathy is the key. Put yourself in the place of the child who is driven to explore… to discover. For her, nothing is a known fact, everything is possible, and her desire to experience and learn is greater now than it might ever be. She can see no reason for restraint in her headlong thrust into the wonderful world of discovery. Yet she knows she is vulnerable: that she needs adults to protect and nurture her, even though her drive for independence makes her resent it, so that in many ways she behaves like a typical teenager.

The child who has not had her needs met consistently, who does not associate her mother or primary caregiver with the relief of distress, or sees her as someone who does not generally respond to her problems positively, will not be able to cope effectively with the challenges and conflicts of the second year. Because this is the time she should be using adults as a resource, and actively enlisting their help – whether it involves her need for food or comfort or as interpreters of the world around her and guides to her place in it.

How the adults, particularly the primary caregiver in her life, meet these needs will colour her nature indelibly. In fact, neurons and synapses – the connecting wiring in the brain – is formed as a result of emotional conditioning and learning. So it is not only academic learning that is contained by the brain, but actual emotional responses.

If she has learnt through past experience that help is not forthcoming within a reasonable time of sending out a distress signal, she will have a distorted idea of how to gain the necessary attention. The baby who has been left to cry unheeded until she finally falls asleep from exhaustion, the infant who was made to wait when hunger signalled, will not see her caregiver as a sympathetic, powerful force.

Supposing you have come through the first year and satisfied your baby's needs to the best of your ability, but now she is showing signs of having a will of her own you are unsure of what line to take. Uncertainty is understandable when you consider that caring for a child between the ages of one and two is a challenge that would test the mettle of the most competent executive, because it requires emotional maturity, insight, foresight, stamina and managerial skills of the highest order.

To form a basis for your strategy you need to know something about the characteristics of children at this age.

UPWARDLY MOBILE. By 13 months most children are starting to take their first steps alone, and even late starters should be on their way not much later than 18 months. But from whatever time the child acquires the ability to move about in an upright position, she is likely to be in almost perpetual motion... it is an intensely physical stage. She needs the opportunity to move in space, to climb, to manipulate. Changing a nappy requires a contortionist's skill as she wriggles and kicks and rolls away...

You will have to out-manoeuvre her by using tactical ploys. Keep a few tempting toys or even a bell near her nappies and whisk one out as you start changing her – it should keep her relatively immobile for a few minutes – then put the toy away until next time.

Pent-up physical energy, especially in boys, needs to be expended. If you do not have the space at home, take a trip to the park and let your child run loose. It is also a chance for you to get to know other mothers and caregivers in your position, exchange ideas and make sympathetic noises. Informal meetings like these have been the start of successful groups that have given housebound mothers the opportunity to enjoy adult company and get a break from the demands of motherhood. For mothers and fathers who work outside the home it's a chance to touch base and tune in to neighbourhood norms.

During the first half of the second year your baby will still spend a lot of time examining things although she will not always automatically put them into her mouth as she did in the first year.

For healthy development at this stage a child needs the opportunity to explore her environment. She needs to touch and take apart and manipulate. She needs as free a rein as possible and should not be trapped in a playpen or other confined space. To keep her occupied while you work in the kitchen, empty a low cupboard and stock it with the kind of play materials children relish: light containers of various sizes, to stack into each other, boxes to pile up in towers, beans to rattle in a tightly closed tin, a bunch of old keys, a box with shapes cut out of the lid and things to drop through – anything and everything as long as it is not dangerous. Expensive equipment is the last thing your baby needs. Pots and pans are far more informative and fun. But you are still her best educational toy. Talk to your baby.

Give her things to feel: a piece of ice, a ball of wool, the roughness of sandpaper. Describe what they are, then play a game asking her to show you what is soft, or blue, or cold or whatever you have been explaining.

Remember it is a game and that your baby will have an attention span of only a few minutes. It is not a test and if you cannot do it in a relaxed way, leave it alone.

You can buy her a cloth book or one with stiff cardboard pages and clear pictures. Or you can make a book out of felt, sewing brightly coloured shapes such as circles, triangles, squares, fruit or anything simple onto the 'pages'. Join them by stitching down one side.

Water play is always a great favourite, especially from a year onwards. Even if you do not have a garden you can probably find a suitable place to put a basin of water with a few kitchen utensils for pouring.

For outings with your child when you will have to spend time waiting, for instance, a visit to the doctor's surgery or hospital clinic, a doll, a car, a few blocks, a light ball, a book or any other plaything your child enjoys, can be a boon.

Besides her newly acquired mobility and her physical discovery of the world around her, the toddler has to learn to cope with the social structure of civilised living.

She is no longer the helpless centre of her universe; she has become a separate entity, a transition that is both fascinating and frightening. How she finds her place in the new world depends a good deal on her inner resources and on the guidance she gets.

Her mother, or her primary caregiver, has the task of helping her find the order of things in her new situation, as she alternates between asserting independence and clinging to the security of babyhood. Sadly, some children never resolve the conflicts of this stage adequately but carry them into adulthood, with unhappy consequences for themselves and others. To help bring order into this state of flux she needs a steady, unambiguous source of security and guidance.

THE 'TERRIBLE TWO'S'. A crisis point in this period usually arises when the child starts to assert her will. Suddenly she seems to want her own way all the time, no matter how unreasonable her desire. Tantrums and negative behaviour could shake your confidence and confuse you.

If you take the heavy-handed 'I'm the boss and you'll do as I say' approach at this stage, backing it up with force whenever you have a clash of wills you may eventually get your child to submit through fear. But one of the things wrong with this approach is that she will eventually grow too big for you to exert your physical influence over her to any effect; and more importantly, she will not develop a healthy self-image, or believe that she can control her own behaviour without fear of punishment. After all, it is self-control you are trying to teach her, not merely that she can be controlled by someone else.

Should your child then be allowed to do as she pleases in the hope that she will eventually resolve her conflicts and learn acceptable behaviour? Certainly not; this would be an abdication of your moral duty and a grave disservice to her.

Whatever happens, you are the final authority in her life, and she should know that no matter how the skirmishes go, you are ultimately in control.

Her behaviour may appear to contradict it, but a little child is terribly afraid that the whole world will go out of control when she does. She needs to know that you are there to put it all together again – that you may reject her behaviour but you are not rejecting her and never will.

HOW TO HANDLE CONFLICTS

- Have as few rules as possible. Stick to the necessary rules consistently.
- Like all people who do not have a secure sense of self, she is very touchy. Don't be bossy, don't put her into situations in which she will 'lose face' by complying.
- Don't look for a fight. This means you shouldn't give too many orders that can be

diseobeyed. For example, you are going out and you tell her to get ready. She refuses, or she decides she doesn't want to wear the shoes you have chosen, or she doesn't like the dress you have put out. Try to circumvent potential flash points like this by simply dressing her without reference to what you are doing, chatting all the while about something else. It won't always work – when a toddler decides to exert her will, she will find almost anything as an excuse – but you can usually handle it better if you expect it and understand that it is a phase of development.

- Before you say no, stop to think if you really mean it. Is it really worth taking a stand on the issue? If not, don't say no. But if you mean it, stick to it and carry it through no matter what diversions crop up. Giving in after she has thrown a tantrum is the worst thing you can do.
- If saying no does not stop the activity; take her away from it physically, instantly. Do it every time. No matter what. If she kicks, restrain her and do not be side-tracked by the fact that you are in a public place or the telephone is ringing or you happen to be drying your hair.
- The sooner she gets the message that you will not tolerate these tactics the sooner she will give them up.
- Your tone of voice is a powerful tool in getting the message through. Use emphasis, not shouting. Children, like most people become deaf to shouting.
- Distraction is still effective in deflecting conflict. Use it.

Don't always expect a young child to comply with your wishes simply because what she is doing is inconvenient or distracting to you. Any child under the age of two is inconvenient and distracting. Her attention span is short, her need for gratification urgent; if she wants to show you something, it is easier to stop what you are doing and attend to her than have her nagging on until you get around to it. It will not be too long (by the third year) before she can conceptualise what 'later' means and she can be expected to wait a little for her needs to be attended to. It is a characteristic of all children to develop an urgent need to hang around their mother as soon as she has guests or becomes preoccupied with something. They simply don't want to share you with anything or anybody. But you will not help matters by shooing her away. You can expect her to be reasonably quiet and not to distract you deliberately without cause; but it is very hard for her to do in the beginning because she desperately needs you to acknowledge her. Unless you lock her away she is going to find some way of getting your attention. And it is usually by doing something 'naughty' so that you are sure to react. Being yelled at or smacked is better than being ignored, in her eyes. So rather include her naturally – let her sit on your lap – give her a reassuring squeeze and a word of interest even if you have company or are busy. She will grow out of the intense need much sooner than if you force her out now.

The lives of many adults are complicated by their need to be the centre of attention and the fact that they become unhappy if their partner does not focus all his or her attention on them all the time. Because the need was not satisfied at an early age and sound self-esteem developed, their emotional insecurity drives them to demand reassurance all the time.

CHANGES IN THE ROUTINE BETWEEN ONE AND TWO

A TIME OF FLUX. Instead of having two naps a day she may only be willing to go down for one, with a stage in between when two naps are too many and one not enough, making her ratty and difficult until she adjusts to the new cycle.

Her eating habits should be more adult now with three meals a day and two snacks in-between. And most likely a bedtime bottle or breast feed. She may need a bottle before her nap, but she should be able to drink out of a cup as well. A lot of children become fiercely attached to their bottle at this stage and are seen trailing it everywhere. It is important to remember that sucking is a pleasurable and comforting habit to a baby and it may have to be continued for a long time before the need is overcome. If she drinks too much juice or milk however, it will spoil her appetite for solids and she could even become malnourished or anaemic.

Some children become attached to a blanket or soft toy they carry around with them and refuse to part with it no matter how grubby it gets. There is no real evidence to prove that this is a bad thing and you will just have to take comfort from the fact that she will eventually give it up.

Don't try to make her grow up too soon. This is often the case if she is physically big for her age, or there is another child on the way and you want to get her over babyhood before the other child is born. Pressuring her is sure to have the opposite effect. It will make her seek the comfort of her bottle or dummy or 'doodoo' even more.

The baby who is constantly drinking from a bottle is looking for security and comfort. Try and discover why this is and rectify the situation if possible.

Is she getting enough stimulation? Are there enough interesting things to do? Is she talked to, played with, hugged and loved? Is she under too much stress in the form of constant brakes on her behaviour? Is she expected to behave in a way that is not appropriate to her age?

There is no harm in letting your child have an occasional bottle if she needs it, as long as it does not become her only source of comfort. By the time she really starts to mix with other children at around three she is unlikely to want to be different or thought a baby. Peer group influence will be far stronger than anything you say in making her give up babyish things.

A BALANCED DIET FOR TODDLERS

Without a balanced diet a child will not get the wide range of nutrients necessary for proper growth and development, and deficiency states of varying degrees of seriousness can result. When assessing whether a child is growing satisfactorily, you must take several factors into account. The sex of the child, the build of the parents and whether the child's height is right for her age given the genetic factors involved. Consult your clinic or Road to Health Card/Growth Chart for more information on the mass variables which are within the normal range.

Boys: *Average mass*
12 months –10kg
18 months – 11.4kg
24 months – 12.6kg
36 months –16kg

Boys: *Average height*
76cm
82cm
87cm
96cm

Girls: *Average mass*
12 months – 9.4kg
18 months – 10.8kg
24 months –12kg
36 months –14kg

Girls: *Average height*
75cm
81cm
86cm
95cm

A BALANCED DIET. For a balanced diet your child needs foodstuffs from the three main food groups plus milk. That is proteins; carbohydrates and fats; vitamins and minerals; plus milk. (*See p. 204 for Vegetarian needs.*)

PROTEINS (body-building foods). Food containing protein is most important in a child's life because it is essential for proper growth and the development of all parts of the body including the brain. A lack of protein and energy foods in childhood can result in under weight and lack of height, to the extremes of kwashiorkor and marasmus.

First class proteins, which is protein that contains all the essential amino acids for healthy growth are obtained from animal sources like lamb, beef, veal, chicken, fish, eggs, cheese, milk and other dairy products. These are called complete proteins because they contain all the amino acids. Incomplete proteins (so-called because they do not contain the full range of necessary amino acids) are cheaper and are found in vegetable sources like dried peas, beans, lentils and nuts. When beans and samp are eaten at the same meal the combination of amino acids is almost complete. Soya beans are a single vegetable source of complete protein. Both vegetable and meat sources of protein should be included in the diet, but children in particular need the complete protein found in animal sources to grow well.

CARBOHYDRATES (energy-giving foods). These foods produce energy and heat. They consist of starches, sugars and cellulose and are found in potatoes and most other root vegetables, cereals, bread (brown, or enriched white is best, whole-wheat has too much fibre and white has too few vitamins unless it has been enriched (check the label), samp, mealiemeel (maize meal), rice, honey, jam, pasta, sucrose (table sugar) and fruit. Carbohydrates and fats are essential to provide sufficient energy for the growing child, and should make up more than fifty percent of the daily diet.

FATS (energy giving foods). Fats are the most highly concentrated source of energy. They supply vitamins A, E and D and are the only source of essential fatty acids. Fats are found mainly in butter, oil, margarine, full cream milk, full fat yogurts, full fat cheese, nuts and meat and oily fish. They add flavour and richness to food.

Do not cut fats out of your child's diet in the belief that this will protect your child against obesity or heart disease unless you have been advised to do this by your doctor. (*See p. 256 Differences between adult and infant nutritional needs.*)

VITAMINS AND MINERALS (protective foods). Fruits and vegetables are an excellent source of minerals and vitamins and should be part of your daily diet as they are needed for the proper utilisation and absorption of foodstuffs and the prevention of deficiency states such as scurvy, beriberi and rickets. A wide variety of fresh fruits and vegetables are needed to provide the various vitamins and minerals not found in other sources. Yellow and dark green vegetables are the most important sources of vitamins and you should try and include servings from each group every day.

Fresh fruit is also a good source of vitamins. Fruits and vegetables also contain fibre (cellulose) which provides bulk and helps prevent constipation. At least one fruit or vegetable should be eaten raw and one should contain vitamin C, or fruit juice enriched with vitamin C should be given. Freshly pressed fruit and vegetable juices taste good and are a source of vitamins and minerals.

IRON, A VITAL ELEMENT. Iron deficiency is the most common nutritional lack in children worldwide and can have serious consequences for mental and physical development. Iron deficiency can result in poor learning capacity and decreased resistance to infection. Iron deficient (anaemic) children are likely to have a poor appetite, be irritable and may be inclined to pica (the eating of substances not normally eaten, like sand). The best sources of iron are meat, especially liver, chicken, fish, eggs, iron enriched baby cereals, and dark green leafy vegetables.

The iron in meat is the most fully absorbed by the body, while the iron in egg yolk is not well absorbed. The tannin in tea (to a lesser extent in Rooibos) hinders the absorption of iron, while calcium, which is found in large quantities in milk also hinders the absorption of iron.

Iron enriched infant cereals are a good source of iron especially if you mix them with vitamin C enriched fruit juice or fruit. This makes the iron three to four times better absorbed. Eight level tablespoons iron-enriched infant cereal (measured dry) will provide 90% of a toddler's daily iron needs.

Besides dietary sources, iron is available as a supplement or as part of a vitamin and iron preparation. Children should not be given iron supplements without a doctor's supervision.

MILK. Milk provides protein, fats, vitamins and minerals, of which calcium is the most important as it is not easily obtained from other sources. From the age of a year children need 500ml milk in 24 hours. More than this will spoil the appetite for other foods which are essential for a balanced diet. Too much fresh cow's milk can also result in gastric bleeding which can contribute to anaemia. Do not give your child 2% or skim milk before the age of two as she needs the kilojoules and the vitamins in full cream milk. Vitamin D is found in cow's milk and fortified margarine. It is necessary to prevent rickets. Coffee creamers are not made from milk and should never be used for children. Do not give milk less than an hour and a half before the next meal as it will spoil her appetite.

HOW MUCH TO GIVE. The amount of food toddlers need depends on their metabolism, mass and activity level. As growth slows down in the second year children need proportionately less food than before, although their protein needs become greater.

This slowing down of food intake can sometimes cause undue anxiety on the part of parents to whom it appears that their child is eating far less than before. Toddlers need three meals a day plus two nutritious snacks and 400–500ml milk. Keep in mind that children's appetites, like those of adults vary from day to day.

Serving sizes: Use the following as a general guide. Think in terms of serving portions as being one tablespoon for each year of the child's age. Thus, for a one year old, one portion would be one tablespoonful. For a two year old a portion would be two tablespoonfuls and so on.

Your toddler needs a minimum of six portions of carbohydrate foods, three portions of vegetables, two of fruits and two of protein every day. You can divide these portions into three meals a day plus two snacks and 500ml milk. Select from the various foods mentioned under the food group headings.

ENRICHING STAPLE FOODS.

A one year old would have to eat 10 cups of soft maize (corn) meal (mielie meel) porridge a day in order to meet her energy requirements. Clearly this would not be possible given her limited stomach capacity. You can double the protein and energy value of maize meal (mielie meel) in the following way:

- 1 cup maize meal (mielie meel porridge)
- 2 teaspoons full cream milk powder
- 1 teaspoon sunflower oil, butter or margarine
- 1 teaspoon sugar

If she is not allergic to it, vary by adding a teaspoon of smooth peanut butter instead of oil.

FEEDING PROBLEMS IN THE TODDLER

WHEN 'SHE DOESN'T EAT A THING'. Eating habits and the amount of food children have during the second year often become a source of conflict and worry for parents. While you should not become obsessive about your child's food intake, more is needed than to simply leave the child to eat 'when she's hungry'.

CAUSES OF POOR APPETITE

TOO MUCH MILK OR JUICE. Very often, this is how things go wrong. During the second year the toddler faces many new challenges. She is becoming mobile, so she touches things and gets hurt frequently. She also wants her own way which is not always possible. Then she wants to be able to do things for which she is not yet developmentally ready. She may be in a crèche, or her mother may be expecting another baby. Infections are more common and frustration is a frequent occurrence. As a result she resorts to breast feeding or sucking on a bottle for comfort a lot of the time.

The milk, tea or juice she has taken this way is enough to spoil her appetite for solids and is also likely to result in anaemia. This makes her crabby, clingy and difficult. Anaemia which results from poor eating habits also spoils the appetite so the vicious cycle is perpetuated.

If your child is having over 500ml milk in 24 hours reduce it by cutting down on the amount, or if she demands the bottle for comfort, mix the milk with water to 'stretch' it. Do the same with juice, which should not be given from a bottle if possible, as taken in this way, it can seriously damage teeth. Too much juice especially that sweetened with artificial sweeteners can result in what is known as 'toddler's diarrhoea'.

Tea, coffee and cola drinks should never be given to toddlers as they do not have nutritional value and contain stimulants which will hype the child up and keep her awake. Rooibos tea does not contain stimulants but has very little real food value, and sucking on a bottle of milky or black Rooibos tea all day will spoil the appetite.

Breastfeeding is more difficult to cut down on, but you will have to be firm and try and use other methods like distraction to keep your child from demanding it so often.

In all cases where a toddler is demanding the comfort of the breast or the bottle for a large part of the day you should look at why she needs this therapy and try and eliminate the need for it as much as possible.

NOTE: Children who seem to be thirsty all the time and drink a vast amount of liquids may have a medical problem and should be examined.

SUITABLE SNACKS. Children who are fed biscuits or sweets whenever they niggle will not feel hungry enough to eat suitable food. Sugary snacks which do not contain other nutrients satisfy the child's appestat (the centre in the brain which controls appetite) so the child does not feel hungry even though her nutritional needs have not been met.

BEHAVIOURAL PROBLEMS RESULTING FROM POOR EATING PATTERNS. Difficult behaviour often has a scenario that goes something like this. The child picks at her midday meal, and then the mother takes her out, perhaps to visit friends. During the afternoon the child begins niggling and whining, and the mother keeps her quiet by feeding her biscuits and the odd sweets. By late afternoon she is totally out of control, crabby and impossible to handle. She is tired and her mother is at the end of her tether too. The child refuses supper because the biscuits have spoilt her appetite and by the time she is put to bed everyone is in a bad temper and exhausted, yet she wakes frequently during the night.

What the mother should have done is given suitable snacks like cheese, a tub of fruit yogurt, a few slices of cold cut meat, a hard boiled egg, a milk pudding, fruit juice or even a peanut butter sandwich, instead of biscuits and sweets.

This will provide her body with protein and fat instead of carbohydrate and sugar which is quickly burnt up resulting in hypoglycaemia or low blood sugar. Blood sugar levels remain constant longer when they are derived from complex carbohydrates, protein and fat instead of fluctuating as they do when you eat foods rich in sugar and little other nourishment. A fall in blood sugar levels can cause faintness, restlessness, agitation, headache and outbursts of temper. If your child has been described as hyperactive it is a good idea to look to her diet for possible reasons for her behaviour.

ANAEMIA. If your child has been eating poorly, have a haemoglobin test done by your doctor. This is a simple test, done in the surgery and will determine what her iron status is. If she is anaemic, the doctor will prescribe the necessary iron medication. Do not give it with milk, but preferably with a meat meal or with vitamin C rich fruit or juice so that it can be well absorbed. Iron can make the stools black, but this is of no consequence. If it makes her nauseous give it at bedtime.

WORMS. You should also deworm your child if she has a poor appetite even if you have never seen her pass worms. Pinworms are all but invisible and are extremely common in all preschool children, as are roundworms and other types. They can cause anaemia, poor appetite and general ill health. Ask your doctor or pharmacist to recommend a broad spectrum anti-worm preparation and dose your child (and the rest of the family) regularly. *See p. 369-374 parasitic infections.*

EMOTIONAL FACTORS. If eating has become imbued with meaning other than that of a simple, enjoyable function, it could become a setting for manipulation on both sides. Right from the start, feed your child placidly and pleasantly even though it is very hard to grin and bear it when she clamps her mouth shut after you have lovingly prepared a meal for her. Take the food away without further comment when she has had enough. Serve small amounts; you can always give more if necessary.

WANTING TO FEED HERSELF. Children with a mind of their own can become very resistant to being fed. This makes for a fight at every feed with no one getting anywhere. Trying to feed herself is a sign of good development and you must encourage it even if it makes for a lot of mess in the beginning. Put newspaper under her chair and give her a spoon. Let her 'feed' herself while you slip in the bulk of the food. Also, let her have 'finger' foods that she can pick up and eat by herself like pieces of chicken, hard cooked egg, little sandwiches and the like.

BOREDOM WITH THE MENU. Children's tastes change and develop in the second year and they may reject foods they previously enjoyed. If you have been making her food 'baby' bland, try a more savoury flavour.

On the other hand toddlers sometimes develop a craze for certain foods. As long as it is not junk food let them go on eating it. On other occasions they may refuse food they used to enjoy. Don't fuss, forget it until later. There is sure to be a substitute for it. It is true however, that it can take up to thirty attempts to introduce a new food to a toddler, so don't give up, but don't force either. Being offered it at a friend's house often does the trick. The rejection of milk and how to substitute for it is discussed on *p.206.*

Remember that most children take years to acquire a taste for strong or highly flavoured foods, such as cabbage, Brussels sprouts, liver and kidneys. Forcing them on her will not make her like them (just as forcing him to eat broccoli in childhood made George Bush, former President of the United States, ban it from the White House). A pity, as broccoli is probably the most valuable of all vegetables, as it is a source of many important vitamins and has been shown to aid in the prevention of cancer.

MANIPULATION. The toddler who develops likes and dislikes daily according to whim and who is rude about the food she gets should be firmly disciplined right from the start. A mother will soon learn when her child is 'trying it on' and she should nip it firmly in the bud even to the extent of removing the whole plate of food without comment and resisting all pleas for snacks in between. It takes more than a few hours without food for a child to starve!

JUNK FOOD SPOILS THE APPETITE. Giving children chips, sweets and fizzy drinks is a sure way to spoil the appetite for healthy food, and it puts them off fruits and vegetables which should be an enjoyable part of the diet. Obesity and type 2 diabetes is affecting children at an ever younger age and this is a result of poor choices in what they eat.

REFUSING HOME COOKED FOOD. Some children get so used to the taste of bottled baby foods that they refuse home cooked food. Simply mix a small amount of home cooked food – for example mashed potato – into the bought baby food, gradually increasing the amount and variety of home cooked food you add until she accepts it plain.

READY MADE TODDLER FOODS. Fresh, cooked toddler meals are available from major supermarkets. They taste good and are nutritious. They are expensive, but can be a boon when you are under pressure.

ILLNESS. During an illness most children go off their food. Offer light, small, attractive meals. Semi-liquid foods like milkshakes, banana, or other fruit shakes, or high energy drinks to help supply the necessary nutrients. Once the child is feeling better try and encourage extra food intake without pressurising her. Your doctor may prescribe a special high nutrient milk.

Give a vitamin and mineral supplement and include dark green and yellow vegetables, as well as milk, liver and eggs in the diet for their vitamin A content which has been shown to help recovery from illness.

EMOTIONAL ISSUES. Puddings, cakes and sweets come to have great significance if they are soon as rewards or are totally forbidden. If they are not made to seem 'special' they will have a natural place in the child's eating habits, not an over-emphasised, out-of-proportion attraction. (This does not mean they should be offered routinely since they are not necessary to the diet.) Similarly, parents who never allow their children sweets, white bread or other 'unhealthy' foods run the risk of making these items emotionally charged and more attractive than necessary.

In the same way, eating all her food does not make her a 'good girl'; nor does not eating it make her a 'bad' girl. Food should not be confused with moral issues. A sense of balance and proportion is needed. Just because a child has not developed a taste for something early on does not mean she will never like it.

Most adults were not exposed to smoked salmon, caviar, or olives in childhood yet they seem to acquire a taste for them without much trouble. If you have remained neutral about the attributes of food, for instance by not coaxing her to eat 'nasty', but 'good for you' foods, she will probably take to them of her own accord.

REJECTING COARSE FOODS. Occasionally a child will reach the second year and refuse food unless it is pureed. The reason for this probably lies in the late introduction of coarse food into the child's diet. (Start at six or seven months with food that is rougher, gradually making it coarser.)

Allowing the child to eat softer foods with her fingers or feed herself with a spoon is usually a good way of getting over this.

Some children who are unable to eat coarser textures have a developmental problem and should be medically assessed.

DIFFERENCES BETWEEN ADULT AND INFANT NUTRITIONAL REQUIREMENTS

CHILDREN ARE NOT LITTLE ADULTS. With greater awareness of healthy eating many mothers are transferring recommendations made for adults directly to their infants. Eliminate salt, sugar, cholesterol and fat as much as possible, and add fibre while cutting down on snacks between meals is a fine dictum for adults but not for children.

Unlike adults, children need concentrated sources of protein and energy foods because of their rapid growth and small stomachs – babies triple their birth weight in the first year – and to do this they need frequent high-kilojoule feeds. Fats and sugars are concentrated sources of kilojoules and should not be eliminated from a baby's diet altogether. Do not give 2% or skim milk to a child under the age of two, and avoid foods that are high in fibre as these are often low in nutrients, and can also hinder their absorption. It used to be recommended that children have no salt in their diets as a way of preventing high blood pressure later on. This has now been discounted as a factor.

Moderate amounts of salt should not be eliminated from a baby's diet altogether as it is needed to replace sodium lost through sweating. Unless advised against it by your doctor cholesterol containing foods like eggs need not be restricted.

Children need three main meals a day plus two suitable snacks, so eating between meals should not be discouraged.

FOOLING THE FADDY FEEDER

TRICK OR TREAT. When feeding your toddler has become a case of more whine than dine – try these tricks. And by the way, the only time you should ask your child what they would like to eat, is when they're buying!

VEGETABLES. Instead of boiled vegetables which most children dislike, try stir frying by cutting any vegetable into matchstick size pieces. Cover the bottom of a heavy based pan with a little oil and cook for a few minutes stirring all the time. Sprinkle with toasted sesame seeds, sunflower seeds or crushed nuts for extra nutrition and flavour.

FOR THE EXTRA FADDY. Cut raw vegetables (all kinds except potatoes) into matchstick size pieces (crudités). Put the different colours into separate compartments of a bright plastic barbecue plate and add a dollop of cream cheese in the middle. Let the child eat by herself dipping the vegetable pieces into the cream cheese. To vary you can flavour the cheese with avocado, fried chipped beef, bacon, spring onions, etc. If she likes a sweet taste mash in a ripe banana, add a teaspoon of peanut butter, or grate apple into it. Add a little lemon when using avocado, apple or banana to stop it discolouring. Dipping an unpeeled avocado in boiling water also works.

The variations are endless and you can make it into a learning event by teaching her the various colours of the vegetables. Fruit is also good like this. Always keep an eye on her in case of choking. If you're not a purist you can let her watch TV or read her a story while eating this way.

You can also disguise vegetables by grating them into a good chicken stock and simmer for a few minutes. Thicken with flour, pea flour, pasta or rice. You can make this soup with a milk base as well.

FOR THOSE WHO HATE EGGS. French toast tastes good and has lots of concentrated kilojoules. Beat an egg. Soak enriched white bread in it until all the egg has been absorbed. Fry in a little butter or margarine until golden on both sides. Sprinkle with brown sugar or golden syrup and cinnamon. Cut into fingers and serve warm.

During cooking mix scrambled eggs with cheese, tomato, spring onions, thinly sliced uncooked spinach, chipped beef or unsmoked bacon, cooked flaked fish, alone or in combination.

Omelette 'Swiss roll'. Make an omelette without salt and pepper. Spread with jam, peanut butter, cheese, avocado or anything else she might fancy. Roll like a Swiss roll and cut into pinwheels.

Beat an egg, add a little grated cheese and thicken with a little dry baby cereal. Season. Spread on bread and grill in the oven.

SUPPER SPECIAL. Slice ripe bananas lengthwise and fry in butter until soft and sticky. Contains plenty of potassium which is needed after a bout of diarrhoea.

'NURSERY FOOD.' Strong men have been known to go weak at the knees with sentiment when it comes to food that brings back memories of mummy or nanny ministering to their little boy needs. Such food is cottage pie. Sauté minced meat and diced onions until brown, add tomato paste or sauce, or a little beef stock. Thicken with cornflower. Top with mashed potato to which a beaten egg has been added. If she hates vegetables you can slip a few peas or grated carrot into the mince mixture. Bake until golden brown.

WON'T DRINK MILK. Add a tablespoon of dry milk powder to soups, stews, anything. Grate cheese over everything.

WON'T EAT MEAT. Make tiny meat balls, roll lightly in flour, fry in a little sunflower or canola seed oil. Spaghetti bolognaise is usually a favourite (add chopped carrots and celery to get in more vegetables). Biltong is an expensive but concentrated source of red meat protein.

MULTIVITAMINS. If you are at all concerned regarding your child's diet, get a multivitamin preparation recommended by your doctor or pharmacist. Omega 3 fatty acids are also desirable as they help brain functioning and may help conditions such as hyperactivity. They are found in oily fish such as salmon, cod liver oil, walnuts, flaxseeds, tofu, cauliflower and broccoli. As these are unlikely to be regular part of a child's diet, use a supplement if your doctor agrees. Omega 3 capsules should be packaged in dark containers.

TOILET TRAINING WITHOUT TEARS

FLUSH WITH SUCCESS. Another area that causes parents great concern is toilet training. Yet, unless there is something wrong with the child they all achieve control eventually, so there is really no need to put so much emotional energy into it.

To become toilet trained a child must have developed enough control over the muscles that contract the sphincter. This enables her to hold the urine in the bladder until the bladder is full, and then release it at will. This ability requires physical maturation. Just as the ability to control the muscles that hold a pen for writing develop only after several years, so control of the sphincter needs time.

Like eating, excreting is a natural bodily function and it should not assume significance beyond that. But for some odd reason, mothers often race to beat the neighbour's child in using the potty. This should only be an event of any significance if it is a milestone in the development of a disabled child. Of course a child who is out of nappies is less work and expense, but to go to the lengths some mothers do to get there is more effort.

Once again it is an area where the normal child will soon sense her power over her mother. It does not take much to feel negative vibes in a mother who is anxious about an aspect of her child's routine and it makes a perfect practice ground for the toddler who is trying to assert herself! But don't get involved in this battle of wits. Rather use your energy in a positive way by helping your child to discover the world around her. Besides, the battle of the pot can cause psychological damage that will need many hours on a psychiatrist's couch in 30 years' time to sort out. Wait until she is ready – sometime around her second birthday – then try using the same philosophy you would when training a puppy (don't rub her nose in it!) – just remember that while it may seem that she will never get the hang of it, they all do eventually.

It is also true that leaving potty training too late, that is, past the stage of the first awareness of being wet (usually between 22-24 months), can drag the whole process out too long and you hit the same kind of resistance as you do in other developmental stages that are missed.

CATCH 22. Forget anything you have been told about babies who were trained before their first birthday. The fact is, if you spent a good deal of your time putting a potty under a baby you would be bound to 'catch' a stool or a flow of urine. This does not mean your baby is potty trained. Others will talk of 'training' their baby at 13 months or so. They may also be spending a lot of time with a potty in their hand and this may coincide with the passing of waste matter. But there is still no conscious control by the child.

Occasionally, a child may get the hang of it around 18 months. But the incidence of regression in children who have been 'trained' at this age is extremely high and the problems encountered in teaching them again when they are older are so numerous that I can see no reason to even attempt it. By the age of two your toddler will be able to understand most of what is being said and will be able to say enough to express the basics. She may also start indicating when she has a soiled nappy. This would be a good time to start potty training. Fads and fashions in potty training come and go! 'How to train your child in a week, a day, etc.' Avoid them. Take your time and do it naturally, normally and calmly and your child will be trained in a sound way that should not leave any scars on either of you. After all you don't learn to drive a car in a day. It takes patience, sensible teaching and time.

Learning in any sphere depends a lot on imitation, so if you can, let your child see a trained child who uses a potty confidently and without fuss.

EQUIPMENT. There are several types of training potties available. The simplest is a small plastic pot with a handle. Others have a pot that slides into the bottom of a small chair; some are shaped like a swan or a car or other novelty. Another kind fits onto the adult toilet seat. In the end, like driving, it doesn't matter what model car you are using, so I see no reason for not using the plainest, cheapest potty. You may be tempted to buy something fancy in the hope that it will 'do the trick' and get the child to sit, but it does not usually work.

Whatever equipment you use the principle is the same, although trying to train a child straight onto an adult-size toilet can be a little frightening for her as she may be afraid of falling in. The trainers that fit onto the adult toilet seat are also not very satisfactory because the child's legs do not touch the ground. The flow directors like the ones for boys can cause injury. In both cases put a box or something firm under her feet so that she can sit securely. If you have managed to expose your child, so to speak, to what sitting on a toilet is all about by letting her see another child in action, you can coax her to try it too. Choose a time when she is likely to have a full bladder about an hour or a little longer after a drink.

Sit her down and encourage her to do a 'wee wee' or whatever name you have for it. If you are in the bathroom, you can open a tap – the sound of running water usually has the effect of encouraging a complementary flow. If she is sitting happily you can chat to her, but do not distract her too much or she will simply forget what she is supposed to do and get up. Remind her now and again what she is supposed to be doing. If after a time (before your patience begins to run out) nothing has happened, take her off, replace her nappy and say something about 'doing it next time'. The minute her nappy is on again she will probably wet it. Grin and bear it and try for success another time.

On the other hand you may have a jack-in-the-box to contend with. Some children shoot up as fast as you sit them down on the potty. If after some coaxing and repeated tries you have no luck in getting her to sit, you will have to put the potty away for a week or two. If the weather is hot, let her play in the garden without a nappy or pants.

Once she connects the feeling of a full bladder with what happens when she lets go, you will be on your way and this is far easier once she has actually seen a flow of urine without a nappy on.

When she appears to have some awareness of an impending flow of urine – which you will usually recognise by the fact that she 'pinches' her legs together for a second or two before letting go – you can put her in training pants. These have a thick towelling gusset, sometimes with a plastic lining. They don't prevent much mess, but they are quicker to pull down than a nappy, unless you are using the special potty training disposables.

Some children achieve bowel control before bladder control, especially if they have a regular pattern of elimination. Babies have been known to put faeces in their mouth, but even though it may take you a while to recover, your child is unlikely to suffer any ill effects. On the other hand, some toddlers become alarmed at leaving part of themselves behind, so you may have to dispose of it while she is not looking. Flushing the toilet can frighten a child, so unless she shows no fear when you do it, leave the flush until she is out of earshot.

Remember to wipe her from the front towards the back. Germs from the anus can easily enter the urethra or vagina and cause an infection if you do it the other way. Washing hands as a hygienic habit should be taught from the start, but there is no need to make out that excretion is a dirty and distasteful business.

Whatever you do, try to keep the whole thing light and relaxed. You would hate to be taught to drive a car by someone who is terribly tense about it so do not inflict powerful pressure on your child.

Be enthusiastic about her successes and stay calm when accidents happen. Initially you will have to let her wear nappies when going out and in the areas of the house where you do not want to get the carpet wet. Incidentally, if you pour club soda water on a urine patch immediately, it should prevent staining and odour. Or use one of the sprays you get from pet shops to neutralise doggy odours.

Going out with a partially trained child can be tricky since you cannot put her on the potty in the middle of a supermarket. I would let her wear a nappy, or pull up disposable, on these occasions, putting it on without comment, so that you can both relax about the possibility of an accident. If you are going to friends where she can use a potty, take it with you and carry on as usual. Occasionally a sensitive child will become mortified if she has an accident even if you don't fuss. It is important to maintain her confidence and dignity, so play it cool and rather err on the side of letting her wear a nappy too often and take it very slowly, than risk regression due to a wounded ego.

NIGHT-TIME CONTROL. Night-time control usually comes much later and you will save everyone, especially yourself, a lot of lost sleep if you do not try to achieve it too soon. To be able to go through the night without voiding, the bladder needs to be able to hold the liquid that accumulates. More importantly, an anti-diuretic hormone which slows down the production of urine at night needs to be secreted. This happens later in some children. You will have some indication of when this occurs when she starts waking with an occasional dry nappy.

Even so, you will still have to take her to the toilet before she goes to bed and possibly during the night. This is done by carrying her to the toilet at least two hours after she has gone to bed.

Hold her on the adult toilet seat and tell her to do a wee. If nothing happens after a few minutes take her back to her room. When you lift her at night, just slip the nappy down if possible, so that you do not wake her completely or you could have trouble getting her back to sleep, although by the age of three or four this is usually not a problem. The reason for taking her to the toilet during the night is so that her bed clothes do not become soaked through her nappy. If she is not getting very wet there is no need to bother.

You may be told that taking her to the toilet when she is half asleep will encourage her to let go when she is in bed. This is not so, she will hold her urine when her bladder is able to and she will let go anyway until it matures. My suggestion is to leave her in nappies at night for even a year or more after she has been toilet trained – that is until she wakes with a dry nappy for a month. The trouble and expense of one or two nappies a day is minimal and far preferable to being woken every night because the child has a wet bed and you have to change the linen. If you find that one nappy is not sufficient to hold the flow, use two or three towelling nappies with a fabric nappy liner next to the skin if it is sensitive; then cover the whole lot with waterproof pants. Or you can use a special highly absorbent disposable.

If you want to keep her from waking up at night if she has wet her bed when she is not wearing a nappy, you can use a genuine or imitation sheepskin bed pad like the kind used to prevent bedsores in patients in hospital. This allows the urine through, leaving a warm area to lie on so the child does not wakeup.

TOILET TRAINING PROBLEMS

WHEN THINGS DON'T RUN SMOOTHLY. There are a number of problems that can arise during toilet training or afterwards. 'Naughtiness' is never the reason for problems although it can seem like it. The reasons for many of the problems that arise are intertwined so read all the sections. Statistically toilet training problems are more common in boys than girls, and they tend to run in the family.

REGRESSION IN TOILET TRAINED CHILDREN. A child who was previously trained suddenly starts wetting or soiling again. Emotional reasons are usually the cause. Is there a new baby on the way or recently arrived? Has the mother gone out to work? Has there been a divorce? Are you making too many demands on the child? Is she under some other stress? She cannot help what is happening – it is a cry for help. Look for the cause and try and rectify it. You can't wish away a new baby, but you can address her fears by working hard to convince her that you still love her and she need not fear that the new baby will change this.

MANAGEMENT. Treating emotional causes takes sensitivity, time and patience. What you are dealing with is essentially insecurity about being loved – even if unfounded. For example, if you put a lot of pressure on a child she could think that you will not love her if she does not perform to your expectations. Teenagers who become anorexic often have the same underlying reasons for their behaviour.

Repressed anger at a new baby is another reason. The child may appear to be loving towards and accepting of the new baby, but turns her resentment and anger inward either by withholding stools or regressing into babyhood. *(See p. 512.)* In some cases regression is due to medical illness. Check this possibility with your medical advisor. *(See p. 265.)*

Once you have sorted out the cause and corrected the problems as far as possible, you can reintroduce her to the potty. If she will allow it, you can put her in nappies again for a time if you feel you cannot remain cool when 'accidents' happen. If you cannot eliminate the cause of regression, you will still have to handle her tactfully and gently. If she can see a child she admires using the potty confidently she might be persuaded to imitate her and begin using it again.

WITHHOLDING STOOLS/ENCOPRESIS/CONSTIPATION/SOILING. Besides the reasons mentioned regarding regression, which sometimes also lead to the withholding of stools, there are physical reasons that can have the same effect. Or a combination of emotional reasons can be complicated by physical reasons. (*See p. 512.*)

Withholding stools or constipation can result in the passing of hard stools that are painful, and this frequently causes a split or fissure in the anus (you could see a little red blood on the pants). Passing of stools becomes very painful and the child then withholds them out of fear. The longer the stool remains in the bowel the more water is absorbed making the stool bulkier and harder. The bulky stools also deaden the nerve endings in the anal sphincter so the child does not feel the urge to pass a stool thus perpetuating the problem.

Some children pass a stool every day but the bowel movement is incomplete resulting in a build up of faecal matter. Soiling may occur when soft matter passes around the hard stool into the pants. This can seem like the child has diarrhoea because the soiling is watery, it is in fact due to constipation. The child should not be scolded for soiling as she is not even aware that it has occurred.

Infestation with worms can also become so great that bowel blockage and constipation occurs.

Some children have a 'sluggish' bowel in that the peristaltic movements that push the stool along are not very efficient and constipation results. Uncomplicated constipation can be treated with extra fluids such as water or diluted juice. Children over two can have additional roughage in the form of fruit with the skin on or stewed dried fruit such as that with yoghurt. A teaspoon of good quality pure flax seed oil daily has the advantage of supplying essential fatty acids as well as lubricating the system. Stool softeners that are not habit forming such as lactulose can be used, or a glycerine suppository can be used under medical advice.

MANAGEMENT. Take your child to the doctor so that she can be examined for an anal fissure. You will be given medication to heal and lubricate the anus. Thereafter keep the area soft by dabbing with petroleum jelly, nipple cream or a product prescribed by your medical advisor. An X-ray or ultrasound scan may be taken to see whether there is a blockage due to worms or an impacted stool in the bowel. The bowel may need to be cleared with a special solution. Thereafter a regular routine for stooling with the help of stool softeners must be instituted until bowel movements are regulated. It may take some time because the nerve endings need to recover and the whole vicious cycle broken. Clearly very sympathetic handling in all respects is needed. If severe, the above cases may need an operation to clear the bowel, followed by stool softeners.

FREQUENT LOOSE STOOLS. (Toddlers' diarrhoea.) If not associated with other symptoms it could be due to too much juice, in particular, juice sweetened with certain artificial sweeteners. These juices should be avoided.

REFUSAL TO SIT ON THE POTTY TO PASS A STOOL. This is often due to fear. Try draping a nappy over the potty and letting her sit with it tucked around her. Make sure the potty is comfortable for squatting. If an adult toilet is used, put a box under her feet so she can sit securely. Ask if she wants you to hold her safely while she sits. If she insists on putting on a nappy you can save soiling it by putting a double layer of paper towel inside it. Or the reward system might do the trick. It often is only a developmental stage and simply needs time.

BED WETTING AND OTHER BLADDER CONTROL PROBLEMS. (Day and night-time enuresis.) It is estimated that 15 percent of boys and 10 percent of girls are still wetting their beds at the age of five. But by the age of nine, however, only about five per cent still have the problem. So, although common, it is a problem usually outgrown in time. Meanwhile, however, it can cause embarrassment and anxiety to both parents and child.

An understanding of what is needed to achieve bladder control can help parents accept and handle any problems that arise.

To achieve bladder control the child's nervous system should have matured sufficiently to enable her to have voluntary control over the sphincter muscles that hold and release urine. This is usually managed by about 30 months, but night time control can usually be expected only some time afterwards.

The time at which daytime and night-time bladder control is gained varies between children; with night wetting (nocturnal enuresis) often running in families, particularly the male line.

Most children are dry by day before they achieve night-time control. During the night, an anti-diuretic hormone vasopressin, slows down the production of urine by the kidneys. Some children simply take longer than others to begin producing this hormone. The bladder also needs to have matured sufficiently to hold the output of urine. Psychological problems, often thought to be the cause of bedwetting, are in fact, more likely to be the result of reactions to the problem. It is also true that some children sleep very deeply and miss the signal of the need to void. Stopping all liquids in the late afternoon places a lot of strain on everyone and does not solve the problem.

Practising stopping the flow of urine midstream will give the child confidence that she can control the function. When sitting on the potty or toilet ask her to try and stop the flow by 'pinching' and then releasing. Do this without pressure and make it seem like fun. She will be delighted to find that she can control voiding at will.

Many parents have unrealistic expectations as far as night-time control is concerned and they label their child a bed wetter unnecessarily – you should avoid labels anyway. Rather keep a child in night-time nappies for longer, than make problems by taking her out too soon. Only when a child wets her bed at least twice a week after the age of five or six is it considered a problem requiring treatment. There are various drugs and devices that can help.

Alarms which alert the child to the start of the flow are available. The ones with wires need to be set by the child, and some sleep through the sound of the buzzer as well. It takes patience and time for this system to work, but it can work well. A newer battery operated device 'pages' the child by vibrating like a silent cellular telephone. This has the advantage of not waking others, and it does not have wires.

Imipramine is a drug that is used in bedwetting. Its use needs to be very carefully monitored. Desmopressin is a nasal spray that mimics the effect of the natural anti-diuretic hormone. This too, needs to be used with great care. Both medication and alarms work, although desmopressin works quicker than alarms.

Diuretics like coffee and tea should be avoided. Pinworm can cause enuresis by entering the urinary tract. Parents need to accept that it is a common developmental problem, not naughtiness. The child needs help and encouragement, not shame or scolding.

Medical problems such as threadworms (see p. 371), diabetes, urinary tract infections (see p. 361) blockage or narrowing of the neck of the bladder, and petit mal epileptic attacks (see p.452), may also result in bedwetting. Therefore a thorough medical examination is essential before you conclude that it is an emotional or maturation problem.

DAYTIME WETTING. Other than for emotional reasons (*see Regression p. 262*) daytime wetting after training is potentially more serious than night wetting. Constant dribbling of urine can be a sign of a deformity of the urinary tract, or an infection or other medical condition, and a doctor must be consulted. The urine must be tested for infection, protein, sugar, blood and other abnormalities. (*See also Bedwetting p. 264.*) Some children become so engrossed in play that they 'forget' to go to the toilet. If you notice your child 'dancing' or squeezing her legs together send her to the toilet.

BETWEEN TWO AND THREE

INCREASING COMPETENCE. By the time your child is in her second year she should be able to use short sentences; identify objects by their use, such as a cup for drinking, be able to understand simple requests like 'bring the cup' or 'put the spoon in the cup'. Remember, too, that she will be able to understand far more than she is able to express. She should respond correctly to these four directions: 'Throw the ball up, down, behind, in front of you.'

She should be able to identify the main parts of her body and name objects such as flowers, dog, cat and so on from life or pictures.

SPEECH AND ITS ACQUISITION. Of all the skills acquired early on, good language development seems to be the best indication of future ability, even though it is said that Einstein was a late talker!

Children who grow up in homes where language is used in more than its basic form and who are talked to in a mature way soon outstrip their peers in development.

In homes where few discussions are held and orders are handed out without explanation, children seldom acquire the ability to use language as a tool to express themselves. Consequently pent-up frustration is often released through physical means, making them disruptive, violent or morose.

Later on it is in the verbal sections of I.Q. tests that these children do badly and which brings down their overall score.

LATE TALKERS. Since almost all information is received and transmitted through verbal or written speech, lack of ability in this area puts a great brake on performance. If your child's language development seems to be lagging in spite of an enriched environment, consider the possibility of a partial hearing loss. Recurrent middle ear infections can leave a gluey residue that can hinder hearing. (*See p. 350.*) If she can't hear properly she will not learn to talk. She will not understand your instructions and this will lead to conflicts. A small procedure can make the world of difference at this crucial learning stage.

SOCIAL DEVELOPMENT AND EMOTIONAL INTELLIGENCE. By now your child should be better able to cope with others and will generally be a pleasant person to be with. Reason, and the ability to foresee consequences, helps prevent frustration, and if her basic learning has been successful she will go onto more complicated modes of thought and action. 'Being with mummy' is no longer a primary concern and much more time is spent in actual play.

Her interest in children around her own age is more mature with the emergence of the ability to play with and not just alongside them. She should be far more co-operative in things like getting dressed, and her daytime bladder control should be good except for an occasional 'accident'. Night-time control is unlikely, and she may still need a bottle or dummy to help her fall asleep. She should be able to follow simple instructions, and will probably enjoy imitating adults at work. Give her practice in the all-important skill of listening and interpreting accurately what she hears by giving her little instructions such as: 'Put the blue mug on the round table.' This may sound perfectly simple but it is not easy for a child to do.

Later on you can make the instructions more complicated, but beware of becoming impatient or scornful if she does not get it right. Simply take her by the hand and, repeating the instruction, go through the required motions. The ability to carry out instructions is vital in the school learning situation and many children cannot do it effectively when they start school, which saddles them with an unnecessary handicap.

IMAGINARY FRIENDS. Imaginative play and 'pretend' games are a sign of developing intellect and many children conjure up an imaginary friend. This is a sign of sound development as long as the 'friend' does not take on the role of scapegoat for all the child's unacceptable behaviour. Although the child should not be allowed to avoid the consequences of her actions by blaming them on the imaginary friend, you must try to sort out the reasons for the behaviour. It could be suppressed anger or jealousy, or some other conflict.

PLAYING WITH EQUIPMENT. All the skills that have been acquired and practised during the first two years of life are now used to greater effect. She should enjoy riding a tricycle, climbing outdoors, playing on a jungle gym, building fairly elaborate structures with blocks or found objects, dressing up and pretend games.

In order to lay the foundations for maths, science and number concepts, you should also acquaint your child with the basic concepts involved in maths, science and numbers, just as you do language. There is no need for these subjects to be thought of as 'only for boys' or particularly difficult. There is nothing really 'difficult' or mysterious about mathematical concepts – they are all around us and we use them every day. The only problem about getting your child started is that she will probably soon outgrow your ability to answer her questions! But that is a kind of privileged situation you will have to cope with later... On the other hand you may not have to spend so much time helping with homework.

Firstly there should be no separate time for 'learning'. It should form an integral part of your everyday living. Although these ideas are placed under the three year old category, they can be started as early as you like, the earlier the better. By three, your child should be initiating many of the directions you take and really consolidating her basic knowledge.

NUMBER CONCEPTS. Right from the start you can watch out for opportunities for introducing numbers into her experience. In infancy, when she is lying on her blanket and you are playing with her feet you could start counting her toes. Do it so that she can see them and squeeze each toe as you go along. One... two... three... four... five... toes. Then hold them all together and say 'five toes'. There's no need to go over five in the first few years. She must really get to understand the fact of numbers in every possible context. This is the important thing, not being able to count to a hundred.

Take every opportunity to point out that five can be made up in different ways. If there are five items on the table, count them separately, then group them together so that they still make five. Ask her to take away two things and show her that three are left. She has done her first sum!

Never make it a test. It is a game, it is fun and it should never become stressful for the child. Work out your own variations. Count the buttons on her clothes, or the steps in the house. You can add other dimensions by counting all the red flowers on a place mat; or the yellow squares on a cereal box. Don't boggle her mind with too much. She needs a lot of repetition and comprehension before you move on to the more complex thoughts.

By the time she is three she should be able to use abstract thought, which is to picture things in her mind without seeing them. Ask her how many dolls she has got when she is not in the room with them. If she says two and it is right, go on to describe them: 'Yes, that's right, two dolls – one with brown hair and one with blonde hair... Susie has the dark hair and Jenny the light hair.' Amplification like this enriches her vocabulary and adds to her store of information.

BASIC MATHS. Number concepts, outlined before, are needed for mathematics. Shapes, classification and mass are also important. The identification of shapes – circles, squares, triangles and rectangles – are all that is needed when a child starts school.

Circles are the easiest for children to draw. Draw a circle then ask her to copy it. Draw two circles, one above the other, and ask her to copy them. Then draw three circles and ask her to copy them. It is difficult for a three-year-old to get the placing right when you have drawn more than one circle.

But if she can draw a recognizable figure by the time she is three or four, even if it is a stick figure, as long as the head, body and legs are in the right place, the chances are that she will not have difficulty in learning to read or write.

Point out shapes in the same way as you pointed out numbers to her: a plate is circular, how many other circles can you see? Children are usually not very good at recognising shapes if they are very large, like a square table, but will pick out the squares on a cereal box or a tiled wall easily. Do not worry if your child cannot do this at three. There is plenty of time. Take it slowly. Even five year olds don't know what a triangle looks like.

You can cut out shapes from cardboard or felt – circles, triangles, rectangles; squares can be used to make figures, houses, hats or whatever her imagination runs to. You can mark out triangles, squares, circles and rectangles of various sizes on stiff cardboard. Then cut out the same shapes the same size from another piece of card board or felt and ask your child to put the shapes into the correct spaces. If you use bright colours she should enjoy doing it. But it is difficult so do not give her too many shapes to start with or she will not be able to do it and lose interest. Gradually build up the number of shapes she has to start with. This is an excellent exercise for spatial perception which is needed for maths, reading and writing.

SCIENCE. We deal with scientific concepts all the time – when we bake a cake, grow a plant, light a fire, or switch on a light. Get the meaning of words like 'big' and 'small', 'short' and 'tall' clear in your child's mind. 'Look at that tall man – next to him you are very short… Draw a big man and a small man for mummy'. 'Feel the empty plastic bottle – it is very light. Fill the bottle with water and it feels heavy. Fill another bottle the same size with sand – does it feel heavier or lighter?' Point out that a small stone is heavier than a large ball of wool. Give her a chance to show you something that proves these principles. She may be five or even six before she can do it but she will still have been absorbing the principles. Bath time provides a great opportunity for pointing out cause and effect. Let her test things to see what will float… the empty bottle with the lid on it will float, because it has air trapped inside it… the empty bottle without a lid fills with water and sinks. A stone sinks, a cork floats.

PHYSICAL SCIENCE. Point out to her that living things need food, air and water to exist. Let her plant a few dried beans between cotton wool in two saucers. See that the one lot is watered regularly. She should do it but you will have to remind and supervise her. Leave the other saucer dry. After a few days she will see for herself that water is necessary for plants to grow. You can carry this experiment as far as you like.

Keep the one saucer in the fridge after it has started to grow. When there is no action after a few days she will have discovered that plants need warmth to grow. Transplant some of the beans into soil and keep some in the saucer. The ones in the soil should grow bigger and better because of the food in the soil, while the one in the saucer will wither once the food stored in the bean has been used up. If the beans in the soil die and others thrive she will have learnt something about the vagaries of life!

If you want to show how plants take up water through their stems, you can colour a glass of water with food colouring or ink and stand a white flower in it. The flower should eventually turn the colour of the water.

To show that people also have a system that flows through their body, you can let her see her pulse beating. Stick a drawing pin into the base of a matchstick and rest the matchstick on her wrist. The head of the matchstick will vibrate with her pulse beats. You can show the existence and movement of air by getting her to hold a piece of paper in front of a hair drier. The force of the air will bend the paper and she will not be able to keep it flat. Better still, make a whirlwind.

You need a sheet of paper about 18cm by 18cm, a dowel or stick about 30cm long and a pin with a big head. Mark out the paper and cut it along the dotted line. Fold as shown and catch all the points together with the pin. Push it into the top of the stick. Let her hold the whirlwind in a draught-free place to show her that it does not spin, then take her into the wind or near the hair drier (not too near) and let her see how the air makes it move even though she cannot see the air.

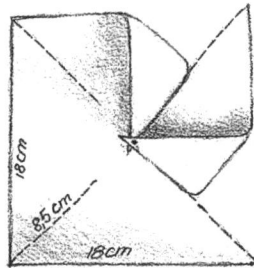

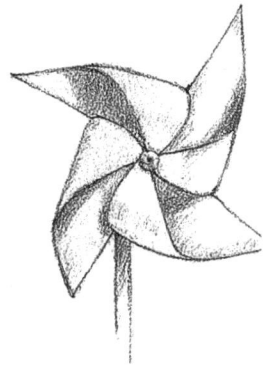

To promote small muscle coordination you can make a threading card out of stiff cardboard with holes punched in a pattern. Thread a thick blunt-ended needle with wool and show her how to 'sew' through the holes. If she is obviously left handed do not try to change her. But if she seems to need to change hands halfway, she may have mixed dominance (*see p. 306*) and she will have to be watched.

The development of touch and taste discrimination is also important and you can encourage this by playing a game of 'guess what you're eating?' Blind-fold her and let her taste familiar things like cheese, sugar, salt; then include less obvious items like grass, vinegar, flour. Learning to describe sour and sweet and raw and cooked, and so on, is good for discrimination. You can do the same with smells. Let hold her nose closed and see how this affects her ability to taste food as so much of flavour is dependent on smell.

Another guessing game you can play is 'what's in the bag?' Put a few objects such as a cotton reel, spoon, lid and bottle in a bag and let her put her hand in and guess what she is feeling. Later on you can try to promote memory by asking her to remember what was in the bag, or how many things. Do not put too many things in the bag or the game will be too difficult.

You can also help her develop classification skills, for instance by letting her sort buttons or cotton reels into colours and sizes. Remember that all these projects need only be done occasionally or they will lose their novelty for you and your child. No mother should feel that she should be doing 'educational' exercises with her child all the time. There is nothing to be gained by forcing yourself or your child. Opportunity for creative play is also important and if your child goes to a nursery school or good playgroup she should have plenty of opportunity for this.

BASIC EQUIPMENT FOR CREATIVE PLAY
- Dressing up clothes
- Dolls
- Blocks
- Sand (washed river sand) used wet or dry. Sieves to encourage the use of fine muscles; funnels, moulds (yoghurt cups work well); plastic spade and spoons are good for manipulating the sand.
- Water. Things to pour it with. Punch holes in the side of a light plastic cup and let her see the water spurt out; make a slide from a plastic tube for things to be 'posted' into the water. Blow bubbles into the water through a straw.
- Junk in the form of milk bottle tops, empty boxes, bits of wool and the like can be used to stick on to stiff paper to form a collage.

HOMEMADE GLUE. Mix white flour with water until it has the consistency of double cream. This will stick most light objects to paper.

VERY ADHESIVE HOMEMADE GLUE. Put a cupful of white flour into a piece of muslin and hold under running cold water. The water will wash away the starch if you knead the bag.

When the water runs clear, put the flour in a glass bowl and allow to dry. Use as needed by chipping off pieces of hardened glue and adding water. Work it until you have the right gluey consistency. This glue can be stored without refrigeration and holds well.

PLAYDOUGH. Moulding and making shapes with the hands is always popular. Bought play dough is good but fairly expensive if you use a lot. You can make your own very successfully with two cups of white flour, half a cup of salt and a few drops of salad oil. Add a little food colouring if you like. Mix to a smooth dough with water and store in a plastic bag in the fridge. A rolling pin and pastry cutters are useful. Spread a piece of oil cloth or have a wooden board for her to work on.

FINGER PAINTS. You will need food colouring or powder paints in the three primary colours, blue, yellow and red, or any colours you have; 1½ cups laundry starch; 1 litre boiling water; 1½ cups soap flakes or finely grated pure green laundry soap. Mix the starch with a little cold water in a pot, add boiling water and soap flakes and cook, stirring all the time, until the mixture becomes thick and transparent. When the mixture has cooled, divide, then pour into glass jars and colour each differently.

Finger painting is great for letting go. Make sure you cover the surrounding surfaces with plenty of newspaper and let the child wear old clothes or an apron. There is no fun in it if she is terrified of making a mess.

BUBBLES. Bubbles have a magic all of their own, and blowing them never loses its charm. You can make your own bubble mixture that makes the bubbles last extra long. Mix washing-up liquid with a little water and add enough glycerine to make it feel slightly sticky. Blow through a wire twisted to make a circle and a handle.

BOOKS AND CDS. By now your three-year-old should revel in story time. Make it a special, treasured time before bed or any other time you want to treat her to the greatest luxury – time with mommy or daddy and a trip into the world of imagery and the magic of words. Recordings of nursery rhymes and stories can be used to add variety and entertain when you are not there. Music recordings for babies and children have become varied and offer an important avenue for learning and brain stimulation.

TELEVISION. In some homes the television is on all day even if it is not being watched. This is not good for children, as it disturbs their concentration, even if it is in the background. This is particularly true for children under the age of two, who have been shown to be distracted from the important business of play. Switch the television off! It is not a good thing for children of any age to be subjected to meaningless noise and pictures. Putting a television set in a child's bedroom at any age is a bad idea.

MADE FOR CHILDREN TELEVISION PROGRAMMES AND DVDS. Nursery rhymes, songs and the ubiquitous Barney are loved by most young children, and are part of the cultural idiom of today. Countless parents have said a silent prayer of gratitude for their power to keep toddlers occupied. But you must limit it and most importantly, watch content. Some cartoons are loud and often violent, and can contain frightening concepts such as abandonment. Make sure that the shows that your child watches are suitable for her age group. Some so called 'educational' DVD's that claim to teach very young children, and even infants, language and other concepts have not been shown to be of any use, and some in the Disney Baby Einstein range have had to be withdrawn, and money refunded. See www.babyeinstein.com

Like most of the other experiences to which your child may be exposed, television can have a negative as well as a positive effect. The younger the child the greater the supervision of viewing is necessary. This does not mean that older children should make their own choices about what they view. If you make a point of being with your child while she watches you will have an excellent opportunity to expand her knowledge and add new dimensions to her concept of the world at any age. Talk to her about what you are seeing, discuss whether what is happening is real or imaginary; use it as a tool to expand the boundaries of her experience. Young children have no idea that what is shown is not real. Use it to discuss moral questions too. For example, 'Should he have hit the other bunny?' and so on.

Remember that her understanding of what is happening is often distorted and can lead to misconceptions that may be frightening to say nothing of encouraging violence. Even cartoons show violence as a solution to every problem. A child has no business watching adult programmes.

ADDICTED TO TELEVISION AND COMPUTER GAMES. If a child is always more interested in watching television indiscriminately than in playing, it is time to review her regimen. If she is not coping well with the business of growing up and learning new skills or practicing the ones she already has, she may spend a great deal of time in front of the TV because it is so easy and undemanding. The same applies to video games and computer games. Don't be misled into thinking that computer games 'encourage eye hand co-ordination' so they are good for your child. In young children, this skill is better promoted by three dimensional, real life games and playing that demands and teaches far more. Computer games can steal away time that should be used in outdoor play, developing imagination and cultivating emotional intelligence through Interaction with peers. These are the skills she really needs for success in the future. The huge increase in childhood obesity has a lot to do with lying in front of the TV, which can often be traced to poor interpersonal skills in the child – a vicious cycle of cause and effect.

VIOLENCE ON TELEVISION. It is a moot point whether violence depicted on television predisposes children to violence; the evidence is that it does in cases where there isn't a strong counter balancing force in the child's life. It is certain that it does introduce an element that should not normally be part of a child's experience. There is also no truth in the idea that watching violence acts as a cathartic that helps get rid of pent up aggression. Studies show that it encourages aggression in both children and susceptible adults. To say nothing of the message conveyed in scenes in which women are physically abused. Young children do not have the capacity to follow a story line in which the perpetrator gets his due in the end. They only perceive the message of the immediate action.

Although you may be able to explain cowboys and Indians shooting it out on the screen as just play acting, excusing the news is not so easy. Don't ignore the issue of violence on your television screen; interpret it in the same way as other issues. Without any kind of explanation, your youngster is likely to grow up thinking that violence is the norm and become conditioned to respond passively when she should be protesting. Popular comic strip characters have been made into movies, some of which are dreadfully violent and even terrifying. Just because a film is based on a comic strip, it does not make it suitable for young viewers.

HEALTH HAZARDS AND TV. If you make sure your child sits the proper distance away from the set according to its size and see that the room is not darkened too much, limited television watching should have no adverse effect on her health. Some parents put infants in front of the television set and although it is unlikely to do any real damage, it can be over stimulating and is certainly no substitute for your attention. Older children who watch a lot of TV often become obese.

A potential hazard of watching TV, especially in susceptible children, is photosensitive epilepsy when the flickering images on the screen trigger epileptic attacks, particularly if the room is darkened, and the child is sitting close to the set. Should the child suddenly seem to go blank and be in a daze and not answer when spoken to, or if she suddenly begins jerking or twitching, switch off the television and support her until the attack passes. Do not try to give her anything to drink until it is over. Warn an older child to cover her one eye if she feels strange when watching television. She should not approach the set or change stations as it is the flickering light that causes the attack. It is more common in girls than boys and later on the lights in a disco could have the same effect on her. There is usually no need for drug treatment in these cases.

CELLPHONES. There is a theoretical possibility that cell phone usage may damage the developing brain cells in children under the age of seven.

THE ART OF COMMUNICATION. At four a child should have enough command of her mother tongue to express her thoughts. Help her practise the all-important two-way exchange that makes for real conversation and communication between people.

Talking with a child should not just be a question and answer affair. It should engage her in exchanges that allow her to express her thoughts and feelings. Tell her what you are thinking; for instance if you are puzzled and wondering what dress to wear, you could say, 'I really can't make up my mind whether to wear the blue or red dress, the red one is pretty but has short sleeves and the weather looks like rain. What do you think I should do?' In this way the child is made to consider alternatives and offer suggestions. You should take her answers seriously and give them due consideration. Discuss her opinions on the matter. She may suggest you wear something over the dress or take an umbrella. Praise her for her good ideas. Showing her you value her opinion will help her react in a responsible way. It also helps her learn to organise her thoughts and present them in a logical fashion. If she comes up with an impractical solution or comment, don't laugh at her, treat it seriously and explain why it will not work.

When initiating a conversation don't just ask her a question with a single yes or no answer. Make it open-ended like, 'Are there any other toys you like playing with besides the doll you're playing with now?'

Help her articulate her fears and anxieties as well as her pleasure. If she is apprehensive or angry don't just ask what is wrong. It is hard for her to put it into words especially if she is not quite sure herself what it is that she is really afraid of. Try and guess what the problem could be and ask her if you are right; it will help her get her thoughts, frustrations and fears to the surface where you have a better chance of helping her. Remember that the art of conversation is complex and vital in human relations. Help her learn it while she is young and you will be doing a great deal towards helping her relate to people effectively. This is a large part of what is regarded as emotional intelligence, as important, if not more important than academic intelligence.

SPEAKING IN TONGUES. Young children are eminently capable of learning two or more languages at a time. If the father speaks to the child in his language and the mother in her language the child will learn both, although she may confuse them at first.

QUESTIONS ABOUT SEX

IT'S SURE TO COME UP. At some stage most children notice the difference between boys and girls and may comment on it. Steer away from any suggestion that either sex is superior because of its particular equipment and explain matter-of-factly when discussing it. A little girl may wonder why a boy has a penis and what has happened to hers. You can explain that boys and girls are different and that they are both beautiful and interesting, and if she still seems to want more you could say that when she is old enough to be a mummy and have a baby in a very long time, she will become fancier and develop breasts and pubic hair. Children love hearing stories about how they were born and this is often a good place to start the explanations, especially since most children think they popped out of their mother's navel! Remember to make the distinction between the special place where the baby comes out and where urine is excreted.

Build up your child's knowledge slowly over the years so that it evolves naturally, rather than launch into a detailed account of spermatozoa, ovaries and fallopian tubes at three. It is all far too complicated for a child to conceptualise in one go, and she could end up with the wrong impression like the four year old who said gardeners were needed to make a baby – because they had to plant the seed!

OEDIPUS AND ELECTRA COMPLEXES AND ALL THAT. There is no doubt that little girls make a great play for their father's attention, flirting outrageously and generally making for more competition than any woman can possibly handle. How he responds will tell her a lot about herself and it is important in building up her image of herself as an attractive, desirable person. Boys, too, often insist they are going to marry their mother when they grow up and telling him you are sure he will make a wonderful husband to some lucky girl should boost his confidence and satisfy him.

MASTURBATION/SEXUAL PLEASURE. Even in the earliest months a mother may notice that her son's penis becomes erect occasionally when he is naked and his exploring hands may reach his genitals. You may feel faintly disturbed by this but it is quite normal and you should not try to prevent it. A little girl, too, may find pleasurable areas but this does not mean she is going to become a rampant nymphomaniac. In fact exploration of the body is not necessarily sexual play. It simply means that she is moving towards the normal use of all the senses she was born with. Stifling it is as unnatural as it is harmful.

Everything you do for your baby tells her something about herself. If you enjoy hugging her and loving her she will get warm, positive messages that will help her grow up with a healthy self-esteem to guide her. It is people who have not being given a positive image of themselves as worthwhile individuals who look for love in self-damaging ways.

Occasionally a child may feel the need to pleasure herself so often that it becomes a dominant feature of her life. The reason why she needs to do this should be sought. If she does it in public, it may be because she finds it a sure way to get attention. You should explain to her that there are certain things that are not done when people are around, and then you should make a concerted effort to establish why she needs to do it.

She may be feeling rejected or jealous or she may not be coping with pressures on her, and be seeking an escape. She may even be bored. Without making her feel guilty or inadequate, gently divert her attention to other things while you sort out the real cause of the compulsion.

A vaginal irritation caused by an infection, worms, or even bubble bath can prompt girls in particular, to masturbate or 'play with themselves'. If her vaginal area is red (most likely due to bubble bath) or if she scratches around the anus (pinworm) take her to the doctor.

SEXUAL PLAY BETWEEN CHILDREN. Playing 'doctor doctor' is almost inevitable amongst children at some time. If you catch them at it, divert their attention matter-of-factly and suggest another game. Occasionally children indulge in more explicit sexual play which includes touching each other. You should remain matter-of-fact but point out that there are parts of our body which are private and which others are not allowed to touch. This message should be part of your normal safety teaching as you would teach about any other aspect of child safety and protection. Sadly, children have been known to sexually abuse other children. Be very careful.

SEXUAL ABUSE. It is sad but true that sexual abuse of children is a worldwide sickness, and its prevention is an essential part of parental care. Firstly, you need to teach both boys and girls that certain parts of the body – say, anything that would be covered by a bathing suit – is a no-go area where only mummy can touch when she washes you for example. They also need to know that touching by anyone that makes them feel uncomfortable is a no-no. And that they have the right to say no firmly to the person doing it – no matter who it is, even if it is a friend or relative – and no matter what reason that person gives for doing it. An exception would be when mummy is with – for a doctor's examination for example. You don't have to make the child paranoid about it, just be simple in your explanation and suggest your child talk to you if she feels the need to tell you something at anytime.

Remember though, that sexually abused children are usually threatened by the perpetrator and sworn to secrecy. Descriptions of sexual incidents by children must always be taken seriously. It is also true that sexual abusers are seldom recognisable as such. They may have high economic or social status, or they may choose a job that gives them access to children. Members of religious orders; 'Father Christmas' figures, school teachers and others have been convicted of sexual offences against children. In other cases drink, drugs or the belief that intercourse with a child (virgin) can cure Aids predicates abuse. Sexual abusers are not always men – women have been known to sexually abuse children too. Sadly, sexual abuse of children by other children is possible especially in cases where the other child has experienced abuse.

SIGNS OF SEXUAL ABUSE IN CHILDREN. These include any sexually transmitted disease; bleeding or damage to the vaginal or anal region; emotional withdrawal by the child and fearfulness; sexual knowledge beyond the child's age, and sexually provocative behaviour.

DRESSING AND UNDRESSING. Until the age of about two, children do not seem to be aware of whether they or others are clothed or not. However, it is not long before they become acutely aware of what they are wearing and develop pronounced likes and dislikes. Whereas before she may have been perfectly content to let you choose what she should wear, your daughter may now refuse point blank to put on anything but jeans or insist on dresses only. A lot of her reaction has to do with her preconceived ideas and what she thinks has the right status. If she decides that girls wear dresses and boys wear pants, she will probably insist on pink frills, no matter how carefully you have avoided sexual stereo typing. She will be getting messages by looking around her. If most of the girls and women she knows and admires wear dresses she will probably want to copy them. On the other hand, if she has an older brother she admires, she may want to wear pants. In other words, children do not like looking different from their peers even though their idea of how this should be achieved is often enough to make parents cringe.

At the other end of the scale, undressing or nudity also has a strong significance for most children. The two or three year old is usually happy to run around naked but there comes a time when it suddenly dawns on her that no one else is doing it and she may become self-conscious.

Insisting that she continue *au naturel* after this stage is not going to 'liberate' her, it is only going to make her more self-conscious. Children are conservative creatures; they like to be like everyone else. It takes experience and intellectual growth before convention can be discarded with equanimity.

However you do not want your child to grow up thinking there is shame in the naked human form. But should parents make a point of going naked in their child's presence? This is not necessary, but natural nudity, especially between the parent of the same sex and the child is healthy and normal. To a child over a certain age when there is an awakening sexuality, nudity of the parent of the opposite sex can be disturbing to the child, and it is as well to handle it discreetly, though not of course fanatically or prudishly.

GO TO www.baby-childcare.com TO WATCH THE FOLLOWING VIDEOS THAT ARE APPLICABLE TO CHAPTER 9

PROF CLAUDIA GRAY	Sleep in babies and children
DR ANUSHA LACHMAN	The first 1000 days of life
	Modern moms
	The role of care givers

Technology

Dealing with conflict

Shared pleasures

Is it okay for my child to be bored?

Toys – less or more?

Boys don't cry – right or wrong?

ANEL ANNANDALE

Reading with your child

Seperation anxiety

Autism spectrum disorder

Dealing with an aggressive toddler

Manners

Discipline for toddlers and pre-schoolers

Single parent

Teaching your toddler to share

Emotional intelligence

Giving children the space to explore

The importance of play

Developing intelligence

Difference between the adult and the child brain

DR. NICOLA DUGMORE

Sibling rivalry

Sharing

Play

LIZANNE DU PLESSIS

What is self-regulation

Sensory regulation

Sensory temprament

JOANNA WILSON

Causes of childhood overweight and obesity

Parent creating healthy homes

Responsive feeding

CHAPTER 10

The Crucial Second Year

TOWARDS INDEPENDENCE

Hopefully, everything you have been doing for your baby has been directed towards making her a self-reliant and independent person in her own right. To achieve this she will need the necessary mental and physical abilities to ensure that her successes outnumber her failures; that she is flexible enough to cope with new situations and endowed with sufficient self-esteem to set herself realistic goals.

This may be far ahead in your child's future, but what you do in the first three years of life has a vital bearing on how she develops later on.

Unfortunately, children are normally at their most taxing during these years and it is hard for new parents to cope with the physical care of a child as well as her emotional, social and mental development. Studies have shown that parents in all cultures do a fine job of meeting their child's physical and emotional needs during the first ten months or so, except in situations where the child may be malnourished or abused through poverty or ignorance. But their handling is often so unsatisfactory after that age that only about one in ten children reach their potential.

This is not meant to induce guilt in parents who have more than enough to cope with, but to help clear away misconceptions about the nature of the child and in particular what promotes sound mental and emotional growth. It cannot be stressed too often that all children are individuals and should be treated as such if they are to flourish. Trying to make your child fit the norm is self-defeating and potentially harmful. Get to know your child, then adapt the knowledge at your disposal to her special characteristics, in the same way as you would approach any challenging and creative task.

But first get rid of any stereotypical ideas of what children are like and how they should be handled. For example, that showing fear is acceptable in a girl; but taboo for a boy; yet the ability to see danger in a situation is a sign of intelligence in any child.

TYPICAL FEARS. If showing fear is natural, should you therefore allow your child to shy away from all situations that induce fear? Not at all; this would be avoiding the problem, not facing or solving it. But before you act when a child shows fear, put yourself in her place. Some children are acutely aware of physical danger. They may be afraid of dogs or even cats – perhaps the noise from a vacuum cleaner fills them with terror. To them these are the things they do not control and whose behaviour they cannot predict. For example, a dog may be twice the height of a toddler and when he 'sniffs' may appear to want to gobble her up. The powerful vacuum cleaner that roars around the house and devours dirt could, to her way of thinking, suck her up too. It you take a little time to look at it her way you will see that this is really not being 'silly', and that forcing a child mercilessly into a fearful situation will only make her fear you more than the original source. Instead of convincing her that you can be trusted to help her, your behaviour will make her insecure and confused in her feelings.

Telling her that she's a baby and that there is nothing to be afraid of may be true, but it will not help solve her problem. Depending on the child's temperament and the degree of her fear, you could help her overcome it by acknowledging it, talking about it and teaching her how to come to terms with it. By helping her to identify her fears and showing her how they can be handled, you will be fulfilling your function as a parent in a positive, meaningful way.

So much of what we do in later life hinges on how we cope with our fears that learning how to recognise and handle them from infancy is one of the most valuable lessons you can teach your child.

HANDLING FEARFUL SITUATIONS. For instance, if she is afraid to visit friends because they have a dog, you can start by identifying her fear. Tell her that you know how she feels when she sees the dog. Describe what he must look like to her: 'He's big and he jumps up on people and his long tail wags and nearly bumps you over, and he makes funny panting noises, and his teeth look as though they can bite hard' Watch her carefully and her face will show if you have touched on her particular fears. Then, having identified the problems, tell her what she can expect. 'Yes, the dog does jump, and he can knock little girls over, but he won't bite and doesn't mean to hurt (presuming that he really is not dangerous). It's just that he is so pleased to see friends that he gets excited and jumps up and wags his tail because he isn't able to talk, he has to use his body to talk' Then, having identified and isolated the fear-inducing possibilities in the situation, tell her what you are going to do. If it is highly likely that the dog will knock her down, you could tell her that you will hold her safely out of the way until the animal settles down and that you will keep a careful eye on him so that he does not get out of hand. This way you will have shown her that you care about and understand her feelings, that you are open to a reasonable expression of her inner thoughts and that you are powerful enough to be able to do something about it. She in turn will not have been humiliated because she has shown fear, her ego will be intact and it will be easier for her to face her problem without developing all sorts of other problems as a result of not being able to handle the original one.

She may not become confident overnight, but she will have learnt that the world is not an entirely illogical place where things happen without reason or sense, and that there are ways of coping with difficulties.

FEAR OF ABANDONMENT. Another fear that is deeply rooted in most children is that of being abandoned. To what extent this fear develops depends largely on how she has been cared for from the first day of life – it is the accumulated effect of many incidents and expressed and implied attitudes. A great number of people grow up never having resolved their fear of being abandoned or alone. It can make them excessively possessive, demanding and lacking in emotional self-sufficiency. Don't think you will teach your child to 'fend for herself' or be self-reliant by pushing her away.

It will have just the opposite effect. She will develop emotional stability only if you give her emotional security and reason to trust. In infancy you can foster this by responding to your child's needs to the best of your ability in the way outlined in the previous chapters. Later on you will have to reinforce it by sticking to your word. If you have said you will be going out and have promised to be back for lunch, be there, or else telephone home at that time so that you can talk to her even if she is under two. Do not appear and disappear unaccountably from her life. Take her with you or say goodbye before you leave and tell her when you will be back. You will have to use something other than a clock to indicate the time you expect to return. Say something like 'before you have your sleep', or 'after lunch… ' Separations for more than a few hours almost inevitably cause some distress before the age of three. Your child may appear to have forgotten you or may reject you when you come back. Unless she has a basically unstable, insecure home life, no permanent damage should be done. But never disappear without saying goodbye, and depending on the length of time you will be away leave a suitable task for her to do while you are away. Painting a picture, doing a puzzle. If you are going away for a few days, call regularly and give her little tasks to do and tell her caregiver about them so that they can discuss you and keep your presence alive. Be sure to acknowledge what she has done while you were away.

Very young children often cry when a parent leaves, causing distress to parent and child. If your child is too young to understand language you can slip away unnoticed, as long as you will be back within an hour or two.

NIGHTMARES. Occasionally, a child who is facing too many stressful situations during the day may relive them in her sleep through her subconscious by having nightmares. She will probably wake in the hours after midnight crying bitterly, not the way she does if she is thirsty, hungry or cold, which usually starts off as a niggly cry and builds up. If this happens, respond as quickly as possible and do your best to comfort and reassure your child. She may not be able to fall asleep again quickly because of fear as she will remember the dream. Try and explain that it is only a dream and that everyone has them and that it is not real.

You should also try to pin-point the sources of stress and eliminate them if you can, although this is not always possible as it may simply be due to an over-active imagination. Some of the possible causes are the arrival of a new baby, a move to a new house, harsh discipline, forced toilet training, conflict between the parents, and unresolved fears, or watching frightening material on television – note that cartoons can also be disturbing. Your child may simply be over stimulated during the day because there is too much happening around her and there is not enough time to assimilate and digest all the stimuli that she is being bombarded with. Children cannot cope with constant chaos around them. As always, try to eliminate the problem if possible and bring order into her life. A dimmed light in the passage will sometimes help with fear of the dark (a nightlight should not be left on throughout the night in her room as it may affect the production of the hormone melatonin). Children derive a lot of security from their surroundings so changing or redecorating her room may not be as great for her as you had hoped.

NIGHT TERRORS. These episodes are characterised by waking an hour or more after falling deeply asleep, sitting up in bed wide eyed, pulse racing, possibly thrashing about and terrified of something unseen.

You child will not seem to know you and may push you away, or point to imaginary 'dragons' or other frightening things only she can see. Her terror will be real and you will just have to console her as best you can. Stay with her and tell her she is safe, hold her if she'll let you and tuck her back in bed when she is calm again. Fortunately she is likely to fall asleep quickly and will have no memory of the night terror the following day. Children grow out of these episodes although they sometimes manifest later as sleepwalking.

HAIR WASHING AND BATHING FEARS. One of the most frequent household dramas in the early years centres on hair washing, with children screaming and mothers tearing their hair out (their own usually although they may be tempted to do it to the child). The fact is that children hate getting water in their faces unless they have been used to it from the beginning.

Playing with a hosepipe on a hot day and splashing her face with water in infancy may help make her more nonchalant about getting water in her eyes and face, although this does not always work.

Always wash her hair with non-stinging shampoo and wrap her firmly in a towel, holding her backwards over the bath or basin. Most children dislike having their hair washed in the bath because the surrounding water makes them even more nervous. Brims, like a hat with the crown cut out, are available and they help prevent water from running down her face. Otherwise you can let her lean over the bath and hold a face cloth to her face so that she does not have water running into her eyes.

Occasionally, a baby may become terrified of bathing and scream as soon as she sees the water. Infants have a very poor sense of relative size and she may fear being sucked down the plug hole. So don't let the water out in her presence. You could give her sponge baths for a while, until she gets over it, without putting her in the water. First lay her on a towel and wash her. Or you can put her in a basin or bath (if she will get in) without water, and wash her that way, using a wet sponge and a jug of water to rinse her. Reintroduce her to the bath after a while using only a tiny bit of water, increasing it gradually over a period of time. Or put the baby bath in the big bath so that she does not feel insecure. Or you could bath with her.

THE SHY CHILD. A child may be shy and withdrawn in the presence of anyone she does not know well because she has not had much opportunity to mix with others, or simply because of innate temperament. As with other fears there is nothing to be gained by pushing her into a stressful situation. Help her to overcome her reticence by

getting her to mix with others on her home ground before facing them on alien territory. Like the truly gregarious who cannot alter their nature, the shy child may not be able to change her temperament radically. But by giving her confidence in herself through tact and understanding you can help her overcome the paralysing grip of her shyness. Many shy children grow up very confident and outgoing in spite of earlier shyness. Medication to alleviate shyness is sometimes recommended. Making a pathology out of what is a facet of human nature seems excessive. Where shyness does present as a life confining problem in extreme cases there may be a place for medication, but only with great caution, after a full investigation into the child's true condition. (See p. 433)

CLINGING. A shy child may cling to her mother when confronted by strangers, but the clinging child hangs on to her all the time. Some mothers are content with this kind of attention, but others swat at their child as though she were a gnat. Both extremes indicate that something has gone wrong in the parent-child relationship and the reasons for the clinging should be looked for.

In some cases the child may never have developed a sense of security about the mother because she has let her down in the past. This makes for a desperate attempt to hold onto her and literally never let her out of her clutches. On the other hand, a child who has not been encouraged to explore her environment may not be able to involve herself successfully in the business of discovery. The clinging child will become more independent if her self-confidence is built up. This cannot be done by rejecting her, insisting on her 'not being a baby' or 'throwing her in at the deep end'. It is a long-term project that needs patience and sincerity. The child whose mother is her only source of interest will have to be introduced enthusiastically to the delights of the world around her. It should be remembered that interest in the mother and desire for her company is natural in the first years. (All too soon you will have to beg or bribe her for her company!) Dependence becomes stultifying only when the child has no other sources of interest.

Children who do not appear to seek their mother out as a source of comfort may be ambivalent in their attachment. This is more problematic.

SEVERE SEPARATION ANXIETY IN THE OLDER CHILD. True anxiety disorders are common in children, yet seldom treated, although they can be the precursor of future depressive and other psychiatric disorders. In cases where a child over six years appears to be truly afraid of normal social interactions, or who has excessive, unrealistic fears, it is wise to consult a specialist in the field. Behaviour therapy and possibly medication are often helpful. (See also p. 433.)

EMERGING INDEPENDENCE. By the time your child is around three years of age you should expect her to be far more interested in doing things than hanging onto you, even though she still likes you to be close. She should also be able to wait for a reasonable period for her needs to be met except in emergencies, for instance if she is hurt; and should be far more co-operative in doing what you want without the negativism of the year before. On your side you should be there to assist and console, but you should not be doing everything for her. She should in fact be on her way to real independence.

DISCIPLINE

GETTING IT RIGHT. Of all the views parents hold about child care, the strongest usually concern discipline. Most of them go along with whatever their own parents did, but others swing the opposite way and reject everything their parents did.

Complicating matters are the couples who differ from each other in their views. This is perhaps the most damaging situation for the child because she becomes confused between loyalty to the individual parent, and not knowing which set of rules really applies. These children are likely to become extra difficult, morose or insecure. It is vitally important therefore for parents to sort out their differences and present a united front for the child's sake.

In general, however, there are three categories: those who believe discipline is the proper submission to authority; those who favour permissiveness and free self-expression; and in the middle, those who vacillate between the two extremes as the spirit takes them.

The old authoritarian approach ('you do as I say or else') succeeded in keeping reasonable order until the child was old enough or shrewd enough to escape its rule. It also kept the timid child suppressed and often alienated parent and child.

Advocates of the totally permissive regimen, on the other hand, have been disappointed to find that it resulted in disaffected, directionless offspring, instead of fostering a healthy self-image and warmth between parents and child. Some parents do not discipline because they are afraid of being rejected by their children, and believe that they should be their child's 'friend'. Sadly, this accounts for some of the worst outcomes. You will hopefully be your child's friend when you are adults, but when they are still young you are the pack leader. And as much as you would rather not have to be the one 'giving the talking to' or laying down the rules, it is a parent's duty and obligation.

Those who vacillate between the two approaches, probably make up the mass of parents, who, unsure of their ground, take whatever line suits them at the time.

THERE IS ANOTHER WAY. How can we effectively direct our children so that they do not become demanding brats or mindless followers? The age-old dictum of 'doing unto others... ' has not lost its validity and like charity, it starts at home.

In the beginning applying this will be rather one-sided with you giving without any possible reciprocal consideration for your needs from your child. But you will be laying the foundation for future reciprocity.

This does not mean total self-sacrifice or becoming a slave to your child, but should be a non-egocentric approach that includes warmth and empathy. During the second year when the child's own ego is developing there will be many occasions when your appreciation of the child's feelings will make clashes easier to understand and, sometimes, prevent.

Understanding how she feels does not mean that you should always capitulate; it means judging a situation on its merits and acting reasonably. Respect for your child's wishes and opinions will set her the example of working with instead of against people. If she has to throw a tantrum to get her needs recognised or whine to get your attention she will understandably keep doing it.

Too often the relationship between parent and child becomes one of a battle between two sides with one always the loser. No conflict between you should ever end with either side feeling defeated. Even if you cannot allow something, or you have had to reprimand her firmly, neither should end up with an ego so bruised that resentment builds up.

THE AUTHORITATIVE WAY. If you say 'no' as seldom as possible, it will be all the more effective when you do say it. You will also be able to stick by your word more effectively so that you can be consistent. If you think about it you will see that most of what your toddler does is not malicious, but the natural exercising of her curiosity or testing of the limits you set.

Diversion is a good way of avoiding an unnecessary clash of wills, since a child has a short attention span and can easily be distracted. For example, supermarket tantrums are common. Yet you can avoid them by giving the situation a little thought. Your child sees you take anything you fancy from the shelves. She sees no reason why she should not do so as well, so why not pass things to her to put in the trolley? Talk to her about them and keep her occupied. If she spies something she likes she is going to want it. Either decide that she can have it quickly or keep her looking the other way when you pass a likely area – the toy or sweet shelves for instance. All you need to say is 'Oh, look at that' and point to something distracting and she will be sure to look that way. It is playing dirty, but every mother is entitled to it sometimes – others call it strategy – or political expediency… If she is getting hungry, buy a few slices of cold meat and let her chew on them. If you really intend buying those sticky sweets let her hold them, or give her one. Don't think that if you are reasonable she will become more and more demanding. It is the attraction of forbidden fruit and the fact that you are unyielding that makes children determined to extract as much as they can out of a situation.

However, if a situation warrants a firm 'no', don't hesitate to say it and follow through effectively. There is no need to be afraid of putting your foot down – limits beyond which your child may not go will give her a feeling of security and make sense out of what would otherwise be a topsy-turvy world. Do not make the mistake of thinking this means hitting your child. If you should happen to lose your self-control and smack her, take her in your arms as soon as you have cooled down, tell her you love her but that she made you very cross. Remind her of what she did and tell her how strongly you feel about it. This way your child will not lose respect for you and herself-respect will be restored. It will make her want to get your approval because there will be no cause for resentment or mixed feelings about you.

When called for, never put off discipline by waiting till you get home or threatening her with statements like 'wait till your father hears about this…' A young child has no sense of deferment, and she will not even relate a delayed punishment to what she has done wrong earlier. You must be really quick off the mark if you want to be effective. There is no point in watching her do something you disapprove of for a while then saying 'stop it', then repeating it if she continues, then going red in the face… until you eventually go blue in the face and slightly mad. You have got to make up your mind quickly. Do you or do you not want to allow something? If you do not, stop it instantly. The conviction in your voice should be sufficient to deter. If it is not, it is probably because you are not really sure of yourself.

KEEP A WATCHFUL EYE. Some situations need a quiet but watchful eye kept on them. If they develop the wrong way, jump in. Don't shilly-shally – you'll make a fool of yourself if you do and your children will take you for a ride. Of course, this is easier said than done! But as you gain experience and confidence as a parent you should be able to assess a situation much more quickly. Get in there; remove her physically if she doesn't listen the first time. Ignore the embarrassing wails and flailing legs and very firmly and as calmly as possible insist that she stop the activity you object to, even if you have to isolate her from the company for a short while. The pressures on parents are often unbearable and an occasional explosion will not harm. But the routine use of hidings or smacking as the means of discipline is damaging and self-defeating.

Humiliation breeds resentment and this will make her want to 'get you back' rather than please you. And in the end this is the only real basis for a lasting and healthy relationship with your child, the kind of love that is based on mutual respect and caring, not fear and dependence.

PLAYING WITH OTHER CHILDREN. The child under two will play alongside another child, but there is unlikely to be any interaction between them, until the one grabs whatever the other is playing with! The victim's response will either be a long silence followed by loud wailing or an attempt to grab it back. The mother will probably react by taking the toy away from the grabber and smacking her, so she will start crying too. Looked at dispassionately, it is a rather comic scene but without any positive results.

The first child was only doing what comes naturally; so was the second. It takes time for the social graces like sharing to develop. The mother is also reacting instinctively by smacking the child, but she should know better.

It would have been better to have prevented the conflict by diverting or separating them as soon as the one started grabbing. Smacking a child as a punishment is not going to teach her to stop using violence as a means to an end. It is only going to teach her that if she smacks she will get smacked and that aggression is used by adults as well as children to solve their problems. You will also have to smack extremely hard for it to act as a deterrent and then you will be making fear your means of discipline. She will soon be too big to spank and when you are not there she will relish 'getting away with it' so you will not have achieved anything.

LEARNING RESPECT FOR OTHERS. When she is older she will learn to respect the rights of others as she matures and is able to put herself in their place. This kind of abstract thought and empathy develops slowly and is not usual until the end of the third year or more likely the fourth. In the same way, she is unable to perceive that when someone hurts her accidentally it was not deliberate, and that they did not mean to do it. When this kind of situation arises talk to her about it, explaining how people feel when their rights are infringed. Children love being talked to like grown-ups, especially when there is no heat in the situation. She will slowly develop the social graces and feelings we associate with civilized living. This is where a good story, role-playing or fairy tales can be a great developer of empathy. Children who have not had this kind of learning do not develop it naturally.

Point out how people give up their seat for others on the train – if this is unusual where you live – be the example yourself; and remind her how nice it is when another child shares her toys or sweets. She may not be able to bring herself to do it yet, but she will be getting the message. You have got to point out the implications of a situation to a child. You cannot wait for her to discover them all by herself, because it could take a lifetime.

AGGRESSION. Aggression is one of the most disconcerting manifestations of early childhood turmoil. Like anyone who is frustrated by their lack of power to get what they want through acceptable means such as talking about their needs, trading services, or even buying their way, children resort to the age old standby, force and aggression. They hit, bite, punch or kick the object of their frustration to get what they want. Temperaments differ and some children have a far lower frustration threshold than others. Justifiable anger is not necessarily bad but frustration is an inevitable part of life and we need to teach our children effective ways of handling it.

The use of language to express feelings and needs is vital. Help your child express what is upsetting her or making her feel inadequate, by verbalising for her if she cannot: 'I know you're angry with Tommy for taking your doll, but you mustn't bite him because of it'.

Excessively aggressive children who bite or hit without immediate provocation are likely to be highly frustrated, resentful and angry children. And they need help. If their life is too full of do's and do-not's without consideration for what they want, if they feel threatened because of a new arrival in the family or because they are being ignored most of the time, they may have a lot of pent up anger that boils over whenever they meet someone they can vent it on.

Do not condemn the child without a sympathetic look at her side of the story. In the normal course of the first three years especially, there will be times when anger and frustration will be inevitable. It is up to you to see that your child finds more acceptable ways of dealing with these feelings. No child should get the idea that it is permissible to hurt others or herself. And remember that you cannot teach her this by smacking it out of her! She will not learn to handle her problems constructively that way. Teach her social techniques such as asking nicely, offering something in exchange for something else, and finally to learn to accept it. Sometimes, even these methods will not get her what she wants, and she will just have to accept this with good grace. Of course you cannot expect this instantly from a two-year-old. It takes time and emotional growth, but at least you will have gone a long way towards developing an adult who can deal with life's frustrations in a non-damaging way.

BITING. It can come as something of a shock to the most gentle of parents to find they have a 'biter' in the family; and it is not confined to boys. Biting is a primitive reaction to competition (ask some famous soccer players!). Do not smack or bite back, as is often advised! This only confirms the action and says that if you are bigger than your opponent you can get away with it.

Say: 'NO!' firmly looking directing at the child, and take her away from the action physically sitting her down quietly elsewhere if possible. Tell her 'biting hurts', or 'it makes sore'... use whatever descriptive language she can understand. It often happens in a playgroup situation and she may have to be taken home with an explanation that she 'can't play if she hurts other children'. Do not tell her she is a 'bad' girl, or label her in other negative ways. Concentrate on explaining the effect it has on others. And try and get her to say sorry to the victim. If not immediately then soon. She may not understand the concept or meaning of the apology, but encourage it. Do not get angry if she refuses. Keep emphasising the principle of not hurting others, and saying sorry if she does. She will get it in due course if her environment reflects this principle.

No doubt mothers' whose children have been victims of the biting will be upset and you will have to apologise profusely. Unless your child shows other aggressive behaviour such as hurting animals or attacking children in other ways, the biting stage should pass before too long. Interestingly, some of the most gentle, caring adults have been early biters.

HURTING ANIMALS. Animals are a great source of fascination for children, but they do not always understand that unlike teddy bears they can be hurt and feel pain. You will need to explain how to touch and handle them. Children are sometimes deliberately cruel to animals. This is an important danger sign and you must not ignore it. See a therapist if the child seems to lack remorse or it happens again.

NEGATIVISM. As discussed earlier you may find yourself knee-deep in negativism from the middle of the second year with your child saying 'no' to almost everything. It's natural for her to object to having to do as she's told all the time, especially when she's trying so hard to develop a picture of herself as a person in her own right. If you win all the arguments she could form an image of herself as a failure and give up trying to succeed in anything. Or she may become aggressive towards others; or become difficult over food, or withhold her stools as a way of asserting herself. Letting her win every battle, however, will give her a false idea of what life is like, and her place in it, and she'll come down with a bump when she comes up against the real thing later on.

So when you really feel a definite 'no' is required stick with it and carry it through. As she becomes more sure of who she is, your child will not need to put it to the test so often and she will become easier to live with.

GETTING ATTENTION. Once a child becomes fully aware that she is a separate being, some time during the second year, she will start to evolve ways of getting the attention of others and using them to her own ends. How you respond to her will tell her a lot about herself and reflect in her behaviour.

A little child's need for attention is immediate. She does not have a concept of time or deferment. Her needs are 'now' – anything other than that has no meaning for her. If she has to get to the extremes of crying, whining, or throwing a tantrum to get your attention, she will eventually resort to those tactics as a matter of course.

Thinking you should teach her to 'wait her turn' or that she will become 'spoilt' if you respond immediately is the surest way of turning a perfectly nice child into a demanding, difficult monster – 'spoilt', in fact. A young child needs solutions to her problems straight away; she needs to know that you will respond without having to be forced to. It is far simpler to interrupt your conversation with an adult to attend to a toddler than to try to carry on while the child becomes more and more agitated and obstreperous. After all, adults should have the maturity to cope with an interruption. Nothing is 'more important' than giving your child your attention when she needs it. You will be surprised how quickly your child will grow up and how much sooner she will become co-operative if you keep your promises and never make it necessary for her to use desperate measures to get your attention.

As she develops a concept of time, and of what happens in the world around her, usually around the end of the second year, she will be able to accept a promise to attend to her as soon as you can. A child has a right to receive your attention fully and freely and without resentment. She will respond by giving you the same consideration as soon as she is able, and you will have a delightful and pleasant companion. It is when our needs are met that we can give in return, not when they are frustrated.

The child who has hurt herself needs your attention and sympathy. Telling her it doesn't hurt and ordering her to stop behaving like a baby is illogical and insensitive. Showing appropriate sympathy and giving her the necessary attention will keep things in perspective. It is a sad reflection if she has to turn every scrape into a major disaster to get a response.

'NAUGHTINESS'. It is easy to label a child's behaviour 'naughty' but when it's examined objectively you will usually find that 'naughtiness' does not come into it at all. A child who is bored, frustrated, neglected, jealous, tired or hungry will often resort to 'naughty' behaviour to draw attention to her problem. A one-year-old who is doing what comes naturally and touching and exploring everything she can is not 'naughty'. The child who wets her bed is not 'naughty'. If you remind yourself to always think of naughtiness as only a symptom you will soon find that you can usually eradicate the cause of the unacceptable behaviour. In an older child it may take time to undo long-standing behaviour patterns, but if you work at it consistently it can be done. Meanwhile you will have to cope with the symptoms.

It is no good feeling guilty and thinking that your child's annoying behaviour is a result of your failings. Everyone makes mistakes and the one big difference between mothers and other executives who have demanding jobs is that mothers feel terribly guilty about their mistakes. You must learn to forgive your own failings and take it from there. Children bounce back intact if you do not keep piling the burden of your guilt on them.

Even if you do realise that there is an underlying reason, you must make it clear that the unacceptable behaviour cannot be tolerated. Understanding the reasons for behaviour does not mean condoning it.

SUGAR HIGH? Sugar has become a sour point with parents today, many of whom believe that it is the cause of 'hyped' up behaviour in their children. Like many urban myths there is some truth in it, but it is not nearly as simple as it is painted. Simple sugars such as those commonly consumed by children in sweets, cool drinks and biscuits give almost instant energy. As soon as that energy is used up there is a quick slump. Sucrose (table sugar) is 99, 5% carbohydrate. Hardboiled and jelly type sweets are 93,1% carbohydrate. Carbohydrates give us energy. From the percentages it is obvious that there is little room for anything other than energy in these 'foods'. If this is what a child has eaten for most of the day then she will certainly be 'hyper, but does this prove that 'sugar' is at fault?

In a well designed medical trial, mothers were given a sweetened drink to offer their children. Half the drinks were sweetened with table sugar, the other half with a sugar-free sweetener. The result: without knowing which drink their child had consumed, most mothers were convinced that the sugar-free substitute had made their child 'hyper'. Conclusion: yes, sweets are 'not good for children' in the sense that they can spoil the appetite, rot the teeth and provide 'empty energy', but they are not necessarily the cause of true ADHD, unless of course, they contain a colourant or preservative to which the child is sensitive, in which case it may be a contributory factor. (*See p. 409 for ADHD*).

It is sometimes thought that eliminating table sugar and substituting it with honey is a better option and 'more natural'. However, a paper published in the Journal of Nutrition which compared the effects of honey, table sugar and high-fructose corn syrup, found that the level of triglycerides, a lipid that can raise the risk of heart disease, had risen for all the volunteers, no matter what sweeteners they had eaten.

Number of calories found in honey: One teaspoon of honey contains 23 calories and 6g of sugar, compared with a level teaspoon of table sugar which contains 16 calories and 4g of sugar. The 'advantage' of honey is that it is sweeter so less can bo used.

NOTE: Honey should not be given in the first year because of the danger of botulism, a serious illness.

HOW TO REALISE YOUR CHILD'S POTENTIAL

THE URGE TO KNOW. There is probably no single factor more crucial to the development of your child's intelligence than curiosity and the urge to enquire into the nature of things.

The question 'why' could almost be called the key to universal knowledge. Fortunately curiosity is a characteristic shown by almost all children who are developing normally. From the first few weeks when your baby starts exploring her surroundings with her eyes, ears, fingers and mouth she is driven by the need to discover and experience. If you feed this initial curiosity in an appropriate way as described in Chapter 8 she will be encouraged to continue developing this trait.

Too many or unsuitable stimuli will not have the desired effect and she will shut them out. Most families provide an adequate environment for babies in the first months unless there is gross neglect. But once a child becomes mobile, a number of other factors come into play that are not always conducive to optimal mental development. The parents' attitude to the child's exploration of her environment, whether she is allowed to touch things, is talked to, and taken out and about, will all contribute to promoting her curiosity or stifling it.

By the time children reach their second year there is usually a noticeable difference between those who come from homes where they are talked to and encouraged to display curiosity, and those from homes where parents are either too pressured by their own problems or believe that children should be seen and not heard.

Encouraging the inquiring mind is no small task and a great deal of patience and sensitivity on the part of the adult is required. But it is fascinating to see the world clearly again through a child's unpolluted view. Strangely, even though the toy industry is a huge money-spinner very few toys have been developed that cater for the real needs of children. Often it is the box, not the contents, that is of most value and interest to a child.

BASIC EQUIPMENT FOR CHILDREN FROM ONE YEAR ONWARDS

THE JOYS OF 'JUNK'. Boxes of every description and size, small boxes to fit into bigger boxes, large boxes that become instant 'houses', 'trucks', 'ships' or anything else the imagination can conjure up.

- Yoghurt containers, cardboard rolls from toilet paper, tins without sharp edges, cotton reels. Water, even a basinful, is always fun and can teach basic science principles. Empty bottles to pour and 'measure' with can teach about quantity and the physics of what floats and what makes things sink. Even a two-year-old will enjoy making these discoveries if you take the time to point them out.
- A box of dressing-up clothes will give pleasure and endless creative opportunity.
- Dolls and soft toys are always useful for adding the human element to a child's play.
- Sturdy puzzles, simple enough not to cause frustration yet challenging enough to be interesting, teach and entertain.
- Toys like 'posting blocks' in which a three-dimensional shape has to be inserted into a matching cut-out promote spatial perception.
- Balls of all sizes.
- Books made from cloth or sturdy cardboard with simple pictures for the child to look at herself from nine months or so. Whenever you have a quiet moment while waiting at the clinic or when she is having a bottle, go through the book with her, talking about the pictures. Point out colours by finding all the reds and blues. Later on you can encourage her to 'find something red' and praise her lavishly when she gets it right. Help her get the right answers by making it easy at first and she will find it such fun that she will want to play along.
- Make up simple learning games along these lines pointing out shapes and sizes – round, big, small, square – there are opportunities for learning to classify all around you.
- Books to read to her. Even before she can understand she will love hearing the rise and fall rhythm of your reading voice. Keep it simple and short – children have a very short concentration span. She will probably only pay attention for a few minutes at first. The warm closeness of the reading ritual is one of the most precious gifts you can give a child.

Don't be misled into thinking that a child who can reel off 'facts' or impress with the ability to count at the age of two is going to be advanced. None of this has any bearing on her future ability. Through repetition you can teach very young children to recognise and repeat words or numbers but this is not really the ability to read, or a sign of a future mathematical genius. You will be doing your child a far greater service if you give her practice in the basic skills that are needed to master these tasks. This way she will have a true understanding of what she is doing not just a superficial ability that is also unfair to her because she will have the wrong impression about it. What you should be aiming to achieve with your child is the continued pleasure and excitement of discovery that is natural in infants. One of the most striking characteristics of children who develop successfully is their desire for discovery and enjoyment of learning, in contrast to the rapid decline in the need to know and the bland acceptance that characterises those whose potential has already been dimmed.

OPPORTUNITY TO LET OFF STEAM IN OUTDOOR PLAY IS NEEDED. Very active children in particular need the opportunity to use up excess energy by running, climbing and jumping. A visit to the playground if you do not have a garden can be a sanity saver when your toddler is bursting at the seams with pent-up energy.

A sand pit, even a small one in an old baby bath, can be set up on a balcony if you do not have a garden. Use washed river sand and keep the pit covered when not in use to prevent soiling by animals.

ATTITUDES THAT HELP CHILDREN GROW UP EFFECTIVELY. There is a fine distinction between helping your child constructively and doing so much that she comes to rely on you completely. When your toddler comes to you with a problem, judge whether it is really impossible for her to cope with it, for example, unscrewing a tight lid; or whether, with a little bit of instruction and demonstration she will be able to manage. It is fine to help in situations where she could not possibly cope and it is good to show her how things are done or work, explaining in a simple way exactly what is happening. But letting your child use you as a tool that does everything for her even when she can manage herself, is unwise. It will increase her dependence on you and will encourage clinging because she cannot cope with anything without you, and will eventually harm her self-esteem.

GO TO www.baby-childcare.com TO WATCH THE FOLLOWING VIDEOS THAT ARE APPLICABLE TO CHAPTER 10

PROF CLAUDIA GRAY	Sleep in babies and children
DR ANUSHA LACHMAN	The first 1 000 days of life
	Technology
	The role of care givers

Dealing with conflict

Is it okay for my child to be bored?

Toys – less or more?

Boys don't cry – right or wrong?

ANEL ANNANDALE

When is the ideal time to send you child to nursery school

Giving children the space to explore

The importance of play

Developing intelligence

Delayed gratification

LIZANNE DU PLESSIS

What is self-regulation

Sensory regulation

Sensory temprament

JOANNA WILSON

Causes of childhood overweight and obesity

Parent creating healthy homes

Responsive feeding

CHAPTER 11

Setting your Child on the Right Track

Besides exhausting their mothers, most children have pretty well exhausted the possibilities offered by their home environment by the time they are three to three-and-a-half. They want to see new faces, new toys and hear new versions of old tales. This is when a playgroup or preschool (nursery school, or kindergarten) can be of great benefit.

It is all very well if your child is way ahead on intellectual skills, but unless she is able to relate to people effectively, she will be sadly handicapped. Learning to mix with and match herself against others in the open market is essential for sound development. This skill has recently been given a name: it is aptly called emotional intelligence, and it is rated as the defining difference between successful people and those who fail despite having intellectual capacity.

PLAYGROUPS. If there are no suitable facilities in your area they can be organised by a group of mothers who want to give their children the opportunity to mix with others.

Playgroups can be run along very informal lines by a group of mothers who arrange to supervise members' children on different days, or one mother can do it every day. There are certain legal requirements for looking after more than six children at a time, so keep your group under that number unless you want to make it more formal and permanent which will mean registering it with the appropriate authority. If you want to organise an informal playgroup with all the mothers taking turns in looking after the children, you must decide on a schedule that suits the ages and routines of the children, keeping the following in mind:

- The mothers should all live in one area because travelling is tiring for youngsters. If it takes you half-an-hour to deliver your child it could defeat the purpose.
- The other mothers in the group should have more or less the same attitude to child-rearing as you do, or it could be confusing and unsettling for the child.
- Work out a duty roster carefully so that public holidays are taken into account, and discuss what arrangements will be made in the event of illness or special occasions, or you could have your friendships ruined.
- Only saints and the senseless should consider including children who are not potty trained. This makes somewhere around two-and-a-half to three years a realistic age for attendance.
- Depending on the child, attendance for a few hours two or three days a week is usually a happy medium at that age.
- The mothers in charge should have sufficient play materials available, especially crayons, paper, building blocks, dressing-up clothes and unless the period is for less than two hours, a garden or some other outdoor play area is essential.
- A small amount can be contributed by each child every term to buy materials. This can be distributed among different homes if there is no fixed venue.
- Each child can bring a piece of fruit that is put in a communal bowl and cut up and shared out at 'break'.
- It takes stamina and determination to make this kind of system work, but if every mother is sufficiently motivated – even if it is only the lure of a few free mornings to herself when she is not on duty that keeps her going – it can be a successful arrangement.
- The more formal playgroup system involves a venue such as a church hall that will accommodate the group on a regular basis. Playgroups of this nature are usually started by one or more mothers who do it because of their training in preschool education or because they see a need for it and possibly want to make a little extra money. Before setting up contact the relevant authority to register if you will be accommodating more than six children.
- Insurance is vital and you should get expert advice on the subject. You may want to offer parents the option of taking part in a scheme that will cover medical costs if a

child is injured on the premises. The cost per child is usually very low and it covers accidents, minor and major, that can happen.

- The playgroup supervisor should take a course in first aid and have a well-equipped first aid kit on the premises.

STRUCTURING THE SESSIONS

- Three hours a day, from nine to 12 is usually long enough.
- Children attend regularly, every morning or less frequently, but it is a good idea to encourage them to attend on consecutive days if not attending every session so that they have some continuity.
- Biscuits and fizzy drinks should not be allowed. Fruit or cheese or raw vegetables and milk or yoghurt are suitable mid-morning snacks.

PRESCHOOLS (NURSERY SCHOOLS, KINDERGARTEN, GRADE N, GRADE R). These schools are the most structured of the pre-school arrangements. Preschools are usually organised and run by church groups or privately. Government sponsored and organised preschools (Grade N, Grade R) are usually attached to primary schools and attendance is often limited to the year before the child enters school.

Private (Independent) preschools are allowed to admit children from any age so long as they have the capacity to provide for their needs. This means that the child may have three or more years of preschool education.

The function of preschools is to develop the skills that will be necessary later for formal learning. Yet some parents still have the notion that sending a child to preschool (nursery school or kindergarten) is not necessary, or an abdication of responsibility and the 'lazy' mother's solution – nothing could be further from the truth.

Preschool education teaches the child to mix with her peers, helps her to develop concentration and encourages the use of the skills needed to learn to read and write, even though there is no formal teaching of letters or numbers. An alert teacher will spot a child who has potential problems, such as poor motor co-ordination, mixed dominance (not clearly left or right handed), ADHD and so on. If they are detected early enough, the child can receive remedial attention before she enters school. School readiness tests are usually administered in the last term before school by a school psychologist or the staff in consultation with a psychologist. If there is a problem the child will either be given remedial attention by the teacher or other professional or, it may be advisable to wait another year before she enters school. All that may be needed is time for the child to mature physically and mentally, or even emotionally. Boys often mature more slowly physically and emotionally than girls.

Children who attend a good preschool or even only Grade R, the reception year before 'proper' school are at a huge advantage compared to those who enter school straight from home, particularly if the home environment is not stimulating. The bright, well-adjusted child may find three years of the same routine tedious and it may be wise to keep her at home for an extra year or half year, provided the home environment is stimulating. The problem is that unless parents can afford to send their child to a private preschool, there are very few Government preschools. This makes a huge difference to how children perform when they get to Grade 1, creating a lag that leaves disadvantaged children behind.

HOW TO SPOT A POTENTIAL LEARNING PROBLEM

DON'T LEAVE IT TOO LATE. It used to be thought that children who did not progress at school were stupid or lazy. Today we know that 10% or more average to highly intelligent children have perceptual difficulties that make it difficult for them to cope with school work unless they receive expert tuition.

Children who cannot keep up with their peers often become aggressive and disruptive. Or they may show symptoms of stress such as bedwetting and depression. Others develop antisocial tendencies like petty thieving and vandalism because of their feelings of inferiority. They may also become bullies or victims of bullying.

Parents are usually aware that there is something amiss in their child's development, especially if it is a second child. Unfortunately, well-meaning friends and even professional people are inclined to reassure anxious parents by saying that the child will 'grow out of it'. Some do, but many do not, and it is unkind to all concerned to neglect what should be remedied, before emotional problems complicate matters.

FACTORS WHICH MAY PREDISPOSE TOWARDS LEARNING DISABILITIES. Although it is known that learning problems tend to run in families, the exact mechanism is not known. It is thought that certain factors may also predispose a child either before birth or later on.

DURING PREGNANCY
- Viral and other infections and illnesses during the first 12 weeks.
- Dangerous chemical substances such as lead and mercury that the mother has absorbed during pregnancy, possibly because of her work. (New legislation protects pregnant women in this regard.)
- Smoking.

- Drinking alcohol. It is best to avoid entirely.
- Use of recreational or hard drugs.
- Poor nutrition, particularly a lack of protein.
- Certain drugs taken during the first 12 weeks of pregnancy.
- Chronic untreated illness in the mother.

DURING DELIVERY. With modern obstetric care these factors are fortunately rare.
- Prolonged or difficult labour may diminish the oxygen supply to the infant.
- Drugs used during delivery may depress the infant's system to a dangerous degree.
- Bleeding into the brain because of pressure during delivery or afterwards particularly in preterm babies, or the faulty use of forceps.
- Deprivation of oxygen to the child either because the cord is around the neck or due to other factors.

AFTERBIRTH. It is not always possible to say exactly what the cause is, and many factors may contribute.
- Very low birth weight because of prematurity or other causes.
- Serious infections such as meningitis or prolonged high fever.
- Poor nutrition, particularly lack of protein and iron in the first two years of life can affect brain growth.
- Hypoglycaemia, untreated low blood sugar levels in the first few days after birth.
- Hypernatraemia, a too high concentration of sodium in relation to body fluids.
- Poisons such as lead (*see p. 304*).
- Brain injury.
- Untreated visual or auditory problems.

WHAT IS A LEARNING DISABILITY? When the central nervous system – the brain and spinal cord which control bodily functions such as sight, speech and movement – does not work perfectly, the child may have difficulty performing certain tasks. This may first become apparent when the child does not reach the normal development milestones at the appropriate age. She may have been slow in learning to hold her head up, or in talking or walking. Or she may not show any symptoms until later when she is unable to do the things other children her age find possible, although you should always keep in mind the fact that children develop at different rates. (*See Chapter 8 for a guide to normal development.*)

Possibly because of their relatively immature neurological development, far more boys than girls are affected. Attention deficit disorder is the term used today to describe children who have problems in processing information, even though they have at least average or above average intelligence. Learning disabilities associated with attention deficit disorder may affect only certain skills, or could be more generalised with an all-over lag in performance. Behavioural problems, particularly hyperactivity, are common; while emotional adjustment, although initially normal often deteriorates due to frustration and loss of self-esteem.

Faulty brain development while in the womb may be a cause in some children as autopsy reports have shown brain abnormalities in some learning disabled children. New research by means of brain scans taken a few hours after birth showed differences between children who later developed signs of dyslexia. Doctors hope to diagnose dyslexia earlier and prevent or reduce problems associated with it.

Slow maturation of the nervous system and defective filtering of information are considered part of the problem. Learning problems with this cause tend to run in families.

The very 'clumsy' child who lacks the co-ordination to do things which other children of the same age do easily should be examined for mild cerebral palsy.

GENERAL CHARACTERISTICS OF CHILDREN WITH ATTENTION DEFICIT DISORDER (ADD) OR ATTENTION DEFICIT DISORDER WITH HYPERACTIVITY (ADHD). Highly irritable, unable to suck properly, extremely restless, poor sleepers, great deal of crying. (These characteristics may also apply to normal or highly intelligent children without the disorder.)

TODDLER STAGE. Extremely clumsy, creates total disorder, excessive temper tantrums, slow to talk coherently.

PRESCHOOL AGE. Destructive, extremely short attention span, particularly aggressive, temper tantrums, unable to follow instructions, hyperactive, mixed dominance; that is not clearly left or right handed, very clumsy.

SCHOOL AGE. Unable to sit still for any length of time, lack of concentration, difficulty in fastening shoe laces, buttons and zips, bad at games that require eye-hand co-ordination such as ball games, unable to control impulses and always having to be reprimanded. Occasionally the child may be 'hypoactive' – slow, placid with little drive and lack of interest in anything. More specifically the child may have problems in the following areas:

Problems of **language and thought processing** sometimes make the child seem particularly disobedient. This may be because she forgets the beginning of a sentence by the time you have completed it.

Spatial and auditory perceptual problems can mean that the information received through her eyes and ears is confused, and she cannot store or recall it correctly. She may not have a true image of the shapes or position of objects she sees, or she may see things as being in the foreground when they are actually in the background.

Her **auditory synthesis** may be faulty in that the sounds she hears seem to be of equal value, that is, background noise may appear to have the same value as close sounds.

Her **interpersonal relationships** with parents and peers are often characterised by extreme aggression and lack of discipline mainly due to frustration and inability to grasp correctly what is expected of her.

Emotionally she has vast mood fluctuations with a very low frustration threshold and many temper tantrums. Because of the nature of the problem that makes it easy to believe that the child is 'naughty' or a 'black sheep' or just plain 'bad', parents may have mixed feelings of guilt and rejection. It is important to understand that what the child is experiencing is beyond her control – for her, life is a terribly mixed up scramble of stimulation that she cannot handle.

As a result she is frustrated and unhappy because she is intelligent enough to understand that she is not coping as well as others.

Because these children cannot sit still they find it difficult to concentrate. Because the information they are receiving is scrambled they cannot make sense of it. Because they cannot process what they are being told, they cannot cope with schoolwork. This sad situation requires understanding and help for both parents and child.

It is vitally important that the child be assessed by experts in this field as soon as possible as the earlier treatment begins the better chance there is of helping the child. These specialists should include a paediatric neurologist, psychologist, paediatric psychiatrist, ophthalmologist and an audiologist, before a diagnosis is made and appropriate treatment applied.

In cases in which true hyperactivity has been established, medication can have a good effect in helping concentration and reducing activity so that the child is able to cope with the discipline of the class room. (*See p. 409*) Because children with emotional problems sometimes show the same symptoms as the hyperactive child, unnecessary medication can be prescribed. Accurate diagnosis is therefore essential before treatment is started.

EMOTIONAL DISORDERS. It is possible for children to have a true emotional disorder such as anxiety or a depressive illness together with ADHD. Unfortunately drugs for ADHD can aggravate these conditions; however, specific treatments for each disorder can be very effective. Early correct recognition of anxiety and depressive disorders is important. (*See p. 432.*)

LEAD. The discovery of lead in the blood of hyperactive children has opened a new avenue for research. It has been found that relatively low levels of lead in experimental animals as well as children result in increased activity.

High levels of lead are known to lead to brain damage and mental impairment. When you consider that it takes only a small amount of lead-based paint, for example, to raise the level of lead in the system, and that it is accumulated by the body, it can be seen that many children may have sufficiently raised lead levels to lead to hyperactivity. Lead is found in water that comes through old lead pipes, in pollution from car exhausts (less so now that lead-free fuel is available), paint and battery casings to name a few sources. Because lead has a slightly sweet taste, children with pica (the tendency to eat unusual substances) will pick at flaking paint and may soon accumulate enough lead to do significant damage. If you have any reason to suspect that your child may have been exposed to lead-based paint or other sources of lead, tell your doctor and ask for a blood test and other tests for lead in the system.

ALLERGY. Some doctors have suggested that hyperactivity is an allergic reaction to substances in the child's diet such as dyes and chemical additives in processed food. Although this has not been proved conclusively, it is worth keeping the possibility of allergy to a particular foodstuff in mind when discussing the problem.

SMOKING. Mothers who smoke during pregnancy are more likely to have children who are hyperactive.

ALCOHOL. Foetal alcohol syndrome that is caused by the excessive intake of alcohol during pregnancy has been associated with hyperactivity, aggression and learning problems.

DRUGS. 'Hard' drugs used during pregnancy can have an effect on the unborn child.

ANAEMIA. Check iron status, as low haemoglobin levels are associated with ADHD.

SPECIFIC LEARNING DISABILITIES

DYSLEXIA, partial word-blindness, is a common problem which reveals itself when the child fails to progress in reading and spelling at school. She may not learn to tell the time and could have a poor auditory memory so that she does not remember what she has heard. Sometimes she learns to cope initially by remembering the shape of the words in her first reader and guessing the rest of the time. But as the books become more complicated and she is expected to read material for other subjects, she lags behind. Remedial teaching is necessary before she gets too far behind the rest of the class and a feeling of inferiority becomes ingrained.

If the parent is able to exercise great patience and refrain from judging or losing her temper, she can assist the child by reading to her and helping her practise her reading.

Although progress is generally slow in the beginning, it does accelerate as the child becomes more proficient. Covering part of the word to split it into syllables helps break it up into easier sections to sound out and using a ruler under the line helps her keep track of her place. Because the child does not have the ability to sound out words in syllables she is very poor at spelling and this is usually most difficult to correct. She needs to sound out the words aloud and then write them over several times without seeing the original. Practise at saying, writing and seeing words will gradually build up her repertoire. Many famous people have succeeded in spite of being dyslexic and if the condition is identified and treated early there is every chance of improvement. The tendency towards dyslexia seems to run in families and is far more common in boys than in girls.

DYSGRAPHIA, the inability to write coherently, is associated with poor fine motor coordination, which is the inability to control the muscles necessary for tasks that require precision. These children are often ambidextrous, that is, they use either hand with equal ease, and they have mixed laterality which means that neither side of the brain has become dominant.

When drawing, the child may use one hand on the one side of the page and switch to the other hand to work on the other side of the page. She may be unable to draw a picture of a man so that there is a head, body and legs even in stick form and cannot copy a triangle, circle or square in any recognizable fashion, even by the age of five.

Although most children use both hands as infants, they should have a preference for either the left or right hand by the age of about two.

Children with learning disabilities are more likely to be left handed, but never force a left handed child to change hands once she has established dominance, as this can lead to stuttering and to mixed dominance. Her learning problems are not due to the fact that she is left handed.

Dysgraphia sterns mainly from poor eye-hand co-ordination, a skill that should be practised by infants from the earliest months. (*See p. 227.*)

Exercises to stimulate visual motor skills, the co-ordination of eye and hand movements, should be part of a child's normal play. These include jigsaw puzzles, 'posting' of various shapes into slots, 'sewing' on a large card with thick needle and wool, threading beads, 'sieving', drawing with pencil and crayons, building with blocks, and cutting out with round-ended scissors.

DYSPRAXIA, is the partial inability to perform coordinated tasks such as tying shoelaces. It is a neurological problem that impairs the organisation of movement and often has no obvious cause.

It is more common in males and at the mild end of the 10% of those affected by it may manifest as nothing more than a general 'clumsiness'. In more severe cases kicking a ball, even walking up and down stairs is difficult in terms of co-ordination. These children can easily become victims of bullying and name calling because they do not meet the popular image of the macho male. Daniel Radcliffe, the actor who played the role of Harry Potter has a mild form of dyspraxia, so there is a successful role model for other so called 'klutzes'.

DYSCALCULIA. Up to seven percent of children, mostly boys, have difficulty doing simple sums. This is sometimes due to an inability to accurately register spoken syllables, numbers and letters so that they are misinterpreted in the brain. In other words, it is a sensory processing problem like many other learning problems.

German researcher Burkhart Fisher emeritus professor of neurophysical biophysics at the University of Freiburg in Germany believes that trouble controlling visual attention contributes towards dyslexia and that another perceptual process called subitizing is lacking in dyscalculia. Subitizing is the knack of recognising quantity by just looking at a group without counting. It is a kind of accurate guessing. This facility helps children recognise the concept of numbers standing for a particular amount. He trains children by doing exercises that improve subitizing ability. He believes that both dyslexia and dyscalculia are partly due to sensory processing problems and that special training in these areas can improve their functioning.

HELPING THE CHILD WITH LEARNING DISABILITIES. As soon as you suspect that your child is lagging behind in any area of development, take her to be assessed by a team of developmental specialists – even if you have to travel. Most large teaching hospitals have a special assessment clinic.

The earlier remedial work is started the better. Before school and even before pre-school is not too early to practise the skills needed later on.

If any of the predisposing factors described on *p. 303* and *p. 304* apply to your child, have her checked regularly to ensure she is developing well.

Partial deafness caused by infections such as otitis media can hamper the child's language development and subsequent ability to express herself and understand precisely what is meant. An auditory test will establish the degree of hearing loss, and a small operation to clear the ears of mucus should improve matters quickly. (*See p. 350.*)

Allergies such as hay fever can make the membranes of the inner ear swell and the eardrums retract so that there are times when the child has a significant hearing loss. Don't ignore allergic symptoms – have them treated. (*See pp. 417–428.*)

Of all the senses, vision requires the largest brain area to control. It is not surprising therefore, that a large percentage of children with learning problems have some visual defect. Correction of the defect results in a marked improvement in the scholastic achievement of children who show no evidence of minimal brain dysfunction – that means that children whose learning disability is a direct result of poor vision are likely to improve. A distinction must be made between 'sight' which may be perfect and 'vision'.

Sight is the ability to see, while vision is the ability to interpret and understand that information which comes in through the eyes.

Children who have visual defects as well as attention deficit disorder are not likely to improve significantly in their learning ability once the visual defect has been corrected. It is worth noting, however, that eye defects are far more common in children with ADHD than in the general population.

Occasionally a child who is having problems at school in which she appears to 'daydream' and as a result misses out on part of the lessons, has in fact been suffering petit mal epileptic seizures or aphasic attacks. This means that she has 'blanked out' for a while without being aware of it. Electroencephalograms (EEG brain scans) can record the brain patterns to show if there is any abnormality, while medication is highly effective in controlling the attacks. Some learning disabilities are caused by inherent sensory processing errors, i.e. an inability to understand sensory information, whereas others are caused by a lack of correct sensory feedback. In such cases, the child has trouble receiving sensory information, and so has little chance of understanding whatever she is presented with. The learning disability she is struggling with is therefore a symptom of an underlying physical problem. Happily, this means that the disability may be temporary, as remedying the physical problem ought to improve the child's learning ability.

HANDLING THE CHILD WITH 'MINIMAL BRAIN DYSFUNCTION'. Concentrate on the positive aspects of your child; making her feel a failure and comparing her with others will only add to her problems.

Many children who have trouble learning academic subjects are extremely good at practical skills – encourage them.

For some children tuition in a special school or class is best; for others, remedial teaching at school is sufficient.

A lot of time, money and effort can be wasted on the wrong treatment – have the child expertly assessed before going to a therapist.

Hyperactive children (ADHD) need a planned, stable routine because they cannot control one for themselves. Make a time for homework, a special time for you to read to her and to discuss the day's events. When you give instructions, keep them simple and precise, repeating the key points. Special schools for children with learning disabilities have been established, and remedial teachers are available at large schools. Private remedial teachers can fill the gap if there is no specialised help at the school.

LEARNING TO BE LIKEABLE

ACQUIRING EMOTIONAL SKILLS. It is not only children with learning disabilities who need tactful handling if they are to reach their full potential. Even children with 'everything going for them' can develop habits and attitudes that handicap them. If you have given your child sufficient opportunity for exploring her environment and finding out about the nature of things, she will, by the time she is three or four, have a fairly comprehensive knowledge of the physical properties of things. She should know what is likely to be hot or cold or dangerous or not to be touched. A single glance or a word or two from you should be enough to check her.

Although she will have made many discoveries by herself, she needs you to guide her too. This is always best done by accentuating the positive. If you want your child to have social graces and good manners you must observe them yourself. If she hears please and thank you, she will learn to say them as well. Nevertheless, children do need reinforcement of any learning. When she remembers what you have taught her, give her an immediate reward by smiling and showing her that you are pleased. There is nothing children want more than to please their parents even if their actions are not always convincing! Don't wait until later to praise good behaviour – children's memories are too short to benefit from delayed reaction – regardless of whether it is good or bad.

Instead of being on the alert for what you can reprimand her for, seek out the times when she is doing what is acceptable, like sharing her toys. Tell her you are proud of her. Everybody wants to be liked and if she finds that she can get your positive attention by straightforward means she will continue to use them. By ignoring a child's good behaviour and picking on the bad, she will simply become conditioned to think that good behaviour is not very important or rewarding, and that bad behaviour at least gets her some attention even if it is negative.

On the other hand you don't need to make it seem as though it is an ordeal for her to behave well and that she should receive a big reward for being 'good'. She will learn to turn it on for the sake of the special treats it supplies. Knowing that she is a nice person and that you feel good about her will build up her self-esteem and make her far happier than will a few sticky sweets.

With this kind of relationship she will not want to let you down, and you will find it easy to give of yourself in time and treats. Don't think you will 'spoil' her by letting her have what you would like to give her. It is only when things are obtained undeservedly or through pressure that the child becomes 'spoilt' and ungrateful. Never try to buy good behaviour or affection – it is self-defeating and degrading for both giver and taker.

Sometimes parents expect too much from a child, so that she fails more than she succeeds. Others feel more comfortable with a child who 'knows her place' and is not too inquisitive or 'cheeky'. Young children are usually totally honest; a trait that makes for bruised egos in adults who feel insecure themselves.

'Children should be seen and not heard' is a convenient philosophy, but not very enlightened. The right to inquire and the need to know is a child's prerogative. What they need to learn is how to do it in a socially acceptable way.

For instance, if a child remarks on the fact that the lady in front of you in the queue is fat and has a big nose, it is no use responding by saying 'You're a horrible, rude child!' She is not. She is an observant, honest child. What you could do is acknowledge the remark calmly, and then as soon as possible, when out of earshot, say something like this: 'Yes, the lady is fat and she does have a big nose, but she probably feels very unhappy about it and when she hears people talk about it, it must make her sad. You wouldn't like people to say you look funny, and so we always try and think about how others feel before we say something that might hurt them.'

By the same token parents should not treat children as though they are deaf and dumb at certain times. Talking about the child to other adults in her company, especially if it is to say how naughty, destructive or difficult she is, is gross bad manners and it is no wonder children respond by being insensitive to their parents' wants. Loyalty works both ways and unsupportive parents get inconsiderate children.

As soon as your child can understand what is wanted, give her responsibility – even if it is just unwrapping a bar of soap. You could say, 'Can you please help mommy by taking the paper off the soap and putting it in the bathroom?' Don't supervise or correct – if she needs help give as little as necessary – and let her finish the job.

Children love being asked to do 'grown up' things and by giving her responsibility you are helping her to develop a good opinion of herself and keenness to do more.

The way parents respond to their child's attempts at doing things is important. For instance, the toddler who is playing with a toy that needs to be fitted together may show her mother what she has done. She has the head attached to the body but it is the wrong way round. Her mother looks at it briefly and says: 'That's nice dear,' and the child goes away pleased. Another mother looks at what she has done and says: 'You've got it all wrong,' and the child goes away disappointed. The third mother says, 'you've got it together, that's nice, but the head is on wrong, let me help you put it right. See, this is the right way.' This child goes away pleased to know that her mother approves of what she is doing and keen to try another task because she has had immediate, positive feedback and correction.

To acquire a positive attitude to problem-solving, a child needs to learn to identify the problem, and then know how to set about solving it. One of the most frequent points of friction between parents and children who are trying to do something together, occurs when the child keeps making the same mistake. Some parents take the line that the child should be forced to carry on until she 'finds her mistake'. Others give up with the child and devalue the task by saying it wasn't worth doing anyway. Still others call the child stupid and throw up their hands in despair. Yet it is a fact that children need to learn how to tackle problems.

Firstly, it cannot be presumed that the child has understood what is required. She may not have sufficient language to grasp the subtleties of what is being asked. Or she may have arrived at a solution that is logical and sound, even though it is nothing like the one required.

LEARNING TO LIKE LEARNING

FINDING OUT IS FUN. One of the saddest situations arises when a child who is lucky enough to be born with all her faculties in sound working order, becomes conditioned to stifling her innate abilities. So much of what we become depends on the attitudes we acquire, and sadly many children get the idea that they are incapable of achieving very much.

Humiliating her for coming to the wrong conclusion is a sure way of stifling any desire she may have to tackle future problems. It is better to ask her to tell you how she worked it out. Listen carefully to her explanation, and then go over it with her telling her why it will not work as well as another solution. Praise her ideas when you can for whatever they have shown... imagination, inventiveness... then, if necessary, tell her why they are not the best or most practical solution. If you respect her attempt, she will be pleased to follow your logic and gain from your reasoning.

Praising a child indiscriminately for everything she does regardless of its value is not a good idea. It will give her an unrealistic picture of her abilities and she will find it hard to accept correction from teachers and peers later on. Yet a positive self-image is essential if she is not to become adept at avoiding problems or cosy in the belief that she is not very bright. Not knowing something is one thing, but being convinced that you can never find out is another – an insidious and destructive attitude that can become ingrained.

From the time an infant first begins to focus and look around her she learns to respond to the attitude of others. When her mother smiles and talks to her she babbles back. However, if she is deaf she will stop babbling and making sounds because she does not hear any response. So throughout infancy, action and counter-action build up a picture of the world for the child. As they grow older the reaction of parents continues to modify behaviour. Children left to discover everything for themselves without encouragement and response show delayed development.

Temperamental differences between parent and child elicit a response as well. The placid mother may make an excellent foil for the over-abundant energy of the active child, keeping calm when all around is chaos, while the placid mother with the quiet, introverted child may be too mild to spur her into action. There is no doubt that some children are born with temperaments that make them more easily irritated and difficult to soothe. As a result mothers are often beset by feelings of guilt and inadequacy. Yet there is really nothing anyone can do that would make them any different. The next child in the family may be calm and cute, sleeping through from six weeks and generally behaving in a more acceptable way. It is easy to think that it is 'experience', that makes the second child less difficult, but it can and does work the other way too, with the first child being a 'pleasure' and the second 'difficult'. The wise parent regards every child as an individual from birth, getting to know her and treating her like the unique individual she is, and avoiding comparisons.

GO TO www.baby-childcare.com TO WATCH THE FOLLOWING VIDEOS THAT ARE APPLICABLE TO CHAPTER 11

PROF ANDRÉ VENTER

What is ADHD and can it be prevented?

Can you be diagnosed with ADHD as an adult?

How does adhd affect my child's learning and development?

Will diet supplements fix my childs adhd?

How is ADHD diagnosed?

ADHD behaviour management

What is the role of medication in ADHD?

The side effects of adhd medical management

Conditions often confused with ADHD

Understanding autism part

ANEL ANNANDALE

When is the ideal time to send you child to nursery school?

Autism spectrum disorder

Bullying

Delayed gratification

JOANNA WILSON

Causes of childhood overweight and obesity

Parent creating healthy homes

Responsive feeding

CHAPTER 12

Moving out into the world

THE WORKING MOTHER. Whether by choice or necessity, more women than ever before are going to work outside the home soon after the birth of their babies. The support of an extended family has virtually disappeared in Westernised societies, although the custom of leaving children with grandmothers is still practiced by many mothers.

The norm however, for the modern nuclear couple is to care for, provide for and nurture their children in unsplendid isolation. And all too often it is the woman who must bear the brunt, and the baby, alone.

We are still taking only the first small steps towards a new social order. Women are now playing multifaceted roles often without the necessary infrastructure to support them. The problem is aggravated by the low value placed on child rearing in many societies. This is probably the result of today's consumerism ethic of glamourising those with the most spending power, and the stay-at-home mother is made to feel inadequate and lacking in status, even though it is generally acknowledged that the first three years of life are of paramount importance to a child. If the foundation for emotional and intellectual growth is well laid in this period, a child is likely to withstand life's battering with greater resilience. However, just because a woman stays at home all day, she is not necessarily a good mother. She may, in fact spend less meaningful time with her children than a working mother does. If a woman has no desire to look after her children herself – and her temperament and circumstances may simply not suit the task – she should pay someone well to do the job. Stay-at-home fathers, are another possible arrangement. 'Grandmother' have been the stalwarts of the traditional African family, giving guidance, discipline and structure in raising their grandchildren. And many do wonderful work caring for more than their share of children. But even they have financial, emotional and physical limitations.

Mothers who dearly long to be with their children yet cannot reconcile their personal needs, such as the desire to maintain a hard-won professional fulfilment or the financial necessity to work, face the greatest dilemma. By choice, a small number of women at the top of their profession in the UK have recently opted to commit fulltime to their families. They have made headlines – but they are the exception. They have proven themselves in commerce, obtained financial freedom and now know what they feel is important for themselves. The key to having choice is hard-to-achieve financial freedom.

Until every mother (or father) is guaranteed the opportunity of spending the first three years with their child – either wholly or partially – with adequate back-up in terms of money, status (inside and outside the home) and no loss of employment privileges – they will have to compromise. And there will be guilt-ridden workers in offices and frustrated women at home...

This is not a simple matter however. In the UK women will soon be getting paid leave of a year off work after every child. It was nine months previously – six months of which can be transferred to the father. There is also talk of allowing women to request flexible working hours until their child is 16. But employers are baulking, saying they can't plan their work force, together with accusations of some binning the CV's of women of child-bearing age. In countries like Sweden, where the state pays transferable paternal and maternal leave for up to 16 months, few children are in nurseries during the first year. Not many fathers take up the full option however as they generally earn more than women. In South Africa, where a small cash grant is payable to indigent mothers until children reach the age of 16, there has been some speculation that it

may induce some young girls to become pregnant. 'You can have it all,' the promise to women by Helen Gurley Brown, doyenne of Cosmopolitan magazine, is clearly not possible. Unless, like her, you have a rich husband and choose not to have children!

THE PRACTICALITIES OF GOING BACK TO WORK

MATERNITY BENEFITS. Different countries have different laws around maternity leave, but in most cases, employers are legally compelled to offer a certain amount of paid maternity leave. The paid leave can start any time from four weeks before the expected date of birth, and continues after the birth. No employee can be forced to return to work less than six weeks after the birth. Benefits for fathers and adoptive mothers of children under two are also available. An unemployed mother might be eligible for government support. Speak to your employer or government representative about the benefits you are entitled to.

TIMING YOUR RETURN. You should not imagine that you will bounce back easily straight after the birth. Having a baby is a tremendous emotional and physical upheaval. It takes at least six months for your body to return to its pre-pregnant physical state, and if you are breast feeding, another three months after you stop. As for the mind – you may think it will never be normal again – but in time it will work as before! One of the biggest shocks that you may not have been prepared for is how tired you will feel. After all, your sleep will be broken for at least the first two months and there is sure to be some emotional tension that is always exhausting.

The instinctive, animal-like protectiveness most mothers feel for their newborn could mean you feel detached, almost resentful of the intrusion of your husband and your other children. You need to work through these feelings naturally by being with your baby and fulfilling your instinctive urge to nurture, or your emotional equilibrium could be disturbed, making the separation more difficult to handle later if you go back to work. Like it or not, your judgement will probably be affected for a while – at least until your hormones settle down. Driving a car again for the first time may seem strangely unfamiliar. Adding a row of figures intensely complicated. Even getting yourself out of your dressing gown before noon may require effort.

In any event, you should not think of going back to work for at least six to eight weeks after the birth if possible. If you have a choice regarding the timing of your return it is probably better to do it when your baby is around four months old. By that time you should have recovered your strength, and she will be at a particularly amenable stage. The four-month-old baby smiles at practically anyone, should be well settled on her feeds and routine, and should adapt fairly readily to being cared for by someone other than her mother.

At around seven to eight months, however, she will start to become wary of strangers and will probably show a good deal of anxiety when her mother leaves the room, so this is not a good time to make a sudden break with her. In fact, any separation from this age onwards can present problems. But a lot depends on the child's temperament and the quality of the alternative care she receives. Going back to work part-time can be the answer, or leaving it until after the age of three when most children have overcome the traumas of the second year and have come to terms with themselves as separate beings from their mother – although they still need security.

For the mother, coping successfully as a working woman depends a lot on how she comes to terms with the conflict and guilt she will feel at times; how supportive her husband is, and on the alternative child care facilities that are available. It is a sad reflection on our society's priorities that the women who have the least choice about going out to work often have the poorest selection of alternative care for their children.

HELPING YOU COPE. The good news is that that there is a growing recognition of the need for employers to play their role and some companies have established daycare on their premises. Alternatively a job near your home is a great advantage and is possibly even worth a cut in salary. Knowing that you can get home quickly in an emergency or in the middle of the day and that you do not have to spend hours in unproductive and expensive travel every day is a big plus.

- Whatever child care arrangement you make, you must keep in mind that when she gets older you will be faced with school holidays when most pre-schools close.
- Try to work for the enlightened firms that allow flexitime. You could then arrange to pick up your child and settle her into an afternoon routine if she is not in all-day care.
- More women are opting to work from home. This can be an excellent solution, especially if you are able to hire more home help as a result. But you could find yourself trying to juggle what amounts to two full time jobs, neither of which you can ever get away from.

BREASTFEEDING. Women who intend to go back to work often ask whether they should breastfeed at all. You may think it would be better to get your baby 'settled' on the bottle right from the beginning, but this is not so. Your child will benefit from the unique properties of your milk even if you feed her for only a few weeks. But more importantly, it will give you a chance to develop a particularly close relationship with her, and you will have the satisfaction of knowing that you are giving her a good, secure start. You can also, if you breastfeed, continue to give one or two feeds a day after your return to work so that your baby can continue to benefit and you can enjoy the feeling of doing something very special for her. (*See p. 150 for breastfeeding while working.*)

THE EFFECT OF WORKING MOTHERS ON CHILDREN. The question most often in the minds of mothers who work outside the home is whether their child will be adversely affected by it. Long term studies have found that in many respects children benefit from having working mothers. Women who work have to be highly organised in order to meet all their commitments, with the result that they make consistent rules for their children's behaviour. Older children are given responsibilities, and when these are reasonable, children's self-esteem is improved and their intellectual performance is enhanced. It must be said however, that an unsuitable substitute (or maternal), care from a young age can have a detrimental effect on a child's emotional and intellectual development.

WHO'LL LOOK AFTER THE BABY?

WHAT TO LOOK FOR. The key to successful substitute care for children lies in finding a situation in which the caregiver is sensitive, stimulating and responsive to each child's particular needs. Knowledge of child development and a warm confident approach with few personnel changes is optimal. There are a number of agencies that provide the services of caregivers in various categories, for a fee. There are also courses in first aid and child care that employees can take. It is a good idea for the child's caregiver to keep a logbook of the day's routine such as eating sleeping etc. so that you can see at a glance how it went.

RELATIVES. A suitable relative could solve the problem of care for your child while you are at work. But you will have to discuss your child rearing ideas with her beforehand so that you do not have too many disagreements later on.

FATHERS. It is not unusual for a woman to earn more than a man today, and to have better career prospects. As a result there is an increasing trend for fathers to stay home and care for the baby. This is a delicate issue and you need to be aware that you may have conflicting emotions in leaving your traditional role to a man. Men too, will need to put up with the inevitable speculation. There is also the question of returning to work at some stage. Women are all too aware of what a gap in their CV can mean to potential employers; as a result both men and women are making strategic plans in order to ease their return. Going freelance, doing volunteer work, distance studies, are some of the ways that a CV can be filled, with an aside that you also raised children.

In terms of parenting style, studies show, that although men's play is more robust than women's, they are just as capable of nurturing a child successfully. The famous 'nanny' school in the UK is now offering training to men as well as women.

HIRED HOME HELP. Before engaging someone you should establish whether she really likes children. If she is expected to look after the house as well, you will have to make it clear that priority number one is looking after the child. If you demand domestic perfection, she could restrict the child's activities to stop her making extra work. You need someone who will provide the child with loving care. She needs to be given comfort and encouragement as well as food. It needs to be someone who will care enough not to let her 'cry it out' when she is distressed, nor isolate her when she needs company. Remember that right from the earliest weeks a baby needs someone to relate to – someone who will talk to her and get excited about her progress. If she is left in the care of a person who keeps the radio or TV blaring and speaks to her in monosyllables she will not be getting the right kind of stimulation. Worse still, an impatient, temperamentally unstable person could become impatient with a crying child and inflict injury. Even shaking a baby can have disastrous results.

DOMESTIC WORKERS. Domestic workers generally come to your home on a daily basis or live-in. Many have no formal qualifications but a real love of children, and an instinctive feeling for child care make up for their lack of training. Although an unqualified person may lack up-to-date knowledge on nutrition, this can be overcome if she is well supervised. She should also be introduced to your neighbours. Involve her in your care of the baby while you are still at home so that she can see how you like things done. Ideally she should know how to handle emergencies such as choking, bleeding, and poisoning. Send her on a first aid course if possible. (*See Dealing with emergencies p. 389*)

NANNIES/AU PAIRS. The famous British nanny of Mary Poppins's ilk who is strict but loving and knows all the tricks required including how to get the medicine to go down, is the genesis of the trained nanny. Standards vary from full, intensive training to a short, superficial course. Check the credentials of the course givers as an impressive certificate can mean very little in reality. Do not expect a well trained nanny to come cheap. Au pairs are often young women who have not found what they want to do in life, or who want to travel and work abroad. A young woman without training is unlikely to know enough about the complexities of child care to look after a young baby properly. In particular she may not have the patience needed to cope with a crying baby. They often do better with toddlers and older children.

TRAINED EDUCARE WORKERS. For those who can afford it there is the option of hiring someone who has undergone several years of training in educare. They are most suited to the care of toddlers or older children. They can usually drive and have training in all aspects of child care and development. To help amortise costs a few mothers may club together.

CHILD-MINDERS/DAY-MOTHERS. Besides live-in nannies or child-minders that come to your home, there are women who take children into their homes and care for them on a daily basis. If they have up to six children in their care their services are not governed by law. If the child-minder is dedicated and not merely swelling her income while she stays at home with her own children, it can provide an only child with company and a chance to mix with others, although there is the possibility that the child-minder will favour her own children. This can lead to emotional problems in the outside child.

The big advantage of nannies and child-minders is continuity of care. The fact that the child has a limited number of people providing for her on-going care means that she can form stable attachments. A big drawback of any large institution's care is the lack of the opportunity to form a one-to-one relationship with a caring person. Negative effects of day care occur when there is a high turnover of caregivers in the child's life, and lack of personal interest or knowledge on the part of the staff. Infections are also more common in children in daycare.

DAYCARE CENTRES (CRÈCHES). If no suitable mother substitute can be found, a daycare centre (crèche) could be the answer. These may be private, church or government sponsored establishments that care for children between the ages of three months (sometimes, one month) and five or six years. Hours vary but are usually from 7am to 6pm Monday to Friday, and 7am to 1pm on Saturday, with meals provided. Not all are open on a Saturday.

Although daycare centres have to be registered and are periodically inspected if more than six children are cared for (the centre is informed of the pending visit!), they vary greatly in quality, and a personal appraisal must be made.

WHAT TO LOOK FOR IN A DAYCARE CENTRE. Pay an unexpected visit. There is no reason to suppose there will be anything to hide, but if there is you will stand a better chance of finding out about it if you don't announce your visit.

Ask to see where the babies are kept. A row of cots with nothing else in sight, even if they are spotless, is a bad sign. There should be mobiles, bright toys and plenty to look at even for small babies.

- Reclining chairs in which babies can be sat in to see what is going on around them should be available. Propping the bottle is dangerous and does not provide the bodily contact babies need to thrive.

- Facilities for older children should include enough play equipment to go around, and sufficient staff to cater for their needs.
- Regulations vary, but usually state a ratio of one qualified caregiver or nursing assistant to eight infants; one adult to 10 children between the ages of one to three years; and one adult to 15 children between the ages of three to six years.
- There should be some structure to the children's day, other than time for sleeping and eating. If there seems to be a great emphasis on sleeping time, stay away. This happens because it is the easiest way of coping with the children.
- There should be a healthy level of noise coming from the older children's area. A group of quiet children is likely to be unhappy.
- Activities during the day should include time for 'free play', more structured activities such as painting or modelling with dough, puzzles and time for gross motor movement (using the large muscles) and outdoor play on suitable outdoor equipment. Beware the supervisor who tells you there are few toys because the children 'break them anyway'. Sometimes toys are kept high up for show, but out of reach. Toys should be safe with no sharp edges, or small components that can be swallowed.
- If the child is to remain at the crèche all day, suitable meals should be provided. Find out who plans the menu and ask for an example of the week's fare. Children need three main meals a day plus two suitable snacks. Some places do not provide this and say it is because children should not eat between meals. This is entirely incorrect. Children's stomach capacity is small and their energy needs high. They need frequent, concentrated, well balanced meals. (*See p. 249.*)
- The gap between the last meal or snack should not be too long. Children are often 'starving' by the time they are picked up and this makes them irritable. By the time they get home things are out of control.
- Enquire how discipline is enforced, and who metes it out. Physical punishment is illegal in many countries, yet there are instances where it is used. Humiliation, shouting, and anger are not suitable forms of discipline. Discuss in detail with the owner.
- Licensing regulations should ensure that safety standards are met, but these can lapse through carelessness. If you see anything obviously dangerous, speak to the supervisor about it and observe her reaction.
- Access to the premises should be restricted. It is also a sad fact that child abuse is most commonly inflicted by persons known to the family. Abuse of children by children is possible. Be alert to any signs of precocious sexual awareness in children.
- Make a point of looking into the medicine chest. Unscrupulous people have been known to dose the babies with painkillers or sedatives to keep them quiet and docile.
- There should be suitable facilities for sterilising bottles, cleaning toys, keeping food chilled, washing hands, and other components of good hygiene.

- You can tell a lot about a place from the atmosphere. If it feels good even if the facilities are not the smartest, follow your instinct.

AIDS AND OTHER INFECTIOUS ILLNESSES. AIDS requires the transfer of body fluids such as blood, breastmilk or other fluids in order to infect another person, so there is minimal risk. If an employee who is HIV positive, or has AIDS is still fit to do the job he or she may not be dismissed on these grounds. Tuberculosis is highly contagious and is easily spread through droplets from coughing. Make sure your child is inoculated against TB (this should have happened in the nursing home).

PROBLEMS IN CHILDREN WHO ARE IN DAYCARE. The most common problem you can expect is that your child will have more frequent colds and other infections passed on by other children. Although no mother likes her child to be ill, she will eventually build up immunity and no lasting damage is likely. You should keep a close check on her hearing if she has frequent colds and ear infections as 'glue' ear can result in partial deafness at a time when crucial language development is taking place. Make sure your child has all her immunisations on time.

Children in daycare may become aggressive because they have to fight for what they want. This is particularly true when there are too few playthings. Talk to the supervisor if this is the case. Learning the difference between assertiveness and aggression is important for both boys and girls. Try and balance it out with emphasis on non-aggressive ways of achieving goals, like negotiation, consideration for others and gentleness in attitude and action while still standing up for one's rights.

EXCUSE MY FRENCH. Your child may also pick up bad language that offends you. Little boys in particular love the effect that an expletive has on the audience. Don't make it more fun by being shocked. Keep a straight face and say, 'What exactly does that mean?' Then matter-of-factly, 'Oh yes, that's the language of people who can't talk properly.' There is nothing as disenchanting as being thought merely pathetic when you expected to be sensationally outrageous. If this does not do the trick just ignore it totally.

SEXUAL ABUSE. Adults are the primary child sex offenders, and they do not preclude professional or wealthy people, and they may be male or female. They may be married, and they are often known to, or they may be related to the victim. Most, but not all perpetrators are male – including a man who posed as Father Christmas – with children on his lap – and most, but not all, victims are female. Anyone seen to be making friends with children should be watched.

A serious, previously rare cause for concern is sexual aggression by children towards children. Children are exposed to sexual scenes on television, and sometimes in the home. They may also be the victims of sexual abuse themselves. Children as young as six have performed acts of sexual aggression on other children. A child, who exhibits sexual knowledge beyond his or her age, must be monitored for signs of sexual abuse. Talk to the supervisor to ensure she is aware of this possibility and that children are monitored at all times. Wendy houses and other spaces in which a door can be closed should not be played in without adult supervision

BABY BURN OUT. Perhaps the most common aspect for parents is being confronted by a demanding, aggressive child when you pick her up after a long day. The day mother says she has been well behaved and a pleasure, but what you get is a kicking, screaming banshee.

Being 'good' all day, and being parted from your mother is highly stressful and so you fall apart when you see her. Partly due to anger at her leaving you, and partly because you are tired and hungry. She should be told that you are going to work and that this is why you cannot be with her all day much as you would like to be. If possible let her see where you work.

She should not be starving when you fetch her. Children should have a good nourishing snack late-afternoon so that they can last until suppertime. Ideally you should also have something ready for her to eat, and you should spend some quality time with her.

This is easier said than done and you will have to use all your organisational skills and muster all the help you can get. What a wonderful world it would be if the man went into the kitchen and you could give your child the tender loving care she needs at this time… or, even if he could give her some quality time. Thankfully more and more men are doing this. She needs it, and it is important for her emotional security – tired though you all are.

WORKING HOUSE MOTHER. Anyone who imagines that a woman who stays at home and looks after a house and children is not a working mother is mistaken. There is probably far more pressure on the housebound mother than in most office jobs. Yet she is unpaid, unsung, and often unhappy.

To the woman who has had a career or at least a job she enjoyed, being at home all day with only a baby for company and stimulation can come as a rude shock. She may become depressed, lethargic and unable to cope simply because she feels worthless and isolated even though she may have longed for the time she could give up work and stay at home.

No matter how much she loves her baby, a steady diet of nappies and gaga talk can wear down the most devoted mother. It is impossible to sustain the necessary enthusiasm and expertise required for good mothering if there is no time to recharge mental and emotional batteries.

Simply talking to other women in the same situation can be a great help. A conversation with the other mothers in the park has been the start of many a sanity-saving friendship. A playgroup formed by friends to mind the child, even once a week, can give a mother time to herself, to follow a hobby, to catch upon reading or simply stare into space...

The 'tired housewife' syndrome is as much a sign of boredom, frustration and lack of self-esteem as of sheer physical exhaustion. Staying home with the children should be a commitment to yourself as well. It is so easy to get bogged down in the nappy routine that you forget yourself as a person. You can bring far more to the task if you have an outlet that satisfies your 'other self'.

Raising a child is the most important, demanding, satisfying, exhausting, challenging, frustrating and creative job there is – take pride in it. The future of the world is in your hands. It does not depend on advances in nuclear technology, but on the kind of people who are growing up today.

PLANNING A SECOND CHILD

MIND THE GAP. It is rather strange that so many women believe that if their children are closely spaced they will be able to get the whole business over with quickly and easily – as though they were building several additions to their house and wanted to get through the mess and bother at once to save themselves trouble later on. It may be a practical decision when it comes to inanimate objects, but children don't function that way. The less effort you put in at the beginning the longer and more difficult the process of raising them is likely to be.

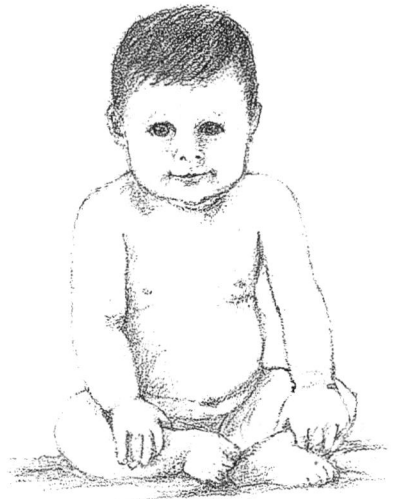

The mother who wants her 18-month-old 'off the bottle and out of nappies', because there is a second one on the way is creating just the kind of complication that is likely to make the child slow to give them up. Anything that tries to force the child's growing up rate is likely to backfire, especially when it concerns emotional development. Every child has the right to be a child, to grow through the various stages with enough time for the stimulation of her cognitive development and the nurturing of her emotional self.

There are adults who remember their large families with nostalgia, and siblings who are close in age and enjoy each other's company. But there are many others who feel cheated of the opportunity to reach their full potential. As soon as another element enters the family mosaic the pattern is altered; inevitably and irrevocably. There are always changes that improve its quality and some that alter it forever.

The arrival of another child is always a shock to the family structure, especially to the child who is already there. Some bounce back fairly quickly, absorbing the impact and expanding to accommodate the new situation. Others are so traumatised that they are altered for life. The damage shows itself in behavioural problems, physical symptoms or lack of self-esteem. The new arrival will clearly never have had the luxury of having the parents' singular attention, and so is less likely to feel aggrieved.

Is an only child the answer then? Not necessarily. Although the only child often does particularly well, there is no need to deny yourself the pleasure of other children. Siblings can enrich each other and their parents' lives immeasurably. But expanding your family is best done sensibly. Spacing children at least three years apart gives each one a chance to develop soundly. It gives the mother the opportunity to nurture them through the all-important first years without short-changing her children, her spouse or herself. Physically it is also better for the mother, and financially it can mean an easier time too. It is however, a matter of personal choice and circumstances – especially since many mothers are having children later, which leaves them little choice but to have them in quick succession.

PLEAS FOR A BABY BY AN OLDER CHILD. Little girls especially go through a stage when they are crazy about babies and visiting someone with a baby may be anticipated more eagerly than the fun fair. She may urge her mother to provide her with a baby, and promise so convincingly to help look after her that you may feel that there will be no problems with the new arrival.

But a child's fantasy of having a baby sister is vastly different from reality. She may think of her as a doll she will be able to play with, or a friend who can share her fun.

When she discovers that the baby is not to be handled, and that her mother is often occupied with the baby when she would like her attention, she will not be impressed. So don't think because your child is enthusiastic about the idea of a baby that everything will go smoothly.

PREPARING A CHILD FOR THE ARRIVAL OF A BABY. Some parents think they should not tell their child ahead of time about the new baby, while others make too much of it. Tell her when you are around six months pregnant, and do not pretend that she will have a 'new playmate who she will love'. The baby will not be a playmate for a very long time, and she may not feel at all loving towards him or her.

Explain that babies are not much fun when they are small – and quite a bother for mothers because they are not able to do anything for themselves.

Tell her stories about the preparations you made for her before her birth, and talk about the preparations for new happenings in her life such as going to pre-school.

Keep as much excitement and attention centred on her life – not around the events relating to the baby. And do not let her get the idea that any changes in her routine – like going to pre-school or moving to a bed – are because of the new baby. Don't choose the month of the baby's arrival to try and potty train her – it is easier to face the fact of extra nappies for a while than to have her regress after she has been trained.

JEALOUSY. If you accept the fact that there will be jealousy, at least for a time, you will find that you understand her behaviour much better. Look at it this way. If your husband announced that he was bringing home a cute young woman who would share your life and all your privileges, and told you that you should love her and be kind to her… you would be furious. Yet a child is expected to be enthusiastic about a rival who turns out to be useless as a companion, yet attracts everyone's attention in the most infuriating way.

It is not surprising that some children resort to crude methods like pinching or slapping their infant siblings in an attempt to get rid of them. Other more sensitive, cerebral children tend to internalise their anger by developing psychosomatic symptoms or regressing to infantile behaviour. Sudden aches and pains, bed wetting, thumb sucking, refusal to eat, holding on to stools, temper tantrums, contrariness, aggressiveness, withdrawal and depression are some of the symptoms of jealousy. (*See p. 512*). (*See p. 512*).

Remember jealousy is about feeling unloved and unlovable. You need to make sure your child still feels accepted and loved. But you cannot make your child feel better by buying her everything she wants or letting her do as she pleases. Behaviour rules do not change. Hurting the baby or others, or being rude – is still unacceptable. But she does deserve a few privileges accorded to her status as the more grown up one. A slightly later bedtime perhaps, more sleepovers at Granny or a friend… going on outings with Daddy…

Doing chores for the baby is not the best way to involve her. Children respond best to siblings when their mother tells them how the baby feels. Say things like 'He's wet so he is feeling a little uncomfortable – I suppose that's why he is crying, what do you think?' Being 'your helper' in this way will make her feel good towards you and the baby. And do not tell everyone 'how much she loves the baby'; rather enthuse about how much the baby loves her. How the baby smiles at her most and so on… Pick her up and hold her close to the baby's face – from around six weeks babies smile at any one at this range… When she sees the baby as a friend, she sees a potential ally, not a rival.

HONESTY. Children are normally perfectly honest in their approach to others. If she says she hates the baby, there is no point in saying. 'No, you don't dear. You love the baby. 'She knows how she feels and making a liar out of her or loading her with guilt is only going to complicate matters. You can acknowledge her feelings without condoning them.

Ensure that she has sufficient opportunities for imaginative play so that she can live out her emotions in an acceptable way. Dressing up and acting like a mother or playing with a doll or pretending to be a superhero can help her come to terms with her feelings. But don't think you can make them go away simply by telling her they are wicked, or that she is not really experiencing them.

GROWING UP TOGETHER. 'Experience teaches' may be true, but the lesson is not always as well taken as it might be. Everyone knows of people who make the same mistakes over and over. Children too, cannot be expected to 'find out for themselves' everything that is to be gained from an experience. They could, and do, spend a lifetime without coming to a conclusion that could have been gained the first time around if it had been pointed out to them.

During the first few years children are intensely receptive to all forms of learning. Your chances of influencing them decrease in proportion to the child's age. It is too late to try to inculcate values and virtues when the child is a teenager.

Say you have a child who is domineering and a bully – it may even be the younger child. Your attitude could be that the other child must learn to fight for herself so you leave them to it. Yet, 20 years later, you will still have a meanie and a mouse. The bullying child should have been intercepted in infancy and the victim encouraged to assert herself by helping maintain her self-esteem.

As much as you are there to bring order into a child's notion of what the world is like, you are there to give guidance on moral issues. Unless the lesson of the experience is learnt, it is a wasted exercise. And it is a very rare individual indeed who can come to the right conclusion without interpretive help. Teasing that is hurtful debases the user and humiliates the receiver. It does not help the one on the receiving end to 'learn to take it'.

Kindness and politeness are even more important within the family than outside. Because the barriers are so much lower, everyone needs to stop themselves from going beyond the point where hurt is felt and goodwill evaporates. More is learnt by teaching the aggressor self-control than by imagining that being hurt will teach the victim to take it. Suffering hunger does not make you less hungry next time. At best the relationships between family members are fragile, tenuous things, and allowing them to turn into a free-for-all-jungle with hurt and recrimination the norm, is savage and stupid.

WHAT FATHERS ARE MADE OF

DAD, remember all those awful temper tantrums? And sulking in the corner? And running away?

...Aren't you glad We've grown up, and you don't have to do that anymore?

ROLL ON THE NEW MILLENNIUM MAN. Cricket and camping and climbing up on the knee… and coming home to chaos and expecting supper on the turn? Oh no, that is a very old scenario. That was when men were living on the outskirts of reality, before they woke up to their rights as fathers and discovered the nucleus of life in their own home. It is not surprising that few fathers bonded with their babies when you consider that they were often kept out of things so efficiently by the maternal mafia. Like mothers, fathers need time to learn to like a child and relate to her. And fathers would learn more quickly if they were encouraged to participate right from the beginning. Even before birth, fathers should be included in preparations for their child.

Antenatal classes which include the father can help make him feel more than a spare part in an unfamiliar ritual. Being at the birth will help overcome the feeling that the child is a stranger who could belong to anyone. Just as a mother must be given the opportunity to handle and re-establish symbiosis with her baby in the first hours after birth, so the father must have a chance to form a bond – so that he can shed his inhibitions and become a primal man and get to the essence of things. There is even some evidence that when males interact with their newborn they experience a hormonal surge similar to that of new mothers. It is now possible for fathers to 'room in' with the mother after the birth if she has a private room, and what better opportunity to become a family unit from the very beginning.

DON'T DROP THE BABY. New mothers are just as nervous of handling their baby as a man might be. Putting down a man for his lack of expertise is a crude old trick used by some women to get men back for making them feel inferior in other ways. Forget it. Games like these are as self-defeating as they are unnecessary. You are both novices and you need all the help you can get, particularly support from each other. Female chauvinism in the nursery has made many men reluctant to become involved. It has encouraged men to denigrate the job of motherhood because they have had no opportunity to discover for themselves what it takes, with the result that women complain about the lack of involvement and feeling in their partners, and the men cut themselves off at a time when they are most needed. Divorce after the birth of a child is depressingly common; it takes a mature couple to cope with the stresses that having a child can place on a relationship. Yet when parenthood is a joint venture, more than just a meeting of sperm and egg, it can be the most enriching experience of all.

Fortunately, there has been a cultural swing across many societies to the notion of the 'new age' man who actively engages with his children. The value of involved fathers cannot be over-emphasised. They can give daughters a warm confirmation of their feminine worth, and their boys training in the true meaning of being a man. One of the revelations of the culture change in many men of today has been the breadth and depth of their natures, which are as complex and sensitive as that of any woman. There have been many trade-offs as a result of the emancipation of women, but this one is an absolute joy. Welcome new age man, we love you!

Pssst… nudge, nudge… wink, wink, Dads. Me-time for moms counts as foreplay and is an excellent aphrodisiac.

THE SINGLE PARENT FAMILY

FLYING SOLO. Even though couples trying to raise a family are often beset with difficulties, the single parent of either sex is likely to have to cope with added complications. As with other realities of life today, such as the need for many women to work outside the home, the problems facing the single parent have still to be adequately overcome.

The single parent's most pressing need is probably the lack of financial security. The difference in outcomes for children in single parent families is largely one of financial resources. Mothers or fathers with good incomes – raising children alone generally do as well as conventional two parent families. Unfortunately, only a very small percentage of women are in the income bracket where money is not a problem, or where they receive a large maintenance from the child's father.

For most single parents, financial hardship is a reality. Maintenance is not always forthcoming from the father of the child even if there has been a court order against him, and he is able to pay. Time-consuming and cumbersome court procedures may be necessary to compel him to comply, and to pursue them requires what the woman lacks most, time and money. The law has been modified to try to make things easier for the plaintiff, and maintenance can be ordered to be deducted from wages (garnishee order), but many fathers simply disappear. Some improvements have been made in payments. Electronic funds transfers (EFT) can be made directly into the bank accounts of beneficiaries, thus saving costly and time consuming trips to collect payments personally. The management of maintenance cases is now an automated process which means that case details can be accessed quickly on the computer, and electronic payments can be made from one court to another and on any day. Welfare grants are available to single parents who are not in a position to support their children on their own. But these are not sufficient, and women often battle along alone.

Lack of adequate day care facilities is a nightmare that plagues men and women who must go out to work and leave their children. Often an inordinately large proportion of their salary is needed to keep their children safe, even if not stimulated, with the result that they become caught in a vicious cycle of poverty, precipitating emotional problems, ill health and insecurity, with negative effects on their children.

BREAKING UP IS HARD TO DO. For the child, there may be the problem of coping with being outside the norm if two-parent families predominate in their area. Remarks by children and even by teachers can be troubling. It is important that the parent should visit the child's school or preschool and talk to the teacher at the beginning of the term or as soon as there is a change of status such as death or divorce, or disappearance of the father or mother. The situation must be explained and the teacher's support enlisted in helping the child cope with possible emotional problems. A sensitive teacher can do a lot to help the child feel less different when home life is mentioned, by including the children who have only one or even no parents at home. Making cards addressed to 'Mummy and Daddy', when the child has never known a father can make her feel deprived and inferior. Tactful handling is even more important to the vulnerable child than the child with the buffer of a secure homelife.

A new school trend in which young children are asked to draw their family tree is unfortunate. Children who are adopted, possibly after the biological mother has abandoned her child; those who have been conceived through a sperm donor, surrogate mother – or other circumstances – that can cause them pain when publicly divulged are placed in an invidious position. The children of same-sex parents could also be subjected to prejudice. There is enough bullying without children being unnecessarily exposed to more of it. While honesty between parent and child is absolutely desirable, sensitivity needs to be exercised when revelations that could be hurtful are made to others.

The other immense pressure on the single parent is simply that of being the only source of emotional and physical comfort to the child. It is at times when the mother or father feels particularly low that the child seems likely to become ill or difficult, prompting them to snap or feel guilty about the care they are providing. Some other person who can lend a hand and an ear is essential in the single parent's life.

Ideally the children's routine should be kept as close as possible to what it was previously. When this is not feasible, creative solutions should be sought. For example combining with other parents in a similar position and sharing a house can offer company, emotional release and free evenings to the single parent. For the child, the chance to mix with children in the same position and to relate to other adults can provide a much needed outlet.

Single parents often worry that their children will not develop an image of the parent who is absent. The boy who grows up without a father will not know how to behave as a man – the girl without a mother image will not know what it is to be a woman. Ideally boys should have a father who can guide them as they are especially vulnerable and susceptible to bad peer influence; and children do model themselves on their parents and acquire a sense of self through them. But if the remaining parent does not paint all men as villains, or all women as man-eaters, and there are enough opportunities for a child to observe and relate to suitable adults of the absent gender, it can help them to develop adequately. Keeping a bad marriage alive for the 'sake of the children' can be a sadly mistaken point of view – rather an absent father or mother than a really rotten one in residence.

Naturally, if visits to the other parent can be arranged and the children handle them well – some children dread visits to the absent parent – a happy relationship can be developed in which the children feel neither deprived nor particularly different.

The children of same sex parents and children in homes where parents have remarried also need sensitive care. The same honest consultation with teachers and care givers applies, while protecting the child.

In all cases it is most important not to use children as a weapon against the other parent. When relationships are breaking up there is usually a lot of anger and acrimony. Children must not – under any circumstances – become pawns in the blame game. Never say bad things about your child's father or mother no matter how angry you are, and even if it is justified. Children need to feel that their parents are good and loving if they are to grow up emotionally stable. They may find out otherwise later, but when they are young they should not see nor hear their parents fighting. Many children are even exposed to domestic violence. Some parents even use their child as a shield from blows. This will do terrible long term emotional harm, and the physical harm is apparent in many hospital emergency rooms. Professional counselling by a family therapist can be helpful.

GO TO www.baby-childcare.com TO WATCH THE FOLLOWING VIDEOS THAT ARE APPLICABLE TO CHAPTER 12

JOANNA WILSON

Causes of childhood overweight and obesity

Parent creating healthy homes

Responsive feeding

ANEL ANNANDALE

School readiness

Emotional school readiness

When is the ideal time to send you child to school?

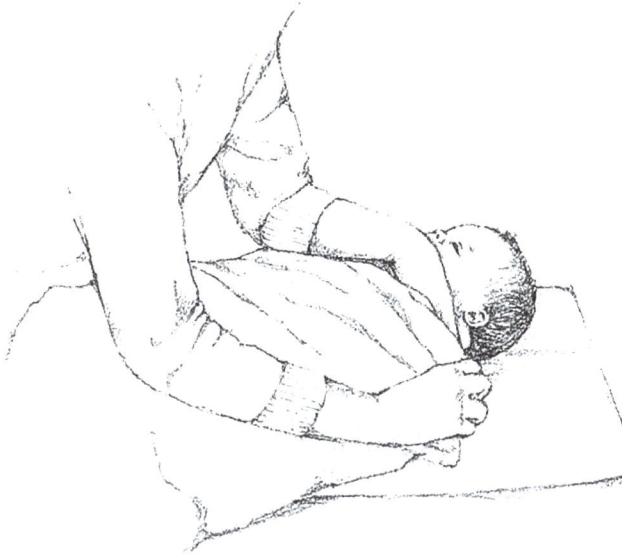

CHAPTER 13

The Sick Child

THE SICK INFANT

FEELING THEIR PAIN. In the first few months it is usually very difficult for a mother to tell whether her baby is ill because she may not have experience of what is normal and what is not. Crying which may be due to colic, hunger or simply loneliness also confuses the whole issue. However, as a general rule, the baby who is gaining weight regularly is following the milestones and reflex patterns described in Chapter 8 and does not vomit or pass abnormal stools, is likely to be well – even if she does cry a lot at times. It is also true that babies under three months old are more vulnerable and you should see your doctor immediately if she has a temperature or you are at all concerned about her. Do not give medication, even to lower a fever, to infants under three months of age without consulting your doctor.

NOTE: You should contact your doctor at any time your baby shows symptoms that give you cause for concern. The younger the child the sooner you should see a doctor. Never medicate a child without your doctor's advice.

SIGNS OF POSSIBLE SERIOUS ILLNESS IN A BABY YOUNGER THAN TWO MONTHS INCLUDE:

- The baby is reluctant to feed.
- She has a convulsion (seizures/fits).
- The baby lies still and does not make movements except when you touch her.
- Her breathing is fast (60 breaths per minute or more).
- Her chest is drawn inwards.
- Her temperature is over 37.5°C (99.5°F).
- Her temperature is under 35.5°C (96°F).

SEE A DOCTOR SOON IF:

- A baby younger than six months old has any sign of a temperature. An older baby has a temperature above 38.5°C (101°F).
- Your baby vomits with great force after every meal and is not gaining weight.
- There is blood (bright red or dark) in your baby's urine or stools.
- Your baby has large, frequent loose stools with vomiting or any of the other abnormal stools including stools described on *p. 175.*
- If vomit is stained green it should be kept and shown to the doctor.
- Your baby is listless and does not take her feeds well.
- There is any swelling that does not appear normal; for example a lump that appears in the groin area when the baby cries could be an inguinal hernia.
- There is weight loss or refusal to feed.
- Bulging fontanelle (soft spot on the head).
- Rapid breathing.
- Noisy or difficult breathing.
- Convulsions (fits).

YOU SHOULD ALSO CONTACT YOUR DOCTOR IF:

- If your child has a fever of 38.5°C (101°F) or higher (*See p. 338* for how to treat a fever.)
- If she loses consciousness, even for a short while. (Breath holding is an exception.) (*See p. 397.*)
- If she has a convulsion (fit).
- If she seems to have trouble breathing. Amongst other things she could have breathed in some milk that has been brought up, or she could have croup, or other serious illness. (*See p. 349.*) Call a doctor immediately.
- If your baby screams with pain and her crying subsides when you pick her up. She may have earache. Rubbing or tugging the ear is not necessarily a sign of ear infection but it may be. (*See p. 350.*)
- If your baby turns blue when she cries or often has a blue tinge.

- If she has constipation with vomiting and swollen abdomen.
- Excessive sweating.
- Abnormal drowsiness.
- A noticeably salty taste to her skin.

THE OLDER CHILD. With the older child it is easier to know if she is ill because she can tell you, but the issue may be confused by psychosomatic pain (illness caused by the mind). The above reasons for seeing a doctor apply to older children as well, and the following symptoms should also be included:
- Painful joints or bones.
- Weight loss and prolonged loss of appetite.
- Burning when passing urine, or discharge or itching in the vaginal area. (Some bubble baths contain detergents that can cause redness and burning in the vaginal area, but infection can have the same symptoms.)
- Swelling in any part of the body.
- A tendency to bruise very easily and the appearance of small bleeding spots in the skin.
- Persistent cough.
- Discharge from the ear.
- Excessive thirst or hunger.
- Recurrent stomachache.
- Constant dribbling of urine. Strong odour or dark colour in urine.
- Headache or stiffness in the neck.
- Periods of breathing difficulty.
- Aversion to bright light.

PSYCHOSOMATIC ILLNESS. This is illness that is caused by emotional factors. Even if you think your child is 'inventing' an illness she still needs treatment. You must find out what is bothering her so much that she needs to express it this way. For instance, a child who is jealous of a new baby may develop a stomachache. To her the pain is real, even though the problem is jealousy. You must treat the symptom as well as the cause. She really wants you to fuss over her – even if she has to become ill to get her message across. This is a real cry for help and should not be treated as 'naughtiness'. It is a signal to you to give her more attention and reassurance of your love. (*See case histories p. 506.*)

Some children have problems outside or inside the home that cause symptoms of stress such as bed wetting, wetting their pants after being toilet trained, destructive behaviour or aggression, or symptoms of illness such as a sore throat, headache or stomachache. Being bullied or teased at playschool, jealousy of a new baby or simply a temporary feeling of insecurity due to a house move for example, can lead to these symptoms and others, like sleeping poorly.

Do not make such a fuss of her symptoms that she comes to rely on them as a means of getting your attention. Concentrate on finding out what is really causing them and try to put it right. If she gets a stomachache every day before school, visit the teacher and find out why. If she is unsettled because of a new baby, reassure her (*see p. 326*). If she is insecure because of a house move, try to keep the rest of her routine as stable as possible.

BETTER SAFE THAN SORRY. By the time your child has passed her first birthday you can expect that most congenital abnormalities will have been detected. Your problems are likely to be centred on the usual childhood infections and accidents and the less common diseases. How can you tell whether the problem will resolve itself without medical help and when you should you call a doctor?

The same general rules as for the sick infant apply: if your child shows any of the symptoms listed in the previous sections, call a doctor. Other situations will have to be judged on merit.

But if you, as a parent, feel there is something wrong with your child, even though her symptoms may not correspond to any of those mentioned, trust your instinct and call a doctor.

FEVERS

One of the most frightening situations parents are faced with is the child who suddenly runs a high temperature. It often happens in the middle of the night and parents wonder whether to call their overworked doctor or go it alone and hope they don't damage their child by delaying unnecessarily in a serious illness.

On the whole, a fever is a sign that a child is fighting an infection and building up resistance to it. The degree of the fever is not necessarily an indication of the severity of the infection, as some serious conditions may have only a slightly raised temperature. A very high fever can cause complications such as convulsions.

HOW TO TELL IF A CHILD HAS A FEVER. A fever is a temperature of 38°C (100°F) or above. Normal temperature when the body is at rest is: 37°C (98.6°F). Even before your child has complained of feeling ill you may notice that she is behaving differently. Perhaps she is flushed and has gone off her food. Feel her forehead – if she feels hotter than normal, take her temperature. Shivering and feeling cold may occur just before the temperature rises. Sometimes a child's skin may feel cool to the touch even though she has a fever. This is because her body is working hard at lowering the fever by sweating, so that the surface of the skin becomes cool. She may be flushed with an unusual redness in her cheeks or she may be unusually pale.

A temperature that is below normal 37°C (98.6°F) can also sometimes mean the child is ill.

TAKING A CHILD'S TEMPERATURE. A baby's hands and feet usually feel cool to the touch, so feel her forehead to gauge if she has a fever. One of the plastic strips that are placed on the forehead can tell you quickly if your child has a temperature simply by the change in colour on the strip. Although not absolutely precise, they are useful as an indication of whether your child has a fever, particularly in a small baby.

As unlikely as the thought is, a good digital thermometer can make a useful baby shower gift: because at some time, you will need one. There is a vast selection of thermometers available for babies – some are fun, others are inexpensive – but what is needed, is a reliable product that does the job speedily, without danger, possible errors and ease of use. Particularly useful, is a thermometer that is non-invasive, gives clinically accurate readings in seconds, stores a memory of previous readings is suitable for use in infants, children and adults without at any time involving the rectal, oral or underarm areas. But, they do not come cheap. Which is why they make a 'suitable' baby shower gift that a few good friends might get together to give you. Or, you can drop a hint to family...

Then, you can be sure that your baby won't have to pull her hair out in horror!

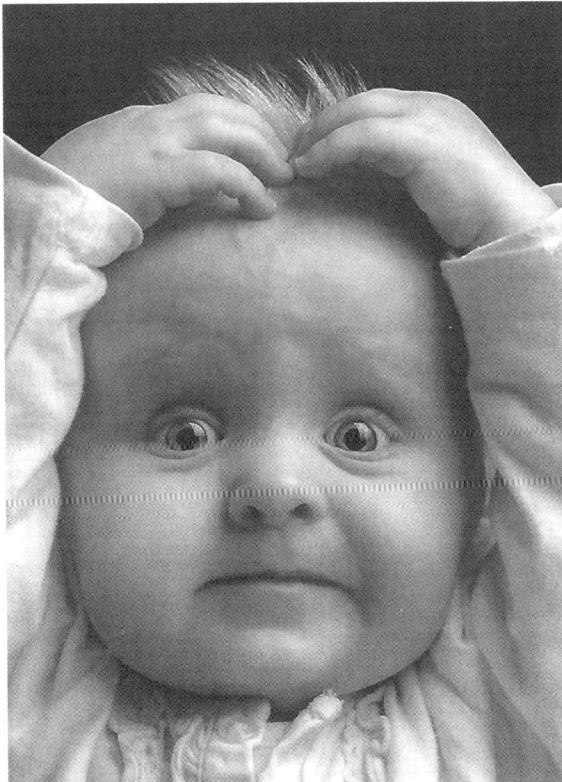

"You are going to put that thermometer WHERE?!"

Not too long ago, glass thermometers were often used under the tongue, in the rectum (anus), or under the armpit (auxiliary) to measure a baby's temperature. Now we know that these thermometers contained mercury, an extremely toxic metal poison. If you still have a glass thermometer, check if there is a visible paper strip inside the glass that has the words 'mercury free', then the liquid in the thermometer should be mercury free. If you do NOT see the words 'mercury free', assume that the liquid is mercury. Contact your local poison centre, or hazardous waste collection for advice on how to dispose of the thermometer. Do not attempt to dispose of it by throwing it in the rubbish or garbage bag, because if it breaks, the mercury can cause serious harm to anyone in the vicinity.

WHAT IS A NORMAL TEMPERATURE IN A CHILD?

A **normal** temperature in babies is considered to be close to 36.4°C (97.5°F) when taken in the **mouth (orally, under the tongue)**. A **fever** is a temperature above 37.5°C (99.5°F), when taken in the **mouth (orally, under the tongue).**

A **normal** temperature is 37.5°C (99.6°F) when taken in the **bottom (rectally)**. A **fever** is a temperature taken in the **bottom** that is above 38°C (100.4°F). The most accurate temperature used by a conventional thermometer, is in the bottom **(rectal)**. Only use a rectal thermometer after the first three months of age.

A **normal** temperature is 35.9°C (98°F) when taken under the **armpit (auxiliary)**. This is two degrees lower than the normal **bottom (rectal)** temperature, and one degree lower if the temperature is taken **by mouth (orally, under the tongue).**

TREATING A FEVER

JUDGE BY BEHAVIOUR. A child who has a relatively low temperature (raised one or two degrees) and is lethargic, off her food and seems to be sick may be more ill than the child with a high temperature who is still active and behaving more or less normally. In other words, be guided by your child's behaviour. Some of the most common causes of a raised temperature are infectious diseases; ear infection (otitis media); tonsillitis; strep throat; urinary tract infection and flu (use index for more details of these diseases).

WHEN TO SEE THE DOCTOR. If a baby younger than three months has a rectal temperature of 37.9°C (100.2°F) or higher call the doctor right away. Infants between 3-6 months with a rectal temperature of 38.3°C (101°F) or more, and if a child older than six months has a rectal temperature over 39.4°C (103°F) they should see a doctor soon.

If the temperature is 38,5°C (101°F) and she does not have any of the symptoms listed on *pages 334, 335* as requiring immediate attention, try to bring her temperature down and wait till morning. **Always consult your doctor straight away if you feel concerned regardless of the degree of fever your child has.**

BRINGING DOWN THE TEMPERATURE

UNDRESSING. The first thing to remember when your child has a temperature is not to overdress her. Piling clothes on when she is hot acts like a tea cosy and keeps the heat in and this could raise her temperature to dangerous levels. Leave her in a nappy and sleeveless cotton top without other covering if she is still an infant. All an older child needs is light cotton pyjamas or just panties. Allow body heat to escape as much as possible. Cotton is better than synthetic fabrics for conducting heat and absorbing sweat. If you take your child out to the doctor, don't bundle her up, even if it is cold outside. Just dress her sensibly as you would if she were not ill. Shivering often accompanies a high fever. This is caused by the body's temperature regulating mechanism reacting to the fever. She should still be clothed to allow air to circulate on her skin. If she feels cold she should be covered lightly.

Do not give medicine to lower a child's temperature without first consulting your doctor. The U.S. Academy of Paediatrics has issued an advisory to parents that a fever is the body's way of fighting an infection. They advise that parents should not immediately give fever lowering medicines as these are easily misused, either by giving two kinds of medication – both of which do the same job – or by giving the wrong dosage. This does not mean that these medications are a bad thing but rather that 'fever phobia' can cause an overreaction, and that great care must be taken to use a correct dosage.

Only medications that have been medically recommended should be used, even if they are available over the counter. For example, aspirin is not recommended for lowering the temperature as it can cause gastric (stomach) upsets, and should not be used in children under 16 years with a viral illness because of potentially serious side effects, in particular Reye syndrome. **Aspirin should therefore be avoided unless your doctor prescribes it.**

Paracetamol or Ibuprofen are usually recommended and are available in a form suitable for children. **Use an accurate measure available from your pharmacy. Wash well after use. Do not exceed the recommended dosage, and give only if directed by your doctor. Do not give to infants under three months of age unless your doctor prescribes it.**

Most medicines, unless otherwise directed, are best taken after meals to avoid an upset stomach. If your child vomits within three quarters of an hour after taking the medicine, give her sips of water or non-acidic fruit juice, and repeat the dose. Medicines are dangerous when taken in excess, so never refer to the flavoured or other kinds of medicine as sweets or candy, as the child could look for some to eat.

NOTE: Indomethacin suppositories should NOT be used to reduce fever, as this is not their function and it can have dangerous side-effects. Use only for juvenile rheumatoid arthritis, or other medications if prescribed by a doctor.

LUKEWARM BATHS. Sponging or tepid baths also help lower the temperature. If she is old enough put her in her regular bath with a small amount of water, about 6cm (2 inches), using a mixture of hot and cold water to make it tepid. (Test it with your elbow so that it is just slightly warm – if you use water that is too cold it will cause shivering which contracts the muscles and generates more heat.)

Let her play in the water for as long as she likes (drop in a few floating toys) and stay with her all the time, while sponging her gently with the water (the evaporation will cool her down). If she becomes restless do not force it. A baby can be sponged down with lukewarm water – don't make it too cold and don't use alcohol as it will cool her down too quickly and may be absorbed which is very dangerous. You can also use a fan to cool her.

FEVERS AND FOOD. There's no truth in the old adage 'feed a cold and starve a fever'. Any sick child with a raised temperature needs to keep up her fluid intake to replace the fluid lost through sweating and the increased rate of body functioning. Let her have anything she fancies: water, fruit juice, cool rooibos tea, high energy 'sports' drinks. Iced lollies made from fruit juice will supply fluid and they also help cool her down. If you give medicine after she has been sucking an iced lolly (popsicle) it will not taste so bad because her mouth will be partially anaesthetised. Don't give very cold liquid to a child who suffers from allergies or asthma, because it can bring on an attack. Milk is fine. The popular story that milk 'produces mucus' is not supported by scientific tests.

Don't force food on a sick child, although a little chicken soup never did any harm and has the advantage of supplying fluid as well as mineral salts and protein. Children often feel nauseous when ill, so a light, easily digestible meal is preferable. Avoid fatty foods. At the peak of the illness a liquid or soft diet will probably be more acceptable than a heavy meal. Meat broths, milk soups, boiled chicken, steamed fish and plain stews are likely to be better tolerated than fried or highly flavoured foods. Plenty of nourishment can be obtained from milk jellies, ice-cream (sorbet does not contain cream so is not as nourishing although it is suitable) and mousses. Vitamin B-producing bacteria in the bowel are destroyed by antibiotics, so give her products that contain the vitamin, such as yogurt with live A-B cultures, milk and cheese or sprinkle a little wheat germ on her food. Vitamin A is a great help in recovery from illness. It is found in liver – not likely to be a favourite food – and in the form of beta carotene, in yellow fruits and vegetables. Carrots, mangoes, spanspek (cantaloupe) all make delicious juice. Green leafy vegetables like spinach and kale are also good sources.

Frequent small, light meals should overcome the problem of a diminished appetite and you will soon be able to tell when your child is well enough to have the usual family meals. This normally occurs when she starts asking for chips and chocolate and generally starts manipulating you. No doubt you will develop a resistance to this at the same rate as she develops resistance to childhood illnesses!

BED REST. Parents often wonder whether the sick child should be confined to bed. In general, it is better to let the child indicate her needs. The child who is not feeling up to it will not insist on getting out of bed. She will be glad to lie there and will be too weak to run around. The child who is moderately ill and wants to rest somewhere other than in her bed should be allowed to do so unless the doctor has specifically ordered her to rest in bed.

If the weather is mild she can even sit quietly outside. There is nothing to be gained by keeping a child in bed against her will. If she doesn't want to stay in bed she will perform and create so much that she will exhaust herself more than if she were up. Certain more serious illnesses such as rheumatic fever, pneumonia and hepatitis may require bed rest, but unless your doctor specifically prescribes this, be guided by good sense and self-preservation (yours as well as the child's). The child who must rest in bed needs a lot of attention and you had better get all the help you can, such as music with ear-phones and plenty to read. If she is too young to read to herself you can try to beg or borrow a small DVD or CD player. Coloured pencils are less messy than crayons and a scrap pad and colouring book are useful.

Knitting wool, beads to thread and sewing cards may keep her occupied for a while. Stamp collecting kits, soccer cards and computer games can also be played while in bed. I wouldn't shower the sick child with gifts – and if you do get some of those mentioned, don't hand them out all at once. Stretch them out over as long a period as possible. What your child really wants is your undivided attention and entertainment. However, since this is impossible, you will have to use some of the ploys suggested to keep her in bed. She needs sympathy and consideration, but being ill should not be the only way she gets them.

RETURNING TO SCHOOL. Most infections become non-contagious after the temperature has returned to normal, so you can let your child return to school or playgroup when you feel she has regained her strength and is able to cope with her usual routine away from home. Consult your doctor when in doubt. *See index for illnesses.*

FEBRILE CONVULSIONS (FITS DUE TO A HIGH TEMPERATURE)

DON'T PANIC. Occasionally a child who has a high temperature will have a convulsion or fit. It is not known precisely why some children react in this way, but it is not necessarily a sign that the child will suffer from epilepsy or convulsions later in life, although a small percentage (2-4%) do develop epilepsy. Generally children who are predisposed to have febrile convulsions have not been shown to have any later physical or intellectual impairment. The tendency towards febrile convulsions appears to be an inherited lower seizure threshold. Febrile convulsions are very frightening for parents and they need to know how to handle the situation so as not to make things worse by panicking.

- The child who is having a convulsion usually rolls her eyes back and starts twitching or stiffens and passes out. She may foam at the mouth and jerk a lot.
- She could pass urine or faeces.
- Call, or get to the doctor, but meanwhile don't try to slap or shake the child out of it, and don't try and give her anything to drink while she is unconscious.
- Keep her out of harms way by lying her on the bed or floor and see that she does not hurt herself against sharp objects.
- Turn her head to the side so that saliva can drain out and make sure her nose is not obstructed. Don't try to put anything in her mouth to prevent her biting her tongue or you could block her airway and do more harm than good.
- As soon as she quietens, place her in the recovery position (*see sketch p. 454*). That is lying on her side as though she is sleeping comfortably.

DO NOT COVER HER WITH A BLANKET. Start peeling off her clothes. Undress her to her underwear and sponge her down with cool water. You can even put a fan in front of her with a basin of ice near it so that it can blow cold air onto her (she will not get a cold). You can also fill a hot water bottle with iced water and put it against her, but don't give her a bath as she may have another convulsion while in the bath. You must get her temperature down as quickly as possible. When she comes round properly you can give her a dose of paracetamol to help lower her temperature. She will not be aware of what has happened after she comes round so don't frighten her by acting in a panicky fashion. She will be sleepy and once your doctor has seen her you can let her rest.

FUTURE OUTLOOK FOR THE CHILD WHO HAS HAD A FEBRILE CONVULSION. Your doctor may order tests if he or she is not quite satisfied that the convulsion was merely the result of a high temperature accompanying one of the more common childhood diseases. There is the possibility of an infection such as meningitis or encephalitis that must be investigated.

Either way you are sure to be advised to keep a close eye on her if she runs a temperature again and to use the measures outlined on *p. 339* for lowering it.

Between two and four per cent of children between the ages of six months and five years suffer febrile convulsions at the beginning of an illness such as an ear infection. The great majority of these attacks do not lead to seizures in later life and pass without problem in five minutes. When the seizure lasts longer than 15 minutes and is repeated within 24 hours there is a possibility of an underlying cause. You must learn to lower the temperature effectively (*see p. 339*), and you may be given something like a diazepam suppository (Valium) to use to prevent or abort an attack if your child develops a fever or seizure in future. In uncomplicated cases the daily use of medication to prevent seizures is no longer advised. Do not let fear of a convulsion make you over-anxious about your child's every symptom – it is not that serious. Your doctor will advise you.

GIVING MEDICINES

I am not sure whether it is good management or good luck that makes some children take medicine like lambs and others fight it all the way. But it is always a wise policy to administer medicine casually and without too much talk, either about how good it is for her or how nice it is or anything else that places too much emphasis on it. Once she gets the notion that it is something you are anxious about she could become difficult. For babies you can use an eye dropper or spoon or a Dinky feeder or a similar device. A clean medical syringe without a needle is handy because it will not spill and you can measure accurately. A universal adapter that fits into the top of the medicine bottle can be used. Turn the bottle upside-down with the syringe pushed into the adapter. Pull the plunger out slowly until the right amount of medicine is in the syringe. You can also crush tablets between the bowls of two spoons, add a little water or juice and suck the mixture up into the syringe. Direct the syringe towards the inside of the cheek and squirt slowly so that she has time to swallow.

When an older child refuses point blank to take her medicine I would not waste too much time on trying to bribe, cajole or threaten her. It seldom has the desired effect and next time you will have to double the stakes. Tell her firmly she has to have the medicine and if necessary you will give it to her by force. Warn her that if she vomits it she will have to have another dose, which will mean double the trouble. Of course it is better not to have to force a child to do anything but here you have no alternative.

Hold her on your lap with your left arm around her (if you are right handed) and with the hand that is encircling her, squeeze open her mouth gently and put the medicine in, using your right hand. Some medicines really taste dreadful and it is a good idea to ask your doctor if he can substitute with something more pleasant if possible. There is no need to impose something really unpleasant on a child if it can be avoided. If she vomits her medicine up within 45 minutes of taking it, give her another dose. Check with your doctor whether she should have it before or after food. If he says it makes no difference, give it straight after meals to avoid stomach upsets. Antibiotics can also cause stomach cramps and loose stools and should not be taken with milk as it hinders absorption in some instances. If necessary, wash down tablets or liquid medicine with plain water. Mashed ripe banana is helpful in making the medicine go down as it prevents tablets from getting stuck.

Tetracycline taken during pregnancy and early childhood can stain permanent teeth brown or yellow so question your doctor about it if he or she prescribes them. They should not be given before the age of six except in cases where there is no alternative. If a child does need tetracycline drugs she should not play in the sun as they can cause a rash.

Antibiotics have no effect on viral illnesses except in very rare instances. Do not badger your doctor to prescribe them as they may do more harm than good. When the doctor is convinced the child has a bacterial infection (a throat swab may be needed to do a culture), an antibiotic will probably be prescribed and is likely to be most effective.

A doctor who prescribes antibiotics for a child by telephone without seeing her and making a diagnosis is not practising medicine properly. The overuse of antibiotics has rendered some of them ineffective. Keep them for when they really are needed.

NOSE DROPS. Nose drops should not be given except on your doctor's orders. If they are used for prolonged periods they can cause the nasal tissue to become sensitised. To give them, get the child to lie down with her head far back off the edge of the bed, for example. Hold her arms down with your free hand and squeeze in the drops. You must then pinch her nose closed gently and hold her head back for 30 seconds. If she lifts her head too quickly the drops will run out. If your baby's nose is so blocked from a cold that she has difficulty feeding, you can clear it temporarily by using a salt-water solution. Dissolve ½ of a teaspoon of salt in 50ml sterile lukewarm water. Or use normal saline drops. Put a few drops in her nose minutes before a feed. You can also buy a nasal syringe to suck up mucus, but do not fiddle a lot with your baby's nasal passages. (*See Colds p. 348.*)

EAR DROPS. Olive oil and other home remedies should never be put in a child's ears as she could have a burst ear drum and drops will complicate the problem.

If your child has a heavy coating of wax in her ears the doctor can remove it with tweezers or flush it out with a syringe. Wax can cause faulty hearing at a time when a child is learning to talk – this can hinder language development. Only medically prescribed ear drops should be given. Let the child lie down with the head lowered and tilted to one side. Put the drops in and give them a chance to soak right into the ear before letting her getup.

EYE MEDICATION. Children seldom need eye drops, but if they are prescribed keep her head back and drop them into the inner corner of the eyes. Eye ointment is sometimes necessary and this comes in a little tube. Just squeeze a little bit into the inner corner of the eye and it will spread by itself.

WHEN IT COULD BE SERIOUS

STOMACHACHES. Like fevers, stomachache is common in childhood and parents are faced with deciding whether it warrants seeing a doctor or if it will pass without treatment. Stomach pain can be a symptom of certain serious conditions in the abdomen; however, some children say their stomach hurts when the cause is elsewhere, so only a professional can judge the situation. To give you an idea of the likelihood of a serious cause, try to answer these questions. A yes answer will indicate the need for medical advice:

- Your young infant cries intermittently and pulls up her legs towards her stomach. This is most likely colic, but it could be a blockage caused when part of the intestine telescopes itself known as intussusception. (*See. p.384.*)
- Is she listless, off her food and obviously in discomfort?
- Does she have diarrhoea?
- Is she vomiting?
- Did the pain wake her up?
- Is she constipated?
- Have her stools been bloodstained or maroon or black? The darker colours indicate old blood while bright red stool would mean fresh bleeding.
- Does she have a fever?
- Does it hurt when she moves, even if she is distracted?
- Does she have a burning sensation when she passes water? Does her urine contain blood? It could be red, orange or brown tinged.
- Is the pain constant or does it come and go? Both can be significant.
- Are there any lumps where there shouldn't be?
- Is her stomach abnormally distended?

GASTROENTERITIS (inflammation and infection of the intestinal tract) is common, especially in summer. It causes cramping pain and is usually accompanied by vomiting, fever and frequent loose stools. The cause is usually viral, but it can be bacterial or parasitic such as giardia lamblia. Because the child is losing fluid top and bottom, she can become dehydrated very quickly. **This is a very serious condition in a young child and a doctor must be seen as soon as possible.** (*See p. 353 for treatment of gastroenteritis.*)

IMPORTANT NOTE: Do not give your child a laxative or enema unless your doctor has prescribed it; because if the stomach pain is caused by appendicitis it could aggravate the condition.

INTESTINAL OBSTRUCTION is another condition that is characterised by cramping pain with vomiting that comes and goes. Between the ages of two months and two years intussusception is the commonest cause of intestinal obstruction: a portion of the bowel telescopes inside another section blocking the passage of food. The child is likely to pull up her legs and cry with pain intermittently because the pain comes and goes. Important signs that help differentiate it from colic and other childhood stomach pains are the presence of small blood-stained mucous filled stools and vomiting of green matter, possibly blood-stained. Caught early, the condition may be treated without surgery, but often an operation is required. **See your doctor immediately.** (*See p. 384.*)

INGUINAL HERNIA. An inguinal hernia generally looks like a marble size bulge under the skin in the groin (the area between the abdomen and the thigh), especially when the baby cries. It can develop when a part of the intestine pushes through a weakness in the belly muscles, especially if the baby was preterm. The child may need surgery to ensure that the blood supply to the intestine is not cut off. **Consult your paediatrician immediately.**

KIDNEY AND URINARY TRACT INFECTIONS can cause pain in the abdomen or back. The child may have a raised temperature and blood in her urine and a burning sensation when she urinates. She may also feel like passing water frequently even though she produces little when she does, or she may revert to bed wetting. In infancy, diarrhoea, vomiting and failure to gain weight may be a sign of urinary tract infection, but often symptoms are very vague. Medical help must be sought as these infections do not clear up by themselves.

Your doctor will want a specimen of urine and this is best taken after washing the vaginal area with soap and water and drying with clean cotton wool. Catch a small amount in a sterile bottle. This needs to be tested very soon afterwards or the normally occurring germs will have multiplied. Keep the sample cold.

APPENDICITIS is probably the most common abdominal condition that requires surgery in children over the age of five. Although rare before this age, it can occur. It is important to be aware of this possibility when a child has a stomachache. Unfortunately appendicitis is not easy to diagnose but it is better to remove an appendix unnecessarily than to leave it until it is too late and have to cope with a generalised internal infection because it has burst.

Usually one of the first signs of appendicitis is loss of appetite. Then the child has pain in the middle of the tummy around the navel. Over the next six to 12 hours the pain usually moves down to the lower right side, which is very sore if pressed or when the child moves. A raised temperature, usually not very high, develops and the child may vomit. The child with appendicitis will usually be more comfortable lying with her knees bent and any pressure on the lower right abdomen produces pain. **Don't take a chance: call or visit a doctor straight away if you suspect she may have appendicitis.**

FOOD POISONING

Stomach cramps, vomiting, diarrhoea and fever can be caused by bacteria that contaminate food. It is usually identified when several people who have eaten the same food become ill at the same time. Staph bacteria transferred by carriers who handle food, salmonella bacteria found in undercooked chickens, meat and eggs; listeriosis is transferred through unhygienic handling of foods including ready to eat deli meats, unpasteurised milk and cheese, refrigerated smoked seafood and raw sprouts are common causes of food poisoning as listeria can also survive in a refrigerator. Careful washing of hands with hot water and cleaning of surfaces on which food is prepared is essential. During pregnancy these types of bacteria can have a severe effect, as the system is extremely vulnerable. (*See Pregnancy p. 19*)

THE DANGR OF HONEY: Botulism is the most serious form of food poisoning and is caused by bacteria that grow in the absence of oxygen. This used to occur in commercial tinned foods years ago – and these days occasionally in homemade products – and in contaminated honey.

Botulinum spores are the most poisonous natural substance known to mankind and are found in dust, soil and honey. While adults who swallow *botulinum* spores are seldom affected, children under the age of a year can become very seriously ill, especially if not diagnosed early. **Raw honey is particularly dangerous, but do not use any type of honey in the first year.**

Before dismissing your child's stomach ache for an ordinary cramp or colic, consider whether she might not have gastroenteritis, an intestinal obstruction, appendicitis, food poisoning, or a kidney or urinary tract infection. A child under the age of a year, who has had honey and is constipated, followed by sucking and breathing difficulty with limpness, **must be treated very urgently.**

INDEX TO CHILDHOOD COMPLAINTS: THEIR SYMPTOMS AND TREATMENT
THE COMMON COLD AND OTHER RESPIRATORY TRACT INFECTIONS

All recommendations are subject to the approval of, and implementation by your doctor.

SYMPTOMS	ILLNESS	TREATMENT	REMARKS
Cough which is hard and dry may become loose and productive, and can last several weeks. May follow symptoms of a cold.	**BRONCHITIS**	If the cough persists see a doctor. Although antibiotics are usually not necessary, a number of organisms can cause bronchitis. Children do not usually spit out mucus but swallow it, which can put them off their food. Keep air moist with a humidifier or boil a kettle in the room with the doors and windows closed.	Cough medicines are not helpful and some are dangerous. No major complications but alert your doctor if the child wheezes or breathes rapidly and does not seem to be getting enough air. 'Chronic' bronchiolitis may be asthma. Give plenty of fluids and a light diet.
Rapid breathing during viral infection in early infancy (below age two). Cough, possible wheezing with mild or high temperature.	**BRONCHIOLITIS**	**See a doctor.** If the pulse rate is over 150/min, and if the child becomes drowsy and is clearly not well, hospital admission for oxygen therapy may be necessary.	In cases where the child has spells in which breathing stops (apnoea) for variable periods, mechanical breathing assistance may be required. Heart disease can present in the same way as bronchiolitis. Respiratory syncytial virus (RSV) is the main cause of bronchiolitis.
Sneezing, watering eyes. Runny nose, sore throat possibly with cough. Babies may cry a lot and be cranky. Feeding may be difficult because of a stuffy nose. Thick yellow or green nasal discharge is a sign of overlying bacterial infection. It may require antibiotics.	**COMMON COLD**	Give paracetamol to ease discomfort and lower fever. Colds are caused by a virus so antibiotics don't help. Moisten air with a cold air humidifier or allow a kettle to boil in the room with the doors closed so that humidity builds up from the steam. Cold air keeps nasal secretions liquid so they don't clog up the nostrils making it difficult to breathe, so don't heat the room and don't be afraid to take your baby outside. If a blocked nose makes feeding difficult, use saline solution drops or a little breast milk in each nostril. Clear thick mucus with a syringe. Squeeze bulb then slowly release the bulb in the nostril to extract mucus. Fluid intake must be kept up. Vitamin C and zinc may shorten the duration of the cold, and a little 'chicken soup' gives nourishment as well as liquids. See a doctor if it is your baby's first cold or if she coughs. Older children may be prescribed a nasal decongestant spray.	Children get more colds before the age of 6 than at any other time because of the many ways the illness can be spread, and their lack of immunity. Most common complication is infection of the short passage between the back of the throat and the middle ear (otitis media). Signs are crying which stops when the child is picked up because ear pressure is relieved when the child is upright. Or sudden screaming in the night with a raised temperature. Never let an older child blow her nose forcefully when she has a cold: it could blow germs straight into the Eustachian tube. Rather hold one nostril closed and get her to blow gently. Bronchitis, tonsillitis, sinusitis and pneumonia are other possible complications. Persistent cold-like symptoms may be caused by allergy (see p. 417). Colds are spread by droplets, touching and other contact. Extremely infectious for two days.

SYMPTOMS	ILLNESS	TREATMENT	REMARKS
Loud, seal-like, barking cough that occurs at night. Symptoms may be sudden, with noisy, difficult breathing in, possibly accompanied by a low or high fever. Croup attacks are usually preceded by symptoms of a mild cold, usually in winter. Most commonly caused by a viral infection in babies older than four months, resulting in swelling of the airway just below the vocal cords making breathing noisy and difficult.	CROUP	**Get medical attention immediately if the child becomes blue, or drowsy with a rapid pulse.** Your doctor may suggest humidifying the atmosphere, or using a nebuliser. Take her to the bathroom and turn on all the hot water taps including the shower. Without frightening her allow her to get as much moist air as possible. If you can stay calm and she is old enough, read her a story in the bathroom. Meanwhile have a humidifier going in her room or boil a kettle with the door and windows closed.	Most cases of croup are caused by a viral infection. If the croup persists until morning and the temperature is high it may be complicated by bacterial infection and an antibiotic may be prescribed. In cases of viral croup, corticosteroids could be prescribed in order to decrease swelling in the airway and lessen the production of mucus secretion. Adrenaline inhalation may be needed in hospitalised cases. In susceptible children croup attacks are possible every winter or whenever the child gets a cold or throat infection especially between the ages of 2 and 4 years. HIV infected children who have severe thrush may develop croup.
High temperature, lethargy, difficult noisy breathing and hoarseness with drooling. Swallowing is painful and the child is reluctant to speak or open the mouth wide.	EPIGLOTITIS	**Emergency! Take the child to the doctor or hospital urgently,** as she may need a tracheotomy to help her breathe (tube inserted into windpipe). **Do not attempt to change the way the child prefers to sit as this helps breathing!** Toddlers usually sit in a characteristic position with their one hand leaning on the floor as they struggle to breathe.	Epiglottis is an acute bacterial infection of the epiglottis (the little 'tongue' that covers the windpipe when we swallow). When it becomes enlarged it can close off the windpipe so the child cannot breathe. By taking a throat swab the exact bacteria causing the infection can be identified. **This condition is serious.** Hib vaccine can prevent the infection.
Chills, headache, pain in the muscles, sore throat, and loss of appetite and feeling of weakness. Mild to high temperature. May feel nauseous and have aching eyes. Nose is stuffy, but there is little discharge.	INFLUENZA (Flu)	Rest, light diet, keep up fluid intake. See a doctor if symptoms persist after 3 days. Paracetamol for pain and fever. Antibiotics only indicated if there are bacterial complications. Flu vaccine is available for vulnerable children.	Common among children aged 5 to 9 and may be complicated by bronchitis. There is no point in administering antibiotics as cause is viral and will not respond to them. Cough may persist and depression is a common after-effect. There is specific anti-viral therapy for H1N1 flu.

SYMPTOMS	ILLNESS	TREATMENT	REMARKS
Earache, possibly with fever following a cold. Lack of appetite and general lethargy. If the eardrum bursts, pus, mucus and possibly a small amount of blood may be seen on the pillow or around the ear.	**OTITIS MEDIA (Middle ear infection)**	See a GP or ear, nose and throat specialist. The appearance of the eardrum gives an indication of the type of otitis media, which will lead to treatment decisions. These include broad spectrum antibiotics. If it does not clear in a month grommets may be needed. These are tiny objects like straws which are inserted in the eardrum, under anaesthetic, in order for the ear to drain. See p. 449. Enlarged adenoids can cause frequent ear infections.	Often follows a cold, when germs spread to the middle ear behind the ear drum. See p. 449. If the earache persists after treatment see a doctor urgently as there may be a serious complication. Hib vaccination helps prevent otitis media although not entirely. Frequent ear infections may result in poor speech development. Infection may persist after the eardrum bursts with resulting discharge, although it is not painful. See a doctor.
Mild to high fever, dry hacking cough, chest pain, nausea, weakness, rapid or difficult breathing. May be blue at fingertips and around the mouth, due to lack of oxygen. This is a serious danger sign, as it indicates that the child is not getting enough oxygen. Child may, or may not have a fever. **Potentially extremely serious in very young children.**	**PNEUMONIA**	**See a doctor very urgently if the child has difficulty in breathing and the lower chest sinks in.** For mild cases rest, paracetamol for fever, extra breastfeeding or other fluids and light diet may be sufficient, but a doctor's opinion is essential. If caused by the pneumococcus and other bacteria it responds rapidly to treatment with a penicillin type of drug. Viral pneumonia is usually mild, but may be complicated by bacterial infection at the same time. Correct antibiotic treatment is indicated if there are bacterial complications.	New state supplied conjugated pneumococcal vaccine (Prevenar), as well as Hib vaccine can help prevent bacterial pneumonia. Overcrowding and exposure to sick children in crèches increase the risk of respiratory infections. Well nourished children with sound immune systems should have no major complications if treated. Pneumonia is a major cause of death in babies from poor socio-economic circumstances, and those who are HIV positive. TB may coexist with viral or bacterial pneumonia. Breastfeeding and immunisation help prevent the disease. Zinc and vitamin A supplements assist recovery. Coughing may continue for several weeks.
Starts off as a cold, and then becomes painful with headache, fever and lethargy. There may be yellow or green foul discharge from the nose, and bad breath. Occasionally there is swelling and redness around the eyes. The child's voice may sound different. Sometimes a foreign body in the nose can cause similar symptoms.	**SINUSITIS**	See a doctor. Antibiotics such as penicillin, amoxicillin or erythromycin are likely to be prescribed. Nasal sprays containing steroids have been shown to be helpful.	Swelling and redness of the tissue around the eyes is potentially serious, as vision may be affected. See an ENT specialist as soon as possible. **Hib** vaccine helps prevent infection. Sinusitis may be associated with allergy.

SYMPTOMS	ILLNESS	TREATMENT	REMARKS
	SNORING *(See Upper Airway Obstruction p. 285)*		
Tonsillitis: sudden fever, chills, headache and sore throat. Nausea and vomiting are common. Loss of appetite during first 24 hours. Temperature usually between 38°C–40°C and could remain high for several days. The skin may be flushed, and there may be some discharge from the nose. Earache is common. Glands under jaw may be enlarged. Throat and tonsils are usually red and may have white patches. Symptoms of pharyngitis are similar but slightly more difficult to diagnose. Pharyngitis is an infection of the throat and surrounding tissues if there are no tonsils.	**TONSILLITIS AND PHARYNGITIS**	**See a doctor.** Treatment started within 24 hours is most effective, but if begun within 48 hours should prevent complications such as middle ear infection, sinusitis, scarlet fever and kidney involvement. Usual medication is penicillin since cause is likely to be a streptococcal infection. A throat swab may be taken to establish exact type of bacteria. Viral infection is also possible in which case antibiotics may not be prescribed. Paracetamol is usually prescribed to ease throat pain, and reduce fever. It is vitally important to complete the full course of medicines prescribed.	**Tonsillitis should not be ignored because of possible complications.** Children may have repeated attacks of tonsillitis. Removal of the tonsils prevents tonsillitis but the infection may then appear as pharyngitis. Any decision to remove the tonsils should be made on an individual basis. A two week course of antibiotics may be prescribed or even longer term penicillin in half the normal daily dose. As the patient may harbour germs for 3 months or longer after an attack, isolation is impractical. Regard child as infectious while her temperature is raised.
Snoring during sleep, and in some children, snoring sounds even while awake. Both loud and soft snoring can indicate a problem. Restless sleep, frequent waking, poor growth and development may be associated with upper airways obstruction that results in snoring.	**UPPER AIRWAY OBSTRUCTION (Snoring)**	An ear nose and throat specialist needs to assess whether removal of adenoids or both adenoids and tonsils is necessary, if snoring persists for more then 6 months or X-rays show severe obstruction. Medication, possibly with steroid drops may be of benefit.	This seemingly unimportant condition affects more than 50% of children under the age of 2 years, and can have serious consequences. Snoring is caused by obstruction of the air passage and this means that the system is deprived of oxygen. **A wide range of problems including poor growth, behavioural disorders, and learning deficits are possible. Can be symptomatic of even more serious problems.**

INFECTIOUS DISEASES

All recommendations are subject to the approval of, and implementation by your doctor.

SYMPTOMS	ILLNESS	TREATMENT	REMARKS
The first symptoms in children are usually recurrent chest infections, or long term or recurrent diarrhoea with weight loss. Prolonged fever (more than a month). Persistent thrush infections. Enlarged glands, cough that lasts more than a month. Skin infections. Repeated infections such as pneumonia. Developmental delays. Liver, heart and kidney disease. Note: Many of these symptoms are common in babies who are not infected with HIV. Severity and duration are key factors.	**AIDS AND HIV RELATED DISEASE**	Properly administered anti-retroviral therapy (ART) can make this a manageable illness, although lifelong treatment will be needed. **Strict adherence to the treatment programme is essential, in order to prevent the development of resistance to the medication.** HIV transmission from mother to child can be reduced to around 2% with triple therapy from 12 weeks of pregnancy. Or AZT can be started at 32 weeks of pregnancy. Or AZT can be started at the start of labour. Bottle fed babies should receive Nevirapine daily from birth to 6 weeks when they are tested for HIV. If the baby is HIV positive treatment is started immediately. Good nutrition and extra Vitamin A is helpful. Timely treatment for any infection is vital. Immunisation against TB, pneumonia, rotavirus and other diseases as per schedule. Consult a paediatrician regarding other vaccines.	HIV is transmitted through bodily fluids such as urine, blood and breast milk. Also from HIV infection in the mother passed on during the birth or breastfeeding. Counselling for care-givers is vital, as good adherence to therapy can reduce mortality. Where the danger of illness is high due to poor hygienic circumstances, breastfeeding only is better. Breastfed babies whose mother is HIV positive should have daily Nevirapine until breastfeeding is stopped. This should be done abruptly and 6 weeks later the child should be tested for HIV infection. In higher socio-economic conditions bottle feeding only is an option. It is legally inadmissible to ask an adult or child's HIV status. Daycare attendance is possible except if there are open sores. **Note: Recommendations are subject to change as new HIV information becomes available. Stay in touch with hospital or other HIV medical advisor.**
The child may have a raised temperature and feel ill for a day or two before the appearance of the spots which are like dark red pimples that develop blisters within hours. Spots first appear on the trunk, then spread to other areas. The blisters dry up leaving itchy scabs.	**CHICKENPOX (Varicella)**	Mild illness caused by a virus associated with herpes zoster (shingles). The spots can become infected by scratching and leave scars. If spots are widespread there may be great discomfort from itching. Half a cupful of bicarbonate of soda added to a lukewarm bath water should relieve itching. Dabbing the spots with calamine lotion containing an antihistamine also helps. If the spots become infected, use an antibiotic cream prescribed by a doctor. Keep fingernails short.	Highly contagious and common in all ages, but most often seen between 5-8 years. **Do not give aspirin because of the danger of developing Reye syndrome.** Child is contagious for eight days after the appearance of new spots, or until all scabs have fallen off. Varicella (Chickenpox) vaccine is available privately. It is serious in HIV positive and other immuno-compromised children who may require treatment with drugs such as acyclovir, or human anti-varicella zoster globulin. Keep infected child away from pregnantwomen.

SYMPTOMS	ILLNESS	TREATMENT	REMARKS
Sudden, copious, very watery stools with white flecks. There is no fever or cramping. Rapid dehydration occurs with dry skin, sunken eyes, weakness and collapse.	CHOLERA	**Seek medical treatment urgently.** Fluids must be replaced rapidly. Use electrolyte solution *p. 178* if not near a hospital. Continue breastfeeding. Antibiotics shorten the course of the disease.	A stool culture can confirm the diagnosis. Cholera is spread through infected water and food sources. Boil all water before use if you are unsure. Wash hands before eating, or preparing food. If there is no possibility of boiling water or sterilising with chemicals, leave water in a closed glass container in sunlight for at least six hours, as it may be helpful.
Headache, lethargy, fever, seizures, severe confusion and coma are possible. This is an infection of the brain which may have mild or extremely serious symptoms and outcome. Similar to meningitis (*see p. 356*).	ENCEPHALITIS	**Should be treated by a specialist in hospital.** Accurate diagnosis is essential in order to identify best treatment.	May have viral origin such as herpes, or infection from adenoids or an after-effect of measles, mumps, chickenpox, German measles or other viral infection.
Possible vomiting followed by frequent, watery stools, possibly with stomach cramps. Usually has no fever, unless caused by Shigella. Severe dehydration due to loss of fluid through vomiting and frequent watery stools causes loss of weight, sunken eyes and sunken 'soft spot' (fontanelle) on the head, lack of tears and general lethargy. The most important signs of life threatening dehydration and shock are lethargy and increasing drowsiness (sleepiness). Stools that have blood in	GASTROENTERITIS Has many causes including Rotavirus, E coli bacteria, Salmonella, Shigella, Giardia lambia, Cholera etc.	**Dehydration is a serious danger, and must be corrected. Children who cannot keep down fluids because of continuous vomiting and those who are becoming quiet and drowsy must be seen by a doctor and may need to be admitted to hospital.** Give breastfeeds or acidified milk feed. In between give electrolyte solution available from chemist. Or make electrolyte solution: 1 litre cooled boiled water + 8 level teaspoons sugar + ½ teaspoon salt. *See p. 178.* The addition of 20mg zinc daily during diarrhoea appears to aid recovery. If child is old enough give mashed banana (for potassium) when she is better. Antibiotics are not indicated except if prescribed by doctor.	**Prevent gastroenteritis by washing hands well after going to the toilet and washing hands before touching the baby or making bottles or food. Sterilise bottles by boiling or use steriliser. Use boiled water for making up bottles. Flies bring disease!** Can have various causes. Including viral e.g. Rotavirus (mainly in winter). Bacterial e.g. E. coli, salmonella, and shigella. For parasitic causes and treatment *See p. 369.* Do not use products that stop diarrhoea in adults, for children. Also see 'toddler's diarrhoea' *p. 264.*

SYMPTOMS	ILLNESS	TREATMENT	REMARKS
them, or are frothy or foul smelling or bile (greenish, yellow) stained need special investigation. Seizures are possible in Shigella.			
Symptoms appear 14 to 21 days after exposure. Lymph nodes behind neck enlarge; then a flat pink rash appears on the forehead, behind ears and on the chest for about 3 days, with possible slight fever and listlessness.	**GERMAN MEASLES (Rubella)**	No specific treatment other than bed rest. Most infectious between 5 days before, and 7 days after rash appears. Rash fades from the face down.	**Pregnant women in contact with rubella should be tested for antibodies, as severe birth defects are possible!** All children should be immunised (see p. 462).
Possible low fever, poor appetite and sore throat 3-7 days after contact. Oval blisters on tongue, throat, hands, buttocks and soles of feet.	**HAND-FOOT and MOUTH DISEASE** (Not related to foot and mouth disease in animals)	Mild illness caused by Coxsackievirus A 16 (more serious form caused by enterovirus 71). Antibiotics are not effective.	Spread by contact with infected saliva, stools or blisters. Wash hands! Common in summer, early autumn. Recovery: 5-7 days. Can complicate existing eczema.
Plus 40°C fever, blisters on gums, lips, tongue, palate and tonsils which become shallow ulcers in a few days. Refusal to eat and drooling due to pain.	**HERPES (Gingivostomatitis)**	See a doctor. May need treatment with antivirals and medication to lower fever. More complicated if HIV positive.	Affects children from 6 mts to 5 yrs plus. Offer non-acidic drinks from a straw, and soft neutral foods. A gel may be used to cover mouth ulcers. Swollen neck glands are common.

SYMPTOMS	ILLNESS	TREATMENT	REMARKS
Red clusters of spots form blisters on the lips and sometimes in the nose. Ulcers develop in a day or two, then dry and form scabs.	**HERPES LABIALIS (Cold sores/fever blisters)**	If antiviral ointment is applied as soon as red patch appears it may be possible to stop ulceration.	Scratching scabs spreads infection: dangerous if it involves the eyes. Children with eczema can be severely affected.
This rare condition presents with very high fever that can last several weeks. The tongue is very red, with a strawberry like appearance and the lips are cracked. Eyes may be red and inflamed while hands and feet are swollen. Skin peels after 10-20 days. There is a bodily rash.	**KAWASAKI DISEASE**	**See a doctor!** Treatment is with intravenous immunoglobulin and high dose aspirin. The danger lies in the serious and common complications including heart disease.	Almost exclusively affects children, mostly under five years. Because it is relatively rare the illness is easily confused with measles, scarlet fever and other infections. Thus patients should be referred to an expert.
Symptoms may only appear 7-21 days or longer after exposure. These include fever, chills, headache, poor feeding, lethargy, diarrhoea and cough. Convulsions and coma, breathing difficulty and collapse may occur. Symptoms may be confused with other severe illness, delaying treatment.	**MALARIA** Malaria is not really an infectious disease but a parasitic disease. It has been placed in this section so that it can be more easily found when you are going through symptoms, as it is potentially serious	**See a doctor! Best treated in a high care unit, as it is life threatening.** Drug treatment begins as soon as blood or rapid antigen test confirms diagnosis: If a child has been in a high risk area tell the doctor, even if prophylactic medication was given as fake drugs are a problem. Once in the bloodstream illness can recur. Babies under 6 mts may be protected by maternal anti-bodies.	Caused by a parasite entering the system through the female mosquito bite in tropical areas: northern KwaZulu-Natal, eastern Mpumalanga, and north-eastern Limpopo in South Africa. Mozambique, parts of Zambia and northern Botswana and Namibia and large areas of Africa, South and South East Asia, parts of Central and South America, the Caribbean, the Middle East and Oceania. About half of the world's population is at risk. Any illness after visiting these areas must raise suspicion of malaria. Use of special nets and spraying is wise.

SYMPTOMS	ILLNESS	TREATMENT	REMARKS
8–12 days after contact the child develops what appears to be a severe cold with dry cough and irritated, red eyes as well as an increasingly high fever. Diarrhoea is common, and convulsions can occur. About 2 days before the rash appears it is possible to diagnose measles by looking for 'Koplik's spots': whitish-blue spots with an inflamed area around them inside the mouth. A day or two later a red, blotchy rash appears, starting behind the ears and on the back of the neck, spreading to the face and then the body, arms and legs. Temperature falls and rash fades. There may be some peeling of the skin leaving a slight brownish stain where the rash was. Cough may persist.	**MEASLES (Rubeola)**	**See a doctor!** Does not respond to antibiotics as it is caused by a virus. Except for paracetamol to reduce fever there is little that eases symptoms. If the light hurts the eyes, darken the room and wipe any crusts away with cotton wool dipped in cooled, boiled water using a fresh piece for each eye; cleaning outwards from the inner corner. Vitamin A supplements should be given to malnourished children. It is also found in milk, eggs, butter, fish and oils. Also broccoli, sweet potatoes, carrots spinach and pumpkin.	Measles lowers resistance to disease and otitis media (middle ear infection), croup, and broncho-pneumonia are common complications. It should always be treated seriously particularly in malnourished children. In very rare cases a child may develop encephalitis that can result in brain damage. Subacute sclerosing panencephalitis (SSPE) is a rare complication that may appear many years after measles, with a slow deterioration in mental ability and loss of control of movement. Weight loss after measles is severe even in well fed children. Babies are immunised against measles at 9 months, or at 6 months in epidemics. Even if a child has the shot at 9 months she can have the MMR vaccine at 15 months which also contains a measles component (*see p.472*).
Fever. Child is drowsy and highly irritable and may be confused, with headache, swollen fontanelle (soft spot on the head), vomiting and possibly, a stiff neck.Seizures (fits) are possible. May lapse into a coma. Meningococcal meningitis may be	**MENINGITIS (Acute bacterial infection, commonly due to Haemophilus influenzae, Pneumococcus pneumonia or Neisseria meningitides.**	**This is an emergency! Get the child to a hospital for treatment immediately, where tests will be performed. This is an infection of the membranes covering the brain and spinal cord.** Antibiotic treatment will be started immediately as it is vital to the outcome. See viral and tuberculous meningitis below.	This serious infection can be prevented by **Hib** vaccination, and by Prevenar (conjugated pneumococcal) vaccines now on the State schedule, but it does not protect against the meningococcal strain. Can originate from TB infection. Deafness, neurological damage,and ga\ngrene are some of the possible serious effects. Infectious for two days from start of treatment.

SYMPTOMS	ILLNESS	TREATMENT	REMARKS
associated with a rash. In young babies and small children there may **not** be stiffness in the neck.			
Fever, vomiting, drowsiness, irritability. Reluctance to feed. Possible neck stiffness.	**MENINGITIS (Viral)**	**All symptoms suggestive of meningitis should be treated urgently.** A lumbar puncture (spinal tap) may be done in order to make a diagnosis. This often relieves the pressure and headache. Should be a big improvement in the patient within a few days. Not likely to be given antibiotics if the origin is viral, unless there is uncertainty regarding the cause.	Viral meningitis is less serious, but until bacterial or TB meningitis is excluded by a blood test, the patient should be treated with great haste and caution including antibiotics.
The onset of symptoms may be rapid (in infants or young children) or gradual. Three phase symptoms: Fever, headache, irritability and drowsiness are followed by neck stiffness, vomiting and convulsions (fits). In the final stage, paralysis, abnormal body posture and coma may precede death.	**MENINGITIS (Tuberculous)**	**It is vital that treatment is started as soon as possible. Get the child to a hospital so that treatment can be started immediately.**	Any child who has come into contact with someone who has active TB is in danger. HIV positive children are at great risk.
Can take 14-21 days after exposure for symptoms to develop. Tenderness or swelling at the angle of the jaw with chills and loss of appetite, followed by a raised temperature. The other side of the face may swell as the first subsides about 5-7 days after onset.	**MUMPS**	Infection does not respond to antibiotics. Treat pain and fever with paracetamol. Chewing may be difficult. Give plenty of fluids and soft food as desired. Acidic foods and drinks may be painful to swallow. Use a straw for liquids.	Spread by saliva droplets. Infectious 1-2 days before and until swelling subsides in about 9 days. Viral meningitis (*see above*) is not an uncommon complication during the acute phase. Mumps in men can be complicated by pain and swelling in the testicles which can result in sterility. It is advisable to have children immunised against mumps. (*See MMR p. 472*).

SYMPTOMS	ILLNESS	TREATMENT	REMARKS
There may be pain in the abdomen if the pancreas is involved. Some children have no symptoms other than swelling of the jaw line.			
Temperature suddenly rises to 39°C or higher, and lasts for 3-5 days, although the child does not seem to be particularly ill. Fever drops suddenly to normal or below and a few hours later a rash of small pink spots appears on the face, body and neck and may spread to the thighs. Rash disappears in a few hours or a day or two and the child is extremely irritable for a few days after the rash disappears.	ROSEOLA INFANTUM	Bring down the temperature with appropriate dose of children's paracetamol. Sponge if necessary with tepid water and keep up fluid intake.	Usually affects babies between 6 months and 2 years. May seem to be a cold at first. Mild disease without complications. But febrile convulsions are possible due to high temperature. (See p. 342). Caused by herpes virus type 6. Contagious until spots disappear.
It is most common between the ages of five and fifteen, and starts with an untreated strep throat infection. Usual first signs are fever and painful joints. Some children may have jerky movements (chorea) and others may have a faint rash. Possible involvement of the heart is the most serious part of this illness.	RHEUMATIC FEVER	**This is a serious illness with potential life long heart problems.** The child may be hospitalised and restricted to bed. Antibiotics and other drugs will be used to treat the joint pain and throat infection. Close observation for possible complications is important; and referral to a specialised hospital may be needed.	This is the most common cause of acquired heart disease, especially among disadvantaged children. Most often following undiagnosed streptococcal throat infections. Sore throats should not be neglected (see Scarlet fever overleaf). Long term preventative treatment with antibiotics is necessary, and especially before the child has dental work done.

SYMPTOMS	ILLNESS	TREATMENT	REMARKS
Develops 1-7 days after exposure. Sore throat and vomiting. Raised temperature 38-40°C. Painful glands in the neck, while the face is flushed and there is a white area around the mouth. Rash appears on face within 24 hours as a mass of small, slightly raised spots against a bright red background then spreads down the back and chest to groin, arms and legs. The throat is bright red and there may be white patches on the tonsils. Tongue has strawberry texture. The child may have stomachache and headache. The skin may peel after the rash disappears. In rare instances an entire skin cast of the hand or foot may peel off. Illness occurs in epidemics, and is less severe these days, than before.	SCARLET FEVER	**Contact doctor immediately.** Caused by group A **beta** haemolytic streptococcus. Early treatment, usually with penicillin is important or complications could be severe. Rest in bed until fever subsides, gargle with mouth wash if the child is old enough. Treat fever with paracetamol. Give light diet including plenty of fluids.	Wash all utensils carefully as illnesses are spread by direct contact with droplets from the throat. Any severe sore throat with nausea should be seen by a doctor so that penicillin or other treatment can be given as soon as possible once strep throat has been diagnosed. A throat swab or germ culture may be required for accurate diagnosis. Complications of untreated scarlet fever and strep throat are: ear infection; swollen glands; pneumonia; kidney disease and rheumatic fever. Contagious until rash disappears, and peeling starts.
Mild illness starting with low grade fever and mild cold symptoms. The illness has a long incubation period of up to three weeks, before the characteristic rash appears on the cheeks, giving them a 'slapped' appearance. Rash spreads rapidly over the body in a 'lacy' pattern. Children do not generally feel ill.	**'SLAPPED CHEEK'** Ery-hema Infectiosum **Also known as "fifth disease' because of its place amongst the common childhood rashes**	No treatment is usually required, but the rash must be correctly identified to rule out more serious illnesses. Immuno-compromised children need special care and treatment.	This is a viral illness. Because the child is infectious long before the rash appears, it is of little use to isolate them. But keep them away from pregnant women as it can have a serious affect on the feotus, and on HIV positive babies and other immuno-compromised children in whom the virus can cause severe anaemia.

SYMPTOMS	ILLNESS	TREATMENT	REMARKS
Symptoms can be mild or severe and appear 5-7 days after being bitten. These include fever, headache, swollen glands and possible rash. Flu-like symptoms of chills, fever and muscular pain can confuse the diagnosis. After a careful examination a painful red bite mark with a black centre may be found where the tick has attached itself. Rash can be confused with measles and other infectious diseases.	**TICK BITE FEVER**	Treatment with tetracycline antibiotics is likely to be prescribed. There are other antibiotics that are suitable for use in pregnant women and very young children.	Wear long sleeves and closed shoes when in areas where it is common like game reserves, peri-urban areas or farms throughout the country. Transmitted by ticks that live on cattle and game. Insect repellents from pharmacy applied to skin and clothes may help. Check carefully for ticks on body and hair after walking outdoors. Note: Ticks may be very small. Even if symptoms are mild a doctor must be seen in order to prevent serious complications. Give travel history to your doctor.
This occurs where eye hygiene is a problem and where access to health care is difficult. It is caused by **Chlamydia** bacteria which infect the roots of eyelashes, causing inflammation of the conjunctiva (the lining of the eyelids and eyeball) with redness of the eyes and a discharge. When healing occurs the eyelashes turn inwards which results in corneal ulcers, which in turn lead to blindness.	**TRACHOMA**	A single dose of azithromycin is recommended by the World Health Organization.	Trachoma is the single most common cause of blindness in Africa. It is passed on by flies that sit on the infected eyes and by poor personal hygiene.

SYMPTOMS	ILLNESS	TREATMENT	REMARKS
The child has a cough lasting more than two weeks, weight loss and a history of contact with an adult with TB. Symptoms are not obvious at first, as they may be mild. Loss of energy and appetite, weight loss, fever, painless enlarged glands in the neck. Cough, night sweats may follow.	**TUBERCULOSIS (TB)**	**Specialist care is needed.** Drugs are available but must be taken regularly for up to 6 months. A small number of TB germs may be resistant to treatment. A year or later symptoms may reappear. BCG immunisation may not provide full protection.	Meningitis and other serious complications are possible. TB is common in HIV positive children. All adults and children in contact with the patient should be tested. Common cause of infection is through infected adults. Spread by coughing. TB germs can live for months in dried sputum from coughing not exposed to sunlight. Skin tests to detect infection take up to six weeks to become positive from the time the child is infected. TB of the bowel can be spread through unpasteurised cow's or goat's milk.
May have fairly non-specific symptoms including increased frequency of needing to pass urine; and burning when passing urine. Blood in the urine will make it a dark colour. If infection moves up the urinary tract to the kidneys there may be a fever above 38°C, abdominal pain, and vomiting.	**URINARY TRACT INFECTION (UTI)**	**Consult a doctor. Urgent management** includes urine tests to isolate the exact organism causing the infection, and antibiotics. Ultrasound examination will identify abnormalities in the urinary tract. Girls aged 3-7 often have recurrent infections and may need long term preventative treatment. Note: UTI's occur at all ages and even in very young babies	Urinary tract infections are common, particularly in girls, but can easily be missed. They can be more serious in boys. There is also a possibility of abnormality or obstruction of the urinary tract. Infection can have serious consequences if untreated. See that children do not 'forget' to go to the toilet. Deworm, and encourage fluid intake. Avoid bubble baths and teach wiping from the front to the back after using the toilet.

SYMPTOMS	ILLNESS	TREATMENT	REMARKS
First signs are like a cold. There is no temperature and a mild cough and irritated eyes. Seven to 14 days later the cough begins to come in violent spasms ending with a loud whooping sound on breathing in. Young babies cough in long bursts without the characteristic 'whoop' and may become blue due to lack of oxygen. Vomiting is common because of the force of the coughing. A raised temperature and rapid breathing could mean pneumonia has developed.	**WHOOPING COUGH (Pertussis)**	**Contact doctor immediately.** Older children who can sit up should do so during coughing spasms. Babies should be lifted out of the cot and held head downwards over your knees to prevent blocking of the air passages with secretions. Frequent small feeds should be given to prevent under nourishment. Fluids are needed to make up for loss through vomiting. If complications set in, hospitalisation may be needed. Collapse of a portion of the lung is common and convulsions may occur. Antibiotics may be prescribed to prevent complications.	Whooping cough is a serious disease, particularly in young children who may become exhausted by the coughing and lose weight because they cannot keep food down. Complications may cause lung and brain damage. Immunisation prevents severe attack. A mild attack is possible even though the child has been immunised. Patient is infectious 4-6 weeks from onset of cough. If on antibiotics, infectious for the first five days after start of treatment. **Whooping cough can be prevented by vaccination (see p. 462).**

RASHES AND COMMON SKIN CONDITIONS

All recommendations are subject to the approval of, and implementation by your doctor.

FEATURES	CONDITION	TREATMENT	INCIDENCE	TRANSMITTED	REMARKS
A **boil** is a small round area of skin that is shiny and swollen and is extremely painful when touched. The spot comes to a head and pain is relieved when it bursts or is drained by a doctor. **Styes** are similar infected areas on the eyelid, usually at the root of the eyelash.	**BOILS AND STYES**	Both **styes** and **boils** are caused by a staphylococcal infection. **Boils:** Apply moist heat to help bring it to a head. If the boil has not opened and drained, or has red lines running from it after 2 days, or the child has a temperature, see a doctor. Do not cover the boil with a sticking plaster, or squeeze it as it can spread the infection. If pus is draining, keep the area very clean by swabbing with a clean piece of cotton wool dipped in antiseptic solution and dress with antibiotic cream. Keep the dressing in place with small pieces of plaster far from the site of the infection. **Styes** can be brought to a head by applying heat. Dip a spoon into hot water (**spoon must not be hotter than is comfortable on your inner wrist**) and hold to the eye. When the stye has come to a head, remove the eyelash with a sterile tweezer which will usually drain the infection. See a doctor.	Common in carriers of staph or strep germs.	A small wound or splinter may be the entry point for germs. A hair follicle may also become infected.	A child who often gets styes or boils should be seen by a doctor for a thorough check-up. A doctor may prescribe an oral antibiotic; or ointment for use on the stye or boil. An ointment that fights staph bacteria may help eliminate the source if it is in the child's nose. All towels and face cloths used should be boiled or washed in a very hot cycle of the washing machine, as they may harbour germs. Keep fingernails short and hands should be washed frequently with soap.

FEATURES	CONDITION	TREATMENT	INCIDENCE	TRANSMITTED	REMARKS
Thick, waxy crusts on the scalp that do not come off with washing. May appear at any time in the first few months of life or later. May spread to the eyebrows, trunk and upper arms. Occurs most commonly between 1-3 months.	**CRADLE CAP Or seborrhoeic dermatitis**	Treat mild cases with a 2% solution of bicarbonate of soda rubbed into the scalp, followed by washing with a mild shampoo. If crusts have become thick, get your pharmacist to make up a 2% salicylic acid, 2% liquor **picis carb** in petroleum jelly. Rub into the scalp and leave overnight, protecting the bedding. If you apply in the morning, leave until evening. Lift off crusts with a clean, fine toothed comb. Shampoo hair. Repeat until all crusts have been removed. If the eyebrows are affected your pharmacist or doctor may prescribe a cream. Wash the area with baby shampoo.	Common.	Not contagious.	Occasionally seborrhoeic dermatitis spreads downwards to the nappy area. The skin feels rough and dry over raised 'pimples'. This may be complicated by thrush (Candida infection). Use a good zinc and castor oil cream (ask your chemist to make it up if necessary). If there is a thrush infection as well (the skin looks scalded), ask for a other cream recommended by your doctor or pharmacist. *See Oral thrush p. 367.*
Patches of red skin which may show scaling, thickening and weeping, but very itchy. Difficult to distinguish from atopic (allergic) eczema.	**CONTACT DERMATITIS**	Caused by contact with a chemical or other irritant. Elimination of the cause is the best treatment. Doctor may prescribe a mild corticosteroid cream. Some lotions and creams may aggravate the condition if they contain irritants. (*See allergies p. 417*).	Common	Not contagious.	Some common causes are soaps containing enzymes, detergents, wool, skin and hair care products, dyes, plants, nickel, latex and animals. Antiseptic soaps may cause photosensitive reaction if the child goes into the sun afterwards. Alkalis such as those found in nappy solution or soaps may also cause a reaction. Babies' clothes should not be washed in detergents or soaps containing enzymes.
Red spots with a pale centre that appear soon after birth.	**ERYTHEMA TOXICUM**	Not required.	Common.	Not contagious.	Appears within hours after birth. It disappears without treatment and is of no significance.

FEATURES	CONDITION	TREATMENT	INCIDENCE	TRANSMITTED	REMARKS
Itchy, scaly skin not associated with illness or a temperature. In children under six months it is mainly on the cheeks. After this in the creases of the elbow, back of the knees.	ATOPIC (allergic) ECZEMA	Corticosteroids in low doses (1%) are usually recommended. Newer non-steroidal products are also effective. Wet wraps may also be recommended. (See Allergies p. 424).	Common skin condition in children.	Not contagious.	Very itchy skin that can become infected with bacteria, virus (herpes), or fungus from scratching. Medical advice and treatment is essential. (See p. 424). Use very mild unperfumed skin products recommended by your doctor.
Red spots on the face, neck and folds of the skin possibly spreading down the back which look like acne pimples. The child has no temperature.	HEAT RASH	Irritation caused by blocked sweat glands. Remove excess clothing and add 1–2 tablespoonfuls of bicarbonate of soda to the bath water or dab with calamine lotion.	Common	Not contagious.	Do not overdress your baby. Feel the stomach to see if she is cold, not the hands as they are normally colder than the body.
Blisters that form on the edge of the lip, or in or around the nose. They heal in 7–10 days. Often confused with impetigo. Can be dangerous if it spreads to the eyes.	HERPES SIMPLEX (Also known as 'COLD SORES' or 'FEVER BLISTERS')	Caused by the common virus, herpes simplex. Does not respond to antibiotics. Acyclovir works well especially if used at the first sign. Camphor stick, gentian violet or lip salve may be soothing but they do not heal.	Common	Spread easily through contact. Do not let anyone with a 'cold sore' kiss your baby.	Some people appear to have a natural immunity to the virus and never develop 'cold sores'. Those who are susceptible develop them when they are run down or have a cold. Prolonged exposure to the sun or cold may also cause an outbreak.
Starts with a slight blistering followed by a discharge which forms a golden yellow crust. Seen mainly around the nostrils, but may spread to the rest of the face.	IMPETIGO (SEPTIC SORES or VELD SORES')	Oral antibiotics should be prescribed. If it recurs, child may need anti-staph cream in the nose.	Common	Easily spread through direct contact.	Usually caused by staphylococcal or streptococcal germs that enter through a small break in the skin. Spreads easily and the infected child should use a separate face cloth and towel which should be machine washed in very hot water, or boiled. Should be changed daily. May be associated with head lice if crusts appear on the ears.

FEATURES	CONDITION	TREATMENT	INCIDENCE	TRANSMITTED	REMARKS
Damp red areas in the creases of the skin. Caused by sweat and not being dried properly, or applying powder to wet skin.	INTERTRIGO	Wash well in creases with very mild product. Dry very well.	Fairly common.	Not contagious unless infected.	May become infected with bacteria or Candida (thrush). See a doctor if there is no improvement after elimination of the cause, i.e. moisture in the skin creases.
Pinhead sized white spots over the nose and cheeks of the newborn.	MILIA	No treatment needed. They will disappear spontaneously.	Very common.	Not contagious.	Caused by blocked oil glands similar to 'whiteheads'.
Flesh coloured dome shaped 'pimples' covering large parts of the body. Child does not feel ill.	MOLLUSCUM CONTAIGIOSUM	Unless infected healing is uncomplicated without treatment. Spots on the face may be removed by the doctor with liquid nitrogen cryotherapy,if unsightly. Or the doctor my recommend using plaster overnight and stripping off rapidly next day.	Common	Virus is spread by contact especially in children until they develop immunity.	To prevent or treat infection of the spots, the doctor may prescribe an antiseptic or antifungal cream. Disease can be especially problematic in HIV infected children.
Bright red rash in the nappy area. A boy may have an ulcer on the tip of the penis and when it heals it could form scar tissue making it difficult to retract the foreskin. Rash does not extend into creases and it may be scaly and swollen. If not treated angry ulcers may appear possibly complicated by bacterial infection. In **ammonia dermatitis** the skin looks shiny and wrinkled.	**NAPPY RASH and AMMONIA DERMATITIS (See also *Oral Thrush* p. 367)**	Clean nappy area well after every stool. Pat dry. Expose bottom directly to the air and sunlight as much as possible. Use a one-way nappy liner with cloth nappies and change nappy often. Use a zinc and castor oil cream to heal or other recommended cream. Best rash prevention is frequent changing of nappies and exposure to the air. Good disposable nappies do not keep urine against the skin helping to prevent nappy rash. Do not use cream when healed as this blocks the nappy lining pores and prevents the urine from going through into the nappy.	Common	Not contagious.	Nappy rash is caused by urine moisture against the baby's skin and the effects of soiling. Wearing a wet nappy for a long time damages the skin, especially if it is held in by plastic pants. One way nappy liner can help keep the skin dry. Wipe the skin with an unscented wet wipe or cloth at nappy changes. Wash nappies in very hot water to kill bacteria. In cases of **ammonia dermatitis** urea in the nappies is changed into ammonia by bacteria. Half a cupful of white vinegar added to the rinsing water when washing nappies will help neutralise the ammonia.

FEATURES	CONDITION	TREATMENT	INCIDENCE	TRANSMITTED	REMARKS
Scaly white patches on the face of young children.	PITYRIASIS SICCA ALBA	Doctor may prescribe a mild cortisone ointment.	Common	Not contagious.	Easily confused with a fungal infection. Doctor will test, and if it is fungal will prescribe suitable cream.
Raised oval areas with a scaly edge appear on the trunk (upper body) after a single patch appears. May be itchy.	PITYRIASIS ROSEA	Doctor may prescribe a mild corisone cream if it itches, but it disappears on its own accord even if not treated.	Fairly common.	Not contagious.	Exposure to sunlight may be helpful. Lasts about 6 weeks.
Circular patches of raised red scaly skin with a whitish centre. On the scalp it causes hair loss.	RINGWORM	Doctor will do a test for fungal infection. Special ointment (Whitfield's) will be prescribed and applied twice a day for up to a month. If scalp is affected an oral fungicide (Griseofulvin) will be necessary.	Common	Highly contagious	The fungus may be transmitted by animals or person to person. Should have no lasting ill effects. Hair grows again.
White patches on the top and sides of the tongue that look like milk. Inside of the cheeks and lips may also be affected. The child may be reluctant to take feeds and the patches cannot be scraped off as is the case with milk residue. There may be signs of intestinal thrush. (*See below.*)	ORAL THRUSH (Candida or Monilia)	Oral medication prescribed by a doctor is effective but reinfection is likely if the source is not eliminated. HIV positive children are at high risk for repeat infection.	Common	Easily spread by contaminated teats, sterilising fluid or dummies or the mother's nipples. Also common after a course of antibiotics.	Caused by a fungus Candida albicans, that is responsible for intestinal and vaginal thrush. The fungus spores are hard to kill and if possible replace dummies and discard any sterilising solution or gripe water that may be contaminated. Boil all equipment for 20 minutes or use a steam steriliser. Breastfeeding mothers should treat their nipples or it will be carried back and forth between mother and child.
Similar to nappy rash but with spots forming a very red sharply demarcated area, making it look as though the	INTESTINAL THRUSH	Treat as for nappy rash but check the baby's mouth for white patches. If the mother has vaginal thrush or the baby	Common	Easily spread by contaminated tests, sterilising fluid or dummies or the mother's nipples.	Vaginal thrush is common during pregnancy because of the altered chemical balance of the vaginal

FEATURES	CONDITION	TREATMENT	INCIDENCE	TRANSMITTED	REMARKS
skin has been scalded. White patches of fungal infection may extend into the skin folds which are also red. 'Satellite' red spots of infection may spread around the main infection.		signs of thrush in the mouth the doctor will prescribe an anti-fungal. (See Thrush above.)	Common	Also commonly after being on antibiotics.	secretions. Signs are a thick, cheesy white discharge that causes itching. It also occurs in diabetics, and after prolonged treatment with antibiotics. The woman's partner should also be treated even though he may have few symptoms. HIV positive babies are often severely affected. Probiotics may be beneficial but not likely to cure thrush.
Raised red wheals on the skin. May be itchy.	URTICARIA (Hives) (See p. 355.)	The substance causing the reaction should be identified and eliminated if possible. Treatment depends on the cause of the allergic reaction.	Fairly common in the allergy prone.	Not contagious.	Common causes are foodstuffs like nuts, chocolate, eggs, fish etc. medications such as penicillin, vitamins etc can cause the reaction. Antihistamines can control flare-ups. Where anaphylactic shock has occurred the child may have to carry a special adrenaline kit, and wear a Medicalert bracelet.
Small areas of thickened skin caused by a virus.	WARTS (Verruca)	No treatment is necessary unless they are very unsightly or get in the way. They disappear when immunity develops. Your doctor may use a special mixture to apply on the warts and then cover them with a waterproof sticking plaster for a week. When it is removed the wart may come off with it. May be removed by freezing with liquid nitrogen. Laser therapy removal is better and less painful.	Common	May be mildly contagious if person has not developed immunity.	Folk remedies are legion in the treatment of warts and may sometimes coincide with their spontaneous disappearance.

PARASITIC INFECTIONS

All recommendations are subject to the approval of, and implementation by your doctor.

Parasitic infection rates are often higher in children and some (e.g. malaria) may be more dangerous for them because of their less developed immunity. Intestinal worms can rob the child's body of nutrients causing anaemia, stunted growth and intellectual impairment.

CONDITION	SYMPTOMS	TREATMENT	INCIDENCE	TRANSMITTED
AMOEBIC INFECTIONS	Stomachache and diarrhoea, weakness, blood and mucus in the stools. Loss of appetite and weight. There may be mild fever. Liver involvement can cause pain on the upper right side of the abdomen.	A doctor must be seen and tests done before treatment.	Common in subtropical areas such as KwaZulu-Natal, in South Africa, throughout Africa, parts of South America, the Caribbean, the Middle East and Asia.	Caused by faeces contaminated water supply and eating raw vegetables grown in infected soil.	Strict hygiene should be maintained and water supplies protected from human waste. Vegetables should be well washed before use.
BILHARZIA (Schistosomiasis)	Blood in the urine or diarrhoea and blood with mucus in the stools, depending on the particular type of infection. In endemic areas many infections are mild or not obvious.	A doctor must be seen in order to do tests and look for possible eggs in the stool or urine before treatment, which is effective.	Common in affected tropical and subtropical areas when sanitation is poor and the snail hosts are present, including parts of South Africa.	Eggs from an infected person pass into water with urine. They hatch and enter certain water snails. From there the infective stages enter humans through the skin and mature to adult flukes that lay eggs in the blood vessels of the bladder and gut. Depending on the type, the spiny eggs damage the intestine, bladder and kidneys or the liver, and sometimes other sites like the spinal cord or lungs.	Do not swim or paddle in rivers, ponds or dams in the areas from the Limpopo River southwards to Gauteng in South Africa, and areas towards Swaziland and the coastal areas of KwaZulu-Natal, as well as the coastal areas of the Eastern Cape as well as areas of the Indian sub-continent, parts of Central and South America and parts of Africa. Swim in the ocean or chlorinated swimming pools. More than 90% of the 200 million people affected live in sub-Saharan Africa and pass infected urine or faeces daily. Can cause pain, anaemia, inflammation and growth stunting in children.

SYMPTOMS	CONDITION	TREATMENT	INCIDENCE	TRANSMITTED	TRANSMITTED
Symptoms vary. Children exposed for the first time often have sudden explosive watery stools, with stomach pains and bloating. Loss of appetite and nausea are likely. Recurrent diarrhoea with weight loss and weakness may follow. Stools may be pale, bulky and smell offensive.	**GIARDIASIS (Giardia lamblia)**	See a doctor who will prescribe medication.	Common in crowded living conditions.	Direct contact, or through contaminated water.	Children in crèches are often affected. Diagnosis may be difficult as excretion is intermittent and several stool tests may be required. Some children are carriers but have few symptoms.
Very itchy scalp. Tiny crusty bite marks can sometimes been seen on the scalp. Small hard white eggs (nits) are attached to the hair and cannot be easily removed.	**HEAD LICE (Pediculosis)**	Doctor, pharmacist or clinic will prescribe treatment which involves applying a special shampoo or spray to the hair and scalp. This may have to be repeated. Comb hair with a fine-toothed comb afterwards to remove nits.	Very common in children in daycare and school.	Head lice are extremely common in all population sectors and epidemics often occur in schools. The length of hair makes no difference. Infection is spread by close contact e.g. when playing. Good personal hygiene prevents body lice.	Very contagious. Passed on by direct contact. Treatment of the whole family is wise. **Do not** use preparations from unregulated sources as they may contain dangerous substances.
Red, itchy areas particularly on the feet where the larvae make their entry. They travel to the lungs during which time there may be coughing and fever. Then they move on to the top of the windpipe and are swallowed. Once in the intestine, the larvae become adult worms about 1cm long with a reddish colour. They fix onto the wall of the bowel and feed by sucking blood. Anaemia, constipation listlessness, stomachache are signs of hookworm infestation in children.	**HOOKWORM**	Doctor will prescribe medication which is effective, possibly followed by a repeat dose. Multivitamin and iron supplements to correct iron-deficiency anaemia and a high protein diet will help restore health.	Very common in tropical areas. Up to 600 million people in Asia and Africa are infected.	Infection is transmitted by touching sand or walking barefoot in soil contaminated by human faeces. Tropical areas with a high rainfall are good breeding grounds for hookworm larvae.	Children should not walk barefoot or play in sand that may be contaminated. Hookworm infestation makes children pale and anaemic and they can have difficulty learning in school as a result of the anaemia. (See p. 430). Also causes problems in pregnancy due to blood loss in the mother and babies may be born with low birth weight.

SYMPTOMS	CONDITION	TREATMENT	INCIDENCE	TRANSMITTED	TRANSMITTED
High fever, chills, headache, severe sweating and exhaustion. **NEEDS VERY URGENT MEDICAL ATTENTION! (See p. 355 under Infections.)**	**MALARIA** Caused by a protozoan parasite which is carried by the **anopheles** mosquito in some hot climates.				
Itching around the anus, restless sleep and, occasionally bedwetting, especially in girls as the worms can irritate the urogenital area.	**PINWORM OR THREADWORM**	Medicine to eliminate the infection should be given to all members of the family, or at least to all children. Children should wear night-clothes that make it difficult to scratch around the anus as this is how eggs can get under the nails and continue the cycle of infection. A morning shower will help rid the body of eggs which have been laid around the anus at night. Repeat medication as advised.	Very common. Up to 97% of children are affected in some areas.	Most common of the worm infestations in man. Occurs in all climates. Transmitted by eggs which are swallowed or inhaled.	Look for tiny white threadlike worms around the anus at night as this is when they come out of the lower intestine to lay their eggs. Or take a piece of sticky tape and blot the area with it at night and have your doctor analyse it for eggs. Pinworm is very common in children. Since the eggs may even be dust-borne and breathed in, very few children escape the infection. Wash hands frequently. Discourage children from putting their fingers in their mouth especially when they are old enough to play outside in the sand. Keep nails short.
Boil-like raised red sore with a yellow head. When the sores are opened a maggot can be seen.	**PUTSI FLY, TUMBU FLY OR MANGO FLY**	Apply petroleum jelly or oil to the sore and the maggot will come out easily. Once the maggot is removed the area heals rapidly, but you can apply an antiseptic cream to ensure that it does not become infected.	Common in subtropical areas.	Eggs are laid by the fly in damp washing, particularly poorly washed nappies as they are attracted by the odour. Once hatched, the maggots burrow under the skin.	Always sterilise nappies with a special nappy sterilising solution, wash in very hot cycle of washing machine if possible, and iron with a hot iron in subtropical areas.

SYMPTOMS	CONDITION	TREATMENT	INCIDENCE	TRANSMITTED	TRANSMITTED
During the larval stage in the lungs, there may be symptoms of wheezing, broncho-pneumonia, coughing and generalised illness. Once the larvae have passed through the lungs they enter the intestine and develop into large pinkish round worms around 10-15cm or even up to 30cm. From there they may travel to other parts of the body and cause a blockage or stomachache. They may be passed in the stools or come up through the mouth or nose. There may be no symptoms until a worm is passed.	ROUNDWORM (Ascariasis)	See a doctor who will prescribe medication to eliminate the worms. It is effective, and should be repeated if necessary. The whole family should be treated. A multivitamin supplement containing iron is useful in restoring depleted nutrients.	Up to 800 million people are affected in Africa, Asia and the Americas.	Spread by contamination of soil and food with human faeces containing eggs, therefore more common in situations of poor personal and environmental hygiene. Do not let a dog lick a child's face, as dogs also harbour a different type of round worm (Toxocara canis) that can cause severe illness in humans.	No one should imagine that their children are immune because of their social status and careful hygiene. Playing on the grass in the park may be all that is needed to pick up eggs. Frequent stomachaches and asthma-like symptoms should alert parents to the possibility of worms, although there are often no symptoms until a worm is passed. **Wash raw vegetables. Wash hands as roundworm eggs are contained in human faeces.** Malnutrition with stunting, and intestinal obstruction are common in severely affected children. Growth and intellectual development can be stunted.
Very itchy red 'pimples' with a yellow head, caused by a small mite that burrows into the skin and lays her eggs. Prefers moist areas of the body especially the groin, hands and feet. Spots may become infected from scratching.	SCABIES	Follow doctor or clinic's instructions. Usually involves washing with a special soap and then a 6% to 12% benzyl benzoate solution according to age, applied and left to dry. After age 2, use 25%. Apply solution again 5 minutes later and leave for 24 hours.	Common in crowded living conditions.	It is highly contagious and easily spreads among children living in over-crowded conditions. If scabies becomes infected, impetigo may result. (See p. 365).	Spread through close direct contact, or sometimes via infected clothing or bedding. Use of a special soap may be recommended to prevent reinfection. The whole family should be treated. Boil all bed linen or wash in very hot cycle of washing machine and press with hot iron.

SYMPTOMS	CONDITION	TREATMENT	INCIDENCE	TRANSMITTED	TRANSMITTED
Diarrhoea, weight loss, irritability, stomachache, nausea and hunger may be symptoms. Segments of the large, flattened white worm may appear in the stool. A different stage of the pork tapeworm can enter the brain causing headache, fits and impaired cognition if infection is severe. This is called cysticercosis.	TAPEWORM (Beef and pork tapeworm, dwarf tapeworm).	Doctor will prescribe medication that is effective, but it may need to be repeated.	More than 40 million people worldwide are thought to be infected.	Avoid eating under-cooked or raw beef or pork. Cysticercosis is not transmitted by meat, but via human faeces. Ensure hands are washed after going to the toilet. The dwarf tapeworm is also spread directly from human faeces.	Beef and pork should be thoroughly cooked as this kills the cysts. Wash hands! Cysts known as 'measles' in meat can be seen. Buy meat from sources where it is inspected before being sold. Freezing at minus 10°C for 10 days kills cysts.
Extremely wide ranging and variable symptoms, some mild others very serious. Swollen glands, sore throat may be the only symptoms in healthy individuals. If acquired early in pregnancy the baby may have severe infection. If acquired in the last three months there may be few clinical signs, although they can manifest later. In HIV- positive children the infection can be severe involving the brain, heart, lungs, skin, eyes and many other organs.	TOXOPLASMOSIS	Special tests can be done before or during pregnancy. If positive treatment will be prescribed. If infection is suspected in a newborn extensive tests will be done and treatment prescribed. Treatment is available at all stages including for eye problems which are common.	Common in many parts of the world especially where raw meat is eaten. Screening is done in France and Germany where there is a high prevalence.	Cysts found in cat faeces or undercooked meat carry the disease. Less commonly transmitted by cockroaches and flies that sit on cat faeces.	Cats get it from eating infected small animals like mice. Feed cats prepared not raw food. Wear gloves when cleaning cat litter. Avoid undercooked meat and wash hands after touching raw meat. The eyesight of up to 50% of untreated babies infected by toxoplasmosis may be seriously affected.
Infected eyes that lead to blindness caused by flies. Not strictly a parasitic infection.	TRACHOMA				

SYMPTOMS	CONDITION	TREATMENT	INCIDENCE	TRANSMITTED	TRANSMITTED
Light infections usually have no symptoms. Blood-flecked stools and severe anaemia may occur if there are numerous worms. Diarrhoea, nausea and abdominal pain can also be present, due to worms that attach to the colon (large intestine) and damage its wall.	**WHIPWORM (Trichuriasis)**	Doctor will look for ova in the stools. Prescribed medication is effective. (Mebendazole or Albendazole.)	More than 600 million people are infected in Asia, Africa and the Americas. Common in KwaZulu-Natal and the Cape coastal areas of South Africa where humidity is high.	Found in soil infected with human faecal waste. The eggs can be swallowed if the child puts her fingers in her mouth after touching infected soil.	Frequent washing of hands and strict hygiene should be observed. Effective human waste disposal is essential in terms of prevention.

CONGENITAL ABNORMALITIES AND INHERITED DISORDERS

All recommendations are subject to the approval of, and implementation by your doctor.

DEFECTS OF THE HEAD, FACE AND SPINAL CORD

FEATURES	CONDITIONS	TREATMENT	INCIDENCE	TRANSMITTED	REMARKS
Normally shaped but large ears that stick out.	'BAT EARS'	Plastic surgery at around six years, when the ears have stopped growing can correct the appearance. Best done before the child start school.	Common hereditary condition, particularly in boys.	Usually an inherited tendency.	This is purely an aesthetic issue that can be corrected with a small operation if desired. Abnormally small or low set ears can be a sign of a genetic defect and should be seen to.
The passage between the eyes and the nose is closed on one or both sides. The eyes water constantly and may become infected. If the lachrymal sac (tear duct) becomes infected there is usually a swelling under the eye.	BLOCKED TEAR DUCT	Blocked tear ducts usually clear up without treatment but massage from the corner of the eye towards the nose is usually recommended. If there is no improvement at 6 months the doctor may insert a probe to open it. This is a simple procedure and the results are excellent.	Very common.	Developmental delay.	Infection as a result of the blockage may need to be treated with an antibiotic ointment. See a doctor. Wash any crusts away with cool boiled water. Wipe from the inner eye outwards to avoid spreading infection.
May be present at birth or develop later.	CATARACTS (Lens of the eye is opaque)	Urgent operation by a specialist to remove the lens of the eyes is likely.	Uncommon. May be inherited or through infection such as German measles before birth.	A lens implant may be done or special glasses prescribed.	Cataracts are usually associated with ageing but may be present at birth.
A split in the upper lip on one or both sides.	CLEFT LIP	Plastic surgery repair is usually undertaken when the child is thriving at about 3 months. The chances of restoring a normal appearance and functionality are excellent. Good advice regarding feeding is essential. The child can swallow normally but sucking may be slow. A bottle with a modified teat or breast milk expressed to the	Most common congenital defect of the face affecting around 1:700 births.	Due to improper fusion of the facial structure of the foetus in the womb. Exact cause is unknown but possible factors may be infections or the effects of medication in pregnancy. There is also an inherited tendency. Occasionally there may be other associated anomalies or syndromes.	Clefts are more common on the eft side, and can vary from a small cleft to a bilateral (double) large or small cleft. Genetic counselling is advisable to ascertain the chances although small, of other children being affected. Clefts can show up on pre-birth ultrasound scans but

CONDITIONS	FEATURES	TREATMENT	INCIDENCE	TRANSMITTED	REMARKS
		back of the child's mouth, or cup and spoon feeding may be advised. Avoid tube feeding as the child needs to learn to suck.			have a 10% false positive/ negative rate. Advice on correct feeding is essential.
CLEFT PALATE	Large or small split in the roof of the mouth that may be combined with a split in the upper lip.	Treatment by a team including a plastic surgeon, orthodontist, speech therapist, maxillo-facial surgeon, geneticist and possibly a social worker and psychologist is ideal. Soon after birth a plate may be inserted in the mouth to temporarily close the gap in the palate. A second operation may be required after the age of nine years to place bone in the gum in order to support the teeth. In the hands of a good team the aesthetic and functional outlook is excellent.	Isolated cleft palate occurs in 46% of all cleft types, and occurs equally amongst all ethnic groups. Cleft palate with cleft lip is most common in Oriental births at around 1:500, and least common in black Africans, at around 1:2000. Caucasians have an incidence of 1:1000 births.	Due to improper fusion of the facial structure in the womb. Exact cause unknown but there is an inherited tendency. Also older fathers. Other causes may be infections or the effects of medication in pregnancy, including acne treatment and anti-convulsant therapy. A lack of folic acid and vitamin B_6 in the diet may also be factors.	Feeding advice is essential and a plate may be inserted in order to facilitate sucking. Bottle feed with breast or formula milk from a special teat. Avoid tube feeding as the child needs to learn to suck. Genetic counselling is advisable so as to ascertain the chances of other children being affected. Occasionally associated with other anomalies or syndromes.
DEAFNESS OR PARTIAL DEAFNESS	Child does not respond to sounds. Does not turn her head towards her mother's voice. Complete or partial hearing loss. Possible lack of external ear or deformity of the inner ear. A deformed external ear may also be a sign of possible hearing problems.	Treatment depends on the cause. When the entire ear is missing there is usually gross deformity of the inner ear as well. Surgery can restore some forms of hearing loss, and a cochlear implant can help some children hear well. Low placed ears may be associated with kidney defects. Early detection of deafness or partial hearing loss improves the chances of successful treatment.	Frequency depends on the cause.	Complete or partial deafness may be the result of a maternal infection such as rubella (German measles) during the first 12 weeks of pregnancy. Other causes include brain injury at birth, exposure to certain drugs during gestation; or damage as a result of a disease such as encephalitis. Very low birth weight and prematurity can be a factor.	Not responding to sounds and late talking are signs that a child's hearing should be checked. Cochlear implants are an expensive implanted device that can restore hearing in certain cases. Deafness can occasionally be associated with other anomalies or genetic syndromes. (*See also otitis media p. 350*).

FEATURES	CONDITIONS	TREATMENT	INCIDENCE	TRANSMITTED	REMARKS
The head is abnormally enlarged at birth or it may become enlarged later, due to the accumulation of fluid either inside or outside the brain. Depending on the cause, other problems such as epilepsy, squint, blindness, paralysis of the limbs and intellectual deficit can accompany the condition. **Early treatment may reduce these problems.**	**HYDROCEPHALUS**	Treatment will depend mainly on the cause, as well as the condition of the child as a whole. Many have a hopeful future, while some have a poor prognosis. A shunt (silicone device) may be inserted to divert the flow of cerebrospinal fluid (CSF) from the spinal cord and brain. A newer treatment – endoscopic third ventriculostomy (ETV) – in which an opening is made to allow fluid to flow freely out of the brain, has not been a great success. Either can malfunction, and regular follow-up is required.	Depends on the cause. Between 0.32 and 2 per 1000 births.	Usually the result of a developmental defect, such as spina bifida (*see pg. 377*), or infection e.g. toxoplasmosis during gestation, birth injury or intraventricular bleed (bleeding into the brain especially after premature birth), tumours or other subsequent brain or head injury. May be inherited by males in a rare genetic condition.	Hydrocephalus means 'water head' and is the result of normal fluid called CSF accumulating in the head due to a blockage. The head enlarges because of the pressure caused by this CSF fluid. A careful watch will be kept on the size of the head so that active measures to relieve the pressure and restore the flow can be taken.
The jaws are not correctly aligned, and when the teeth come through, the top or bottom teeth protrude. ('buck teeth'.)	**MALOCCLUSION OF THE JAW AND TEETH**	Assessment by an orthodontist (dentist who specialises in correction of dental defects) should be made at the age of 9–10 years. Treatment usually consists of bands worn to pull the teeth into place at the start of adolescence.	Up to 6:10 births.	Inherited tendency, but can be influenced by habits.	Mainly inherited tendency. Bottle feeding and mouth breathing due to enlarged tonsils, and dummy sucking are minor possible contributory causes. Forceful thumb sucking after the age of five or six has negative effect.
'Spina bifida' simply means an opening in the back of the spine, which is very common and usually not a problem. Sometimes however, this occurs with abnormalities of the spinal cord: there are a number of variations,	**SPINA BIFIDA: MYELO-MENINGOCELE (open: more complicated due to spina cord being exposed at birth). OCCULTA (closed: varies from mild to moderate). MENINGOCELE (closed: very rare form where the spinal cord is not involved .**	Treatment depends on the type and severity of the condition. Surgery to repair open spina bifida may need to be done very soon after birth. Closed forms of spina bifida may need surgery but this is done later. The main issue here is the fact that the spinal cord is 'tethered' i.e. stuck down, which may lead to later injury.	Incidence varies in different parts of the world but averages 1:900 births for open spina bifida and 1:5000 for closed spina bifida.	May be genetic with a 10% recurrence rate. A lack of folic acid in the diet is an important causitive factor. Daily (0.4g) supplementation of folic acid a month before becoming pregnant and for the first 12 weeks of pregnancy cuts the incidence drastically. Some epilepsy medications can	Genetic counselling is advisable if there have been spina bifida defects in the family. The alpha- fetoprotein blood test during pregnancy can help detect the possibility of spina bifida in the unborn, and an ultrasound scan and amniocentesis can establish with greater certainty if this is the case.

FEATURES	CONDITIONS	TREATMENT	INCIDENCE	TRANSMITTED	REMARKS
some more serious than others. These are either 'open', where there is a sac at the bottom of the spine that contains part of the spinal cord, or 'closed', where the only outside sign is a lump, a hairy patch, or simply a small dimple. An MRI scan is needed to evaluate the spinal cord. Bladder and bowel problems and leg weakness may occur in either form, while hydrocephalus may occur with open spina bifida.		Urinary problems due to nerve damage can be a problem but new surgical techniques can greatly improve outcomes. Hydro-cephalus is associated with open spina bifida and CT and an MRI scans can give essential information.		hinder the absorption of folic acid, so inform your doctor if you take them and are considering becoming pregnant.	
Condition in which the eyes do not move together, that is one turns out or in. Many newborn babies squint but they should be able to focus properly within the first six weeks. Squinting after that needs a specialist's assessment. Occasionally squinting may only become apparent in the second year.	SQUINT (Strasbismus)	Treatment may involve covering the 'good' eye to strengthen the muscles of the weak eye. An operation to correct the squint may be needed. Glasses may also be prescribed.	Depends on the cause. Relatively common.	Depends on the cause, may be the result of a developmental fault, birth injury or other condition.	Epicanthic folds (the skin fold at the inner corner of the eye) can give the illusion of a squint, but an assessment must be made by an expert. Children do not outgrow true squints and the sooner treatment is begun the better, preferably before the age of a year, as improvement after age six is unlikely.
One or two teeth are present at birth.	TEETH AT BIRTH	If the teeth are loose they may be removed. If they are well rooted they may be left in place.	1:2000	Not known.	Of no particular significance although teeth can interfere with breastfeeding.
A piece of skin ties the tongue to the base of the mouth.	'TONGUE TIE'	No treatment is necessary except in a very few cases. Best left alone unless a doctor is convinced that surgery is indicated.	True 'tongue tie' is rare.	Not known.	Feeding and speech problems can occasionally be ascribed to 'tongue tie'. This is very rarely the cause, although it is possible.

DEFECTS OF THE LIMBS

All recommendations are subject to the approval of, and implementation by your doctor.

FEATURES	CONDITION	TREATMENT	INCIDENCE	TRANSMITTED	REMARKS
Child's legs appear to be 'bowed' (bend or curve outwards).	'BOW-LEGS', AND RICKETS	Children usually outgrow 'bow-legs' and 'knock-knees' in the first few years. But if due to rickets, it will not improve unless vitamin D, which helps calcium absorption needed for strong teeth and bones is supplemented. If only one leg is affected it may be due to other causes and need more complex treatment.	Depends on the cause. If due to rickets up to 10% in some countries. Used to be even more common before vitamin D was added to foods. May also be due to a genetic mutation.	Genetic, or more commonly due to a lack of vitamin D in the mother's diet, or lack of vitamin D in child's diet or lack of exposure to sunlight which makes vitamin D in the system which in turn helps the absorption of calcium.	Breast milk has low vitamin D content and supplementation is usually recommended. (See p. 147). Formula has added vitamin D, and many foods are supplemented, including milk, bread and margarine. Causes of a lack of vitamin D include: Concerns about skin cancer mean fewer babies are exposed to sunlight. Less vitamin D is absorbed by dark skins. Cultural practices of keeping the body totally covered. Vegan diets and the use of unfortified soya and rice milk. The use of maize meal without milk as a weaning food. (See p. 251).
When one or both feet are turned to an abnormal position and cannot easily be brought to a natural position. The most common position is inwards.	CLUB FOOT (Talipes)	Diagnosis at birth and early treatment bring the best results. Occasionally massage or strapping may be recommended. But more likely a plaster moulding splint will be used. If discovered late or if there is not a satisfactory response to splint treatment, surgery may be undertaken. Results are generally good.	1:700 births. Chances of having another child with a club foot when one is affected are 1:30. Twice as common in boys.	May be an inherited tendency. The position in which the baby lies for a prolonged period in the womb can also be a factor. Or if there is very little amniotic fluid. May also be associated with spina bifida. Less commonly, infection during a critical developmental stage may be a factor.	See a specialist early. If it is possible to position the affected part without much effort there may not be a need for splinting, however a child with club foot who 'toes in' markedly when she starts to walk will not 'grow out of it'. The earlier treatment is started, the more effective.

FEATURES	CONDITION	TREATMENT	INCIDENCE	TRANSMITTED	REMARKS
Fingers that are joined by webbed skin or at the bone.	**DEFECTS OF THE HANDS (Syndactyly)**	Surgical treatment is usually undertaken between 1 and 3 years. Results are usually good.	Second most common defect of the hands. Between 1:2000 births. Occurs twice as often in Caucasian as in black Africans.	Inherited tendency or part of a congenital syndrome. Can also occur by chance.	May be associated with various other defects if part of a genetic syndrome. Or due to infections or medication in pregnancy, or medical conditions in the mother.
Medical examination at birth may reveal dislocation of one or both legs at the hip joint. If missed at birth, symptoms may later include a limping walk and extra creases in the skin folds of the upper leg on the affected side. If both sides are affected the walk has a characteristic 'waddle'.	**DISLOCATED HIP ON ONE OR BOTH SIDES**	An orthopaedic surgeon must be seen and an ultrasound scan done for accurate diagnosis. X-rays are only helpful after 6 weeks. A special splint or harness will be used. The earlier treatment is started the better. If started after six months an operation may be needed.	Inherited tendency, or sometimes breech birth.	If one child is affected the chances of subsequent children being affected is 1:20. If one parent is affected the risk is 1:2. Three times more common in girls, and firstborn breech delivery.	When the hips are examined at birth there may be a 'click' sound which could signify a dislocation. However, this may not be a true symptom and at further examination at three weeks may show the hips may have stabilised. Sometimes the hips only dislocate later between 4-12 months. An ultrasound scan will indicate this.
Extra fingers and/or toes.	**EXTRA FINGERS (Polydactyly)**	In simple cases the extra digits can be easily removed at an early age. More complex correction is usually done by the age of two years.	Most common defect of the hand 1:700 births. Ten times more common in Black and Oriental births than Caucasians.	Inherited condition or part of a particular genetic syndrome. Can also occur by chance.	The more complex deformities are usually associated with a genetic syndrome.
Child's knees seem to 'knock' together when learning to walk.	**'KNOCK KNEES'**	Not treatment is needed in the vast majority of cases as the child outgrows it by the time they start school at around seven.	Common in the early years.	No treatment is needed unless rickets or other condition is suspected. (*See 'bow' legs p. 379*).	This is very common in children learning to walk but should correct itself over the early years.

DEFECTS OF THE TRUNK AND ABDOMEN

All recommendations are subject to the approval of, and implementation by your doctor.

FEATURES	CONDITION	TREATMENT	INCIDENCE	TRANSMITTED	REMARKS
Vomiting milk, especially when the infant is placed flat, or after a feed. Not associated with temperature, diarrhoea, or generalised or specific illness, and is not very forceful. Some babies cry a lot because of the burning pain in the oesophagus. Sometimes there is cough or wheezing due to inhaling of milk.	GASTRO-OSEOPHAGEAL REFLUX	Ultrasound and X-rays may be done to access what is causing the problem. In uncomplicated cases the treatment is usually thickening of the feeds, or a product that stops acid production in the stomach. The baby should not be changed after a feed, thereby avoiding pressure on a full stomach. Feeding and even sleeping in a fairly upright position may be necessary. A suitable baby reclining chair is useful. Frequent small feeds are advisable.	Fairly common, but sometimes confused with colic if there is crying and pain but no vomiting.	May be a genetic tendency or developmental lag	The condition usually rectifies itself by 18 months and with careful handling the inconvenience can be minimised. If the vomiting is forceful or the baby begins to lose weight, or gets frequent chest infections urgent medical attention is required. Vomiting can be due to diseases and the cause must always be investigated. **Episodes of wheezing, croup, pneumonia are danger signs and need urgent medical attention.**
Symptoms vary with individual defects, but generally include: breathlessness, especially on exertion; the baby sweats a lot and tires easily when feeding; may become blue when crying; breathes rapidly and seems weak and may refuse feeds or feed poorly. Older children may adopt a characteristic squatting position when resting.	HEART DEFECTS (Various types	Treatment will depend on the defect. The baby may be given oxygen to facilitate breathing. Any anaemia or infection will be treated, and feeds are likely to be small and frequent. If surgery is indicated, doctors will assess whether to wait until the child is older or if an immediate operation is necessary.	8:1000 births. Women who have had a child with a heart defect have a chance of giving birth to another child with a heart defect. Get genetic counselling.	Genetic tendency. Some deformities are the result of maternal infections such as German measles during early pregnancy. Certain medications can contribute, as can alcohol, warfarin and other substances.	Some defects due to a developmental lag may be healed with medication. Rapid progress has been made in the surgical treatment of children with heart defects and the prognosis for a normal life is good if surgical repair is possible. Get the child to a large specialised hospital if possible. Occasionally more than one operation may be necessary.

FEATURES	CONDITION	TREATMENT	INCIDENCE	TRANSMITTED	REMARKS
Abnormal sounding heartbeat.	**HEART MURMUR**	No treatment necessary if the murmur is physiological – that is, due to natural causes.	66:100 births.	Developmental.	Heart murmurs are of no significance in most cases. But a careful examination is necessary to exclude significant causes.
Hernias occur when part of an organ protrudes through a weak area in the wall of the structure that contains it.	**HERNIAS (See various types below)**	The child's general condition will be assessed before deciding whether surgery should be done.	Hernias are congenital in most children but can be acquired after other operations.		
Breathing is likely to be difficult due to pressure on the lungs. Chest may be distended. Caused by organs pushing up through an opening in the diaphragm – the muscular partition between the thorax (chest) and abdominal (lower) organs.	**DIAPHRAGMATIC HERNIA**	An assessment of the child's general condition will be made before deciding to operate in order to correct the problem.	Not common. Incidence depends on the type. Occurs more commonly on the left side of the body.	May be genetic or developmental error.	Severity depends on the mass of organs that have pushed up through the diaphragm and how much they have impacted on lung development. Ultrasound scan may detect the problem before birth.
A swelling on one or both sides of the groin or scrotum that becomes enlarged when the baby cries.	**INGUINAL HERNIA**	Refer to a doctor immediately if the swelling cannot be reduced by pressing with the fingers, as strangulation may occur and the blood supply to the bowel may be cut off in the hernia resulting in tissue decay with possible serious consequences. An operation is performed immediately. Even if the swelling can be reduced, a doctor should be seen to decide if an operation is needed. Recovery is usually quick and uncomplicated. The doctor may operate on both sides as the opposite side may be affected even if there are no symptoms.	Fairly common. Nine times more common in boys. Inguinal hernias are the most common cause of intestinal obstruction in babies.	May be genetic.	The swelling may disappear when the child is lying down and enlarges when the baby cries. Inguinal hernias may be associated with hydrocele and undescended testes. In girls there is usually an ovary in the hernia, or in very rare cases, a lack of internal female genital organs.

FEATURES	CONDITION	TREATMENT	INCIDENCE	TRANSMITTED	REMARKS
A soft swelling at the navel which enlarges when the baby cries. Caused by an opening (hernia) in the abdominal wall.	UMBILICAL HERNIA	Binding of the navel, pressure with a coin and other methods of trying to reduce the swelling are useless. The muscles usually close in time and no treatment is usually necessary. If it becomes painful, red or hot it needs urgent medical attention.	Common. Around 5:100 white births and about 38:100 black births.	May be genetic or developmental error.	Strangulation of an umbilical hernia is very rare. The hernia may enlarge when the baby cries but this is not dangerous. If there has been no improvement by the age of 2-3, or even 5 years, an operation may be performed. It is a simple procedure and the stitches are hidden in the navel. Hernias above or below the navel should be seen by a doctor.
The baby suffers from severe constipation, vomiting and has a very large abdomen. A section of the bowel lacks the nerve cells that promote peristalsis (the movement of food and stools towards the rectum). Part of the bowel becomes distended while the section that is affected narrows.	HIRSCHSPRUNG'S DISEASE	After diagnostic tests including barium enema and a biopsy are done surgery may be needed to ease the immediate problem. At six to nine months surgery to remove the affected portion of the bowel may be done. Modern management may involve only one operation if the condition is diagnosed in the first or second week of life.	More common in boys.	May be genetic.	Treatment by a specialist paediatric surgeon is desirable. Keep a sample of the vomited matter especially if it is stained yellow with bile. This will help with the diagnosis. Condition can be confused with meconium plug syndrome thus it needs careful evaluation.
A soft swelling of the testis due to an accumulation of fluid, usually on the right side but may occur on both sides.	HYDROCELE	The hydrocele usually reduces without treatment by six months but may sometimes persist for longer. A small operation will then be performed requiring hospitalisation for a day or less.	Common.	Caused by fluid that accumulates around the testis if the passage through which they descend during formation in the womb does not close.	An operation may be needed if the swelling is large and tense, or if it persists beyond 12 months. If it develops later in childhood or is associated with abnormal testes, an operation may be needed. Care must be taken not to confuse this condition with an inguinal hernia where the swelling enlarges and reduces with crying and sleeping. If in doubt seek medical attention.

CONDITION	FEATURES	TREATMENT	INCIDENCE	TRANSMITTED	REMARKS
HYPOSPADIAS and CHORDEE	The urethra opens on the underside of the penis. The penis may also bend downwards (chordee).	May be surgically corrected after the first year. Frequent reassessment by a paediatric urologist is wise as there may be intersex problems present.	Fairly uncommon	Developmental anomaly in males. In females may present as the urethra opening into the vagina.	Best to complete correction before school age to avoid teasing. This condition is not an indication for circumcision in males and circumcision in the repair.
INTUSSUSCEPTION	Sudden crying and pulling up of the legs. Red-current jelly coloured stools develop later, followed by vomiting.	An ultrasound scan will confirm the condition and an air enema may unlock the gut. If not, an operation may be needed. Most common between ages 6 – 18 months.	Second most common cause of intestinal obstruction in infancy. Inguinal hernia being the most common.	May be caused by a growth in the intestine, but usually occurs due to swollen glands in the bowel because of infective diarrhoea. Occurs when a portion of the intestine telescopes in on itself.	If it develops after the age of 2 years it is likely to be more complicated. Usually occurs in otherwise well babies after or during an episode of diarrhoea.
MALROTATION WITH VOLVULUS	Bile stained, yellow to green vomit usually in the first week after birth. Older infants may present with recurrent colic-like abdominal pain.	X-ray with contrast to determine the cause. **Immediate operation if Malrotation with Volvulus is diagnosed, as delay results in death of the bowel.**	1:2500 births	Developmental error	This condition occurs when the bowel never develops into its correct position in the abdomen. This results in the bowel twisting 180° - 360° and cutting off the blood supply.
MECKEL DIVERTICULUM	Blood in the stools, abdominal pain and restlessness.	Tests will be done to confirm the diagnosis followed by surgery to remove the diverticulum. Can be done with 'key hole' surgery in some hospitals which is less invasive and makes for quicker healing.	Three times more common in boys.	Developmental error.	Caused by an intestinal passage (diverticulum) that normally disappears during growth in the womb but may remain. This allows gastric juices to pour into the ileum (part of the small intestine) and cause an ulcer which may bleed.
MECONIUM ILEUS; DUODENAL ATRESIA; JEJUNAL ATRESIA.	Bile stained vomiting soon after birth with or without a distended (swollen) abdomen. May not pass meconium (the first very dark stools babies pass) due to malformation and blockage of the bowel.	In meconium ileus, once the child is stabilised and ultrasound and other tests are done treatment with water soluble enemas may be tried before surgery. In jejunal and duodenal atresia surgery to resection and repair the affected part of the bowel is likely.	Around 1:10 000 births.	Developmental error, prematurity, or part of a congenital condition. Duodenal atresia may be associated with a number of other congenital conditions. Meconium ileus may be associated with cystic fibrosis. (*see below*).	Ultrasound scans may pick up the abnormality before birth. Polyhydramnios (too much amniotic fluid during pregnancy), is often an alerting symptom. See also malrotation w with volvulus above. Also oesophageal atresia.

FEATURES	CONDITION	TREATMENT	INCIDENCE	TRANSMITTED	REMARKS
The baby vomits when given the first feed. There is also likely to be drooling. This condition is usually picked up within hours of birth.	**OESOPHAGEAL ATRESIA**	The child will be placed in a semi-sitting position so that she does not regurgitate, and any fluids will be aspirated (sucked out). If necessary she will be fed through a tube inserted through the stomach wall. Surgery to repair the faulty internal structures will be done.	Uncommon.	Developmental error.	Women who carry a lot of amniotic fluid (water surrounding the baby) during pregnancy should have an ultrasound examination as this can show this defect which is commonly associated with the problem.
Classically between 4 and 6 weeks after birth (although it may be earlier or later), vomiting of milk begins which gradually becomes forceful, shooting out soon after a feed, or just before a feed. The baby remains hungry, loses weight and may be constipated.	**PYLORIC STENOSIS**	Because there is a narrowing of the exit from the stomach, the passage of milk is obstructed to a greater or lesser degree. Ultrasound scan barium meal test may be done to confirm diagnosis. An operation to widen the gap is likely to be performed with good results.	May be inherited. Occurs in 1:500 births. Four times more common in the first born boy.	Genetic tendency	Urgent medical treatment in cases of persistent vomiting must be sought or the child could become dehydrated and lose a great deal of weight. **Potentially serious if untreated.** Operation can be done with minimally invasive 'keyhole' surgery.
Testis that have not descended into the scrotum by six weeks after birth.	**UNDESCENDED TESTES**	An operation may be performed to position testes correctly if they do not descend spontaneously. Often done at the same time as an inguinal hernia operation if they occur together. Hopeful prognosis for future functioning if treated in the first year.	Occurs in 3.4 percent of newborns and only 0.7 percent after age one year.	Developmental delay. May be genetic.	Infertility in adulthood is possible, but less likely if an operation is performed by the second year. If the baby was preterm time must be given for the testis to descend spontaneously. Long-term follow up advisable because of possible malignancy. There is no place for hormonal therapy.

GENETIC AND CHROMOSOMAL DEFECTS

All recommendations are subject to the approval of, and implementation by your doctor.

FEATURES	CONDITION	TREATMENT	INCIDENCE	TRANSMITTED	REMARKS
In infancy, chronic chest infections, salty taste on the skin, poor weight gain due to malabsorption. Thick mucus clogs the lungs making breathing difficult.	CYSTIC FIBROSIS	Child should be under specialised care in a unit that has all the necessary disciplines such as a pulmonary (lung) specialist, geneticist, gastroenterologist, liver and other specialists.	Common autosomal recessive genetic condition. Occurs in around 1:2000 Caucasian births. Less in Southern European countries, and far less in Asians and black Africans.	When both parents are carriers of the gene the risk is 1:4. There are a number of genetic variations with some being milder than others.	Although cystic fibrosis is a serious condition, with good care in infancy and later, survival has increased dramatically. Schooling and independent living is possible.
Body tone is poor and the child is floppy. Skull is small and the eyes have prominent folds across the inner corners. Neck may be short and the ears deformed. Hands and feet are broad and there may be a single horizontal crease on the palms. The tongue may protrude. May be associated with heart defects. Eyesight and hearing problems are common.	DOWN SYNDROME (See p. 448)	Any associated health problems must be treated. Depending on the type, varying degrees of intellectual lag may occur. Some high functioning children can be educated in mainstream schools, while others benefit from special schooling. Most children are able to walk at approximately two years and learn to talk to a certain extent. Toilet training is possible. (See p. 456).	1:600 births. Occurs at random in all maternal ages – with most in the younger age group due to the greater number of births. However older mothers have higher risk. At age 35 it is 1:180, after the age of 40 it beccmes 1:60 increasing each year.	Inherited tendency, age of mother in particular is an important factor. But it also occurs as a random chromosomal defect in the children of young mothers.	Fathers over the age of 55 have a greater risk of fathering a Down syndrome child. Females with Down syndrome are fertile but males are usually sterile. Down syndrome can be diagnosed before birth through various tests including ultrasound, and amniocentesis. (See p. 456).

FEATURES	CONDITION	TREATMENT	INCIDENCE	TRANSMITTED	REMARKS
The baby shows signs of jaundice (yellowness) and anaemia within the first day of birth, possibly with an enlarged liver and spleen, as well as generalised oedema (swelling due to fluid retention).	**RHESUS DISEASE** **(Rh incompatibility or pathological jaundice)**	The mother's blood group will be checked, and a Coombs test done on the baby's blood. Depending on the severity of the symptoms, the baby may be put under the special lights that reduce jaundice, or a blood transfusion may be necessary either a partial exchange of the baby's blood, or if the baby is anaemic, a straight transfusion may be given.	Uncommon in areas where women's pregnancies are well monitored. Thus if she has been pregnant before or had a miscarriage she will be tested for antibodies.	Rhesus disease occurs when a mother who is Rh negative carries a baby that is Rh positive. Some of the baby's blood passes into the mother's bloodstream and she makes antibodies because it is different from her own blood. When she becomes pregnant again the antibodies begin to destroy the baby's blood. As a result the child is jaundiced and anaemic due to the breaking down of red blood cells. If the mother's antibodies are allowed to build up over several pregnancies the effect becomes progressively worse and the child may die in the womb.	Physiological jaundice i.e. 'normal' jaundice occurs on the second or third day after birth. Rhesus disease can be prevented if the mother is given an injection within 72 hours of the birth of her first baby, or after a miscarriage. This injection will destroy the foetal cells that have entered the bloodstream. Urinary tract infection in the baby must be tested for as it can cause jaundice.

GO TO www.baby-childcare.com TO WATCH THE FOLLOWING VIDEOS THAT ARE APPLICABLE TO CHAPTER 13

PROF CLAUDIA GRAY

Coughs and colds

Common skin conditions

Febrile convulsions

Stools

Side effects of commonly used medications

Reflux and vomitting

Common general illnesses

Rashes

CHAPTER 14

Dealing with Emergencies

DO A COURSE IN FIRST AID. Do not wait for an emergency before learning about first aid. Reading about it cannot replace practical training. Anyone who has children in their care should do a course in first aid, it is a skill that may one day save the life of a loved one. Contact your local Red Cross Society or St John Ambulance, or other Registered First Aid Training Organisations for information on courses.

THE FIRST AID KIT. Every household should have a properly stocked first-aid box that is kept fully equipped. You can obtain one ready made up or buy your own supplies. If you make up your own kit you can keep it in a sturdy box with a lid, or a fishing tackle box or something similar. Ideally, it should have a child proof lock and it must always be kept right out of reach of children. Mark all supplies with the date of purchase and details of contents.

BASIC CONTENTS FOR A FIRST AID KIT

- Scissors
- Tweezers
- Eye cup
- Sterile, individually wrapped gauze dressings (7.5cm squares)
- Roll of cotton wool
- Bandages (two rolls 2.5cm wide and two rolls 5cm wide)
- Adhesive tape 2.5cm wide
- Sticking plaster strips (various sizes)
- Thermometer
- Two triangular bandages for slings (can be made from an old, clean sheet by cutting a triangle with each side measuring about 1 metre).
- Antiseptic solution

- Adult and children's paracetamol
- Petroleum jelly
- Calamine lotion with antihistamine
- Bicarbonate of soda
- Ammonia

INTRODUCTION TO CARDIO PULMONARY RESUSCITATION (CPR)

If the patient is not breathing for whatever reason, you will have to keep the circulation going and try and re-establish breathing.

RESUSCITATION

CAB–CHEST COMPRESSIONS, AIRWAY AND BREATHING are the basis of all major life saving procedures. This replaces ABC (Airway, Breathing and Circulation) the order in which it was previously done.

RESUSCITATION OF AN INFANT UNDER ONE YEAR

WARNING. If there is a possibility of a spinal injury do not move the patient unless they are in danger.

1. Lie the baby down on her back in a safe place on a firm flat surface. Check her response by tapping the feet. She should move or make a sound.
2. If not, shout for help and get someone to call for an ambulance immediately.
3. Place two fingers on the chest in the centre of a line just below the nipple line.
4. Compress the chest with your two fingers to a depth of one third to a half deep (4cm).
5. The rate of compressions is 100 per minute or almost 2 compressions per second. Lift your fingers rapidly after each compression so that the blood can circulate.
6. After 30 chest compressions take a normal breath and seal your mouth over the baby's mouth and nose, while lifting the chin with one finger.

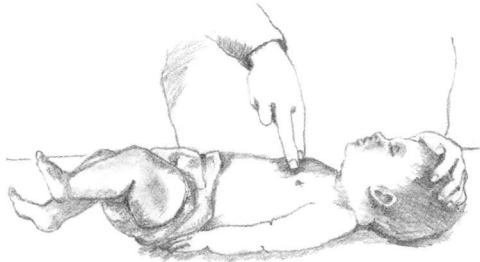

7. Give 2 gentle, slow breaths, each breath should take 1 second.

8. Watch that the chest rises with each breath. If not, be sure that you have a good seal over her mouth and nose.

9. After the breaths have been given immediately continue with chest compressions. Continue giving 30 compressions and two breaths until someone takes over or the baby starts to breathe on her own.

Chest compressions are the most important.

RESUSCITATION OF A CHILD OLDER THAN 1 YEAR OR AN ADULT.

1. Ensure your own safety.

2. Try and get a response by tapping the shoulder and asking: 'Are you okay?'

3. Shout for help and get them to call for assistance.

4. Lie the child on her back on a firm flat surface and lift her chin with two fingers.

5. Begin chest compressions immediately using the heel of one or two hands. Placement of the hands is in the centre of the chest between the nipples. Rate is 100 compressions to a minute Compress chest to a depth of 1/3 (5cm).

6. After the first 30 compressions seal your mouth over her mouth while keeping the nostrils pinched closed. Blow gently into her mouth for about 1 second. Look to see if the chest rises.

7. Give two breaths and begin chest compressions again immediately. Do 30 chest compressions to 2 breaths.

8. Once breathing has started put her in the recovery position.

Chest compressions are the most important. Continue until help arrives.

RECOVERY POSITION

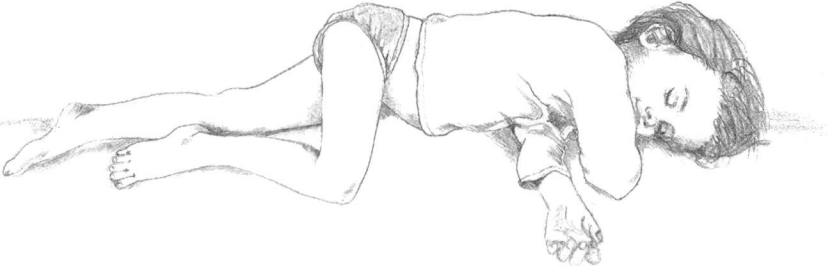

- Place the child in this position if she is breathing but still unconscious.
- Is likely to vomit
- If she has had a convulsion

ANIMAL BITES

All animal bites should be treated as a potential rabies risk. High risk bites include those from stray animals, any animal with abnormal behaviour e.g. stray or wild animals that appear tame or aggressive.

1. Flush wound well with soap and water or water for 5 minutes then apply disinfectant e.g. 70% alcohol or iodine solution. Avoid having the wound stitched.
2. Doctor will prescribe an antibiotic such as amoxicillin clavulanate, and give a tetanus booster shot. If possible, find out if the animal has been inoculated against rabies. Get the SPCA or police to assist in catching the animal if necessary.
3. Depending on the nature of the wound – a scratch on the skin, lick on the mouth or nose, lick on broken skin – the doctor will either give a full course of rabies vaccine, or rabies immunoglobulin or both.

Note that it is too late to treat rabies once any symptoms become apparent.

HUMAN BITES

Human bites are always dangerous because they can easily become infected. Wash well with soap and water if the skin is broken, and apply a sterile dressing. Any bite that shows signs of infection such as redness, swelling, or pus must be treated by a doctor. See individual entries for insect, snake bites, etc.

BLEEDING

1. Bleeding usually stops soon because of the body's clotting mechanism. If it is profuse or does not stop quickly dangerous shock can set in.
2. Wear rubber gloves to avoid contamination if possible.
3. Do not put antiseptic on the wound.
4. Wash with water if the wound is dirty.
5. Press the edges of the wound together for a few minutes.
6. If the bleeding does not stop, pad with a sterile dressing or, if the wound is large, use a folded clean cloth.
7. Apply firm pressure directly on the wound. Hold in place for 15 minutes.
8. If the bleeding has not stopped and the pad is soaked, put another pad on top of it.
9. Do not remove the first pad, but continue to add pads and keep up the pressure on the wound.
10. Do not apply a tourniquet.
11. If bleeding does not seem to be stopping, even with continuous firm pressure, get to a doctor or hospital immediately if you are not on your way already.

Treat for shock if necessary. (*See under Shock p. 404.*)

BLOWS TO THE NOSE

BLOWS to the nose can result in displacement that needs expert attention, otherwise permanent damage such as a skew septum can result. Keep the child calm and apply a cold cloth to the area to reduce swelling. If the doctor suspects there may be a fracture he will want to X-ray the area. If necessary a surgeon will set the nose, usually waiting for the swelling to subside before treating the injury. Two black eyes can indicate a broken nose.

BROKEN BONES (FRACTURES)

FRACTURES. A bone is likely to have been broken if there is a lot of swelling, or the child cannot move that part of the body, or if it is very painful. There is often some deformity and the bone may stick out of the skin. There is usually redness or bruising in the area. Sometimes the joint is loose and wobbles.

1. Do not try to make the child use the hurt limb.
2. Do not try to straighten the limb whether it is dislocated (pulled out of joint) or broken.
3. Do not move the child unless absolutely necessary, and only if you have immobilised the joint.

4. If there is bleeding or the bone is sticking out do not attempt to push it back, but get to a hospital emergency room immediately.
5. Do not give anything to eat or drink in case an anaesthetic is necessary.
6. If the back, neck or pelvis (hip) is injured do not move the patient at all.
7. Make sure she is breathing adequately. (*See p. 390.*)

Make a splint to keep the injured part steady so that no further damage is done. A pillow tied firmly in place around an injured part makes a good temporary splint; or use a thick folded pad of newspaper and keep it in place by knotting several strips of material or handkerchiefs around it, especially on each side of the break.

If the arm is injured you can make a sling by using the triangular bandage. Tie the long ends around the child's neck and fold the point at the elbow back, and catch with a safety pin; or simply pin the child's sleeve to her dress with safety pins so that the arm is kept steady.

See a doctor soon, and meanwhile apply cold compresses by dipping a clean cloth in water and holding lightly to the affected area if it is not already in a splint.

BUMPS AND BRUISES

Apply a cold compress wrapped in a cloth for at least half-an-hour to relieve pain and swelling. See a doctor if pain persists as there could be a broken bone. Two black eyes in a child can indicate a broken nose. If the bump was on the head, watch out for signs of concussion (*see p. 397*).

BURNS

1. Immerse the burnt area in cold water immediately.
2. If a large area of the body is burnt put the child into a bath of tepid (lukewarm) water.
3. Do not pull off any clothes that are sticking to the wound.
4. Do not put anything at all on the burn, just cover with a sterile dressing or clean wet sheet.
5. Get her to the hospital emergency room or doctor straightaway.
6. Treat for shock until the ambulance arrives or you leave for the hospital. (See p. 404).
7. Any burn on the face, neck or genitals must be seen by a doctor, as should any minor burn that does not heal in a few days or becomes infected.

MINOR BURNS

1. Hold the area under cold running water for 20 minutes.
2. If the burn is small and not deep, with the skin red and painful but not blistered and weeping, you can wash it with water.
3. Take care not to break the skin or any small blisters.
4. Only apply medication that has been prescribed by your doctor or chemist.
5. Do **NOT** use home remedies, fats or other ointments.
6. Small burns do not need a dressing, unless they are in a position that is likely to be easily bumped or infected.
7. Use sterile gauze and keep in place with sticking plaster far away from the burnt area.

Any burn on the face, neck or genitals must be seen by a doctor. Any minor burn that does not heal in a few days or becomes infected must be seen by a doctor.

CHEMICAL BURNS

If it is dry lime or any powder, brush this off before rinsing with water as the powder can react with water.

1. Wash away chemical with a hose pipe or lukewarm shower for at least five minutes.
2. Do not use anything but water and do not touch the burnt area.
3. Do not let the child rub her eyes if any chemical has entered; wash the eye quickly with clear water making sure you do not wash any into the unaffected eye.
4. Continue to bathe the eye with clear water for at least 20 minutes, making sure you run water under the eyelids as well. Find out what the chemical was and get medical advice from the poison unit or doctor immediately.

POTENTIALLY SEVERE BURNS

1. Immerse the burnt area in cold water immediately.
2. If a large area of the body is burnt, put the child into a bath of tepid (lukewarm) water.
3. Do not pull off any clothes that are sticking to the wound.
4. Do not put anything at all on the burn, just cover with a sterile dressing, clean wet sheet.
5. Get her to the hospital emergency room or doctor straight away.
6. Treat for shock until the ambulance arrives or you leave for the hospital.

CHOKING

Remove any visible objects from the mouth. If the child is conscious do not put your fingers in her mouth as reflexes could cause her to bite you. If the child can cough or talk and she is breathing do not interfere but get her to hospital immediately

If she is struggling to breathe and is unable to make much noise except a high-pitched sound or she is turning blue or you cannot feel her breathing, take emergency action at once (*see below*) to dislodge the object she is choking on, and, if necessary, to resuscitate her.

CHOKING INFANT (UNDER ONE YEAR OLD)

Get onto your knees, and hold the baby over your forearm with her head downwards, supporting the head.

BACK SLAPS AND CHEST THRUSTS FOR A CHOKING INFANT

1. Call for help. With the heel of your hand strike sharply five times between the shoulder blades. Do not simply slap with your flat hand, using the heel of your hand do it firmly enough to jar the child without causing injury.

2. After five backslaps turn the baby over and check if anything has been dislodged.

3. If not, give 5 chest thrusts using your middle and ring fingers placed in the centre of the chest just below the nipples, and look for any dislodged object.

4. If this does not work, repeat steps 1 and 3 again. Summon help immediately.

5. Continue with the above procedures until the object has been dislodged or the baby becomes unconscious.

6. If the baby becomes unconscious begin CPR immediately. (*See p. 390*).

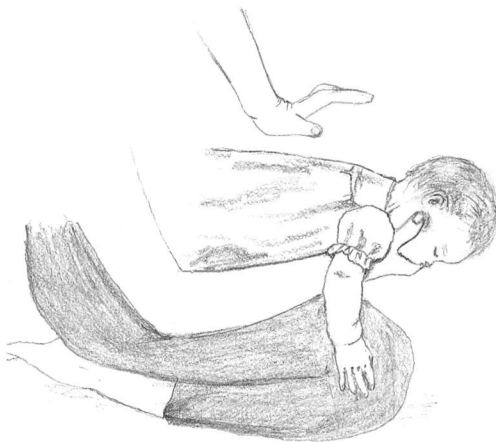

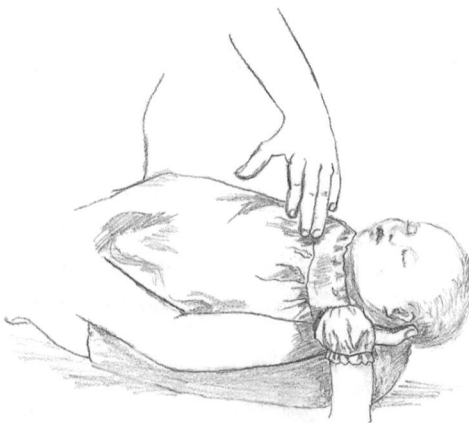

CHOKING IN AN OLDER CHILD

1. If the victim is wheezing and spluttering while clutching at the throat and unable to cry out, there is likely to be something obstructing the windpipe. Ask: 'Are you choking?'
2. If they nod, do the 'Heimlich manoeuvre'.

HEIMLICH MANOEUVRE FOR AN OLDER CHILD

1. **Call for help.** Stand or kneel behind the child with her back against you and encircle her waist with your arms.
2. Make a fist and cover it with your other hand. Using the thumb side of the fist push your fist sharply inwards and upwards into the diaphragm just above the navel. The object should be pushed out with the air in the windpipe.
3. Repeat the manoeuvre in sharp, distinct movements – if necessary administering up to five thrusts. Check to see if anything has been dislodged into the mouth.
4. When the object has been dislodged, begin mouth-to-mouth immediately if the child is not breathing (*See p. 390*).

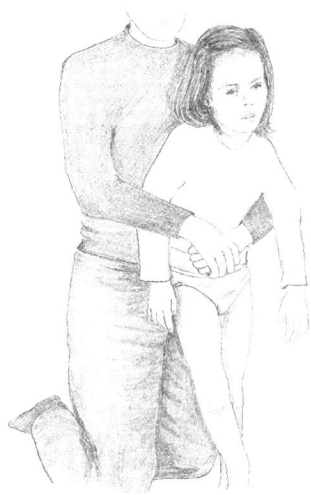

If the child is unconscious perform CPR and keep on with CPR indefinitely until help arrives even if the object has not been dislodged (*See p. 390.*)

CONCUSSION (SEVERE BLOW TO THE HEAD)

Watch the child carefully. If she begins breathing in an odd way, if she seems confused or irritable, vomits, becomes sleepy or does not stop crying within 15 minutes, **get medical help immediately**. Anyone losing consciousness even for a few seconds must go to hospital.

1. Let her lie on her side in case she vomits and inhales it (*see sketch of recovery position see p. 398*).
2. Keep her warm but not overheated.
3. Try to keep her awake until help arrives by talking to her gently and getting her to reply to you.

If a child who has had a bump on the head complains of severe headaches, is dizzy, is unable to move a limb, falls into a deep sleep, has enlarged pupils or pupils of differing sizes, or becomes very pale, keep her quiet and call a doctor immediately or take her to the hospital.

CONVULSIONS (FITS)

1. Do not restrain the child but see that she is in a safe position.
2. Do not try to 'bring her round'. She will come to when the convulsion is over.
3. Do not try to give her anything to drink during the attack.
4. When it is over lie her on her side for a minute in case her tongue has slipped back into her throat. She will be confused and sleepy, so allow her to rest in the recovery position.

RECOVERY POSITION

Place the child in this position if:
1. She is unconscious
2. She is likely to vomit
3. She has had a convulsion

Find out if she has taken anything that may have poisoned her and call the emergency poison centre for advice. (*See p. 401.*)

1. If she feels very hot it is likely that she has had a febrile convulsion caused by a high temperature. Strip her clothes off and cool her down with tepid water (lukewarm). (*See p. 339.*)
2. Call a doctor or take her to hospital.

CRAMP

This is a painful contraction of muscles that may occur while swimming, during exercise or through loss of body salt.

1. Stretch the shortened muscles by straightening the affected limb, and then knead and massage it.
2. Give drinks of water.

CUTS

Examine the wound. If it is less than 2.5cm long, has straight edges, is easy to clean, and does not go so deep into the skin that yellow fat shows, and is not on the face or in a joint, it probably does not need stitching.

1. Wash the cut well with soap and cool running water.
2. Stop the bleeding by pinching the edges together and applying pressure.
3. Hold firmly until bleeding stops (it may take 15 minutes or more).
4. Cover the cut with sterile gauze and hold in place with a strip of sticking plaster across the cut so that the edges are held together.

SEE A DOCTOR IF:

- The cut is deep, even if it is small.
- You cannot stop the bleeding within 15 minutes (*see bleeding, p. 393*).
- The edges are ragged.
- The wound is dirty and you cannot clean it.
- The child has not had a tetanus injection within the last 12 months and the wound was caused by anything that was in contact with soil.
- The injury is on the face, or in a joint, or there is a possibility that a bone may be broken, or the injury causes weakness or numbness.
- Cuts on the hands are especially likely to result in damage to the nerve or tendon and these must be seen by a doctor.
- Cuts on the scalp bleed a lot but if they are small and there is no sign of concussion you can stop the bleeding by applying pressure and closing the wound with sterile gauze and a sticking-plaster dressing.
- If a wound becomes infected, see a doctor immediately.

THE SIGNS ARE: Redness, pain, swelling and heat in the area. Red streaking from the wound, pus and a raised temperature are danger signals. See a doctor immediately.

Do not try and squeeze out pus, and do not touch the wound with your fingers.

DROWNING

1. Make sure the airway is not obstructed.
2. Begin mouth-to-mouth immediately (*See p. 390*).
3. Turn her on her side intermittently to allow water to drain. Summon help.
4. Ensure the child is lying on a firm flat surface and if she is not breathing do CPR. (*See p. 290*)

EARS

FOREIGN BODIES. Do not attempt to remove objects like beads, nuts, insects, etc. from the ear. Get the child to a doctor.

ELECTRIC SHOCK

1. Do not touch the child.
2. Switch off the electric current.
3. Follow the CPR steps. (*See p. 390.*)
4. Summon help.

NOTE. An electric shock that has caused the body to become rigid, even if the child appears to have recovered quickly, may have caused internal damage.

EYES

If something penetrates the eyeball do not attempt to remove it. Cover both eyes with a clean dressing and a light bandage and see a doctor immediately (preferably a specialist at a large hospital).

BLOWS TO THE EYE

Blows to the eye should be treated by laying the child flat on her back and closing the eye. Apply a pad of cotton wool and a light bandage. Get the child to a doctor.

Specks of dirt or small insects that enter the eye should be removed (*see below*) if they do not penetrate the eyeball and if you can get them out without fiddling too much. If something penetrates the eyeball, do not attempt to remove it. Cover both eyes with a clean dressing and a light bandage and see a doctor immediately (preferably a specialist at a large hospital). If a lot of dirt has entered the eye or you cannot get it out within a short time, see a doctor. If the dirt has scratched the eye it may be uncomfortable for some time. Keep the eye covered with a light dressing and see a doctor if it is not better within a few hours or it worsens.

REMOVING SPECKS IN THE EYE

1. Wash your hands thoroughly.
2. Fill an eye bath with cool boiled water and let the child use it with her eye open. Many children are reluctant to do this so do not force her.
3. Or get her to stand with her eye open under running water. The affected eye must be closer to the ground or the grit could run into the other eye.

IF THE GRIT IS STILL NOT OUT, TRY THE FOLLOWING PROCEDURE

1. Stand behind the child with her head resting against you.
2. Hold a matchstick lengthways along the upper lid close to the lashes.
3. Hold the lashes and roll the eyelid back over the matchstick.
4. Remove the speck with a damp twist of cotton wool or the corner of a soft clean handkerchief.
5. If you have not found the speck, repeat the same procedure with the lower lid.

If you cannot find the speck or cannot remove it gently, see a doctor.

FAINTING

Fainting is caused by a temporary shortage of blood to the brain. The child may become very pale, break out in a sweat and start swaying, or she may say she feels dizzy.

FEELING FAINT

1. Tell her to breathe normally
2. Let her lie down with her legs raised.
3. Reassure her and loosen any tight clothing.
4. If the room is stuffy move her to a cool draughty spot.

IF SHE HAS ALREADY FAINTED

1. Loosen any tight clothes.
2. Open the doors so that fresh cool air reaches her, or take her into the fresh air if possible.
3. Lift her legs up high while she lies on the floor so that blood can go to her head.
4. When she has recovered, give her sips of water if requested.
5. Keep her lying down for at least ten minutes.
6. If there is no obvious cause for the faint such as a very stuffy room, prolonged standing or a missed meal, have her examined by a doctor.
7. If it is not your own child, check for a Medic Alert disc that may give a clue to the cause of the collapse, for example, diabetes or epilepsy.

FOOD POISONING

Cream cakes and the like, as well as meat or other foodstuffs that have been contaminated by bacteria, can make a child ill. Symptoms may show within an hour of eating the food or even 12 hours later.

Vomiting, diarrhoea and stomach cramps are the most common signs of food poisoning. Give frequent sips of electrolyte solution (*See recipe p. 178*). If this is impossible, give plain water; although this is not ideal, it can help prevent dehydration in an emergency if the vomiting and diarrhoea are severe. See a doctor if the symptoms do not pass in four hours, or if the child does not seem to be improving, or cannot keep the electrolyte solution down.

HEAT STROKE

This is a very serious condition and may develop after a child has been playing or running in the hot sun for a long time.

- Heat stroke is caused by the body's inability to control the internal temperature regulating mechanism.
- The victim is hot and flushed with a dry skin.
- Breathing is rapid.
- She may rapidly become unconscious.
- A conscious child may complain of headache, nausea, dizziness, and feeling hot.

THIS IS AN EMERGENCY. GET THE CHILD TO HOSPITAL IMMEDIATELY.

Apply as many of the following procedures as possible before or during the trip.

1. Bring her temperature down by taking off her clothes and wrapping her in a cold, wet sheet.
2. Direct as much cold air on her as possible. Place a fan near her with a bowl of ice in front of it.
3. Keep wetting the sheet with cold water until the temperature is down to 38°C (100.4°F).

NOSE

Unexplained drainage of foul-smelling pus from one or both nostrils may indicate that a foreign object like a pea or bead has been pushed up the nose. See a doctor.

A hard blow to the nose can result in displacement that needs expert attention so that there is no permanent damage. Keep the child calm and apply a cold cloth to the area to reduce swelling. If the doctor suspects there may be a fracture, they will want to X-ray the area. If necessary, a surgeon will set the nose, usually waiting for the swelling to subside before treating the injury. Two black eyes can indicate a broken nose.

NOSEBLEEDS

1.   Place the child in a sitting position leaning forward slightly.
2.   Tell her to breathe through her mouth.
3.   Pinch the nose closed just below the bone on the soft part of the nose, for at least ten minutes.
4.   You can hold a pad of cotton wool under her nostrils to catch the blood but do not push it up her nose as you will dislodge the clot every time the pad is changed.
5.   Do not let her blow, sniff, pick at or touch her nose for a few hours after the bleeding has stopped.
6.   Allow her to spit out any blood that collects in her mouth.

If you are unable to stop the bleeding within 40 minutes, get the child to a hospital.

POISONING

It is important to recognise the symptoms of poisoning as soon as possible so that treatment can be given without delay.

SUSPECT POISONING IF

■   You find a container that is out of place.
■   You smell a chemical odour on your child's breath.
■   There are burn marks around the mouth.
■   The child develops sudden severe stomach cramps or convulsions not associated with a high fever. The child becomes drowsy suddenly or lapses into unconsciousness.
■   Sudden vomiting with pain and, possibly, diarrhoea occurs.

WHAT TO DO

■   Try to establish what the child has taken, remembering that if you panic she may be afraid to tell you.
■   Look around and try to find an empty container and take it with you to the hospital.
■   Try to establish how much has been taken.
■   Phone your poison unit or doctor, preferably after you have established what the child has taken.

GENERAL TREATMENT FOR POISONING

■   Do not give her anything to drink or try to make her vomit unless instructed to do so by your doctor.
■   If she vomits catch it in a bowl and show what she has brought up to the doctor.

Do not make the child vomit unless directed to do so by the doctor as this could cause more damage!

If the child is not breathing, or if she is unconscious make sure the airway is clear and start CPR immediately. (*See p. 390.*)

COMMON POISONS INCLUDE: rat bait, cigarettes that have been eaten, iron tablets for anaemia, aspirin, sleeping tablets and other medicines as well as plants and berries.

CHEMICAL POISONS include both acids and alkalis: ammonia, bleach, battery acid, cleaning fluid, benzene, drain cleaner, furniture cleaner, floor cleaner, lime, motor oil, methylated spirits, paraffin, oven cleaner, paint stripper, petrol, pesticides, rust remover, toilet cleaner, thinners, turpentine, kerosene and washing soda.

WHAT TO DO
Do not make the child vomit unless directed to do so by the doctor as this could cause more damage!
1. Wash away any chemicals around the mouth and wash the child's hands with plenty of water.
2. See that she does not rub her eyes.
3. If there is any chemical in her eyes keep pouring cool water over them, letting it flow under the eyelids as well taking care not to let contaminated water run into the other eye.
4. Take the child to hospital

SCORPION STINGS
Usually, the thicker the scorpion's tail, the more dangerous the sting. Scorpions with large nippers are less poisonous than others. The child may have difficulty breathing and become paralysed.
- Get the child to hospital immediately.
- Give CPR if the patient stops breathing. (*See p. 390.*)
- Apply crushed ice in a cloth to the bite to delay absorption of the poison.

SHOCK
Shock can result from any injury, loss of blood, severe pain or fright.
- The child will be very pale, with a clammy skin. She will sweat and may feel faint or giddy. Breathing is rapid and shallow and the pulse is quick and weak.
- She is likely to be confused and may become unconscious.

IMMEDIATE TREATMENT IS VITAL.

GET HER TO HOSPITAL AS SOON AS POSSIBLE.

1. Keep her warm but do not pile on blankets.
2. Do not give anything to drink, merely moisten her lips if she complains of thirst.
3. Do not give alcohol.
4. Let her lie down and lift her legs higher than her body unless there could be spinal or head and chest injuries.
5. If she is likely to vomit or becomes unconscious, lie her on her side in the recovery position (*See illustration p. 390*).

SNAKE BITE

Unless you have witnessed the incident, it is not always easy to diagnose a snake bite as there may not be any marks on the skin. Occasionally there are scratch or puncture marks made by the fangs but not always. In the case of most adder bites, there will be pain and swelling at the site of the bite. However, severe symptoms can occur without much reaction at the site of the bite, especially in the case of some cobra bites.

1. Try to identify the snake so that the correct treatment can be given. However, even if this cannot be done the snake will be able to be identified from the patient's symptoms and most antidotes are effective against all kinds of bites except the boomslang.
2. **Contact the nearest poison centre immediately and follow instructions.**
3. Clean any venom away from the wound.
4. Do not apply a tourniquet or cut the wound and attempt to suck out the venom.
5. Apply a clean gauze and pressure bandage to the site taking care not to make it too tight. Then bandage the whole limb working from the fingers or toes upwards. Make sure the fingers and toes are visible so that feeling and circulation can be monitored.
6. Keep the patient as quiet as possible in a neutral position, and if the bite is on a limb, immobilise it by splinting against the body.
7. Loosen the bandage if the limb becomes cold or blue.
8. Should the patient collapse and stop breathing do CPR. (*See p. 389.*)
9. If the child is breathing but unconscious put her in the recovery position (*See p. 398.*) to prevent suffocation while you get help.

THERE ARE 2 TYPES OF ANTIVENIN: Polyvalent, effective against puff adder, Gaboon adder, spitting cobra, non-spitting cobra, mamba and rinkhals bites. Monospecific antivenom is only effective against boomslang bites. Antivenin must only be given in hospital and not in the field, as it is given intravenously and a severe allergic reaction is possible.

SPIDER BITE

You should suspect your child was bitten by a poisonous spider if the child complains of a burning area of skin (the site of the bite) which may or may not be red, swollen and later become ulcerating. Poisonous spider bites may cause muscle pain, difficulty breathing, facial swelling, cramping pain, sweating, fever, nausea, rapid heartbeat, and even collapse.

SYMPTOMS OF BUTTON SPIDER BITE

The **Button spider's** venom is neurotoxic, that is damaging to the nervous system. First signs are likely to be burning pain at the site of the bite. Followed by muscle pain, difficulty breathing, facial swelling, cramping pain, sweating, fever, nausea and vomiting, rapid heartbeat, and collapse.

SYMPTOMS OF VIOLIN SPIDER BITE

The **Violin spider** is also very dangerous. It is brown to reddish in colour with dark markings on the body. The legs are long and thin in relation to the size of the body. They have only three pairs of eyes, rather than four pairs as most spiders have.

This bite is cytotoxic, that is damaging to cell tissue. There may not be pain at the site, but symptoms appear within a few hours, with the area becoming red, swollen and painful. The bite area forms a large ulcerating wound with a danger of infection.

GENERAL TREATMENT OF SPIDER BITES

1. Try and identify the spider.
2. Apply a cold cloth or wrapped ice to the site of the bite to delay absorption of the poison.
3. Contact a poison centre for advice and get the child to a hospital immediately. Give mouth-to-mouth resuscitation if necessary. (*See p. 389*.).
4. Wash the area of the bite. Do not apply a bandage, dressing or medication to the wound.
5. Get your child to a hospital or poison centre immediately.

SPRAINS

Treat as a fracture until X-rays have been taken.
1. Apply cold compresses or immerse in cold water.
2. Raise injured area and do not let the child use it.
3. Seek medical assistance.

STINGS

BEE, WASP, HORNET AND BLUEBOTTLE STINGS

1. Remove the sting (if present) by scraping out with a credit card or the back of a knife.
2. **Do not** try to pluck it out with your fingers as more poison could be released.
3. To reduce pain and swelling apply ice cubes wrapped in a cloth.
4. Calamine lotion with antihistamine applied immediately will lessen the reaction. A weak ammonia solution may also be applied.
5. In the case of bluebottle stings first remove tentacles from the skin, then immerse the part that has been stung in water as hot as the patient can stand it.

Contact a doctor or take the child to hospital immediately if there is any sign of an allergic reaction such as dizziness, severe swelling, difficulty breathing or collapse!

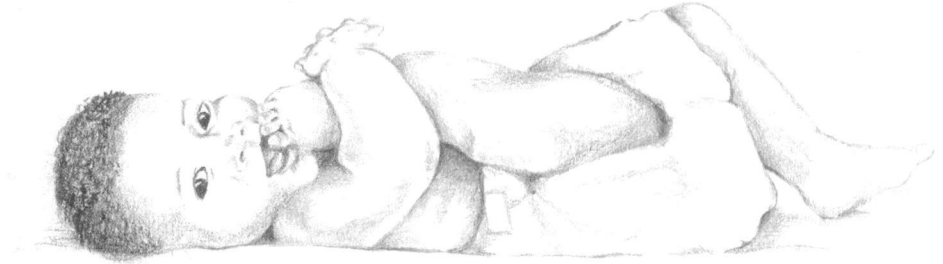

CHAPTER 15

A-Z General Reference

ADENOIDS

THE ADENOIDS are situated at the back of the throat near the nasal passage. They may become enlarged due to infections or allergies. Sometimes they are enlarged without symptoms, or the symptoms go away when the swelling subsides. When they become persistently enlarged they can cause mouth breathing, particularly at night, and snoring. Snoring is a potentially serious symptom as it indicates that there is obstruction of the airways making breathing difficult. Some children develop sleep apnoea in which breathing is so difficult that the child does not get sufficient oxygen during sleep. They wake exhausted and lethargic because they sleep so badly. Mouth breathing can cause the structure of the mouth to change so that the teeth become displaced. If mouth breathing persists orthodontic treatment may be required when the permanent teeth come through.

Enlarged adenoids are also a common cause of recurrent middle-ear infections. If they become greatly enlarged, they can block the bottom end of the Eustachian tubes that go up to the inside of the inner ears. The Eustachian tube allows air to enter the cavity behind the eardrum to equalise the pressure on both sides of the drum. Because air pressure vibrates in the Eustachian tube when sound waves hit the eardrum, any blockage of the Eustachian tube can result in deafness and infection. If the adenoids remain enlarged their removal is normally recommended. The operation is simple and requires a day or less in hospital. The child may speak with a nasal tone for many months after the operation but the pitch of the voice returns to normal in time.

TONSILS AND ADENOIDS. Allergy-prone children frequently have enlarged tonsils and adenoids. Enlargement of the adenoids often results in middle-ear infections and obstruction of the Eustachian tube which can cause partial or complete deafness. It is therefore important to treat a child with chronic hay fever, or partial deafness could result. This in turn may mean that the child misses out on all-important language development, causing problems that are difficult to solve later on. If the adenoids and tonsils of an allergic child are removed and the allergy is not treated and controlled, they may enlarge again so that there is no long-term benefit from the operation.

The question of whether to remove infected tonsils and adenoids or to treat them with medicines does not always have a simple answer. While most children will outgrow their tonsillitis by the age of eight, waiting this long can mean years of frequent infections.

When enlarged tonsils or adenoids make breathing, speech or swallowing difficult, removal is usually recommended. Various criteria are applied for the removal of tonsils after repeated attacks of streptococcus or other substantial infection.

These include: repeated infections (four or five in a year, or three a year in consecutive years), an abscess on the tonsils, or sleep apnoea (short stoppages of breathing during sleep). Heavy snoring, severe mouth breathing, persistent enlarged lymph nodes at the base of the jaw, and ear infections that continue even after grommets have been inserted are all reasons to consider surgery. Each case must be assessed individually by an ear, nose and throat specialist taking all factors into account. In certain cases where the child has epilepsy or asthma or may suffer from rheumatic fever, the tonsils are usually removed without hesitation.

ADHD (ATTENTION DEFICIT HYPERACTIVITY DISORDER)

ADHD is the most common neuro-behavioural disorder in children – affecting between 5 to 7 per cent. If your son – I refer to boys, because ADHD is four times more common in males although it does occur in girls too – shows the following symptoms or some of them, you should have the child carefully assessed by experts.

- Is the child's attention span very short compared to others in his age group?
- Does he become frustrated easily?
- Does he have sleeping problems?
- Is he very impulsive – interrupting repeatedly when someone is talking, and won't wait for his turn?
- Is he aggressive?
- Is he destructive?
- Is he very easily distracted?
- Does he run, fidget and move excessively?

- Is he forgetful and unable to concentrate on tasks?
- Does he have little sense of danger?

Before a child is labelled ADHD or 'hyperactive', a very careful evaluation must be done, preferably by a specialist in this field; including a child psychiatrist (not just a paediatrician, unless it is his or her particular field of expertise). Great care needs to be exercised in diagnosis and treatment because the same symptoms may indicate poor handling, emotional problems or possibly even a highly gifted child. But investigate you must because, whatever the cause, the child needs help and so do the parents.

You may find when looking into the family background that there are others who were affected by the same problem, as it is an inherited disorder to a large extent. It is important to remember that the child cannot control himself, and that the problem is not due to your parenting. For children with ADHD, the world is a muddled, unclear place over which they have no focus or control.

All aspects of the child's medical history and behaviour should be assessed by a specialist in the field. A physical examination should also be done to rule out hearing loss, eyesight and other possible factors such as epilepsy.

Once a full picture of the child's condition is obtained treatment options are discussed. These could include behavioural skills training so that the child can learn to modify social and school interactions; and advice to parents and teachers on handling of daily routines, behaviour, etc. Although behaviour modification is helpful it is seldom entirely effective without the use of medication.

Medication choices for the treatment of ADHD have advanced to the point where symptoms can be controlled for short or long periods during the day. And there is also a choice between 'stimulant' and 'non-stimulant' drugs. The best known drug (methylphenidate, commonly known as Ritalin) that is used as a stimulant in adults, has a calming effect on some hyperactive children. It can be valuable in helping children calm down enough to bring order into their life and aid concentration at school, so that the emotional problems that could complicate things are hopefully prevented. However, no child should be given these drugs lightly as they need careful supervision over time so that the best dosage and type can be established in each case. The drug can act as an appetite suppressant and may retard growth if used for several years without a break. It does not, however, have addictive effects or lead to substance abuse. The use of these medications in children under four is not recommended. Rather, behavioural modification training for parents and child has been shown to be helpful.

A non-stimulant treatment, atomoxetine HCl (Strattera), offers once-a-day dosage. Atomoxetine blocks or slows reabsorption of noradrenaline, a brain chemical considered important in regulating attention, impulsivity and activity levels, and does not have addictive or abuse potential, although there are some reversible side effects. Other treatments are available, and a careful assessment must be made. Sometimes a combination of treatments is necessary in order to effect a change. ADHD is challenging for parent and child, but exceptional achievements are possible, such as that of the United States swimmer Michael Phelps who won eight gold medals at the Beijing Olympics. Dr Craig Venter, the US medical scientist who – in a race against a US government-sponsored project in 1990 – mapped the human genome by sequencing the entire human DNA structure in record time, had childhood ADHD. Until this day he races ahead where others fear to tread. His latest iconoclastic venture is 'creating a new life' form.

Besides the inherited tendency, other possible contributory causes for ADHD are being investigated including high levels of lead in the child's system, and a low iron status, as well as certain vitamin deficiencies and a low intake of essential fatty acids. Speak to your child's medical adviser about possibly adding omega-3 fatty acids to the child's diet, and testing for iron-deficiency anaemia. In one study, 84% of ADHD sufferers had low iron levels. The effect of certain foods such as sugar and food additives is sometimes cited as a factor by parents. (*See sugar high p. 293*)

Now a study published in the medical journal *The Lancet* has demonstrated that for some ADHD children – not all by any means – a variety of common food dyes and preservatives do increase distraction and activity in susceptible children. Food colourants are found in many sweets, cheeses, jams, soft drinks, including some fruit juices, chips and other snack foods, convenience meals, as well as soups, puddings, baked goods and ice cream. Sodium benzoate, the preservative that was studied, is commonly used, particularly in soft drinks and squashes. It is worth checking labels and avoiding products to which your child appears to be sensitive. For those children who show a definite improvement when certain products are avoided it is worth paying more for products that are free of colourants and additives. Following a restrictive diet if there is no real evidence for it is not a good idea however, as it is sure to make for friction between parent and child, and will not show benefits. See also the sections on learning disabilities (*p. 305*) and hypoglycaemia (*p. 253*).

HANDLING THE CHILD WITH ADHD. Once you have a diagnosis and advice on possible medication and treatment find out as much as you can about ADHD. It is important that your child lives in an organised, structured environment. Like all children, those with ADHD need rules and clear direction, for them; it is absolutely essential. Although their behaviour can be annoying and frustrating, remember it is not their fault and they need praise for what they do right rather than reprimanding for what they do wrong. Draw up a daily schedule and post it where your child can see it. If he (or she) is too young to read remind him every day what the rules are, and ask them to repeat them if possible. They should know what the consequences of breaking the rules are and they should be enforced. Try not to shout or become angry. Simply enforce 'timeout', or loss of a treat.

Look for behaviour to praise – this is the strongest form of reinforcement. Make star charts, give rewards. A structured behavioural support programme at school or preschool, plus carefully prescribed and monitored medication can make a great difference. (*See also dyslexia and dysgraphia p. 305. See Tourette's p. 502.*)

ADOPTION

THE GIFT OF LOVING ANOTHER AS YOUR OWN. The word adopt is derived from the Latin *optare* – to choose. When you choose to take the child of another and raise him or her as your own, you consciously perform an act that involves personal choice on every level. Each individual or couple will have their own reasons for doing it. Women have said they are so desperate for a child they will 'take anything'. Others have sought out children who are as similar to themselves as possible. Some will choose a child who is HIV positive, or who has a disability regardless of the pain this may bring. Many will choose cross-cultural or cross-racial adoption. Whatever the reasons for their decision, parents who choose to adopt display an unusual willingness to love the child of another as their own – surely one of life's most selfless acts.

You can adopt through a non-governmental agency such as Child Welfare, who have many years of experience, or through a private agency, which may be church-affiliated, or through a registered social worker. Either way, you will need information and continuing support from experienced child-placement social workers. You will be screened for suitability and, depending on how wide your brief is, you may get a child quickly or have to wait a long time.

The legal issues involved in adoption vary from country to country and need to be checked carefully. Only registered adoption agencies and social workers registered with child protection agencies should be consulted.

Adopting a child does not generally allow you to adjust to and prepare for the huge changes in your life in the same way as if you are pregnant. But somehow parents fall in the deep end and swim. Some even prepare for breastfeeding without knowing when they might receive a baby. (*See p 124.*) A big difference between adoptive parents and biological parents is their attitude to the inevitable difficulties of looking after a baby, especially in the early months.

Few adoptive parents ever complain about a lack of sleep, colic or the strictures that babies impose on parental lifestyles. This may be based on the fear that they will be found to be 'unsuitable' parents and that the child will be taken away. Don't worry, it won't happen! Allow yourself a night out. Complain occasionally. Join a support group of other adoptive parents. Long-established adoption agencies like Child Welfare have parents who adopted children that are now adults; they love sharing their wisdom and experiences. Most adoptions work out well, at least as well as biological parent-child relationships.

Possibly the biggest mistake adoptive parents make is over-compensating and spoiling their children.

Years ago adoption was shrouded in secrecy, and children might never have been told that they were adopted. These days there is far greater openness, and parents are encouraged to tell their child sooner rather than later. There are also many 'obvious' adoptions where the child is clearly not biologically that of the parents. People will not always be tactful, not least because they are unthinking. The same applies to adoption by single and same-sex parents. There is no evidence that these adoptions work out less well than any other form of parenting by committed and caring parents. There is evidence that the younger a child is adopted the easier the adjustment. Children of adoptive parents generally do better academically than might be expected if they had stayed with their biological parents.

Adoption can be 'open' or 'closed' with the identities of the parties known or kept confidential. Adopted children have the right to seek out and meet their biological parents when they reach the age of 18. This can be hurtful to the adoptive parents who have done so much for the child. But the urge to know our origins is natural. Sometimes there is disappointment and disillusionment and you will have to help your child accept the loss of a dream. As one girl said, 'I had built up a picture of my biological mother as a very special person who had sacrificed for me. She turned out to be uncaring and nothing like my expectations.' Another young woman finally met her biological father only when he was in his eighties. For him it was a joy to finally meet his daughter together with her husband and son. They were all well served by the meeting. Children in cross-cultural adoptions may feel the need to partake in or get to know their biological heritage and culture. Advice from experienced social workers is often helpful with this. Meeting a biological parent is best facilitated by a social worker.

As an adoptive parent you should not imagine that had you been the biological parent you would 'instinctively' have known what to do in every situation. This is not so: all good parenting comes from commitment, experience and endless love no matter who you are.

AIDS

HIV INFECTION AND AIDS. HIV is transmitted through bodily fluids such as urine, blood and breast milk, as well as birth. Once a person has been infected with the human immunodeficiency virus (HIV) the virus remains in the body for life. If untreated, at some point it is likely to develop into full-blown AIDS (acquired immunodeficiency syndrome) in which the virus breaks down the body's defence system so that the patient is susceptible to any infection, and death will be the likely result. In well-nourished patients that are treated with an antiretroviral (ARV) therapy carefully adhered to, the disease becomes a chronic, yet manageable condition with which the patient is able to live.

Generally, pregnant women are given ARV's regardless of their CD4 count. Antiretroviral therapy is now being started much earlier in the progression of the disease, and this helps to make the illness more manageable, although lifelong treatment will be needed. Strict adherence to the treatment programme is essential in order to prevent the development of resistance to the medication.

About one in three children whose mothers have the AIDS virus can be infected in the womb, during the birth or through breastfeeding. They generally show symptoms before the age of two, although it may sometimes take years longer. Transmission of the virus from mother to child can be reduced to around 2% by the use of antiretroviral medication from the fourth month of pregnancy and at the onset of labour and then given to the child immediately after birth and for a period thereafter. Safe delivery practices and Caesarean section can also limit transmission. Since there is a chance of transferring the virus through breastmilk, a decision must be made as to whether an HIV-positive mother should breastfeed or not. Where the danger of illness is high due to poor hygienic circumstances, breastfeeding only is better. After the birth the breast fed baby must be tested frequently and brought for immunisations. Regular visits to the clinic are essential for both mother and child during pregnancy and after the birth in order for them to receive ARV medication and check-ups.

It is essential that mother and child keep all clinic appointments as they are vital to ensure regular testing and correct medication.

In higher socio-economic conditions, bottle feeding only is an option.

If you are HIV positive and you are in a position to bottle feed your baby without a problem (and you have decided to do so in consultation with your medical advisor), then you should not put your baby to the breast at all. Your expressed breast milk or colostrum should also not be given. In this way, if your baby is not HIV positive, you will hopefully safeguard her. Mothers who are not breastfeeding need ongoing guidance with regard to the introduction of suitable solids and the prevention of infection since the protective properties of breastfeeding will be missed.

Or there may be a recommendation that HIV-positive mothers or their infants take antiretroviral drugs throughout the period the child is breastfed and until the child is 12 months old. Breastfeeding mothers should also be supported with practical advice regarding the introduction of suitable solids and other measures to sustain health. Breastfeeding should be exclusive because the risk of the transmission of HIV infection to the baby is much higher when the mother mixes breastmilk and formula feeds. Studies show that if the mother breastfeeds, weaning should be rapid and complete when she decides to stop.

Children who are infected with HIV fail to thrive and lose weight; have frequent respiratory and other infections; may have a temperature and diarrhoea for periods of longer than a month; and may have thrush, enlarged glands or persistent cough, repeated infections such as pneumonia, developmental delays, and liver, heart, or kidney disease. *Note that many of these symptoms are common in children not infected with HIV.* If the baby is HIV positive, treatment is started immediately. Good nutrition and extra vitamin A is helpful. Timely treatment for any infection is vital. Immunisation of HIV positive children is important and your clinic will guide you.

The virus is not spread through normal contact and HIV-infected children need the same loving attention as any child. They are, however, very susceptible to infections and may need medical care more frequently. Day care attendance is possible, except if there are open sores. (*See p. 467 for immunisation and HIV infection, and p. 119 for breastfeeding, and enrichment of food.*)

NOTE: Recommendations are subject to change as new HIV information becomes available. Stay in touch with the hospital or other HIV medical advisor.

AIR TRAVEL

HIGH FLYERS. Travelling anywhere with young children is never easy, but going by air is probably the most convenient if you organise yourself properly. Start by checking the website of the airline you are using for information about their services for travellers with children. You may, however, not be able to rely on this information, so it is best to be prepared. If you are travelling with a very young baby (infants can travel by air from the earliest weeks) ask for one of the front seats so that you are first to be served and are near the toilet. Sky cradles are available on international flights but they must be booked well beforehand and are only suitable for small babies.

A lightweight compact pushchair or baby buggy is handy for getting the baby to the plane since there is usually a very long walk from the departure point at international airports. (Check if you can take the fold-up baby buggy aboard the plane.) Ground hostesses are there to help you but it is better if they carry equipment rather than the baby who may start screaming at the sight of a strange face.

When travelling with a baby it is wise to take a supply of disposable nappies in case supplies run out in the plane, and bring your own bottles, ready made with teat covers on. Restrictions on carrying liquids in hand luggage may however preclude this, so find out beforehand. You may have to take powdered milk and have it made up on the plane. Although baby foods are carried on board they may not be the kind your baby is used to, and getting them from the crew can sometimes mean a long wait, with a crying baby. Pack a light hold-all with everything you will need for the flight: nappies, bottles, spoon, jars of baby food, wet wipes, a change of clothes for the baby in case she gets sick over what she is wearing, and a clean top for you in case she gets sick over you!

Remember a small bottle with doses of painkiller – paracetamol is best. Take her favourite small toy or cuddly. The change in air pressure on take-off and landing can cause a sharp pain in the baby's ears – let her suck on a dummy so that the swallowing action will help equalise the pressure. (An older child should hold her nose and swallow to relieve pressure in the ears.) You can also ask your doctor or pharmacist for a suitable nasal decongestant, which will help relieve pressure. Don't give her a bottle as she could bring it up again a few minutes later. If you are breastfeeding wear a suitable dress and carry a large light shawl so that you can cover yourself and the baby when feeding on board.

TRAVELLING WITH OLDER CHILDREN can be made reasonably painless with a little forethought. Again, ask for a seat near the front and ask if you can have a few seats left unoccupied around you if the flight is not full. Explain that it is for the comfort and safety of the other passengers as much as for your own. Pack a small, light case with goodies for your children on the flight. Some airlines have novelties for children, but they cannot be relied on and are not always available when you need them. A small box of crayons, a thin colouring-in book, some glucose sweets for take-off and landing, any other noiseless novelties like finger puppets, magic slate, a small doll, car game or whatever… The toys should preferably be new so that they have the attraction of novelty, but include an old favourite and don't leave the security blanket (if she has one) behind! You will also need wet wipes for the inevitable sticky hands and mess.

Waiting for a flight and going through customs can take hours, so make sure your children have had a good meal before you leave for the airport: it could be a long time before they get another, so include a dried fruit stick or cheese wedges in their cabin bag. If you request vegetarian, halaal or kosher food when you make your booking on international flights you will be served first.

SHOULD YOU MEDICATE? It is not wise to give children a sedative before a flight as it often has the opposite effect of making them belligerent and groggy, but not enough to send them to sleep. Some children get airsick, so you may want to travel prepared with airsickness medication and, before the flight, dose her according to the manufacturer's instructions if you think it will be a problem. But, as always, it is preferable not to take medication unless it is really necessary. Ginger helps nausea so perhaps a few ginger biscuits will do the trick. Do not suggest that she may get airsick, as it will probably give her an instant queasy feeling.

ALBINISM

THE COLOUR OF DISCRIMINATION. Albinism is a hereditary disorder in which there is either a partial or total absence of melanin, the colouring pigmentation in the skin, hair and eyes.

Albinism is far more common in dark-skinned people – around 1:4000 compared to light-skinned people who live in cold climates such as Denmark, where only 1:60 000 is affected.

The type that most affects dark-skinned Africans results in yellow hair at birth, and very light skin and eyes. They do develop pigmentation (skin colouring) to a certain extent as they grow older but always have distinctively light skin and hair. Because of their very light skin and inability to tan, people with this condition are more susceptible to burning in the sun and developing skin cancer. While there are some forms of albinism which also include serious health problems, in the more common form weak eyes are the biggest medical issue. People with albinism look different in their colouring, but other than poor eyesight they are no different to anyone else in intelligence and feelings.

Unfortunately, because they look different, they are often victims of discrimination and even violence. Some even accuse them of witchcraft or of being bewitched. Murders of people with albinism for *muti* (potions that people believe have the power to improve a person's health or fate) are distressingly common – particularly in Tanzania – and have also occurred in Swaziland. The birth of a child with albinism can happen to anyone, as it is not possible to tell beforehand whether the parents are carriers of the gene that causes it. It has nothing to do with whether one parent was light-skinned and the other dark.

ALLERGIES

FOOD ALLERGY AND INTOLERANCE. It has become common to put down many childhood problems to allergies. There is some basis for this in that allergies can cause illness, particularly in young children that are more susceptible. However, it is also true that allergy is over-diagnosed and blamed for many problems it does not cause.

More than 20% of adults believe they are allergic to certain foods, yet the incidence of true allergy is less than 2%. Children have a higher incidence of around 7 to 10 per cent, although in some areas it is said to be around 20%. Allergies can cause much discomfort and ill health and their possibility should be considered in cases where the symptoms indicate it.

HEREDITARY INFLUENCES IN ALLERGIC RESPONSES. The tendency to develop allergies runs in families. If one parent is affected the likelihood that a child will be allergic is 40%; if both parents are allergic the child has a 70% to 80% chance of developing symptoms, although not necessarily to the same substance.

VARIOUS TYPES OF ALLERGIC RESPONSE ARE POSSIBLE. IgE is the antibody which is mainly responsible for allergies. IgE-mediated food allergy (immediate, or immediate plus an on-going reaction) occurs when the body's immune (defence) system 'fights' a normally harmless substance that has been eaten, touched or breathed in. It is usually a food protein that causes this type of allergic response, although the reaction is not necessarily experienced in the stomach but anywhere the blood carries the substance. During this defensive reaction the body releases histamine into the surrounding tissues. This results in swelling, spasm and the secretion of watery mucus. (The popular belief that milk 'makes mucus' is not true, but rather a false perception in allergic individuals, and others.)

Common causes of IgE-mediated food allergy in babies are: cow's milk, peanuts, egg white, fish, wheat and soya. More than 50% of children outgrow allergy to cow's milk, soya and egg by three. Peanut and seafood allergy may be lifelong and life-threatening.

Some food allergies are due to a response other than that of the immune system and are known as non-IgE-mediated and usually involve T-cells. These reactions are also commonly to cow and soya milk and eggs, as well as pork and food additives and many other substances. The symptoms are likely to be gastrointestinal, that is, in the stomach and digestive system. Skin allergies such as eczema are also possible.

THE FEAR OF FOOD ALLERGIES. Childhood allergies have become a major concern for parents in recent years. The emergence of serious reactions to foods such as peanuts, which can result in death through anaphylaxis – a severe, potentially life-threatening allergic reaction – is understandably frightening. To complicate matters, the earlier recommendation to delay the introduction of any food that may cause a reaction has not proven to be the answer. To the extent that doctors are seeing malnutrition in middle class children who are not getting the nutrients they need, because parents are cutting out so many food groups. It is also true to say that many more people believe they have allergies than are substantiated by tests.

Susceptibility to food allergies is largely genetic but there is also a difference in allergens in various countries. In Europe, the US and UK, cow's milk and eggs are the most common problems which are typically outgrown. Yet in Korea, wheat and buckwheat is known to cause life threatening allergies, while bird's nest soup, a delicacy in Singapore in the most common food allergen.

Generally however, 85% of food allergies are caused by the protein in cow's milk, egg, peanut, tree nuts, shellfish, wheat, sesame seed and soya.

The correct diagnosis of allergy requires a detailed history and testing by an expert allergy physician. Unfortunately there are a number of tests which are touted to be effective for which there is no scientific evidence. These include the Vega test, York hair follicle test, acupuncture and homeopathy, 'energy blockage' and home testing kits.

The American Academy of Paediatrics latest recommendation is in line with the European, in saying that there is no advantage in delaying the introduction of solid foods beyond 4-6 months in a bid to prevent allergies. In fact, it appears that the introduction of potentially allergenic foods before 16 weeks may decrease the chances of allergy. A comparison of peanut allergy in Israeli children who have a low incidence – and Jewish children in the UK who have a 10-fold higher incidence of peanut allergy – indicates that the early introduction of peanut products, and giving them more frequently, may be a better option. Another study showed that children introduced to cereals before six months had a lower prevalence of wheat allergy than children who started later than six months. Introducing eggs from 4-6 months was also associated with a lower prevalence of egg allergy. It was also found that infants were far less likely to have an adverse reaction to well cooked eggs, and extensively heated cow's milk. **Warning: Do not try and desensitise a child who has had a previous reaction to a food allergen. This must only be done under the close supervision of a medical allergy specialist.**

For those parents who have been fed the mantra to avoid the early introduction of potentially allergenic foods, it may be disconcerting. But the proof is in the pudding – avoidance or late introduction of eggs, wheat, peanut or milk – has not helped, as food allergies have escalated.

Intolerance is not the same as allergy. Lactose intolerance which is sensitivity to lactose in milk is uncommon in north European countries in which milk and cheese products are a regular part of the diet. In countries and communities in which milk after infancy is not a part of the diet, lactose intolerance is common. In many cases the affected person may not be aware that they are intolerant because they seldom drink milk or eat milk products such as cheese.

LACTOSE INTOLERANCE is caused by the permanent or temporary lack of the lactase enzyme needed to digest the natural sugar in milk, known as lactose. This also applies to breastmilk. (*See p. 127.*)

WHEAT ALLERGY is caused by intolerance to the gluten in wheat, and is usually outgrown. However, there is an inborn condition called Coeliac disease that is lifelong, and which needs a seriously modified diet for life. (*See p. 196.*) Allergy to wheat that begins in adulthood is rare.

PREVENTING ALLERGIES DURING PREGNANCY. If both parents and a previous child are allergic it is sometimes recommended that the mother exclude milk and dairy products from her diet during pregnancy. The evidence that this works is not conclusive however, and a restrictive diet in pregnancy is not recommended. There is some evidence that taking probiotics and fish-oil supplements may be helpful, while avoiding smoking and smoky environments is highly recommended.

PREVENTING ALLERGIES AFTER THE BIRTH. Until recently, it was recommended that the best way to prevent the development of allergy is to avoid sensitising foods or other substances. And in particular, that certain foods should not be introduced before six months of age because the infant digestive system is porous and sensitising substances could cross the gut barrier. These include cow's milk, wheat, eggs, peanuts and fish. Yet the cases of childhood allergy continued to increase.

This has led to a number of scientific studies in an effort to find the reasons for this escalation. The results have been counter to previous thinking, but the evidence is convincing.

Allergy to peanut affects 1 in 50 school age children in the USA, Canada, UK, Australia, the EU, and many others, with huge implications. Not only is it potentially life threatening, but great care must be taken by food producers to ensure that there is no 'contamination' by peanuts during the manufacture of any foods.

Peanut allergy is less common in children born in Israel where they eat peanut containing foods from early in life; whereas Jewish children, of similar ancestry living in the UK, have a far higher incidence of peanut allergy. This prompted a closer look, and the **Learning Early about Peanut Allergy** known as the **LEAP,** study was instigated, and the results after five years of testing were known in 2015.

Six hundred infants aged between 4 and 11 months of age, at high-risk for peanut allergy were randomly assigned to either avoid peanut or to regularly eat at least 6 grams of peanut protein per week. The avoidance and consumption regimens were continued until 5 years of age. The children who were introduced to peanut products and had continued eating them, had an 81% reduction in the subsequent development of peanut allergy, compared to those who avoided it.

At the time Anthony S. Fauci, M.D., Director, National Institute of Allergy and Infectious Diseases (NIAD), who in 2018 ranked as the 26th most highly cited researcher of all time, declared that *'For a study to show a benefit of this magnitude in the prevention of peanut allergy is without precedent. The results of which have the potential to transform how we approach food allergy prevention.'*

In August 2015 the following international associations issued a consensus communication endorsing the new recommendations and made policy statements supporting early, rather than delayed, peanut introduction when starting complementary foods in infancy.

They include the World Allergy Association; American Academy of Asthma, Allergy and immunology; American Academy of Paediatrics; the European Academy of Allergology and Clinical Immunology; European Society for Paediatric Gastroenterology,

Herpetology and Nutrition; Australasian Society of Clinical Immunology and Allergy; Canadian Society of Allergy and Clinical Immunology; European Academy of Allergy; Israel Association of Allergy and Clinical Immunology and the Japanese Society for Allergology; Academy of Allergy and Clinical Immunology; Society for Paediatric Research USA.

THESE ARE SOME OF THE COMMENTS THEY MADE:

'Do not delay the introduction of any specific solid food beyond six months. Later introduction of peanut, fish or egg does not prevent, and may even increase, the risk of developing food allergy.'

'There is no evidence that avoiding milk, egg, peanut butter or other potential allergens during pregnancy helps prevent allergy, while the risks of maternal under-nutrition and potential harm to the infant may be significant.'

'Breastfeeding for at least six months may be more protective than exclusive breastfeeding for six months.'

'Formula fed babies: Extensively hydrolyzed casein formula is likely to be more effective than partially hydrolyzed whey formula in preventing atopic dermatitis (skin allergies). There is no role for soy formula in allergy prevention.'

'Regular ingestion of newly introduced foods (several times a week and with a soft mashed consistency to prevent choking) is important to maintain tolerance.'

'Routine skin or specific IgE blood testing before first ingestion is discouraged, due to the high risk of potentially confusing false positive results.'

NOTE: It is essential to consult a paediatric medical allergist or your paediatrician for specific advice regarding your child.

There has also been evidence for a while now that early exposure to a potentially allergenic environment, such as that found on farms (a so-called 'dirty' environment), as well as animal dander (especially cat fur), moulds and the house dust mite (found in house dust), may help to activate the immune system in the prevention of allergies other than food. Cigarette smoking and smoky environments are a no-no.

BREASTFEEDING. Breastfeeding may help avoid – or at least delay – the onset of most allergies (food and other). Seven times more bottle-fed babies than breastfed babies develop allergies early on. Breast milk also contains Immunoglobulin A (IgA) which makes it more difficult for allergens to pass through the gut wall of the infant directly into the bloodstream.

SYMPTOMS OF ALLERGY TO COW'S MILK. The baby with allergy to cow's milk or cow's milk formula is restless, with recurrent vomiting, diarrhoea and colic-like cramping. The stools are watery and may contain small amounts of fresh blood. The baby fails to gain weight normally and may develop anaemia. If the diarrhoea and vomiting are severe the child may become dehydrated and this can have serious consequences. Because the baby is sensitive to the protein in the milk it is not absorbed, leaving the baby hungry and malnourished.

Colic also causes restlessness and crying, so it should not be assumed that the baby is allergic if there is no diarrhoea and if the baby gains weight. Other common symptoms of allergy to cow's milk are excessive sweating from the head, especially when the baby is feeding, watery discharge from the nose, and noisy breathing.

Young babies often sneeze and this should not be seen as a sign of allergy, but if the child's nose appears to be itchy and runny it could point to an allergy. The child who is allergic to cow's milk often has rashes and dry rough patches on the face, arms and legs, and eczema often develops later, sometimes followed by asthma.

TREATMENT OF COW'S MILK ALLERGY. Milk and milk products such as cheese must be avoided, while breastfeeding should be continued for as long as possible and solids introduced with care between four to six months.

Testing for cow's milk allergy can be done, preferably by an allergy specialist, but it is possible to make a diagnosis by giving the child with suspicious symptoms a substitute to cow's milk. If there is a marked improvement within 24 to 48 hours it is an almost certain indication that the problem was indeed cow's milk allergy. However, if there is not a quick improvement, the cause is probably not cow's milk allergy and there is no point in subjecting parents and child to the expense and inconvenience of providing a substitute to cow's milk. Some doctors prescribe soya milk formulas as a substitute to cow's milk, but they can produce unpleasant symptoms such as windiness and some children are allergic to it as well. If it is tolerated, however, it may be a better option than the more specialised milks which are very expensive. Soya milk is not recommended for cow's milk allergy not associated with IgE.

Goat's milk, or goat's milk formula is sometimes suggested for babies who are allergic to cow's milk. The differences between the protein in cow's milk and goat's milk are not substantial. Do not use fresh unpasteurised, goat's milk because of the danger of brucellosis, a serious long-term infection. Goat's milk formulas are not suitable for infants with cow's milk allergies.

A hypoallergenic formula in which the protein has been hydrolysed and acidified may be preferred. There are several forms of hypoallergenic milk formulas ranging from partially modified to extensively modified. An amino acid based formula may be needed for children who are highly allergic to cow's milk. It is extremely expensive, however, and it may not be halaal or kosher. (*See p. 159.*)

WHEN TO TRY COW'S MILK AGAIN. If cow's milk allergy has been proven it is necessary to cut it out of the child's diet in all forms for at least six months before trying it again. But it could take a year or two, perhaps longer, before the child outgrows the allergy. *Offer cow's milk again only under your doctor's supervision.*

TEMPORARY LACTOSE INTOLERANCE after a bout of severe diarrhoea can also mimic the effects of cow's milk allergy. In this case the child is not allergic to the protein in cow's milk, but sensitive to the lactose in milk because the enzyme lactase needed for its digestion has been diminished (*See pp. 162, 195 for lactose intolerance.*) Stools are watery, frothy and acidic. Tests for lactose intolerance must be done and if they are positive, try soya milk, which does not contain lactose. Cow's milk formula in which the lactose has been removed is also available.

ECZEMA AND ALLERGIC RASHES. Eczema or atopic (allergic) dermatitis is one of the earliest signs of allergy and may appear in the first few weeks of life as rough red patches on the child's face, or rashes and rough patches on the arms and legs. Later on the eczema develops in the creases of the arms and legs. Eczema may be caused by an allergic reaction to substances in the child's diet and is characterised by redness and small areas of blisters. There may be weeping when the blisters break and the area will be itchy. When this dries out the skin becomes scaly and rough. While the tendency to get eczema is inherited, it is not contagious and there is no danger of it spreading to other children.

Although its exact causes and mechanism are not precisely understood, its symptoms are probably the result of the release of histamine into the surrounding tissues. This causes redness, swelling and the secretion of fluid. It is important to remember that eczema-like symptoms may be caused by a number of conditions and your doctor will have to establish whether it is true eczema before prescribing treatment.

Some infants become sensitised to foods, including formula through their gastrointestinal tract which is normally protected by 'good' bacteria. There is some evidence that pre-biotic supplements, added to infant feeds may stimulate the growth of 'healthy' bacteria in the digestive tract and thus prevent, or at least improve eczema. Harsh soaps, chemicals, heat, humidity, stress, house dust-mites, animal dander (hair) and inhalant allergens such as grass and other pollens are also potential causes, as is atmospheric pollution.

IDENTIFICATION AND TREATMENT OF ECZEMA. Nappy rashes and other forms of dermatitis (skin problems) should not be confused with eczema, which does not commonly occur in the nappy area. The child with eczema is likely to be sensitive to extremes of temperature and should never be overdressed since sweating irritates the condition. Use baby clothes and blankets of pure cotton or synthetic materials rather than wool, and use only pure soap (not the usual household soap powders) for washing the baby's clothes and linen. Wash new clothes before use.

Soaps, creams and lotions should be used with caution since they may contain potential allergens such as perfumes, lanolin or peanut oil. It is worth remembering that ointments and creams for nappy rash may themselves contain substances that could irritate the child's skin, even if not used on the eczema itself.

Emulsifying ointments that contain a mixture of paraffin oils may be recommended, or a mild corticosteroid cream or one of the non-steroidal creams to relieve the itchiness and rash. **ONLY USE PRODUCTS PRESCRIBED BY YOUR MEDICAL ADVISOR.** (If possible, eczema is best treated by an allergy specialist.) Oral antihistamines are sometimes used at night, as they can make the child drowsy and relieve the itchiness.

Because eczema is so itchy the baby is likely to be restless and irritable, making life difficult for everyone. Understanding the child's distress and inability to stop scratching is important to prevent a vicious cycle of recriminations and frustration. Do not cover the child's hands with mittens to stop her scratching but keep her nails clean and short to prevent infection, although it might help at night. Infected eczema can be serious and needs medical treatment. (*See p. 365.*) The parents of a child with eczema need a lot of support from each other as well as their doctor. There is some consolation in the fact that the condition improves in time and waxes and wanes of its own accord so that there are periods of relief, even if only temporary. Most children grow out of it by their teens. Many children with eczema also develop other allergic conditions such as asthma and hay fever.

Causes. Harsh soaps, chemicals, heat, humidity, stress, inhalant allergens such as grass and other pollens, the house-dust mite, animal dander from pets, and foods including eggs, wheat, peanuts, soya and cow's milk are common culprits. In babies, diet is one of the main causes of eczema and it is worth trying to establish if the condition improves when certain foodstuffs are eliminated. **AN ALLERGY SPECIALIST SHOULD BE CONSULTED SO THAT RELIABLE TESTS CAN BE DONE.** Cow's milk should be the first to go and preferably milk in which the protein has been hydrolysed to the point at which it is no longer allergenic should be substituted. Other possible allergens such as orange juice, wheat (in cereal or baby foods) and even vitamin supplements (if they contain colouring and flavouring) should be eliminated. It takes a few days before any improvement is noticed, so do not reintroduce the food too soon in the belief that it is harmless. Egg white is a common cause of allergic reaction and you should remember that it is used in cakes, ice-cream, baby foods (read labels) and other foodstuffs.

Handling and treatment. Wash your baby with an allergy-tested no-soap wash. Some doctors recommend using an emulsifying ointment in the bath water. Dissolve one or two tablespoons of the ointment in a litre of boiling water and mix into the bath water, which should be tepid (blood heat).

Any other creams and lotions should be used with caution since they may contain potential allergens such as lanolin or peanut oil. It is worth remembering that ointments and creams for nappy rash may themselves contain substances that could irritate the child's skin even if not used on the eczema itself. Only use allergy-tested products.

The main way to treat eczema in infants is to use an effective emulsifying cream or moisturiser every day, as advised by your doctor. Your doctor may prescribe a *mild* corticosteroid cream or one of the newer non-steroidal creams to relieve the itchiness and rash, if necessary. Use only as prescribed and as soon as a flare-up appears. If used correctly for up to a week at a time the skin should clear without problems. Thereafter a moisturising cream recommended by your doctor should be applied. Oral antihistamines are sometimes useful at night as they can make the child drowsy and relieve the itchiness.

If the eczema is infected an antibiotic may be needed. A high temperature with blisters and weeping sores and enlarged lymph nodes can be a sign of herpes simplex infection and this is potentially serious. Keep anyone with cold sores from having close contact with your child. Bacterial infection is more common, especially with organisms known as streptococcus ('strep') and staphylococcus ('staph'). Any medication for eczema should only be used under a doctor's supervision.

Some claims have been made for the use of gamma-linolenic acid products (evening primrose oil, or borage seed oil) for eczema. Although some patients do see an improvement the results are not conclusive.

Other skin rashes in infancy that have not been diagnosed as eczema and are not associated with a specific illness such as chickenpox may be allergic. As a general rule, if there is no temperature and the rash itches but does not change much or develop into a specific disease, it is likely to be caused by something the child comes into contact with, breathes or eats. Pin-pointing the offending substance is not easy, since there may be two or more items that can precipitate the rash. However, it is wise to try and eliminate the most likely causes through medical testing.

CONTACT DERMATITIS. Just lying with her cheek against her mother's clothes if they have been washed with certain washing powders can sometimes cause a rash on a baby's face. Lotions, shampoos, soaps, ointments such as those used for nappy rash, oils, and even petroleum jelly can cause a rash. Watch for a reaction so that you can identify the offending substance. Occasionally a child will develop a rash after using antiseptic soap and then going into the sun. Antiseptic soap should be avoided, unless prescribed.

URTICARIA (nettle rash or hives). Urticaria is characterised by itchy, pale raised swellings with red edges due to histamine release in the skin. These symptoms usually disappear within 48 hours without treatment, although scratching may lead to infection, and you will need medical advice.

Common causes of urticaria are:

- Reaction to medicines such as aspirin, penicillin or almost any other drug.
- Internal parasites such as round worms and whipworm.
- Bites caused by fleas, or bee stings.
- Food such as cow's milk, chocolate, egg white, strawberries, nuts, mushrooms, pork, fish, shellfish, food additives, preservatives and colourants.
- Substances that are breathed in like house dust, sprays, feathers, cat fur (dander) or dog or horse hair.
- Extreme temperature changes during exposure to heat, sunlight or cold water.

If a cause can be established, elimination should solve the problem. However, often no cause for the urticaria is found and antihistamines may be needed if the symptoms and itching are severe. The use of calamine lotion containing an antihistamine dabbed on the swelling may help reduce the itching. **CONSULT YOUR MEDICAL ADVISOR AS IT IS NOT GENERALLY USED BEFORE THE AGE OF 2 YEARS.**

PAPULAR URTICARIA (with extreme itchiness and weeping of the skin) is often caused by flea bites. Treating the symptoms with calamine lotion containing an antihistamine helps relieve the itchiness, if the child in older than 2, while thiamine (vitamin B_1) taken orally is said to make the skin bitter, with the result that the fleas don't bite. Garlic in the diet also discourages fleabites.

ANAPHYLAXIS. This is the most severe allergic reaction. It can be a reaction to drugs, especially antibiotics such as penicillin, and insect bites and stings are also common causes. Foods can also result in a severe reaction, in particular shellfish; while peanuts and sesame seeds have become a problem recently. The child goes into shock and breathing may stop within minutes. This is an emergency and immediate treatment is essential. After one such episode a Medic-Alert disc should be worn and emergency medication carried at all times.

BEE STINGS. Severe reactions to bee stings usually develop only after the person has been stung several times and sensitivity has been built up. If your child shows signs of a severe allergic reaction that includes swelling of the face or mouth, noisy or difficulty in breathing or swallowing, get medical help immediately. A doctor may undertake a desensitisation procedure in severe cases, and you may have to keep a kit that contains adrenalin or other emergency medication for use in any future emergency.

ASTHMA. Asthma in childhood is often missed during examination, and it is always worth considering in cases where the child coughs even if there is no wheezing. The cough of asthma most often comes at night, but it also occurs at dawn, after mild physical exertion, during a change in season or weather, after contact with an allergen like the house-dust mite, sulphur dioxide or cigarette smoke, and often after viral chest infections. *Children whose symptoms are relieved by a bronchodilator can be assumed to have asthma.*

The child with asthma experiences recurrent episodes of tightness in the chest, difficulty in breathing, and coughing or wheezing during an attack because the smooth muscle of the airways of the lungs goes into spasm and swells. The membrane lining the airways becomes swollen and inflamed. Thick, sticky mucus is released which blocks the bronchial tubes. This causes coughing and makes it difficult to breathe air out. Note that wheezing does not always accompany asthma, and wheezing can have a number of other causes. Ninety-five per cent of children who suffer from asthma also have allergies. More boys than girls are affected and most children with asthma have eczema at some time. It is not clear which children will outgrow asthma but those who require only intermittent treatment are likely to outgrow it by their teens.

Of those who respond to treatment such as montelukast (Singulair), or inhaled corticosteroids and bronchodilators, more than half are better by their teens. Interestingly, girls are more likely to continue to need steroid therapy into adulthood to control their symptoms. Although asthma can appear at any time, if wheezing starts before the age of two the chances of the child out-growing it are less than if it starts later. It is a potentially serious condition but regular treatment can prevent attacks and the lungs from becoming weakened. Asthmatic children should grow and develop normally, play sport and attend school with little or no disruption. **The aim of modern treatment is to provide children with asthma a completely normal and good quality of life.**

Management. The house-dust mite is an extremely common trigger of asthma and strict measures are needed to keep it under control. (*See house-dust mites p. 429*) Common grass pollens and fungal spores are more difficult to avoid, and can cause seasonal flare-ups. Pets, especially cats, should be kept out of the asthmatic's room. Asthma sufferers should not be exposed to cigarette smoke or smoke from fires. When foods, which commonly provoke allergies, such as egg, milk, soya, wheat, fish, tree nuts, peanuts and shellfish are identified, they should be avoided. Sulphur dioxide and other sulphites used as preservatives in some cold drinks, dried fruit and vegetables cause a reaction in 20% of young asthmatics. Tartrazine, the yellow food colourant, is often thought of as an asthma trigger, but this has not been shown.

In most cases asthma attacks are mild, respond to simple treatment and never develop into anything serious enough to require hospitalisation. Even if attacks are mild and infrequent it is important that they be treated so that the lungs are not damaged.

When laughing or crying triggers an attack it is probably due to the sudden inhalation of cold or dry air rather than the emotion itself. Exercise can produce narrowing of the airways and precipitate an attack. However, suitable treatment will allow a child to participate in sport and many great athletes have been asthmatics. Soccer star David Beckham is an example of someone with asthma reaching the top of his sporting field. UK long-distance and marathon runner Paula Radcliffe still defies the odds by winning world championships, and swimmer Mark Spitz won nine Olympic Gold medals! Swimming is an excellent form of exercise for asthmatics. They don't come bigger or tougher than multi-capped Springbok rugby player Schalk Burger, who is also an asthmatic.

Treatment. There are a number of excellent drugs without side effects, which – if correctly used – can control asthma. These include bronchodilators (beta2-antagonists), possibly combined with an anti-cholinergic drug, which relieve symptoms at once. Montelukast is a new non-steroidal asthma treatment. Steroid drugs can control more severe asthma and early treatment is recommended. It is *not true* that asthma inhalers are harmful to the heart, and used properly are an excellent remedy. Asthma is best handled by a medical specialist in the field who will prescribe suitable treatment.

Do NOT use patent over-the-counter 'cures' as they often contain substances which can be harmful. Antibiotics, cough syrups, breathing exercises, mucus-dissolving medicines and ionisers are not effective in treating asthma.

ALLERGIC RHINITIS (HAY FEVER). In some babies allergic rhinitis is triggered by a food allergy, most often cow's milk, but egg white, wheat, peanuts and soya are also culprits. Because of the runny nose it is easy to see the problem as a hard-to-get-rid-of cold. Removal of the trigger food from the diet should 'cure the cold'. The older child with any nasal allergy usually has dark rings and puffiness under the eyes making her look as though she lacks sleep. Creases in the lower eyelid, from the inner corner towards the nose, are common in severe cases, and a white line across the top of the nose, known as the 'allergic crease', are signals that the child is allergic. This whitish line does not tan and is caused by the child continually pushing up her nose because it itches, in a movement known as the 'allergic salute'. Mouth breathing is common due to swelling of the mucus membrane of the nose and this can result in a high arched palate and subsequent malocclusion (displacement) of the teeth. Symptoms are seasonal

LET'S GET RID OF THE KIDS. THE ANIMALS ARE ALLERGIC TO THEM

or year-round sneezing, and itching of the nose with a watery discharge. Hours later the nose seems to be blocked and the eyes water and itch.

Up to 20% of all children have some degree of allergic rhinitis and many of the recurrent 'colds' reported in toddlers are in fact allergic reactions.

When allergic rhinitis or hay fever is year-round, the symptoms are less obvious. The eyes may not become red and the nose may not be itchy but there may be a headache, pain in the sinus cavities under the eyes, with a dry cough owing to the nasal secretions dripping into the back of the throat. Seasonal rhinitis (hay fever) has more noticeable symptoms of sneezing, itchiness and nasal discharge.

Common causes of allergic rhinitis are grass and other pollens (in seasonal rhinitis) and house-dust mites, moulds, particularly in damp homes and on rotting kelp (seaweed) that are blown about when dry. Sudden changes of temperature, cigarette smoke, food allergens, and the prolonged use of nose drops which require larger and larger doses to produce an effect can be a problem in perennial rhinitis. As is the case with all allergies, the best treatment is to remove the cause if it can be found. In low-lying, damp areas house-dust mites are a particular offender and every effort should be made to keep them to a minimum, particularly when the child suffers from hay fever or asthma.

Treatment. There are a number of very effective treatments including antihistamines that do not sedate, nasal sprays, and immunotherapy in which desensitisation against the allergen is done. Allergy treatment is a highly specialised area and it should be undertaken by an expert in this field.

HOUSE-DUST MITES. The house-dust mite is a tiny organism, invisible to the naked eye that is found in all households although it does not like high-lying, dry areas like the Karoo or semi-desert areas. It lives on human skin which is continually being shed, and likes dark, humid places like mattresses and dusty book-shelves. The droppings of the mite are the main cause of their allergenicity.

How to limit the house-dust mite population/infestation and allergy producing moulds. Dust collectors such as carpets, fluffy toys, artificial flowers and dried flowers should go. No feather pillows, eiderdowns, feather flowers or birds should be kept. The child's room should be kept as simple as possible with an easily washable, smooth bedspread; no bookshelves; toys should be wood, not wool or fabric-covered (soft toys are sometimes filled with cat fur making them doubly allergenic). Curtains should be washable, and clothes should be kept in a closed cupboard. Humidity should be kept low by using an oil heater if the room or house needs to be heated.

The floor should preferably be tiled or linoleum-covered or wood laminate so that it can be wiped down. If not, it should be vacuumed daily. Wallpaper and wood panelling can harbour mould. Humidifiers and steamers will promote the growth of mould. The mattress should be covered with a special impermeable synthetic fabric that helps keep the house-dust mite and mould growth down. It should be aired, wiped down and turned as often as possible – at least once a week. Once a month the room should be emptied and cleaned with a damp cloth, wiping all walls, woodwork, the floor and cupboards, indeed every surface that it is possible to reach.

Vacuum cleaners should have a HEPA filter for mite infestation. Anti-allergy protective bedding covers made from a special fabric that 'breathes' create a barrier against allergens like the house-dust mite. Before purchasing, speak to your doctor about sprays that claim to be safe for use in the air and on cots, carpets and beds against the house-dust mite, as few have been tested in clinical trials.

POLLEN-INDUCED HAY FEVER. The child should not play in grass during the pollen season and stay indoors while it is being cut. She should always sleep with her windows closed. Desensitisation by injecting extracts of grass pollen is effective if the cause of the allergy is known, but it is not recommended for children under six. Skin tests for sensitivity can help pin-point allergens. There are also a number of very effective new inhalants for allergic rhinitis. Desensitisation to mites and pollens using an oral solution known as SLIT (sublingual immunotherapy) is highly effective in treating allergic rhinitis.

NASAL POLYPS. These are soft and grape-like and may be found in the nasal cavity or the sinuses. Their significance in allergies is not clearly defined but children who have them tend to be mouth breathers and cough at night owing to the mucus that drips into the throat. Fortunately, nasal polyps are rare in children. Discuss all medication with your medical advisor.

ANAEMIA

IRON-DEFICIENCY ANAEMIA. This is the most common form of anaemia affecting children and babies born prematurely in particular. Iron is needed to produce haemoglobin, the pigment in the red blood cells that carry oxygen to all parts of the body for growth and proper functioning. Iron-deficiency anaemia is an extremely common condition in children world-wide and is often undiagnosed.

SYMPTOMS. One of the reasons for anaemia being missed is that the symptoms are not easily detected. In mild cases there may be nothing more obvious other than a little paleness (pull down the lower eyelid to see if the membrane is pale). Long-term iron-deficiency anaemia can result in poor mental development and functioning, susceptibility to infection, irritability and lack of energy. In severe cases there could be shortness of breath, swelling of the hands and feet and an increased heart rate, with resulting poor growth and development. It is therefore an important area of concern.

A child may be lacking in iron without actually being anaemic. The symptoms of iron deficiency include poor appetite, irritability, susceptibility to infection, particularly ear infections, and delayed development. Many behaviour and feeding problems, including lack of appetite, are part of the vicious cycle of poor eating habits and resulting iron deficiency. It is important therefore not to assume that a child whose diet lacks iron will still remain healthy.

PICA. Sometimes anaemic children will eat strange substances like sand, chalk, dog biscuits, dirt or paint flakes (very dangerous if it is lead-based) because they are anaemic.

CAUSES. There are various forms of anaemia. It can be caused by blood loss through internal or external bleeding. Haemolytic anaemia is a condition in which red blood cells are easily destroyed for various reasons. A severe inherited disorder called sickle-cell anaemia is a condition which mainly affects people of African-American origin. And, most commonly, anaemia is caused through a lack of iron or folic acid. Your doctor must identify the type before any treatment is started or you could mask serious conditions.

Iron-deficiency anaemia, which is the most common form, can result when children are fed fresh cow's milk early on. Cow's milk lacks iron and can also irritate the gut lining causing bleeding. It is recommended that a formula enriched with iron and vitamins be used, preferably until the child is a year old or at least until the child has a good mixed diet.

Iron is stored in the baby's body before birth and this lasts for the first three or four months. Babies born prematurely lack these iron stores and are more vulnerable to iron-deficiency anaemia. They normally receive iron supplements and an iron-enriched formula. Breastmilk has small amounts of iron but it is well absorbed. Iron-rich foods such as fortified cereal should be started from four months and meat added by at least six months to ensure that dietary iron intake is good. Some doctors recommend iron supplements for all babies. Do not use them unless prescribed.

If your child does not eat well, in particular red meat and green leafy vegetables, you should consider taking her for a haemoglobin test to establish her iron status. It is easily done in your doctor's rooms.

IRON IN THE DIET. The best source of iron is red meat (haem iron), 25% of which is absorbed by the body, whereas only 10% of iron from plant sources (non-haem iron) is absorbed.

Liver is high in iron as are other forms of red meat. Chicken and fish have lesser amounts. Plant sources include iron-enriched breakfast cereals and green leafy vegetables like broccoli and parsley. Spinach, the food that gave Popeye his strength, got its reputation in error when a scientist put the decimal point in the wrong place giving spinach ten times more iron than it has in fact!

Other plant sources include whole-wheat bread, enriched white bread, lentils and beans, oats, nuts, dried fruit, in particular apricots, and potatoes. Egg yolk has good amounts of iron but it is not very well absorbed due to the fat content. When taken at the same meal vitamin C increases the absorption of iron from plant sources. Serve fruit juice or fruits rich in vitamin C with meals. High levels are found in oranges, strawberries, kiwi fruit and blackcurrants.

NOTE: The tannin in Ceylon tea inhibits the absorption of iron. Check labels of herbal teas. Rooibos has low tannin. For more information about iron in the diet (*See p. 171.*). If an iron preparation is prescribed do not give it with milk as the calcium in milk hinders absorption. Raising a child on a vegetarian or vegan diet requires a sound knowledge of the supplements needed to safeguard them from developing iron-deficiency anaemia.

WARNING: Iron preparations are extremely poisonous in excess. Keep all medicines away from children. Iron preparations can stain teeth and stools black. Iron supplements should only be taken if prescribed by your paediatrician.

ANXIETY AND OTHER PSYCHOPATHOLOGICAL CONDITIONS

CHILDHOOD LOST. It is estimated that up to 20% of children worldwide suffer from some form of psychological or emotional disorder, many of them undiagnosed and untreated. In children, the symptoms of these disorders are easy to misdiagnose because the child may complain of recurrent stomachaches or other physical symptoms, rather than show clear-cut anxiety or other problems. It is thought that psychiatric conditions which originate in childhood may be precursors to adult problems if they are not treated.

ANXIETY DISORDERS are the most common non-physical illnesses in childhood and adolescence, robbing the young of the freedom to be joyful. Possibly the first time parents become aware that their child is capable of anxious feelings is during separation anxiety, which typically occurs at around eight months. Babies cry when their mother or other primary caregiver leaves the room. They may also become fearful of strangers. The common response of parents is that the child has been 'spoiled' by being given too much attention. In reality, this fear is normal, and it is a sign of good development in that the child is slowly becoming aware of being a separate entity. Later on, kindergarten children may have a fear of the dark or monsters, people in fancy dress or animals, but this normally passes with reassurance and time.

Anxiety in some children may be missed because they are compliant and withdrawn, and always wanting to please, although they have high levels of internalised tension. They may have frequent nightmares, periods of weepiness, stomachaches, bed-wetting and other psychosomatic symptoms of stress. (*See p. 326, 335*). Anxiety disorders are more common in girls.

THE TIE THAT BINDS. True separation anxiety disorders (SAD) in children can sometimes be related to parents who also have an anxiety or depressive disorder. These children show excessive fear of being without the parent, and are often fearful of letting them out of their sight in case something happens to the parent or themselves. Sometimes this follows a domestic trauma such as divorce, death or violent crime.

Stressful situations such as these understandably cause feelings of anxiety, but with time and support, the child should return to normal. Family or individual cognitive-behaviour therapy is often very effective. There is some evidence that faulty fear-circuit functioning in the brain is a factor in true anxiety disorder.

There are also children, who through various scenarios discover that they are able to exert huge power over their parents through their anxiety and separation fears, with negative results all round. (*See Tyrannical children p. 510.*) However, these are not the children of whom we are speaking, but others who have a real pathology.

During the Cold War between the USSR and the USA in the 1960s many US children showed severe anxiety symptoms due to the prevalent fear of nuclear war. School children did drills in how to get to shelters and parents and television frequently mentioned the danger. Today, many children experience violent crime either directly or through the media and parental talk. This has resulted in a reported surge in anxiety symptoms in South African children. We all need to be aware of how our own fears are expressed in the presence of children.

SOCIAL PHOBIA. In recent times, shyness has been labelled as 'social phobia' or 'social inhibition' and has been listed as a mental illness. It is true that some children and adults are painfully shy, while others blush or become embarrassed easily. (See *the shy child p. 284.*) There are also children who do not 'join in' readily in play situations, and seem to prefer to observe from the perimeter of the action. This can be a sign of a problem, but it may just be the child's nature to observe rather than participate actively. Treat with caution and respect – you may have a thinker – rather than an indiscriminate doer. (*See Slow to warm up children p. 524.*)

True social phobia based on extreme anxiety can be a serious problem however. One of the most debilitating symptoms is mutism, in which the child is able to speak, but does not to do so except in circumstances in which they are not afraid.

SELECTIVE MUTISM. This condition was previously called *elective* mutism, which gave the impression that the child chose not to speak. This is not the case however – the child does not *choose* not to speak – she is actually paralysed by fear of speaking, even though she is able to. This may be with strangers, or at school, or even with other children. Yet they are perfectly able to talk to their parents or others in a 'safe' environment.

SYMPTOMS. Although it is common for children to cry when they start at kindergarten or school, they soon get over it, and are happy for the parents to leave. Others may not be outgoing at first but it changes, usually when they make a friend or a few weeks have passed. In cases of selective mutism, however, it does not pass even after months or years, and the child remains 'frozen' when in situations that require a response, even to a simple 'how are you?'. Clearly this is a problem that has a negative impact on schooling and socialisation. It is not effective to try and 'cure' the child by getting cross with her or demanding she speak. It is like expecting someone who is afraid of heights to do rock climbing. Cognitive behaviour therapy (CBT) can be helpful, while in rare extreme cases medication such as selective serotonin reuptake inhibitors (SSRI) may be indicated. It is more common in girls.

RITUALS WITHOUT MEANING. Obsessive-compulsive disorder might require rituals like obsessive hand washing or saying the same words or counting, or arranging before being able to move on to doing something. Or the child experiences irrational but compulsive thoughts. Children often know that these obsessions do not make sense and may hide them from their parents.

Of course, children have always played games that touch on the outskirts of these behaviours such as not stepping on the cracks in the pavement, and it is fair to say that many of these 'habitual rituals' are transient in children. It is when normal tasks cannot be done *without* the ritual that it becomes a problem.

There is some evidence of a biological basis for the disorder in that it may be an after-effect of a streptococcal infection. Faulty circuits in the brain have been shown occasionally and there is an inherited tendency to the disorder. Treatment is likely to be based on a combination of medication and cognitive behavioural therapy, which may need to be long-term. Some children report a 'trigger' for their behaviours such as seeing a door they feel they have to go through repeatedly. They may improve with behaviour desensitisation in which they are exposed to the trigger and taught how to overcome the compulsion. Parents may need to be deterred from playing a part in reinforcing the compulsion by aiding the child in the ritual in the belief that this will ease the problem. (*See Tourette's p.502*).

FEARS AND PHOBIAS. Children who experience feelings of panic, for example if they see a spider, or have to get into a lift, or water, or fear loud sounds, experience real distress when confronted with the prospect of having to deal with the stressor. They will cry, scream, run away or freeze; they are not aware that their fear is unreasonable, and they need help.

Treatments shown to be effective include: cognitive behavioural therapy; modelling, in which the child is shown someone else happily doing what they fear, and gradually encouraging the child to do the same; as well as reinforced exposure in which the child is gradually encouraged and rewarded. It is particularly effective when parents are involved in the treatment. Note that panic is not the same as having an aversion to something. A woman, who as a child discovered that her soft-boiled egg was bloody inside, will not eat eggs at all. But this is an aversion, not a phobia: she does not run screaming at the sight of an egg.

POST-TRAUMATIC STRESS DISORDER. It is shameful that children are still so often exposed to violence, both domestic and external. Rape, war, crime, accidents, natural disasters do not draw the line at the young. Children may show symptoms such as nightmares, re-enacting the event in play and drawings, sleep disorders, distress at anything that reminds them of the event, withdrawal, startling easily and a watchful wariness that is inappropriate for their age. Possibly the most common feature is regression. The child reverts to behaviours that are more appropriate in a much younger child.

Older children may relive the event and show lack of interest in activities they enjoyed previously. They are likely to be anxious, irritable, angry, depressed and even suicidal. Their experience brings home an awareness of their own mortality, and that of loved ones. It is understandable that stressful events have emotional consequences. In order for them to be overcome, sensitive handling is needed. This is often not available to children for they are the unrecognised victims in many cases. Children may be reluctant to talk to their parents for fear of upsetting them, and others may feel it is not polite to ask as this will upset the victim. This may be seen as rejection on the part of the victim. We need to show understanding and give effective treatment. Treatment that involves reliving the event has become controversial, although older children may be grateful for the opportunity to talk about their feelings, if not the facts about the experience. Reactions amongst children vary with some apparently coping well. A supportive family is invaluable; while trauma-focused cognitive behavioural therapy has been shown to be useful.

DEPRESSION. It is almost unthinkable that young and even preschool children could possibly be affected by depression, and the last thing that should happen is that unnecessary interventions and medication is prescribed. Yet depression does occur even in the very young and they need help. Although traumatic events can result in depression, this kind of situational depression is usually overcome with time, empathy and good support. Anxiety and depression often go together and this is both genetic and environmental; children imitate their parents and if they suffer from depression, children may learn to deal with life events in this way too. It is also a fact that children, in circumstances where there is parental drug or alcohol abuse, criminal behaviour or violence, are understandably likely to be depressed and anxious. Parents who have a warm and involved relationship with the child, have clear behaviour expectations, spend time with their child and engage in family home and leisure activities are a protective factor. Those with ADHD (Attention Deficit Hyperactivity Disorder) may become depressed due to rejection as a result of their behaviour.

SYMPTOMS. Children who are depressed have a lack of interest in activities that normally bring pleasure. They may also experience anxiety. Depressed people have no sunshine in their lives, only various degrees of cloud.

What you should watch for are changes that make you uncomfortable and concerned about your child, especially if there is a family history of depression. For example, pervasive sadness that does not lift, irritability, increased or decreased sleep, changes in appetite and a lack of interest in play need closer examination.

TREATMENT. In cases where there is a chemical malfunction in the brain with low serotonin and norepinephrine levels that affect mood, appetite and sleep, medication may be needed. Various therapies such as cognitive-behaviour therapy can have a positive effect when combined with the correct medication.

LET THEM TELL THEIR STORY. Since young children's behaviour is often unpredictable and evolves according to developmental stages, as well as sometimes being a mystery to parents anyway, it is unwise to ascribe random behaviours to psychological problems. However, you should not shrug everything off as 'just a stage'.

If you are concerned about your child's behaviour in any respect, take the time to observe him or her at play. Set aside at least an hour in a quiet place where you will not be disturbed and let your child play with his or her choice of toys. Sit on the floor or low chair, and interact only when invited to, letting the child lead the play. In this safe setting it is often remarkable what is revealed through play. Do not be disapproving or comment even if a doll gets beaten or a car smashed. Suppressed fear and anger often come to the surface, and incidents of abuse may be enacted. What you see will help inform your discussions with a therapist.

SEEKING TREATMENT. Unfortunately there is still some stigma attached to mental illness, even though it is no different to having a broken leg. In both, timely and suitable treatment will usually fix the problem. Get advice from a developmental paediatrician, psychologist and or a child psychiatrist. The good news is that two thirds of children with anxiety or similar disorders will improve over time. This does not mean you should ignore it in the hope that it gets better. Rather seek advice. With suitable treatment, those who do not improve spontaneously can become much happier and better functioning. Psychological problems are not a sign of 'weak character'.

NOTE: Treatment and medications used for child psychiatric problems and other medical conditions must be prescribed by and carefully supervised on an individual basis by a suitably qualified professional.

AUTISM SPECTRUM AND OTHER PERVASIVE DEVELOPMENTAL DISORDERS

THE APPARENT EPIDEMIC OF AUTISM. Note that autism (Autistic Spectrum Disorders), Asperger's syndrome and pervasive developmental disorder often have overlapping symptoms, with Asperger's generally considered as being the mildest form. Autism (and the conditions clustered under the name pervasive developmental disorder or PDD) have become a common area of concern for parents today. Not too long ago, the fear that their child may be autistic was virtually unheard of even amongst informed parents. These days it is as much a secret fear of sophisticated parents as HIV may be in the minds of those most likely to be affected.

Autism diagnosis has increased enormously worldwide to the extent that it is postulated that 1:150 children are affected, although some experts doubt this figure. Is autism growing, or showing? The high numbers may be due to a greater awareness and therefore more diagnosis or a broader definition of 'autism'. It might also be true to say that until the condition was given a name in 1943, it existed but was hidden in dark places. It could even be ascribed to the fact that today children on the autism spectrum in the United States and other developed countries rightly have access to good social services, grants and special schools.

ASPERGER'S SYNDROME. First described by an Austrian paediatrician, Dr Hans Asperger, in 1944, it was only officially included in text books fifty years later. Asperger's is no longer regarded as a separate entity.

CHARACTERISTICS OF ASPERGER'S SYNDROME. The differences between children who have Asperger's syndrome and those who are developing normally may not be obvious at first. Children with Asperger's often talk early and well, and are usually bright; thus their unusual behaviour may not be readily picked up or seen as a problem. It is in their social behaviour that there may be a clue, especially as they get older. Sensory overload is a big issue in that they may be highly sensitive to certain lights, sounds, smells, tastes and touching; causing them to become agitated. They are able to speak well, but often talk in a flat expressionless monotone, standing too close and not interacting with any sensitivity to the feelings of others. They get stuck on a subject that interests them and talk about its minutiae endlessly and without expression. They are prone to temper tantrums, which may be violent as they get older, and are socially isolated although they would like to have friends. They are inclined to walk 'funny' and are generally physically clumsy. In some respects their behaviour may be called 'nerdish' in that they don't seem to care how they look, sound or interact.

If they are at the high end of functioning, they may simply fall into the category of what most people think of as 'weird' or eccentric or even as geniuses. Many brilliant or creative people such as the composers Wolfgang Amadeus Mozart, Erik Satie and Béla Bártok, as well as the artists Andy Warhol and Vincent van Gogh may have had Asperger's syndrome. Their awkward social manner and problematic personalities were regarded simply as 'part of their genius'.

Sadly, without the compensation of exceptional talents society does not readily accept these personality types, with resultant unhappiness and unfulfilled hopes. Children diagnosed under the various labels of pervasive developmental disorder need help. They need training in developing good communication, positive habits, and adequate social skills. Dr Temple Grandin, an autism advocate and animal science professor at Colorado University, who has Asperger's herself, emphasises that good, old-fashioned manners are an excellent starting point to better socialisation. Teach children to take turns, in speaking and playing, and encourage friendships with others with the same interests, she says. For parents who worry how their children will be treated when they are no longer there, good manners at least evoke a positive response in most people. Although it seems simplistic, good manners oil the wheels of social interaction, and make things easier for those with social or physical deficits.

CAUSES AND TREATMENT. There is no medical drug treatment as such for Asperger's syndrome and a definite cause has not been found, although certain aspects may be treated by medication. There are many theories, from defective chromosomes to pollutants in the diet and mercury previously found in vaccinations. Unfortunately the only credible cause at this time is gene patterns and faulty brain development. It would be a good thing if a man-made cause was found because we could then eliminate it but extensive research has not found credible proof. (*See p. 463.*)

High-functioning people with Asperger's syndrome are usually able to be well-educated and live independent lives.

AUTISM. It is a sad reflection on medical services worldwide that the parents of an autistic child often know that something is wrong, yet they are sent from pillar to post, sometimes for years, before they get a diagnosis and help.

CHARACTERISTICS OF CHILDREN WITH AUTISM. 'Classic' autism is also known as 'Kanner' autism, after the Austrian-born doctor who first described it, Dr Leo Kanner (pronounced 'conner'). The autistic child does not make eye contact, and does not enjoy the usual cuddling interactions with parents. They may not learn to speak, or they simply repeat a sound without understanding, or any acquired language may be lost by the age of two or three. Games babies love like peek-a-boo seem to have no meaning, and pointing at something does not bring a reaction.

Later on they may develop repetitive actions known as *stimming*, such as hand flapping, rocking,or lining things up. These repetitive actions appear to comfort the child when stressed. They have unusual compulsions. It is as though their brain is scrambled, and the senses are over-loaded. The may experience soft sounds as overwhelmingly loud, causing them to withdraw defensively into behaviours that 'deflect' this assault. A significant proportion develop epilepsy.

Possibly the biggest social problem is their seeming lack of understanding that people have feelings and how to interact with them. For those who love them the apparent rejection of affection that is given can be heartbreaking. Autistic children seem to inhabit a world of their own.

Recently a lot of attention has been focused on the importance of emotional IQ as a component value of intellectual IQ. It is incredible that it has taken us so long to 'discover' this aspect of human functioning. Many so-called normal people have very low emotional intelligence levels, yet they are accepted because they do not have the obvious mannerisms and extreme emotional isolation of the autistic person.

CAUSES AND TREATMENT. Autism is four times more common in boys, and although there may be earlier signs it often becomes apparent only at around eighteen months, when speech that has been acquired is lost. This is one of the reasons why it has become associated with the MMR vaccine which is given at that time. In Yokohama, Japan, a study of the total population was done before the MMR vaccine was introduced, and again after it was discontinued. The incidence had continued to rise. Andrew Wakefield, whose 1998 paper in *The Lancet* medical journal made an apparent connection of autism with the administration of the MMR vaccine, was barred from practising medicine in the UK in 2010. After vaccines containing thimerosal (mercury) were discontinued in Denmark, there was an increase in autism spectrum disorders (ASD). We are thus no closer to finding an easily fixable cause. (*See p. 463.*)

In physical terms, the brain of autistic children is often enlarged due to an excess of white and grey matter; by the age of four the head circumference may be that of a 13-year-old. Magnetic resonance imaging (MRI) studies of the functioning brain show that autistic children appear to make different 'connections' including in the areas used in social responses. Put simply, they do not make the right connections when responding to people. It is estimated that 30% of autistic persons have normal intelligence, while 40% are intellectually impaired.

Scientists everywhere are searching for a cause for autism in the hope that it will lead to a better understanding of the condition and effective treatment. Many popular theories of causation exist, and understandably parents explore every avenue for a cure. Some 'causes and cures' include 'leaky gut' syndrome in which food 'poisons and toxins' enter the bloodstream due to permeability of the intestine. A diet free of gluten and casein has been tried, as has secretin – a hormone said to have an effect on the brain; and supplementation of vitamin B_6 and magnesium. These interventions have not been scientifically proven to be effective. There has been some reported improvement with the use of essential fatty acids but this has also not been generally accepted as a treatment. While there is no drug treatment for autism as such, medication for some of the more difficult aspects such as compulsive and repetitive behaviours, self-harming and aggression is available.

Some researchers have found anomalies in the immune system of autistic children that may involve an abnormal response to viral infections, but like all aspects of this complex disorder there is no clarity yet. What does seem to be clear is that children who develop autism have a greater incidence of problems before birth and during delivery. Yet this too is mired in a multitude of possible reasons for the effects.

That there is a strong genetic influence in autism seems apparent in that siblings and identical twins are often affected. A comprehensive study in 2009 indicated that DNA changes which affect genes involved in early brain development are responsible for up to 15 per cent of autism cases. Called CDH9 and CDH10, on chromosome five, they play an important role in forming nerve connections in the part of the brain responsible for speech and the ability to interpret social interaction. These genes do not directly cause autism but appear to have an influence. The immune system is involved in some cases with children's brains showing signs of chronic inflammation. Faulty serotonin synthesis in the brain has also been implicated. Research on the hormone oxytocin and a receptor gene looks promising but there is no recommendation for treatment as yet. Recently, researchers have tested the urine of children diagnosed as autistic and compared it with that of non-autistic controls. There have been some chemical differences, but far broader and more intensive studies need to be done before any conclusions can be reached.

A number of rare genetic disorders including Fragile X, Angelman syndrome and Rett syndrome (which almost exclusively affects girls) may be associated with or sometimes misdiagnosed as autism. Older fathers do have a higher incidence of autistic children possibly due to mutations in the sperm. *What has been thoroughly discounted is that the parenting of these children is faulty in any way.*

Autistic Spectrum Disorder is a complex cluster of symptoms. The main features are: impaired social interactions, a restricted range of interests and verbal and non-verbal communication outside of the norm. From this broad definition it can be seen that ASD has a wide a range of attributes and symptoms. Treatment and diagnosis thus needs to be informed and personalised.

Autism affects people in all income spheres and those with high-achieving and famous parents. Early diagnosis with intensive treatment, specialised schooling with a structured approach and parent support and training can improve the quality of life of many autistic children. In the long term some autistic adults can find employment and live fairly independently.

MYSTERIOUS GENIUS. An intriguing aspect of ASD is the mysterious talent of savants. These are rare people who have amazing capacities such as the ability to do spectacular mathematical calculations in their head, or play classical music without being taught, or create remarkable paintings. Even more astonishing are the individuals who after a brain injury or stroke display savant-like abilities. This reveals one of the most remarkable secrets of the human brain: a 'savant capacity' for genius buried within us. We may have a kind of genetic memory to do things we have never learned.

There are people diagnosed as autistic in childhood who have overcome huge obstacles to lead normal or near-normal lives. They have written their inspiring stories. It is not an easy path for anyone, including siblings and parents. One day the workings of the mind will be unravelled and the key will be found. Each advocacy group will have stories of therapies that work, and they can make a difference. But care needs to be taken not to 'buy into' just any and every one of these. Good professional advice and support for both parents and child is essential.

BABYSITTING

PARENTS' PLAYTIME. All parents need a chance to get out and enjoy themselves together without worrying about their children, but unless you have a live-in relative or nanny you will have to make arrangements for the children's care. Some parents take their young baby with them in a carry cot and this can work if you are going to friends and the baby is small. However, as the child grows older and becomes aware of her surroundings you could create sleep problems. Your baby who could sleep anywhere can change drastically as she goes through the various developmental stages, so don't rely on her previous behaviour. Some babies are able to sleep virtually anywhere, but for some a secure and set environment is necessary to avoid sleep problems. Unfortunately you won't know what category your baby falls into until things go wrong.

Another method is to get a babysitter to come to your house. This can be less disruptive to the child if she knows her and is asleep before you leave so that if she does wake up she will at least see a familiar face. When the child is at the difficult age around two and three it will probably be easier for all concerned if you do not leave until the child is asleep. If you have made a habit of keeping your child to a regular bedtime at a reasonable hour you should be able to get away in time for most social occasions.

Some children start playing up when they get wind of the fact that mummy and daddy are going out. It is natural not to want to be left behind, but unless the child is ill, allowing her to blackmail you into staying will not do her or you any good. Assure her that you will be back soon and give her something to do while you are away, such as a drawing. Tell her she will see you in the morning, then leave. Do not creep out while your child is awake. This can lead to insecurity. Always say goodbye if she has not fallen asleep. If she performs, be firm, cheerful and confident and leave. Students and others wanting to earn a little extra money are often happy to baby-sit. Contact them through a university residence or church groups.

You could start a baby-sitting circle. This is formed by a group of several families who live within reasonable distance of each other, have their own transport and telephone. Someone is chosen to act as secretary to coordinate the calls. His or her job is to keep a list of members and find someone from within the circle to baby-sit when requested. A note is made of the number of hours the person has baby-sat, and he or she is then in credit for that number of hours. The system works on a reciprocal basis with no payment in cash for baby-sitting, but the sitters are paid in kind by someone within the group. The secretary changes every month so that one member is not burdened with having to do it too often and with the expense of the telephone calls. It is better if members are not chosen with too many interests in common. For example, if they all have children at the same school it would be a problem finding a babysitter on the night of the PTA meeting. But if the group is well-mixed in interests, it is normally possible to find a reliable babysitter without having to pay for the service.

Before leaving your child with a babysitter make sure there is an easily accessible list (posted near the telephone) with your doctor's name and number – including the night number and emergency number. The numbers of the security company, if you employ one, the police, flying squad, fire brigade and poison unit should also be listed, as well as your cell phone number. Tell your sitter if your child has been ill or has been immunised and what to do if she becomes restless. You should also know your sitter's name and address and telephone number. If your sitter does not know your house, take her on a quick tour so that she knows where exits and other key points are.

Chances are that they will not need to use any of this information, but you will rest easier knowing that you have most potential hazards covered. It is a reality of life that you need to check personal credentials before hiring anyone to look after children.

It is also sadly true that you need to be careful when leaving a child with someone whom you know. Most sexual abuse and molestation is committed by someone known to the family.

LEAVING CHILDREN IN THE CARE OF OLDER SIBLINGS. It is tempting to leave younger children in the care of older siblings, but this is seldom a good idea. Even a twelve-year-old is easily distracted by a telephone call, the television or simply 'making something to eat'. Some parents even think that a seven-year-old is capable of looking after a four-year-old. This is not possible. They are all far too young to maintain the concentrated effort it takes to watch and control young children. They would also not know what to do in an emergency, for example should the child swallow a coin or pull on the tablecloth and get burnt. Fifteen or sixteen is probably the minimum age at which siblings can been trusted to care for one another.

BIRTHMARKS AND NAEVI (MOLES)

'STORK BITES', MOLES AND OTHER MARKS. The skin of the newborn baby is seldom flawless, what with pressure marks from the birth, rashes and various moles and marks. Most birthmarks consist of an abnormal collection of small blood vessels just below the skin. Most disappear in time but some remain and may increase in size.

'STORK BITE' marks or *salmon patches* are commonly seen on the eyelids, forehead, nose and especially at the back of the neck. They become darker during crying. They look like flat pink spots and disappear eventually, usually within the first year if they are on the face, and are of no consequence. 'Stork bites' at the back of the neck usually persist.

'SPIDER' ANGIOMA looks like cobwebs of small blood vessels under the skin. If pressure is applied they fade temporarily and usually disappear by the second year.

'PORT-WINE' stains are deep pink or purple marks present at birth, usually of a different texture to normal skin and although they do not grow, they will not disappear. Paler marks may fade in time. Port wine stains may sometimes be removed, or covered with a special cosmetic preparation. Pulse dye laser (PDL) therapy has been successful in removing dark stains.

'STRAWBERRY' *haemangioma* usually appear in the first few weeks of life and look like raised, strawberry-textured lumps as the name implies. They can grow quite rapidly in the first year and this is a sign that they are also likely to reduce and usually disappear by the time the child starts school. A sign that the mark is on the decline is the appearance of pale grey areas. If it is in an awkward place or there is danger of haemorrhage they may require treatment. There are a number of effective options, but in most cases none is necessary, and they are best left alone. Some doctors do however; recommend surgical removal because they feel the final appearance is better. In very rare instances the naevi may be internal and in a dangerous place such as the trachea (air passage through which we breathe). Fortunately innovative treatment with steroids and beta-blockers may be effective.

Even though you may be anxious to have these marks disappear immediately through surgery, it may be better to allow them to resolve naturally in most cases. Your medical team will advise you after an examination. By five years half have disappeared and by the age of seven around 90% have disappeared.

'PIGMENTED' naevi are brown patches on the skin that often increase in size. The skin texture is the same as normal skin and they are not usually unsightly.

HAIRY OR WART-LIKE MOLES usually appear after birth and should be left alone. Particularly unsightly moles may be removed surgically. Any change in a mole should be investigated immediately, although the small common brown mole from which a few hairs grow is unlikely to become malignant. Large hairy moles must be examined by your doctor.

MONGOLIAN SPOTS are flat blue-grey patches like a bruise sometimes found on the lower back of babies born to dark-skinned parents. They are of no significance and usually disappear by the age of three or four.

VITILIGO are white spots or areas that lack pigment in the skin and cosmetic preparations are used to cover them. Similar areas on the scalp may result in patches of white hair. Usually this is of no significance but may be associated with congenital defects.

CEREBRAL PALSY

This is a non-specific term used to describe the most commonly occurring disorder involving the way muscles work due to damage that has occurred in the brain. This includes spasticity with uncontrollable muscle movements, and may also involve deficits in speech, vision, hearing and intellect. Some children develop epilepsy. Because the spectrum of symptoms under the name cerebral palsy is wide this label is usually only given at around the age of two when the problems are more defined. They can include normal intelligence, together with severely abnormal motor movements involving the large or small muscles; or minor physical effects together with severe intellectual disability. Up to 2:1000 children are affected due to a wide variety of causes before or after birth. Eighty percent of the damage occurs during pregnancy because of reasons such as infection of the amniotic fluid surrounding the baby, or the umbilical cord, illness in the mother with high temperature at birth or other possibly unnoticed medical problems. It is not always possible to establish the precise reason for the condition, especially since most babies who subsequently show symptoms of cerebral palsy are born at full term with uncomplicated labours. A small percentage of children have had a difficult birth possibly with oxygen deprivation and a resultant low Apgar score (*See p. 66*). Preterm babies are at particular risk, especially those with a very low birthweight (under 1.5kg), as they are vulnerable to bleeding into the brain a few days after birth (intraventricular haemorrhage, a kind of stroke). Depending on the degree of bleeding, brain cells may be damaged and if there is a resultant blockage of the flow of spinal fluid circulating into the brain the head can become enlarged due to the collection of fluid. (*See hydrocephalus p. 377*).

Cerebral palsy is characterised by several categories of abnormal physical and intellectual functioning. Palsy (paralysis) of varying degrees and types as well as uncontrolled movements (spasticity) can affect one or both sides of the body. Infants with spastic hemiplegia show an early preference for using one arm and hand and may only have limited use of the other arm. They may walk on tiptoe due to contractures (tightening) of the Achilles tendon at the back of the foot. Children with spastic diplegia may only be identified when it is noticed that they crawl dragging their legs rather than using them independently. Spastic quadriplegia affects many areas of functioning including legs and arms and there is often difficulty with swallowing. Intellectual handicap, seizures and speech and vision defects are possible. Athetoid or dyskinetic cerebral palsy affects a small number of children possibly due to a lack of oxygen during the birth or other reasons. In infancy they may be characterised by very low muscle tone and cannot hold their head upright. Speech development is slow with words being slurred and with poor tonal quality due to the lack of muscle development in the mouth and nasal passages, which also results in uncontrolled drooling. These children may have normal intellectual functioning.

Before a diagnosis of cerebral palsy is made the child must be extensively examined for possible central nervous system or metabolic disorders, genetic syndromes, tumours or muscular dystrophy. These are only some of the possible alternative diagnoses. Should cerebral palsy be diagnosed a wide range of professionals including a neurologist, speech therapist, physiotherapist, occupational therapist etc. should be consulted in order to help optimise individual potential.

Treatment. Custom made leg splints and walking frames can be helpful in aiding the child to learn to walk. Or, depending on the area of spasticity an operation to loosen the muscle spasm may be done. In select cases an operation (dorsal rhizotomy) can greatly assist walking. Muscle spasm around the hip girdle may need a surgical procedure to release and correct displacement. In other cases botulinum toxin (bee venom) commonly known as Botox, injected into specific muscles can have a positive effect on muscle spasm and contractures (tight muscles), and also on drooling. Where only one hand is used, movement constraints (splints) applied to the unaffected side can help develop functioning on the weak side. While children who have severe uncontrolled movements that spoil their quality of life may undergo a delicate operation called deep brain stimulation which serves to control the unwanted actions.

Despite high hopes – and many advertisements claiming otherwise – hyperbaric oxygen therapy in which the patient is placed in a so called decompression chamber (normally used for deep sea divers who have ascended too quickly and get 'the bends') has unfortunately not shown satisfactory clinically proven results. Stem cell therapy has also not as yet produced lasting improvements and can be dangerous. (*See p. 493*).

(*See p. 493*).

Horse riding for the disabled, swimming and other physical exercise can be psychologically and physically beneficial. Bliss symbols, talking typewriters and specially adapted computers are some of the means used to assist language development and motor functions. Physiotherapy or occupational therapy cannot 'cure' cerebral palsy but it is helpful in optimising physical functioning and preventing deterioration of muscle tone and functionality.

Children with severe physical deficits may have high intellectual functioning, while others can have minor physical dysfunction with more severe intellectual deficit. Parents will need to be advised on how to handle the child so as to help optimise development. Fortunately we now know that the brain is plastic and that if stimulated, undamaged parts may take over the functions of damaged areas. In time to come, scientists will surely overcome the challenges of renewing brain cells so that functioning can be assisted.

CIRCUMCISION

CIRCUMCISION is an operation to remove the prepuce (foreskin) of the penis. Jewish and Muslim religious law requires that it be done in infancy, while some African cultures do it ritually in early adulthood. The practice of circumcision in Western cultures, in particular the US, became necessary when men serving in the Western desert during World War II suffered penile infections due to a lack of water for washing. On their return home many chose to have their infant sons circumcised in order for them to 'match'. But the practice has now fallen out of favour as a routine procedure because many physicians feel that there is no compelling reason for it and it is wrong to subject babies to unnecessary trauma. The final decision lies with parents who should have the medical pros and cons explained to them.

Medical reasons for circumcision include far less urinary-tract infections in infancy, a lower incidence of penile cancer in later life and possibly less cervical cancer in the partners of circumcised men, as well as a lower incidence of some sexually transmitted diseases in men. There is new evidence that circumcised men are up to 60% less susceptible to infection from HIV-positive women; thus there is now a drive to circumcise men in areas where there is a high incidence of HIV infection. It is not, however, a guarantee since there is still at least a 40% chance of becoming infected; additional means of protection such as condoms must therefore still be used.

Medical reasons against the practice include prematurity, illness in the baby, possible complications such as haemorrhage, scarring and an unsatisfactory cosmetic outcome. One such case, in which the operation was so badly botched that the boy's penis was mutilated, resulted in one of the most far-reaching medical and psychosocial misrepresentations in recent history. (*See p. 483*).

On the surface it appears that there are many more reasons for circumcision than reasons against it. It is not entirely that simple however.

Although there is less cancer of the penis among circumcised men, regular washing under the foreskin is thought to offer equally effective protection against this disease. Men in countries with high levels of personal hygiene also have a low level of penile cancer without being circumcised. The theory that circumcision protects the female partner from cervical cancer is also disputed and may have more to do with the lifestyle of the partners of men who are traditionally circumcised. (A vaccination against the Human Papilloma virus (HPV) that causes cervical cancer is now available). (*See p. 475*). Phimosis, the inability to retract the foreskin, is avoided if the child is circumcised but in most cases this condition is outgrown in due course.

Circumcision is a relatively simple procedure in expert hands, but it can lead to complications such as bleeding and infection, or an ulcer can form at the tip of the glans owing to the irritation of wet nappies. If the operation is to be done, it may be best a week after birth, so that bleeding is less likely and the infant's condition has stabilised. It has been shown that giving the baby half a teaspoonful of sugar just before the procedure lessens crying considerably. Some practitioners use a local anaesthetic, depending on the circumstances. Your doctor or whoever does the procedure – be sure to get an experienced person – will advise you on how to treat the area, and when it is best done. Keep it clean by wiping gently with soap and water during nappy changes. If there is swelling, yellow crusted sores or anything else which worries you, consult your doctor.

Because it is such a personal issue, parents will in the final analysis probably make a decision based on emotional and social factors as much as anything else.

DIABETES MELLITUS

TYPE 1 DIABETES MELITUS. There are various types of diabetes with a number of differing causes. Type 1 diabetes mellitus (formerly called insulin-dependent diabetes mellitus or juvenile diabetes) is due to low or no insulin secretion from a very early age. The reasons for this vary from a genetic predisposition, autoimmune disease or developmental error. Other possible causes include infections during pregnancy, viral infections in childhood and genetic syndromes.

Insulin is made by cells in the pancreas and is released after a meal so that glucose (from sugar) can be stored for energy, and proteins, fats and other food substances can be effectively utilised. Insulin performs an extremely sensitive and important function in the maintenance of well-being. Without the glucose it metabolises the body and brain is starved of the fuel it needs to function, and the patient can go into a coma.

The main symptoms of type 1 diabetes are likely to be a raging thirst and frequent urination. Children have been known to try and drink water from the toilet because of severe thirst. Their appetite is likely to increase although they do not gain weight. Urgent expert medical evaluation and lifelong treatment is necessary.

TYPE 2 DIABETES MELLITUS (formerly called non-insulin-dependent diabetes mellitus or adult onset diabetes) has increased alarmingly in the past twenty years and it now seen from the age of around ten years into adulthood. Symptoms include tiredness and weight gain, although the patient is likely to have been overweight in any event. Many remain undiagnosed until symptoms such as failing eyesight or an unrelated infection prompts a general health investigation. Type 2 diabetes mellitus is a disease related to lifestyle, although there may be an inherited predisposition. A sedentary lifestyle and bad eating habits – high in saturated fats and sugar – are at the core of the problem. At the time of diagnosis medication may be needed in order to stabilise glucose levels, but with adherence to a correct diet and an effective exercise plan, it may be possible to discontinue medication. There has been a huge increase in type 2 diabetes in the present generation due to lifestyle, with a greater prevalence in Black Africans and African Americans, Alaskan Natives, Indians, and Pacific Islanders although it is common in all ethnic groups with the common factors being genetic, incorrect eating habits and too little exercise. Uncontrolled, type 2 diabetes can lead to serious health problems.

DOWN SYNDROME

MOST COMMON CHROMOSOMAL DISORDER. Down syndrome is the most common chromosomal disorder and it occurs approximately once in 750 to 1000 live births. However, it is present in around one in 375 conceptions. This rate is reduced by either spontaneous abortions (miscarriage) or elective terminations after being diagnosed early in pregnancy.

Although Down syndrome is best known for occurring when the mother is over the age of 35 (at the age of 42 the risk is 1:65), it also occurs at random in much younger mothers. Half the number of Down-syndrome babies is born to young mothers due to the greater number of births in this age group. In the vast majority of cases (95%) Down syndrome is the result of three copies of chromosome 21 (trisomy 21). In the remaining cases it is a result of the 21st chromosome becoming attached to part of another chromosome in what is called translocation. The mildest form is called mosaic-pattern Down syndrome because not all the cells have the defective chromosomal make-up.

Children born with Down syndrome have distinctive physical features. They are short and stocky in build with broad hands and feet with a wide gap between the first and second toes. Their eyes are almond-shaped and the nose is small and flat-bridged. The tongue is enlarged and this may make speaking difficult. Some have congenital heart defects, and depending on the severity and type of the condition, they may be prone to a variety of other problems such as diabetes mellitus, leukaemia, obesity, hypothyroidism as well as hearing and vision defects. Previously Down-syndrome children seldom lived past the age of twenty but these days their lifespan has increased vastly due to better care. However, after the age of forty Alzheimer's occurs in many with Down syndrome. They have varying degrees of mental deficit, but most can be educated, some in mainstream schools.

Like all deviations from what we call perfect, those with Down syndrome do come with challenges. But they can also be amongst the most lovable and loving of children with or without problems.

Down syndrome can be detected by antenatal testing, made easier these days by an ultrasound test for distinctive folds at the nape of the neck (nuchal folds). Alpha-fetoprotein blood tests and amniocentesis can confirm whether there is a problem. (*See p 456.*)

EARACHE

EAR INFECTIONS. These are common in the first few years and are generally due to inflammation of the middle ear (otitis media), but may be due to a boil in the outer ear, colds or throat infections, or pain referred from elsewhere as in mumps. Babies with ear infections may pull on the ear or cry when they feed, but this should not be used as a diagnosis. Sleeping or feeding can be a problem because lying flat or swallowing changes the pressure in the middle ear, causing pain. Although common in childhood, earache may not always be recognised for what it is. The baby may wake up screaming, but calms down when picked up. As soon as she is put down she may start screaming again. This is because ear pressure is relieved when the child is upright.

Sometimes it is obvious that the child is ill because she has a fever and her face is flushed. But often there is little to tell parents that the child is in pain and they can be misled into thinking she is merely being difficult or 'spoilt' because she stops crying when she is picked up. If there is any suspicion that your child may be suffering from earache, see a doctor as soon as possible.

Middle-ear infection (*otitis media*) is very common in children who are in daycare because of the frequent infections they pick up. It may be a complication accompanying colds, enlarged adenoids, infected tonsils or allergic reactions such as hay fever. A child who has frequent colds, allergies or any of the other problems mentioned, should therefore be examined by a doctor for signs of an inflamed eardrum. The peak incidence of otitis media is up to the age of three. Episodes decrease with age, and there is a familial tendency.

SYMPTOMS. Acute otitis media occurs when fluid accumulates in the middle ear and this becomes infected causing pain and inflammation. Pus may be visible behind a red and bulging eardrum, and the child has a fever. Special instruments can confirm a true ear infection by painlessly measuring eardrum movement. Fluid in the middle ear without an infection occurs in children who are suffering from upper respiratory-tract infections such as colds. This fluid may remain visible up to 12 weeks after an infection has been successfully treated. Prolonged fluid accumulation can cause hearing loss and this is a major concern.

TREATMENT. When discovered early, otitis media usually responds well to antibiotics (and decongestants if it is caused by allergies) although it may take a few weeks to clear up completely. Your child should feel better on an antibiotic within three days, but make sure you follow instructions exactly and give her the full course. Traditionally this has been ten days, but recently there has been discussion of using a shorter course of five to seven days for certain indications. This shorter course is not recommended for children under the age of two or children with a burst eardrum or for more serious cases with underlying medical problems. Occasionally the infection does not respond quickly and your doctor may suggest taking a sample of the infected fluid to see exactly which germ is causing the problem. **Your medical advisor will decide on the treatment.**

SURGICAL PROCEDURES. Myringotomy and the insertion of grommets (tiny tubes) in the ear drum can help drain the ear and restore health to the middle-ear mucus. This procedure needs a general anaesthetic and a short stay in hospital.

PREVENTION. Ear infections are five times less likely in breastfed babies because breastfeeding provides protective antibodies that help fight ear infections. The DTaP-IPV/Hib combined vaccine and the Pneumococcal Conjugated Vaccine may be helpful in preventing middle ear infection. While the flu vaccine can help children who suffer repeated upper respiratory infections. Smoking in the vicinity of children is responsible for a huge number of respiratory tract infections and subsequent otitis media. Allergies need to be treated, as they cause 35–40% of ear infections. Dummies (pacifiers)seem to be implicated in many cases. Propping the bottle when feeding a baby is also a potential cause of otitis media, because milk can easily flow into the Eustachian tube from the back of the throat. Blowing the nose hard through both nostrils simultaneously can also force infected mucus into the ear passage. Children in large daycare centres are exposed to many sources of infection. If possible choose a smaller group.

'GLUE EAR' AND HEARING LOSS. Ear infections can become chronic, with a gluey substance collecting behind the eardrum, and the only signs of its presence may be loss of hearing or excessive irritability. A young child may have a severe hearing loss without anyone being aware of it, with the result that language development is handicapped. Since the child cannot hear, she cannot imitate sounds. She may even be noisier than most because she is unaware of the pitch of her voice. Any child who seems to be slow in learning to talk should have her hearing tested because she could be missing out on a crucial stage in her language development. In extreme cases of hearing loss the child may even appear to be backward and, if the real cause is not discovered before school, she could be held back by her inability to hear. It is essential that hearing is clear from 8 to 24 months because this is critical for language development.

If on examination by a doctor the eardrum is not shining and mobile, there is a possibility that the back of the drum is gummed up. If the condition is left for too long, permanent deafness can result, but a simple procedure called a myringotomy, in which a small hole is made in the eardrum and the 'glue' is sucked out, restores hearing very well. Because there is always the danger of 'glue' building up again as soon as the eardrum heals, a procedure in which a tiny plastic tube like a straw is inserted into the eardrum has been devised. This tube, called a grommet, allows secretions to drain and hearing is maintained by preventing the accumulation of 'glue'. The operation is simple and the child usually spends only a few hours in hospital. The fact that it is done under anaesthetic, and that the long-term benefits are not conclusive, makes this a somewhat controversial procedure. After the operation water must not be allowed into the ears. Ear plugs should be worn when washing the hair or swimming, and the child should not put her head under water. As the child grows the grommets may pop out without anyone being aware of it, or they may be removed and the hole then closes. Laser-assisted myringotomy (LAM) offers a quicker and easier procedure but is not always available. A local anaesthetic is applied in the child's ear and a tiny hole is made in the eardrum by means of a laser beam. The whole procedure takes about five minutes in the doctor's surgery. Extended treatment with low doses of antibiotics is sometimes preferred to myringotomy. **Consult your medical practitioner.**

'BURST' EARDRUM. Sometimes infected secretions cause the eardrum to burst or perforate and there is a discharge from the ear which you notice only when you see a bloody, yellowish stain on the bed linen. The infection must be treated and a doctor will mop up the discharge with a swab and may prescribe medication. The hole usually heals without complications but water must not be allowed to enter the ear. Travel by air is allowed.

However, if the source of the infection, for instance tonsils or adenoids, is not treated, the problem is likely to recur. When the discharge from the ear has a bad smell and the child feels ill, has a temperature and pain behind the ear, a doctor should be seen immediately. (A doctor should be seen for all ear problems but this is the most urgent because the infection could spread to the brain.) A bad smell from the ear may also mean a 'foreign body', such as a bead or matchstick, is lodged in the ear. Never put drops in your child's ear unless instructed to do so by a doctor.

Although ear infections are almost inevitable in children under three years, they diminish in frequency as the child builds up immunity to infections and the inner ear grows, thereby reducing the likelihood of blockage. (*See p. 462 for a vaccine that can be helpful.*)

EPILEPSY

CONVULSIONS, FITS, SEIZURES, EPILEPSY. The tendency to have seizures is one of the oldest and most common medical problems, and can occur as a result of many different causes. The convulsion or seizure is not a disease, but a symptom of what happens when the brain is stimulated by an abnormal 'electrical' impulse. This results in a 'blackout', or stiffening of the body with uncontrolled muscular movements or jerking. Diagnosis and treatment will depend on the cause of the seizure.

When convulsions occur soon after birth they are likely to be caused by an imbalance of chemicals in the blood, kernicterus (severe jaundice within 36 hours of birth), brain damage before or during birth, bleeding in the brain due to prematurity, or drug dependency in the mother. Diseases such as meningitis, encephalitis, and bleeding in the brain through injury from blows and other reasons can cause brain-cell damage.

Other infections, dehydration, hydrocephalus, brain tumours, accidents and poisons such as lead can also cause damage that results in convulsions. Certain rare genetic syndromes and, occasionally, pervasive developmental disorder (autism) or cerebral palsy may include epileptic seizures. There is also the inherited or idiopathic tendency towards seizures with no apparent brain damage although the electrical impulses from the brain may show an abnormal pattern.

Any child who has a convulsion should have a thorough examination by a specialist to establish the cause. Febrile convulsions due to a high temperature (*See p. 341*) are common in childhood and do not mean the child has epilepsy.

DIAGNOSIS. Modern techniques such as computer-assisted tomography (a CAT brain scan) can give a comprehensive picture of the brain and its workings. Other procedures such as lumbar punctures to examine spinal fluid, skull X-rays and electroencephalograms (ECG's, which trace the brain's electrical impulses) can give a picture of the actual working of the brain and of damaged cells or other abnormality.

Epilepsy occurs in various forms, and it is most common after the age of five years. Grand mal or major epilepsy is the most obvious type. More than half those affected by it experience a warning sensation or 'aura' before an attack, in which they become aware of a strange smell or a light or stomach pain. This is followed by a 'tonic' phase when the body becomes rigid and breathing stops briefly, followed by violent muscular contractions that cause jerking of the limbs and possibly foaming at the mouth. The attack lasts a few minutes, after which consciousness is gradually regained. To the onlooker this form of epilepsy can be frightening and has resulted in many of the myths and misconceptions about the condition. But it is nothing more mysterious than a kind of short circuit in the brain as happens when wires are brought into accidental contact.

FOCAL attacks are those which begin in one of the limbs and spread throughout that side of the body, usually on the opposite side of the brain that has been damaged. In young children there is sometimes temporary paralysis on the involved side.

PSYCHOMOTOR attacks are epileptic reactions that do not result in a convulsion but in changed behaviour. The child may do the same thing over and over, or her actions may have nothing to do with her situation. Thought processes are confused and she may become impulsive and unreasonable because of the 'internal' seizure she is having.

IN PETIT MAL or 'absences' the symptoms consist of a very brief loss of consciousness sometimes accompanied by slight twitching of a few muscles, usually of the face and head. Petit mal or absences are often so mild that they are not noticed by parents and the child may miss out on learning because she has blank spots. In school, too, many children suffering petit mal attacks are thought of as dreamers or as inattentive and they may fail to make progress. When they are diagnosed as suffering from petit mal and receive medication to eliminate the attacks they often make great strides at school.

PHOTOSENSITIVE EPILEPSY occurs when the susceptible person watches a flickering image, for instance on a television screen (*See p. 274*) or a line of trees from a speeding car or a train passing at a station. Soccer star David Beckham's middle son Romeo has this type of epilepsy and he and his wife Victoria have had to shield their son from the camera flashlights that follow them wherever they go. In many instances the pattern of epileptic seizures is not confined to one type but is a mixture of several.

HANDLING A SEIZURE. Once the attack has started it cannot be stopped. Do not try to 'bring the child round', hold her down, or unclasp her hands. Make sure she does not hurt herself on hard or sharp objects. Loosen the clothing at the neck and lay her on her side with her head lower than her hips so that saliva does not flow into her wind pipe and she chokes. Don't try to give her anything to drink. The attack will take its course until finished and will stop spontaneously in a few minutes. As soon as the attack settles, lay her in the recovery position. She is likely to be exhausted and fall into a deep sleep.

RECOVERY POSITION

If an attack lasts longer than a few minutes and there is difficulty breathing, choking or blueness she may be in *status epilepticus*, when one seizure follows another without a period of consciousness in between. **This is an emergency and medical help should be called for immediately.**

Treatment in epilepsy does not consist of doing something when an attack occurs, but in preventing it as much as possible. Epilepsy is a chronic condition and must be treated as such, or repeated seizures can do more damage. New drugs as well as a well-tried range of medicines can eliminate or greatly reduce attacks in many forms of epilepsy. Several types of epilepsy that typically occur in childhood are outgrown. Surgery can also be helpful, with up to one in six cases being treatable with specialised intervention. In those focal epilepsies which are not responsive to drug treatment, up to 50% can be helped through surgery.

Children who suffer from epileptic seizures should be integrated into normal schools unless they have several attacks a day or are unable to cope with the curriculum. The child with good control of seizures needs a minimum of supervision. Swimming should be closely supervised and other potentially dangerous situations limited. All other activities, including sports (some very famous sport stars have epilepsy) should be encouraged. Parents, a doctor or the social worker should explain to the teacher that the child may have a seizure and how it should be handled. There is no reason why a child who can cope with normal schooling and has only occasional attacks should be isolated. For those who cannot be integrated into the ordinary classroom there are schools which provide excellent facilities.

An important aspect of caring for a child who has epilepsy lies in preventing emotional problems from developing.

Even though many people are now aware of the facts concerning epilepsy, there are still those who view it with fear and superstition. If parents and those around the child are careful not to isolate and stigmatise her, the epileptic child has a good chance of growing up with a normal sense of self. Many great figures have suffered from the 'falling sickness' – Pythagoras, Dante, Vincent van Gogh, Emmanuel Kant and Dostoevsky to name a few – so there is no reason to try to hide the condition. On the local front Jonty Rhodes, one of the greatest fielders in cricket ever has epilepsy.

FOETAL ALCOHOL SYNDROME (FAS)

HOW DRINKING ALCOHOL IN PREGNANCY HARMS BABIES. South Africa has the highest rate of children worldwide (more than 14 000 new cases per annum) who are born with severe problems caused by their mothers drinking alcohol during pregnancy. Children with FAS have characteristic facial features and small stature. More importantly they often have low birth weight, heart, kidney and brain damage and emotional and behavioural problems that make it very hard for them to fit into society. Some of the behaviour problems associated with FAS include lack of concentration, aggression and poor impulse control. These make learning difficult, as well as the fact that their intellect is also often below average. In addition they mostly come from low-income families where nutrition is poor and good role models are scarce.

This disastrous combination of circumstances makes for a very poor outcome both for the individual and society. The women who drink while pregnant are mostly poor and come from a culture of binge drinking, especially over weekends. Studies reveal that contrary to what is generally assumed they mostly drink beer, followed to a lesser extent by wine. Changing this behaviour pattern is not easy and attempts so far have not been very successful.

Low-income women are not the only ones who drink alcohol during pregnancy. Although most middle-class women know that it is not a good thing, they may not be aware that they are pregnant. Some choose to drink regardless. The greatest danger period for drinking during pregnancy is in the first three months when foetal development is at its most critical. There is no safe period for drinking during pregnancy however.

GENETIC DEFECTS AND DEFECTS OCCURRING DURING PREGNANCY

INHERITED DISORDERS. Genetic abnormalities are responsible for a number of birth defects and in many cases they can be prevented by adequate counselling and the use of modern diagnostic techniques. Any mother who has had a baby with an inherited defect should seek counselling to advise her of the chances of other children being affected. Counselling is also indicated if there is an inherited condition on the mother or father's side of the family.

Among the diseases that can run in families are: spina bifida, Down syndrome, porphyria, Tay-Sachs disease, haemophilia, diabetes mellitus, sickle-cell anaemia, thalassaemia, anencephaly and cystic fibrosis.

Simple tests have been developed to identify the carriers of Tay-Sachs disease, a fatal condition that affects the offspring of Jewish people of Ashkenazi descent. Gaucher's disease is an enzyme deficiency that also occurs in people of Jewish origin, and can be detected by means of amniocentesis.

Thalassaemia, a blood disease, and deficiency in G-6-PD (an enzyme involved in the metabolism of red blood cells) are inherited disorders that mostly affect people of Greek and other Mediterranean descent.

One in four Nigerians carries the gene for sickle-cell anaemia, with the result that over 90 000 children born annually are affected. It is also common in African-Americans, the gene having been carried through the slave trade. Diabetes mellitus is common in the Indian community, while Huntington's chorea and phenylketonuria (PKU) mainly affect people of British and Huguenot origin. Porphyria, cancer of the colon, sclerosteosis, high cholesterol and cystic fibrosis are common in the Afrikaner population.

Among Xhosa people there is a defect known as 'Transkei foot' in which the little toe bends outwards, while some members of the Zulu population are affected by Mseleni joint disease and osteoarthritis. In general though there are few genetically transmitted diseases among black South Africans.

The incidence of other congenital abnormalities such as Down syndrome increases with the age of the parents (if the mother is over 35 and the father over 55). Tests such as ultrasound, followed if necessary by amniocentesis should be done, especially if parents have had a previously affected child or there is a case in close family. Down syndrome can also occur randomly with young parents. An ultrasound should be done if you are at all concerned.

Techniques in the diagnosis of genetic diseases, including the isolation of the causative gene, have improved greatly. It is always worthwhile finding out if there is a test for a particular abnormality if there is any indication that it may occur in your family.

SOME OF THE AVAILABLE TESTS INCLUDE: AMNIOCENTESIS. For this test, a little of the fluid surrounding the baby in the womb is drawn out through a hollow needle inserted through the wall of the abdomen. Local anaesthetic makes the procedure painless. The test is usually done between the 14th and 18th week of pregnancy and the amniotic fluid is cultured for signs of certain chromosomal abnormalities such as Down syndrome, anencephaly and spina bifida. Because this test reveals the sex of the baby, diseases that affect only males or females such as haemophilia and Duchenne muscular dystrophy can be identified. Rhesus incompatibility can be assessed, as well as the maturity of the baby's lungs in case an early birth is advisable (*See p. 479*). There is a small chance of abortion as a result of amniocentesis.

ALPHA-FETOPROTEIN TEST. This is a simple blood test done during pregnancy that can detect the possibility of spina bifida and other neural tube defects. If the alpha-fetoprotein is above a certain level amniocentesis will tell for sure whether the child is affected.

ULTRASOUND. By ultrasound or sonar scan, a technique for examining the baby in the womb, it is possible to find out whether it is developing normally. Unlike X-rays, ultrasound is safe for use throughout pregnancy, and can indicate the maturity, size and the heartbeat of the foetus. The sex of the child can often be revealed, but this is not always possible. The position and size of the placenta is also shown and this has taken much of the guesswork out of the management of pregnancy. Ultrasound scans also show the position of the baby before amniocentesis in later pregnancy so that the needle is inserted safely. By taking certain measurements at the nape of the neck an expert can also tell from an ultrasound whether a child is affected by Down syndrome while developing in the womb.

X-RAYS. In late pregnancy X-rays are considered safe and can reveal bone deformities such as anencephaly and microcephaly, and an abnormal position of the baby. These conditions are also usually visible on ultrasound scans.

AMNIOGRAPHY. In this test a dye is injected into the womb that sticks to the vernix (fatty coating) covering the baby. This enables X-ray pictures to be taken of the outline of the baby to indicate whether it appears normal. When the baby swallows some of the harmless dye the X-ray shows whether there are defects of the intestinal tract. Cases in which this test may be used include polyhydramnios (too much amniotic fluid) which is often associated with defects of the gut.

FOETOSCOPY. A very fine instrument is inserted into the womb through which the doctor can look at the baby and take samples of fluid, skin and blood. Photographs of the baby can also be taken through the foetoscope.

CARDOCENTESIS. This is a less invasive procedure than fetoscopy in which a needle is guided to the base of the umbilical cord with the aid of ultrasound. A sample of blood is taken and this can be screened for a number of problems including haemophilia, errors of metabolism and platelet disorders.

CHORIONIC VILLUS SAMPLING. A sample of chorionic villi can be sucked up and tested for many possible defects early in pregnancy. However, there is a greater risk of abortion and birth defects after this sampling technique than is the case with an amniocentesis. Anyone who has an inherited disease in the family should be referred to the nearest genetic counselling centre to learn if there is a likelihood of a child being born with the disease. If the counselling service is attached to a provincial hospital costs are very low. If abnormalities are found, parents are counselled and may be given the option of a termination.

GENE THERAPY. Possibly the biggest advance to come will be treating the source of the problem, that is treating illnesses such as cystic fibrosis and other inherited conditions at the gene. Experiments in mice have been successful and it is only a matter of time before many serious inherited diseases will be able to be prevented by altering the genetic code through gene therapy. (*See p. 493*).

DEFECTS OCCURING DURING PREGNANCY. Around 50% of defects, including heart malformations in the unborn child are of unknown origin, while only around 2% happen due to factors brought about by functional effects like bleeding. Less than 10% are due to teratogens, agents such as mercury, radiation, or medicinal or recreational drugs. Women who are on long-term medication for conditions such as epilepsy should consult their doctor before becoming pregnant. Illnesses the mother may have, such as German measles, uncontrolled insulin-dependent diabetes, syphilis, toxoplasmosis and HIV, can also have unfortunate effects. Sometimes defects are caused by both genetic and environmental factors. In South Africa, the most common cause of preventable physical and mental defects is foetal alcohol syndrome caused by excessive alcohol consumption during pregnancy, with 14 000 children affected annually. HIV transmission from mother to child is also a tragically common occurrence but it can largely be prevented (*See p. 413*). Smoking during pregnancy increases the chance that you will develop heart disease, chronic lung disease, stroke, lung cancer, and have a low birth weight baby. Much can be done through genetic counselling, medical and psychosocial support for parents and children.

'GROWING PAINS'

GROWING OUT OF IT. So called 'growing pains' are common in children between the ages of four and around eight years. The child complains of pain at the back of the thigh or the calf muscles, after going to bed at night, especially after a lot of running around during the day. They are able to walk and there is no swelling, and they do not have a fever. Rubbing the affected muscles with a menthol ointment, and applying warmth, can bring some relief. 'Growing pains' occur intermittently and pass without complications by the age of around eight.

It is important to differentiate this painful but harmless condition from the more serious possible causes of limb pain in children, in particular rheumatic disease and bone tumours. Morning stiffness, limping, facial rashes, joint pain or weakness, fever, swelling or tenderness of a joint or limb must be taken seriously and be seen by a specialist.

HABITS

COMFORT HABITS. Habits such as nail biting, thumb sucking and hair twirling are irritating but not necessarily a sign of disturbance. They may have been started in times of stress and continued because they provide comfort and pleasure. It is not worth making a fuss about them because then you create tension that will need to be relieved by the habit!

SUCKING COMFORT. Sucking is a primary source of comfort and is clearly shown in pictures of babies still in the womb. The problem arises when it continues beyond what parents consider appropriate for the child's age. To help them relax most children need to suck on a bottle or breast well into the second year and even longer. This is not a problem if it is confined to sleep times. Children who demand the breast or bottle as a source of comfort very frequently – some virtually every hour – may be under stress, bored, frustrated or jealous. One of the main reasons for discouraging this is the fact that it can contribute to malnourishment because the child drinks too much milk or juice, spoiling the appetite for solids. You must try and find the reason for the need for constant comfort and do something about it rather than simply breaking the habit.

EFFECT ON THE TEETH. Parents are concerned that thumb sucking will cause malocclusion of the teeth and jaw. Prolonged thumb sucking, in particular past the age of four or longer, can push the teeth forward and distort the palate. While this is obviously undesirable, malocclusion of the teeth can be an inherited tendency and occurs in babies who have never had a bottle, dummy or sucked their thumb. Tooth decay can rapidly result when juice or sweetened drinks or even milk is washed over the teeth.

DUMMIES (PACIFIERS). As the name implies dummies, and the thumb, are surrogates for the nipple. They are a form of sucking comfort, and the child comes to depend on them for emotional 'survival'. Deal with the reasons for the need and gently encourage the child towards finding other ways of coping. Often there is little real reason for the need and once she realises she is stronger than she thinks, she will cope without it. But forcing the issue by throwing the object away is likely to cause greater tension, unless she chooses to do so herself.

Try and get her to leave the dummy at times when she is having fun. She doesn't need it plugged in all the time. Get her to leave it to one side and distract her through rewarding play. Point out to her afterwards that she can have fun without the dummy. The same applies to the bottle. Some parents do a deal with older children in which the bottle or dummy is 'donated' to another younger child who 'needs' it. Some children go along with this but then scream for it later. It often takes a number of tries before the object is given up permanently. Gentle encouragement with a firm belief that she can do it will help give her courage. The most successful ploys are those in which the child is truly ready for the big 'sacrifice'. Often it is peer pressure that makes the child give up because she does not want to be seen as a 'baby' by her friends.

NAIL BITING. This common habit can become entrenched and is sometimes caused by underlying tension but can also simply be a habit that starts by imitating other children. Discourage it from the beginning but do not over react as this will just give the child a reason to continue.

TRANSITIONAL OBJECTS. Giving up a comfort habit 'cold turkey' is sometimes too much to handle. A transitional object that takes the place of the less acceptable habit can do the trick. A cuddly toy can develop into that 'friend in need'.

SECURITY BLANKETS. As cartoon character Linus will tell you, survival can depend on a blanket. The 'doodoo', 'blankie' or, more correctly, scruffy piece of rag can be an object of affection like no other. All you need worry about is not to lose it!

Most children outgrow their habits; others carry them through to adulthood and resort to them in times of stress, or cultivate adult comfort habits. Habits are developed in order to provide comfort and solace. We all resort to them in some form now and again. It is not worth worrying about unless it comes to dominate the child's behaviour. The good news is that in the long term children who have security objects are no less emotionally mature.

FOOD. Eating for comfort is a common habit amongst adults, and we need to guard against cultivating it in children. Never use food as a reward.

GRINDING OF TEETH during sleep is sometimes said to be caused by worms, but this is not the case, although the child may in fact have worms, since they are so common. Teeth grinding is not a serious problem but check with your dentist in case her teeth become worn down. Deworm her and check for stress.

NOSE PICKING. This comes naturally to children (and many adults!) but you still need to control it for the sake of social acceptability. Some children pick their nose at night as well, causing it to bleed. Try putting a little petroleum jelly around the nostril to keep the area soft so that crusts that are tempting to pick are less likely to form.

HAIR PULLING AND HAIR TWIRLING. Many children – and adults – twirl a lock of hair between their fingers when they are tired. Some love to play with their mother's hair before they fall asleep. This is simply a habit done for the relaxing pleasure of the tactile experience. Hair pulling, in which the child tugs at her hair forcefully and pulls out chunks, is more problematic. It could seem as though she is getting bald patches for no reason. This can be a sign of stress and sometimes occurs when there is a new baby and the jealousy is internalised. Other causes should also be considered and she needs comforting and not scolding. Plenty of tactile stimulation in the form of massages, hugs and kisses will do a power of good. This applies to boys and wells as girls.

BREATH HOLDING. Some children have a frightening tendency to force air from their lungs while crying, and are then unable to breathe again for what seems an endless period. Their pulse slows down and they may pass out. But they regain consciousness quickly – as soon as the amount of carbon dioxide in the blood is too high – and start breathing automatically again with no harm done. It is difficult for a mother to stand by idly while her child goes blue in the face, and a sharp smack, holding her upside down or splashing her with cold water is often recommended. These measures will not help shorten an attack and she will recover with or without them.

The best thing you can do is lie her on her side and ensure that her airway is not blocked. Luckily children who hold their breath soon grow out of it, and until then their parents should cope with each attack as calmly as possible. Do not become so terrified that you allow her to do anything she pleases in order to prevent an attack, because then you will have a long-term problem! It is worth checking to see if your child is anaemic as this often predisposes them to these attacks.

MASTURBATION. Self-stimulation is not abnormal in children and it should not be forcibly discouraged. Some children seem to do it so much, however, that it assumes a dominant part in their life. Others make a point of doing it in company. In others it is a comfort habit with the same basis as any other. Sometimes the reason for it is simply an irritation in the genital area. This itchiness may be caused by bubble bath or thrush or pinworm, which is then scratched. It may then become a pleasurable habit. (*See pp.367, 371 for thrush and pinworm treatment.*)

If masturbation is due to an emotional need caused by jealousy, feelings of rejection or insecurity, provide emotional reassurance. Children who masturbate in front of others inevitably do so as an attention-getting gambit. Take her by the hand and lead her to her room explaining that it is something that may be done but only in private. Then get to work on the reasons for her need for attention.

HEAD BANGING AND RHYTHMIC ROCKING. Banging the head against the side of the cot or other surface, with or without rhythmic rocking, is one of the more worrisome habits. It is often a sign of a lack of the tactile stimulation given by holding and stroking, and is more often seen in boys, probably because parents think they do not need so much touching. Any child who has to self-stimulate and obtain comfort in such a negative way is likely to be severely deprived of sensory stimulation. This in turn can lead to depression. Do not be afraid to hug your child, give loving massages and lots of tender loving care every day. It is as important as food, possibly more so. (*See case study of Daniel p 517*)

HAND WAVING, TICS OR OTHER MOVEMENTS. This involves repetitive movements in which the child spins in circles or waves a hand in front of their eyes, or flaps an object rhythmically, or makes other meaningless repetitive movements or jerks involuntarily. This can be a sign of a severe disorder and you need to consult a developmental specialist. (*See also Tics p. 502, Pervasive developmental disorder p. 437*)

IMMUNISATION

Immunisation is a way of providing protection against disease. A small amount of vaccine (a preparation made from the germs – either live attenuated (weakened), or inactivated – that cause the particular disease) is given to the child, either by injection or by mouth. This prompts the child's body to make antibodies (cells that fight the disease). These antibodies are then ready to offer resistance if the child comes in contact with the disease. Booster shots or extra doses of vaccine are needed to produce and maintain a sufficiently high level of antibodies for certain diseases.

The number of vaccines given to children has increased over the past four decades, and vaccines for six or more diseases may be given at the same time. As a result parents have understandably wondered if it is a good thing. They ask whether it will overload or weaken the child's immune system; and if they should rather delay or space immunisation, or even whether they should take an alternative route.

The human immune system is an extremely intricate and miraculous structure. Before birth, 'passive' immunity to diseases the mother has had or been vaccinated against, is transferred to the baby. Breast milk and colostrum (the yellow milky substance secreted before breast milk comes in three days later) also provide a certain amount of protection. However, this fades after a few months and is not as effective as the protection offered by an infant's 'active' immune response.

During and after the birth the neonate's system is exposed to a vast numbers of germs, and the immune system must kick in. The vaccination schedule is timed around the age-specific risk of a particular infection, and the ability of a baby's system to respond effectively. Immunisation covers diseases such as diphtheria, meningitis, pneumonia, polio etc – all too awful to contemplate – some of which are fortunately no longer part of living memory. Yet some are still killers in our midst.

The reason why vaccines do not overwhelm a child's immune system in the same way that being exposed to the actual disease would, is because the 'germs' in the vaccine are modified. A child's immune response can also cope with an enormous number of challenges in terms of producing antibodies to vaccines. Every millilitre of blood contains ten million white blood cells which are sufficient to cope with an estimated 10,000 vaccines given simultaneously. The number of antigens, that is the ingredients in vaccines that tell the immune system to make antibodies against a disease, has also been dramatically reduced over the years.

CONTROVERSIES AND QUESTIONS AROUND VACCINES. Smallpox, a disease from which millions died until 100 years ago, has been eradicated worldwide. Yet many were not believers in the beginning, including Benjamin Franklin – one of the Founding Fathers of the United States – who lost a child to smallpox. As he observed in his autobiography:

> *"In 1736 I lost one of my sons, a fine boy of four years old, by the smallpox, taken in the common way. I long regretted bitterly, and still regret that I had not given it to him by inoculation. This I mention for the sake of parents who omit that operation, on the supposition that they should never forgive themselves if a child died under it; my example showing that the regret may be the same either way, and that, therefor, the safer should be chosen."*

Polio, a lethal and crippling disease until fifty years ago counts among its victims Franklin D. Roosevelt President of the United States, who contracted polio at the age of thirty-nine. Polio is now on the list of illnesses that are targeted for eradication. But there has been a resurgence of polio cases recently because of rumours in some countries that vaccination is being used in a plot to sterilise women, with Nigeria, Pakistan and Afghanistan still outstanding due to poor vaccination rates.

Some parents are also not immunising their children in the belief that the effect of generalised ''herd'' immunisation will protect them. Others believe that it is better for the immune system to develop on its own without immunisation, or to postpone immunisation until the child is older.

The "sterilisation" story is clearly mischief-making by cynical forces. As for "herd" immunisation offering protection, this is rather short-sighted, since "herd" immunity breaks down once the number of unvaccinated children reaches a critical point. The unprotected will also not be able to travel to other countries, and are likely to be exposed to serious illnesses. As for the infant's system developing immunity on its own, the fact is that three million children still die every year as a result of diseases that could have been prevented by vaccination. Postponing immunisation in the belief that an older child will be protected against "possible harm" caused by immunisation is not a valid medical reason no matter how well meant, as the severity of the diseases against which it protects are life threatening from a very early age.

Perhaps the most emotive issue surrounds the MMR vaccine and whether it causes autism. It is understandable that such a condition would push parents to seek a cause. The MMR theory was given impetus when a study published in the prestigious Lancet journal in February 1998 in the UK, claimed such a link. However, the study was debunked after it was shown that the doctors involved had taken money from a group of lawyers who were suing the manufacturers on behalf of parents.

The journal has since distanced itself from the research and apologised. Dr Andrew Wakefield, who instigated the study, was found guilty of serious medical misconduct in February 2010, with more than 30 charges proven against him. He was barred from practising as a doctor in the UK in May the same year. Mr Wakefield now lives in Texas in the USA.

Since then, tens of thousands of children in Japan, Canada, the UK and the USA have been involved in trials seeking a link between the MMR vaccine and autism, but none has been proven. All aspects of possible links such as enterocolitis (inflammatory bowel), abnormal immune response, and persistent measles infections were explored. No link was found.

As with almost all medications and procedures, there are occasional adverse effects after vaccinations, but the vast majority are mild. What cannot be denied, is that immunisation has cut the rate of infant mortality and disease worldwide by huge numbers, and is surely the single greatest advance in preventative health care. There is also personal peace of mind in knowing that your child is protected when epidemics occur.

For more information on autism see page 437.

INGREDIENTS IN VACCINES. Aluminium salts are incorporated into some vaccines in order to enhance the immune response and have been used for over sixty years. We are all exposed to aluminium in drinking water and food.

Antibiotics are used in very small amounts in some vaccines in order to reduce bacterial growth in nonsterile substances such as eggs used in the manufacture. The antibiotics that are most likely to cause severe allergic responses such as penicillin, cephalosporins' and sulphur drugs are not used, and allergy to eggs is not regarded as a contraindication, unless anaphylaxis (very severe allergic reaction) has occurred previously. The antibiotics that are used are reduced to very small or undetectable amounts during processing.

Formaldehyde is an organic compound found naturally in many living things and is used to inactivate viruses and bacteria in some vaccines so that they don't cause disease. The amount of formaldehyde is so diluted during the manufacturing process that it is far smaller than the amount that occurs naturally in the body. Even a newborn baby naturally has between 50-70 times more formaldehyde in their body than they would get from all their vaccinations together, and even a fresh pear contains more than fifty times the amount of formaldehyde than is found in any vaccine. When the body breaks down formaldehyde it does not distinguish between that which is naturally produced, environmental or from vaccination.

Thimerosal, a mercury-based preservative that prevents the growth of bacteria, fungus and germs that was used in some vaccines, has also caused concern in parents because mercury has the potential to damage the nervous system. Although studies have found no evidence of harm when used in vaccines, it is no longer in vaccines given to children under six years, due to rumours that have disturbed parents.

Consult your medical advisor if you have any concerns regarding having your child immunised. Either because they have a particular medical condition; or if you have safety concerns, or the child has had a previous adverse reaction.

As with almost all medications and procedures, there are occasional adverse effects after vaccinations, but the vast majority are mild.

WHY VACCINE SCHEDULES DIFFER AROUND THE WORLD. There are differences in the immunisation schedules in countries around the world. Reasons for this include: The vaccine is no longer necessary because the illness has been eradicated in the area due to immunisation. Or, it is still required because of a high incidence of a disease that is preventable through immunisation. Or the vaccine is not yet listed for use in the country, usually due to budget constraints. The Bill and Melinda Gates Foundation contribute millions of dollars to assist with global immunisation.

Immunisation schedules may also vary according to a country's demographic profile. There is a common thread of around fourteen vaccines that are given in middle to high income countries. In middle to low income countries where there is a different profile of childhood illness and levels of immunisation, there are likely to be additional vaccinations. For example, the need for the BCG vaccine against tuberculosis in countries such as Latin America, Asia, Africa, South Africa, Eastern Europe and the Caribbean where there is still a high incidence of the disease.

A vaccine against meningococcal C (infection of the membrane around the brain and spinal cord) has been on the schedule for a while now, but not for the most serious form, meningitis B which caused the most deaths in children under five years in the UK. There is now a vaccine for meningococcal Group B for two of the most lethal forms of bacterial infection: meningitis B and meningococcal septicaemia (blood infection).

It has been licensed by the FDA in the US and in another 34 countries, and it is also authorised by the European Commission, thus member countries can choose to introduce it. Australia, Italy, Germany, the UK, Ireland, France, Canada and the US were amongst the first to make it available. In the USA it is also offered to students entering university, as meningitis B commonly occurs in dormitories.

VACCINATION IN SPECIAL CASES. The vaccination schedule may be different for ill children or children with special conditions or circumstances.

PRETERM BABIES. You may wonder when your premature baby in special care should be vaccinated. The schedule may be started as though the child was born at term, if your paediatrician advises it.

VACCINATION IN PREGNANCY. Vaccination against pertussis (whooping cough) and other childhood illnesses is being offered during pregnancy in some developed countries. Passive immunity is then passed from the mother to the unborn child. There has been a resurgence of whooping cough, which is an extremely dangerous illness particularly in infants as they can only be given the whooping cough vaccine from two months. Tdap= (tetanus, reduced diphtheria-reduced- acellular pertussis), inactivated polio, inactivated influenza vaccine are amongst those offered.

PREGNANCY AND IMMUNISATION. Live vaccines such as the BCG= (against TB), the live vaccine against influenza that is used as a nasal spray, MMR= measles (rubeola), mumps and rubella (German measles), oral typhoid, chickenpox (varicella), yellow fever and the OPV live polio vaccine, are not generally recommended in pregnancy. **Consult your doctor or clinic for information and advice.**

MEDICAL CONDITIONS IN CHILDREN WHICH MAY NOT PRECLUDE VACCINATIONS: In general, illnesses with a temperature below 38.5°C, diarrhoea, coughs and colds, asthma, hay fever, localised skin infections, malnutrition and heart, kidney, liver and lung problems should not preclude children from having vaccinations. General allergies should not be a problem, although previous anaphylactic reactions would preclude some vaccines. Consult your medical practitioner or clinic.

UNKNOWN STATUS, MISSED OR DELAYED VACCINATION. Should a child have missed a scheduled immunisation, it should be resumed as soon as possible. There is generally no need to begin the course from scratch again as their system will have a "memory" of it. Inform your clinic or doctor who will advise you. In cases where there is uncertainty whether the child has been vaccinated or followed the immunisation schedule, obtain professional advice in order for the child to be given suitable catch up immunisation.

HIV-INFECTION. The use of antiviral drugs during pregnancy can and has reduced the mother-to-child transmission of HIV to many unborn children. However even uninfected babies born to HIV positive women are very susceptible to childhood infections including pneumonia, whooping cough and meningitis. This is possibly because the natural antibodies transferred from HIV positive mothers are not as effective. The good news is that these babies usually respond well to immunisation and it is therefore important that they receive appropriate vaccinations.

HIV positive children do not produce antibodies as effectively as healthy children. Nevertheless, the World Health Organization recommends that they be immunised where possible. They should also be given the influenza and pneumococcal vaccines before AIDS symptoms appear, however the BCG vaccine should be avoided in confirmed HIV-positive children. Children on antiretroviral therapy (ART) usually respond well to vaccinations. **It is important that an HIV specialist is consulted who will decide which immunisations should be administered.**

CHILDREN WITH SPECIAL CONDITIONS AND CIRCUMSTANCES. In general children with non-progressive medical conditions such as Down syndrome should be vaccinated. Children with certain progressive central nervous system conditions; children with cancer and those being treated with cytotoxics (cancer drugs), radiation therapy, or steroids (other than low dose or inhaled); immunisation with live vaccines should be avoided until at least three months after therapy has stopped. Children with sickle cell disease are usually given all the vaccines on the schedule, as well as special pneumococcal vaccines and the flu vaccine. They will probably be on a daily regimen of antibiotics such as penicillin as well. Vaccination for MMR may need to be delayed for three months in children who have received immunoglobulin or plasma. Serious allergic reactions to neomycin and streptomycin mean vaccines containing these antibiotics should be avoided.

NOTE: That all the above information is a generalisation and in all cases you should follow the advice of your medical practitioner.

INTERNATIONAL TRAVEL IMMUNISATION. Children in particular, need to be protected against diseases endemic to other countries. Check with your local health department or the consulate of the countries you intend to visit for specific requirements. Some international airlines have an advisory immunisation service. Women who are pregnant must tell the vaccinating officer of their condition as it is not advisable for them to have certain vaccinations.

RABIES. This vaccine is given if and when required. There is normally no reaction in children. Ensure that your animals are vaccinated yearly. Rabies is usually fatal in humans unless treated immediately.

SMALLPOX. Smallpox vaccination is no longer required since the disease has been eradicated worldwide due to immunisation. The threat of biological warfare may make it necessary in future.

POSSIBLE SIDE EFFECTS AFTER VACCINATION. Mild fever, irritability, pain and redness at the injection site are the most common. See under each type for specific side effects to the vaccine. Notify your doctor of any severe reactions such as abscess at the injection site, swollen lymph glands, high fever, fits or severe swelling. Any other troubling reaction must be reported.

GENERAL IMMUNISATION INFORMATION AND POSSIBLE SIDE EFFECTS

BCG (BACILLUS-CALMETTE-GUERIN) = VACCINE AGAINST TUBERCULOSIS (TB). In countries where vaccination against TB is still required, the first shot of BCG which is a live vaccine is normally given as soon after birth as possible while the mother and child are still in the hospital where the baby was born.

REACTION. The BCG vaccine is usually given in the right upper arm and a normal reaction would be a hard raised red lump at the site of the injection. This should develop between four and six weeks after the vaccination, and disappear in about three months, leaving a white scar. Ulceration at the site that does not heal quickly is a complication that occurs mainly in HIV-infected children.

PRECAUTIONS. Children with eczema and open sores should be vaccinated on an area of healthy skin. The BCG vaccine is not generally given to children with impaired immune systems or active HIV infection (AIDS).

OPV (ORAL POLIO VACCINE) AGAINST POLIOMYELITIS. In under-developed areas the oral polio vaccine (OPV) which is a live vaccine against three types of polio virus, is given by mouth and thus does not need to be administered by medics. Polio is life threatening and causes paralysis.

REACTION. If the child vomits within an hour of taking it, you should let the clinic know so that they can repeat the dose. If you cannot get to the clinic on the same day, make a note of it and tell them the next time. A small number of serious reactions to this polio vaccine have been noted, but they are extremely rare.

PRECAUTIONS. If the child is ill, check with your clinic or medical adviser before having the vaccination done. The virus is live and is passed into the baby's stools soon after vaccination, so anyone handling the stool should be careful if they have not been immunised. Immuno-suppressed individuals are particularly at risk.

NOTE: It used to be thought that breast milk interferes with the efficacy of the polio vaccine. This is not so and you can breastfeed your baby before or after the vaccine is given. The same applies to giving any other feed.

POLIO = IPV INACTIVATED POLIO VACCINE GIVEN BY INJECTION. The inactivated (IPV) polio vaccine is used in developed countries where polio has largely been eradicated. It has very few side effects.

DIPHTHERIA DTAP = THREE-IN-ONE VACCINE. DTaP combines protection against diphtheria; tetanus and acellular (inactivated) pertussis (whooping cough).

DTAP-IPV/HIB = FIVE-IN-ONE VACCINE. This single injection protects against diphtheria, tetanus, acellular pertussis (whooping cough), polio and *Haemophilus influenzae* type B (against some strains of meningitis and pneumonia).

Pertussis (whooping cough) is an extremely serious illness in young children. Not having the pertussis injection according to the schedule can expose children to a potentially fatal illness. Tetanus (lockjaw) is an equally severe disease and half the people who get it and have not been immunised, die. You can get lockjaw through a cut or a scratch. It used to be recommended that people have a booster shot once every 10 years, but it is now recommended only after the age of 50 years, unless a booster has been given within the previous 10 years.

HAEMOPHILUS INFLUENZAE type B (Hib) component protects against Hib-induced meningitis, pneumonia, and epiglottitis, and may offer some protection against otitis media (middle-ear infection).

REACTION. The injection may cause pain, redness and swelling at the site. The child may have a mild fever and be irritable. Your doctor or clinic should advise you on any treatment that may be required. It is unfortunately not as effective in HIV-compromised children and a repeat shot may be needed.

PRECAUTIONS. The five-in-one combined vaccine should not be given if the child is ill or has a temperature over 38,5°C (101.3°F) or other signs of illness. In rare cases of anaphylaxis (severe allergic shock reaction), high fever, previous poor reaction to vaccination, or convulsions, you should consult your doctor before having the vaccination done or repeated.

SIX-IN-ONE VACCINE (DTAP-IPV/HIB/HBV). This six-in-one vaccine has the advantage of reducing the number of injections infants require as it targets six illnesses at once: diphtheria, tetanus, pertussis (whooping cough), polio, *haemophilus influenzae* type B and the sixth addition is against hepatitis B (liver disease) see HepB below.

HEPATITIS A VACCINE. This form of jaundice (liver disease) is relatively common in children where there is poor sanitation and overcrowding. Although they may be extremely lethargic and off their food, they usually recover well. When deemed necessary in children, two doses of the vaccine are usually administered, with an interval of six months between them. Because it is such a debilitating disease in adults it is generally advised for health care and day care workers who are easily exposed to the virus to be inoculated.

REACTION. Potential reactions include pain at the site, low fever, and loss of appetite.

PRECAUTIONS. If the child has a moderate to severe illness, delay the immunisation. Serious allergic reaction to any of the ingredients would be a contraindication. **Be sure to consult your medical provider in all the above vaccination questions and issues.**

HEPB VACCINE AGAINST HEPATITIS B. This vaccine is generally administered to all newborns before discharge in the USA. This is a highly contagious infection which leads to untreatable liver damage, including cancer and cirrhosis of the liver. If the mother is infected with hepatitis B, the baby will likely receive the vaccine within 12 hours of birth as well as a 0.5ml (0.017 fluid ounce) dose of hepatitis B immune globulin. Thereafter the usual HepB schedule is followed.

REACTION. Reactions may include low-grade fever and soreness at the site of the injection.

PRECAUTIONS. Most hepatitis B infections are caught in childhood, usually without symptoms. The virus has a seven-day life outside the body so it is easily transmitted, especially in places of child care. It can be caught through a skin puncture such as a human bite or broken skin in the mouth or nose. Adults at risk can also have the vaccinations.

ROTAVIRUS= (RV) AGAINST GASTROENTERITIS. Gastroenteritis caused by the rotavirus typically occurs in winter in mild climates. The symptoms are low-grade fever, vomiting, and frequent, watery stools. Children aged between three months and five years are most susceptible and can become extremely ill due to dehydration. The vaccine is given in a liquid form by mouth.

REACTION. An earlier rotavirus vaccine that was occasionally associated with intussusception has been discontinued. The present version has no serious side-effects.

PRECAUTIONS. The rotavirus vaccine is given before the age of eight months and no later.

MEASLES VACCINE. Measles (rubeola) has raised its ugly head in some areas due to missed immunisation. It is a serious disease and can cause complications such as pneumonia, encephalitis, brain functioning problems and chronic lung disease. It also lowers the body's resistance to disease and makes the child more susceptible to tuberculosis and other illnesses. Subacute sclerosing panencephalitis (SSPE) is a dreadful condition that can occur years after a bout of measles, in which the child gradually loses all functioning.

Even well-fed children lose a lot of weight, and deaths from complications following measles are common, even in children over the age of ten. In infants, the death rate is extremely high. Although the vaccine works better if given at 12 months, medical authorities in high risk areas may decide to give the measles vaccine earlier in order to reduce the infectious pool and protect those at risk. The MMR vaccine can be given even though the child has had the measles component previously. **Check with your doctor.**

Roald Dahl, author of children's books including *Charlie and the Chocolate Factory, James and the Giant Peach* and *Matilda* lost his seven-year-old daughter to measles.

> *Olivia, my eldest daughter, caught measles when she was seven years old. As the illness took its usual course I can remember reading to her often in bed and not feeling particularly alarmed about it. Then one morning, when she was well on the road to recovery, I was sitting on her*

bed showing her how to fashion little animals out of coloured pipe-cleaners, and when it came to her turn to make one herself, I noticed that her fingers and her mind were not working together and she couldn't do anything. "Are you feeling all right?" I asked her. "I feel all sleepy," she said. In an hour, she was unconscious. In twelve hours she was dead."

Dahl's daughter died when her measles progressed to a disease called measles encephalitis. In 1962, no vaccine existed for measles, but by 1986, one had been developed and Dahl advocated for its use. *"It really is almost a crime to allow your child to go unimmunised,"* he wrote.

PRECAUTIONS. Provided it is given within 72 hours, the measles vaccine can be given after contact with an infected person. Measles vaccine can be given at any age if not given in infancy, but women who receive the measles vaccination should not become pregnant for three months afterwards. Amongst the conditions which would contraindicate the vaccine are leukaemia and Hodgkin's disease, or if the patient is on high-dose steroid drugs or has severe immune deficiency such as AIDS.

Delay the immunisation if the child has an illness of which one of the symptoms is a high temperature. In general HIV-positive children should be immunised; but your clinic will advise you. There should be a gap greater than one month between the measles vaccine and the BCG vaccine as they are both live vaccines.

Even though the presently used vaccine is grown on chick embryo cells, egg allergy is no longer considered a contraindication to the measles vaccination. Severe allergy to any of the components of the vaccine, including neomycin and gelatine, is a contraindication. **However, you should consult your doctor in all respects.**

REACTION. Between 5 and 12 days after the immunisation, the child may develop a fever and a rash similar to measles. This is not serious or contagious. Give infant paracetamol (acetaminophen) or ibuprofen if advised by your doctor.

Febrile seizures (fits due to a high temperature, or as the temperature comes down) occur very occasionally 8–10 days after the vaccination. **Report any such reaction to your doctor.** Do not give the child anything to eat or drink during seizures. **Lower the temperature with children's medication recommended by your doctor, and do not over-dress.** There is no evidence that these events lead to epilepsy or seizures in future.

MMR=COMBINED VACCINE AGAINST MEASLES, MUMPS, AND RUBELLA (GERMAN MEASLES). MMR vaccine is given at 12–15 months so that the measles component is given at the most effective time. Even if your child has had the single measles vaccine earlier, it can be repeated in the MMR. A woman having either the rubella injection against German measles or the combined injection should not become pregnant for at least three months afterwards. Children who have had the Rubella (German measles) vaccination do not pose a threat to pregnant women.

REACTION. Because the MMR vaccine combines three separate vaccines in one injection, each vaccine can cause side effects that occur at different times. Consult your medical adviser. There is less chance of side effects after the second dose of MMR than the first.

About a week to 11 days after the MMR injection, some children develop a measles like rash with fever and loss of appetite. This should pass after two to three days, and it is not generally serious or contagious. Febrile seizures (fits) are rare but possible, and may occur more than a week or two after the vaccination. If this does happen, do not try to give the child anything to drink until the seizure has passed. **Report a high fever or seizure to your doctor.**

The mumps component occasionally causes swelling of the glands in the cheeks, neck or under the jaw lasting a few days. One to three weeks after the vaccination, the rubella (German measles) component can cause some adult women to experience painful, stiff or swollen joints, which can last up to three days.

In very rare cases, a child may develop a small rash of bruise-like spots about two weeks after having the MMR vaccine. It usually passes without treatment **but as always you should report it to your doctor.**

PRECAUTIONS. Breastfeeding mothers can have the MMR vaccine, but it should not be given during pregnancy. Allergy to egg is not considered a contraindication. However, a history of anaphylactic reaction to neomycin or other vaccine component, or previous reaction to MMR may indicate it should not be given **again.** Consult your medical practitioner who will advise you.

Children who are severely immune-suppressed, either because of an illness or its treatment should not be given the vaccine. Siblings and other members of the household should be vaccinated in order to protect the child. The MMR vaccine is one of the few live vaccines that are recommended for use in HIV positive children. However it is important to take the child's CD4 count and previous reactions to immunisation into consideration. **Consult your HIV clinic or doctor.**

HAEMOPHILUS INFLUENZA TYPE B) (HIB) AND MENINGOCOCCAL CONJUGATE SEROGROUP C = (MENC). Although the name sounds as though it is against influenza (flu), it actually protects against far more serious infections that caused the death of thousands of children before the vaccine was introduced in 1992. The Hib vaccine offers safe and effective protection in the very young against pneumonia, epiglottises (both of which can cause life-threatening breathing problems) and meningitis (a very serious infection of the covering of the spinal cord and brain). The disease may not have serious symptoms until the infection enters the bloodstream (septicaemia) making it particularly dangerous. It can be spread by unvaccinated carriers coughing and sneezing who are unaware they harbour the germs.

REACTION. Redness, tenderness and swelling at the sight of the vaccination are common but not serious. Less commonly, there may be a slight temperature with irritability, diarrhoea and vomiting. Your doctor may suggest a dose of children's paracetamol or ibuprofen. **Report any side effects that cause concern to your doctor.**

VARICELLA = (CHICKEN POX). Varicella vaccine (VZV) is routinely given in most high-income countries. Although generally considered a relatively mild illness in children, the virus stays in the body and can cause painful variations of the infection throughout life, including shingles. A serious complication of chickenpox in boys and older males is the possibility of orchitis (swelling of the testes) that can result in sterility.

Although rare, kidney problems, difficulty with balance, brain inflammation, heart problems and encephalitis are possible. It is not uncommon for bacteria such as streptococcus and staphylococcus aureus to take hold, possibly due to the child scratching the itchy skin. Scars left by scratching are permanent. If caught during pregnancy it can have serious effects on the unborn child.

The vaccine is highly effective for use in healthy children. Provided it is given within 36 hours of exposure to chickenpox, the vaccine can be given and may prevent infection. The problem is that chickenpox is contagious before the rash appears. **Get advice from your medical doctor.**

REACTION. Possible reactions include redness at the injection site and a slight fever.

PRECAUTIONS. Do not give during pregnancy and advanced immunosuppressive disorders. Children whose immunity is still sound, including HIV-positive children, should be considered for immunisation. Consult your medical caregiver.

Never use aspirin to treat a fever in a child with chickenpox, or the side effects of chickenpox vaccination, as it is a viral illness and can lead to Reye syndrome; although very rare, it is an extremely serious and potentially fatal illness in the young.

PNEUMOCOCCAL CONJUGATED VACCINE = (PCV) AGAINST PNEUMOCOCCAL INFECTIONS. This vaccine is a significant step towards protecting babies against very severe illnesses including pneumonia, meningitis and septicaemia, a kind of blood poisoning caused by the pneumococcus bacteria. It may also have a preventive effect against middle-ear infection which can cause deafness. All these infections are a huge problem in children under five years of age, and in particular those under two. These illnesses pose a serious threat because the disease has become resistant to some of the medicines used to treat it. The vaccine is given before two years of age when children are the most vulnerable to the disease and protection lasts for at least three years.

Delay if the child has an illness with a high fever. The vaccine is recommended for children between two and five years of age who have certain medical conditions such as sickle cell disease; HIV-positive children, but the effectiveness may be reduced. **Always consult your medical advisor.**

REACTION. Possible reactions include slight pain, redness and swelling at injection site, and mild fever. Severe allergic reactions (anaphylactic) are rare. Should a child have difficulty breathing, wheezing, hives or appear distressed contact your doctor immediately.

PRECAUTIONS. The vaccine may have reduced efficacy in children with impaired immunity, either through genetic causes, HIV or other reasons. As always, these children should be assessed by a doctor beforehand.

INFLUENZA VACCINE AGAINST FLU. Flu 'shots' are commonly given to older people, but in some countries they are also recommended for children six months and older. Because the strain of influenza virus varies from year to year, the World Health Organization (WHO) makes recommendations annually regarding the type posing a threat and a suitable vaccine. Consult your doctor.

HPV (HUMAN PAPILLOMAVIRUS) VACCINE AGAINST CERVICAL CANCER. The human papillomavirus causes 99.7% of cases of cervical cancer. The virus is transmitted during sexual intercourse. Years after infection, changes in the cervix take place that can indicate precancerous abnormal cells. Pap smears are a way of identifying these early warning signs, even though there may be no other symptoms. However, an aggressive type of cervical cancer, adenocarcinoma, may not be detected by a Pap smear as it occurs high up in the cervix. The vaccine is administered to females before they become sexually active, offering protection to the second-most common cancer in young women worldwide. Research is being done on its possible use in males.

REACTION. Very mild soreness at the site may occur.

PRECAUTIONS. Having the vaccination does not mean total protection, although it does protect against the most common strains of the virus (there are over 100) which can cause infection. Regular screening should still be done.

Vaccination should not be done during pregnancy, as the effects have not been studied. Women who have an abnormal Pap smear can have the vaccination. Although it will not cure any present infection, it may protect against other strains of the virus. Allergy to yeast or other ingredients of the vaccine require caution. **Speak to your medical advisor.**

SPECIAL VACCINATIONS FOR EPIDEMICS. During epidemics you may read or hear about the use of medication that may be used. Your medical practitioner will guide you as to whether you should take preventative medication, and which product.

A meningitis vaccine which is effective against four strains of meningococcal meningitis can be given to children over the age of two years (it is not very effective under two years). There is also a pneumococcal vaccine that can be given in epidemics of pneumococcal bacterial meningitis to babies as well as older children. A vaccine against meningitis B, the most serious form of meningitis was approved in 2015.

MAKING VACCINATIONS EASIER FOR YOUR BABY. Dress your child in clothes that make it easy to access the thighs and upper arm areas, and try to keep the visit relaxed. You may have to wait a while, so take soft toys or other comfort items such as a dummy (pacifier) and "blankie". Many children do not feel the shot being given; and others cry only for a short while. Comfort your child and it should all be over soon.

OVERWEIGHT
WHAT IS THE EXTENT OF THE PROBLEM?
In 2016, The World Health Organisation released the Ending Childhood Obesity (or ECHO) report, highlighting the extent of the problem of childhood overweight and obesity, the proposed causal mechanisms driving the problem, and the proposed strategies to address it.

In 2014, an estimated 41 million children under the age of 5 were affected by overweight or obesity. In South Africa, the prevalence of childhood overweight and obesity has reached epidemic proportions, having doubled since the 1990s to an estimated 13.5% among children between the ages of 6-14 years. Interestingly this spans across all ethnic and socioeconomic groups.

WHAT FACTORS ARE CONTRIBUTING TOWARDS THE PROBLEM?
Childhood overweight and obesity is a complex issue, involving environmental, socio-

economic, familial, and cultural factors. According to the WHO, obesity is caused by children being exposed to an unhealthy, or obesogenic environment. In addition, individuals' behaviour within this environment, as well as biological factors during early life exert a strong influence on the development of overweight and obesity.

WHAT IS AN OBESOGENIC ENVIRONMENT?

An obesogenic environment simply means an environment which encourages weight gain and obesity. As countries undergo rapid urbanisation and socio-economic transition, food availability and choice increase. Children are exposed to processed, energy-dense yet nutrient-poor food. In addition opportunity for physical activity both in an out of school time decline, with increasing time spent in front of screens, and on other sedentary activities. As a result, children are increasingly exposed to this environment which promotes an energy imbalance where more energy is being consumed than is being utilised.

WHAT ABOUT THE EFFECT OF CULTURE?

Cultural values and norms are known to influence people's perception of health. National data released in 2014 showed that in South Africa, an astonishing 87.9% of the population identified a 'fat' body shape as ideal, with a larger body size being associated to health, dignity, and affluence. This suggests that cultural and ethnic influences are strong, and could prevent many parents from recognising childhood overweight and obesity as a problem.

WHAT ABOUT FAMILIAL FACTORS – CAN OBESITY BE PASSED FROM PARENT TO CHILD?

Yes, the risk of obesity is frequently passed from one generation to the next, as a result of behavioural and / or biological factors.

From a behavioural perspective, children inherit their parents' socioeconomic status, cultural norms, eating habits and activity patterns which could perpetuate obesity.

Biological factors too, can lead to increased risk of obesity in children. Developmental factors during preconception, pregnancy, and infancy (known as the first thousand days of life) can change the biology of individuals, placing them at greater or lesser risk of developing obesity. This is thought to occur through two major developmental pathways.

(i)   The first is called the "mismatch" pathway, in which a child's early environment does not match the environment in which they later grow up in.

Malnutrition during the foetal period or during early childhood is thought to exert an influence on a child's gene function. In short, that child's biology is prepared for a harsh environment. So, when exposed to energy dense food and sedentary environment later in life, children who were undernourished during early life are at far greater risk of becoming obese.

(ii) The second is called the developmental pathway, in which a mother enters pregnancy with pre-existing obesity or diabetes, or develops gestational diabetes during her pregnancy. This predisposes her child to increased fat depositing which is associated with metabolic disease and obesity.

As a result of these developmental aspects, there is increasing focus on obesity prevention from preconception, and throughout the first thousand days of life.

HEALTHY CHOICES

- Breastfeed your baby if possible as this allows babies to take as much as they need rather than a set amount in the bottle.
- Do not think that giving children younger than two years 2% low fat or skim milk or yogurt and other dairy products is a good way to prevent them becoming overweight. They need full-cream products for their essential fatty acid content which is vital for brain development.
- Some fast foods are not suitable for young children as their preparation methods are likely to destroy the vitamin and other nutritional content. The oil used in fast foods that are fried may not be fresh, and many fast foods are extremely kilojoule-dense. Children also develop a taste for these foods, which seldom include fresh vegetables or fruits. It is very difficult to change food preferences once children have become used to them.
- Young children need three meals a day plus two healthy snacks.(See *p. 249)* for suitable foods. This should prevent them filling up on cakes, sweets, chips and the like.
- Weaning babies and putting them on foods such as mielie meel can result in malnourishment. This is turn predisposes them to obesity later on. *See p. 251* for how to enrich mielie meel.
- Children get to like what they are used to. You do not have to serve Brussels sprouts and broccoli at every meal, but vegetables, salads and fresh fruit should be part of their regular diet. And it is possible for them to acquire a taste for any food if it does not come loaded with emotion.
- It has been speculated that children become overweight due to a lack of exercise. This is partially true, but not the only reason. Young children naturally like to run around. Encourage this. Keep TV watching and computer games to certain times.
- Avoid deep-fried foods.
- Some mothers are so afraid of making their little girls fat that they never give sweets, biscuits and so called 'treats'. This is counterproductive because it simply gives these foods an emotional attraction. (*See pp. 191, 255.*)

- Do not confuse what is a desirable diet for an adult with that of a child. (*See p. 256.*)
- Many children eat out of boredom. Keep them busy.
- Do not expect children to 'clean their plate'. Yes, they should eat what is offered, but be sure they are hungry enough and do not offer rewards for finishing their meal.
- Respect real preferences. Do not put up with manipulative rejection of food.

HOW SLIM PEOPLE STAY SLIM

Studies on people who are 'naturally' slim revealed that they seem to have an internal 'off switch' that stops them from eating more than they feel like. They had to *force* themselves to eat more than they wanted to in order to see whether eating more would make them gain weight. It did.

Kindergarten children were offered a selection of biscuits and other 'treats' after they had had their snack break. Some children continued snacking from their plate while drawing. Others had a taste then left the rest. This indicates that continuing to eat after you are full is programmed from a very young age.

Once extra fat cells are formed in childhood it is very difficult to stop them being 'filled'.
- Obese adults have great difficulty in keeping weight off when it is lost. It appears that once an internal point for satiety – the feeling of being more than fully satisfied – is set high, it is very difficult to reset it at a lower point. The appestat is the centre that controls appetite. Appetite and hunger are different.
- Slim people move quickly and use many more movements in doing ordinary tasks than overweight people. They walk on the escalator; wave their arms when talking on the telephone; they even move more on the tennis court.
- Doing more exercise in order to lose weight only works if you eat less as well. Unfortunately exercise also gives you an appetite, and any kilojoules that are burnt off can quickly be added again by eating a 'reward'. Exercise- induced anorexia (lack of appetite) occurs with extreme exercise, for instance amongst long-distance runners.
- In rare instances obesity is associated with hormonal problems such as hypothyroidism or hyperthyroidism. Consult your doctor.

PREMATURITY

BORN EARLY. When a baby is born after being in the womb for less than 37 weeks it is termed premature or preterm, as it is more usually called today. Between 38 and 42 weeks newborns are regarded as being full-term, and after 42 weeks, post-term. Up to 20% of babies born in underdeveloped areas are preterm, while the incidence is around 6% in more affluent areas. Although there are a number of reasons why babies are born before their time, doctors are not able to pinpoint the exact cause in up to half the cases. Certain factors are known to cause early labour. One of these is poor nutrition.

Other important causes of premature birth are placenta *praevia* and *abruptio* placenta, when the placenta is placed over the mouth of the womb, or starts to come away from the womb. With good antenatal care, and diagnostic techniques such as ultrasound, doctors can tell if a woman has any of these conditions and can treat her (usually with bed rest) so that early birth can possibly be postponed.

Maternal illness such as diabetes, heart or kidney disease, infections and toxaemia can also bring on, or necessitate early labour. But with good antenatal care these conditions can be treated. Twins are often born early due to the size of the uterus. Premature labour can also result if the baby has certain abnormalities.

In the 50% where the causes of early labour are not known, factors such as smoking, lack of vitamins and minerals, and taking certain drugs are implicated. With modern techniques, smaller and younger babies are surviving with a good chance of growing up normally. Babies born at only 26 weeks have done well with specialised care.

Hyaline membrane disease, which causes lung problems – until relatively recently one of the main reasons why preterm babies did not survive – is treatable with CPAP (Continuous Positive Airway Pressure) which keeps the baby's lungs expanded. Tests can show if the baby's lungs have produced surfactant, a substance that prepares the lungs for breathing outside the womb. If the substance is lacking and labour can be delayed for 24–48 hours, the mother can be given certain drugs to help the baby's lungs manufacture surfactant so that the infant can be born safely. The administration of artificial surfactant after the birth may help preterm babies with lung problems.

The old tale that babies born at seven months do better than those born at eight months is not true and the nearer to term the baby is born, provided there are no complications, the better. More important than the gestational age of the baby is the child's weight.

Babies with a low birth weight (below 2 500g or 5lbs 8oz) are usually at greater risk than heavier infants. However, with modern techniques, smaller and younger babies are surviving with a good chance of growing up normally. Babies born at only 26 weeks have done well with specialised care.

PRETERM BABIES LOOK DIFFERENT. When you see your tiny baby with her transparent skin, fragile features and seemingly disproportionately big head in relation to her body you will understandably be filled with emotion. She will be thin because fat is only put on towards the end of pregnancy, and her head will be longer and her features sharper and less rounded than babies you have been used to seeing. Some babies' wrists are so tiny that a man's wedding ring fits over it like a bracelet. She will probably have fine, downy hair on her face and body, but no eyelashes and eye brows. Her ears are thin and pressed close to her head, and her nails are very soft and short.

There will most likely be many tubes strapped to her little features because she needs to be tube feed, as she cannot suck well yet, and her breathing may need assistance. Because she has no insulating fat she is very susceptible to cold and will have to be kept warm on a special heated bed. When she breathes her chest may sink right back so it seems like it will cave in. She will seldom cry, and she will sleep a lot.

There will be the beep and hum of monitors and the urgent sounding of alarms, and the doctors and nurses will gather round. You will probably feel that she belongs to them more than she does to you because they can help her and you cannot. Nothing could be further from the truth. Your baby needs you more than anything. She needs to hear your voice and to feel your touch and love.

ADJUSTING TO YOUR PREEMIE. For the parents, premature birth is always a shock. You will experience conflicting emotions and feel cheated of the last few months of pregnancy, the time in which the mother prepares herself and her home for the arrival of the baby. Instead of ready love and acceptance there is the conflict of fear of getting too close to your baby in case she does not survive. Ask the doctors and nurses your questions, and be positive. Your baby needs you. Handle her as soon as you can, even if it is only a touch with a finger. If you are allowed to, carry her close to your body 'kangaroo mother care' style. Your breathing, warmth and the sound of your voice will create a bond that is therapeutic, and stimulate growth.

FEEDING. Some mothers are able to produce breastmilk and can express it so that it can be given to their baby in the incubator, and even keep their milk supply going until the baby is strong enough to suck. This has health benefits for the child, and can give great satisfaction and alleviate some of the feelings of failure that plague many mothers who have given birth prematurely.

The ability to suck and swallow is present at 28 weeks of gestation, but is not fully coordinated until 32 to 34 weeks of gestation. Thus very preterm babies are not likely to be able to suck from the breast or bottle. Since sucking is such an important part of development, both physically and emotionally, giving a dummy can be helpful, in particular during tube feeding. Although dummies are frowned on by some institutions because of the belief that they interfere with breastfeeding, the evidence for this is weak. Preterm babies given dummies were less restless and left hospital earlier. These tiny dummies must be ordered by your doctor. Another practice that is meant to protect breastfeeding is to feed the babies from a cup rather than a bottle or tube. Babies who have been fed from a cup are more likely to be exclusively breastfed when they leave hospital, but are no more likely to be breastfed three or six months later. Their stay in hospital is also 10 days longer on average.

YOUR BABY'S PROGRESS. Touching, stroking and other tactile stimulation has been shown to release brain chemicals that support growth. Preterm babies receiving this stimulation early on gained weight faster than those who did not. A year later they also showed better mental and physical development than unstimulated babies. Preterm babies need extra iron from birth since they have not had time to store it while still in the womb. Although they gain weight rapidly they may not catch up in growth to other babies until they are three or four years old.

When judging a preterm baby's progress and milestones you should keep in mind the date on which the baby should have been born. For example, if she was born six weeks early she will behave like a six-week-old baby when she is three months. Nevertheless, most preterm babies do catch up developmentally as well as physically and there should be little difference after the first few years.

By the time the child is ready for nursery school there should be no lag. If there do appear to be learning or other problems they should be investigated and it should not be presumed that the child will 'catch up'.

SEXUAL DETERMINATION AND ORIENTATION

BOTH SIDES OF THE COIN IN ONE. The first question parents ask after the birth of a child is usually this: is it a boy or a girl? Yet the answer to this simple question may not always be straightforward. Disordered sexual differentiation, when the genitalia are not obviously male or female at birth, is not that uncommon. The rate for children worldwide who are born with ambiguous internal and external sexual characteristics is estimated to be around 1:2000, with certain conditions such as true hermaphrodites, said to be much higher in certain parts of southern and central Africa.

The birth of a child with sexual organs that are not clearly male or female is a huge shock for parents. To provide reassurance the utmost sensitivity is needed, as well as support by a team of specialists experienced in this field, even if it means transferring the child to another hospital. Comprehensive testing must be done, including chromosomal analysis, hormonal functioning and pelvic ultrasound before conclusions are reached, as there are many possible variations.

Before any corrective surgery is done, it is essential that all possible medical reasons for the condition are explored. For example, some infants who may appear to be more female at birth, are raised as girls yet develop male characteristics during the teenage years, and then feel and behave more like males. The human hormonal system is complex, and there are numerous chromosomal defects that affect the growth and development of sexual characteristics before and after birth. Later on, hormones also influence the development of secondary sexual characteristics and orientation.

Assigning gender at birth and doing invasive and definitive procedures immediately is now being questioned by activists who would like to postpone surgery until the child can participate in the decision. Thus a highly experienced team including a paediatric endocrinologist, surgeon, geneticist, social worker and family practitioner are needed to work together with the family and the child if he or she is old enough. This does not lessen the fact that both child and parents will have a difficult path to tread. The psychological welfare of the child is extremely important and everyone concerned will need the very best help and advice possible.

Research is ongoing and already much is known regarding the various medical conditions involved and how they play out. But it is a specialised field and the best advice must be obtained. Psychological care is desirable.

SEXUAL ORIENTATION. During the height of the feminist revolution in the 1960s and 1970s parents were urged to avoid giving their girl children dolls, and rather go for cars, blocks and other toys which might be considered gender 'neutral'. This was done so that girls would not be 'conditioned' into the conventional roles assumed by the 'weaker' sex.

Despite this, any experienced parent will tell you that little girls have an impulse of their own and a natural propensity towards pink, Barbie dolls and kitsch. They may grow up to be engineers and pilots, but they start off with fairies, frills and fantasy castles. The same applies to boys. Spiderman, bikes and skateboards are desirable. Barbie dolls are not. Just how strong this impetus is was played out in a tragic tale of genital mutilation and medical mismanagement.

NATURE OR NURTURE? Twin boys, Brian and Bruce, were born in 1965 to a young couple in Winnipeg, Canada. At six months the twins were having difficulty urinating and doctors suggested circumcision. Things went horribly wrong, however, and Bruce's penis was badly mutilated. One night his parents saw an interview with a professor at a very famous American medical university. He argued that nurture, not nature, determines a child's gender. A boy could live happily as a girl if caught early. His distraught parents decided immediately to visit the professor in Baltimore, USA.

For the professor, this was an ideal opportunity to test his theories on gender. At the age of 21 months, Bruce's testes were removed, and his parents were told to go home and raise him as a girl. All the while the professor wrote medical research papers claiming that all was going well with the experiment, and that it was a resounding success. This spread the idea that nurture is more important than nature, in terms of whether we behave like males or females. Meanwhile Bruce had become Brenda, while his 'control' in the experiment, his twin brother Brian, developed like a typical boy.

But Brenda was not doing well. Although he was given female hormones, dressed as a girl, had long hair and was treated like a girl by his parents, he walked like a boy and played like a boy. It was clear all was not well, yet the professor continued to claim academically that the experiment was a great success, and pressured the parents to allow doctors to operate and create a vagina.

It was at this stage that Bruce ('Brenda') threatened to commit suicide and his father broke down and confessed the whole story. When Bruce was 14 he doused his female clothes with petrol and set fire to them. He then changed his name to David and had an operation to remove his breasts and form a penis. The idea that you could alter the gender of children simply by raising them as a boy or girl was discredited. Tragically it was too late for David, who committed suicide in 2004 at the age of 38.

A new angle to the question of the emotional differences between males and females seems to be all in the genes, and not the hormones. The culprit, it is thought, is the X chromosome – one of the two sex chromosomes. Both men and women have the gene, but it is only 'switched on' in women. This makes women able to 'read' non-verbal behaviour: the so-called 'women's intuition' that makes women aware of social norms and non-verbal signals in others. Men can become more sensitive to these cues, but in them it is a learned skill. 'New age' men therefore are seemingly made, not born.

SLEEPING PROBLEMS

HOW TO AVOID AND TREAT SLEEPING PROBLEMS. There is probably no aspect of the early years of raising children that demoralises parents more than the child who does not sleep. There are a number of reasons why some children sleep less than their parents would prefer. Disruptions are sometimes due to the child's internal sleep rhythms, but some are due to habits and faulty management. The best cure for sleeping problems lies in prevention, and in understanding what sleep is and how this mysterious function works.

Sleep centres in the brain control the human circadian rhythm of 24-hour cycles of sleep and wakefulness. As pregnant women will attest, babies have periods of rest and activity while still in the womb. After birth, sleep patterns are divided into four stages, moving from the lightest to deepest sleep repeated several times a night.

THE EARLY WEEKS. Soon after birth babies spend more time in deep sleep, which explains why they are able to sleep through a lot of noise and wake less frequently. Newborn babies sleep from eight to 16 hours out of 24, which unfortunately is nothing like the old myth that babies sleep 23 out of 24 hours! Babies who were born preterm and those who have had a difficult birth are often more restless.

In the first few weeks or sometimes months babies wake during the night because they cannot go through the night without nourishment. So give a breast or bottle feed during the night as demanded in the early weeks. Giving water instead of a feed will simply mean that your baby wakes again a short while later. Breastfed babies are likely to wake within four hours of being put down to sleep, but they do not wake more often during the night than bottle-fed babies at this stage. Later on breastfed babies are more likely to wake more frequently at night and continue do so as long as they are breastfed.

HOW TO ESTABLISH A GOOD SLEEPING ROUTINE FROM THE BEGINNING

- Try and put your baby down to sleep while she is still awake so that she gets used to falling asleep without you. She needs to learn to self-soothe.
- It has been shown that babies wake when they get too hot, so do not think your baby needs to be smothered in blankets to sleep comfortably. Overheating a baby has also been associated with cot death. Feeling cold will also wake a baby, so a happy medium must be found.
- Be calm but distant when you feed your baby during the night. Do not talk to, or play with your baby. Just make the age-old schussing sounds that have lulled babies through the ages.
- Always put her to sleep in a darkened room so that she does not confuse day and night sleep cycles. Do not leave a night light on as it can affect the secretion of melatonin, a vital hormone.
- Put your baby to sleep in the same place every time if possible and with the same routine.
- Some babies fall asleep when listening to a sound like a telephone dialling tone, vacuum cleaner or other 'white' noise. While this may be harmless it does not seem ideal. Better to make or buy a recording of soothing lullabies or classical music specially recorded to help babies fall asleep.
- If your young baby is a restless sleeper try swaddling her before you put her in her cot. (*See p. 81 for how to swaddle.*)
- Allow your baby to settle herself – don't rush into her room immediately – she may need to make a little noise before she relaxes into sleep.
- Parents should take turns in putting their baby to sleep so that she gets used to someone else at night.
- Sucking or rocking helps babies settle into sleep but this could develop into a need that involves breastfeeding, replacing a dummy or rocking your child for many hours every night. Try and avoid a settling routine that involves your presence at length.
- This may not always be possible as some babies need help in order to relax into sleep. Gently bouncing on a large exercise ball such as those used in Pilates, while holding your wrapped baby, can be very effective.

BABIES' SLEEP NEEDS. Young babies do not stay awake out of 'naughtiness'. They will sleep when they need to unless they are in severe discomfort from hunger or colic, for example. Newborn babies sleep an average of 16 hours out of 24, and by four months the average time spent awake is 10 hours, which may come as a rude shock to many mothers. Between 12 and 16 weeks the average child should be able to go for at least six hours between feeds at night. Some considerate children sleep through sooner. Try and 'stretch' the time between feeds if you are still feeding at night.

WHY BABIES WAKE. Babies, like adults, have sleep cycles in which brain activity is increased or decreased. There are four sleep stages, from wakefulness to stage four, the deepest. Everyone goes through the four sleep stages several times during the night. Rapid eye movement sleep (REM), when dreaming occurs, is the lightest stage. We all rouse on several occasions during the night in periods of light sleep but quickly drift back to sleep unless we are anxious or kept awake by other stimuli. Instead of slipping back into sleep some children are unable to self-soothe and need outside help to settle again. This is why your baby should be encouraged to learn to settle by herself from the beginning.

HANDLING NIGHT-TIME WAKING.
- The very young baby will need a feed. (*See p. 95.*)
- There is no consistent evidence that it is better to go to your older baby the moment she wakes or to let her try and settle herself. This is because the possible reasons for waking in the older baby are so numerous. What is important is to try and learn to differentiate between a distress cry and a demand cry. After a quick check, it is worth giving her up to ten minutes to try and settle herself before taking action. The child who wakes in the natural cycle and can't get back to sleep by herself usually niggles for some time before crying. A child who is ill or in pain will probably wake crying, and of course you will go to her immediately.
- A child who is ill will probably be hot to the touch and flushed. Earache is made worse when the child lies down so picking the child up may stop her crying, leading you to think she is being 'naughty'. Teething can be treated by rubbing the gums with a suitable teething product but note that some 'remedies' may be potentially harmful, so get medical advice before using a teething product.
- Do not give a painkiller routinely to help your child sleep. Drugs prescribed to help your child sleep can help get you some rest in the short term but hardly ever change sleeping patterns in the long term.
- Do not make a habit of giving the older child milk or juice during the night when she wakes. If she is hungry, make sure she has frequent high-kilojoule meals during the

day and investigate whether she is anaemic by having a haemoglobin test done by your doctor.

- Make sure she has a good meal before putting her to bed and don't make it too early. Babies cannot be expected to go for 12 or more hours without food as their growth needs are great. If you are giving milk or juice during the night water it down until it is plain water and then stop giving it as soon as you can.
- Babies' sensitivities vary. Some are disturbed by being wet, others by loud sounds or a tense atmosphere. Change nappies with as little disturbance as possible.
- Pinworm (Threadworm) infestation can wake a toddler due to severe anal itching.
- Toddlers derive emotional security from their surroundings. Try not to change her room's furnishing even if you move.
- After infancy, do not take your child into your bed unless you are willing to keep her there for the foreseeable future; any change is likely to be seen as rejection and be resisted. (*See p. 490.*)

THE BEDTIME ROUTINE

- Do not let your baby get over-tired or over-stimulated before bedtime. Have a predictable routine and a time for going to bed that is followed regularly.
- Being read a bedtime story is a wonderful custom that creates a warm and pleasant end to a child's day, and builds a bond between parents and child. If you do it with commitment and care this is truly what quality time is about. In comparison, watching a TV programme offers nothing as good.
- Working parents sometimes allow extended bedtimes because they have not seen their child during the day, or through guilt. Chances are that you will become resentful of her presence rather than giving her any meaningful attention. Rather spend a lot of time with her over the weekend.
- Sucking on a dummy, stroking a soft toy or blanket often helps the older child relax into sleep. Don't let your child get used to playing with your hair or you will be anchored.
- You can give a bedtime bottle of plain milk if your child cannot fall asleep without it.
- Dress your older child for bed just before bedtime so that it forms part of the sleep routine.

RESISTANCE TO GOING TO SLEEP IN THE OLDER CHILD

- Toddlers are notoriously good at manipulating parents. Calling for a drink or for Daddy or just one more story or another kiss and cuddle are all ways of keeping you around and staying awake. Be firm, pleasant and absolutely resolute about not giving in to these games. If you give in after resisting initially she will have learned that she only has to persist and you will crumble eventually.

- If she is having too many sleeps during the day, try to change her routine. Even a short nap can leave a toddler refreshed. There is sometimes a point at which two sleeps is too much – and one, too little – but this should adjust quite soon.

- If your child has been staying up very late, set a slightly earlier bedtime every day, after checking the rest of her daily routine, especially sleeping and over-stimulation. Do not let her sleep late in the morning.

- Older children respond to rewards like stars, stickers and the like for modification of their behaviour. Do not make the initial goal for earning a star too hard to achieve. Behaviour modification can be gradual so long as it is in the right direction.

MODIFYING FREQUENT WAKING

- Some children seem never to have achieved the goal of sleeping through the night. Go through the information on the previous page and see whether you have been doing things wrong. You may have an easy waker who cannot relax back into sleep without help until she learns how to do it. Try the strategies described to modify this.

- Keep a diary of exactly when your child wakes during the night, and when and how she goes back to sleep. This will give you a clearer picture of the problem and you will be able to chart changes.

- Children who have never learned to settle themselves when they rouse at night, or who have developed a habit of waking for a drink, must be helped to modify their behaviour. You can leave a bottle of watered-down milk or preferably plain water in the corner of her bed – show it to her and she will hopefully do the necessary without waking you. Most children lose interest if there is only water in the bottle. Be sure to use only sterilised bottles, water and milk.

- Should this not work, check to see if she is alright, while being firm about not picking her up. Then go through the usual routine you have developed for getting her to sleep again.

- To be successful you will have had to make up your mind that you mean what you say and you will not weaken. Once you have made up your mind that things have to change and you really mean it children often sense it and stop their demands. But you must really want to change things or you will do more harm than good.

- Discuss your strategy with your partner and make a pact to support each other when either of you weakens. If you undermine each other by suggesting that you may be doing the wrong thing, you will fail.
- When your child wakes, go in as usual and reassure her calmly and with confidence. Tuck her in but do NOT pick her up. Leave the room even if she starts crying. Wait five minutes. Go in and repeat the procedure. Wait five minutes every time. If you have really made up your mind not to pick your child up, chances are she will settle in a few nights. But it may even take two weeks and getting up twenty times a night initially, for changing behaviour can take time. But it has been shown to work and you will not have damaged your child emotionally, which is the fear that keeps good and caring parents from being resolute.

WILL THINGS GET BETTER NATURALLY?

About 20% of one- and two-year-olds wake regularly. At three, 14% still wake at night and at four years only 8% wake regularly. By the time they are teenagers you can expect to spend half the night waiting for them to come home and then you can't get them up in the morning!

MORE ABOUT SLEEPING AND WAKING PROBLEMS

CRYING FROM PAIN. Around six months, and then perhaps in the middle of the second year, a child may wake from pain caused by teething. The area around the mouth is usually red because of dribbling and she will be restless and may wake often. If you suspect this to be the cause, buy a teething product from your chemist or doctor and rub it on the child's gums. Some old remedies contain harmful substances so go for a safe, recommended product.

Night-waking from this cause should not last for more than a week or two, and if it does, it is probably due to something else. A common cause for waking during the night from pain is middle-ear infection. If she is flushed and has a temperature she probably has otitis media. (*See pp. 350, 449.*) If she has suddenly started screaming and seems to be relieved when you pick her up, do not think she is 'spoilt'. The pressure in the ears changes in the upright position, easing the pain. Give children's paracetamol and call a doctor in the morning. Any discharge from the ear could be a sign of a burst eardrum. Keep water out of the ear and see a doctor.

COLD. Your child could also be waking because she is cold. If she kicks off her blankets you can try putting her in a special baby sleeping suit or bag, or sew tapes on the corners of the blankets and tie them around the bars of the cot. It is also possible to buy clips that serve the same purpose. Remember that overheating her at night could also make her uncomfortable and wake her. Duvets are not recommended for babies.

WORMS. Although tiny, only about a centimetre long, threadworms cause intense itching in the anal area when they come out to lay their eggs, mainly at night. They may occasionally travel into the vagina and cause irritation that results in bedwetting – besides waking the child because of the terrible itching. These worms are extremely prevalent in toddlers and are no reflection on your standard of hygiene: they are spread by microscopic eggs that can be dust-borne and breathed in.

You can check to see whether your child is being worried by worms by looking at the anal area a few nights running about two hours after she has gone to bed. They look like very fine white threads about 1cm long. The whole family should then be treated with a suitable mixture from your pharmacist. It is pleasant tasting and needs only one initial dose, to be repeated a few weeks later according to the instructions. (*See p. 372.*)

GETTING INTO BED WITH YOU. Some children wake without crying and want to get into the parents' bed saying they are 'scared'. This is usually enough to make parents take the child into their bed for comfort. It can be the start of a habit that is very hard to break, presuming, of course, that you do not want to share your bed with a rather damp and restless toddler who is likely to hog most of the available space. Rather spend the night in her room. If she comes to your bed immediately take her back every time. If both you and your partner enjoy the company then you do not have a problem – there is something to be said for the family bed. And many children do come to the parent's bed because they enjoy it.

However, you might not be able to get a good night's sleep, and feel tired and crotchety in the morning. If you are breastfeeding she may wake even more often for a feed. It can also inhibit your sex life. But having to drag an unwilling toddler back to her room is also going to interrupt your sleep, so the best solution is to find the reasons for the problem and try to solve them.

The most likely cause is night fears and a basic sense of insecurity. If your child is waking for these reasons and you cannot resolve them during the day, it may help to overcome them sooner if you welcome her into your bed. Children develop quickly and if you give her intensive care for as long as necessary – it may take weeks or months – she will most likely return to the attractions of independence, which are also strong.

You should encourage her very gently, as soon as you think she may be ready, by getting her a new cuddly toy to 'keep her company'.

Don't forget the value of a dimmer switch which turns the light down low in the passage so she's more secure. Do not keep a bright light on in her room as this can inhibit the production of melatonin, as this hormone is needed for growth and development in children. It also regulates sleep cycles which is why we feel 'jet lagged' when we have travelled across time zones.

Having a friend to sleep over can sometimes be the catalyst a child needs for sleeping in her room, but very young children will often resist this.

WHEN THREE'S A CROWD. On the other hand, if you are quite sure your marital bed could not cope with another addition, you will have to be firm the first time she tries to get into bed with you, and in many ways this is a justified position to take. But it is no good allowing it once or twice, or sometimes; you will just frustrate and confuse her. Take her back to her bed in a reassuring but firmly confident way. Tuck her in and kiss her goodnight, assuring her that you will hear her if she needs you. If she turns up at your bedside again, go through the same procedure. If she has the least indication that there is any chance of sleeping with you, you will never persuade her back to her own bed. Be firm, reassuring and friendly. But do not weaken.

One way of keeping a toddler from wandering in the night is to keep her in a cot with high sides for as long as possible. You will of course go to her at once if she is really unhappy. But leave her to try and settle herself for a few minutes before you go in. Graduating to a bed is far easier from the third year when the conflicts of the toddler stage are less troublesome.

Single mothers are sometimes quite happy to have their child in bed with them. This is a potentially fraught situation. You may in time prefer to share your bed with someone else and you can be sure that your child will not want you to. Children have been known to hog the parental bed until their teens in an effort to keep mummy to themselves.

COMING TO YOU EARLY IN THE MORNING. If you are an early bird and happy to spring out of bed at the first chirp, then why not enjoy time with your toddler. But if you wake like a bear with a sore head and can't stand the thought of the day before your coffee, then make a plan. Put a radio clock in her room and set it for the time she is allowed to come through to you. No music, no mummy. She can even learn to read the magic spot on the clock. Until then she plays with toys you've left at the bottom of the bed. If she comes through take her back and explain the rules again. Be firm but friendly. It will work if you are prepared to be consistent.

BATTLES AT BEDTIME. You may have a child who refuses to go to bed and ends up roaming the house, when you and your partner should be unwinding and catching up on adult conversation. It usually starts insidiously without your realising that it is happening. There is no reason to suppose that your toddler will go to bed without protest if you have never had a stable routine. Children need and thrive on the kind of snug security they get from a regular pattern in their lives.

Keeping to a schedule means you will have to be adaptable and arrange your life so that you or Dad can go through a bedtime routine regularly. Give your child a basic pattern in her life, while being as flexible as possible in between.

This does not imply an arbitrary, insensitive approach. Ordering a toddler who has just started a game to come in for a bath is looking for trouble. It is up to you to keep an eye on the time and start winding her down slowly. Bedtime, too, should not be a kind of punishment; it should be the cosy conclusion to a full day. If you make it an unfailing rule to read or tell your child a story while she is tucked up in bed it will not be so hard for her to give up the day's activities. A recording of lullabies or music specially designed to stimulate alpha brain-wave patterns can help your toddler release into sleep.

Pleas for one more story or one more glass of water must be resisted. Although bedtime can be flexible on certain occasions it should not be a daily negotiation. Agree on a number of stories and stick to it if you do not want to be there for half the evening. Do not allow your toddler to fall asleep in the sitting room with you. Do not lie down with her on her bed. Her place is tucked up cosily in bed. You will all be happier for it.

For the system to work you will have to discipline yourself to keep to it. Remember too that a toddler, unlike a tiny baby, is able to keep herself awake until she is beyond sleep. Over-tiredness can keep a child up long past her natural sleep time, so don't wait until she starts to get crabby before the bedtime routine. Rough-house play with Dad is great but not just before bed. Rather have him tell a story or read to her. She should preferably not run around in her night clothes. They are part of the sleep routine and should be put on close to bedtime. (*See p. 517.*) Many children need the comfort of a bottle, dummy or 'doo-doo' to get off to sleep – don't deny it to them.

HOW MUCH SLEEP DO CHILDREN NEED? Between ten and twelve hours a night. They need sleep more than adults do for their bodies to grow and renew themselves. Children who constantly get less than the sleep they need become stressed and difficult. They stay awake not because they are not tired but because they want to be with their parents for emotional reasons. Find ways to fill this need rather than through losing battles at bedtime.

CHILDREN WHO NEED LITTLE SLEEP. There are rare children who do not need a lot of sleep and these are usually very bright. They are the ones who wake early, even if they go to bed late, and do not fade during the day. Don't confuse them with the child who likes to stay up late and wakes early, but is grumpy and difficult during the day. Overtired children often become hyperactive rather than sleepy because they become more tired. The children who genuinely and consistently need little sleep are bright-eyed and bushy-tailed on far less sleep than other children need.

These children should be allowed to play quietly in their rooms until they want to sleep and encouraged to stay in their rooms if they wake early. After all, you need your sleep to keep up! Do not have a television or computer games in a child's room.

NIGHTMARES. NIGHT TERRORS. (*SEE P. 283.*)

STEM CELL THERAPY

Looking back at mankind's development we seem to have gone forward in some respects and backward in others. But we have made it possible for humans to live far longer through medical discoveries. Anaesthesia, antibiotics, immunisation, organ transplants – are among the advances made and now the awesome possibilities of stem cell and gene therapy are in view.

I have no doubt that within the next fifty years the blind will see, the paralysed will walk and the brain will be rejuvenated. Inherited conditions will be prevented, and defective organs will be regenerated. Fortunately, I will not be here for you to hold me to account! It will not be easy as the challenges are immense – but the key has opened the door – and progress is being made.

IN THE BEGINNING. One of the first breakthroughs came in 1981 when scientists discovered a way to extract stem cells from mouse embryos. This led to a method to derive stem cells from the human blastocyst in 1998.

The use of these blastocysts has been controversial, and the United States Government refused to direct federal funding for the research although private funding was allowed. This led to a great deal of controversy and concern, and even ostracism from some people at the thought that stem cells would be removed from the human body, and then fertilised outside the body. (This policy has since been reversed.) These cells are called human embryonic stem cells and they give rise to the entire body.

A blastocyst is an embryo which has 5 or 6 days to form a complex cellular structure of approximately 220 cells. (The blastocyst phase is the development stage before implantation of the embryo in the mother's uterus.) These 3-5 day old eggs were fertilised outside the woman's body in what used to be called 'test tube baby' procedures, which was part of the reason for the outrage among some people. 'Test tube babies' was an unfortunate title for the name, as it did not correctly describe the development and use of stem cells. Today it is known as 'in vitro fertilisation'.

DIFFERENT TYPES OF STEM CELLS USED IN RESEARCH. Embryonic stem cells can become one of about 200 types of tissue found in the body and are called pluripotent stem cells (i.e. human cells that self-replicate and are derived from human embryos or human foetal tissue and are able to develop into cells and tissues of the three primary germ layers.) In these cells, gene signals trigger the cell to change in what is called differentiation to become a particular cell type. Once this process has started, it cannot be reversed. But because they contain the master information to develop into every tissue and organ of our being – bone, muscle, blood, brain, nerves, skin etc – they are of great interest in terms of research and therapy. Stem cells removed from a single blastocyst can be cultivated in a Petri dish in a laboratory, multiplying endlessly to provide a supply of stem lines for many years of research.

Work is being done to try generate specific types of differentiated cells including heart muscle cells, nerve cells, blood cells – by changing the chemical composition of the culture medium in which they are grown – or inserting specific genes.

Heart disease, hearing loss and vision defects have made progress, but conditions such as Parkinson's disease and Duchenne's muscular dystrophy, in which muscle weakness begins around the age of four in boys and worsens quickly, has not seen any progress. Sadly, these are complex disorders that have not yet been cured.

However, the good news is that stem cells have been used to successfully grow a section of windpipe for transplantation in patients. While embryonic stem cells have also been used to grow a type of eye tissue known as retinal pigment epithelium for transplanting in patients who have a common degenerative eye condition that causes blindness.

Stem cells also exist in adult tissue and these are called multipotent. Their main function is to repair and maintain skin, fat, gut, bone, teeth, heart, lung, bone marrow etc. Sixty years ago – researchers presented evidence that brain cells could also renew themselves despite accepted scientific wisdom – but they were ignored. We now know that the brain is plastic and that the three main types of brain cells can be generated.

In 2006 researchers made another breakthrough which allows some adult cells to be 'genetically reprogrammed' to assume embryonic stem cells properties. There are only a very small number of stem cells in adult tissue however, and their capacity to divide outside the body, is limited. Scientists are trying to generate greater amounts of adult stem cells and persuade them to become specific cell types. For instance, insulin-producing stem cells could treat type 1 diabetes – heart muscles could be repaired following heart attacks – broken hearts, not so easily…

The oldest treatment using stem cells is that of blood cells (haematopoietic stem cells), in bone marrow transplants. Umbilical cord blood is also a source of stem cells, and a new type of stem cells is found in amniotic fluid.

There are exceptional researchers such as Professor Shinya Yamanaka and his colleagues, who has received ten major scientific awards. A UK scientist Sir Martin Evans received the Nobel Prize for his work on identifying genes in mice (strangely, mouse and human genomes are almost identical). It is now possible to produce almost any type of DNA modification in the mouse genome, allowing scientists to establish the roles of individual genes.

The negative news is what has been called one of the greatest medical frauds in recent times. A highly regarded South Korean stem cell and cloning researcher at the Seoul National University, Woo Suk Hwang, resigned from his post when a journal found anomalies in his work suggesting that he had faked results. He was tried for fraud and convicted.

In China, some purveyors of stem cell therapy have been arrested. In the US a number of medical doctors have had their medical licence rescinded. A South African on the US 'most wanted list', who offered stem cell treatment on the internet from a US base, fled to Cape Town where he continued to offer stem cell therapy. A clinic in Germany that gave stem cell injections for cerebral palsy, muscular dystrophy, Alzheimer's and other serious conditions and illnesses, was closed down after a child died and others were damaged. It had been doing huge business because of a loophole in the law, with clients from around the world impressed by its seemingly solid credentials. The owner has since stablished a similar business in Lebanon.

The field is ripe for unscrupulous exploitation because it offers hope and for this, desperate parents will pay anything. But the internet is an ungoverned advertising medium where unsubstantiated claims can be made with no recourse. To compound matters some countries do not have clear legislation as to what is allowed in terms of experimentation and treatment.

POINTS TO KEEP IN MIND. Like all medical procedures, stem cells treatments must be proven safe before that are accepted into general practice. Clinical trials must be done, and peer review of results must be obtained. 'Testimonials' from patients are not scientific proof of their effectiveness.

Independent clinical trials, publication and replication of the results by other laboratories, and treatment methods must be scrutinised by credible scientists before a treatment can be deemed safe and effective. If they are, the world will certainly hear of them and your doctor will be able to look them up in medical publications.

It is vital to know the source of the stem cells or tissues being used as there are many ways in which claims can be made that skirt the truth. For example, stem cells that are not pure enough for human use have been used. Even animal stem cells have been injected for use in humans.

Experimental therapies offered may be claimed to be far more advanced than they are. Infection, immune system rejection and cancer (because stem cells can easily go on replicating themselves as do cancer cells), are some of the dangers.

Stem cells can remain in the body for many years with unpredictable results. Others die soon after treatment. Some replicate uncontrolled like cancer cells do.

Before embarking on treatment discuss all options with a medical specialist who has no affiliation with the treatment provider.

We stand on the brink of the next breakthrough in the prevention and treatment of human disease. When treatments are tried and tested with credible results, we will all hear about it, until then, take great care where you put your money and most of all, your hope.

SUDDEN INFANT-DEATH SYNDROME (SIDS) OR COT DEATH

'COT DEATH'. The thought that their child could die an unexplained sudden death without a sound is one of the night mares that haunt parents. Yet there is no way they could have foreseen the tragedy. Fortunately, the percentage of children affected is relatively small and scientists are slowly finding clues to the mystery. A number of possible causes and reasons as to why children between the ages of one month and a year or a little older, sometimes die suddenly and without a sound are being investigated.

One theory has it that SIDS is due to sleep apnoea (the tendency to stop breathing for a period during sleep). These babies seem to have an abnormality of the mechanism in the brain that modifies breathing in response to levels of oxygen and carbon dioxide in the blood. Thus a baby may go to sleep and never awake simply because she has stopped breathing for too long.

The SCN5A gene that regulates heart rhythm has also been linked to SIDS. The gene uses sodium to regulate the heart's electrical rhythm, and it is associated with long-QT syndrome, a heart irregularity that can cause fainting or sudden death during rest or sleep. Unfortunately screening for the gene is not commercially available at this time.

Certain mattress types have been implicated in cot death. The regulations for these items have changed over the years in order to make them safer.(*For more information see The Consumer Safety Protection Commission, www.cpsc.gov.*) A researcher has found that the chemicals used to produce some foam mattresses react when in contact with the body's moisture and heat, and as a result a normal house fungus produces three toxic gases, including a poisonous nerve gas. Autopsies on babies who died from cot death revealed these gases in the babies' lungs. Overheating, a lack of oxygen and inhalation of toxic fumes may therefore be implicated.

PREVENTING SIDS

- Put your baby to sleep on her back. Sleeping on their back has reduced the incidence of SIDS by more than half in some countries.
- Do not allow smoking anywhere near you baby. This increases the risk by 80%. Do not smoke during pregnancy.
- Do not use a duvet, or pillow.
- Do not use an old mattress – it may harbour dangerous toxins.
- Do not overheat your baby, since this has been associated with cot death. The ideal room temperature for sleep is around 18°C (65°F). Your baby only needs one more light layer of covering than you do when sleeping. Feel her stomach to see if she is cold, not her hands as they normally feel cold even if she is warm enough.
- If your baby seems off-colour, contact your doctor as some babies have been found to have underlying infections or abnormalities.
- Do not cover your baby's head when she sleeps.
- Her feet should almost touch the bottom of the cot so that she cannot move down under the covers.
- A monitoring device that sounds an alarm as soon as a baby stops breathing for 20 seconds or if her heart rate slows has been devised. They can give false alarms though and may also not go off when necessary. They are therefore not foolproof. Consult your medical advisor.
- Do not put your baby to sleep with you if you use alcohol, sleeping pills or recreational drugs.

Breastfeeding provides some protection from disease and together with immunising according to the recommended schedule lowers the risk of SIDS by about 50%.

Sucking on a dummy (pacifier) has been shown to help prevent cot death. After you have fed, burped and changed you baby put her to sleep on her back with a dummy to suck. Do not dip it in anything other than a little breast milk, and keep it clean. There are some concerns about giving a dummy before the second month as this might cause nipple confusion and rejection of the breast, but babies are generally smarter than this.

Don't give honey to an infant under 1 year old. Honey can lead to botulism in very young children and the bacteria that causes it may be linked to SIDS.

Some experts believe that babies may die as a result of a fault in the electrical impulses that stimulate the heart to beat, resulting in a kind of 'heart attack'. In spite of these theories, sudden infant death remains a mystery.

The sympathetic understanding of others who have been through the same agony can help them come to terms with it.

STUTTERING

Stuttering or stammering when learning to talk is common and is outgrown in 75% of cases. It is usually caused by the 'brain running ahead of the tongue' before children become fluent. True dysfluency (stuttering) is linked to chromosome 7 and is more common in boys. In girls, it is linked to chromosome 21. Thus there is an inherited tendency, although environment also plays a role.

Anxiety, blinking, movements of the head and limbs often accompany stuttering. Do not hurry a child when he or she is trying to express something. Do not finish their sentences. Allow the child time to become relaxed when trying to express something.

Stuttering beyond the age of seven is difficult to correct. The Michael Palin Centre in London – (he starred in *A Fish Called Wanda*) – www.stammeringcentre.org focuses on reducing speaking pressure on the child. Behavioural modification therapy can also be useful. See a speech therapist if you are concerned.

TEETH AND TEETHING

STRONG TEETH. A baby's teeth are formed before the birth while still in the mother's womb so what the mother eats can affect them. Calcium is needed for tooth formation, and strong enamel, so extra calcium is advisable if the mother's diet does not include sufficient milk or dairy products.

If you live in an area where the water has low fluoride content, or does not have fluoride added to the water, you may be advised to take fluoride supplements. Consult your dentist. Too much fluoride and certain drugs such as tetracycline can stain teeth brown, so make sure your health advisers know you are pregnant before prescribing medication or supplements. (*See p. 171.*)

Occasionally, babies are born with one or more teeth, or they erupt during the first month. These teeth do not usually have proper roots and if they interfere with breastfeeding your doctor or dentist may remove them. However, it is not always easy to tell whether they are, in fact, rudimentary teeth and the dentist or doctor will want to be sure of this before removing them. There may not be other milk teeth under them waiting to erupt at the normal time. However, it is a rare occurrence and most babies' first teeth appear at the expected time, around six months.

The first teeth to appear are usually the lower central incisors (sharp cutting teeth in the front), followed by the two upper central incisors and then, on either side of these, the second incisors, with the lower ones coming before the upper two. The molars (the big grinding teeth towards the back of the mouth) appear next, around the first birthday, and then the cuspids (or canine teeth which are pointed like the teeth of a dog), between 14 and 20 months.

When the child is around 18–30 months the second molars appear and the child has the 20 teeth that make up a full set of 'baby' or 'milk' teeth. These are also known as deciduous teeth because they eventually start falling out at around six years of age as they are pushed up by the permanent teeth.

The order and timing in which the teeth appear does not always follow this pattern, and variations of six months and more are possible. Early or late teething is not a sign of intelligence, nor has it any other significance; and it often runs in families. So, unless your child shows no sign of teething after the age of a year, do not become concerned. In this case your dentist will advise you and may take X-rays to establish if there are teeth in the gums, but this is seldom necessary.

TEETHING SYMPTOMS. Because teeth appear at intervals throughout the first three years, it is inevitable that their eruption will coincide with some of the ills babies' experience. Although teething does produce certain symptoms, it is wrong to put every ailment down to teething and leave it untreated.

To emerge from the gum, teeth have to force their way through tissue, and as they do this the tissue is stretched and torn, causing pain and inflammation. Although the development of the teeth takes a long time, it normally takes only between three and 10 days before the tooth erupts. During this time you can expect your baby to become irritable, with disturbed sleep and a lot of drooling. The drooling can cause a rash and the increased activity in the area can result in an angry red patch on the baby's face.

The increased secretion of mucus can also make it seem as though the baby has a cold and the stools may become slightly loose. It is vitally important, however, that you do not put diarrhoea with vomiting down to 'only teething' as it is an extremely dangerous condition that needs prompt treatment. (*See p. 353.*)

A high temperature is also not simply due to teething. The swelling of the mucous membranes in the area as well as the increased mucus secretion can affect the

Eustachian tube leading to the ear drum, causing ear problems. Whether the problem is caused partly by teething or not, it still needs treatment.

To treat the general effects you can rub your baby's gums with a very clean finger to relieve itching and help the teeth cut through. Do not buy old folk remedies for teething as they may contain potentially dangerous substances. If your child's sleep is being disturbed (this is very common especially around six months and again when the second molars appear around 20 months), you can rub the gums and give a dose of paracetamol to ease the pain and inflammation. It is important to be reasonably sure that the child's wakefulness is indeed caused by teething (the gum area is normally raised and red) and not by something else. (*See waking at night p. 489.*) Rubbing the gums with an ice cube is also a good way of offering temporary relief. Babies who are teething like to bite on something hard – it helps get the tooth through and eases the irritation. Give your child a special teething biscuit or very hard rusk to bite on. Do not give hard fruit or vegetables for a teething baby to chew on as a piece may break off and choke the child. Teething rings made from hard rubber can be useful. There has been a recent alert against chemicals called phthalates that are used to soften hard plastics like PVC for toys, so don't let your child chew on these. Liquid-filled teething rings have been associated with infection if the liquid escapes.

Don't let her chew on furniture or toys that may have been painted with toxic or lead-based paint. (*See www.cpsc.gov/Going off her food.*) Many babies and toddlers go off their food when teething and some reject the breast because their gums hurt when they suck. Use a teething jelly 15 minutes before a feed, or rub her gums with an ice cube directly before a feed. Make her meals more liquid than usual. Serve yogurt, milk jelly and pudding, ice cream, puréed milk soups, mashed banana and other soft foods if she will not take her usual meals.

CAUSES OF MALOCCLUSION. Parents often worry that the child who sucks her thumb or dummy will end up with buck teeth. Although these habits can certainly encourage the teeth to protrude if carried on after the age of four or five, there are other many other factors that influence the placement of teeth. Bottle-feeding is one of the most important because the child uses a different action when sucking on a teat than if she were sucking on the breast. At a time when the jaw and mouth structure is at its most malleable, the constant application of pressure on the wrong areas can cause the structure of the mouth to assume a different shape. Enlarged adenoids or allergies that cause mouth-breathing at night also have a bad effect on the placement of the permanent teeth. (*See p. 408.*)

Keeping the milk teeth until they are ready to fall out naturally is important, because early loss of teeth can cause the gums to shrink, leaving too little space for the permanent teeth which may, as a result, come out crooked. Care for your child's teeth by avoiding sweetened drinks, especially from a bottle (fruit syrups and acid fruit juices are known to decay teeth rapidly, but milk and even breastmilk can do so too). Basically, tooth decay is caused by an acid found in plaque – the colourless pulpy material that develops around teeth. This acid results from the breaking down of starches and sugars in food by bacteria. The acid acts on the tooth enamel, breaking it down. By strengthening it with fluoride, tooth enamel is made less susceptible to the action of the acid.

Besides giving your child extra fluoride if you live in a low-fluoride area (*see pp. 149, 171*) you can help reduce tooth decay by brushing the teeth with toothpaste which contains fluoride. Do not let your child swallow fluoride toothpaste – it's not good to take in so much fluoride. Avoid giving biscuits, chips and other starchy food between meals and brush the teeth after eating. If the teeth cannot be brushed, a piece of cheese is a good way to end the meal.

CARING FOR THE TEETH. Make a practice of brushing your child's teeth. Using a soft brush, clean from the gum towards the tooth edge. Do this on the inside of the teeth as well as the outside. The biting surfaces should be scrubbed backwards and forwards. Rinse without swallowing the toothpaste. You can also wipe a small baby's teeth with a piece of clean gauze wrapped around your finger. Children should be taught to floss their teeth so that the areas between the teeth are cleaned. Floss is a fine thread, flavoured or plain, that may be waxed for easier use, to get rid of food particles and plaque. Ask your dentist to demonstrate the right action because incorrect flossing can damage the gums. You can also ask your dentist to apply a fluoride gel to the teeth so that the surface concentration of fluoride is built up. Another means of fighting tooth decay is to have your child's teeth sealed with a special adhesive material that is painted on. It seals the tiny crevices in the teeth so that plaque cannot get into them and cause decay.

PREMATURE LOSS OF A TOOTH. If your child loses a tooth by having it bumped out, your dentist may be able to replace it in the socket if you see him within an hour. When retrieving the tooth be careful not to touch the root end since the root damages easily. Hold it gently on the enamel and if you have a sterile saline solution, place the tooth gently in it. The tooth should not bump against the sides of the container, but rest in a net or gauze fabric inside the saline solution. Take care not to damage the delicate root until you get to the dentist.

If the child is old enough to cooperate and there are no other injuries that need priority treatment you can rinse the tooth with saline (sterile salt water) and replant it in the child's mouth. The child should bite on a clean piece of gauze or hanky until you reach the dentist. If a tooth cannot be saved the dentist may use a space maintainer to keep the space open so that the permanent teeth do not become crowded. Teeth that are chipped should also be seen to as they can go black if the nerve dies.

VISITING THE DENTIST. The sensible mother will never refer to doctors or dentists in a way that implies they will hurt the child, or as a punishment. Take your child to visit the dentist around the age of two-and-a-half or three, before there should be any need for fillings, so that he or she can check that all is well and the child can build up a friendly relationship. A new invention identifies cavities with ease simply by being placed close to the teeth, removing some of the potential for trauma.

TOURETTE'S SYNDROME; TICS

Tourette's syndrome is named after the doctor Gilles de la Tourette, who first collated and described the symptoms in the 19th century, although it was known for millennia before then. The condition is twice as common in boys and becomes apparent between the ages of three and ten years. The early symptoms are involuntary twitches of the head or other part of the body, eye blinking or jerking. They may be mild and can easily be confused with other conditions such as epilepsy or the uncoordinated movements that are sometimes part of cerebral palsy.

However, around a year or two after the tics first manifest, the child begins to make unusual sounds with the tics – repeating words or shouting suddenly or making animal noises or even swearing. This is extremely distressing for parents and child, especially when it is intense. Fortunately the symptoms often improve spontaneously, although they often come back in a waxing and waning pattern such as allergic conditions like eczema do. Just as stress exacerbates eczema but does not cause it, there is no indication that Tourette's itself is caused by stress. As in epilepsy, in which sufferers may become aware of an 'aura' or feeling that an attack is imminent, Tourette's sufferers may experience an 'impulse' that an outburst is coming. For some this can help give them control.

TREATMENT AND CAUSES. There is no standard treatment for Tourette's syndrome although interventions can appear to work – or not – mainly because the condition waxes and wanes without a set pattern. Tourette's syndrome is sometimes associated with obsessive compulsive disorder and attention deficit hyperactivity disorder (ADHD). (*See p. 409*) Thus the patient's history needs to be established and a thorough examination done. Medication is sometimes prescribed for ADHD and obsessive compulsive disorder but this too must be very carefully prescribed. Behaviour therapy that has shown some favourable results is 'habit reversal training' in which the child is taught to respond to the urge by doing the opposite until the urge passes.

For adults with severe tics deep-brain stimulation, which involves the placement of an electrode in the brain, has shown some success. This is sometimes also used for people with severe uncontrolled movement disorders in cerebral palsy. Botox injections that temporarily paralyse the muscles that are used in severe tics have also been helpful in some cases.

The cause of Tourette's syndrome is not known but there is an inherited tendency with complications during pregnancy and birth a common feature. Many other possible medical and genetic factors are being studied but no conclusive evidence has been found.

When you consider the social and behaviour problems which accompany Tourette's, it is not surprising that depression and anxiety is common. Children are likely to be teased at school and teachers and even parents sometimes believe that the vocal outbursts are intentional, all of which add to the child's stress. When parents and teachers as well as peers and patient receive sound information about the condition they often deal with it in more effective ways. For example, allow the child to do oral exams in private or to take a short break outside when tics become extreme. Explanations of the condition to peers and monitoring by a suitable adult on the playground and elsewhere can help defuse teasing and the child can maintain self-esteem.

Tourette's syndrome is not a well-mapped disorder and neither outcome nor cause is certain. Like all conditions that are far from the norm of the behaviours usually considered socially acceptable, Tourette's brings it own burdens. The acclaimed television series *Boston Legal* made a brave attempt at familiarising the public to persons with the condition. One of the star lawyers in the firm supposedly suffered from Tourette's with its accompanying tics and verbal outbursts. Despite severe problems his character was endearing.

TWINS

TWINS, TRIPLETS AND MORE. Although diagnostic machines like ultrasound scanners (*see p. 456*) can usually tell if there is more than one baby, a small percentage of twins arrive unexpectedly and throw everyone into a state of confusion! The incidence of twin pregnancy varies in different ethnic groups, with black Africans and East Indians the highest at 1:60, while amongst Chinese it's the lowest at 1:300. Women of North European origin are somewhere in the middle, producing twins at a rate of around 1:80 on average. Triplets occur once in every 8 000 to 9 000 births and quadruplets once in every 700 000.

The greater the number of babies the higher the number of females in the group. Non-identical twins are more likely to be born to older mothers with a history of twins in the family, a tendency that is carried through the female line. These days many instances of multiple births are associated with treatment for infertility, and three, four and even more babies born from one pregnancy is no longer uncommon. This has somewhat skewed the ethnic basis for the rate of multiple births. Many countries have stopped placing more than two or three eggs during fertility treatment.

MONOZYGOTIC OR IDENTICAL TWINS originate from a single egg, fertilised by one sperm as normally happens in a single pregnancy. Early in its development, however, the egg splits in two and identical, same-sex babies are created with one placenta.

DIZYGOTIC OR NON-IDENTICAL (FRATERNAL) TWINS result when two eggs are released at the same time and are fertilised by two spermatozoa. Two placentas are formed and the babies are as different as if they had been born years apart, like any other siblings. In very rare cases dizygotic twins can have different fathers if the mother has intercourse with different men within a few hours.

Giving birth to more than one baby at a time is challenging and a little frightening. The chances of complications at birth are greater than a singleton and twins are often born prematurely due to the increased size of the uterus.

THE MYSTERY OF TWINING. Everything about the idea of producing more than one child at a time, in particular identical twins, captures the imagination and teases our thinking. Identical twins are after all clones of each other. Twenty-five percent of all identical twins show signs of mirror imaging – some even have organs on the opposite side of their body. How identical twins look may be connected to the time separation takes place in utero. Early division of the egg seems to make for a greater variation in characteristics. This may explain why some monozygotic twins are as different as ordinary siblings. Conjoined (Siamese) twins occur when separation is incomplete.

Despite their increased incidence and survival rate, huge excitement surrounds the birth of triplets, quadruplets and other multiples. Remarkably parents survive, and somehow cope. Practical advice from parent-support groups can be helpful. Helping hands are worth gold.

THE SPECIAL NEEDS OF MULTIPLES. Twins are often born early because of the strain on the womb and the mother should be given every opportunity to bond with her babies. (*See Prematurity p. 479 and Bonding p. 34.*) They are likely to need extra vitamins and minerals, but breastfeeding is possible so you may want to keep your milk going by expressing if they are not strong enough to breastfeed at birth (*See p. 121*). They can still receive your milk which may be fortified if they are very premature.

Most mothers today do not dress their twins alike so that a sense of separate identity can be fostered. Encourage each child to develop their own strengths and personality, and try and refer to them as individuals rather than a single entity.

CHAPTER 16

Case Histories

'They f**k you up, your mum and dad,
They may not mean to, but they do.
They fill you with the faults they had
And add some extra, just for you.'
Philip Larkin 1922 – 1985

Before you have a child of your own, it is easy to be sure that you would do things better than others. But once in it, it is awfully difficult to get things right even with the best will in the world. Fortunately the human infant is generally forgiving, and most children are sufficiently robust to survive even our worst errors of judgement; unlike some species.

Three goldfish pushing their heads out of the water and snapping their mouths open and shut, seemed hungry to me. So I fed them. Frequently. Then why am I now standing at the toilet bowl, flushing away the dear departed with a muttered apology?

It is because I had misread their signals – they were not hungry in fact – but gasping for air... Reading the signs and learning the lessons of caring for another creature is not easy, and we should not be too hard on ourselves for the mistakes we make.

Fortunately the care and feeding of children is generally less knife edge than goldfish. For one thing, children seldom eat themselves to death. But circumstances often arise when it is difficult to read the situation and know what to do.

BEHAVIOURS AND BRAIN TUMOURS

Pumla is a caring mother who is worried sick about her youngest son Mandla, and the effect his behaviour is having on the family. This is their story. Four-year-old Mandla's behaviour is becoming so erratic and difficult that everyone is at their wits end, including his grandparents. He is destructive, explosive and refuses to go to bed. At other times, he is an angel – notably when his father – who works on a fishing vessel is home.

Mandla has been severely punished for his behaviour, but the more he is spanked, the worse he seems to become. Pumla, who works as a doctor's receptionist has even considered the possibility that Mandla has a brain tumour that is causing his unpredictable behaviour.

WHERE MANDLA IS AT. Mandla is an angry and unhappy little boy. He cannot understand why his father disappears out of his life, particularly because his father leaves in the early hours of the morning while Mandla is still asleep. Mandla's dad is at sea for up to six weeks at a time and then has a break of four weeks at home, during which he devotes much of his time to his young son. Ironically, had Mandla been less bonded with his father, his absences would not have been so traumatic.

Mandla's verbal development is not sufficiently advanced for him to talk about his anxieties, and so he acts out. Fear of abandonment is one of the strongest possible threats in childhood. Children are entirely vulnerable when abandoned and everything in their being is dedicated towards holding the attention and commitment of their primary caregivers. The large appealing eyes of children are just one of the ways in which nature begs to seduce the adults on whose care they must depend.

WHAT CAN BE DONE FOR MANDLA. Mandla's father was told to explain to him that his work took him away for long periods and that it meant that he had to leave while Mandla was asleep. He promised to warn his son when he was going away. The day before he was due to go to sea again Sipho said goodbye to Mandla and asked him to draw him pictures of what he did when he was away. They also made a wall chart in which the days could be marked off so Mandla could feel he had some control in his father's absence.

Most importantly, the whole family was encouraged to stop treating Mandla as a 'bad boy' and concentrate on positive reinforcement. Every possible opportunity to praise him for good behaviour, was taken; even his grandparents made a point of praising him in front of others for things he did right. Soon his temper tantrums had lessened and he became a far better balanced child. Dad made a point of looking at the 'work' assignments Mandla had done while he was away and discussed the 'drawings' in detail.

Trust in their parents is vital for children, and when parents appear to break that trust albeit inadvertently, children can become highly agitated and their stability is threatened. Older children should be encouraged to talk, but young children sometimes need to have their actions deciphered by entering into their inner world.

In preverbal children, divorce is sometimes the trigger for behaviour such as Mandla's. This is made worse if the child has to move to unfamiliar surroundings. Try and keep as much as possible of the child's regular routine intact, and do not argue in front of the children! Reassurance and a calm and loving atmosphere, despite underlying tensions must be maintained as far as possible.

Like the father who told his son that he would catch him if he jumped off a low wall, and then allowed him to fall in order to 'teach him a lesson from life', parents are sometimes very misguided in their perceptions of what their children will benefit from. Trust is vital in any relationship. More so between parent and child as it is the foundation for lifelong attitudes. This includes knowing that there will be consequences for actions. So do not make promises that you do not intend to keep – including promises of punishment.

Children also need to trust in themselves. This is how confidence is built. One of the things that worries parents most as their children get older is that they will drop out of school, take drugs or end up lost to their influence. This is not unrealistic given the statistics. The foundation for prevention is laid long before you think. It is during that innocent period when your child is adorable and you are not thinking about anything that will affect this idyll. While the use of drugs and dropping out of school has a lot to do with peer influence, the reasons why you lose your personal influence over your child may never be clear.

DESPERATE TO PREVENT THEIR CHILDREN FROM GOING WRONG

Aziz is a messenger for a legal firm. He has high moral standards and a sincere love for his two young sons. He is desperate to ensure that they escape the lure of gangsterism that is rife in the neighbourhood where the family live. He is perplexed that despite the numerous 'hidings' his boys are given they still disobey him and his wife Shaida.

'I don't want my boys to go bad' he says, almost weeping with emotion. 'But I don't know what to do anymore; they just don't want to listen… ' Watching them interact is a sad revelation. Aziz and Shaida are always on the look-out for 'naughty' behaviour from their three- and five-year-old sons, who are normal, spirited youngsters. Their parents are so strict that not even the slightest challenge is tolerated. No discussion is allowed, and 'do as I say' is the order of the day.

Are Aziz and Shaida's boys doomed to follow the neighbourhood path of school drop-out and a life of crime? Will these caring parents be disappointed, and what can they do to help prevent their children from being sucked into the morass around them? What are the differences between these caring parents and those in more privileged neighbourhoods? Certainly it is not motivation or love for their children.

Aziz and Shaida mean well, but they are caught in the common misperception that only by being extremely tough on their boys will they learn to obey, and stay away from the ways of their peers.

The fact is that the most telling difference between successful parenting and that of less successful parents lies in punishment and communication. Researchers found that the more spankings children received as toddlers; the lower they scored on IQ tests four years later. It was not that they became less intelligent, but that their intellectual development was slowed. Successful parents talked to their children in more elaborate ways than merely giving orders or punishment. They explained the reasons for their rules and allowed children to participate in making choices that affected them, while setting clear and consistent boundaries.

Language development was the key to much of the successful children's academic superiority, which was an important reason they stayed in school and did not drop out. Their parents talked to them in sentences rich in descriptive language and reasoning, which in turn helped develop moral reasoning and depth of thinking.

Aziz and Shaida were unused to this kind of communication but they were given a list of books to read to their children, and encouraged to discuss what they had read with them. Rather than have the expectation that their children would behave badly they were told to treat them as though they expected them to behave well. Slowly the parents learned to be less controlling and the boys became more self-controlled. Internalised moral standards and good self-esteem now stand a chance of being developed which will help the boys resist negative peer pressure. (*See Authoritarian parenting p. 286, Authoritative parenting p. 286.*)

THE SADNESS OF THE GOLDEN BOY

Richard and Margaret are a golden couple who have everything money can buy. Richard has made a fortune in publishing and Margaret is famed for her charity work and glittering parties. Their son Jared was born after two daughters when Richard was at the height of his push to become an international media mogul. He was overjoyed at the birth of his son and every possible luxury was lavished on him. Whenever Richard returned from an overseas trip in the company jet Jared received another planeload of presents.

Strangely, Jared was not a happy child. He had a habit of sitting under the dining room table and barking whenever guests were present. People were too polite to comment, some even thought he was autistic. Richard and Margaret chose to ignore him until his nanny took him away. He was a withdrawn child and at four he began withholding his stools. At seven years he started stealing money from his mother's purse.

WHERE JARED IS AT. Although he is well loved, Jared has had everything a boy could wish for except the attention of his parents. It is not that they do not care – it has simply not occurred to them that he needs more than gifts and the best of everything money can buy in order to satisfy his needs.

Margaret's social life and fundraisers take so much of her time that she is hardly ever at home. And Richard has so many balls in the air something always gets in the way of spending time with his son. The nanny, the cook and the chauffeur are effectively the people in Jared's life. Formal and distant, they never really make meaningful contact with him. The two girls are by nature more outgoing and they have each other, while Jared is excluded from their life as well. His nature is such that he has sought comfort through means other than human contact.

By the time he was fourteen Jared was stealing to support a drug habit. Margaret and Richard were devastated. The utter irony of her fame as a charity fundraiser and her inability to do anything for her son burned deeply into Margaret's soul. She established a drug rehabilitation centre and devoted herself to the care of drug addicts. But by then Jared was HIV positive due to dirty needles.

It hardly seems possible that well-meaning parents with every resource at their disposal should become part of a tragedy such as this. The hard thing about raising children is that they need our attention most, when we are least able to give it. They need our love when they are at their most unlovable. And no matter how much money can buy, it cannot replace the lost opportunity.

TREVOR THE TERRIFIED TYRANT

As though to negate the lessons of Margaret and Richard's tragedy of unwittingly not meeting their child's need for attention, John and Brenda were too accommodating and let their son dominate them, to everyone's detriment.

Trevor was a bright five-year-old who was conceived after his parents had given up hope of ever having a child. He walked and talked early, and his parents, who are highly educated professionals, doted on him. Trevor was a demanding child but his parents were happy to indulge him. Part of the way his parents showed Trevor how much they 'loved' him was to make sure that his life was always pleasant and free of frustration. When he did not want to go to kindergarten, they kept him at home. He was not yet fully toilet trained as his parents had given up when he resisted. His every whim was indulged. His parents became concerned when he developed overwhelming fears: of the dark, or being alone even in his room, of animals, of going to school, of strangers.

When he started expressing fears, they worked at reassuring him, sometimes even before he expressed a fear. They promised him rewards in order to get him to 'face' the simplest thing like entering a room. Trevor ruled the roost. He determined his bedtime and the foods he would eat. And he kept his parents prisoner because he was too afraid to be left in the care of anyone else.

When he did not immediately get what he wanted he would shout and scream, and his parents would comply immediately. In this topsy turvy situation the child had assumed the role of decision maker and dominated his family. His parents felt helpless and despite their obsession with keeping him happy, they began to resent their child.

POOR TREVOR, POOR PARENTS. Because Trevor had never been allowed to suffer even mild discomfort or anxiety, he never developed the basic skills that come from meeting the learning challenges every child must go through in growing up. He did not know how to cope with novelty, or deal with situations of even mild frustration.

Outside the home where his dependence and his parents yielding pattern was not followed, he became extremely anxious and fearful. His dependence on his parents increased and they in turn were so panicked by the thought of their child experiencing any pain that they made him even more afraid.

Trevor's early promise of brightness was lost when his intelligence was relegated to a secondary skill, his skills being emotional manipulation rather than mastery of a situation. He was functioning way below his intellectual ability. All he knew how to do was make demands.

On the one hand Trevor felt omnipotent – he was master of the universe when he could make his parents do anything he wanted – but he had never learned to tolerate frustration or delay gratification. This gave him unrealistic fantasies of power. He even declared that he had the 'right to do anything he wanted'. But in time his parents could not protect him from the realities of the real world. Trevor became angry and hostile when he was frustrated and responded with sulking and temper tantrums. Even small expectations of him were met with fury as he made every minor thing into a drama.

Ironically, Trevor knew that he was dependent on his parents and resented them for this. Some days he even wished they were dead. These thoughts terrified him and made him cling to them even more. This vicious cycle spun around and around, bringing grief to all concerned. Trevor's parents had yielded their authority and role as parents of a child. Children need parents who behave as adults in that they take control and ultimate responsibility. This gives children the emotional security they crave.

John and Brenda had to take on their appropriate adult roles in the family. They had thought they were being 'democratic' and caring by never imposing their will on their son, or making any demands or setting boundaries. They were in fact, being more protective and 'kind' when they took charge. Before long Trevor had become toilet trained, and accepted his role as a child rather than that of a mini-dictator. In time, everyone was happier and Trevor's irrational fears retreated as he mastered tasks.

TOO MUCH, TOO SOON

Linda is a caring single mother whose ex-husband is also close to Kimberley, their four-year-old daughter. Linda's family are emotionally close and as the first grandchild, Kimberley has received a lot of attention. Kimberley is always treated in an adult way and been given a choice in everything she does. She is intelligent and articulate, and makes the most of her position as the centre of her extended family's universe. Within this connectedness, Linda is the emotional glue that holds them together. Due to her gentle and non-confrontational nature she is often put upon and manipulated by others – especially her needy mother. So she is determined not to 'impose' anything on her child.

The result is that Kimberley is used to endless attention. Her doting family have complied but now an inexplicable problem has arisen. Outwardly 'grown-up', Kimberley has declared that 'she wants to stay a baby'. She is refusing to become toilet trained, and won't give up her dummy.

Rather than give her freedom, allowing her to make every choice herself has made Kimberley insecure about being 'grown up'. She enjoys the advantages, but deep down she lacks the protection that comes with having an adult in charge of her life. Too many choices, too much freedom to dictate, have given her more than she can handle. She is, after all, just a young child and she needs direction and protection from herself as much as anything else.

First Linda has to change her mindset about what is best for her child, but suddenly becoming firm with her will only result in resistance from Kimberley. It often happens that those who feel resentful of the way they are treated by their own parents act in the opposite way with their children. But the 'opposite' is not necessarily the best way. A considered middle path is often better. Linda needs to first distance herself from her extended family's demands by not being so available. In this way, she too will grow up. Emotional blackmail is one of the most common 'weapons' family members use to get what they want. It is probably the lowest means civilized people employ – but they do it all the same.

Once she sees that it is better for Kimberley to have a mother who is ultimately in control, rather than merely a compliant handmaiden to everyone, Linda will find it easier to assert herself.

Linda was advised to inform her daughter matter-of-factly that she cannot just be a 'baby' in some areas only, but will have to relinquish all the fun and privileges of being a 'little girl'. Thus if she reverts to being a baby, she will have to do as babies do including going to bed early, and no TV.

They set a deadline for the discontinuation of disposables, and the start of the use of the potty. Together with Kimberley, Linda counted the disposables on hand and made a chart ticking them off as they were used. She made it clear to Kimberley that once they were finished there would be no more. She had to steel herself not to buy any 'just in case'. The dummy was allowed only at bedtime as it was an effective way of helping Kimberley relax into sleep.

The day before the disposables were due to run out Kimberley urged her mother to buy more. 'The shops don't have your size any longer because you are a big girl now,'

Linda replied. Surprisingly Kimberley accepted this and was well on her way to growing up just as Linda has done.

SUPPRESSING THE GREEN EYED MONSTER

Lucy is another bright little girl who was three-and-half when her brother Guy was born. Articulate and highly intelligent (she was later classified as gifted); Lucy never showed any aggression towards her new brother. She was often around his crib trying to kiss him and wanting to hold him. Everyone remarked on how much she loved her sibling.

But soon she was withholding her stools and getting a lot of attention because of the problem. Nothing would persuade her to use the toilet which she had previously done competently. In time she had to have a procedure to remove impacted faecal matter.

Only when a therapist was consulted did it become clear that Lucy was withholding her stools in protest against the birth of her baby brother and it became possible to begin to address the issue. Lucy was extremely jealous and threatened by her brother's arrival, and rather than externalising this she suppressed her feelings by withholding her stools. When she was 'given permission' to acknowledge her resentment and fear of being displaced, things improved and she stopped withholding her stools in protest.

THE VICIOUS CYCLE OF DEPRIVATION

Maria lives in fear of her child's father who abuses her when he is drunk. He is particularly prone to violence when she feeds the baby or plays with him. As a result she tries not to show Jan too much attention or affection, and often sobs in terror while holding him.

Tsepo was born as a result of rape and his 16-year-old mother often lets him cry because of her anger and resentment at all she has lost. She handles him roughly and seldom reacts to his smiles.

These babies are learning not to trust through their conflicted emotional experiences. The wiring for emotions in the developing brain is dependent on experience. These two children's future emotional health will be fragile. Just as early warm and caring experiences inoculate against future stress, bad emotional experiences literally shape the brain. Both Tsepo and Jan could become bullies, and then abusive, emotionally handicapped adults. And so the sad cycle of a bad background affecting future functioning, is continued.

Sara does the best for her six children but there is never enough money in the house she shares with her sister and her children, despite the child grants she and her sister get. She does not have the emotional energy to stop the older children from fighting, and it is a free for all most of the time. She finds herself shouting at the little ones for messing and the older ones for making too much noise. Her solution is to send them all to play in the street outside.

In these two families, no one ever gets any emotional nurturance, including Sara and her sister. Some of the older children are becoming bullies and this too impacts on the vicious cycle of not enough food or emotional care to feed the desperate need.

DEPRESSION DARKNESS

Jeanie had looked forward to her baby, although as an only child she was a little apprehensive because of her lack of experience with children. She was never close to her mother who died suddenly during Jeanie's pregnancy. Being closer to her father, she seemed to recover quite quickly from the loss. But after the birth Jeanie slipped into a depressive state in which she was unable to relate to her baby, and became steadily more withdrawn until she only responded to the child in a leaden manner. She had always been a rather reserved, private person who suffered occasional bouts of depression, and her partner thought she was still mourning and very tired.

Although Jeanie had not been very close to her mother, pregnancy had created an unidentified need for her to be mothered by her own mother. Not only had Jeanie suffered an unresolved loss, but she was in a deeply depressed state and unable to help herself.

It was only when the clinic picked up that Jeanie's baby was not making babbling sounds that more questions were asked. The babies of mothers who are severely depressed do not imitate their mother's vocal tones, and may not get the kind of varied emotional feedback needed to build healthy emotional wiring in the brain. With psychotherapy and medication Jeanie made a good recovery, and her baby responded to intensive, but sensitive stimulation.

WHERE IS YOUR CHILD AT

Everyone knows how important it is to always know where your child is and with whom. But it is just as important to know *where your child is at.* Knowing where your child *is at* in his head and heart; now this is valuable information. If you keep tabs on this throughout your child's life, right into adulthood you will indeed be well informed. One of the most successful ways of doing this is by taking regular family meals together. This basic custom is a sure way to tap into the mood – both good and bad – of family members. A study of students at Harvard University in the USA revealed that what the best students had most in common was having grown up having regular family meals together. Who would have thought?

In order to know where your child is at you must have a good idea of what can be expected at the various developmental stages. Thus when people mutter, 'It's just a stage he is going through' you will know whether this is true or one of those old, or new wives' stories which should be avoided. In order to know where your child is in his heart and head, you will have to look into yours. You need to put yourself into his shoes and feel what he is feeling. Not how *you* would feel if you were he, but how he feels it himself, which is likely to be very different.

THE MYSTERY OF MEL

Mel's mother cannot understand how her sweet baby has suddenly became so difficult at 16 months. He often throws tantrums and has frightening breath holding spells, and now he is starting to bite other children. They tell her he is a 'good boy' at crèche apart from this new thing of biting, but by the time she and David get him home at 6pm he is beating them with his fists and behaving so badly they wonder whether they should see a therapist.

WHERE MEL IS AT. His first year went well. His mom was able to be with him for six months and then his Granny looked after him. All those neurons and axons that were ready for joining up with his brain's taste, smell, sight, and hearing senses connected effectively through the stimulation he received. His emotional wiring was well advanced by the warm attachments he had with his Mom, Dad and Granny.

But by the time he started walking Granny could not cope, and anyway he seemed to need the company of other children; it would be good for his social development. Being at the crèche was not the same for Mel as being at home. There was lots of noise and although the staff played with him and organised games he really missed being on Mom or Granny's lap when he needed to. Being 'good' all the time was hard work and he got very tired.

He wasn't always hungry when it was time for meals because he had resorted to sucking juice from his bottle a lot of the time. There were toys to play with but other children grabbed them and this made him so angry he sometimes lashed out and sank his teeth into them. By the time Mummy and Daddy picked him up after work he was weak, exhausted and emotionally spent. Over tiredness made him hyperactive and unable to release into sleep, and his poor nutritional state created a similar paradox in his eating patterns.

Mel had become iron-deficient through his poor eating habits and this was part of the problem. Many toddlers with access to enough food become malnourished through filling up on liquids because of comfort needs. Some children demand the breast almost constantly, others are given tea or juice in a bottle to pacify them and the result is often iron deficiency anaemia and under nutrition. Iron deficiency anaemia is the most common nutritional problem in children world-wide. It can stunt intellectual growth and indirectly cause behaviour problems. Toddlers who have breath holding tantrums in which they pass out are often found to be iron deficient. There is even new evidence that hyperactivity and learning difficulties (ADHD) are associated with iron deficiency anaemia.

At 16 months Mel is barely out of babyhood. He cannot talk well enough to express his needs and the fine-motor co-ordination he needs to control his fingers is still developing. He is unable to skip yet and even walking up and down stairs is done by putting two feet on each step. He does not yet understand the principle of sharing, nor do his play companions. If someone bumps him he assumes it is deliberate, as he cannot yet understand the principle of accidental cause and effect.

He only has a hazy idea of what is and what is not allowed. He is not yet old enough to conceptualise and respond to rules. He finds it very difficult to contain his impulses. He will only be able to control his sphincter and anal muscles in four or more months so he is not yet toilet trained.

WHAT CAN BE DONE FOR MEL? Punishing Mel for biting would only possibly be effective if it was so harsh that it instilled an overwhelming fear in him – it would also not foster desirable traits. It is virtually impossible for such a young child to understand why he is being punished, or to be able to remember for what it was. Some people even suggested to his parents that they bite him back so he would know what it feels like. This would only teach him that in order to get away with violent acts you have to be bigger than the person to whom you do them – the basis of bullying behaviour.

Because he had had effective early parenting that was nurturing and warm Mel will soon be able to show empathy with others. He had already brought his mother his favourite toy when she had burnt her hand. Rather than try and deal with the aggression that was a symptom of his underlying stress, Mel's Mom and Dad looked at the whole picture.

Although it had seemed good enough when they enrolled him, the crèche had lost staff and broken toys were not replaced so there were too few to go around. They were also cutting down on overheads, and they had dropped the mid-afternoon snack the children had been given. By the time Mel got home he had been without a meal for many hours.

The doctor found him to be anaemic and a suitable iron supplement was prescribed. He was no longer given a bottle of juice whenever he became crabby, and as his appetite improved he began eating the foods he needed to fuel his mind and body. Mel's mother arranged to work half days. And although this meant the family's finances were stretched, all agreed that Mel's welfare was vital. He was placed in a morning's only day care in his neighbourhood. This had the added potential of forming friendships that could be cultivated afterhours.

Handling Mel's tendency to lash out when frustrated was another priority. His new day mother was warned of the problem and she promised to look out for signs of trouble brewing. She put Mel with older children who were less inclined to grab things at playtime and made sure there were plenty of toys. Although Mel and the other children were still inclined to want what others were playing with, she used distraction to cool things down.

Mel's behaviour was frequently reinforced with words such as 'play nicely', 'don't grab', 'that hurts'. Most of all he was praised when he behaved well. When he did break down occasionally and lash out he was sharply told: 'No that hurts!' and he was picked up and taken away. Once he had calmed down he was taken to the child who had been hurt and told to say sorry.

Although his language is still rudimentary his brain is computerising the expressions he is hearing. Slowly he will learn to say them too, and when this happens in what is known as 'private talk' he will begin repeating them out loud to himself. His Mom was delighted when she heard him say 'don't hurt' under his breath some months later as she knew this was the beginning of self-discipline.

DANIEL'S DISTRESS

Sally's son Daniel is a 14-month-old toddler but unlike Mel he is withdrawn and often sits in a corner rocking himself. He has even started banging his head against the cot before he goes to sleep at night and Sally is afraid he will hurt himself. She has no choice regarding her work arrangements as she is a single mom, and she is worried sick about his lack of socialisation with other children.

WHERE DANIEL IS AT. Daniel's personality is different to Mel's. Whereas Mel externalises his problems, Daniel internalises them. Because Sally has had to leave him in care since he was a few month's old, Daniel has not had constancy of caregivers. Other than his Mom, there has not been a single figure in his life that has developed a close relationship with him. He has not enjoyed the interplay of one-on-one eye contact and loving gazes. He has a mobile to look at but no one has played peek-a-boo with him until he has giggled with delight. Nor rolled a ball on the floor, nor sung him a lullaby. He has not developed stranger anxiety because he sees so many people come and go. He was put in a walking ring at eight months to 'make him mobile' but he has not started walking at 14 months.

WHAT CAN BE DONE FOR DANIEL? Daniel is a sad little boy who needs tactile stimulation to provide the physical and emotional comforting he needs. His rocking and head banging are primitive responses to a lack of being touched. Sally was taught how to massage him every day before bed time while playing relaxing music and singing to him softly. She found this de-stressed her too, and soon he was smiling up at her more than he had ever done before.

Sally's bed time routine with Daniel was extended to reading a story, and over weekends she made a point of playing rough and tumble 'wrestling' games with him, in order to give him the kind of play that comes naturally between fathers and sons. The walking ring was banned, and before long Daniel was walking around holding onto the furniture. A few tumbles later – to his mother's delight – he was taking his first steps.

MANIPULATIVE MANDY

Gary and Sharon are a highly educated and financially secure couple who should, in theory have had an easier run with their toddler Mandy. Gary and Sharon want everything of the best for their little princess and booked a place for her in an expensive pre-school before she was born. Sharon is a stay-at-home mom and has household help. Yet Mandy has become impossible and even her doting parents are becoming tired of pandering to her, and exhausted by her refusal to go to bed at night. Mandy has never had any limits placed on her. She has been allowed to do anything she pleases and her parents believe it will develop her imagination and encourage creativity. Her 'art work' on the walls bears testimony to this.

At night she refuses to go to bed and stays in the TV room with her mother and father until she falls asleep there eventually. She wakes frequently at night and sleeps late in the morning.

Sharon has never been a particularly organised person herself and spends a lot of time socialising with her friends at the tennis club and spa. The staff has been made to understand that they are there to do Mandy's bidding and they act accordingly, while privately describing her as a 'spoilt brat'.

WHERE MANDY IS AT. Despite a stay-at-home mother and live in staff, Mandy has never had any real intimacy in her life. She was bottle-fed and although her nursery is a cornucopia of dream toys no one has really played with her. Her parents talk past her and the staff is fearful of making real contact with her. For all practical purposes Mandy is a neglected child. The more she feels pushed aside the more demanding and disruptive she becomes in order to get some attention. Her playing up at bedtime and er night waking are all part of this ploy.

WHAT CAN BE DONE FOR MANDY? Hard as it is for Sharon and Gary to set limits on Mandy, they must or she will become more difficult and explosive when expected to conform to societal norms. Sharon was also urged to spend more time with her on a one to one basis. A new bedtime routine that involves both parents was instituted and her parents were warned that she would not take to it easily but that they should be consistent in their approach.

Once she had bathed and put on her night clothes Mandy was taken to her bedroom for a story without an intervening period of running around. She was not told that she was not allowed to run around as this would have made her defiant, but the new routine was to be instituted firmly but cheerfully. She was also not allowed to sleep late in the mornings.

Mandy was put to bed and Gary read her a story. When she begged for another she was told that there would be a story again tomorrow night. A warm kiss, a soft toy to cuddle and Mandy was bid goodnight. But before long Mandy had appeared in the TV room – would Gary or Sharon weaken? When after the third time of taking her back to her room, Mandy began to wail inconsolably Sharon made a fuss of her and allowed her to stay with them until she fell asleep. When Mandy refused to have her story read to her in her room the following night and demanded it in the TV room Gary and Sharon accused each other of being at fault. Shrewdly, Mandy realised that she had learned a lesson in how to manipulate her parents. Mandy's parents divorced within a year and Mandy is still playing them off against each other.

CHAPTER 17

The Hopes we have for our Children

'I've got a hundred bucks that says my baby beats Pete's baby.' Andre Agassi tarnished tennis player, winner of eight Grand Slam titles, predicting his unborn child with Steffi Graf winner of 22 Grand Slam tennis titles will play better tennis than the offspring of 14 times Grand Slam tennis winner Pete Sampras.

WE ALL HAVE HOPES AND DREAMS FOR OUR CHILDREN. Pictures we conjure up in our mind. Our son being capped at university… or at the helm of his transatlantic racing yacht… perhaps being honoured for his energy saving research. Our daughter, the Marie Curie of her time, receiving the Nobel Prize for discovering a cure for cancer… Ah, the dreams we have for our children…

If we do not go that far, at least we picture a good life for our children. If only we could be sure that if life has been a struggle for us, at least it will be better for our children. And because we believe that the world is becoming increasingly competitive, we push our children hard, and fill their lives with activities that read like a roster for superkid.

In all honesty we want our hopes fulfilled as much for our own – as for our children's sake – as validation for a job well done. There is nothing wrong with that. It is our duty as parents to give our children every opportunity to reach their full potential. This is a sacred trust, and we may have to sacrifice for it. But our prime duty, our absolute imperative and *raison d'être* should be to prepare our children for life. A life which has value for them.

GETTING WIRED. As a mother I have often complained that human babies come into the world raw and ill-equipped for survival compared to other species. If only they could pull themselves upright after birth, like deer do on their shaky marionette stringed legs and wobble over to find the teat. If babies could just say – even in a few words – what the problem is.

If only, during the millions of years it has taken to develop the opposing thumb that makes it possible for us to use tools so successfully, our digestive system had worked out a way around colic. Surely it is not too much to ask that this highest form of life require a little less commitment in order to thrive? Clearly Mother Nature has been so busy making us complex that she has not had the time to make us easy. *But then, a woman's work is never done.*

Although there are many cultural differences in raising children, Indian or Caucasian, African, Inuit or Arabian; they all learn to walk, talk, laugh and behave badly within a similar loosely defined time frame. Yet they eat different foods, experience different handling and dance to another tune.

No culture has managed to radically change the pace at which children go through the various physical developmental stages. Even if they are swaddled for months, or carried on the mother's back they still learn to walk at an appropriate age. *Nature sets the parameters of what nurture can do.*

The great debate as to whether we are purely a product of our environment or purely the result of our genetic material is no longer an either or one, although the idea that nurture is paramount in terms of gender has been discounted. (*See p. 482*.) We are only just becoming aware of another dimension to the eternal riddle of what makes us who we are – it is in fact a triangle. There is a third force that shapes us: it is the interaction of genes and our environment together with our individual character traits that ultimately defines us.

TEMPERAMENT AND BEHAVIOUR: or is it entirely the fault of parents? The more we learn about what affects children's development the more it seems as though parents are to blame for all their children's problems. Not so. Children are not only the product of the way they are raised, but of many intertwined factors including inborn temperament and genetic predisposition. One of the gifts we should ask for when we make a wish upon a star regarding our children's characteristics is that we are blessed with a 'goodness of fit': that is, that we are temperamentally compatible with each other.

When it comes to lovers we all know the old adages: 'opposites attract', 'like peas in a pod'; 'different strokes for different folks… every which way'. But the most successful unions are those in which our partners bring out the best in us. We are all strange in our own way, with quirks and complexes and baggage. What a comfort it is to have someone who understands, who says the right thing when we are down, against whom we can lean for strength, and who finds us attractive and even funny. Such a luxury is the cashmere of a truly good fit between partners. It is so much easier too, if there is a 'goodness of fit' between you and your child.

INBORN TRAITS. As many parents soon become aware, babies are born with distinctive temperamental characteristics. Irritable, placid, hard to soothe, anxious… and we are often quick to identify them with family members that we know. Sometimes we put it down to gender; 'she's a really fussy little lady', 'He's irritable like his father,' we moan.

Rather than being only gender bound, although it does count, researchers now think that specific genes make for particular traits, including distinctive male or female ways of being. *See p. 482.* Even more intriguing is the finding that metabolism and flow rate of brain chemicals such as serotonin and dopamine influence characteristics. Amongst other things serotonin inhibits impulsiveness, and when the transporter gene is short – resulting in less serotonin reaching the cells – aggression, impulsiveness and even a tendency to drink too much alcohol is a possible outcome. Calm and rational characteristics apparently flow from the longer version of the gene that releases more serotonin.

As proof of the genetic base of traits, lab monkeys have been selectively bred to be shy, including the faster heart rate that distinguishes them. Now a controversial experiment with a drug usually used in adults suffering from depression has been shown to reduce anxiety and social inhibition in children. The desirability of such tinkering with the mind in order to give us uniformity seems like a nightmare to some. For others, the debilitating effect of pathological shyness is a greater evil. (*See the Shy child, Anxious children and selective mutism pp. 432-437.*)

We need to remember too, that one man's shy child is another's duly respectful and socially adept treasure. In China adults view cautious, withdrawn children as socially mature! Teachers and peers see shyness and sensitivity as leadership qualities. Cultural values play a huge role in what we see as desirable characteristics; and who is to say that the Western model is the only desirable one? Japanese mothers for example, believe that children are born independent and must learn to rely on their mothers. This is done through gentle persuasion and nurturing with lots of hand movements. While Caucasian mothers believe the opposite; that babies must be encouraged to become independent of their mothers with many verbal commands. German mothers are amongst the most forceful in the belief that children should become independent as early as possible, and they act accordingly. In many African cultures an assertive child who looks his elders in the eye and speaks first would be considered totally out of line, and a shameful reflection on his parents and ancestors. The Xhosa people, of whom Nelson Mandela is a royal chief, consider it unacceptable for a younger person to even greet an older person first, regardless of stature.

Thus while certain characteristics may be innate, the way a child is handled has an effect in modifying behaviour. But do we want one homogeneous, world-wide no name brand of humanity? Is our individuality not what makes life worthwhile? Are the terracotta warriors and horsemen created more than 2,000 years ago in Xi'an, China not as magnificent as the work of Michelangelo in Rome's Sistine Chapel? Different, unique, seductively beautiful and the product of minds and cultures with their own norms and values; we are all our own distinctive works of art.

While there is room for people with all kinds of natures in this world, some youthful temperament traits can signal potential problems that require careful handling if they are to adjust well in society.

NOTE: Use only as a guide. Never allow a label to define your child. There are advantages and disadvantages in all temperaments and characteristics. Your child is a unique, evolving being who should not be boxed, labelled and categorised. The good news is that behaviour can be modified and sensitive handling can make for positive change.

THE NATURALLY EASY CHILD. With a cheerful disposition, these children quickly adapt to routines and new experiences such as feeding, settling into sleep and responding to others; which in turn easily elicit warm, responsive care. Fortunately forty percent of children fall into this category.

DIFFICULT CHILDREN. These are children who seem to be at odds with the world; they are hard to settle, react negatively to new conditions and experiences, and need sensitive handling in order to overcome their disposition. These are the ten per cent who may become aggressive or anxiously withdrawn in childhood. Because they are relatively unrewarding and frustrating, it is hard for parents to always respond adaptively. Many times parents find themselves reacting with anger and frustration towards the difficult child causing higher levels of difficult behaviour.

NOT SO JOLLY JOSIE. Josie was a colicky, difficult baby and nothing Mary did seemed to calm her. Her friends gossiped that her baby's behaviour was a result of her anxious parenting. But who would not be stressed by a baby that cries incessantly and cannot seem to be calmed by her mother's care? Josie's difficult temperament brought out the worst in Mary who was driven to distraction by her daughter's seeming rejection of everything she did for her. Even the food she painstakingly prepared was spat out. In trying to get her to sleep Mary would march up and down patting her vigorously which merely made Josie tense rather than helping her relax into sleep.

Once she had been told that Josie was a difficult child by temperament it was easier for Mary to respond in a more relaxed manner. She stopped seeing rejection in everything Josie did and became more philosophical in her reactions. If she did not like the new food Mary had cooked, she would simply put it away in the freezer and try again another time. Mary became less intrusive in her attempts at soothing and allowed Josie to calm herself down by swaddling her and playing soothing music. (*See p. 81.*)

THE SLOW TO WARM UP CHILD. David is one of approximately fifteen percent of children who are distinguished by a minimal reaction to stimulus, and who are rather negative in mood, taking a long hard look before participating in new experiences. Because they seldom fuss these children present few problems. Later on they may become 'outsiders' watching from the sidelines, rather than participating in children's group activities. Although Western society generally values 'team players' more highly, observers on the fringes are often thinkers who become creative problem solvers. Some children may display excessive fearfulness in participating in games and they need to be gently encouraged to play in small groups.

CHILDREN WITH MIXED CHARACTERISTICS. The remaining thirty-five percent of children, who do not fall into ready categories of temperament, display mixed characteristics. Although temperament seldom changes radically from early parameters, environment has a distinct influence.

DEVELOPING HEALTHY HABITS

Parents often under-estimate the influence they have in their own homes. In reality, parents are strong role models for their children. The evidence is clear that parents are the major agents of change within households, and have the potential to significantly influence their children's behaviour over the short and the long term. Parents need to take charge and become authority figures in creating healthy environments for their children. This simply means creating an environment which helps rather than hinders children in developing healthy habits.

Here are several key points which parents can focus on to help them achieve this.

ADOPT A FAMILY APPROACH

It is essential for parents to adopt a family approach to health. In this way each and every member of the family is included, and no individual is singled out. This kind of team approach enables parents to keep the focus on health rather than on appearance or on weight. This can appear exciting to children, rather than it seeming like a punishment.

LIMIT SCREEN TIME

Screen time simply means sedentary time spent in front of the TV, computer, tablets, mobile phones and alike. There is a clear link between childhood obesity and the amount of time children spend in front of screens. As a result, reducing screen time has become a major international priority in obesity prevention. The American Academy of Paediatrics recommend that children under the age of 2 to be exposed to no screen time at all. A study conducted in the UK found that significantly more 3 year olds who spent 8 hours or more in front of a screen per week were overweight or obese by the age of 7 years.

ADOPT AN HOUR A DAY FOR PLAY

Children need at least an hour of moderate to vigorous activity each day. For younger children, this can be broken up into shorter bursts of 10-15 minutes of active play several times per day. Children also need to learn that activity is part of a normal day and normal family activity. Parents play a crucial role in shaping this learning. As far as possible, parents can aim to include the whole family as this will make it fun for children. New family rituals can be adopted, for example Friday night cricket or football games, Saturday bike rides, or Sunday hikes or brisk walks together. It is useful to make some equipment readily available to children, like bats and balls, skipping ropes, hula hoops, trampolines or bikes which again make outdoor activity more appealing.

RESTOCK THE CUPBOARDS

Parents are the gatekeepers of what enters their households. As a rule of thumb, parents should only stock food in the house which they want their children to eat on a regular basis. The reasons for this are simple. Firstly, what your children see in your cupboards and fridge will be what they learn to consider as normal. This is how they learn what everyday foods are versus foods which we only enjoy occasionally. They are highly likely to adopt the same approach in their homes later in life. Secondly, children (and many adults) find temptation difficult to deal with. It is far easier for certain foods to simply not be in the cupboard. In this way, parents don't have to adopt a restrictive, militant approach to their child's eating which we know is not helpful, and in fact makes these foods seem even more appealing to children. It is such a valuable exercise for parents to re-evaluate their food cupboards and consider what their children are learning from them.

SERVE HEALTHY PLATES

Mealtimes are a time for learning. Children learn about what type of food is offered, what a healthy plate looks like, what portion sizes are normal, and what setting meals take place in. Parents can aim for colourful plates – this ensures that a variety of nutrients are being offered from fruit and vegetables sources. For learning purposes, it is essential for children to see fruit and or vegetables on their plates every day, even if they are not initially accepted.

RESPOND TO SATIETY

Many of us were brought up being taught to finish what was on our plates. We now know that this strategy is not helpful when trying to prevent overweight and obesity. Instead, children must be encouraged to respond to their own satiety cues. When they are full, they should be allowed to stop eating without repercussion. In this way children don't learn to override their own satiety and continue eating. Most children are good at regulating their intake, and parents must allow this.

PROTECT FAMILY MEALS

There is such interesting research highlighting the importance of shared family mealtimes. Some of the benefits associated to regular family meals include children having healthier BMIs, being able to make healthier food-related choices, and having a lower incidence of disordered eating later in childhood or adolescence. Mealtimes have also been identified as an important time for children to communicate with their parents.

Practically, parents need to protect specific times in the week to sit together and eat. This can be at any meal, for example breakfasts or dinners during the week, and lazy lunches or dinners together over the weekend. The aim for family mealtimes is for a social, relaxed, chatty atmosphere, in which TVs, phones, and tablets are turned off. This environment slows down the pace of the meal and allows each person to actually register what they are eating and when they are full. This prevents what is called mindless eating – eating in front of the TV in which we eat too fast, have no idea what we've eaten, and immediately feel hungry once our plates are finished. This is a major contributor towards over-eating in both children and adults.

THE VULNERABILITY OF BEING A PARENT

YOU WILL NEVER KNOW HOW VULNERABLE YOU ARE UNTIL YOU HAVE A CHILD. Everything you have previously believed about yourself means nothing now. You may think you have felt pain, fear, love, but it is nothing compared to the intensity of feelings a child elicits. Especially when your child is ill, or suffering, or not perfect. It can destroy your relationships, your joy and your life. When fear for your child squeezes your heart and shards of metallic ice gut your belly, you know you will protect this child with your life and shamelessly bargain with any god for mercy… *But the human spirit has no boundaries and it is possible to overcome.*

TRIUMPH OF THE SPIRIT. Kyle Maynard is a congenital amputee in that he was born without arms or legs above the elbow and knees. He is, in effect, a body with stumps for arms and legs. He is also exceptionally good-looking. Kyle could have spent his life railing against the injustice that cut him off from normal life. Or he could rise above it. Although he 'walks' like an animal on his four stumps, he walks taller than the tallest man.

He is a Greco-Roman wrestling champion competing against able-bodied competitors. Yes, really. He says he just works harder in order to compete and win. He is an inspiring motivational speaker, and male model. He can type 50 words a minute, and eats without the help of the prosthesis that was made for him as a child. 'We kept losing it when we went out', says his father. Kyle remembers his father saying kindly, 'You had better learn to eat on your own or you'll starve'.

So he did. He beat every neighbourhood kid at video games. He writes holding a pen with his stumps. Kyle says the challenges that he faces in life have made it possible for him to achieve what he has achieved.

How did Kyle's family, mother, father, and two sisters treat him as a child? From the time he was born, 'we let him do what he could', they say. His mother 'focused on his gorgeous face', and also told him to be sure not to go over the lines when he coloured in. There was very little, if anything they believed Kyle could not do. And he too, did not for one moment allow himself to believe that there was anything he could not achieve as long as he put in the effort. What of people outside the family? After all, it's a big cruel world. 'By accepting myself, I believe other people will accept me', is Kyle's credo.

Kyle and his family have religious faith, and this has, no doubt, helped sustain them. But they have not relied on it to sort out their problems. They have all refused to succumb to either pity or self-pity. They did not believe in protecting their child from the pain of failure. They had expectations. 'Colour between the lines,' is a remarkably direct instruction. Rather than make the huge allowances that might be expected in Kyle's case, his parents gave him the credit and the dignity that comes from being treated as a worthy person, rather than someone without mettle. Kyle himself chose to compete in able-bodied wrestling, an individual sport where, when you lose, you lose alone.

Contrast this with the current vogue for 'protecting' children from every possible challenge in life. Praise a child for every effort, no matter how meagre. Find excuses for every cop-out. But children are not incapable of effort, or resilience. No child will ever thank his parents for making them less than they could be. Please do not misinterpret here. Pushing a child is not the same as having loving expectations. Parents need to encourage their child to reach for the stars, but always be there for them as an emotional and physical safety net.

'Loving expectations' is the perfect phrase to describe the way caring parents gently, but firmly move their children towards competence and a robustness of spirit. It's not the same as 'tough love' which sometimes has an element of rough stuff in it – often with good cause. This is more suited to older children who might need it.

I have described the primary 'instinctive' drive of new parents as one of protection. And this is a healthy and necessary imperative in the preservation of the species. But now that most of us are past the immediate needs of staying alive, we need to look at the other biological determinant – survival of the fittest. We are past the stage of throwing our children to the wolves and seeing who makes it. What we should be doing is making our children 'fit for survival'. Just like Kyle and his parents did.

Parents with loving expectations do this not by shielding their children from every adversity or challenge, but by 'holding their hand' as they test the water and themselves. You want to protect your children from failure and humiliation, so you set their sights low. You are in effect, writing a metaphorical note to excuse them from participation in the challenges of life.

THE CHALLENGE OF HANDICAPS. We all know the story of champion swimmer Natalie du Toit who lost her lower leg in an accident. With remarkable resilience of spirit she has continued to compete in both the able bodied Olympics and the Special Olympics.

James Baillieu was so uncoordinated he could not catch a ball or play any of the usual games boys play. At twelve, his handwriting was virtually illegible and complaints from his teachers made his mother seek the help of a physiotherapist, who recommended piano lessons. 'For months, I banged on the piano like a pig,' is James's rather quaint analogy of his playing. And then slowly he improved.

Fortunately James's problem occurred 'BC', that is, in the era before computer games when, rather than piano lessons he may have been prescribed a PlayStation. Today James is a young prize winning pianist who has played before the Queen of England, and is rapidly making his name on the international stage. He has come a long way, but he ruefully says he still needs regular physiotherapy on his thumbs. *How the sweet serendipity of life plays out when we give it everything we've got.*

THE SECRET OF SUCCESS. Now there's a telling line. Actually, if you are a middle class child today you could easily think that you have it, the secret of success, that is. After all, you are constantly praised for whatever you do. Like Rose, a four-year-old in kindergarten who came home clutching a certificate for 'sitting nicely on the carpet'. Not a day goes by without her getting a smiley face or star for some 'achievement' no matter how inane. While many children still experience hunger and deprivation and brutality, the culture of protecting children from every reality has become pervasive in some societies.

No competitive games are allowed in preschool because this will mean someone will lose. No egg-and-spoon, no three-legged race… none of the old stalwarts of childhood fun. Publishing the results of children's under-eight football matches has been banned in the UK in case this puts the players under too much pressure if they lose a match. In a perverse way this makes winning everything, and having competed count for nothing. But children are not that delicate unless we make them so, either through implication or over commiseration. So you lost? Try again next time.

In Japan, a kindergarten production of Snow White featured 25 Snow White leads, no dwarfs and no wicked witch. Yet the point of fairy stories down the ages has been to teach empathy. By identifying with the fears, hopes and dreams of the characters in the tales, children experience strong emotions and realise that others have them too. In turn they learn to feel for others.

The seven dwarfs that social correctness left out of the performance have personal characteristics just like anyone else, despite looking a little different. Happy, Sneezy, Grumpy, Bashful, Sleepy, Dopey and Doc – are a mini panoply of any population. Perhaps Sneezy has allergies, and Dopey is not too bright, and Bashful is rather shy but there is always sensible Doc... and with Happy around things are sure to be fun. How many lessons could be learnt!

FEELING FOR OTHERS. Empathy is a learned trait and the window for acquiring it is in the preschool years. Hundreds of years of fairy stories and traditional oral tales evolved and were loved for good reason. Through them, children experienced a metaphor for life from the safety of their homes. The trials and tribulations of Hansel and Gretel being lost in the wood express the basic fear of abandonment, with a happy ending. Witches exemplify the kind of threatening character that is sure to come into everyone's life sooner or later. They inevitably get their comeuppance. Ergo: living through bad experiences is not the end of the world; stay strong and you will overcome. Rather than an over emphasis on personal feelings; how much better to cultivate feelings of empathy with others.

THE EYE OF THE BEHOLDER. Of all the attributes generally considered desirable, being popular amongst their peers is possibly the most important to young people. When preschoolers were asked who they liked in their class, and who they preferred playing with; and then who they were not keen on and even actively disliked, certain characteristics were clearly identified. Physical attractiveness, especially a good-looking face was the one sure thing in terms of assuring popularity. This applied even when they were only shown pictures.

While a trim female body and rippling muscles may be important in terms of attractiveness to Westerners, this is culturally influenced and largely a learned response. Certain ethnic groups may prefer a more rounded female shape and a ripped torso may not make a male attractive. To say nothing of bones in noses and discs in ear lobes, tattoos and scarring – this isn't a value judgement, honestly!

What is astonishing is that even babies as young as three- to six-months-old look longer at attractive people. This applies regardless of race, sex and age of the person. Preschool four-year-olds respond similarly when rating people. Attractive people are good, kind, clever and desirable as friends, while unattractive people are seen as horrible and not nice to have as a friend. Studies were done to try and disprove this apparently unfair characterisation. But by the age of five unattractive children often did behave in less than desirable ways.

What comes first in the chicken or egg conundrum? It seems the 'egg on your face' is the culprit. By the age of five less attractive children began responding in unattractive ways, because of how they have been treated since they were little. As unfair as it seems looks do count and they make for a self perpetuating polarity. For all my lauding of the value of fairy tales I must admit to sanitising the 'ugly' sisters' looks in Cinderella when relating it to my grandchildren. 'Evil' stepmothers may also need a clean up. 'Big bad' wolves are okay so long as the animal rights people don't hear you.

POPULAR CHILDREN AND PUSHED OUT PEERS. In terms of social acceptance certain traits besides looks make for top popularity. Predictably friendliness, consideration, being able to disagree without upsetting others and going with the flow in games makes for popularity even amongst kindergarten children. It all makes perfect sense that they would be liked. These children are likely to have been guided by their parents and teachers in positive behaviours and taught how to interact positively. Warmth, good verbal interactions in terms of instruction and consistent discipline characterise these families. (*See p. 286.*)

Then there are the children who have *ambivalent* characteristics. Liked by some and rejected by others, they have both positive and negative traits in that they can be aggressive occasionally, and at times kind and considerate. They make up about a third of a typical group of youngsters, and are generally happy with the number of friends they have and their acceptance. Because of their variable natures their social acceptance can change over time, becoming better or worse according to their circumstances. Inconsistent parenting styles and unclear expectations with unsure guidance is the norm. (*See p. 286.*)

The point of identifying these various groups is not to state the obvious: that children from well balanced homes develop good social skills and those from the more usual mix are something like the curate's egg – good in parts and not so good in others – same as the average Joe Soap. But to alert us to the serious prospect of vulnerable children becoming victims of things they cannot help, and to ensure they are protected and nurtured.

THE TRULY VULNERABLE. These aggressive outsiders or socially rejected children are those who virtually no one likes. Unattractive, pushed aside and not easy to love. Their behaviour is hostile, aggressive and impulsive so they often misinterpret the actions of others and are quick to blame them, which leaves them socially isolated and lonely. They may seek out younger children or only find company with similarly isolated children so they do not learn effective social skills. Complicating matters for some of these children is that they may have the disadvantage of problems such as ADHD (Attention Deficient Hyperactivity Disorder) which makes them disruptive, unable to wait their turn, clumsy and forceful.

NOTE. ADHD behaviours can be treated. (*See p. 409.*)

The home life of typically rejected children is likely to be filled with stress through parental problems such as violence, alcohol abuse and financial insecurity. Their parents' interactions consist of demands in which the child has no voice. Discipline is likely to be harsh. (*See p. 286.*)

There is little justice in the apparent truth that the 'good and the beautiful' are loved and the 'bad and the ugly' are rejected. Even worse, peer rejection makes innocent children unhappy and depressed and cultivates in them feelings of worthlessness and low self-esteem. As they reach their teens they tend to drop out, do drugs and in general turn out badly. Some may seek out the dubious 'acceptance' of gangs.

THE BULLYING BURDEN. Then there is another group of children who are rejected by their peers. They are passive and socially timid. They cry easily and are overwhelmed by feelings of anxiety (*See p. 432.*). These unfortunate traits make them prime prey for bullies who see their submissive, fearful natures as easy targets.

They give the aggressor the satisfaction of not fighting back and by showing signs of distress and giving up whatever is demanded. This is not to say they are to blame. They need to be taught the skill of standing up for themselves and reasons for their anxiety must be addressed. Yelling at such a boy 'to be a man' is a form of bullying in itself. According to some studies, in the case of victimised boys they may have over controlling and over protective mothers, with parenting styles that provoke anxiety and dependence, resulting in a passive, vulnerable demeanour.

However, small stature and a naturally fearful and inhibited temperament are innate. A child cannot be expected to grow a head taller overnight – although some do seem to. Children can be taught non-reinforcing ways of responding to their attackers, and their self confidence developed possibly by means of self defence classes or other assertive but non violent means. Girls too can bully and become victims of bullying. Typically they use words, ostracism or text rather than physical means.

Parents can help by facilitating the development of suitable friendships for the bullied child. Even one good friend can be helpful. It may involve offering desirable bait: such as inviting a child in the same class to join the family on a fun outing; coming over to play with a new puppy… Think of it as *realpolitik* – that is a reality based on practical rather than ideological considerations. Having a good friend can boost a child's image to others as well as to him or herself. Teach your child how friendships are cultivated.

CYBER BULLING is a curse of the 21st Century. Talk to your children about it. Make it clear that it is done by cowards and that they should tell you if they experience it. Do not say they have become 'victims' of bulling; the bullies are the victims because they are emotionally handicapped. If possible discuss it at home, and get your child to talk about what she is feeling. Bulling of boys takes a different line, but the aim is the same. Without dismissing or making less of the hurt, try and show how pathetic those who do it are, and if they become a laughing stock in your home, then you have overcome.

There are also children who through various scenarios discover that they are able to exert huge power over their parents through their anxiety and separation fears, with negative results all round. However, these are not the children of whom we are speaking, but others who have a real pathology.

THE GREEN EYED MONSTER. Sometimes jealousy can prompt a vicious reaction towards academic or sporting achievers. The UK Olympic contestant and 10m board world diving champion, 15-year-old Tom Daley was forced to change schools after bullies threatened to break his legs. However, it is usually not successful children that are targeted but children with poor social skills or attractiveness such as the passive or obese child

Bullying behaviour has become prevalent in schools and even preschool, and it damages the spirit of many children – some with lifelong effects. It is significant that both bullies and the bullied have high rates of depression and feelings of rejection.

Teachers may have difficulty in handling it unless they have been trained. Developing a school code against bullying, involving parents of both bullies and the bullied, can go a long way towards dealing with it effectively.

Bullies are a reflection of their background and we need to look at how the child was raised to get to the core of the problem, before we can effect change. We need to instil values in all children that prompt them to intervene when they see bullying. After all, the majority of children are not bullies. If bullies were censured by their peers or excluded they would find it counterproductive. The culture of egging a perpetrator on is not new – it is an expression of our inner barbarian – but like any popular culture it can be changed. But it needs to start early. Preschoolers are highly malleable; they can be taught through play acting how it feels, how to react, and what to do in various scenarios.

Studies have revealed that primary school children who do intervene do so because they say their mother or father would want them to – they have clearly been taught right from wrong – some children are not so fortunate. This is not dependent on social status or income as bullies come from privileged homes as well. It is about the value systems and behaviours they have acquired. As much as the bullied child needs help so do those who bully.

RAISING RESILENT CHILDREN. As previously discussed emotional characteristics are hardwired into the brain through the experiences a child has from birth, possibly before. This is why early positive nurturance is so important, although innate temperament and genetic predisposition play a role too (*See p 521.*) Strangely enough this is not usually a result of receiving a great deal of praise and constant assurance that we are wonderful. It is helpful to know we are loved.

The warm embrace of family love is a precious gift that can help shield us from the arrows of the outside world. But in the end it is how we feel about ourselves in the dark cave of our inner being that makes or breaks our psyche. According to the child's temperament they may be over confident or easily crushed. A realistic assessment rather than a 'save their self esteem' at all costs response is more useful. Often it is about 'picking yourself up, dusting yourself off, and starting all over again'. Being able to do this will build your child's self esteem more meaningfully than endless empty praise and affirmation.

BEING THE BEST YOU CAN BE. Steven sailed through his early schooling until the sixth grade. He was the 'clever' boy in class earning top marks and praise from his teachers and parents. His parents had always told him he was naturally gifted and as it was easy for him to get good marks Steven got used to coasting. But as he reached the higher grades and greater application was needed to get good marks he began neglecting his homework and did not study for tests. The more his parents told him he was naturally brilliant and should be achieving, the less interest he showed in school. Steven was not doing drugs or mixing with the wrong crowd, he was just demotivated saying school was a waste of time and boring. Steven had become cosy in the belief that being 'clever' meant he did not need to make an effort.

The new challenges to his ability were perceived as threats to his sense of self-worth. He had developed a mindset that said he was a natural winner, and that his innate intelligence meant that he did not have to make an effort. He believed only weak students had to try hard. He had never learned that effort is always necessary for success. He was afraid of the challenges posed by the more difficult work and so he denigrated school. Steven had given up on learning. From now on, if he did not change he would be surpassed by children who believe that progress comes from hard work rather than innate ability. Steven's parents were told that 'boosting his self esteem' was not the route to take, but rather to commend him for the effort he puts in. Effort is controllable, it is up to you, but believing that you have a fixed level of intelligence no matter how high tells you that there is a ceiling to what you can achieve.

Studies show that children who believe that success comes from innate ability rather than effort, often acquire 'learned helplessness' when they are faced with a difficult challenge. 'It's no use, I can't do maths', they wail. Girls in particular favour this reaction. It may be partly due to a desire to 'fit in' with a particular culture of clever females not being attractive, or it can be a learned reaction. It even manifests in very young girls.

Preschoolers of both sexes whose parents are highly critical of their performance in tasks take their criticism to heart. They do not have the capacity to objectively judge themselves but rely entirely on outside evaluations of their capacity and self worth. They believe they are being punished because they do not live up to their parents' expectations. When they succeed they believe it is due to luck rather than effort. Parents who offer information on how to do something such as a puzzle which requires persistence, while patiently explaining and encouraging are likely to produce children who are enthusiastic and motivated to try and master tasks, and they are likely to acquire persistence.

WHAT CAN BE DONE ABOUT STEVEN? Steven's parents were told that while their child was talented he had to learn that it is application that is the key to success. His mindset had to change from one of a belief that there is a set limit to intelligence and that he has reached its limit; to one in which he understands that ability grows with application. The brain needs to be stretched through meeting challenges. That the 'learning' neurons in the brain that are formed (and pruned), in the very early period can grow new connections at any age. It was also explained that praising a child's intelligence by saying how clever they are, is not necessarily a boost to their self esteem. In fact it can be counterproductive. Rather praise the effort that is made. 'I like the way you drew the buttons on the man's shirt and the lady's earrings are very pretty, they look like flowers. You put in so much detail!' 'Let's see what we can find that's a little harder because it will be more fun to do!' This gives a positive view of challenges and the process of learning.

Contrary to what people imagine, the most successful people in any sphere inevitably have self doubt. They constantly question what they are doing and strive to do better, they experience many ego wobbles and sleepless nights. They make mistakes, they have failures, but they soldier on. They give themselves good advice: 'Slow down and look at it again… ' The one constant in their lives is never giving up and always applying themselves to the maximum. They know that the effort they put in is the route to mastery. Self-discipline is the key. If you have to stay up all night to study or to finish that project then so be it. The good feeling that comes from knowing you can discipline yourself and put in the necessary effort is a reward in itself.

THE KEY TO FUTURE ACIEVEMENT. A test was devised in order to find a predictor of future success. Four-year-olds were put alone in a room with a marshmallow. 'If you don't eat it before I come back, I'll give you another,' said the researcher, before slipping next door to observe them through a one way mirror. Some children could not hold out at all. They grabbed the treat immediately and gobbled it down. Others held it, smelt it, or licked it working hard to resist the temptation to eat it. They lasted a few minutes. Yet others closed their eyes, or put their head down. Some hid the marshmallow out of sight; others sang a song, using everything they could think of to resist temptation because they were determined to wait. When the researcher returned they got their well deserved reward.

Years later these same children where followed up. Those who had given into temptation had a short attention span and few friends. They could not handle stress and found challenges burdensome. The children who were able to wait for the second marshmallow turned out to be high achievers, popular and confident. As glib as this seems these conclusions bear a basis in science. Being able to defer gratification and discipline oneself to work towards a future goal has clear advantages. It is the basis for the kind of psychological profile that makes for mastery and success in life.

PERFECT PARENTING. Raising a child is a Homeric epic adventure tale of spirit soaring heights that are almost too much for the heart to contain, and sometimes brutal challenges. My thoughts are constantly with all the wonderful committed parents who do everything they can to meet their children's needs whilst juggling many balls in the air, often under difficult circumstances. I see them everywhere – the rich and the desperately poor – they try so hard, and yet I know they often experience doubts and I feel for them. The irony is that there are no prefect parents, only acceptable outcomes for which we can hope.

For in the end as the ancient Greek philosopher Heraclitus said:
'*Character is destiny… '*

CHAPTER 18

MARINA PETROPULOS'S EXPERT SPEAKERS

QR CODE

Use your device to scan the QR code for free access to **www.baby-childcare.com**. You will then be able to hear renowned paediatric specialists in a variety of fields give you the latest information on child care, including radical changes that have overturned previous thinking.

INTERNATIONAL PAEDIATRIC EXPERTS

It has been a privilege for me to know exceptional medical professionals whose heart is a significant part of that which feeds their medical expertise; as well as the sensitivity they feel for the human child and their parents... From them, you will hear a plethora of subjects that inform you and hopefully bring insight on what matters in your life.

ANEL ANNANDALE

Anel Annandale is a Registered Child and Educational Psychologist Specialising in Children from year 2.

She has 15 years' experience in the field of education and has been practicing as an educational psychologist for the last 10 years.

anel@childpsych.co.za; www.childpsych.co.za

QUALIFICATIONS:

B.Soc.Sci (psych) University of Pretoria

B.Soc.Sci (hons) University of South Africa

B.Ed (hons) University of South Africa

M.Ed. University of South Africa

DR NICOLA DUGMORE

Dr Nicola Dugmore is an Educational Psychologist and has a Ph.D. in early Childhood Development

QUALIFICATIONS:

PhD (Psychology) (Wits)

M Ed Psych (Wits)

H Dip Ed (Wits),

B Soc Sci Hons (Psych) (UCT)

Nicola works as a psychologist in private practice in Cape Town. She sees adults and adolescents for individual psychotherapy and works with children in a play therapy setting. Nicola sees adults and adolescents for private consultations and sees children in a play therapy setting. She offers couple counselling and parental guidance, and she also consults to families. Her doctoral dissertation focused on parent-child psychotherapy for infants/children between 0 and 5 years of age. Nicola is an Extraordinary Lecturer in Psychiatry, Stellenbosch University where she teaches on the MPhil Infant Mental Health programme.

dugmorenicola@gmail.com

LIZANNE DU PLESSIS

Lizanne du Plessis received her Bachelor's degree in Occupational Therapy with distinction and completed post-graduate training in Ayres Sensory Integration, DIR Floortime model and Therapeutic Listening. She has worked for over 20 years both in the private sector in London (UK) and in South Africa and currently works part time in her private practise in the northern suburbs of Cape Town. She has a special interest in treating fussy infants and young children with sensory processing disorders.

Lizanne has extensive experience in presenting workshops and lectures for professionals, teachers and parents on the subject of sensory processing and general parenting topics.

Lizanne is passionate about empowering parents, and her work has enabled thousands of parents and professionals to discover and understand their child's true nature, support their development, manage daily challenges and build strong relationships. She is the author of *"Raising Happy Children: The Key to a Calm, Connected Child'*, and her second book will be released in 2019. Lizanne shares her insights into motherhood and combines it with her knowledge in the field of child rearing and development at **www.lizanneduplessis.com**.

ASSOCIATE PROFESSOR CLAUDIA GRAY
QUALIFICATIONS:
MBChB (UCT, summa cum laude)
FRCPCH (London)
MSc (Clin Pharm.) (Univ. Surrey, *with distinction*)
Diploma Paed Nutrition (London)
Diploma in Allergy (Southampton), PhD.
PhD (Paediatric allergy)
FAAAAI (USA)

Claudia Gray is a paediatrician with subspecialist accreditation in allergology. She undertook her medical degree at the University of Cape Town and specialised in paediatrics, paediatric allergy and paediatric clinical pharmacology in London.

Claudia has a private paediatric and allergology clinic at Vincent Pallotti Hospital in Cape Town. She is also a part time consultant at the Allergy and Asthma clinic at Red Cross Children's Hospital, and an Associate Professor in Paediatrics at the University of Cape Town. Her research interests are in allergy pharmacology, and in food allergies in eczema patients, on which she based her PhD.

Claudia has over 70 publications in the fields of allergy and pharmacology in local as well as high-impact international journals, and presents regularly at local as well as international conferences. She is on the editorial team of the journal "Current Allergy and Clinical Immunology" and co-editor of the new 2017 South African Allergy text book. Claudia is a regular examiner at the postgraduate Diploma in Allergy and Allergy

Fellowship exams, and a member of the executive committee of the Allergy Society of South Africa, as well as a director of the Allergy Foundation of South Africa.
reception@kidsallergy.co.za; www.kidsallergy.co.za

DR SIMONE HONIKMAN

Dr Simone Honikman is a Medical Doctor specialising in Paediatrics, Obstetrics, Gynaecology and Psychiatry and has a Master's degree in Maternal and Child Health and is a Perinatal Psychologist.

QUALIFICATIONS:
MBChB (UCT)
MPhil (UCT)

She is founder and director of the 16-year old Perinatal Mental Health Project (PMHP) based in the Alan J Flisher Centre for Public Mental Health, department of psychiatry at the University of Cape Town. The Project has received formal commendation by the World Health Organisation. Simone received the international Ashoka Fellowship for Social Entrepreneurship, collaborates with several international research consortia and has published academic papers, editorials, book chapters and training manuals. She designs and conducts training for a wide range of healthcare and social service providers and consults to health policy and programme processes provincially and nationally.
simone.honikman@uct.ac.za

DR ANUSHA LACHMAN

Dr Lachman is a Child and Adolescent psychiatrist and a lecturer at the Department of Psychiatry, Faculty of Medicine and Health Sciences Tygerberg Hospital Adolescent Unit.

QUALIFICATIONS:
MBCHB (UKZN)
DCH Diploma in CHILD HEALTH
Diploma in Child and Maternal Health – CMSA
FCPSYCH (SA) – CMSA
MMED (Psych) (SU) cum laude – CMSA
MPhil (Child & Adolescence) cum laude (US)

EXECUTIVE COMMITTEE MEMBERSHIPS

- National Secretary, BOD South African Society of Psychiatrists, 2016–2018
- HREC 1-Health Research Ethics Committee member, Stellenbosch University, June 2015 ongoing
- SASOP Biological Psychiatry congress planning committee, 2012 to date
- Western Cape Subgroup SASOP, 2014 to date
- SASOP national treasury subgroup, 2015/16

INTERNATIONAL SOCIETY MEMBERSHIPS

- World Association for Infant Mental Health (WAIMH)
- Marce International Society for Perinatal Mental Health
- World Biological Psychiatry Association

anusha@sun.ac.za

EMMA NUMANOGLU

Emma Numanoglu is a Registered Nurse, Midwife and Internationally Board Certified Lactation Consultant and Childbirth Educator.

QUALIFICATIONS:

BA Psychology and Communication Science
BScHons Psychology,
IBCLC
SACLC
emma@breastfeedingmatters.co.za

PROFESSOR ANDRÉ VENTER

Professor André Venter is Academic Head, Department of Paediatrics and Child Health Medical School, University of the Free State, and a registered Paediatric Neuro-developmentalist with a special interest in ADHD and Autism.

QUALIFICATIONS:

MBChB (UP)
DCH Diploma in CHILD HEALTH
FCP (Paed) SA
M.Med (Paediatrics) (WITS)
PhD (Paediatrics) (Univ. of Alberta, Canada)

- He is one of the founder members of The Paediatric Neurology and Developmental Association of Southern Africa (PANDA, 1996- current) and currently its national chairman.
- He is an elected and active member of the International Child Neurology Association (1997- current);
- Fellow of the American Academy for Cerebral Palsy and Developmental Medicine (1991-current). He is a member of the South African Association of Sensory Interpretation.
- He is an elected member of the Executive Council of the International Paediatric Chairs Association (August 1998-current).
- Immediate past President and co-founder of the African Child Neurology Association
- Elected as an active member of the International Child Neurology Association (1997-current)
- Founder and director of the Mother and Child Academic Hospital Foundation.
- Member of the Executive Committee of Senate of the UFS
- Chairman of the Committee of all academic Paediatric Departments of South Africa
- Member of the South African Association for Medical Education (1992-current)
- Appointed to the Advisory Board of the South African Institute for Sensory Integration (1993-current)
- National Chairman of the Paediatric Neurology and Developmental Association of Southern Africa (PANDA) (1996-current)
- Chairman of PANDA-SA Bloemfontein Branch (1996-current)
- Elected as an active member of the International Child Neurology Association (1997-current)
- Member of the Committee for Research Grant Applications of The South African Association for the Scientific Study of Mental Handicap (1997-current)
- Elected as a member of the Executive Council of the International Paediatric Chairs Association (August 1998-current)
- Committee member of the Bloemfontein branch of the Hyperactive Parent Support Group (1996-current)
- 2006 – International Health professional of the year.
- Award – 2000 Outstanding Intellectuals of the 21st Century.

gnpdav@ufs.ac.za

DR BAVI VYTHILINGUM

Dr Bavi Vythilingum is a Psychiatrist and Specialist in Postnatal depression, Eating Disorders, and Post-Partum Psychiatric Disorders. She holds a Fellowship of the College of Psychiatrists of South Africa.

QUALIFICATIONS:

MBChB (UKZN)
FC Psych (SA)
MMed Psych (SU) cum laude
DCH Diploma in CHILD HEALTH

Dr Bavi Vythilingum obtained her MMed (Psychiatry) cum laude from Stellenbosch University. She worked at the MRC Anxiety Disorders Research Unit, where her work focused on OCD and Social Anxiety Disorder. She then went on to establish the Women's Mental Health service at Groote Schuur Hospital. She also ran the Eating Disorder service, and developed the subspecialist degree program in Liaison Mental Health for UCT. Dr Vythilingum is currently in private practice in Cape Town and remains an honorary lecturer in the Department of Psychiatry at UCT.
drbavipractice@gmail.com

JOANNA WILSON

Joanna Wilson is a Registered Specialist Neonatal and Paediatric Dietician with a special focus on maternal, neonatal and infant and child nutrition.

QUALIFICATIONS:

BSc Human Life Science at Stellenbosch University
BH Hons (Psychology)
BSc Medical Honour (Dietetic) in Nutrition and Dietetics at Cape Town University.

She is currently enrolled in an MSc Advanced Professional Practice in Paediatric Dietetics through the University of Plymouth.

She is a member of the European Academy of Paediatrics and Child Nutrition.

Joanna spent 5 years in London working in neonatal and paediatric units in leading specialist tertiary hospitals. During this period she gained invaluable experience in general paediatrics, neonatal nutrition, gastroenterology (including allergy), enteral and parenteral nutrition and behavioural feeding difficulties.

She also had the opportunity to lecture to a variety of audiences from medical colleagues to parents and children.

Joanna currently works in private practice, where she offers advice to pregnant and breastfeeding mothers, and guidance on infant and toddler nutrition, weaning, fussy eating, gastro-oesophageal reflux, IgE and non IgE mediated food allergy, nutritional deficiencies, management of over and underweight, special needs, Inflammatory Bowel and Coeliac diseases, post-surgical nutrition, and enteral feeding. She is passionate about helping parents navigate the challenges of early feeding!

eatliveplay.dietitians.co.za

VIDEOS

These videos, presented by experts in their fields, are complimentary to Marina Petroplulos's BABY AND CHILDCARE HANDBOOK and can be accessed on her website by means of the QR code on page 536.

PREPERATIONS TO MAKE BEFORE BIRTH

EMMA NUMANOGLU	Why you should do a hospital tour
	Breastfeeding questions before the birth
	The father's role
JOANNA WILSON	Causes of childhood overweight and obesity

PREGNANCY

PROF CLAUDIA GRAY	Allergy prevention stategies
EMMA NUMANOGLU	Common birthing fears
DR SIMONE HONIKMAN	Anxiety disorders and pregnancy
	Management of anxiety disorders
ANEL ANNANDALE	The psychology of pregnancy
DR. NICOLA DUGMORE	Sibling rivalry
	Fathers
DR BAVI VYTHILINGUM	Prenatal depression

THE BIRTH AND AFTERWARDS

PROF CLAUDIA GRAY	Colic
	Sleep in babies and children

Common skin conditions
Developmental milestones
Stools
Rashes

DR ANUSHA LACHMAN

The first 1000 days of life
Good enough parenting
The role of care givers
Bonding with a premature baby

DR BAVI VYTHILINGUM

Can fathers experience postnatal depression?
Postnatal depression
Prenatal depression

EMMA NUMANOGLU

A message to new mothers
Birthing options
Preparing for a ceasarian
Common birthing fears
What happens if things do not go as planned
The hours after your baby is born
Breastfeeding questions after the birth
Giving your prem baby the benefit of breast milk
Taking your baby home
Induction
Circumcision
Take home info when you are discharged
The father's role

DR SIMONE HONIKMAN

Management of anxiety disorders

ANEL ANNANDALE

Traumatic birth
Brain boosters
Attachment bonding
Brain development
Neuroplasticity

DR NICOLA DUGMORE

Parental self reflection
Transitional objects
Fathers

BREASTFEEDING

PROF CLAUDIA GRAY

Reflux and vomitting

Stools

Rashes

Milk and weaning

Introducing solids

EMMA NUMANOGLU

Breast feeding concerns

Expressing breast milk

Giving your prem baby the benefit of breast milk

JOANNA WILSON

Responsive feeding

BOTTLE FEEDING

PROF CLAUDIA GRAY

Reflux and vomitting

Rashes

Stools

Milk and weaning

EMMA NUMANOGLU

Bottle feeding

INTRODUCING SOLIDS

PROF CLAUDIA GRAY

Introducing solids

Rashes

Milk and weaning

Gluten free

THE FIRST YEAR

PROF CLAUDIA GRAY

Sleep in babies and children

Developmental milestones

Potty training

Bed wetting

DR NICOLA DUGMORE

Toilet training

DR ANUSHA LACHMAN

The first 1000 days of life

The role of care givers

Modern moms

Technology

Dealing with conflict

Shared pleasures

Is it okay for my child to be bored?

Toys – less or more?

ANEL ANNANDALE

Developmental delays

Reading with your child

Seperation anxiety

Understanding babies social development

What babies need in their first few months of life

Autism spectrum disorder

Being a single parent

The stages of play for babies

The importance of play

Developing intelligence

Difference's between the adult and the child brain

DR NICOLA DUGMORE

Play

Transitional objects

JOANNA WILSON

Causes of childhood overweight and obesity

Creating healthy homes

Responsive feeding

THE TODDLER AND BEYOND

PROF CLAUDIA GRAY

Sleep in babies and children

DR ANUSHA LACHMAN

The first 1000 days of life

Modern moms

The role of care givers

Technology

Dealing with conflict

Shared pleasures

Is it okay for my child to be bored?

Toys – less or more?

Boys' don't cry – right or wrong?

ANEL ANNANDALE

Reading with your child

Seperation anxiety

Autism spectrum disorder

Dealing with an aggressive toddler

Do manners manner?

Discipline for toddlers and pre-schoolers

The single parent

Teaching your toddler to share

Emotional intelligence

Giving children the space to explore

The importance of play

Developing intelligence

Difference between the adult and the child brain

DR. NICOLA DUGMORE

Sibling rivalry

Sharing

Play

LIZANNE DU PLESSIS

What is self-regulation

Sensory regulation

Sensory temprament

JOANNA WILSON

Causes of childhood overweight and obesity

Parent creating healthy homes

Responsive feeding

THE CRUCIAL SECOND YEAR

PROF CLAUDIA GRAY

Sleep in babies and children

DR ANUSHA LACHMAN

The first 1000 days of life

Technology

The role of care givers

Dealing with conflict

Is it okay for my child to be bored?

Toys – less or more?

Boys don't cry – right or wrong?

ANEL ANNANDALE

When is the ideal time to send you child to nursery school

Giving children the space to explore

The importance of play

Developing intelligence

Delayed gratification

LIZANNE DU PLESSIS   What is self-regulation

Sensory regulation

Sensory temprament

JOANNA WILSON   Causes of childhood overweight and obesity

Parent creating healthy homes

Responsive feeding

SETTING YOUR CHILD ON THE RIGHT PATH

PROF ANDRÉ VENTER   What is ADHD and can it be prevented?

Can you be diagnosed with ADHD as an adult?

How does adhd affect my child's learning and development?

Will diet supplements fix my childs ADHD?

How is ADHD diagnosed?

ADHD behaviour management

What is the role of medication in ADHD?

The side effects of ADHD medical management

Conditions often confused with ADHD

Understanding autism

ANEL ANNANDALE   When is the ideal time to send you child to nursery school?

Autism spectrum disorder

Bullying

Delayed gratification

JOANNA WILSON   Causes of childhood overweight and obesity

Creating healthy homes

Responsive feeding

MOVING OUT IN THE WORLD

JOANNA WILSON   Causes of childhood overweight and obesity

Creating healthy homes

Responsive feeding

ANEL ANNANDALE

School readiness

Emotional school readiness

When is the ideal time to send you child to school?

THE SICK CHILD

PROF CLAUDIA GRAY

Coughs and colds

Common skin conditions

Febrile convulsions

Stools

Side effects of commonly used medications

Reflux and vomitting

Common general illnesses

Rashes

INDEX

NOTES

NOTES

NOTES

NOTES